D1234453

# The Pattern
# of Our
# Salvation

# The Pattern of Our Salvation

## A Study of New Testament Unity

### Ronald A. Ward

Word Books, Publisher
Waco, Texas

*Whether a man is an evangelist or not depends ultimately on his theory of the atonement.*
—P. W. GIBSON, D.D., late Bishop of Jamaica

Printed in the United States of America.
ISBN 0-8499-0002-6
Library of Congress catalog card number: 77-075454

Quotations from the Revised Standard Version of the Bible, copyrighted 1946, 1942, © 1971, 1973 by the Division of Christian Education of the National Council of the Churches of Christ in the U.S.A., are used by permission.

Quotations from the *New English Bible,* © The Delegates of the Oxford University Press and The Syndics of The Cambridge University Press, 1961, 1970, are reprinted by permission.

Quotations from *The Jerusalem Bible,* copyright © 1966 by Darton, Longman & Todd, Ltd. and Doubleday and Company, Inc., are used by permission of the publisher.

# Contents

# ABBREVIATIONS

Besides the standard abbreviations for the books of the Bible, the following abbreviations have been used in this volume:

| | |
|---|---|
| ASV | The American Standard (Revised) Version of 1901, published by Thomas Nelson |
| JB | *The Jerusalem Bible* |
| KJV | The King James or Authorized Version |
| LXX | The Septuagint, Greek translation of the OT completed by the Christian era |
| NEB | *The New English Bible* |
| NT | The New Testament |
| OT | The Old Testament |
| RSV | The Revised Standard Version |
| RV | The Revised (English) Version of 1881 |
| Moffatt | *A New Translation of the Bible* by James Moffatt |
| Goodspeed | *The Bible, An American Translation,* by Edgar J. Goodspeed, et al |
| Arndt-Gingrich | *A Greek-English Lexicon of the New Testament* by W. Bauer, translated by W. F. Arndt and F. W. Gingrich |
| *Begriffslex.* | *Theologisches Begriffslexikon zum Neuen Testament* Lothar Coenen, et al, eds. |
| Blass-Debrunner-Funk | *A Greek Grammar of the New Testament* by F. Blass and A. Debrunner, revised by Robert W. Funk |
| Brown-Driver-Briggs | *A Hebrew and English Lexicon of the Old Testament* by Francis Brown, S. R. Driver and Charles A. Briggs |
| Liddell-Scott | *A Greek-English Lexicon* by Henry G. Liddell and Robert Scott |
| Moulton-Milligan | *The Vocabulary of the Greek New Testament* by James H. Moulton and George Milligan |
| *NBD* | *The New Bible Dictionary,* J. D. Douglas, ed. |
| *TDNT* | *Theological Dictionary of the New Testament,* Gerhard Kittel and Gerhard Friedrich, eds. |

# Foreword

THIS VOLUME IS BASED on a study of the Greek text of the New Testament. Translations are largely my own, with occasional side glances at modern versions. Scholars engage in research and publishers make known their results. The work is subject to consideration and comment and thus discussion proceeds. Public acknowledgment is due to publishers, who understand the situation. They facilitate the advance of learning by looking with a kindly eye on the frequent references made by scholars to their publications. Without this assistance progress would be severely hampered. The "grapevine" would not be a very useful medium. I am especially grateful to T. & T. Clark of Edinburgh for their indulgence. They put all scholars in their debt, not least for their prestigious International Critical Commentary, recently augmented by C. E. B. Cranfield's massive work. In the fall of 1970 the *Southwestern Journal of Theology* published an article of mine on "The Theological Pattern of the Johannine Epistles," and I acknowledge to them with thanks that I have drawn on it for my relevant chapter. Five years later the same Journal published my "Quotation Marks as an Aid in Interpretation," and reference has been made to it in this book.

I owe much to many friends and want to place my debt on public record. Mr. W. C. Guise, M.A., sometime Scholar of Christ's College, Cambridge, shared my schooldays. He went on to Cambridge and I did not. But I watched his career and example with admiration and in a sense entered sympathetically into his experiences. At any rate he fired me with the determination to write "alpha proses." Classical scholars will understand the allusion to Greek prose composition at a high honors standard.

I am grateful also to the Rev. Cuthbert McEvoy, M.A., sometime Scholar of Christ's College and Gaisford Prizeman in the University of Cambridge. He was my form master for two years and left a lasting impression. Tall and gaunt, with neat and short white hair, he had a commanding presence which made it hard to misbehave. Yet he was always approachable and understanding. His Christian life was manifest and his superb scholarship

[7]

in many fields unfolded in his general conversation. He inspired respect and admiration for remarkable gifts of intellect and grace. He made learning attractive and hard work an opportunity to be taken, not avoided. It was rumored that he rose at five in the morning in order to add Hebrew to his languages. (He told me years afterwards that it was six, not five.) He revealed in class one day that with his knowledge of Latin and "about as much French as you have," he could beguile the hours in a continental train by reading an Italian novel.

Professor E. H. Warmington, M.A., showed me many kindnesses. When I first met him he was Professor of Classics in the University of London and editor of the Loeb Classical Library. For some years he supervised my work for the M.A. and Ph.D. degrees. He encouraged me when academic officialdom could not understand, and would not at first accept, the subject of my thesis ("they don't really know anything about it"), set me off on Aristotle's *Generation of Animals* and saw me through, even at times overruling my own doubts and assuring me that I had a case.

The Rev. P. W. Evans, D.D., was principal of Spurgeon's College, London. His Greek New Testament lectures were always a joy. He combined massive learning with wit and spiritual intelligence. With rare insight he opened up for me the scriptural territory which waited to be explored. He not only gave the treasures of the hour. His whole method could be carried away and applied throughout the New Testament. Few New Testament lecturers today are so relevant to the preacher's needs.

Miss Mary Ruth Howes, M.A., is the senior editor of Word Books. In the toilsome task of transferring typescript to print I have been grateful for her alert mind and helpful ideas, her uniform kindness and patience. She toiled and aided the "transference." I have reaped the benefit. When I visited Waco some little time ago, Mr. Floyd Thatcher and his staff received me with great courtesy and I blush when I recall the length of time which they so freely accorded me.

My wife has sustained me for many years and I acknowledge with thankfulness all her helpfulness. Apart from criticism and suggestion, both literary and otherwise, she has compiled the indexes and written many letters. In the proofreading she generally carries the heavier load: she reads out loud—and I listen and occasionally correct.

To all these I owe a debt for precise and definite help. And there are many others, known and unknown, who generously share their knowledge and insight, add their encouragement and their prayers, and confirm with "seals of ministry" the preacher, teacher and writer.

RONALD A. WARD

*St. Stephen, New Brunswick*
*Canada*

# Introduction

It is a commonplace of New Testament scholarship that there are different theologies within the compass of the one book. Thus men speak and write of the Johannine theology, the Pauline theology, the Petrine theology, and so on. Emphasis is sometimes laid on the view that the New Testament is not a book but a library and that it is therefore quite natural for the various authors to differ in their approach to the subject and in their doctrinal views. This outlook has been familiar to me from early student days. It did not receive any undue stress and to some extent it merely pointed out the obvious. I suppose that I accepted it or at any rate went along with it. It did not affect my preaching. I never found myself saying that "John says this and Paul says that and because of their mutual contradiction they cannot both be right." It is plain that differences can be discerned in apostolic language, category and spiritual experience, but I think that I must have unconsciously assumed that in spite of varieties the New Testament writers were ultimately saying the same thing. The subject never became an issue with me.

Occasionally it came out into the open and was thoroughly ventilated. In the graduate school—I think that it was just after we had been examining a thesis submitted for a higher degree—a colleague hammered home to me that "there *are* different theologies, you know." Without being obscurantist I took the observation from whence it came. I hope that my work of exegesis in lectures and seminars was faithful but it never occurred to me to go to the students with the zeal of an evangelist and demonstrate conflicts in apostolic theology.

Then the subject blew up in my own mind. A few years ago, in circumstances which are of little importance or relevance, I felt that I had to examine the question for myself. The risks are great. For the work had already been done. I remember the joy with which the present Archbishop of Canterbury held up to me Professor A. M. Hunter's study, *The Unity of the New Testament*. It still has value. And there is also the possibility of what Professor Oscar Cullmann calls "the common suspicion of any thesis which harmonizes the different elements of the New Testament." [1] But necessity was laid upon me. I had to find out.

I began by going through the Greek of the Epistle to the Hebrews with a fine tooth comb, noting everything which was said or implied about the character of God. The results were put into some sort of logical order. The metaphysical qualities led up to judgment; and there was also the other side of grace and mercy. Then I studied in the same detail the work of Christ for us and in us and again similarly formulated the evidence.

What had been learned was tabulated in a column on the left hand side of the page under the heading of "Hebrews." First came the character of God, summed up in a word or two (living, conscious, righteous, etc.), and the appropriate references. This took up the left hand side (a third) of three pages. There followed another page devoted to the "other side" and the problem involved in law and grace, justice and mercy. Three more pages (still in the left hand column) were required for similar treatment of the answer to the problem, Christ's finished work for us and his continued work in us.

This done, I started off afresh by going in detail through the Greek of the Epistle to the Romans, putting the results in the right hand column of the same pages. Thus were created two columns of parallels. For example, the first item on the first page on the left side, under the general heading of "Hebrews," read "Living 3:12." On the same line on the right side of the same page, under the general heading of "Romans," was the entry "14:11."

I was on the point of saying that "everything that Hebrews says, Romans says, and vice versa" but one point eluded me. Hebrews speaks of sin as defilement and no satisfactory parallel in Romans seemed available. I therefore examined the rest of the Pauline corpus—and found the reference in 1 Corinthians 8:7 and 2 Corinthians 7:1. Detailed study of the Pauline correspondence (apart from Romans) enabled me to fill up the intervening space between the columns on the left and on the right.

In consequence I had seven pages, each with three columns, headed "Hebrews," "Alia" and "Romans." In spite of differences of language and approach and framework, in spite of the cultic in Hebrews and the law court in Paul, it seemed that what one said the other said. Even the cultic Hebrews knew about redemption (9:12, 15).

This was all very exciting. When I told the Archbishop of Fredericton that "what Hebrews says, Paul says," he at once replied that Paul did not write Hebrews. I agreed—and found it all the more significant. It was therefore necessary to start with a chapter on Hebrews, expounding in detail what had been found. This was followed by one on Romans. I

---

1. Oscar Cullmann, *The Christology of the New Testament*, p. 68. Cf. James Barr, "Trends and Prospects in Biblical Theology," pp. 270–71; E. Käsemann, "The Problem of a New Testament Theology," pp. 235–45; G. E. Ladd, *A Theology of the New Testament*, p. 33. Full bibliographical information on these and all works cited in the text or in the notes is given in the bibliography.

similarly went through each individual book of the New Testament, finishing with the Book of the Revelation and the Acts of the Apostles.

The task has taken over three years. The formulation of the Appendix was laborious—it took up to nine weeks—but I felt that it had to be done. There is something to be said for seeing one's results in a comprehensive glance.

The parallels are not by any means always linguistic. Sometimes an inference has to be drawn and sometimes the opposite of what is said must be considered. For instance, Paul calls Elymas a "son of the devil" (Acts 13:10). Whose son is Paul? We are reminded of his doctrine of adoption (Rom. 8:15) and of John's distinction between the children of God and the children of the devil (1 John 3:10). In some instances we have to see a parallel in spiritual experience and the doctrinal implication.

I cannot quite remember why I started on the Epistle to the Hebrews. It may be that at the time I was already working on Hebrews; or it may be that the epistle which is particularly the one concerned with the finality of Christ was the obvious point of departure. At any rate I found it a fruitful beginning; and it was not unwelcome to end with the Acts.

The study has confirmed my belief that there is a plan of salvation, a divine plan which is reflected throughout the New Testament. We must now investigate in depth and our first chapter will deal with the Epistle to the Hebrews.

Perhaps a word of explanation ought to be given of the omission of the four Gospels from our survey. At present I have nothing to add to my earlier book, *Royal Theology: Our Lord's Teaching about God*. Its more than kindly reception by no less a scholar than the late Dr. Vincent Taylor in *The Expository Times* (Jan. 1965) encouraged me to continue with the rest of the New Testament.

In case anyone thinks that we are concerned merely with the academic, a theoretical study with little bearing on life, I ought humbly to make one addition to this introduction. Every night of my life, in my final devotions before retiring to sleep, I offer the following homemade prayer:

> I thank Thee for the blood of Christ. It
> availed and avails for me. Forgive the
> sins of today of thought, word and deed,
> and give me grace to take the proffered
> grace to rise victorious over all temp-
> tation, through Jesus Christ our Lord.

Without this and all that it stands for I could not face the practical business of living; without it I should shrink from the fearful prospect of dying. But thanks be unto God for his unspeakable gift.

# A Note on the Greek Tenses

As we shall have occasion from time to time to consider the doctrinal or spiritual significance of the tenses, it may be an advantage briefly to review them.

The *present* and *imperfect* tenses indicate a *process, continuity,* "something going on." For example: the Greek for "he reads" means "he is reading." The imperfect means "he was reading." They may also imply *repeated action,* possibly a *custom* or *habit.* For example: "he reads (every day, every week)"; "he used to read (every day, every week)." Sometimes these tenses are *conative* ("striving") or *inceptive* ("beginning"). For example: in Romans 2:4 we see the apparently simple statement in the present tense, "it leads." We must take it as conative, however, and translate: "the kindness of God is trying to lead you to repentance." Similarly in Acts 7:26 we must render the imperfect by saying that "he was trying to reconcile them."

The *aorist* tense expresses the bare action: "he read the book." It might have taken him a month to do it, but the act of reading is concentrated into a single point. This is how a speaker views it, though he does not suggest that a month's reading has been reduced to a mere second of time. Sometimes the aorist is *ingressive* and marks the beginning of an act or state. We can distinguish "he was ill" (imperfect) from "he fell ill" (aorist). In Romans 13:11 salvation is nearer than "when we believed," i.e., nearer than when we began to believe.

The *perfect* tense expresses the abiding result of a past act. A starving man could say, "I ate," meaning that he did it a week ago. If we say "I ate" (aorist), anything can have happened since then—even starvation. If we say "I have eaten" (perfect), we imply that "I am now full" and not hungry any more.

# 1

# The Epistle
# to the Hebrews

## THE NATURE OF GOD

THE AUTHOR OF THE Epistle to the Hebrews is concerned with *the living God*. "It is a fearful thing to fall into the hands of the living God" (10:31). In spite of the fact that both the NEB and the JB retain the definite article, its use here may be questioned. There is no article in the Greek and there is no more need to supply it here than in 1:2. The earlier varied and piecemeal revelation has been replaced—or fulfilled—by God's final revelation "in a Son." "The emphasis is not on the identity of the revealer, but on his filial nature; the question is not *who* but *what* he is" (Peake, p. 73).[1] Revelation in Christ is "complete, final and homogeneous" (Moffatt, p. 2).

The situation is similar in 10:31. Identity has already been established. "We know the One who said, 'Vengeance is mine, I will repay'" (v. 30). The matter now turns on *what* rather than *who*. Will he act? Will he judge? An emphasis on the adjective will supply the answer. "It is a fearful thing to fall into the hands of a *living* God." This is in striking contrast to the idols who may have human form but no life. "They have hands, but they handle not" (Ps. 115:7). They neither touch nor feel. They do nothing. Not one of them is a living god. Idolatry is indeed dangerous,[2] but the menace of idols is not derived from their actions. God, by contrast, has his own inherent vitality. From it flows all his activity. Without it "he" would be locked up in the universe, a mere principle.

The expression "living God" occurs also in 3:12 and 9:14. In neither text does the Greek have the definite article and it may well be true that in these two instances the presence or absence of the article makes no difference. The living God is clearly meant. Moffatt sees no real distinction but Peake prefers "a living God" in 10:31.[3]

---

1. Full bibliographical information on all books is given in the bibliography. Where only the author's name is given, the reference is to his commentary on Hebrews.

2. J. A. Motyer, "Idolatry," *NBD*, p. 553.

3. Moffatt, p. 47; Peake, p. 206. But see James H. Moulton, *A Grammar of New Testament Greek*, vol. 3, Nigel Turner, *Syntax*, p. 174. (Hereafter referred to as Moulton-Turner.)

The living God is *eternal*. This may be inferred from 1:8, 10 ff. "Thy throne, O God, is for ever and ever." The Old Testament quotation (Ps. 45:6) is indeed applied to the Son but it would be very odd if eternity were possessed by the Son and not by God. And it would similarly be strange if sovereignty (thy throne) were eternal and God not.[4]

It is not necessary for us to enter the contemporary debate between James Barr and Oscar Cullmann.[5] Eternity may mean the whole of time, unlimited time; we can look back into an infinitely remote past or forward into an everlasting future. On the other hand eternity may mean that which is qualitatively different from time. God is thus "above" time. We can speak of his having an infinite time-span or his being Lord of time.[6]

However this question is finally resolved we can say that at whatever points we like to choose in the past or future history of the universe, God is the living God. He is further not limited by time as we are. The frustration of being too early or too late is not part of his experience.

The living, eternal God is *greater than all*. When he gave his promise to Abraham he reinforced it by an oath. This creates no difficulty for our author, who sees no impiety in an oath as such and no impropriety in the thought of God's swearing an oath. On the contrary: the divine oath explicitly brings out the reliability of the promise. The very naïveté of the story enhances the reverence (6:13–16).

For the writer does not merely mention the oath; he reflects upon it. Normally men swear "by the greater"—by God. How then can God swear? Since he cannot swear by anyone greater, he took the oath by himself. There is nobody greater than God.

This is expressed in another way when reference is made to Melchizedek, "priest of God Most High" (7:1). "God Most High" comes from Genesis 14:18, lxx, where it represents the Hebrew *El Elyon*. There is much to be said for A. B. Davidson's view that the words are not used in a comparative sense but mean "God the supreme" (p. 130). Even so a man who regularly quoted the Septuagint would not fail to see the significance of the superlative. Either it originally implied that God is the highest of gods or it was elative from the beginning. In his day the author would not take kindly to the view that God is only the highest of all divinities. Hence "Most High" can be regarded as evidence for belief in the purest monotheism. Whatever it may have been, it is now elative. Not only is there nobody, god or man, higher than God. There is nobody in the same class or category. It may be that in certain missionary contexts the superlative sense may receive a new emphasis, but for the author God is alone in his greatness and his height.

The same thought is reflected in 1:3 and 8:1, the Greatness, the Majesty, which is a periphrasis for God. It is immaterial whether we translate

---

4. See the perceptive note in Nigel Turner, *Grammatical Insights into the New Testament*, p. 15.

5. See for example, James Barr, *Biblical Words for Time*, pp. 50–85.

6. W. R. Sorley, *Moral Values and the Idea of God*, p. 465; Emil Brunner, *Dogmatics*, 1:266–71.

" . . . sat down on high (in the heavens) on the right hand of the Majesty" or " . . . sat down on the right hand of (the throne of) the Majesty on high (in the heavens)." Perhaps the best comment would be the quotation of Acts 17:25 and Amos 7:2, 5. God in his greatness does not lack anything and does not need anything. By contrast Jacob is *small*.

Here then are the categories of size, and altitude. A "superior" person may criticize their use but the writer to the Hebrews never meant them to be taken literally. They express the "position" of God.

God is *invisible*. Moses "held out, in the conviction that he was seeing the Invisible One" (11:27).

*Living, eternal, supreme, invisible:* these words, taken together, rule out any crude anthropomorphism. They point rather in the direction of the famous saying, "God is Spirit" (John 4:24). For God is *conscious*. It may be that John's emphasis is not on the metaphysical and that the term *spirit* refers to God's creative and life-giving power.[7] But even so the expressions "God is Spirit," "God is light," and "God is love" (1 John 1:5; 4:8, 16) need not be restricted to God's relation to, and activity within, the world. They describe his being as it is active in the world; but it is still his being. Admittedly we must use concepts and symbols drawn from our own world as pointers: no human statement could comprehend the fullness of the divine being. It is illustrated by, for example, the natural light.[8]

God is *conscious* because he remembers. "What is man that thou rememberest him?" (2:6; cf. Ps. 8:5, LXX). "Their sins I will remember no longer" (8:12; 10:17; cf. Jer. 31:34; 38:34, LXX). It is granted that God's remembering is not an exclusively mental process. When God remembers, he acts, either in mercy or judgment. Otto Michel can even call God's remembering an event, actual, concrete, efficacious and creative. "If God remembers His servant, there comes a new turn in the situation. . . . "[9] All this is true but it is not the point here. The concrete divine act arises out of the divine "mental process." If this is not so, it is difficult to see how any event can come from God except mechanistically. But he is the living God.

There may be some support in the second part of 2:6, "(What is) the son of man, that thou visitest him?" The NEB translates this verb *(episkeptēi)* "hast regard to him" and the JB "care for him." Arndt-Gingrich (p. 298) renders it "be concerned about." These suggest mental activity.

A negative example adds its confirmation. "God is not so unjust as to forget your work and the love which you demonstrated for his Name" (6:10). Only consciousness can forget; only consciousness can notice work and recognize love.

The conscious God in fact *has knowledge*, for he speaks (1:1–2). "The Word of God (4:12) is God speaking" (Moffatt). His Word discerns and sifts and judges the reflections and thoughts of the heart. Nothing in

---

7. C. K. Barrett, *St. John*, p. 199; cf. A. Schlatter, *Der Evangelist Johannes*, p. 126; R. H. Lightfoot, *St. John's Gospel*, p. 134.

8. Cf. J. Schneider, *Die Kirchenbriefe*, pp. 144–45.

9. TDNT 4:675-6; cf. Alan Richardson, *Introduction to the Theology of the New Testament*, p. 368.

creation is invisible to (not "it" but) him. Everything is naked and exposed to his eyes (*autou* twice refers to God 4:13). God is thus conscious; he remembers, knows, sees all, speaks and witnesses (2:4; 11:4).

God *has power*. In the complicated situation when God seemed to be contradicting himself, Abraham in faith reasoned that God was able even to raise from the dead (11:19). It makes little difference whether we interpret in particular "raise (his son) from the dead" or generally "raise (people, any he chooses) from the dead." The point is the power of God. It was not exercised literally but only as a "parable" of the resurrection of Christ.

God was able to raise; he was also able to prevent the necessity of a resurrection. Our Lord prayed in Gethsemane to "him who was able to save him" (5:7). God was able to do for Isaac what he actually did for Jesus (13:20); He was able to do for Jesus what he actually did for Isaac. God has power and he exercises it in history. Hence we read of his "manifold works of power" (2:4; cf. perhaps 6:5).

The exercise of God's power is not limited to history. He is *the Creator*. "The one who built everything is God" (3:4). The simple illustration of house building plainly refers to the act of creation. More explicit is the statement that God "made the worlds" (1:2). He did it through the Son, but he nonetheless did it. The Son was God's Agent. It is instructive to quote here the statement that "by faith we understand that the worlds have been created by the Word of God" (11:3). This not only recalls the "God said" of Genesis 1 and "By the word of the Lord were the heavens made" (Ps. 33:6) but shows that either God had two "agents," the Son and the Word, or one only: the Son and the Word are identical. This reflects Johannine thought. "All things came into being through it" (John 1:3). In contrast to the rendering of the NEB, "through him" should be reserved for a second reading.

The worlds, then, have been created; the visible has been brought into being but not out of observable materials (11:3b). The perfect tenses are suggestive. The implication is that the universe is still in existence. This is not pointing out the obvious. An aorist tense would have left the door open for the author to have pointed out some modification. As it is, the perfect implies that the universe is in existence but is not self-existent. It still exists in virtue of a power outside itself.

This suggests that the God who is the Creator is also *the Sustainer*. Having created the universe he keeps it in being. This is in itself reasonable or why should it have been created at all? But in addition God had plans for it. He appointed his Son heir of all things (1:2). He would not, like some negligent trustees, let the estate go to rack and ruin and disintegration. Once more God's method is mediation. As the Son was his Agent in creation, so he is God's Agent in sustaining the universe. He bears all things by the word of his power (1:3). He is not an immobile Atlas, bearing a dead weight; he is rather to be seen as one who bears the universe and bears it on to its appointed goal. But it must not be forgotten that this is figurative language. He is not literally whirling it through space to a distant end. He made the worlds and hence knows them in their details and he sustains them in their particulars.

We can perhaps make the meaning plain by taking an illustration and then discarding it. As a boy I used to watch my mother using a sewing machine. As she held the handle and turned the wheel, the needle went rapidly up and down and the cloth was stitched. When the wheel stopped, the needle stopped. Its "impulses" were transmitted through the machine to the needle and as long as the wheel went round the needle worked. If we regard the universe as a machine, then all the time God is "turning the handle" which works it.

But the illustration must be discarded or impossibly amended. It would serve if we could imagine that God is not merely turning the handle but present at every part of the machine. Every part of the universe, down to its infinitesimal details, is the scene of God's sustaining, though not localized, presence. He not only "works" it or "operates" it in whole and in part; he keeps it in being. Apart from this the universe would disintegrate into nothingness.

This line of thought may be discerned in the expression "for whom the universe and through whom the universe" (*di' hon ta panta kai di' hou ta panta*, 2:10). The reference is undoubtedly to God. Charles B. Williams in his *New Testament: a Private Translation in the Language of the People* renders "who is the Final Goal and the First Cause of the universe." This is Westcott's final cause and efficient cause. But is the meaning exhaustively given thus?

The phrase *di' hon* means "on account of whom," "because of whom." The preposition with the accusative can look backwards or forwards. If it looks backwards, then all things are "because of him"—he made them. If it looks forwards, then all things are "because of him" in the sense that they are "with a view to him"—they are for him. (The dual use may be seen in Rom. 4:25.) The two uses, consecutive and final, backwards and forwards, are not restricted to things. Persons may be indicated. A consecutive example occurs in Mark 6:26, "The king was very distressed because of . . . the guests." For final or purposive examples see Matthew 24:22, "for the sake of the elect"; Mark 2:27, "the sabbath was made for the sake of man"; John 12:30, "this voice has not come for my sake [Jesus himself] but for your sake."

It seems not impossible that the author of Hebrews had both senses in mind. "The dominant, though not exclusive, idea of *di' hon* here is final, 'for whom' " (Moffatt on 2:10). Room is thus left for the additional meaning of "because of whom" in the consecutive sense. God made the universe and it is for him. It may be of some significance that in quite another context Alan Richardson can "entertain the possibility that a phrase . . . may contain not merely one meaning but several meanings and several reminiscences and overtones of different biblical themes and passages." [10] In view of Moffatt's "dominant idea" it is worth recalling the other "biblical theme,"

---

10. Richardson, *Introduction to the Theology of NT*, p. 368, note.

which appears in Revelation 4:11, "Thou didst create all things [*ta panta*], and because of Thy will they were and were created."

This leaves us with *di' hou*, which seems to be redundant. If the universe is "because of him" in the sense that God made it, there would be little point in adding that it was "through him" except for the sake of paronomasia or assonance or because the double expression had become stereotyped. But this is to forget an important factor—the verb.

In fact there is no verb. This may be due to the author's style, though the explanation is only partial. The verb is omitted because two verbs must be understood and it would be too cumbersome to insert both. If we translate "because of whom (consecutive) the universe" we must add "came into being" *(egeneto)*. If we say "for whom (final) the universe" we must add "has come into being and still exists" *(gegone)* or else the mere "continues to exist" *(esti)*. Perhaps the bare *egeneto* would serve both purposes; but surely "through whom" requires *esti*. It is through him that the universe goes on in being. He who created the universe, he for whom it was created, he has it all "at His command and under His control" (Moffatt). Its continued existence depends on him. "He can create and he destroy." God is both Creator and Sustainer of all; and he is the final Owner.

We have inevitably had to anticipate in our references to the Son but it should be remembered that at present our main object is to discover what the author of Hebrews thinks about God.

God sustains all things in their details and in particular the spiritual development of men. In his investigations the scientist can regard the world as a closed system.[11] Growth takes place according to nature and without the necessity of divine intervention. The Christian, even the scientist who is a Christian, knows that it is *di' hou*, "by means of him, through him," but it has no prominent place in this method of research. He is seeking earthly causes for earthly events. The world has a relative independence and the Bible is not unaware of this. "Of its own accord, by itself, the land produces a crop, first the blade, then the ear, then the full grain in the ear" (Mark 4:28). Now however true this may be in the realm of physical nature, it is not so in the world of the spirit. Moral and spiritual maturity or ripeness does not come by nature. Seeds germinate and crops grow of themselves, but if a newborn Christian is left to himself he will not of himself, "automatically," develop into a mature believer.

The author of Hebrews is alarmed at the spiritual immaturity of his readers. Time has passed and they have not grown. They ought to be able to teach. By contrast, so dull are they that they need "someone" again to teach them the elements of the faith. They are "retarded children." And yet he does not again take them over the old truths. His method is bolder. Though they are babes in need of milk he will give them solid food. And he will not shout at them from the sidelines. They and he will march together. "Therefore leaving the primary word of Christ let us press on to maturity. . . . And this we shall do, if God permit" (6:1–3). (The omitted

---

11. Cf., for historical research, Jeffrey Burton Russell, *A History of Medieval Christianity*, p. 3.

words might well be bracketed in the text. See Hermann Strathmann, pp. 103–4.)

"If God permit": the words are conventional and on first appearance seem very much like the "D.V." (*Deo volente*—God willing) used by some Christians today. Such expressions were widespread in the private letters of pagan antiquity.[12] But the author is not merely observing the pious conventions. He writes in the deepest reverence. He is far from denying his readers' need of intellectual effort in order to avoid moral and spiritual ruin. But all their effort will be in vain if God does not permit their advance. But would he refuse permission? One would hardly think so. But it cannot be ignored or taken for granted. Spiritual growth is not unlike that of the harvest. Without man's effort there will not be a harvest; without God there cannot be a harvest. The author is thus not raising questions about whether God will give his permission or not. He is reverently recognizing that God through whom the universe continues in being likewise sustains the spiritual life of men. The human soul must be nourished and cultivated but God gives the blessing (cf. 6:7).

A step further may now be taken. *God has a will.* Salvation was proclaimed at first through the lips of the Lord and was confirmed "to us" by his hearers. Their preaching was attested by God. In their striking and varied nature, his mighty works demonstrate in themselves that he is the living God. In particular the distributions of the Holy Spirit took place according to his will (2:3–4). This is the sole occurrence of the word *thelēsis* in the New Testament. The distribution is not the crude sharing out of an equal quantity of the same "thing." What is meant is that believing men receive the Holy Spirit; they are now able to do what previously they could not do in their own strength; but they do not all do the same thing. For example, one man now has wisdom and another the gift of prophetic utterance. This is more than a natural talent. It is because he has received the Holy Spirit that a man has a new wisdom or can preach or exercise whatever gift has come to him with the Spirit. But who decides what gift a man shall exercise? It is God who decides, because it is "according to his will." The gifts vary at God's sovereign pleasure but each gift is a manifestation of the one and the same Spirit. (Cf. 1 Cor. 12:7 and context, and note v. 18, "as he willed.")

Will, *thelēsis*, means the general mental faculty of willing. A cognate word, *thelēma*, means rather what one wills to happen. Thus the prayer is offered (13:20–21): "May the God of peace . . . equip you with everything good so as to do his will [*thelēma*]," i.e. what he wills you to do. Thus when God wills, he discriminates and chooses. There is a certain action or there are certain actions which he wills this or that man to do.

The logical consequences are interesting. God is the Sustainer of the universe; he wills to keep it in being. In particular he wills to keep men in being and once more in particular the members of his church. He wills to keep in being the tools whereby they may do what he wills: either their legs for visiting the poor and needy, their arms and hands for acts of

---

12. Adolf Deissmann, *Bible Studies*, p. 252.

service and their brains and minds for the necessary thinking; or the instruments which they must use such as money, food or even cooking utensils. But will they actually do what he wills them to do? This will ultimately depend on their own will and its response in obedience. Thus a new factor is introduced: although nothing can happen apart from God's will, much may happen (in disobedience) which is contrary to God's will. The sustaining activity of God may be misused by disobedient men. He keeps them and their tools in being even when they disobey him. The elaborate consequences of this will be seen later.

A similar use of *thelēma* may be seen in 10:5–10, 36.

God thus has a will. If we may speak in human terms, he exercises his will in general in sustaining the universe and in particular in the day-to-day imposition of duty on men, who are to do what he wills. If (still in human terms) we think of God looking a long way ahead and planning and willing that something may take place in the distant future, the event in question would still be his *thelēma*. His persistent willing *(thelēsis)* of the distant event is long-term and in this connection we may say that *God has purpose*.

This is illustrated in 11:39–40. The Old Testament saints were men of faith but did not receive the promise. They did not attain to "perfection," the putting away of sin (9:26; 10:4, 11) and the new covenant with God (7:22; 8:6). It was not that their faith was defective or that God was impotent or ungracious. It was because of "His far-reaching purpose in history" (Moffatt). His "design," as A. B. Davidson calls it, was to deny them exclusive privileges. It was not that they needed "us" but that God reserved his salvation until we could share it with them and they with us (9:15; 12:23). The fulfillment of the Old Testament promise in Christ was postponed by God, "His plan being to make room for us as well" (Moffatt). If the "perfection" had come earlier, the later generations would not have been—which conflicted with the will of God (cf. Strathmann, p. 146). "God had made a better plan" (NEB). The historic Jesus came to do God's will and he did it (10:9–10). By God's provision salvation is now to be enjoyed by his one people, Old Testament saints and Christian believers alike.

We must not be misled by the preposition *peri* (11:40). "For us to have something better" (JB) suggests that Christians are better off than the Old Testament believers. Those who actually saw the fulfillment are obviously possessed of something better than those who had merely hoped (cf. Luke 10:23–24). The disciples were better off than the Old Testament saints were *in their day*. But in Christ the situation has changed. Old and New Testament saint *now* have the same salvation. A little literality may help here. The word *peri* at heart means "around." (Hence "about," "concerning.") Therefore "God provided something better 'around' us." If it is thus *around* us, then we are *in* it. A paraphrase would state that "God provided something better by including us." The "improvement" does not mean the advantage of our quality; it means a bigger church!

It is clear that the work of Christ, which opens up the access of men to God and establishes the new covenant, was "what God willed." As the Old

Testament centuries unfolded, God was willing this to take place. Such a long-term will is a sign that God has purpose.

Some confirmation of this is given in the divine attestation (2:4). This, like the preaching ("to us"), can hardly have been on only one occasion. The present tense of the participle is that of repetition. God was carrying out his purpose. We were being brought in.

For God is consistent. *He does not change his mind.* He demonstrated "the unchangeableness of his purpose" through "two irrevocable acts" (NEB), the promise and the oath (6:17–18). Moulton and Milligan cite examples of the Greek adjective in association with the other adjectives "immovable," "unshaken," and "authoritative" and note that it was used as a technical term in connection with wills. Our author quotes Psalm 110:4 with approval: "The Lord swore an oath and will not change his mind [his purpose, NEB]: thou art a priest for ever" (7:21). "For ever" heightens the effect. God will never change his mind.

This does not really conflict with Old Testament examples of God's "repentance." They imply a change of treatment rather than a change of mind. Thus Meredith G. Kline on Genesis 6:6 in the *New Bible Commentary Revised:* It was the unchangeableness of the divine purpose . . . that paradoxically required the change in divine government." This point was noted by A. Cruden in his *Concordance* as long ago as 1737. "God is not capable of repentance. . . . But sometimes He changes His conduct towards those that are unfaithful to Him. . . . "

God's consistency of purpose is not the inflexibility of a machine. *God is righteous.* The evidence for this in Hebrews is indirect but it is there. In his first chapter the author quotes Psalm 45:7–8, which he regards as messianic. He uses the nominative *(ho theos)* as a vocative [13] to address the Son. He thereby implies that "what God is, the Son is" (cf. John 1:1, NEB). It would be strange if we had to say that "what the Son is, God is not." When therefore the text continues, "Thou didst love righteousness and hate lawlessness," we are hardly wrong in ascribing righteousness to God. It was in any case because of this loving of righteousness that God anointed his Son (1:8–9), "in acknowledgment of His vindication of divine justice" (F. F. Bruce). Bruce notes that righteousness and justice are the foundation of the throne of both God and the Messiah (cf. Ps. 89:14). Hence the author can say that "God would not be so unjust [*adikos*] as to forget" their love of him in their service of his people (6:10). He further attested the righteousness of Abel (11:4).

The proof that God is righteous is not so weighty in Hebrews as in Romans but it is strong enough to show that though it does not figure so largely in the "system" of Hebrews as in Paul, it is nevertheless there and the author was familiar with it. (Cf. 12:11.)

It is a natural step from here to say that *God does not lie.* In the irrevocable acts of the promise and the oath "it was impossible for God to lie"

---

13. Cf. C. F. D. Moule, *Idiom Book of New Testament Greek,* p. 31 f.; J. H. Moulton, *Grammar of New Testament Greek,* vol. 1, *Prolegomena,* p. 70. Moulton's remark is very suggestive: *"Descriptiveness* is the note of the articular nominative of address."

(6:18). In this connection Old Testament passages are frequently observed, especially Numbers 23:19; 1 Samuel 15:29. An even closer connection with righteousness may be discerned in Proverbs 17:7, LXX, "Lying lips will not suit a righteous man." The author of Hebrews knew and quoted the book of Proverbs, as we see from his twelfth chapter (12:5–6, 13). It is not impossible that he knew the text just quoted. At any rate he would have sympathized with the thought that the righteous God does not lie.

If the promise were not carried out there are three logical possibilities to explain it, and all must be rejected. Either God could not fulfill it—but he has power; or he would not—but he does not change his mind; or he did not intend from the beginning to keep his word—but he cannot lie. The way is thus open for the author to say that "he who promised is *pistos*" (10:23), to be believed and trusted. The *God* who does not lie *is trustworthy*. This was Sarah's motivation. By the exercise of her *pistis,* her credence and indeed her faith, she received power to meet *(eis)* the emission of seed, since she deemed him who had made the promise to be *pistos,* credible and trustworthy. When we say that a man "commands respect" we do not mean that he has ordered us to respect him ("Say *sir* when you are speaking to me!"). We mean that he is of such a nature that we are compelled to respect him. So when it is said that God is *pistos* we mean that his nature entails his credibility (11:11). Hebrews 10:23 is quoted by 2 Clement 11:6 in an exhortation against doublemindedness, "being of two minds," indecision.

Central to the author's concept of God is holiness. *God is holy.* The purpose of the divine chastisement or discipline is the true welfare of men, namely that they may "share his holiness" (12:10). This was in origin a cultic concept and it denoted a quality whereby its possessors (things as well as persons) could approach God. Things which are holy are dedicated to God and are for him and his service alone. Holy men are consecrated to God and his will.

If holiness thus means "reserved for God alone," how can we speak of God's holiness? We do so by proceeding to the logical end. As P. T. Forsyth says, God is holy as he is set apart for himself. He is transcendent or separate from the universe of men and things, not only as a fact but because he wills it. He is the self-sufficient, self-existent and self-determined moral reality of the universe. Men stand under their conscience, recognizing a universal, moral claim. God is his own conscience and the moral order is alive in him.

Whereas God's glory means God as he has revealed himself, his being, his character, his majesty and his might, "His holiness denotes His innermost and secret essence." [14]

The stress on holiness runs through the epistle. Reference is made to the Holy Spirit (2:4; 3:7; 6:4; 9:8; 10:15). God's people are called "holy brothers" (3:1) or simply "the holy ones" or "saints" (6:10; 13:24). The reason for this will appear later. The sanctuary of the older covenant is

---

14. Otto Procksch, *TDNT,* 1:93; cf. Arndt-Gingrich, p. 9; John H. Rodgers, *The Theology of P. T. Forsyth,* pp. 31–33.

well known, with its outer tent or Holy place and the inner tent or Holy of Holies which symbolized the very Presence of God (9:2–3). *God is himself holy and he requires holiness in men.* He himself disciplines men so that they may share his holiness (12:10), and they are themselves to "pursue" it. They must take it so seriously that they aspire to it, earnestly seek it and make it their supreme goal. For everything depends on it. Without it nobody will see the Lord—enter his Presence and have fellowship with him (12:14).

It should not be overlooked that the reference to holiness occurs in a context of respect and subordination. To be holy, to be set apart for God, means obedience. He who is holy must reverence God and be subject to him (12:9). Both activities are important, the religious and the moral. For the moment we draw attention to the call for reverence.

For *God is to be worshiped.* Following his pastoral purpose (cf. 6:1) the author invites his readers to join him in what he is going to do. "Let us worship" (12:28). The implication is: "I am going to; come and join me." This is a sort of first person imperative. The constituents of worship are thanksgiving, reverence and awe. The language of New Testament worship is colored by that of Old Testament practice, which was sacrificial. The writer therefore again invites his readers: "let us offer to God continually the sacrifice which consists (not of animals but) of praise" (13:15). The JB rightly recognizes that this is a "verbal sacrifice." It is what the lips utter when they "confess his Name." This must not be regarded as "nominal religion." It is reinforced by active good works and the sharing of resources (13:16).

This is admittedly Christian worship. But even in Old Testament times God was to be worshiped and indeed he required it. There were regulations for worship (9:1), "which God himself had enacted" (Strathmann). It is important for the purpose of our argument to establish the fact that the "regulations" *(dikaiōmata)* were given by God. If he gave them, he clearly demanded worship.

The evidence which we seek is to be found in the Septuagint, with which the author of Hebrews was familiar. "The form in which the Old Testament is quoted throughout the epistle is regularly that of the Septuagint version." [15] " . . . all his knowledge of the Jewish ritual is gained from the LXX and later tradition" (Moffatt, p. xvi). Now the use of the word *regulations* or *ordinances* in the LXX goes far to confirm the statement of A. B. Davidson (on 9:1) that "the term *ordinances* implies that the arrangements and actions so called were of divine appointment." Of particular significance is Deuteronomy 10:12–13, LXX. "And now, Israel, what does the Lord thy God ask from thee but to fear the Lord thy God . . . and to worship [*latreuein*] the Lord thy God . . . , to keep the commandments of the Lord thy God and all his ordinances [*dikaiōmata*] which I command thee this day." Worship itself is asked for, and the ordinances are commanded—in a context of commandments. This passage from

---

15. F. F. Bruce, p. xlix; cf. p. 287; R. V. G. Tasker, *The Old Testament in the New Testament*, p. 114.

Deuteronomy is taken from a chapter which immediately follows one to which the author of Hebrews makes allusion (Deut. 9:3, 19; Heb. 12:29, 21). This is not an isolated instance. "Thou shalt keep his ordinances and all his commandments which I command thee this day" (Deut. 4:40). Our author alludes to verse 24 of this very chapter (Heb. 12:29). Could he possibly have missed the force of *dikaiōmata?* (Cf. Deut. 6:1-2; and see also Exod. 15:25-26; 21:31; Lev. 25:18; Num. 15:16; 27:11; 30:17; 31:21; 35:29.)

The author accordingly sees worship being offered "according to law" (8:4-5). In the cultic framework the priests discharge their ritual duties (9:6; cf. vv. 9-10). Old Testament worship only foreshadows (10:1-2; 13:10) Christian worship (9:14).

What follows might perhaps have been expected but it must be stated explicitly. *God has an attitude.* The author of Hebrews prays that God will equip his readers to do his will, producing in us "what is well-pleasing in his sight" (13:21). The term *(euareston)* is "always used (except Titus 2:9) of God's attitude towards human conduct" (Werner Foerster, *TDNT* 1:457). He calls them to join him in a worship which will be well-pleasing to God (12:28). In such sacrifices as good works and the sharing of resources God takes pleasure (13:16). Enoch had given pleasure to God, an impossibility apart from faith (11:5-6). It is unlikely that the author of Hebrews knew the Old Testament in the Hebrew, but it is at least interesting that his Greek verb *(euaresteō)* is used in the LXX of Genesis 5:24, which he quotes, to render the Hebrew verb of the text, "he walked with God." Faith is necessary if a man is to please God, for the man who approaches God must believe that he exists and that he rewards his seekers. To approach God and to walk with him are not quite the same. Our author may not have seen the connection between walking with God and pleasing him—at any rate not as a linguistic matter. But the argument is not invalidated. If God is pleased with human conduct, he not only knows about it but he has an attitude to it. He does not dwell in the *intermundia* or *metakosmia,* in the spaces between the worlds, like the Epicurean gods, unconcerned and uninterested in the affairs of men. He knows all and he sees all; and he has an attitude to what he sees.

God's attitude is discriminating. He does not merely observe trends or the spirit of the age. *God deals with individuals.* This is clear in the warning which the author gives. "See to it, brothers, that there is not in any one of you [*en tini humōn*] an evil heart of unbelief . . . but exhort one another . . . to prevent any one of you [*tis ex humōn*] from being hardened" (3:12-13). "Let us fear lest . . . some one from your number [*tis ex humōn*] may seem to have come too late" (4:1). After speaking of "the man who entered into his rest" the author continues: "Let us show speed and zeal to enter into that rest, in order to keep any one [*tis*] from a fall into the same pattern of disobedience" (4:10-11). The failure of even one individual will not be unobserved by the living Word of God. It penetrates to the depths of personality and judges even secret thoughts and purposes. No creature is invisible to him. Everything lies open to his eyes (4:12-13). It is with affection that the author says that "we desire each of you [*hekaston humōn*] to demonstrate the same swift zeal for the certainty of hope until the end." Such zeal will manifest *makrothumia*, an ability to hold out, "not vexed by waiting" (6:11–15, J. Horst, *TDNT* 4:386). Each individual who so behaves will be like another individual, Abraham.

Another example from the Old Testament (12:14–17) shows that it is not only in the Christian dispensation that God deals with individuals. The readers are to pursue holiness, without which no one (*oudeis*) will see the Lord. They are to take preventive measures against individual failure: note the significant *tis* (any) and its occurrence three times. The individual may fall short of the grace of God. The individual may be a faithless and selfish root whose growing tendrils weave themselves round the community and poison it. The individual may be a secular man who prefers the sensuous to the spiritual, either from insensitiveness or from policy, like Esau—and awaken too late.

*God is the Author of law.* Legislation is based on the priesthood (7:11–12) and gifts and sacrifices are accordingly offered *kata nomon*, according to law. But the priests serve the shadowy copy of the heavenly realities. This is in line with the revelation [16] given to Moses (8:4–5). "See to it, he (God)[17] says, that you make everything according to the pattern shown you in the mountain." The inference is obvious. The law comes from God. The high priest is called by God (5:4) and appointed by the law (7:28).

At the inauguration of the first covenant Moses read every commandment to the people, so that they "might clearly understand the obligations they assumed on entering the covenant" (Marcus Dods). He acted thus "as the Law directed" (NEB).[18] According to Hebrews he sprinkled the book itself, "the scroll containing the primitive code" (Moffatt), "containing the divine commandments which constituted the basis of the covenant" (Bruce). While Moses sprinkled, he spoke: "This is the blood of the covenant which God commanded you." The author changes the *dietheto* of the LXX into *eneteilato*, cognate with the preceding *entolē*, commandment. This is significant. Behind the covenant, behind the blood, behind the book, stands God. According to the law, pretty well everything is purified with blood and without it there is no forgiveness. Therefore of necessity the "copies" must be purified by these means. The blood has piacular efficacy. Moffatt notes that the author does not ask why sacrifice was essential. "It was commanded by God in the bible; that was sufficient for him." Any other divergences from the LXX do not here concern us (9:18–23; Exod. 24:1–8).

---

16. *Chrēmatizō* is used, "as often in the LXX and the papyri, of divine revelations as well as of royal instructions" (Moffatt, pp. 105–6). Cf. Acts 10:22. In Acts 11:26 the "same" verb is really a different word. See Moulton, *Grammar of New Testament Greek*, vol 2, J. H. Moulton and W. F. Howard, *Accidence and Word Formation*, pp. 265, 408. (Hereafter referred to as Moulton-Howard.)

17. Partly understood from *kechrēmatistai*, and partly from the text quoted from the Septuagint *and its context*: Exod. 25:1, 8–9, 40.

18. The Greek is *kata ton nomon*, which is rendered *sicut erat (scriptum) in Lege* by Max Zerwick, *Analysis Philologica Novi Testamenti Graeci*, p. 508. This no doubt explains the "all the commandments of the Law" of the JB, and justifies the *legis* of the Vulgate. The *scriptum* refers to the commandment, *mandatum*.

Other passages yield their supporting evidence by their coherence with what has already been said. *Commandment* is almost a numinous word and priests have a *commandment* to tithe the people *according to the law* (7:5). The law appoints high priests (7:28), and what a solemn task was laid upon them (9:6–8)! The sacrificial system was not God's last word but it was according to law (10:8). To set the law aside—even by an individual *(tis)!*—brings the punishment of death (10:28). The immediate allusion is to Deuteronomy 17:6, LXX, but it is unlikely that the author was unaware of Numbers 15:30, LXX. (In 3:17–18 he refers to the previous chapter of Numbers.) The offender not only formally breaks the law; he provokes God to wrath. Perhaps we might add 1:9, "Thou didst hate lawlessness" *(anomia)*, and 10:17, the acts of lawlessness which will be forgiven under the new covenant. The "ordinances" of 9:1 have already been considered.

### Man Against God

Even though God himself gave the law for men to obey, *he is the object of revolt. Men rebel against him.* The verb in 3:12 may be rendered by "revolt." "See to it, brothers, that there is not in any one of you an evil heart of unbelief in revolting [epexegetical] [19] from the living God." How far the metaphor was still a living one is hard to say, as in a religious context we tend to think of "apostasy." But F. F. Bruce can speak of "the rebels in Moses' day" and of the "latter-day rebellion" which the readers must avoid. "Falling away . . . denotes rebellion against God." "Unbelief involved disloyalty." The point is that the rebels were supposed to believe, were called on by God to believe, and they did not. Unbelief is a form of disobedience and of insubordination. They heard; they "provoked"; and they were punished. They did not enter into the Promised Land because of unbelief (3:19; 4:2) and because of disobedience (3:18; 4:6). It is of some significance that the *parapikrasmos* of Psalm 94:8, LXX, which the author quotes (3:8) is translated by "rebellion" in Arndt-Gingrich (p. 626) and the NEB. (Cf. Exod. 17:7.) The LXX has replaced the names of localities by "generalizing moral terms" (Moffatt).

It is admitted that the author is warning professed Christians against rebellion. His example, however, is taken from pre-Christian times.

Not far removed from the concept of rebellion is that of hostility. In 10:13 the author of Hebrews quotes Psalm 110:1. After offering his one sacrifice Jesus "took his seat at the right hand of God, from then on waiting until his enemies should be placed as a footstool of his feet." The passive voice does not state who will so place the enemies. In other contexts it might be argued that the passive was used from motives of reverence, to avoid the actual naming of God.[20] But God has just been mentioned ("at the right hand of God"—contrast 1:3) and in any case the active voice is used in 1:13, "until I place your enemies . . . ," where the same

---

19. Moulton-Turner, *Grammar*, 3:146.
20. Cf. Gustaf Dalman, *The Words of Jesus*, p. 224.

Psalm 110:1 is quoted. Or is it a quotation? Either the author had two different manuscripts with differing texts or, more likely, he is not quoting precisely but giving the general sense and, like John Bunyan, "speaking in Bible language." The human footstool is pictured in Joshua 10:24.

The enemies are the enemies of Christ. But as God will deal with them it can hardly be supposed that he is impartial. The enemies of Christ are the enemies of God. This must be so, because Christ is the Son (1:2, 8–9) and "'Son of God' means complete participation in the Father's deity." [21]

Moffatt points out (p. 140) that the author never identifies the foes. Stauffer bluntly calls them "the powers of hell" and Cullmann somewhat similarly speaks of "the unseen powers" in contrast to the earthly enemies of Israel of which the Psalm thinks.[22] This is probably the right verdict, though men must not be excluded.

The author thinks of everything without exception, the totality, being subordinated to Christ. We do not yet see it, but we do see Jesus crowned with glory and honor (2:8–9; cf. 12:2–3). What should we see if in fact we did actually see the totality in subjection to Jesus? Are we to omit the men who inspired and actualized "the contradiction of sinners"? The first thought may well be Cullmann's "unseen powers," but their human henchmen should not be forgotten. Rebels and enemies are after all not very far apart. Cf. 10:27, "the adversaries" (of God—Arndt-Gingrich, p. 846).

The rebellion and the hostility of men are not to be considered merely on the political level. God is unutterably holy and he has the moral right to impose his demands or laws on men. Their refusal to obey is therefore not merely opposition. *God is sinned against.* It is true that there are what are called the sins of society but ultimately sin is to be found in "an evil heart" (3:12), the heart of the individual. This is the seat of unbelief, which in itself is rebellion against God.

The heart denotes the inner life of man, intellectual and volitional as well as emotional. It can stand for the man himself: "harden not your *hearts*" (3:8); "in order that *some one* of you may not be hardened" (3:13). The author desires his readers to exhort one another in order to prevent the "hardening." If they fail, some one will be hardened. This means that he will become set in his thinking and persistent in his doing—and all on wrong lines. All the suppleness, elasticity and flexibility which are implied by the possibility of repentance or conversion will have gone. And it will have been caused by "the deceit of sin," perhaps "the pleasant illusion of sin." He foolishly enjoys his self-expression beyond the point of no return.[23]

The author speaks of having "the temporary enjoyment of sin" (11:25). In spite of its short-term advantage—enjoyment—it impedes progress (12:1) either as a long cloak would enfold and trip the runner who tried

---

21. Oscar Cullmann, *Christology of the New Testament*, p. 305,
22. Ethelbert Stauffer, *New Testament Theology*, p. 138; Cullmann, *Christology*, p. 223.
23. See H. Wheeler Robinson, *The Christian Doctrine of Man*, pp. 22, 78, 105–6; W. D. Stacey, *The Pauline View of Man*, ch. XIV; A. Oepke, *TDNT* 1:385; Arndt-Gingrich, "*apatē*," p. 81.

to wear it, or as a distraction [24] from what should be a dominant purpose. But it is not merely a negative impediment. Sin is disloyalty (8:9). It "contradicts" (12:3). It excites God's anger and counteraction (3:10–11, 17). It needs gifts and sacrifices (5:1). Its seriousness is revealed by the fact that men must repent of it (6:1, 6). There is a remedy for it, as the gifts and sacrifices suggest, and there is hope that God will not remember sins (8:12). Those who go on sinning deliberately have rejected the only remedy (10:26) and their predicament is sore. Only one was without sin (4:15).

The manifold nature of sin is brought out by the variety of terms used to describe it. *God is sinned against* as men are guilty of *disobedience* (2:2; 3:17–18; 11:31). When they disobey the law of God they commit *lawlessness* (1:9). Acts of lawlessness are associated with sins in 10:17. Disobedience to an individual commandment is a *transgression* (2:2, *parabasis;* cf. 9:15), "overstepping the legal limit" or "getting off the track"; or "falling off the track" (*parapiptō,* 6:6), where the emphasis is not so much on the fall as on being beside, not on, the track. If the fall is regarded as final, a helpful imagery would be that of falling off a viaduct or bridge. The man is "beside" the track and has no prospect of climbing up to regain his former position.

A general example of this is *erring* or wandering (3:10; 5:2), with its implication of being in the wrong place. Another form of sin is *ignorance* (3:10). It is to be observed that it is combined with the previously noticed "erring." "They are always wandering in their hearts [25] and they did not know my ways." If the ways are not known, wandering is the consequence. The same juxtaposition appears in 5:2, "the ignorant and erring." This is one group, not two (which would be "the ignorant and *the* erring"). The erring results from the ignorance. Moffatt's suggestion of hendiadys (one thing through two) is almost certainly correct. There is an ignorance which is culpable and it has culpable consequences. Hence the *agnoēmata* of 9:7, "the sins of ignorance" (Bruce), "the unconscious mistakes" (R. Bultmann, *TDNT* 1:115). Sin so affects the mind that it prevents the entry of knowledge or obliterates it if it has entered. Men who persist in sinning deliberately cannot plead ignorance (10:26).

Sin is also characterized as *weakness* (5:2–3; cf. 7:28). It is because of his weakness that the high priest has to offer sacrifice for his own sins. "Our weaknesses" (4:15), in contrast to the strength of him who was tempted yet without sin, must refer to our sins. Weakness implies that we are unable to withstand temptation.

It is sometimes felt that the strong cannot really sympathize with the weak. The point is that the strong endure much longer. For example, the weak succumb to torture after five minutes; the strong endure for five days. They know only too well what even the weak suffered. Our Lord never gave in—and understands the experience of those who do.

24. Cf. G. Zuntz, *The Text of the Epistles,* pp. 25–29.
25. Literally "heart." The singular is used distributively. "Something belonging to each person in a group of people is placed in the sing.: as . . . Lk 1:66" (Moulton-Turner, *Grammar,* 3:23). This reflects the "inner" meaning of "heart."

Sin *(hamartanō)* has been traditionally described as "missing the mark," as in the story of Adrastus. He aimed his javelin at the boar and *missed it,* but hit the son of Croesus (Herodotus I.43). Similarly sin is pictured as *coming too late (hystereō)* and so *to miss, to be excluded* (4:1; 12:15). If the "lateness" is blameworthy it may suggest the neglect of opportunities. The promise of entering remains open: do not fail to enter.

Failure in discharge of duty towards man is *unrighteousness* (8:12, "acts of unrighteousness"). Failure in duty towards God is *impiety.* Hebrews does not use this word *(asebeia)* but the thought is present when the author speaks of unconcernedly disregarding so great a salvation when more, not less, attention should be paid to it (2:1–3). It was spoken through the lips of the Lord and attested by the living God. If the disregard of such witness is not impiety, what can be? The two concepts are together illustrated in 12:16, "(See to it) that nobody is a *pornos* or *bebēlos* as Esau. . . ." (The reference of only the second adjective to Esau does not affect the illustration.) *Pornos* describes the person who engages in illicit sex. His activity is clearly unrighteousness (13:4). The *bebēlos,* "common worldling," is deaf and blind to spiritual realities, and "degrades religion" (JB). Strathmann renders the word by *gemeiner Weltmensch.*[26] Such a man is clearly guilty of impiety.

Sin may also be described in a more or less cultic sense. The previous discussion of God's holiness and his demand that men should be holy prepares for the definition of sin as *unholiness.* "Without holiness nobody will see the Lord" (12:14). It could be argued that the whole of the Epistle to the Hebrews is a statement of the unholiness of men and the final and perfect way of attaining to it in Christ. More about this will be said later. For the moment the fact of human unholiness must be noted. It is in direct contrast to the holiness of our High Priest (7:26, *hosios*). The concept here—or rather its opposite—overlaps that of "impiety."

Sin is regarded in addition as *uncleanness.* This is suggested by those passages which speak of purification (9:13–14, 22–23; 10:2). The religious and ceremonial and the moral; cultic violations and criminal offences—all were taken together in Judaism as sins against God because "the Old Testament is the unconditional Word of God . . . as a book which contains religious demands and as a valid code of civil law and penalties" (G. Stählin and W. Grundmann, *TDNT* 1:289.) This all-embracing conception of sin, in which uncleanness is largely ritual and cultic, is reflected in Hebrews. The author uses the cultic category but deepens it by contrasting the purification of the flesh with that of the conscience. This is the "supreme cleansing," accomplished by the death of Christ. (See F. Hauck, *TDNT* 3:426. Cf. Heb. 1:3.) "It gives access to holiness and enables man truly to live in the presence of God."

*Sin is defilement.* In the Old Testament this is a cultic term. Defilement, the opposite of holiness, incapacitates for fellowship with God (cf. 9:13).

---

26. Esau's act shows "dass er ein frivoler Weltmensch war, der sich um Gott nicht kümmert"—"that he was a frivolous worldling who does not trouble his head about God."

Once more the cultic category is deepened. It leaves behind the ceremonial and becomes moral and spiritual. Or perhaps it would be better to say that the ceremonial is used as an illustration of the moral and spiritual. For example, one man by example and precept can grievously affect his fellows and "defile" them (12:15). This means that by his influence, consciously or unconsciously exercised, the many are led to be "failures in faith" just as he is. He takes away from them what they have. They cease to believe. They not only do not try to approach God but they are not entitled to try (cf. 11:6). They have become incapacitated for fellowship with God. They are "defiled."

The natural married life does not in itself separate from God (13:4).

The man who tramples on the Son of God and deems the blood of the covenant common, profane, defiled, will receive the severest punishment (10:29). He has shown contempt for what is of no service to him (cf. Matt. 5:13). He has wantonly reversed the function of the blood. It is the blood of him who offered himself in sacrifice to God (9:14) for the putting away of sin (9:26) and who now appears before the face of God for us (9:24). It is the blood which cleanses the conscience and so qualifies men to approach the living God in worship (9:14). That blood he has regarded as ineffective and in itself disqualified from the presence of God. Such is his blasphemy: the sanctifying blood is itself contaminated with sin—defiled.

Our high priest was himself undefiled and separate from sinners. This does not mean that he was in quarantine from men. He was rather wholly other in character as he stood among men. Even in the midst of the world Jesus had nothing holding him back from fellowship with the Father (7:26).[27]

*Sin may also be called hardening.* We have already considered this (3:8, 13, 15; 4:7). It is enough at this point to say that it marks the final state of the man who resolutely sets his face against God and persists in his own way. Its essence is the disobedience of *utter unbelief* (3:12, 19; 4:2).

With sin in its many forms *God is not pleased.* This is particularly clear when we think of sin as unbelief, because "apart from, without, faith it is impossible to please him" (11:6). The absence of faith implies the absence of the divine pleasure. This is expressed in another way when reference is made to the "provocation" (3:8, 15–16). Moffatt regards the verb (*parapikrainō*) as a LXX neologism "to express 'rebellious' with a further sense of provoking or angering God." Although he is quoting Psalm 95 (94, LXX) the author of Hebrews may well have Deuteronomy 31:27 running in his mind in addition. The presence of both "hard" and "provoke" in the same verse is at least suggestive. In Deuteronomy 32:16 the verb (in the text of Codex Vaticanus) is parallel to *paroxunō.* The author of He-

---

27. The separateness from sinners is not to be explained solely by reference to the following phrase, "higher than the heavens." See Arndt-Gingrich under *chōrizō,* p. 898, and Herodotus I. 140, "Magians are very different from priests in Egypt especially"; I. 172, "laws very different from . . . "; IV. 11, "their opinions were different"; IV. 28, "this [Scythian] winter is different from all winters that come in other places."

brews was familiar with both of these chapters in Deuteronomy (Deut. 31:6, 8/Heb. 13:5; Deut. 32:43/Heb. 1:6).

Mention of the "temptation" (3:8–9) coheres with what has been said. The term suggests that men put God to the practical test by "seeing how far they can go with him." Will he really act in accordance with his revealed nature? Let us try him and see! Faithlessness and defiance are clearly combined. God is not pleased with such an attitude and such conduct. (See Exod. 17:2, 7, LXX; Ps. 77:17–19, 41, 56, LXX.)[28]

The author's use of the verb *eudokeō*, "take delight in," points in the same direction. In 10:6 (cf. v. 8) he quotes Psalm 39:7–9, LXX ("whole-offerings and sin-offerings thou didst not delight in"—NEB) but instead of reading the LXX, "Thou didst ask for" ("Thou didst seek" is read in Codex Sinaiticus and Codex Alexandrinus), he writes *eudokēsas*. In this he may have been influenced by Psalm 50:18, LXX. The ancient sacrifices of the old covenant have been replaced by the one sacrifice of Jesus (cf. 10:9–10). If, notwithstanding, any man tried to perpetuate the old sacrifices, he would be trampling on the Son of God and deeming the blood of the new covenant ineffective (10:29). For now that the new covenant has been inaugurated, God is not pleased with the temporary activity of the old one.

The same Greek verb is used in 10:38, "if he shrink back, my soul takes no pleasure in him." F. F. Bruce speaks of "the divine displeasure which will rest upon anyone who draws back."

God is not pleased with men, and he does not remain silent. *He blames men and he utters his blame.* The long quotation from Jeremiah 31 is introduced (8:7–8) with a striking use of cognate words and a sudden and unexpected change of expression. "If that first covenant had been without flaw [blameless, *amemptos*], no place would have been sought for a second. (But it was not flawless, though the defect was not in the covenant itself but in the people who were partners in it.) For[29] it is in blaming [*memphomenos*] them [not "it"] that he says. . . . " The Lord is speaking ("saith the Lord," v. 8), and "blaming them" he states his charge. "They did not abide by my covenant." God's covenant was not set up as a result of negotiations. It is unilateral rather than bilateral. Even so there is a curiously familiar ring about the words. If it is a serious charge to break the covenant of the United Nations, how much more serious is it to break the covenant of the living God? For *God is the One "with whom we have to do"* (4:13). We have to reckon with him. Christian leaders keep vigil over their flock, conscious that (*hōs*, subjective) they will render an account (13:17).

There is an adverbial phrase (*ta pros ton theon*, 2:17; 5:1) which possibly expresses the fact of human responsibility. The same phrase is translated

---

28. Cf. S. R. Driver's useful note on Deut. 6:16 in his commentary on *Deuteronomy* (ICC), p. 95.

29. The *gar* justifies, because it explains, the "understood" words given above in parentheses.

from Romans 15:17 by F. F. Bruce, "regarding those things for which I am responsible to God." [30] If men are responsible to God, they have to reckon with him.

## God Against Man

It is over forty years since C. H. Dodd first stated [31] that "such an archaic phrase [as the Wrath of God] suits a thoroughly archaic idea." Dodd's approach to this subject has by no means won universal acceptance and the debate still continues. We consider elsewhere (pp. 85–88) the evidence from the Epistle to the Romans and at present confine ourselves to Hebrews. The relevant passages are 3:10–11, 17–18; 4:3; 12:25. These show that for the author of Hebrews *God is a God of wrath.*

Two words are used, *prosochthizō* and *orgē,* both expressive of anger. It should be carefully observed, in this interpretation of the wrath of God, that three factors are involved: attitude, decision and action. At the time of the Provocation and the Temptation "your (fore)fathers" tried and tested God. *Therefore (dio)* he was angry. This inferential conjunction, as it has become, has been deliberately inserted by the author of Hebrews into the text of his quotation from the Septuagint (Ps. 94:7–11, LXX). The rendering of the JB, "that was why I was angry with . . . ," is more explicit than the bare "and so, I was indignant with . . ." of the NEB.

It is clear that *God took up an attitude* to human conduct: the people were erring and ignorant. *He made a decision:* he swore an oath that they should not enter the land. *God acted:* the people in question did not in fact enter the land. "Their bodies fell in the wilderness" (3:17).

Note the three logical stages. God was angry with those who sinned (3:17). This is attitude. He swore an oath to those who disobeyed (3:18). This is decision. They were not able to enter in because of unbelief (3:19). This marks the action of God. The author means that God prevented the people from entering. It would have been unthinkable to him to banish God from the scene. An oath, especially a divine oath, is an oath (cf 6:13–18; 7:21; 11:11, 19). What God had decided to do, he would do. He would not be unfaithful to his "negative promise"; he would not change his mind; and he would not be foiled by inability. For disobedient, unbelieving and sinful people there would be no escape (12:25; cf. 2:2–3; 10:29–31).[32]

The concept of wrath leads up to, and is summarized by, the statement that *God is a God of judgment.* "The Lord will judge his people" (10:30; cf. Deut. 32:36, LXX). "God will judge fornicators and adulterers" (13:4).

---

30. *An Expanded Paraphrase of the Epistles of Paul,* p. 235. See his note in his commentary on *Hebrews,* p. 52, and the authorities there cited.

31. C. H. Dodd, *The Epistle of Paul to the Romans* (Moffatt), pp. 20–21.

32. For somewhat different treatment see Anthony Tyrrell Hanson, *The Wrath of the Lamb,* pp. 132–33. But he makes a significant admission. ". . . the attitude of the writers of the NT to the OT was that of the orthodox Jews of their day, and hence if the OT recorded an event as having taken place because of the wrath of God they would accept it without question. The author of the Epistle to the Hebrews adopts the same attitude: see the discussion of Heb. 3:7–4:13" (p. 76).

*The judgment may be executed in history.* The people did not abide by the old covenant and God "disregarded" them (8:9). His action is vividly illustrated by the "dramatic contrast" (Moffatt) of the use of the same verb in 2:3. If men neglect so great a salvation, God neglects them.[33]

On the other hand *the judgment may be executed on the Day of Judgment.* It may throw its shadows backwards into time so that "you see the Day drawing near (10:25)." The eschatology is not realized but the Day is indeed coming. For those who are not swept along by the crowd or by uncontrolled passion but deliberately persist in sin, no sacrifice remains (10:26). It might be argued that the one sacrifice of Christ stands fast and that the offer of the gospel is still open. After all, a sabbath rest "remains" (4:9). This is true. The point, however, is that a sacrifice does not "remain" (*apoleipetai*) for the deliberate and persistent sinner. It remains indeed; but it does not remain for him. He has rejected it. There is for him nothing left but "a fearful expectation of judgment" (10:27).

We have seen that the wrath of God arises from a situation which he has apprehended (*"therefore I was angry,"* 3:10). It follows that *"God's judgment is logical.* This is confirmed by the reference to Noah (11:7). In Noah's response to the revelation he manifested the active obedience of faith, and through his faith he "judged adversely [gave sentence against—Liddell-Scott], condemned the world" (note *krinō* and *katakrinō*). The question arises about the sense in which Noah can be said to have judged.

The NEB renders the phrase "he put the whole world in the wrong." It is an attractive translation and understandable. But this kind of expression always reminds me of a footballer who unobtrusively moves up the field and so puts an opponent offside. (It used to be called "playing the one-back game" in soccer.) To begin with, the opponent was not offside; he was made so without his having done a thing. Now it was different with Noah and his contemporaries. They were in the wrong already.

It is nearer the mark to say that Noah showed up the world, the sinful humanity so characteristic of the Fourth Gospel. In contrast to that dark background, his faith shone forth. In contrast to that brilliant light, the world appeared *for what it was.* Noah did something: he built an ark. But he did not do anything to the world. And yet he adversely judged it.

This might have been Noah's unconscious attitude. But it is more likely that he discerned the situation. He believed that the flood was coming, and though deep inland he built something which would float. He looked upon the heedless world as destined to receive what was coming to it. He did not cause the flood but he saw that it would destroy the world. This shows that the adverse judgment or condemnation was purely mental. Hence according to the meaning of the word, God can judge now but carry out the condemnation later at the Day of Judgment. (Cf. Strathmann, p. 142. Cf. also Matt. 12:41-42; Luke 11:31-32).

---

33. Strathmann's translation (p. 115), "so dass auch ich mich nicht mehr um sie kümmerte" ("so that I likewise did not trouble my head about them anymore"), is more vigorous than Luther's "so habe ich ihrer auch nicht wollen achten" ("so likewise I did not wish to pay attention to them"). Its apparent lightness must not blind us to its severity.

*Judgment is the personal prerogative of God.* "To me (and to no other) does vengeance belong; I (and no other) will repay" (10:30; cf. Deut. 32:35). This is emphasized by the words of introduction: "we know the Speaker." (It is put like this in order to avoid the apparent dependent question of "we know who said.") This interpretation carries with it the interpretation of the previous verse. "Of how much severer punishment do you think he will be deemed worthy who trampled on the Son of God . . . ?" If we ask, "Be deemed worthy by whom?" there can be only one answer—by God, who is the Judge of all (12:23).

The idea that God "deems worthy" and that he thinks before he punishes may seem oversimple but it safeguards a truth. God's judgment is not mechanical. As he "thinks" he takes every individual factor into account. The agent of every transgression and every act of disobedience receives a *misthapodosia*—reward, retribution (2:2). Arndt-Gingrich note that the word is restricted to Hebrews and ecclesiastical literature, but that its constituent phrase, *apodidōmi ton misthon,* is quite common. This gives us something on which to work.

The word *misthos* means "pay," "wages." The employer does not "give" his workmen their wages. They are entitled to their pay because it is not calculated on a basis of favor but "as their due" (cf. Rom. 4:4; Arndt-Gingrich). The *misthos,* then, is what is due to a man. "What is due" is not given to a man; it is paid back (*apodidōmi*). This has a wider reference than that to mere wages. Consider, for example, the story of the two debtors in Matthew 18:23–35 with *apodidōmi* used seven times and *opheilō* (or a cognate) six. Or, perhaps even clearer still, consider the question of tribute to Caesar (Mark 12:14, 17). "Is it lawful to give [*didōmi*] tribute to Caesar or not?" "Give back [*apodidōmi*] to Caesar what is Caesar's. . . ." The verb used by Jesus, says Vincent Taylor, following an observation of H. B. Swete, "implies that the tribute is a debt." [34] Caesar supplied the amenities of the Roman state—government and administration, public order, roads and such like. In return the people must pay back what is due to him.

When, then, the transgressor receives the *misthapodosia,* he is receiving precisely what is his due (2:2). *God's judgment is deserved.* As a comment on this we can draw attention to the adjective *(endikos). God's judgment is just.* It is based on what is right. The NEB boldly translates "due retribution."

If God is all that we have seen him to be: if power is his and if he deals with individuals; then it follows that *God's judgment is inescapable* (2:3; 12:25). They did not escape; we shall not, if . . .

The careless and the heedless and above all the man who has rejected finally the gospel message make light of the prospect of judgment. This they do in their blindness, for there is nothing left to them except "a terrifying expectation of judgment and a blaze of fire intent on devouring the adversaries" (10:27). This awe-ful symbolism is intensified by the use of the word *zēlos,* the meaning of which comes close to the modern "en-

---

34. Vincent Taylor, *The Gospel according to St. Mark,* p. 479. Cf. C. E. B. Cranfield's similar title, p. 372.

thusiasm." The fire "appears like a living being" (Arndt-Gingrich) with one absorbing purpose. This "enthusiasm of fire" is no doubt figurative here, for the fire is personified. But it might well point to the literal, for "our God is a consuming fire" (12:29). "It is a terrifying experience to fall into the hands of the living God" (10:31).

T. R. Glover used to say that if Paul had been writing he would have said that it would be a terrifying experience to fall *out of* the hands of the living God. David would have agreed with him, for God is more merciful than man (2 Sam 24:14). But the two positions are not contradictory. It would be fearful for the believer to fall out of the hands of God (cf. 13:6; John 10:28–29). It will be fearful for the unbeliever to fall into his hands. For *God's judgment is terrifying.* Let us therefore worship God "with reverence and fear" (12:28). "Let us fear, lest . . ." (4:1).

Judgment comes to its climax in the concept of perdition. The defiant offender against the law of Moses was punished with physical death (10:28). The man who finally rejects the gospel will be deemed worthy of much more severe punishment (10:29). The previous reference to a terrifying expectation of judgment and to "the enthusiasm of fire" (10:27), in conjunction with the "severer punishment," prepares for the summary "perdition." "We are not the sort of men to withdraw—into destruction" (10:39).

The content of being lost (*apōleia*), when salvation was possible, is too terrible for further description. Strathmann (p. 138) contrasts the two sure prospects, eternal perdition and eternal salvation.[35]

## THE OTHER SIDE—GOD FOR MAN

This is a frightening picture: an all powerful and an all holy God, who will execute judgment upon men. But there is another side, equally authentic. We shall try to trace the evidence in the Epistle to the Hebrews. If at first it is thought that the space taken is small in proportion to what has been written already, the answer is found in the second half of this chapter. All of it in a sense is "the other side."

To begin with, reference is made to *"those who are going to inherit salvation"* (1:14). Perhaps judgment may be avoided. Perhaps even God the Judge has some wider purpose. It is for the sake of those who are to inherit salvation that angels or ministering spirits are sent forth. Who sent them forth? It can be only God himself. The present participle (*apostellomena*, "sent") is one of repeated action. If the angels are repeatedly sent forth for the sake of those who are intended to be heirs (not earners!) it suggests a consistent purpose of God.

In the symbolism of the tabernacle there is yet another ray of hope to be discerned. The Holy Spirit himself indicates that the way into the very

---

35. "Unsere Sache ist es nicht, schwachmütig zurückzuweichen—mit der sicheren Aussicht des ewigen Verderbens, sondern zu glauben—mit der ebenso sicheren Aussicht des ewigen Heiles." "Our business is not to fall back weakly—with the certain prospect of eternal perdition, but to believe—with the equally certain prospect of eternal salvation."

presence of God [36] has not yet been opened up (9:8). Not yet: *God has still held his hand* and has not swept away the whole human race in judgment. Perhaps a door for our escape remains open. It does indeed remain open. *God again appoints a day of invitation*, "today"; let us show swift zeal to enter in (4:6–7, 11).

For it seems that there is another prospect besides that of judgment. The law, which is God's law, foreshadows *coming blessings (ta mellonta agatha* 10:1). There is the thought of *the removal of sin* (10:4, 11) and the mysterious utterances about "canceling the first system in order to establish the second" (10:9). Is there any hope for us in the "second"?

According to the evidence there is hope. The impossible has become the possible. The God of judgment is also the *God who loves*. "Whom the Lord loves he educates" (12:6). The training may be strenuous and even painful but it is the training of one whom the Lord "receives favorably." This is in direct contrast to God's exclusion of the unholy.

## Mercy

For behind judgment lies mercy *(eleos)*, which is something which we may "get" (4:16). In other circumstances we might explore the meaning of this word by going back to the Hebrew which it translates, but such a proceeding is not open to us. "The writer [to the Hebrews] knew no Hebrew" (Moffatt, p. ix). We must banish all thought of Hebrew from our mind, except possibly to help elucidate the meaning of a difficult passage of the Septuagint, and try to find out what *eleos* meant to our author. We have available the whole usage of the LXX before us. It is better, however, to concentrate on the use of the word in chapters which he actually quotes or to which he alludes, or in chapters close to them. It is reasonable to suppose that he did not pick out special texts all the time in complete ignorance of everything else. His very habit of allusion rather points to the fact that he read his Bible generally. What is more natural than to think of his reading in the wider context of the text which he quotes or recalls?

We are indebted here to the index of Old Testament passages appearing in some form in the New Testament which is given at the end of the Nestle-Aland Greek Testament (25th edition). We hope to find out by this means something of what might have been in the mind of our author when he used the word *eleos* and we shall list the meanings or implications. We shall add questions and comments which might have arisen in the mind of a man who had been awakened by the thought of the power, the holiness and the judgment of God.

To begin with, *eleos* is found with God (Num. 11:15). (The next chapter was known to the author of Hebrews: Num. 12:7/Heb. 3:2, 5–6.) Will this temper his judgment?

Next, our author would understand that *eleos* implies that God acts, that he "does" something. In Genesis 24:12 (cf. vv. 14, 44), LXX, *poiēson eleos* may well be a literal, even a slavish, translation of the Hebrew, but the author was not to know that. For him *eleos* is something which God does. (The wider context was familiar territory: Gen. 22:16–17, LXX/Heb. 6:13–14;

---

36. *Ta hagia* for the inner shrine, as clearly in 9:25; see also 9:12; 10:19–20; 13:11.

11:12. Gen. 23:4, lxx/Heb. 11:9, 13. Gen. 25:33–34, lxx/Heb. 12:16.)

The divine activity is implied in Psalm 24:6–7, lxx, "Remember, O Lord, thy acts of compassion and thy acts of *eleos*[37] .... According to thy *eleos* remember thou me. ..." (The nearest "context" seems to be Ps. 21:23, lxx, quoted in Heb. 2:12, cf. 17.) The same implication is seen in Psalm 97:1–3, lxx, "the Lord did wonderful deeds . . . he remembered his *eleos*. ..." (Ps. 96:7, lxx is quoted in Heb. 1:6.)[38]

Perhaps the clearest example of divine activity is furnished by Psalm 32:18–19, lxx, "Behold, the eyes of the Lord (are) upon those who fear him, those who keep their hope upon his *eleos* to deliver their lives from death and supply them with food in famine." (Ps. 33:15, lxx echoes in Heb. 12:14.)

A man under deep conviction might well ask if God would act on his behalf instead of executing judgment upon him. Will he "do something" for me? He might derive some encouragement from the reflection that God's *eleos* extends in his actions to thousands (*eis chiliadas*). The same Greek expression is used in Exodus 20:6; Deuteronomy 5:10; Jeremiah 39:18 (all in lxx), and it is hard to imagine that the author of Hebrews had not come across it. In Exodus he has allusions to the wider context (Exod. 17:1–3, lxx/Heb. 3:16; Exod. 19:12–19, lxx/Heb. 12:18–20; and especially Exod. 24:6–8, lxx/Heb. 9:20; 10:29). In regard to the passages just mentioned in Deuteronomy and Jeremiah, Hebrews has striking quotations from the immediately preceding chapters (Deut. 4:24, lxx/Heb. 12:29, God . . . is a consuming fire; and Jer. 38:31–34, lxx/Heb. 8:8–12; 10:16–17, the great passage about the new covenant [Jer. 31:31–34, kjv]). Is the number "thousands" high enough to inspire a well-founded hope?

God's *eleos* is great. "Have *eleos* upon me [*eleson me*], O God, according to thy great *eleos*" (Ps. 50:3, lxx). The second part of the verse conveys the atmosphere, "and according to the multitude of thy acts of compassion." The previous psalm (Ps. 49:14, 23 lxx) is quoted in Hebrews 13:15, "sacrifice of praise to God."

Reference is made to the great *eleos* in Numbers 14:19, lxx, a chapter which is itself quoted in Hebrews 3:17. In Isaiah 54:7, lxx it is contrasted with the divine abandonment. "For a short period I abandoned you and with great *eleos* I will exercise *eleos* upon you" (*eleēsō se*). No more than seven verses away (Isa. 53:12) the author of Hebrews can see a text which he can use (Heb. 9:28) to describe the work of Christ, the Suffering Servant who "bore the sins of many." Hebrews 13:20 may contain an allusion to Isaiah 55:3.

Is the *eleos* of God great enough to deal with judgment? "All the ways of the Lord are *eleos*" (Ps. 24:10, lxx). (A nearby psalm [Ps. 21:23, lxx] is quoted in Heb. 2:12, cf. v. 17 almost perfectly.) And his *eleos* which he "does" is for ever (2 Sam. 22:51, lxx). Hebrews 2:13 may quote verse 3 of

---

37. Plural of abstract noun to indicate a plurality of concrete instances. See Blass-Debrunner-Funk, para. 142. When God remembers, he acts.

38. Note that the chapter and verse in the Psalms may not always tally between the lxx and the English version which are based on the Hebrew. They may be one number off.

this very chapter, though the words appear also in Isaiah 8:17, LXX. Hebrews certainly quotes the book (2 Sam. 7:14/Heb. 1:5). Psalm 135, LXX, rapturously praises God for what he has done in creation and redemptive history, and every verse contains the refrain, "because for ever is his *eleos.*" The previous psalm (Ps. 134:14, LXX) is accurately quoted in Hebrews 10:30.

We have just spoken of Isaiah 54:7, LXX. Verse 8 of the same chapter contains the expression "eternal *eleos*" and the Lord goes on to say in accordance with his oath that "the *eleos* from me to you will not fail" (vv. 9–10). (Cf. Ps. 99:5, LXX, near to Ps. 96:7, LXX [Heb. 1:6].) It will not fail because he is "God the faithful, who keeps covenant and *eleos* with those who love him" (Deut. 7:9, 12, LXX). (Deut. 9:3, 19, LXX nearby is quoted in Heb. 12:21, 29.) "My *eleos* I will not withdraw from him" (2 Sam. 7:15, LXX). This verse must have been known to the author of Hebrews, as he quotes the previous one accurately (Heb. 1:5). In the same vein are two further passages. "For ever will I keep for him my *eleos.* . . . My *eleos* I will certainly not scatter from him" (Ps. 88:29, 34, LXX). There is an allusion to Psalm 88:51–52 in Hebrews 11:26.

God's *eleos* is for thousands and it is great. The fact that it is "for ever" may lead the man under judgment to reflect that he may not be too late; and the fact that it is associated with the faithfulness of God may inspire the hope that God may not finally give him up. For God's *eleos* is no improvization; it is no flash in the pan. It not only lasts for ever; it is from eternity. "The *eleos* of the Lord is from eternity [*apo tou aiōnos*] and unto eternity" (*heōs tou aiōnos,* Ps. 102:17, LXX). The author of Hebrews seems to have been well acquainted with this particular part of the Psalter. He quotes the previous psalm at some length (Ps. 101:26–28, LXX/Heb. 1:10–12) and a whole verse of the one which follows (Ps. 103:4, LXX/Heb. 1:7).

In fact the earth is full of the *eleos* of the Lord (Ps. 32:5, LXX; Ps. 118:64, LXX). (For "surrounding" passages see Ps. 33:15, LXX/Heb. 12:14; Ps. 117:6, LXX/Heb. 13:6.) If God's *eleos* is ample enough, great enough and persistent enough, it would seem that it is now near enough. It would be small wonder if the man under judgment joined the psalmist in saying, "We thought, O God, of thy *eleos*" (Ps. 47:10, LXX).

For it is the object of his hope. "May thy *eleos,* O Lord, come [*genoito*] upon us, just as we set our hope upon thee" (Ps. 32:22, LXX). Such a hope expressed to God is a prayer, and the psalmist prays accordingly. "Extend thy *eleos* to those who know thee" (Ps. 35:11, LXX). (The author of Hebrews alludes to an intervening psalm, Ps. 33:15, LXX/Heb. 12:14.) Has the convicted man any chance? It would seem that he has, because it is God's *eleos* which suggests that he will answer the prayer. "Hear my voice, O Lord, according to thy *eleos*" (Ps. 118:149, LXX). The previous psalm is quoted by our author (Ps. 117:6, LXX/Heb. 13:6).

It all depends on God's will. "The Lord will command his *eleos* . . ." (Ps. 41:9, LXX). The author of Hebrews quotes at some length from a nearby psalm (Ps. 39:7–9, LXX/Heb. 10:5–10) and draws attention to the will of God in the quotation. The psalmist himself has not hidden God's *eleos* from the large congregation: he has told them of his experience. God's *eleos* constantly came to his aid (Ps. 39:11–12, LXX). There is a measure of support for associating the will of God with his *eleos* in Jeremiah 38:20, LXX, a text which is but a dozen verses away from the celebrated prophecy of the new covenant which Hebrews quotes (Jer. 38:31–34, LXX/Heb. 8:8–12; 10:16–17). "I exerted myself upon him [*espeusa ep' autōi*], I will certainly have *eleos* [*eleōn eleēsō auton*] upon him, says the Lord."

The man under judgment has even deeper grounds for hope. There is good reason to inspire an appeal to God. "Hear me, O Lord, because thy *eleos* is kind [*chrēston*]; according to the multitude of thy acts of compassion look upon me" (Ps. 68:17, LXX). (Ps. 68:10 may be recalled in Heb. 11:26.) "And thou, O Lord, O Lord, do *eleos* upon [*meta*] me for the sake of thy Name, because thy *eleos* is kind" (Ps. 108:21, LXX). The next psalm is frequently quoted in Hebrews (Ps. 109:1, 4, LXX).

The kindness is shown in the divine activity. "If I said, My foot (has been shaken, i.e.) has slipped, thy *eleos*, O Lord, helps me" (*boēthei moi*). It is a simple picture which is drawn: a man suddenly loses his balance and is about to fall. A divine hand is there to seize him and hold him up. It is a sign of the "helpfulness" of *eleos* (Ps. 93:18, LXX). Four verses of the very next psalm are quoted consecutively in Hebrews (Ps. 94:7–11, LXX/Heb. 3:7–11, 13, 15; 4:3–11, passim).

If the man under judgment feels that "help" is precisely what he needs, and begins to hope that it may come to him, his heart must surely leap when he learns that God's *eleos* is great in forgiving sin. "Forgive this people their sin according to Thy great *eleos*" (Num. 14:19, LXX). The writer to the Hebrews was familiar with this chapter (Num. 14:22–23, 29, LXX/Heb. 3:17–18). A step further is taken in Psalm 50:3, LXX, the chiasmic parallelism of which should be noted.

Have *eleos* upon me [*eleēson me*], O God, according to thy great

                                                           *eleos*

And according to the multitude of thy acts of compassion blot

                                     out my act of lawlessness.

"Great" and "multitude" both suggest a high degree of quantity, the former suggesting size and the latter plurality. We can see that *eleos* is synonymous with "compassion." But what does it do when it compassionates? It blots out lawlessness. The author of Hebrews might be unaware of Hebrew parallelism, but as an educated speaker and writer of Greek he could surely recognize chiasmus [39] and feel its effect.

"(Doing) *eleos* and compassion" are associated in Zechariah 7:9, LXX. (Zech. 6:11, LXX may be recalled in Heb. 10:21.) They are linked again in Psalm 24:6–8, LXX, "Remember thy acts of compassion, O Lord, and thy acts of *eleos*. . . . Remember not the sin of my youth and my ignorance; according to thy *eleos* remember thou me for the sake of thy kindness, O Lord. The Lord is kind and upright." (Ps. 21:23, LXX is quoted in Heb. 2:12, 17.) The psalmist prays that in compassion God will act on his behalf and in compassion will refrain from acting against his sin. The "kindness" is a sort of comment on the *eleos*.

---

39. A diagonal arrangement of terms, e.g., **A B**.
                                     **B A**

The climax of this study of *eleos* is reached in salvation. The psalmist prays, "Save me for the sake of thy *eleos*" (Ps. 6:5, LXX); "save me in [*en*, possibly instrumental] thy *eleos*" (Ps. 30:17, LXX); "help me, O Lord my God, save me according to thy *eleos*" (Ps. 108:26, LXX).[40] He virtually identifies *eleos* with salvation in Psalm 118:41, LXX, "Oh that thy *eleos*, O Lord, might come upon me, thy salvation [*to sōtērion*] according to thy Word." (The nearest psalm quoted by Hebrews is Ps. 117:6, LXX/Heb. 13:6.) The two concepts are again closely associated in Isaiah 56:1, LXX, "Thus [*tade*] saith the Lord . . . My salvation has drawn near to appear on the scene and my *eleos* to be revealed." (The nearest text is Isa. 55:3, LXX/Heb. 13:20.)

If any soul was awakened to the fearful prospect of the doom which awaits the man under judgment, if he sought desperately to find out if it would be possible for him to "get *eleos*" (Heb. 4:16) even from the Judge himself, and if he stumbled across the rich meanings and implications of the word which we have discovered, then his heart might leap with a new hope. Judgment threatens but *eleos* is available. "Let the earth bring forth *eleos*" (Isa. 45:8, LXX). (Hebrews alludes to this very chapter: Isa. 45:17, LXX/Heb. 5:9.) Whether a person lives on the rocky ground of New Brunswick or amid the Arctic snows of the far North, God has commanded the earth to bring forth a crop hitherto unknown. Everywhere and anywhere on earth there are to be the colorful flowers and the kindly fruits of *eleos*. There is plenty.

The initiative is not with man, even with desperate man. "Thy *eleos* will follow hard upon me, will pursue me, all the days of my life" (Ps. 22:6, LXX). (Ps. 21:23, LXX/Heb. 2:12, 17.) It might be that the convicted man started by trying to run away from judgment and then found that it was mercy which was in pursuit.[41] It is hot on his heels. But it comes closer still. This mercy overtakes, passes, wheels and returns: *eleos* "will encircle him whose hope is set upon the Lord" (Ps. 31:10, LXX). (Ps. 33:15, LXX/Heb. 12:14.) If we abandon the thought of the gathering of the armies of *eleos* (cf. Luke 21:20) in favor of those armies actually in position, we see the convicted man hemmed in.

Thus the earth is to bring forth mercy, even in unlikely places—everywhere. It is at the man's feet. It pursues him. It is therefore behind him. It is all around him. In whatever direction he looks he sees mercy. All round him, it fills the horizon.

This is the "other side." Judgment and mercy: which is to have the last word?

---

40. The nearest psalms from which Hebrews makes quotations or allusions are as follows: Ps. 2:7, LXX/Heb. 1:5; 5:5; Ps. 8:5–7, LXX/Heb. 2:6–9; Ps. 33:15, LXX/Heb. 12:14; Ps. 109:1, LXX/Heb. 1:3, 13; 8:1; 10:12-13; 12:2.

41. Cf. Francis Thompson's moving *Hound of Heaven:*

    I fled Him, down the nights and down the days;
      I fled Him, down the arches of the years;
    I fled Him, down the labyrinthine ways
      Of my own mind.

## Grace

There is one more term to be considered, *charis*, generally translated "grace." It appears in Hebrews 2:9, "by the grace of God" (*chariti theou*).[42] The death of Jesus was not an accident or a setback. It was "for every man" —by the grace of God—and every man's salvation depended on it (cf. Strathmann).

The writer to the Hebrews urges his readers to join him in an approach to "the throne of grace" (4:16) in order that we may "find grace." This is an Old Testament expression to which we shall return. "Grace" is a term which is taken with the utmost seriousness. Dire punishment is the fitting treatment for one who has insulted "the Spirit of grace" (10:29). A man should guard his conduct and see to it that he does not fail to reach, and so be excluded from, the grace of God (12:15). But what exactly is "grace"?

We must not begin either by assuming that the author of Hebrews knew all the technicalities associated with grace in the history of the church, or, on the other hand, by foisting on him any of the misunderstandings of the term which later arose,[43] or by reading into his Greek word the meaning of the Hebrew *hen* which it frequently translates in the LXX.

Our author did not know Hebrew and we should therefore search in the Greek literature which we know he read. We shall accordingly try to find passages in the LXX which afford some clue to the meaning of *charis*, and to assemble them in logical order.

We begin with the story of the encounter of Jacob with Esau. Jacob had no reason to expect a kindly welcome from his brother. He had taken from him both birthright and blessing (Gen. 27:36, LXX) and was in danger of a murderous attack (v. 41). He sent messengers to Esau to report "to my lord Esau, in order that thy servant may find grace in thy sight" (Gen. 32:6, LXX). Their return with the news of Esau's approach with four hundred men did not add to Jacob's peace of mind. When the two brothers did meet, Jacob prostrated himself seven times (Gen. 33:3, LXX). Similar obeisance was done by his handmaidens and their children, Leah and her children, and Rachel and Joseph (vv. 6–7). Jacob explained that all the accompanying "host" was for the purpose of finding grace with Esau, but his brother generously declined (vv. 8–9). Esau had already run to meet him, had enfolded him in an embrace, had kissed him and had fallen upon his neck in tears (v. 4). It is impossible to keep Luke 15:20 out of our mind.

Thus Jacob found grace. He "gained" it; he "secured" it. ("Find" is no

---

42. There is a textual difficulty here, to investigate which would take us too far afield. A variant reading, *chōris theou* ("apart from God") may be a marginal comment (cf. 1 Cor. 15:27) which crept into the text and was then altered to "by the grace of God." See R. V. G. Tasker's note in *The Greek New Testament* (the text translated in the NEB), p. 441. The evidence is fully set out in the Aland-Black-Metzger-Wikgren Greek text. Most of the Greek manuscripts support "by the grace of God." Strathmann (pp. 85–86) regards the reference to our Lord's cry of dereliction (Matt. 27:46) as out of context. But see G. Zuntz, *The Text of the Epistles*, p. 34; and J. K. Elliott, *The Expository Times* 83, No. 11 (August 1972):339 ff.

43. See T. F. Torrance, *The Doctrine of Grace in the Apostolic Fathers*, pp. 133–41. Contrast Michael Green, *Evangelism in the Early Church*, pp. 132–36.

more than a literal translation of a Hebrew idiom and should not be pressed. The author of Hebrews just took it from the LXX.) Some reflections may reveal to us something of what grace really is.

Jacob was the offender. By sheer trickery he had outsmarted his brother. He recognized Esau's superior position by the use of such terms as "lord" and "servant" and by his prostration before him—"upon the ground seven times." His fear is eloquent. By contrast Esau was the offended party. He had good reasons for complaint. He occupied a superior moral position. He was under no obligation to Jacob and was influenced by no gift. The acceptance of gifts came after the reconciliation (Gen. 33:10–11, LXX).

It would seem that grace is an attitude which is expressed by welcome and kindness. Its occurrence is contrary to reasonable expectation, contrary to the natural demands of the situation. It is quite spontaneous: it is not subject to persuasion, still less to bribery. It does not arise as a result of negotiation. It is undeserved. (For the "timely" help of Heb. 4:16, cf. John 4:52–53.)

The absence of reasonable expectation is illumined by the story of Joseph. He had been sold and brought down to Egypt (Gen. 37:28, LXX) and then resold to Potiphar (v. 36). The latter was thus his *kurios*, his slave-owner (Gen. 39:1 ff. LXX). In ordinary circumstances Joseph could expect nothing more than the usual hard life of the slave. But there was a point in his favor, though Joseph did not originate it. His master recognized that the Lord was with Joseph and was leading everything he did to success. It is small wonder that Joseph found grace in Potiphar's eyes, though it would have been very surprising in any other slave. Joseph's acceptability was not of his own doing. Thus grace is contrary to normal expectation and it cannot be attributed to any quality in its recipient.

These two factors are brought out even more clearly in a later incident. As a result of the unpleasant episode with Potiphar's wife, Joseph was thrown into prison (Gen. 39:20, LXX). He was now not only a slave but a criminal. Mr. Derek Kidner suggests in his perceptive and penetrating commentary (*Genesis*, p. 191) that death was the only penalty which could be reasonably expected and that the reprieve may be due to Joseph's reputation and Potiphar's uneasy misgiving. This is probably true. Even so, Joseph was still a slave, was in prison, and his good name was sullied by a serious charge. His prospects can hardly be described as brilliant. Yet the chief jailer looked upon him with favor and committed the prison to his care. The prisoners and their activities were in his hands. Joseph virtually ran the whole concern. The story is a study in the unexpected, and the favor which he received was not due to anything in Joseph. The Lord was with him (this is stated twice) and gave him grace in the sight of the chief jailer (Gen. 39:21–23, LXX).

This may now be considered in a theological setting. Just prior to the Flood, the Lord God saw that the misdeeds of men had multiplied and that without exception and without intermission men were purposing and planning evil. In wrath he determined on universal obliteration. "*But* [the *de* is surely adversative] Noah found grace in the sight of the Lord God" (Gen. 6:5–8, LXX). As this narrative is read in the LXX, the final verse comes as a complete surprise. Sin and punishment, universal wickedness and universal doom, it is all leading up to a shattering climax—which does not come. At any rate it does not come in the way which might have been expected. Instead, "Noah found grace. . . ."

The kindness of God consisted of the warning in advance and instructions on how to proceed. The initiative was with him and his revelation to Noah was spontaneous. He was not asked for anything and his word was not therefore in any sense a response to Noah. It was certainly not the result of negotiation.

Study of the eleventh and twelfth chapters of the Epistle to the Hebrews makes it almost certain that the author was acquainted with the Old Testament passages just considered in our search for the meaning of *grace*.

Thus the character of God leaves us with a problem. He is unutterably holy and he reacts to men's sin in wrath and judgment. He requires holiness in men if they are to approach him, and they lack holiness. His attitude to them is therefore: "Keep out." But he is also loving, compassionate and gracious and desires them to "come in." How can this dualism be resolved?

## God at Work For Us—The Work of Christ For Us

In seeking an answer to the problem we must first clear the ground. The solution will not be found in the realm of law. The author of Hebrews is insistent on the ineffectiveness of law. The Levitical priesthood, on which the law was based, failed in its purpose (7:11). The commandment was weak and unprofitable and the law fulfilled nothing of its purpose (7:18-19). During the existence of the first tabernacle the way into the Presence of God was closed; the offering of gifts and sacrifices could not bring the worshiper to that state of conscience which they were designed to do (9:8-9). The law foreshadowed the coming blessings indeed, but it could not provide the reality. The annual sacrifices which it prescribed in perpetuity could never bring those who were trying to approach God into his Presence (10:1, 8). They occasion an annual remembrance of sins, not their removal (vv. 3-4). The old system of sacerdotal drudgery to no purpose must give way to a new—by the will of God (10:9-11). The first covenant thus had its defects. Hence the new covenant will not be on the lines of the old (8:7-9). A new way is envisaged (10:20).

The answer to the problem raised by the character of God falls into two parts. They may be comprehensively described as (a) Christ's completed work for us; and (b) his continuing work in us. We now look for evidence in Hebrews which will enable us to trace out, step by step, what is involved in this finished work. We have called it Christ's work and such indeed it is. But it originates in God, and we must start with him.

To begin with, *God has a gospel and it is no afterthought.* In exhorting his readers to maintain their faith the author illustrates his theme by recalling the experience of the children of Israel in the wilderness. They had God's promise that they would enter into the land of Canaan, into his "rest," but they failed to enter because of their disobedience and unbelief. So too "we" should be on our guard. A promise has been left to us of entrance into God's rest, into the gospel Canaan. We should fear lest some one of our number be excluded from it. "For we have been evangelized just as they were" (4:2). "They" obviously were not told of the gospel as it is understood by the author, but they did receive good news (cf. Exod. 19:1-6; 23:20-33); "we" did not receive good news of a literal land which was opening to us but we did receive the good news of the gospel. The "spiritual Canaan" is still open even though "those who had earlier been evangelized" (4:6) did not take the opportunity to enter. In fact a "sabbath rest" remains for the people of God (v. 9). This is far removed from judgment and perdition.

The author of Hebrews does not use the noun "gospel" (*euangelion*) but he does use the cognate verb (4:2, 6). He clearly has a gospel and he does not regard it as God's sudden improvization. Even the Old Testament believers did not receive the fulfilled promise because, as we have seen (p. 19), God delayed his action until we could be included (11:40). God knew his own purposes, but he did not reveal his gospel until "our" time. Something has happened, and happened also to the readers. It occurred so long ago that by now they ought to be teachers of the subject instead of needing "someone" (any new Christian?) to instruct them in the ABCs, the elementary principles, of the oracles of God (5:12). The light of gospel truth had dawned (10:32) upon them; they had savored the heavenly gift; they had found the Word of God good to their taste, to say nothing of the powers of the coming age and sharing in the Holy Spirit (cf. 2:4; 6:4-5). All these blessings came to them because they had believed what they had been told and by faith had received what they had been offered. The Word of God was—and is—centered in Christ, but it was no innovation. It was the climax of the centuries. For the Word which was centered in Christ had been spoken earlier. It had been fragmentary and varied in the prophets; it was one, unbroken whole in the Person of Christ and in him it admitted of no variation, because he is the same yesterday, today and for ever (13:8; cf. 1:12).

God was not silent throughout the Old Testament period and then suddenly broke the silence in a comprehensive revelation (1:1-2). He had been speaking repeatedly and the author of Hebrews refers frequently to the oracles of God. In his proof of the superiority of the Son to the angels (1:5-13) he quotes what God said to, or in reference to, the Son. It could no doubt be argued that "we were not there" when God thus spoke and that his Word is not for us. But it is enshrined in the Old Testament, from which God still speaks. "The Word spoken through the medium of angels" (2:2) was valid and allowed no exceptions: penalties were involved for infringement. It was a weighty Word, uttered in past history. The Word is still spoken in the written record: "just as the Holy Spirit says" (3:7). "The Holy Spirit testifies to us; for after having said . . ." (10:15).

The author can even see Christ speaking in the Old Testament. He is not ashamed to call the sanctified his brethren, and he does so call them ("saying"). At this point (2:11-12) the author gives Christ's actual words: "I will declare thy Name to my brethren" (Ps. 21:23, lxx). Two further quotations (2:13) from the Old Testament follow, and Christ is still the

Speaker. A remarkable example is given in 10:5–9, with its quotation at some length from Psalm 39:7 ff., LXX. "When entering into the world he says, '. . . a body didst thou prepare for me. . . .' " It would not be a valid criticism to say that this is not the language of a newborn baby. That would demand the expression, "after he had come into the world." The present participle denotes the transition from heaven to earth, not the arrival, and could point as appropriately to last words in heaven as to first words on earth.[44] The main point, however, is that the author of Hebrews finds no difficulty in the thought of Christ speaking in the Old Testament.

The Father speaks to the Son and addresses him as such; and addresses him as a priest for ever, ranking with Melchizedek (5:5–6, 10; cf. Ps. 2:7, LXX: 109:4, LXX). He speaks to Abraham and gives his promise (6:13–14; 11:8–12) and puts him to the test (11:17–19). He gave a revelation to Moses when he was about to erect the tabernacle (8:5) and to the people at Sinai (12:25). (See note 16 in this chapter and Bruce's comments on 12:25.) He spoke the creative Word at the creation (11:3) and revealed his will to Noah (11:7).

All these divine utterances are recorded in Scripture and they still speak to us. Exhortation may be based on them. For example, when the people earlier did not enter in and the way is still open, "again he fixes a day, 'Today,' saying in David after so long a period. . . . Let us therefore show swift zeal to enter in . . ." (4:6–7, 11).

Thus God spoke through the centuries and the record still speaks. But all the broken pieces of divine revelation, all the varied styles and imagery, have been concentrated in the one comprehensive utterance: God spoke in a Son (1:1–2). We can thus take our earlier statement further. God has a gospel. As an expression of this, *God has a Son.*

This is no mere honorific title; and it implies more than the sonship of those who are brought by God to glory (2:10) and in the meantime receive the discipline from him which a loving father gives to his sons (12:5–11). The Son is superior even to the angels, in spite of their exalted position in the thought of the author's day (1:5–14). They are to worship him, for he is *the* Son. Like Moses he is faithful; but whereas Moses was a servant in the house, he is a Son over the house (3:2–6). For he is the Son of God (4:14; 6:6) for ever (7:28). It is because of this that the clause, "though he was a Son," achieves its force (5:8). The Melchizedek of Scripture appears in lonely prominence. He is related to no family and he has neither beginning of days nor end of life. As such he resembles the Son of God (7:3). As F. F. Bruce finely says (p. 138), "It is the eternal being of the Son of God that is here in view; not His human life." To trample on the Son of God is an enormity, for it casts contempt on both his Person and his work (10:29).

Bruce's use of the word *eternal* is apposite. Hebrews points to the eternity

---

44. I am not unaware of "myth" and "demythologization." But if we believe that Jesus is the eternal Son of God; if we believe him when he speaks of heaven as where God's will is done (Matt. 6:10); and if we infer from this that there are personalities in heaven who actually obey: then the language and the interpretation given above, even if symbolic, are not out of place.

of the Son, and in both directions, future and past. The Son is the Heir of all things (1:2). God says to him: "Thy throne, O God, is for ever and ever" (1:8), and it is not an unoccupied throne. ". . . Thou remainest . . . thy years will not fail" (1:11–12). We can never put the Nicene watchword of anathema into the future tense, *estai pote hote ouk estai* ("there will be a time when he will not exist").

Similarly, if we look backwards, there never was a time when the Son did not exist. It was through him that God made the worlds (1:2). It was he who laid the foundation of the earth, and the heavens are the products of his hands (1:10). The author can consider and reject the possibility that Christ suffered (9:26)—or would have had to suffer—time and time again from the foundation of the world, but the reason for his rejection should be carefully noticed. It is because the all-sufficiency and the *Einmaligkeit* (once-for-allness) of his sacrifice ruled out the repetition of his sufferings, not because of his nonexistence in the past. The preexistence of the Son is but a limited statement of the eternity of the Son. He not merely reflects the glory of God; he is that very glory shining forth. He is the stamp of God's real being (1:3).

### Christ Our Apostle

The Son of God came into the world (cf. 10:5). But he did not merely appear on the scene, nobody knows why. He did not come out of curiosity, like a tourist. He came because he was sent. To single out a descriptive word, he was "the Apostle" (3:1).

For a long time the field of inquiry concerning the meaning of this word has been influenced by the work of K. H. Rengstorf. He links "apostle" with the Jewish technical term *shaliach* (from the Hebrew *shalah*, to send), an accredited representative with power to act in the name of the authority which sent him, individual or corporate (like the congregation of a synagogue). His position is summed up in the rabbinic statement that a man's emissary is as the man himself.

The connection of the Jewish *shaliach* with the New Testament "apostle" is hard to prove conclusively. Examples of its use in postbiblical Hebrew texts seem to be too late (2nd cent.) to influence the New Testament development and usage. The office of *shaliach* is a Jewish legal institution, it lasts for a limited period of time and it is not related to missionary activity or prophetic utterance. The apostolate by contrast is spiritual and religious and it is held for life: the missionary commission is never withdrawn. The message of the *shaliach* may not carry the weight which it should; but the apostle's message itself proves his apostolic authority. In the New Testament the apostolate is not ecclesiastically instituted and it is not transferable. Schmithals goes so far as to say that apart from the fact of being sent, the *shaliach* and the apostle have nothing to do with each other.[45] C. K. Barrett is nothing like so drastic.

In view of the uncertainty, it seems wiser to follow the hint of D. Müller

45. K. H. Rengstorf, *TDNT* 1.398–447. But see *Begriffslex.* 1.31–38; C. K. Barrett, *Romans,* p. 16; and Stephen Neill, *The Interpretation of the New Testament 1861–1961,* p. 90. A fresh approach to the problem has been made by J. Andrew Kirk in his article "Apostleship since Rengstorf: Towards a Synthesis," pp. 249–64.

in the *Begriffslexikon* and pay more attention to the cognate verb, *apostellō*. Rengstorf would not dissent from this (*TDNT* 1:435–36). The author of Hebrews, who knew no Hebrew, should not be uncritically credited with a knowledge of the *shaliach*-theory of the apostolate; but he did know the LXX. In this Greek version of the Old Testament there are some very interesting instances of the use of the verb.

The question of Moses (Exod. 5:22, LXX), "Lord, . . . for what purpose [*hina ti*] hast thou sent me?" implies that the person sent is to carry out the purpose of the sender. This is first of all to speak. David's deed was evil in the sight of the Lord, who "sent Nathan the prophet to David, and he went in to him and said to him. . . . Thus saith the Lord the God of Israel . . ." (2 Sam. 12:1, 7, LXX). The divine voice said to Ezekiel "I am sending you[46] to the house of Israel . . . and you will say to them 'Thus saith the Lord . . .'" (Ezek. 2:3–4, LXX). Jeremiah said to the rulers and all the people "The Lord sent me to prophesy . . . all these words which you heard . . . in truth the Lord has sent me to you to speak in your ears all these words" (Jer. 33:12, 15, LXX. See also Jer. 19:14–15, LXX; 50:1, LXX).

The divine purpose, then, is that the sent man should speak. But he not only speaks; he is a means through which God himself speaks. This is apparent in Exodus 7:16, LXX, ". . . the Lord . . . has sent me to you saying . . ." Whom are we to regard as "saying"? The Hebrew (*lē'mōr*) implies Moses ("sent me to bid you," NEB; "has sent me to say" JB). But the Greek of the LXX is *legōn*, a nominative present participle agreeing with the subject, the Lord. The author of Hebrews knew nothing of Hebrew construct infinitives and he would take the Greek as he found it—as Greek. Now if we give due weight to the perfect tense, which expresses the abiding result of a past act, we should have to interpret the sentence thus: "The Lord has me here on a mission, (he, the Lord) saying. . . ." God is speaking through Moses.

This may seem over subtle, though I think that a Greek would understand it. The LXX translators may have used the nominative participle deliberately; elsewhere they can use the genitive. "Jacob heard the words of the sons of Laban, (the sons) saying . . ." (Gen. 31:1, LXX).

At any rate there is confirmation of this interpretation. "If you do not hear me . . . to hearken to the words of my servants the prophets, whom I send to you early in the morning and I sent (them) and you did not hearken to me . . . " (Jer. 33:4–5 LXX). "And I sent to you my servants the prophets early in the morning and I sent (I, *legōn*) saying . . . . And they did not hear me . . . (Jer. 51:4–5, LXX). The prophets are sent; and when they speak, the Lord speaks.

Thus the divine purpose is that the Sender may himself speak through the sent speakers.

But he also sends his servants to act. Thus in the case of Joseph, "God sent me before you with a view to life." The two years famine would continue for another five and Joseph would handle the situation. It is not his brothers who "have sent me here but God, and he appointed me . . . master

---

46. *exapostellō*. The double compound has "essentially the same meaning as *apostellein*. In the LXX it is fully interchangeable with, though not so common as, the latter, as the many variants show." Rengstorf, *TDNT* 1:406.

of all (Pharaoh's) house and ruler of the whole land of Egypt" (Gen. 45:5–8, LXX). God sent Joseph to do something.

The same is explicitly stated with regard to Moses. "By this you will know that the Lord sent me to do all these deeds, that (they are) not from me myself" (Num. 16:28–29, LXX). Moses did not plan them and do them; he did not invent them. He was sent to do them. This is expressed in a final tribute to Moses at the end of Deuteronomy. ". . . all the signs and wonders which the Lord sent him to do in the land of Egypt . . . " (Deut. 34:11–12, LXX).

Moses, sent as he was, was able to act because of the divine presence. "And now, come, I will send [*aposteilō* [47]] you to Pharaoh . . . and you will lead out my people . . . I will be with you and this will be the sign to you that I am sending you: when you have led out my people . . . I will bring you up from the oppression of the Egyptians . . . and they will hearken to your voice" (Exod. 3:10–18, cf. vv. 7–8, LXX). Whom are we to regard as acting? "The Lord sent Moses and Aaron and he led out [48] our fathers from Egypt and he settled them in this place" (1 Sam. 12:8, LXX).

Thus the prophet is sent; and when he acts, the Lord acts. The divine purpose is that the Sender may himself act through the actions of those whom he has sent.

Word and action are combined in the prophet Samuel. "And Samuel said to Saul, 'The Lord sent me to anoint you king over Israel, and now hear the voice of the Lord; thus said the Lord of Sabaoth . . .'" (1 Sam. 15:1–2, LXX). The same combination is to be observed in the servant-passage of Isaiah 61:1, LXX, "He has sent me to bring good news to the poor, to heal those who are shattered in heart." Speech and action are the function of the one who has been sent.

With Isaiah the prophet the actual sending was preceded by a call. "And I heard the voice of the Lord saying, 'Whom shall I send, and who will go to this people?' And I said, 'Behold, I am (here); send me.' And he said, 'Go and say to this people . . .'" (Isa. 6:8–9, LXX).

If, then, the use of the verb is a safe guide to the meaning of the noun, and if the author of Hebrews had sufficiently studied the LXX to observe the usage of the verb, then his concept of an *apostolos* might include the following points. An apostle is one who has received a divine call. On his response to the call he is sent by God to fulfill a certain divine purpose. He is to speak and he is to be a means through which God speaks. He is to act and he is to be a means through which God acts. His message is not his own invention and his action is not his own choice. Inasmuch as he says what God tells him to say and does what God tells him to do, he has authority for speech and action.

We must now gather up all this material and apply it to the Son of God.

---

47. Futuristic subjunctive: a 1st person singular hortatory, "let me send," would be as out of place with regard to God as a 1st person plural like "let us pray." See Moulton, *Grammar*, 1:185, 240.

48. Codex Vaticanus (B) reads "they led out." But "as the emphasis is laid upon Yahweh's activity all through, *exēgagen* may be right." H. P. Smith, *The Books of Samuel* (ICC), p. 87.

He who is sent is sent by God with a purpose. If the Son, like Moses, had asked the question, "For what purpose hast thou sent me?" the divine answer could have drawn on Hebrews 3:1 and said, "to be high priest." The single article (*ton*) unites the two nouns in one person. It is as if the author had written "the apostle-and-high-priest"; or "the apostolic high priest" or "the high priestly apostle." The duty of high priest will appear later. It is sufficient for the moment to observe that Jesus embodies the purpose of God.

The call of the Son does not appear so vividly as in, e.g., the call of Isaiah, but the concept is not alien. The author of Hebrews takes pains to point out that the high priest is not self-appointed but takes office because he is called by God. So it is also with Christ: he did not put himself into the glory of the high priesthood. He was installed by the One who addressed him as Son (5:4–5). The parallelism between the two verses suggests that when God said, "Thou art my Son . . . ," he called him.

The Son "learned obedience from what he suffered" (5:8). There must have been a first occasion on which he felt the pull towards suffering, the first summons to this obedience. It could be argued that, as God was calling his Son thus to obey, it constituted his call. This is not wrong, though it might be better to regard it as a renewal of a prior call. For such an experience is deeply rooted in history, and the man who wrote of the entrance of the Son into the world (10:5) would look further back. The One who was sent did not start his mission at some time during his earthly life, and his call must be prior to his mission. This takes us back into eternity.

There is something bordering on anthropomorphism in the thought of the eternal Son being "called" by God in a past eternity. And yet John can speak of the fact that God sent his Son into the world (John 3:17). The sending is no less anthropomorphic than the calling. The matter to be considered is not an imaginative reconstruction of a scene in heaven in which God "calls" and "sends" his Son—though a preacher might not disdain to attempt the task with care and with good taste—but what is the meaning implied by the calling and sending.

These two concepts—or pictures—are theological safeguards. To speak in very earthly terms: they ensure that we do not ascribe "private enterprise" to the Son of God. They prevent us from thinking that he saw a situation of need and like an alert businessman stepped in to meet the need and from a small beginning built up (not an industrial but) a spiritual empire. They close the door to all thought of the love of the Son rising up to counter the righteousness and holiness of God.

The fact that the Son was called and sent by God means that the initiative was with God. This is of the utmost importance. The God of righteousness and holiness who looks with displeasure on the deeds and lives of sinful men and would move on to judgment and destruction—he it is who of set purpose called and sent his Son to carry out his purpose.

With authority, then, the Son speaks and he says what God wills him to say (2:3); and when he speaks, God speaks (1:2). With authority he acts, and he does what God wills him to do (5:8). When he acts, God acts. Word and deed, and God and his Son, are exquisitely brought together in 12:24–

25, "the sprinkled blood (of Jesus) speaks better than the blood of Abel. See to it that you do not refuse him who speaks."

Our *apostolos* is no mere *shaliach*, yet in one point at least he resembles him. The sent one, "acting for his principal, committed him irrevocably." [49]

The uniqueness of our *apostolos* should not be unobserved. A whole succession of ministering spirits had been "sent" by God for the purpose of service, each one of which could have been termed an "apostle." But he who was sent to be high priest was not just "an apostle"; he was "the Apostle." They were merely angels; he was and is the Son (1:14).

The Son of God, then, was sent by God into the world (10:5) and men knew him as Jesus (2:9; 3:1). Our high priest is clearly designated by the author as "Jesus the Son of God" (4:14). The historical Figure (2:9–10), though humbled for a season (cf. 10:19), did not begin his life on earth. Yet his incarnation was real. Since his "children" (cf. John 21:5) share in the common humanity of blood and flesh, he also correspondingly partook (*meteschen*—ingressive aorist) of the same constituents when he entered the world. This makes his work possible, as we shall see. The purpose of his incarnation and by implication of his mission on which he was "sent," was by means of his death to put an end to the activities of the diabolic blackmailer who wields the threatening weapon of death. Thus he would deliver all those whose lives are spent in the slavery of the constant fear of death, of which they are constantly reminded by the blackmailer (cf. 2:14–15). The sharpness of his weapon is the subsequent judgment (9:27). It is the purpose of the incarnate Son through his death to make the devil's suggestions futile. Does he point to sinful acts as a means to avoid death? Death now need not be so avoided as it has not the power to terrorize. Does he urge the temporary enjoyment of sin (cf. 11:25) before the final judgment ends it all? His argument carries no conviction with those who look forward to glory (2:10).

The Sent One may also be described as the Destined One. In making allusion to Habakkuk 2:3, LXX, the author of Hebrews adds the definite article to the word "coming" in his text. This has the effect of altering "coming he will come," i.e., "he will surely come," into "the Coming One will come." "The Coming One" is a Messianic title, and a highly significant one. The Messiah is described not by the work which he will do but by the fact that it is certain that he will come to do it. The Messiah is thus "destined"—though not by fate or any other secular principle. God will send him (10:37).

The incarnate Son was sinless (7:26–27) but God did not spare him. He could have saved him from death, but did not (5:7). As we have just seen, the Son became incarnate to carry out a purpose by means of his death (2:14).

### Christ Our High Priest

The author interprets the work of Jesus by reference to the Day of Atonement of Leviticus 16. Into the outer tabernacle or holy place the priests

---

49. Richardson, *Introduction to the Theology of NT*, p. 324.

are constantly entering, in discharge of their ritual duties. But the inner tabernacle or holy of holies was separated from the outer one by a veil or curtain. No man could go beyond the veil; the holy of holies symbolized the very presence of God. But there was one exception. Once a year the high priest, and he alone, could enter, provided he entered "not without blood which he offers for himself and the sins of ignorance of the people" (9:6–7). It was this office which our author had in mind when he said that God appointed Jesus (3:2). God appointed him apostle and high priest. The former term lays emphasis on the commission and the authority and the latter draws attention to what the envoy had to do: he had to be high priest. The author seems to use priest and high priest interchangeably, but dominant in his thought is Jesus as high priest.

God appointed Christ as high priest (5:5–6), though not as a member of the Aaronic order. This would have been superfluous. There are Aaronic priests to offer sacrifice already! If he were on earth, he would not be a priest (8:3–4). As it is, he has a superior ministry (8:6). If the Aaronic order had been adequate, his higher order would not have been necessary (7:11). But his higher order was necessary and it was instituted even at the expense of changing the law (7:12). The tribe to which Jesus belonged was not priestly, but this is overruled by the change of law (7:13–14). The higher order is not based on the weakness and unprofitableness of the old law, which can safely be set aside as a failure (7:15–19a).

Jesus is high priest "according to the order of Melchizedek." This man appears in scripture (Gen. 14:17–20) as "priest of God Most High." His greatness is apparent to those who will consider it: he took tithes from Abraham and he blessed him (7:1–10). The greater blessed the inferior. By implication the descendants of Abraham, the levitical priesthood, must share his inferiority. From the short record of Melchizedek in Genesis the author of Hebrews draws the conclusion that he stands out alone, belonging to no family and knowing neither birth nor death, comparable to the Son of God. "He remains a priest in perpetuity." Sigmund Mowinckel's words (*He That Cometh*, p. 75) are helpful here: "When the Epistle to the Hebrews speaks of his having neither father nor mother, this is scarcely an invention of the author based on the fact that the Old Testament does not mention his family, but rather an ancient tradition which survived in Judaism and was really intended to express his close relation to the deity."

This is the climax of the comparison. When the author of Hebrews describes Christ as a priest "according to the order of Melchizedek" he means that the weaknesses of the old Aaronic order have been transcended and that he remains in office for ever. The older priesthood was a kind of procession through the years. The "wastage" caused by death required constant replacement and hence there was a "plurality" of priests. But "because he abides for ever he has an unchanging priesthood" (7:23–24; cf. 6:20). He is living (7:8, 16), qualified (7:28) and in office for ever.

It is of some importance to recognize this. We have all met "retired priests." They may even be invalids or incapacitated but they still belong to their order. They are alive—but not in office. Jesus is alive. His resurrection is not perhaps woven into the texture of the main argument but it is necessary. Jesus died, and however much we lay stress on his ascension and exaltation in Hebrews, to pass from the tomb to heaven directly would leave a hiatus. God raised him from the dead (13:20). He is alive but he is not only alive; he is in office as a priest for ever.

Two further characteristics must be mentioned before we pass on to consider what specifically our high priest actually did. He was sinless. He can sympathize with our weakness; He was tempted in every point as we are, "without sin" (4:15). Notice that it is not only the Man, Jesus, who was thus tempted without falling into sin. We have a high priest without sin. This is no mere negative virtue. He was holy and undefiled, with the innocence which never stoops to trickery or cunning, utterly different from men even as he stood among them (7:26; cf. p. 30). He had no need, as other priests did, to offer sacrifices for himself as well as for the people (7:27–28). He was without blemish (9:14). His sinlessness is reflected in 1:8–9.

He was sinless; and he was obedient. In a moving reference to Gethsemane, the author of Hebrews tells us that Jesus' prayer was heard "on account of his godly fear" (5:7), "the godly fear which leaves everything to the will of God" (Moffatt). "Son though he was, he learned obedience from what he suffered" (5:8). It might have been expected that the Son would be exempt but it is not so. Each pang of suffering was an item of raw material on which he could work: he could avoid it; he could complain about it; or he could accept it. Without the raw material there would have been no finished product. As each challenge came, as each choice was presented to him, to accept or to refuse, so at each stage he accepted the suffering which was involved, because God asked it of him. Thus as he went along, stage after stage, point by point, he constantly obeyed and constantly accepted the suffering. Thus in his experience he learned obedience from what he suffered. We may think of him in his earlier earthly days dedicating himself to his task. "I have come . . . to do thy will, O God" (10:7). When he suffered he did God's will, and this was obedience. He learned it by doing it.

Our sinless and obedient high priest was of the higher order of Melchizedek; his work, however, resembles that of the high priest on the Day of Atonement, though there are some striking dissimilarities. As high priest he offered sacrifice indeed, but unlike the Aaronic high priest he did not repeat the sacrifice. "He offered one sacrifice for sins" (10:12). "(He did not enter) in order time and time again to go on sacrificing . . ." (9:25). This is what is done every year by the high priest on the Day of Atonement. Our high priest did it once, once only, and once for all (9:26–28).

Again, unlike the Aaronic high priest, he did not have the necessity of first offering sacrifice for himself and then for the people. He was sinless, obedient, and by his obedience made perfect (5:8–9; 7:27–28). All men who were appointed to the high priesthood were beset with weakness: He was not and consequently needed no sacrifice for himself.

A third and vital difference is concerned with the nature of the offering. In other sacrifices animals were offered. He offered himself. "He offered himself to God, an offering without blemish" (9:13–14). (Cf. Num. 6:14;

19:2, LXX for the use of the term *amōmos* to denote the absence of defects in sacrificial animals.) The author can speak of "the offering of the body of Jesus Christ once for all" (10:10). This means that the passion of Jesus Christ was not merely a passion, a *pathos*, something which was done to him; it was his action. He sacrificed himself. The high priest is also the victim.

Our sinless and obedient high priest sacrificed himself once for all, and in so doing he bore the sins of many (9:28; cf. Isa. 53:12, LXX). This was the purpose of his sacrifice. "Having been offered once [*prosenechtheis*] with a view to bearing the sins of many. . . . " The verb used for "bearing" (*anapherō*) is a technical term of the sacrificial system and is used in Hebrews for "offering sacrifices," "offering himself" (7:27) and "offering the sacrifice of praise" (13:15). It can hardly mean "offering the sins of many" in 9:28. What then does it mean?

Liddell and Scott give the meaning of *anapherō* as "take upon one," citing Isaiah 53:12, LXX and Hebrews 9:28. Accordingly Moffatt can say (p. 134) that "He took upon Himself the consequences and responsibilities of our sins." Peake (p. 194) suggests as one possibility "to bear the punishment of sins." For Bruce (p. 223) the bearing of sin means its removal from others. Strathmann (p. 127) speaks of being sacrificed "*zur Beseitigung der Sünden vieler*"—"for the removal of the sins of many."

The removal of sins is the consequence of the bearing of sins. The verb in question is used in Numbers 14:33, LXX (a chapter quoted in 3:17–18), "they will bear your *porneia*," with the idea of "bearing the penalty." A passage frequently mentioned in this connection is 1 Peter 2:24 and E. G. Selwyn's treatment is relevant here. He quotes with approval Archbishop Leighton's "masterpiece of rich and flowing exegesis." This is what the Archbishop wrote: "The sins of all, in all ages before and after, who were to be saved, all their guiltiness met together on His back upon the Cross." Selwyn himself says that Christ bore our sins "in the sense that He took the blame for them; suffered the 'curse' of them (cf. Deut. 21:23, quoted in Gal. 3:13), which is separation from God; and endured their penal consequences." [50]

Some people today would regard this as very robust language. It may therefore be of some value to quote the view of yet another churchman. "I do not think that we need shrink from saying that Christ bore penal suffering for us and in our stead." [51]

It is remarkable that no mention is made of the "scapegoat" of the Day of Atonement. As Moffatt says (p. xxxvii), the author "never alludes to the famous scapegoat, which bore away the sins of the people into the desert" (cf. Bruce, p. 193). It may be that he is concentrating on the sanctuary and its ritual. Even so the coincidence is remarkable. Aaron will lay his hands on the head of the living goat and confess upon it all the sins of the people and he will lay them (the sins) upon the head of the living goat and will send it out . . . ; and the goat will take (*lēmpsetai*) upon itself

50. E. G. Selwyn, *The First Epistle of St. Peter*, pp. 97, 180.
51. J. K. Mozley, *The Doctrine of the Atonement*, pp. 216–17.

their iniquities (Lev. 16:21–22, lxx). The goat "symbolically carried away the sins of the Israelites." [52]

Christ bore our sins; the goat bore the sins of the Israelites. Christ died in order that he might bear them; but we cannot say that the goat died in order to bear the Israelites' sins. Is it naïve to think that the two goats were necessary to the original purpose, one to be a sacrifice and one to bear the sins?

The author of Hebrews may not have mentioned the scapegoat but there may be a conscious or unconscious allusion to it in 9:27–28. Note the comparison: it is appointed to men to die once; then comes judgment; correspondingly Christ was offered once; then comes—what? "The usual human death is the passage to judgment. This death means deliverance from judgment" (Strathmann, p. 127). His people eagerly await his second appearance for their salvation, just as the Israelites waited for the emergence of the high priest from the holy of holies. Now if Christ has borne their sins and if he comes for their salvation, why should it be necessary to add the phrase "without sin" (chōris hamartias)? This is generally interpreted as "not to deal with sin," because he has already dealt finally with it. This interpretation is probably correct; but I wonder if the author of Hebrews had a further picture in his mind? If the goat which had carried away the sins of the Israelites ever came back, it would still have been loaded with their sins. To avoid any possibility of misunderstanding our author rules out the question. The sacrifice has been offered; the sins have been borne; the Savior will come back to his waiting people with final salvation for them.

Our high priest sacrificed himself in order that he might bear our sins. In so doing "he endured a cross, despising shame" (12:2). The Greek aorist participle may be that of coincident action: all the time that he endured he was despising the shame. On the other hand it may well denote prior action: he faced what was coming, thought little of the shame and went on to endure. This would place some emphasis on the positive side of Gethsemane. "Thy will be done." But what is meant by "shame"?

In a useful study of verb and noun Rudolf Bultmann (TDNT 1:189–91) tells us that the substantive "is very seldom used for the 'feeling of shame.' It mostly denotes 'disgrace,' . . . Its primary reference is to the shame brought by the divine judgment." In 12:2 the "shame" is not brought on Jesus by himself. Who then are the "others" who bring the "disgrace"? Moffatt, in considering the text, speaks of the "stinging indignity" (not the torture) of the crucifixion, and refers to Galatians 3:13 "for an even darker view." Bruce similarly, and quite rightly, sees crucifixion as "the lowest depths of disgrace," "a punishment for sub-men." The "others" would then be all the human beings who were involved in the Lord's death. But if Bultmann is right, the disgrace is not untouched by judgment. This again raises a question. Would our Lord "despise" God's judgment? As P. T. Forsyth said in The Cruciality of the Cross (p. 213), he stood with men in the dock but was with God on the issue. He would not "despise" that with which he agreed.

---

52. R. K. Harrison, Introduction to the Old Testament, p. 602.

Moffatt's observation that this "is the only place in the NT where *kataphronein* is used in a good sense" may save the day. If the concept of judgment is relevant here, we are not to suppose that Jesus rejected it with contempt. What he did do was to look at it full in the face, with all its dark awesomeness, and decide: I will not let this deter me from the endurance to which God calls me. In reference to 12:2, Arndt-Gingrich can translate the verb by "care nothing for," "disregard," "be unafraid of."

According to the reasonable view of Moffatt, "the writer [of Hebrews] assumes, as in 5:7f, a close knowledge of the Passion story." On the strength of this we may see in our Lord's repudiation of the use of force an example of his "contempt" for the stinging indignity devised by men. "Do you think that I cannot appeal to my Father and he will at once put at my disposal more than twelve legions of angels?" (Matt. 26:53).

But what about his attitude to the divine judgment? He did not deserve it and without doubt shrank from it. But he did not seek to avoid it. He held fast to his obedience to God's call to endure the cross, including the judgment, and by contrast thought lightly of judgment as an alien thing (cf. Matt. 6:24). It should be particularly noted that this is a comparison and is relative. We do not mean that our Lord regarded divine judgment as a trifling matter. It constituted the horror of the cross. But to hold to his task in obedience meant more to him than to escape judgment.

Our high priest, then, sacrificed himself and bore our sins with all their disgrace. He has in so doing wrought redemption. This category is perhaps more congenial to St. Paul than to the author of Hebrews and it does not easily cohere with the dominant category of sacrifice. Its use, however, suggests that our author knew of this manner of interpreting the death of Christ and that though he did not develop it he was sympathetic to it.

In language reflecting the ritual of the Day of Atonement, the author says that "Christ, appearing on the scene as high priest . . . through his own blood entered once for all into the holy place, having found eternal redemption" (9:11-12). Dr. David Hill is of the opinion that such a background of ideas prevents us from regarding the term "redemption" (*lutrōsis*) in terms of ransoming, especially as the phrase "through His own blood" is unlikely to express price or cost.[53]

Now it is clear that we are here concerned with two quite separate categories. We have the thought of the cultus in general and the sacrificial system in particular; and the slavemarket and emancipation, or in more general terms, deliverance. It is open to question whether the interpretation of one category should be modified because as it stands it does not apply to the other. It is quite right to say: "Ransom is not a term which should be applied to the animal sacrifices; therefore it should be eliminated from the interpretation of redemption when redemption is mentioned in association with sacrifice"? Cannot the two terms be used side by side, each with its own meaning?

It would seem that each term could retain its full meaning, even if the two categories overlapped and the second one was introduced because of some common factor. This sort of thing is not uncommon in everyday life.

---

53. David Hill, *Greek Words and Hebrew Meanings*, p. 68.

During World War II there was a celebrated expression used by General Montgomery, "We shall hit them for six." (He was referring to the enemy.) It would be neither relevant nor in good taste for a pompous feminist to say, "*Mr.* Montgomery, you are not playing a game of cricket." The acidulated comment has missed the point. Two concepts are being used side by side, war and cricket. A crushing victory will drive the enemy from the field of battle. A mighty hit (which scores six runs) drives the ball right out of the field. The common element is the mighty hit; but war and cricket each retains its separate meaning.

In North America this kind of expression is frequent. In all sorts of situations we speak of "not getting to first base" (from baseball) or "not getting off the ground" (flying), when we mean that the enterprise could not even get started. A skilled surgeon, who faced failure from the very beginning because his patient was already in the advanced stages of terminal cancer, would not even get off the ground. Yet we should not say that the concept of flying would have to be amended. The two concepts, surgery and flying, remain intact but in this particular instance they have something in common—failure. If we turn to the happier side we could point to the brilliant surgeon who has saved his patient's life after an operation lasting six hours. A friend might congratulate him for scoring a home run. Surgery and baseball may not have much in common, but here they have. The difficult has been achieved. The surgeon (or "medical player") has reached the point he wished to reach.

These illustrations are not used in a spirit of levity. They reveal rather how men think and speak, and at the least afford an analogy to what the author of Hebrews has done. Leaving the concepts of sacrifice and redemption intact he has been so impressed by what he has said about the sacrifice that he exclaims: "a redemption indeed!" For there is a common element, "through his own blood." We do not have to bring in ideas of cost, price, cash or commerce when we dwell on what this meant for Jesus. During the War I heard a news broadcast which told of a Polish fighter pilot who in the heat of a dogfight in the sky gained the victory by ramming his German opponent. "It cost him his life." Must what he gave for victory be reduced to price? Through the blood of the sacrifice so freely given, our author is reminded of redemption. Others, like St. Paul, can work out the details.

At the risk of being charged with mixing metaphors we may put it like this. The author uses the word *redemption* as if it were a sort of Niagara Falls. It appears on a comparatively narrow front ("the common element"), but behind it are the vast resources of the lake above which pour over it to fill the lake below. This may or may not be scientific exegesis but it seems to me to be common sense.

As the eternal Son, Jesus had—and has—the right of access to God at all times. As the high priest and representative of men he entered the presence of God "through his own blood." The language, as we have seen, is here sacrificial, with an added comment drawn from another field, redemption. A few verses later (9:15) the author can speak of redemption without creating the apparent difficulty that *dia* plus genitive cannot express price or cost. "A death having taken place with a view to [*eis*]

the redemption of the transgressions involved in the first covenant. . . . "
If we must have some reference to cost, the genitive absolute is broad
enough to cover it.

We have translated by the traditional "redemption of the transgressions."
Strictly speaking we should not think of redeeming transgressions. We do
not scrub dirt; why try to scrub a dirt floor? It may be doubted if the word
*redemption* governs an objective genitive. The genitive is more likely to be
a general descriptive one ("transgressions-redemption") or a genitive of
separation ("redemption from transgressions"). There is an analogous expression in 1:3, "purification from sins."

The mention of transgressions implies a broken law. Law gives a precision
to God's requirements. In transgressing, men have not merely failed to be
their better selves or to manifest a vague goodness. In their deeds they
have given a flat contradiction to what God has asked of them.

The author regards this matter as one of great importance, perhaps
because of his pastoral experience. There could be a shallow presentation
of the Christian faith, on the lines of "come with Jesus back to God." But
what about past sins? Moffatt notes that our author, without actually saying
so, is close to the Pauline view that sin became guilt in view of ·the law.
Are sinners who come to God with Jesus still guilty? The author has given
the answer in terms of both sacrifice and redemption. Christ was offered
once for a specific purpose: to bear the sins of many. Their sins have been
taken from them and laid upon him. They are therefore not now guilty
(9:28). (Care should be taken to distinguish the question of fact from that
of the divine attitude. When believing men "come to God with Jesus" they
are not treated as guilty men by God. How could he still regard them as
guilty when their high priest has taken their responsibilities upon himself?
On the other hand it is true, and will be true for all eternity, and God
knows it to be true, that in actual fact these same men did sin. But their
sin does not now determine God's attitude to them.)

As with sacrifice, so it is with redemption. They have been redeemed
from their transgressions. They can "come to God with Jesus" without being
burdened by their sins. If there had been no redemption, their former
transgressions would have lived on in them as guilt. But they have been
redeemed, delivered from their guilt. When therefore they come to God,
they come as sinners whose sin has been dealt with, not merely forgotten
or ignored.

The redemption is thus retrospective. But it is also an eternal redemption
(9:12). It is therefore prospective as well. The death of Christ is not to be
repeated. Apart from his second and final appearing (9:28), he does not
come back from the heavenly sanctuary to renew his work annually, as if
he were an Aaronic high priest whose work at best lasted only for a year.
He has taken upon himself responsibility for sinful men—for ever. (This
absolute statement will have to be considered later in the light of Christ's
continuing work in us. See p. 43.) "The single sacrifice of Christ . . . [is]
availing for all sin, past as well as present and future" (Moffatt, p. 133).

It is therefore in accordance with this wideness of application of the
sacrifice that our author can say that Christ "has been manifested once with

a view to the setting aside *(eis athetēsin)* of sin through his sacrifice"
(9:26). The meaning of the "setting aside" must be examined with great
care. Any quick decision merely to say "removal" must face the fact that
the author sees sin as still an active, deceiving power (3:13) which impedes
or can impede Christian progress (12:1). It has not been removed from
the human scene.

The basic idea of the word is that of "putting aside from its position."
There are men who thus set the law aside (Isa. 24:16, lxx; Ezek. 22:26).
But they only set it aside from its position in their own minds. The law
itself still stands fast with its claims, its authority and its sanctions. They
remove it from the center of their attention as an authority to be obeyed.
We can say much the same if the object is not the law but God's Word
(Isa. 31:2, lxx) or his words (Jer. 15:16, lxx). Men can even set God aside
(Isa. 1:2, lxx) as object of trust and obedience, or a sacrifice to him as
an action which demands reverence. God can set aside the reasonings of
peoples and the counsels of rulers (Ps. 32:10, lxx) as no longer worthy of
attention: their schemes are brought to nought. The promises which emerge
through his lips he will not set aside from his own attention in forgetfulness
or unfaithfulness (Ps. 88:35, lxx), nor will he set aside the truth which he
swore to David but keep it "in position" in his mind (Ps. 131:11, lxx).

Having asserted that the word implies removal from its position in the
mind we must go on to say that such a mental "removal" is followed by
appropriate action. The man referred to in Hebrews 10:28, who sets aside
the law of Moses and is executed for it, not only dismisses the law from his
mind but disobeys it. It must be similar in 7:18. The old law failed. God
therefore appointed another, non-Aaronic, high priest with the rank of
Melchizedek, Jesus. As he did not come from a priestly tribe, the change
of priesthood involved a change of law to authorize it (5:4–6; 7:11–17).
God thus sets aside the earlier commandment from his mind; he no longer
views it as other than weak and unprofitable; and he proceeds in actual
fact to alter the law. The mental "setting aside" is followed by action
(7:18).

With this background we turn to consider the "setting aside of sin"
(9:26). First we must notice that Christ "has been manifested." The perfect
tense expresses the abiding result of a past act and can always be reinterpreted as a present. Here the meaning is not "he is now visible" but "the
effectiveness of his work continues." He was manifested by God, because
he is God's Apostle, sent by him to be high priest (3:1–2). In particular he
was sent with a view to the "setting aside" of sin. God's purpose was this
"setting aside," and it is brought about by Christ's sacrifice.

It would seem that there looms before the very eyes of God the mass
of human sin. It engages his attention. As long as it occupies that central
position it will determine what God will do with men—he will judge them.
But God has another purpose, linked with Christ's sacrifice. He was offered
to take the sins of the many upon himself—this was God's purpose. He has
taken the sins upon himself. He has thus fulfilled God's purpose. God
therefore no longer looks at the mass of human sin. It does not occupy the
center of his attention and it does not therefore determine what God will

do with men. What God now sees is human sin laid on Christ. God has "set aside" human sin from its dominant position in his mind. Through the sacrifice of Christ the hindrance to divine forgiveness has been removed. God is free to act and he does act in receiving sinners.

It must not be forgotten that the "setting aside" is done by God. He manifested his Son in order that he himself might do it, and it remains effective for all eternity. This reflects the retrospective and prospective aspects of redemption, and the fact that God no longer remembers sins (8:12; 10:17).

The "setting aside" reappears in slightly changed figures, notably in 10:4, 11, though by implication rather than explicitly. If the annual, "shadowy," sacrifices, argues the author, could have "perfected" those who try to draw near to God, they would have come to an end. The worshipers, once purified, would no longer have had any consciousness of sins. As it is, however, the annual sacrifices mean no more than an annual remembrance of sins. The blood of animals cannot remove *(aphairein)* sins (10:1–4).

According to the picture thus presented to us, the worshipers look back over a year of their lives; they review their moral past. As they do so they are conscious of the sins of the past year; they do what they have not been doing all the time: they remember them. But the actual sins were committed in the past. Do they not therefore belong to the past? Are they not over and done with, apart from their unpleasant memory? They are certainly "over": the theft, for example, took place six months ago; but they are not done with. Is it not therefore merely a question of finding out how to banish the sins from consciousness and how to avoid remembering them? If they only matter to this extent, then would some spiritual drug be enough to meet the case?

Our author would not be satisfied with such a remedy. It is not merely the problem of banishing the thoughts from the minds of the worshipers. The past sins live on, as we have earlier seen, as guilt. Drug the worshiper if you will; you have not solved the problem. For God still remembers the sins. It is not enough to put the worshiper into a state of moral unconsciousness. The sins have to be "removed" from God's sight and memory. This, it is implied, has been done through the sacrifice of Christ. The blood of animals cannot take sins away; the blood of Christ can.

Similarly the daily, sacrificial offices of the priest cannot take away *(perielein,* 10:11) sins. Christ's one offering for sins can take them away.

The verb *aphairein* is used in Exodus 34:7, 9, LXX, for taking away sins. It seems to emphasize the fact that through the sacrifice of Christ the sins of men have really gone. It is used in Genesis 40:19, LXX, for what looks like beheading, and certainly so in 1 Samuel 17:46, 51, LXX. By contrast *perielein* draws attention to the fact that apart from the sacrifice of Christ men have no escape from their sins. They are closely surrounded by them and cannot break out from their guilt. As the infant Jesus was wrapped in swaddling clothes (Luke 2:7) which wrapped him round as with a long bandage, so sinful men are in the encircling bands of their adult swaddling clothes— their guilt. God sees them in these swathing bands. Only the sacrifice of Christ can unwind them and take them off. This "circular removal" is illustrated by the act of Pharaoh (Gen. 41:42, LXX) in taking off his ring. The "setting aside" of sin removed it from the central position in the mind of God; its "removal" takes it from men as they are in the sight of God. The effect is the same: God is free to forgive men.

Two consecutive actions are recorded in 1:3. "Having made a purification of sins he sat down on the right hand of the Majesty on high." The purification is completed before the exaltation takes place. There can be no question here of men being purified at their conversion or baptism or anything like that. The work was finished before our Lord left the earth at the ascension.

"Purification of sins" does not mean that sins have been made "good" or black turned into white. The genitive is not objective but "has the force of an ablative of separation in Latin" (J. Héring, p. 6). Our Lord effected a purification *from* sins. Who then was purified? The world, says Héring. Without necessarily dissenting from this we can but observe that the empirical situation hardly tends to confirm it. The world is far from being purified in the ordinary sense of the term.

In purification two factors should be discerned. First of all, purification depends on the sacrifice of Christ. If he had not offered himself there would have been no purification (9:13–14, 22–23). Secondly the author speaks also of sprinkling and of the purification of the conscience (cf. 10:2). The blood must first be shed and then sprinkled. If in any sense sinful men must be sprinkled with the blood of Christ—as we shall have to consider later—before their conscience is purified, then at the death of Jesus nobody had yet been sprinkled and purified.

When the author speaks in 1:3 of our Lord's making a purification of sins immediately before the ascension, he has only the first factor in mind. The world has not been sprinkled and its conscience has not been purified. But in some manner purification applies to it. "Our Epistle uses the noun *athetēsis*-'abolition' (9:26) in an analogous sense," as Héring observes. In Aristotelian language the world has been purified potentially. God looks upon the world and what does he see? He sees a mass of sinful men. But this their uncleanness does not now determine his attitude to them or his treatment of them. Through the sacrifice of Christ it is as if they had been purified. They will be actually purified and their conscience made clean when they are sprinkled with the blood of Christ. In the meantime, God holds his hand of judgment. He is free to forgive.

The term, "purification from sins," is used in Exodus 30:10, LXX. "This combines a ritual and a moral concept of sin. . . . The more inward concept of sin [in the NT] gives it greater depth than in the OT" (F. Hauck, *TDNT* 3:429–30). Hauck sees the two factors but links the second with baptism. Even so he notes that "this *katharismos* still seems to refer essentially to a single act of purification." The single act is the cross. The rest, whether baptism or being sprinkled with the blood of Christ, is but the appropriation by men of "the benefits of His passion."

Our Lord also made propitiation for the sins of men. The linguistic evidence in Hebrews is not great (2:17; 8:12; 9:5). We rely, therefore, partly on Dr. David Hill's study and partly on the general thought of the Epistle to the Hebrews.

At the close of his perceptive investigation, Dr. Hill says that "in the case of the *hilaskesthai* words, the frequent references to divine wrath and its turning aside which are found in their contexts suggest that the idea of propitiation belongs to the terms." [54] This coheres with what we have found in Hebrews. God is not pleased; he blames men and he utters his blame, for they are responsible to him. Scripture speaks of his wrath, in which may be discerned attitude, decision and action. This merges into the judgment of God: it is deserved, just, inescapable and terrifying, and it leads to perdition or destruction (pp. 30–35). If we ask what is the reason which has "prevented" God from acting fully in accordance with what we have just said, there can be only one answer: the cross of Christ. There is a reason why God does not act in wrath. He did not merely forget or lose interest or cool down. The reason is our great high priest, whom God himself sent. God himself provides the sufficient reason. This is what is meant by propitiation.

Our high priest, then, obedient and sinless as he was, has offered himself in sacrifice. He bore our sins and he redeemed. It is through him that sins have been set aside and removed. He made purification and he propitiated. All this may be summed up in the statement that "he has perfected for ever" (10:14). To elucidate the meaning we must go back to the ninth chapter of Hebrews.

The author makes plain that the gifts and sacrifices of the old order cannot "perfect" (9:9; cf. 10:1). He at once contrasts this with the work of Christ, who has appeared on the scene as high priest. By implication, what he has done will "perfect." This is elaborated by the compact argument of 9:13–14, in which the old order is compared with the new. Attention is drawn to five points of the old sacrificial system and we list them as follows:

1. If the blood of goats and bulls and the ashes of a heifer
2. by sprinkling those who have been defiled
3. exercises hallowing power
4. with a view to the purity
5. of the flesh.

It is suggested that the other side of the contrast (9:14) implicitly though not explicitly follows this scheme.

1. The blood of Christ "means His life given up for the sake of men" (Moffatt). He offered himself to God as an unblemished sacrifice. He resembled sacrificial animals in being unblemished, but there the likeness ends. It was not a reluctant death and not the death of the irrational victim which does not know the purpose of the sacrifice: "in return for the joy which was set before him" (12:2). This is brought out in the phrase "through eternal spirit." There may be in the background an allusion to Isaiah 42:1, LXX, but it is doubtful if the main reference is to the Holy Spirit. A clue to the meaning may be found in the variant reading of Luke 9:55, appearing in the footnotes of critical Greek texts: "you do not

---

54. Hill, *Greek Words*, p. 47. Cf. Norman H. Young, "C. H. Dodd, 'Hilaskesthai' and his Critics" pp. 67–78, and Roger Nicole's reply in the *Evangelical Quarterly* 49, no. 3 (July-Sept. 1977): 173–77.

know of what spirit you are." This may well be "a copyist's addition. . . . It is a clarification of what already is implicit in the text." [55] The motive of James and John in inquiring whether they were to command fire to descend from heaven and consume the inhospitable Samaritans was punishment and destruction, perhaps tinged with personal ambition. (It reminds us of the message of the blood of Abel, 12:24.) The motive of Jesus by contrast was to spare and to save. It was the eternal motive of the eternal Son, and he went to the cross in full consciousness of it. We thus know "of what spirit he was." (It does not matter that the text in question is not authentic. We are here concerned with linguistic usage, even of anyone who happened to use the Greek language.)

"Spirit" here means "spiritual state," "state of mind," "disposition" (cf. Arndt-Gingrich, p. 681) as in 1 Corinthians 4:21; Galatians 6:1, with perhaps a side-glance at "will" as in "the spirit is eager but the flesh is weak" (Matt. 26:41; Mark 14:38). The preposition *dia* plus the genitive will express manner (as in Rom. 8:25; 2 Cor. 2:4; 6:8).[56] The reference to the will, with its exclusion of the flesh (see again Arndt-Gingrich, p. 681), would fit in admirably with the context. The high priest was not aiming in his sacrifice at the purification of the flesh, and his own disposition was not "fleshly."

2. Sprinkling is not specifically mentioned but it is an essential part of the author's scheme. The ultimate object of the "how much more the blood of Christ . . . " is worshipful service *(latreuein)* to the living God, a sacerdotal term implying the right of access to God. Another sacerdotal metaphor is used in 10:22, "let us draw near" *(proserchōmetha)*. But what entitles us to draw near? Our hearts have been sprinkled. Moffatt says that Christians may approach God "on the basis of Christ's sacrifice, since they have been sprinkled (and so purified . . . )." He sees an allusion to baptism in the next phrase and says that "once and for all, at baptism [cf. 1 Pet. 3:21] Christians have been thus purified from guilty stains by the efficacy of Christ's sacrifice." The actual cleansing, then, took place at baptism; but in a significant footnote Moffatt (p. 144) adds "more specifically, by the blood of sprinkling of 12:24" (cf. A. Oepke, *TDNT* 2:66 for "a real sprinkling.")

It is not our present purpose to embark on a discussion of baptism. But it should be observed that in the missionary environment of the New Testament church, it was converts who were baptized; and converts are people who have already come to God through Jesus Christ. The logical order would therefore be, first sprinkling, then baptism. The blood of the covenant is spiritually sprinkled (9:19–20), the blood of the new covenant in which a man was sanctified (10:29). The blood of animals was visible to the human eye; the blood of Jesus is applied invisibly as spiritual reality.[57]

---

55. E. Earle Ellis, *The Gospel of Luke*, p. 151.

56. Cf. Moulton-Turner, *Grammar*, 3:267.

57. F. Laubach, *Begriffslex.* 2:134. The New Testament use of the words for sprinkling "is controlled by the cultic use of the O.T." "Sprinkling with sacrificial blood brings the power of the sacrifice to bear on the objects sprinkled," C.-H. Hunzinger, *TDNT* 6:980–81.

3. The expression (9:14), "how much more the blood of Christ . . . will purify," is a telescoped one and corresponds to the fuller statement of the previous verse, "will exercise hallowing power with a view to purifying." The blood of Jesus certainly sanctifies, as we have just seen (10:29). Jesus suffered, in order that he might sanctify the people through his own blood (13:12). To be holy means to be qualified for entering into the presence of God. Without holiness no one will see the Lord (12:14). I am not sure that it is here just "a social virtue" (Héring, p. 114); too much is at stake. When telling his readers to "pursue" holiness, the author does not mean that they should earnestly seek the qualification to enter God's presence but that having entered it they should make it their goal to live "as in his sight."

4. It is because the blood of Christ exercises hallowing power that it purifies. It was done in principle at the cross, as we have seen (pp. 59–60 on 1:3).

5. But when it makes its impact on men it cleanses the conscience. The sins of men have been "set aside," and "removed." They have been borne by Christ. God is free to receive men and men may draw near to him. But men may still hold back; they know that they have sinned and that they are guilty. When they are "sprinkled" with the blood of Christ their sense of guilt is taken away. This does not mean that they merely forget that they are sinners. They realize that their sins have been laid on Christ and that he has taken them away: the sinner is clean in God's sight and he draws near to serve the living God.

Thus "by one offering he has perfected for ever" (10:14). We reserve discussion of the object, "those who are sanctified," until later. "To perfect" does not here mean anything like "to bring to moral and spiritual perfection or maturity." It means "to bring to the appropriate end or goal." The goal is a right relationship to God.

It would seem that there are two stages in thus bringing men to their goal. It must never be forgotten that our Lord became "the Author of eternal salvation to all who obey him" (5:9). There are those who do not obey him—persecutors, adulterers and false teachers for example (13:3–4, 9). Yet the one offering stands fast. In its lonely eminence it may be regarded as abstract, formal and potential in its relation to men. (It is far from abstract in its relation to God.) Until they "obey him," the blood of Christ does not purify their consciences and they do not draw near to serve the living God. But when they do obey him, the abstract becomes the concrete, the formal becomes the material, and the potential the actual. For then by the one offering of himself he has brought them to the goal in view—into the very presence of God.

For our high priest has himself entered once and for all into the heavenly sanctuary (9:12). This is the genuine tabernacle, the "original," pitched by God and not by man, of which the Mosaic tabernacle is but a shadowy copy (8:1–2, 5). Once a year the earthly high priest went through the veil into the holy of holies which symbolized the very presence of God. Jesus has passed through the veil into the heavenly holy of holies, there to remain—for us (6:20). As the eternal Son he has this right in himself always; as our high priest he entered in virtue of his own blood which had been shed in sacrifice. It was not into an earthly sanctuary that Christ entered, materially constructed to correspond to the genuine pattern. He entered—we expect the author to say "within the veil" or "the real holy of holies," but this time he says—heaven itself. This must mean just where God is, on the lines of the Lord's Prayer: "Our Father, Who art in heaven." His purpose is, "now [i.e. after the sacrifice of the cross] to appear before the Face of God for us" (9:24). Again come the significant words, "for us."

There he represents his people. Who they are will be discovered later. But this is not the end of the story. Jesus entered for us as a Forerunner (6:20). Does this mean that somehow a way into the presence of God has now been opened up (9:8; see p. 35)? It does indeed. Jesus has inaugurated (cf. 9:18) for us a new and living way of entrance through the veil (10:20). Entrance into the holy of holies is "in the authority of" (*en* instrumental) the blood of Jesus (v. 19). It is in virtue of his sacrifice. But the author means even more. The "living way" is Jesus himself, Jesus our crucified high priest. There may here be an unemphasized contrast between the living way and the dead animals of levitical sacrifice or the hard floor trodden by the high priest once a year through the veil.

Access to God is now a possibility. It is new in that it is through Jesus. It is not direct but is mediated. This is the blessing of the new covenant: "I will be their God . . . and they all will know me" (8:10–11). Hence Jesus is the Mediator of a better covenant (8:6; 9:15; 12:24). Men come to God "through him" (7:25). Worship, or the sacrifice of praise to God, is to be offered through him (13:15). God works in his people through Jesus Christ and whatever in them is acceptable to him is through him (13:21). The Mediator of creation is also the Mediator of salvation (1:2). He is the Guarantee that the promises of the better covenant will be fulfilled (7:22; 8:6). For he is Lord (7:14).

## God at Work in Us—the Work of Christ in Us

If there had been some unseen but all-seeing witness of the death and resurrection and ascension of our Lord, and if it had been given to him to have understanding of the things of God, then he might have made a comment on these events which we have tried to expound. All this, he might have said, has been done. In other words, the stage is set. Christ has done his work for us. He has died and has appeared before the face of God for us. The stage is set. The evangelistic drama can now begin. For until men are told the good news of all that Jesus has done for them they are still in their sins.

This brings us to the second part of our study (see p. 43). We now have to consider how the author of Hebrews sees men taking hold of the blessings of the gospel; to consider, in fact, Christ's continuing work not only for men but in them.

We notice, to begin with, that our high priest is able to save. This should put us on our guard against the tendency in some quarters to say that nothing remains to be done. Our Lord has done his work indeed. But his work in itself did not automatically save all the world. "He is able to save . . . " (7:25). There are certain necessary steps which have already been referred to as the evangelistic drama and as Christ's continuing work in us.

The author urges his readers to remember their leaders, "who spoke to you the Word of God" (13:7). Men have to be told what God has done for them in Christ.

But it is one thing to tell men and another to be told. They "must pay attention to what has been heard" (2:1). If they do this they "receive the knowledge of the truth" (10:26). The expression probably includes faith in Jesus Christ[58] but an ingredient of this is knowledge of the facts of the case—which they have been told.[59] The truth must not only be known, in the sense that they have been informed of it, but it must be obeyed (cf. 5:9). The first step of obedience is repentance. "Repentance from dead works" is part of the "foundation" (6:1, 6). A complete break with sin must be made—and maintained (12:1). The second step, logically but not necessarily chronologically, is faith in God (6:1). Repentance and faith may begin at the same moment. Faith in God is faith in the One who spoke in a Son (1:2) and commissioned him to be our high priest (3:1).

According to our author, faith is absolutely vital. Even the Word can fail to profit if faith is absent. It can be heard, but this is not enough. It must be met with faith or it accomplishes nothing (4:2). It must be mingled with faith in the hearers; or it must be mingled with the hearers by faith. (Cf. Blass-Debrunner-Funk, para. 202, "many variants," "but the sense is plain enough," Bruce, p. 70.) The preaching of the Word was attested by God and believing men received the Holy Spirit (2:3–4 and p. 19).

So vital is faith that the author can regard it as distinctive of Christians. "We are . . . a people of faith" (10:39). The outcome of the way of life of Christian leaders should provide food for thought: "imitate their faith" (13:7). "Let us draw near (the object of the whole enterprise!) with full assurance of faith" (10:22), for faith is "man's genuine answer to the realities of divine revelation" (Moffatt, p. 144). In fact without faith it is impossible to please God; for he who approaches God must believe that he exists and proves to be the Rewarder to those who seek him (11:6). This is not so theoretical and sterile as it might seem. For one thing, the man is already approaching God. He is not going through the farce of drawing near to a nonentity. In his heart is the conviction that God is responsive. This touches on the work of the high priest. Apart from his sacrifice, the way in has not been opened and God would not be responsive.

Faith, as we see illustrated in the eleventh chapter, is total commitment to God, before whom Jesus appears for us. And we have him as our exemplar. He has run the full course of faith and has completely actualized

---

58. See Bruce's note, p. 259.
59. Cf. Strathmann, p. 135, "Er weiss, was Christus und sein Werk bedeuten"; "He knows what Christ and his work signify."

it. In him it was no mere pious hope or religious talk. He committed himself utterly to his Father, both in Gethsemane and on the cross. In the concrete historical situation of the active contradiction of sinners he set up something for us to see: faith in God as actual, real, true and sustaining.

All that we have said is in the realm of what we often call "personal religion." I do not know if there could be an impersonal religion worth the name, but the expression is used to describe the sincere dealings of an individual with God. For example, he does not go to church to be sung to, prayed over and (as he thinks) to be bespattered with words, the whole proceeding having no effect on him at all. Personal religion means that a man obeys the Lord and enters his private room and prays to his Father in secret. When he goes to church he "participates" in the worship. He may or may not sing the hymns, but he follows their words with sympathy. When the lesson is read he pays attention, and when the sermon is preached he listens for the message: for he is eager to receive God's Word. In Christ he has encountered God and he walks with him.

This implies no rejection of the corporate. But a Christian community made up of individuals who did not each believe the gospel would not be Christian and would be worthless. The author of Hebrews starts with the preaching of the Word to the individual. This accords with the promise of the new covenant. God's laws will be in men's understanding and written on their hearts. Each and all will know the Lord (8:10–11; 10:16). It is because the new covenant is individual and intimate that it can be universal.

The use of the word "confession" (homologia) by our author has some significance here. "Let us hold fast to our confession" (4:14) is sometimes taken in the sense of holding fast to "our religion." Jesus is the Apostle and High Priest of our religion (3:1). Through him we are to offer worship to God, that is, "the fruit of lips confessing to his Name" (13:13). The last text shows us that we must not translate homologia by "religion" without further comment. Our religion, in fact, has been described by its characteristic activity. It is not the secret thought of individuals. Christians confess Jesus Christ; in him they have hope for the future (10:23).

They have not always had the hope; they have not always confessed Christ. There was a time when they did not confess him. They did not believe in him. They did not even know about him. It is plain that there is such a thing as a Christian beginning, the start of the individual Christian life. The readers could each look back to the time when they heard the Word (2:3) for the first time, repented of their sins, put their faith in Christ and confessed him.

The beginning of the Christian life is reflected in other expressions. They were once enlightened (6:4): "once for all men enter Christianity" (Moffatt, p. 78). The expression is often referred to baptism,[60] but this is an over-

---

60. E.g. G. R. Beasley-Murray, *Baptism in the New Testament*, p. 221; A. George and D. Mollat in a Roman Catholic symposium, *Baptism in the New Testament*, pp. 20, 82–83; R. Schnackenburg, *Baptism in the Thought of St. Paul*, p. 81, "with Paul the expression has no firm relation to baptism. It is different in Heb. 6:4 and 10:32. . . . "

simplification. In the New Testament church men were baptized because they had been enlightened. The term *enlightenment*, noun and verb, was used for baptism in the middle of the second century ("zuerst nachweisbar bei Justin," "first of all demonstrable in Justin"—Strathmann, p. 104) but I am not convinced that it was used *simpliciter* in the New Testament in the same way.

They had tasted the heavenly gift. They had experienced its full flavor—the stress is on form, not matter. They knew what God had given, for they had felt it in their lives.[61] They had become partakers of the Holy Spirit—and of Christ (3:14). They had savored how good the Word of God is even as their high priest had savored how bitter the taste of death was (2:9). The coming age had wrought proleptically within them (cf. 2:4) already. At a tense moment of decision they had fled—to take refuge (6:18). There may be here a faint allusion to the cities of refuge of the Old Testament (Deut. 4:42; 19:5, LXX).

All these diverse expressions speak of the time—and the experience—when heathen and unbelieving men put their faith in God through Christ; or when Jews received the full light of the messianic message and turned to Jesus. When they thus first believed, something happened. It did not occur apart from their believing but it is to be distinguished from it.

## Sanctification

The author of Hebrews encourages his readers to do that which each one could and should do. We have confidence for entrance into the sanctuary, he says, into the very presence of God, as we are so authorized by the blood of Jesus: let us draw near (10:19–22). This is to exercise the high priestly privilege.[62] But how does such privilege work for "us"? What was objectively wrought through the deed of Jesus is subjectively applied to the readers. (Cf. Strathmann, p. 133.) Their experience is analogous to that of the Old Testament priests, who were consecrated through the sprinkling of blood and washing with water (Lev. 8:6, 30; 16:4). The sprinkling of blood "was because [the priest's] way to the inner altar had to be ritually cleansed." [63] "When the readers became Christians," says Strathmann most significantly, "they came under the operation of the blood of Christ. Through its sprinkling they were inwardly liberated from an evil conscience. . . . "

This seems to me to be a sound insight. The readers are urged to join the author in drawing near with sincerity of heart (NEB; without any hesitation or doubt—Moffatt) and certainty of faith. This is a mark of spiritual experience. And their hearts, they themselves in their inner life (cf. 3:8, 13), have been sprinkled from an evil conscience—not a bodily uncleanness. The whole has been reflected in the submission to bodily baptism in water.

When they first put their faith in Christ, then they were sprinkled with

---

61. Cf. I. Howard Marshall, *Kept by the Power of God*, p. 137.
62. Cf. Otto Michel, pp. 273, 276; and Ronald Williamson, "*The Background of the Epistle to the Hebrews*," pp. 232–37.
63. Norman Snaith, *Expository Times* 82, No. 1 (Oct. 1970):24.

the blood of Christ. This is a concomitant of believing, for "you have drawn near . . . to the blood of sprinkling" (12:22–24).

This rounds off the discussion which had to be begun earlier (p. 62). It should be observed that the reference to "heart" and probably that to sprinkling as well must imply individual, personal response to the gospel. It might happen that ten or twenty or even a hundred men might thus respond in faith at the same time. Even so each man would have to believe for himself. He might conceivably be influenced by what his neighbors were doing, but if the "heart" is any guide to our thought, if it really means the man's own inner life, then he in his heart must himself believe. And when he believes, then he is sprinkled with the blood of Christ.

The pattern is emerging. Christ shed his blood for sinners and thus did his work. The sacrifice was offered to God and sins have been set aside from his sight; but the benefits are received by men when they believe. Then they are sprinkled with the blood already shed; their hearts sprinkled from an evil conscience. The washing in the water of baptism is an outward and visible sign which points to the inner cleansing of conscience. Heart and body together point to the unity of the human personality. Note the two perfect participles (10:22). The cleansing is complete and lasting. Guilt is gone.

The process may be analyzed in more detail. The sprinkling exercises a sanctifying power with a view to cleansing (9:13–14). If a man is sanctified or made holy, he is qualified for God's presence. The unclean conscience, i.e. the conscience with guilt, is made clean by the fact that the sprinkled man knows that his high priest has taken responsibility for him. He can thus offer sacerdotal service to the living God: he can draw near to him. All this—being sprinkled, sanctified and cleansed—takes place when a man first believes, and it is in virtue of the shed blood of Jesus.

Our author can therefore regard the sanctifying of the believer through the blood of Jesus as His characteristic activity. He suffered in order that he might sanctify the people through his own (sprinkled) blood (13:12). He came to do God's will and in the sphere of that will we have been sanctified (perfect: therefore we are now holy) through the offering of the body of Jesus Christ once for all (10:10). The blood has been sprinkled upon us. Hence the author can address his readers as "holy brethren" (3:1; cf. 13:24). If a man with faith received the knowledge of the truth, he was thereupon (note the aorist) sanctified by the blood of the covenant (10:26, 29).

"He who sanctifies and they who are sanctified are all of one origin (—God)" (2:11). The tenses of the participles are often ignored: "timeless designations" (A. B. Davidson): "devoid of reference to time" (Moffatt). I can understand this as a principle of grammar but doubt its applicability here. Surely the present tenses denote repetition, not repetition by "resanctifying" anyone, but the repetition which takes place as men one after another put their faith in Christ—and are sprinkled with his blood. Thus the text means: "He who keeps on sanctifying one man after another and they who are sanctified one after another. . . . " The means is Christ's sprinkled blood. This is brought out beautifully in the tense arrangements of 10:14, "by one offering he has brought to the goal for ever those who one after another are sanctified." If men hear the gospel and repent and believe, they are sprinkled with the blood of Jesus. By this means they are sanctified, ready for God's presence. It was not their own doing. If Jesus had not died for them there would be no blood with which to be sprinkled. As it is, he has died and by his one offering he has brought them to the goal of the whole operation—into the presence of God. Moffatt (p. 32) quotes Numbers 16:5, LXX, "where the holy are those whom God brought to Himself."

It would seem that the thought of the sprinkling of the blood of Jesus when a man first believes fills what would otherwise be a lacuna in the author's thought. Jesus suffered to sanctify the people through his blood. If by the fact of dying he *ipso facto* sanctified them there and then, then they are already holy and nothing more needs to be done. They do not need to be told of the gospel and they do not need to believe in Christ. They are already holy! This cannot be right and it does not fit the author's scheme anyway. Christ has done his work once for all *for* men; in his mercy he continues to work *in* them. The benefits of his work have to be received.

A judicious comment by A. S. Peake on 10:14 seems to favor our interpretation. Christ has only to wait for the subjugation of his enemies, since "His single offering has this never-ending efficacy, that those whom it sanctifies are made by it for ever complete."

We meet with a change of expression when we learn that through the sacrifice of Jesus comes forgiveness. Pretty well everything is purified (as the result of sprinkling: cf. Moffatt, p. 130) by means of blood, and apart from the shedding of blood forgiveness does not take place (9:22).[64] Forgiveness is described by Arndt-Gingrich (p. 124) as cancellation of guilt. If this took place at the cross (as opposed to "in virtue of the cross"), it is the same as the "setting aside" or the "removal" of sin. But it seems to occur when a man believes in Jesus, for the word appears again in a context of experience (10:18).

The author has already spoken about the permanent "perfection" which our high priest has wrought by his one offering in those who one after another are sanctified (10:14). He goes on to speak about the new covenant and what is sometimes called the religion of the heart. God will no longer remember the sins and the lawlessnesses of men. He will no longer call them to account. Their sins will no longer determine his attitude towards them. For these men have been forgiven, in virtue of the one offering of their high priest. There is no further need of any other offering.

The forgiveness is not universal. It is in virtue of the cross, but it did not "happen" on the cross. The forgiveness of sins, made possible by the cross, is actually given to those who have been sanctified—to those who believe in Jesus. For the author continues with references to sincerity of heart and certainty of faith, and being sprinkled in heart from an evil

---

64. Dr. Frances M. Young speaks of "the indispensability [of the blood] under God's law for purification" and observes "a stress on the seriousness of God's wrath, especially in Romans and Hebrews." See her article "Sacrifice" in *The Expository Times* 86, No. 10 (July 1975):305–9, especially p. 305 and n. 31.

conscience. He considers the case of those who deliberately sin after receiving the knowledge of the truth. The consistent atmosphere of the passage ( 10:15–22, 26) is "the heart," the inner life of men. The forgiveness of sins, then, depends on Jesus and his sacrifice: without the cross forgiveness would not be possible. But it is received when men believe in Jesus. Without the cross there could not be forgiveness. Without faith there will not be.

We now proceed a step further in the simple summary statement that Jesus "invites us in." He already appears before the face of God for us (9:24). He has inaugurated a new and living way for us through the veil (10:20). As we run the race set before us we are to look away unto him (12:2). He is the pioneer of faith as of salvation (2:10). He has blazed the trail into the very presence of God. Can men follow him thither? Hope, as well as a race, is set before them and it is anchored within the veil (no dragging anchor, this!). It cannot slip: it is constituted by what our high priest has done for us in the eternal order. Jesus is already there, beckoning men to follow him, for he entered "for us" and as a forerunner. He would not be the first—and only—member of a procession, a leader without a following, a pioneer who did his work in vain. The very word "forerunner" holds out hope (6:19–20).

And it is no vain hope. The law "perfected" nothing, but the introduction of a better hope does: through it we actually draw near to God. Jesus is the ground of the hope, for he is the Guarantee of the better covenant (7:19, 22). Shall we say, let us draw near in the certainty of faith, knowing that when we come to God through him, he has the rich treasures of his presence for us (10:22; 7:25; 11:6)? It seems hardly necessary, because we have drawn near . . . to God the Judge of all (even to the Judge, safely through Christ) . . . and to Jesus the Mediator of the new covenant (12:22–24).

If it be true that Jesus Christ is the same yesterday and today and for ever (13:8), then what we have said about his "inviting us in" and beckoning us is no more than saying what he said in the days of his flesh. "Come unto me" (Matt. 11:28). He who comes finds his rest—in God.

And when he comes to God, what then? It may be that he is solemnized by the august presence, encouraged by the company, and even entranced by the scenery (12:22–24). He knows that he is entitled to be there, because he is authorized by the blood of Jesus who has inaugurated a new and living way through the veil (10:19–20) for him to use. In addition to all this he finds that Jesus has mediated the adoption. He is not just another member of the human race who has come home to God from afar. He is one of many sons whom God has been leading to glory (2:10). Jesus, who sanctifies all those who put their trust in him, and those who are sanctified when they put their trust in him, are all derived from a common origin—the living God. Hence Jesus the Son is not ashamed to call them his brethren (2:11–12). But they are hardly this by nature. Jesus had to be made like them in everything, in order that he might become a compassionate and faithful high priest in matters for which they are responsible to God (2:17). They are therefore sons, and it is through the work of their high priest.

This thought is taken up when the author dwells on the strenuous side of the Christian life. The exhortation in scripture speaks to his readers as sons. Whom the Lord loves he trains, and scourges every son whom he receives—and he does receive those who come to him through Christ (7:25). "God is dealing with you as sons," he says. Paternal discipline is universal. If you, my readers, are complete strangers to it, then you are not sons at all. God's purpose in the exercise of discipline is to profit his sons; to bring them to share his own holiness—a purpose as sublime as that in giving Jesus as their high priest to sanctify them (12:4–10).

This again is an "inside" view. The author is not speaking of men in general but of those who have received the gospel. Through Christ they find themselves sons of God.

Explicit reference ought to be made to what has all along been implicit. Our high priest gives a lasting possession to those who put their trust in him. He himself is high priest for ever (5:6; 6:20; 7:3; 7:17, 21, 24). He is qualified as high priest for ever (7:28). As high priest he offered himself once for all (7:27; 9:26), to bear the sins of many (9:28). When this work had been done he sat down on the right hand of God (10:12), never to leave it until he comes finally ("the second time") for those who eagerly await him (9:28). By his one offering he has for ever qualified the sanctified for God's presence (10:14).

The point which the author wishes to make is that the blessing of the gospel, the removal of sin and guilt and the welcome which God gives to the returning sinner who puts his trust in Christ, is not given on a temporary basis. At this particular stage the question of apostasy is not relevant. God does not forgive sins—for a period. He does not welcome sinners into his presence—for a limited time. All sins have been "set aside," and when a man puts his trust in Jesus all his sins are forgiven. That is to say, he is not given merely a temporary respite.

This is reflected in the language of the epistle in its various figures. The readers had joyfully put up with the plunder of their possessions because they knew that they had a better and a lasting possession (10:34). Christians, like the patriarchs, may have on earth only the temporary residence of tents, but they expect the city with foundations, whose architect and builder is God. He has indeed already prepared it (11:9–10, 14–16; cf. 13:14). We receive an unshakable kingdom and what is unshaken lasts (12:26–28). God will never leave and never abandon his people: there is no fear of it, no question of it, no possibility of it (13:5).

The permanence of the possession depends on the permanence of the high priest. All who come to God through him, whether for the first time in conversion or all their lives in the relationship which he has established through himself between them and God, come through One who is living always. And he intercedes with God for them. He entered the holy of holies of heaven itself to appear before the face of God for them. As long as he lives(!) he continues thus to appear for them. He is their Representative before God himself. And if God looks upon their sins, he sees them as sins which have been borne by their high priest. There is a Voice on the throne of heaven itself to speak with convincing eloquence for them. And God will for ever listen to the Son whom he sent as high priest (3:1; 7:25; 9:24, 28).

## Salvation

All these blessings are comprehensively summed up in the word *salvation*, which is the very opposite of judgment and perdition. So great a salvation was the subject of the Lord's utterances in the days of his flesh, was confirmed by his hearers and was attested by God (2:3-4). It is man's only hope. If it is disregarded there is nothing else and there is no escape from judgment and perdition. It is dependent on Christ and on him alone. He alone is "qualified" to give it (5:9). It does not come to men automatically or mechanically. It is given to those who obey him. This does not so concentrate on Christ that it omits God. It is God who sent his Son and appointed him and addressed him as high priest (5:10).

The mighty attestation of God (2:4) suggests that salvation is received by believing men here and now. They do not have to await the day of judgment. "Things connected with salvation" (note that salvation is the opposite of "curse" and "burning") reveal the difference which it has made in the readers' lives: their work and the love which they had demonstrated towards his Name. They had loved and served God and they had ministered to his "holy ones," to those sanctified by their faith in Christ. This they were still doing. The text (6:9-10) must not be so interpreted—or so secularized—as to teach that service to one's fellows is the only way of loving God. It is a way but it is not the only way. The fruit of salvation is later described in greater detail (10:32-34).

Salvation is given and received in principle when a man believes in Jesus. Like certain forms of inheritance, it falls to a man, but he does not yet have the "handling" of his salvation in its entirety. It will be given in its fullness when Christ appears a second time (9:28). In the meanwhile he is able to save to the uttermost those who draw near to God through him: to the last syllable of recorded time—and beyond; to the inmost reaches of character; and to the depths of despair (7:25). Salvation is a present possession and a future denouement and it is all due to him who is our high priest who suffered for us.

## Holiness

A further feature of Christ's continuing work consists of the fact that he begins a discipline in believing men, the purpose of which is to train them in holiness. He is their Sanctifier (2:11) and in consequence they can be addressed as "holy brothers" (3:1). Through his sprinkled blood (13:12) He sanctifies those who put their trust in him and thus "qualifies" them for their approach to God. They are thus already holy. The life of discipleship has begun.

They are addressed as sons and God deals with them as sons. Because they are his sons, he trains, educates, disciplines and sometimes chastises them. This is the universal custom in the life of the Roman world. In the exercise of the authoritative *patria potestas* (power of the father), fathers disciplined their sons in accordance with their more or less arbitrary power until the sons were adult. This might conceivably serve the interests—or whims—of the father rather than the welfare of the son. But God disciplines his sons for their profit, their advantage: his purpose is that they may share his holiness. The process at times may be painful but it yields fruit to those "who have profited by the education," who have been trained by it. Their relationship to God is peaceful (12:4–11).

In all the changes and chances of this human life there is a divine providence which uses the varied experiences of God's sons for their discipline. Its purpose cannot be to make them holy in the sense of being qualified to draw near to God. They are that already. Through the discipline, faithfully accepted even if painful, they grow in holiness of character. They become more and more "set apart for God," to love him and serve him and do his will.

This distinction between holiness as a qualification for the approach to God and holiness as a state of character achieved in believing men by God's discipline of them is sometimes expressed on the popular level in vivid terms. The first is called a "ticket of admission" into the divine presence. The second is likened to a medical certificate which states exactly the present health of the subject. The two should never be confused. Holiness is given by Christ to believers, and through him they may draw near to God. This is their only "ticket of admission." Holiness of character is produced through the divine discipline, but however holy a man becomes in this sense it never "qualifies" him for the divine presence. For he has grown in holiness because he has been in the divine presence all the time of his "education."

In holiness of character there are differences of degree. One man may be more holy than another (though he ought not to know it; this is for God alone) or he himself may become holier. But there are no differences of degree in the holiness which Christ gives to a man who puts his faith in him. A man is either holy or he is not. He is either entitled to draw near to God or he is not. The man who was not far from the kingdom of God may have been very near but he was still outside. The man who is on the brink of faith may be on the very verge of being sanctified through the blood of Jesus; but until he puts his faith in him he is still unholy. But when he does trust him, in true repentance and faith, he is given a holiness which throws open the door into God's presence. In the discipline of the Christian life with all its variety of experience he becomes progressively more holy in character, more and more at home in the presence and fellowship of his holy Father.

Not all discipline is "chastisement," symbolized by the scourge (12:6). There is a divine pastoral care. "The Lord is my Helper" (13:6) even when enemies threaten. The quotation from Psalm 117:6, LXX, may be construed in two different ways according to the punctuation adopted. The question may be dependent or direct. But the meaning is plain. God is the Helper of his people.

It must be God in Christ who thus helps, for Jesus is Lord (7:14). The throne of grace (4:16) is the place where Christ represents his people and it is the source of timely help. He is ever the same (13:8), and the grace mentioned in the following verse cannot be unrelated to him. What would be more natural than for this to be reflected back to the Lord (13:6) who is our Helper?

The "help" which is part of the discipline may take the form of strengthening. "It is good for the heart to be strengthened by grace. . . . "

God works in his people through Jesus Christ (13:20–21), completing in them what is incomplete, and "mending" them for their obedient service to his will.

God's discipline thus educates and trains his people, sometimes giving them a lesson in the painful experiences of their life, sometimes helping, strengthening and "mending." It is all for their profit, that holiness of character may grow in them. It could not even start if they had not been made holy at the outset through the blood of Jesus.

The discipline ought not to raise questions in the minds of believing men. Christ has brought certainty to his people in their dealings with God. In him we have boldness for entrance into the presence of God (10:19). The blood of Jesus ensures that God will not turn us away. As we have been given such boldness, then, let us "use" it. "Let us draw near with boldness to the throne of grace" (4:16). It is not for some specially endowed men, for the select few, for the aristocrats of the spiritual life. It is for "us." We have it, logically; we ought to "use" it, practically; and "we," every individual member of the believing community, ought to keep it (3:6). "Do not throw away your boldness" (10:35)!

An interesting coincidence leads us on to a further consideration. We have noticed that "the Lord is my Helper" (13:6). The Greek word for "helper" *(boēthos)* is used for the "helpmeet" given to Adam (Gen. 2:18, 20, LXX). Thus a husband has two helpers, God and his wife. No contradiction is involved. The wife may "help" just by being the wife; or she may be regarded as a means—not the only means—through which God helps. This is a useful fact to remember, for it will provide an analogy.

The author of Hebrews tells his readers that Jesus founded the household of God, "whose household we are" (3:3, 6). The individual believing Christian who has been sanctified by the blood of Christ is thus not isolated from those who have traveled the same way as he has done. Each and all are members of God's household. The "benefits and responsibilities" of church membership (for the author is speaking of the church without using the name) are not formally listed, but they may be discerned (10:33–34; 12:15–16; 13:1–3, 7, 15–19), including "meeting" (10:25). From this evidence we can see that it is in the fellowship of the family of God that the individual members give and receive help and encouragement. The Lord is my Helper—and so are my brethren in the family (cf. 2:11–12). The analogy holds. Just as a husband can say that the Lord is his Helper and that his wife is his helper, so a Christian man can say that the Lord is his Helper and that his fellow Christians are his helpers. In other words, part of Christ's continuing work is to set those who have come to him in a context of likeminded men, each of whom owes his very life to Christ and is under obligation to him. Christ has set his people in a situation "for the mutual society, help and comfort that the one ought to have the other."

The man who comes to Christ out of heathenism or Judaism thus finds himself in a new fellowship. The Jew may have belonged to the "people" of God (e.g. 5:3) but "the law perfected nothing" (7:19). Now in Christ he shares the blessings of the new covenant wherein "God will be their God and they will be his people" (8:10), newly constituted.

In this company both Jew and Gentile find that they are surrounded by "helpers" who are more than the ordinary earthly helpers of a kindly neighborhood. They have anticipated heaven itself. They look for a city, which God has already prepared, and find that already they have come to "Zion, mountain and city of the living God, to the heavenly Jerusalem and myriads of angels, to the festal gathering and church of the firstborn registered in heaven, and to God the Judge of all, and to the spirits of just men made perfect, and to Jesus the Mediator of the new covenant and the blood of sprinkling that speaks more eloquently than that of Abel" (12:22–24). How could any sane Christian who has entered into these glories ever consent to the secularization of the church?

The cup which he has tasted will never be dashed from his lips. All that he has received so far he owes to Christ: the blessings of his one work, completed on the cross, and the blessings of his continued work in those who put their trust in him. The foretaste will be followed by the fullness of heaven. It was through the Pioneer of their salvation that they became sons of God; and it is through him that God will bring them to glory (2:10).

# 2

## The Epistle
## to the Romans

WE BEGIN OUR STUDY of this epistle with the search within it for evidence concerning the character of God. We desire to answer the question, What can we say about God?

### THE NATURE OF GOD

God is *the living God*. This is shown in Romans 14:11, where St. Paul quotes Isaiah 49:18, LXX, "I live, saith the Lord." It accords with this that he can say, "the God of peace (be) with you all" (15:33). Clearer still, because the verb is expressed, is the prayer, "the God of endurance . . . give to you . . . " (15:5). Any reference to prayer (8:26) or to God as witness (1:9-10) must carry with it the implication that God is the living God.

God is *eternal*. Paul speaks definitely of "the eternal God" (16:26) and of "his eternal *(aidios)* power and divinity" *(theiotēs)* 1:20). He is "the imperishable God" (1:23).

God is *the only God*. There is no other God. He is "the only wise God" (16:27). It is unthinkable that Paul meant that there are other gods but that God alone is wise. He is the only God; he alone is God; and he is wise. The heathen gods are regarded as gods by the darkened and unintelligent hearts of men. They may have an objective existence as images and idols, but they have no existence as God. If they exist at all they belong to the realm of creation. Not one of them is God. Even a deified man is no more than a living god and not God. And he will perish in the grave (1:21-25). Cf. 3:29-30; 11:34-36.

God is *invisible*. "His invisible nature *(ta aorata)* . . . is discerned *(kathoratai)*, his eternal power and divinity." We do not discern directly; our apprehension comes from the objects of God's creation.[1] This explains

---

1. The construction of "apprehended by the things he has made" may be elucidated by the analogous "the jug is grasped (by me) *by the handle*."

the fact that what may be known of God he has made subject to our awareness (1:19-20).

God's invisibility may also be inferred from Paul's horror of idolatry. Men changed God's glory into the likeness of an image *(eikōn)* of man and birds and animals and reptiles (1:23). Although he was exposing the sinfulness of the Jew, it cannot be doubted that Paul was sympathetic at least in this one point with his countrymen who abominated idols (2:22).

The one, living, eternal and invisible God is *conscious.* He has mind. "Who knew the mind of the Lord? Who became his counselor?" (11:34). He who has mind *(nous) has knowledge.* He searches the hearts of men, and when the Holy Spirit intercedes for the saints, God knows his attitude and aim. Before he called and justified his people he foreknew them (8:27, 29). Cf. 11:2. "O the depth . . . of God's knowledge" (11:33)! He must know, because he judges the secret broodings of men (2:16). Similarly he who has knowledge knows how to use it: God *has wisdom.* "O the depth of God's wisdom" (11:33-34)! The unaided human reason cannot search out his judgments or find a trail left by his journeys. Such is his wisdom that he needs nobody to advise him. He is the only wise God (16:27).

*God has power.* "With a view to this very purpose I raised thee (Pharaoh) up, namely that I might demonstrate my power in thee" (9:17). The "speaker" to Pharaoh is the scripture, but Paul means "God as recorded in scripture." A few verses later he asks, "What if God, willing . . . to make known his ability . . . ?" (9:22).[2] The exercise of God's power may be analyzed into four main divine activities.

God is *Creator.* This is shown in the contrast which Paul draws between the creature and the Creator (1:25). The whole of creation, the universe *(ta panta),* has its origin in him (11:36). All things are derived from him *(ex autou).*

God is also *Sustainer* of the universe. It is through him *(di' autou)* that it continues in existence. If God were to cease to exercise his sustaining power it would vanish completely into nothing. This is reasonable, because the universe is "for him" *(eis auton),* and he keeps his own property in being.

Within this broad activity God *exercises providential care.* We see his hidden hand in the traditional rendering of 8:28, "all things cooperate with those who love God—for good." ("With" may be replaced by "for.") Either events work with believers or they just "work together" for their benefit, for good. A secular interpretation would do violence to Paul's deepest beliefs. If events or things work together, it can only be because God in some inscrutable way causes them to work together.

The hidden hand comes out into the open in a second interpretation. There is a reading, not without weight (p46, B, A, etc.), which inserts "God" *(ho theos)* into the text. This means that "God cooperates in all things with those who love him—for good." He could hardly do this if he

---

2. *to dunaton autou:* "how powerful He is"—Moulton-Turner, *Grammar*, 3:14. For the introduction of "what" in "what if . . . " cf. John 6:62 and perhaps Acts 23:9. "Power" is normally *dunamis*, as in 9:17.

were not in control. The difficulty here lies not in the textual authorities but in the Greek: "God" appears twice in a short space and the result is awkward. A third interpretation, favored by the NEB, rejects the insertion and takes the subject of the verb to be "the Spirit" continued from the previous verses.[3] In any case we see the divine providential care. He is the One who arranges different chains of causation so that they have to intersect;[4] for our good.[5]

In the secular realm God *exercises his power in the civil authority*. All supreme authority has been ordained by God and should be obeyed, not resisted. The state is a divine institution and the ruler is God's agent—for good. He does not bear the sword in vain. The restraint of evil, if necessary by force and by punishment, is for the purpose of social preservation, not spiritual salvation. The spheres are distinct but both are under God. The state is part of God's providential order. He exercises his providential care of those who love him (8:28) in all things and of all men particularly through his agents, the rulers (13:1–7). The authorities are not the demonic powers behind the state, as Dr. Oscar Cullmann suggests. Paul would not advocate obedience to such; and bearing the sword pictures the human magistrate who is one of the authorities. On the contrary the state exists as a divine institution to act as a dam against the inrushing demonic flood. (Cf. C. K. Barrett, pp. 244, 249.)[6]

In exercising his power, God does not act like a machine nor is he subject to pressure from outside. *God has will*. The Jew thought that he knew God's will (2:18). It is more than a "general" will, for example that the universe might continue to exist. It descends to the details of human life. Thus Paul can pray that he may succeed in visiting the Roman church. But it is "in the sphere of the will of God" (1:10). If his journey is against God's will he will either abandon the attempt in obedience to God's known will or (if he does not know it) he will be prevented by God from visiting Rome.

Paul earnestly calls upon his readers to join him in strenuous prayer to counteract[7] human disobedience and lack of enthusiasm, in order that he may come to them in joy "through the will of God" (15:30–32). If the prayer is answered the will of God will bring him to Rome. The will of God may be described as that which is good, well pleasing to him and perfect (12:2).

The will of God, then, is related to different situations in human life

---

3. See R. V. G. Tasker, *The Greek New Testament*, p. 434.

4. Cf. Helmut Thielicke, *I Believe: The Christian's Creed*, pp. 48–49.

5. It ought to be added that C. E. B. Cranfield finally favors the interpretation of the Latin Vulgate, and of the Revised and Authorized Versions (RV, ASV, KJV). "All things work together for good to them that love God." His exhaustive treatment of Rom. 8:28 antiquates all prior discussions. See his commentary (ICC) 1:424–31.

6. Where only an author's name is given, the reference is to his commentary on Romans.

7. *Sunagōnisasthai*, a metaphor from a contest in sport, suggests rivalry or competition, not between Paul and the Roman church but between these two parties and the opposition. The joint prayer is a contest: Paul and the Romans versus the disobedient and the unenthusiastic.

and without inconsistency may vary from time to time. It might be the will of God that Paul should not go to Rome now but a few years later it might be his will that he should go. It could, of course, be rightly objected that God is not in the dark "now" about what he wills in a few years' time. This raises the question of a "long term" will. To put it very simply, can we point to anything which God willed a few thousand years ago and still wills? Is there any one *thelēma* of God which has never been changed?

There is such a will and it is described by the term "purpose." *God has purpose.* After speaking from the human side of "those who love God" Paul describes them from the divine side, "those who are called according to his purpose" (8:28). He proceeds in the next two verses to trace the outworking of God's purpose and it is more than a matter of a few thousand years. Pretemporal, temporal and posttemporal are covered in one broad sweep. God's purpose begins in eternity, is implemented in history and is completed in the glory of eternity. It is not determined by human ancestry or conduct (9:11). Before birth Jacob was distinct from his twin Esau. If ancestry were the decisive factor, Esau would have had to be included. If conduct decided, the distinction was made too soon. "God has a purpose; it works by a process of election; and it cannot fail" (Barrett, p. 182).

God's purpose is reflected linguistically in the use of the prepositions *eis* . . . *pros* . . . *eis,* and perhaps also in the verb *proetheto* (3:25–26), and in the purposive expression *eis auto touto* . . . *hopōs* . . . *kai hopōs* (9:17).

God has a purpose; and *he does not change his mind.* "The gracious gifts and the calling of God are irrevocable" (11:29). His purpose persists (9:11; cf. 11:7).

God has power and persistent purpose. How does he use his power and in what manner does he carry out his purpose? What is the content of his conscious mind? This brings us to the question of the character of God. *God is righteous.* Paul speaks quite definitely about "the righteousness of God" (1:17; 3:5, 21, 25–26; 10:3). There is no unrighteousness in him (9:14). The text of 3:26 has some significance in the fact that the adjective, noun and verb of the *dikaios* group all appear together. Their meaning interlocks. We shall later have to go more deeply into this subject but for the present we must be content to affirm that God is righteous.

*God is true.* The Jews possessed the advantage of having the scripture, with all that it told them of the mind and claim of God. Jewish unbelief does not nullify the faithfulness of God. He stands by what he has said. He keeps his promise and acts in accordance with his revealed character. He is to be believed, even if every man in the world deny what he has said. For even in these circumstances he is to be regarded as true. It is those who deny who merit the designation of "liars" (3:1–4). They are opposing "the truthfulness of God" (3:7). By contrast Christ has become the Minister of the circumcision (a Servant of the Jews?) "for the sake of, for the vindication of, the truthfulness of God,[8] namely to confirm (by

---

8. "Of God"—subjective genitive: A. T. Robertson, *A Grammar of the Greek New Testament,* p. 499.

fulfilling) the promises made to the fathers" (15:8). If God is thus true, *he is faithful.* He is reliable, credible and trustworthy.

*God is to be worshiped.* This is plain in Paul's reference to those who in idolatry worshiped and served the creature to the neglect of the Creator (1:25), who is blessed and praised for ever. Men did not glorify God as God or give him thanks, though they should have done, an omission which is indefensible (1:20–21). Paul himself worships God (1:9), as a true Israelite might be expected to do (9:4), and Gentiles also should likewise worship him (15:6, 9).

The point is proved negatively in what Paul says about impiety *(asebeia),* the failure to render one's duty to God. All impiety, including the refusal to worship, excites the wrath of God (1:18). Christ died for impious men (5:6) and God justifies them when they believe (cf. 4:5). A practical illustration is given in the doxology of 16:27.

Invisible though he is, *God may be known.* What may be known of him is manifest among men, perhaps even in them, in their conscience. What is "manifest" is subject to man's awareness, if he will but pay attention. This is due to God's activity, "for God manifested it to them." The evidence is in the works of creation. What cannot be seen by the eye can be discerned by the mind's eye (1:19–20, 32; 2:15). God may be known, and *he should be known,* but men did not deem him fit to be continued in their knowledge (1:28). This is not the intimacy of devout religious experience but even so Paul says that *God is known* (1:21). This enhances human guilt.

It might be regarded as an inference from the fact that God has mind, but whether it is an inference or not, St. Paul makes it perfectly plain that *God has an attitude.* He is far from being uninterested in men. "Those who are in the flesh cannot please God" (8:8). They are not "in the spirit," their standards are not God's standards and their attitude to God is one of enmity; they are not subordinate to his law and cannot be. If they cannot please him, then clearly they do not. God is not pleased.

On the other hand there are those who can and do please God. "The man who serves Christ on this principle is pleasing to God" (14:18). God is pleased (cf. 12:1).

Thus the conduct of men may please or displease God. He obviously has an attitude.

For *God himself is holy and requires holiness in men.* Paul exhorts his readers to present their faculties as slaves to righteousness. They will then, as it were, obey the commands of righteousness. The result of this will be holiness. The apostle proceeds with a slight but significant change. Liberated from sin and enslaved to God (not explicitly to righteousness), "you have something to show for your service"—holiness (6:19, 22; W. Sanday and A. C. Headlam, p. 167). God now gives the orders to those who have moved from the false servitude to the true one. The resulting holiness can hardly be an accident. It has been God's purpose. He has required it. The call to holiness would not come from an unholy God. The Spirit of God (8:9, 14) is the Holy Spirit (5:5; 9:1). God's oracles (3:2) are the holy scriptures (1:2). His law and his commandment are holy (7:12). His people are holy by vocation (1:7; cf 8:27). Their living sacrifice should be holy (12:1) and their kiss of mutual greeting should be holy (16:16). All this derives from the fact that God himself is holy.

Though separate from men in his utter holiness, *God deals with individuals.* This is palpably plain in the second chapter. Although universal sin is the theme, Paul is not considering merely the collective sin of humanity. Not only is society corrupt; each individual man is a sinner. His address in the second person singular to "Mr. Everyman" (2:1) is designed to bring home his point to each man. "Do you think, sir, . . . that you will escape . . . ?" It is the individual who has the unrepentant heart. God will render to each man according to his works (2:3, 5–6). There is no righteous man, not even one (3:10). A man (singular) is justified by faith (3:28). Cf. 9:13, 18. And if a man *(tis)* has not the Spirit of Christ, this man *(houtos)* is not his (8:9). God not only sees the sin of the human race; He discriminates and evaluates in reference to individuals.

There are those who do not take kindly to all this because they are strong critics of "individualism." It should therefore be remarked that Paul was deeply aware of the church. The word itself *(ekklēsia)* appears only in the last chapter (16:1, 4–5, 16, 23), a fact which might pose problems for those who do not believe that "15:1—16:23 is undeniably Pauline." [9] But could it be doubted that when he writes to all God's beloved people in Rome, holy by vocation, and greets them in his manner of addressing a church (1:7; cf. 1 Cor. 1:3), he has the church in mind? His treatment of baptism suggests the church (6:3–5). "We, the many, are one body in Christ" (12:5). The readers should have unanimity in their fellowship and offer their praise as one man (15:5–6). Cf. 15:14, 24 for a closely knit community. They should watch those who cause divisions and avoid them (16:17–18).

Paul glories in the church but not at the expense of its members. He would scrutinize and expound carefully any emphasis on "the faith of the church" with its possibility of individual vagueness and even insincerity.[10] For him the one body is made up of individual, believing men in their relationship to one another in Christ. His position is illustrated by his address to the church at Corinth: "to the church of God (singular), men (plural) sanctified in Christ Jesus" (1 Cor. 1:2). This is no more "individualism" in the bad sense than the answer given in the Anglican Catechism, ". . . I was made a member of Christ, the child of God. . . ." Bonhoeffer was no "individualist." God does indeed deal with individuals.

*God is the Author of law,* which is binding upon all, as the treatment of any individual offender shows. Paul speaks of "the law of God" (7:22, 25; 8:7) to which men should be subordinate. Its commandment is holy, righteous and good (7:12). The law comes from God, for it is "spiritual" (7:14). As the law is good, it might be thought that men would be glad to do what God commands.

---

9. W. G. Kümmel, *Introduction to the New Testament*, p. 222. Cf. p. 226.
10. Cf Dietrich Bonhoeffer, *Letters and Papers from Prison*, pp. 165–66.

## Man Against God

But *God has enemies*. Here we must touch on Paul's use of the term "flesh" *(sarx)*. As merely material, flesh is morally indifferent. It can indicate the relation of kinsmen or ancestors (9:3, 8). But Paul uses the term in a further sense. The flesh is weak (6:19). It is not to be our standard (8:12); we should walk according to the spirit (8:4). Failure here leads to death (8:6, 13), for those who are determined by flesh cannot please God (8:8). Flesh as such is not evil in the Gnostic sense that matter is evil,[11] but sin has won a beach-head in it. Because of "the flesh of sin" (8:3) Paul can say that he is "fleshly, brought under sin as a slave that is sold" (7:14) to a new master. "In my flesh there dwells nothing good" (7:18). Hence man's "moral incompetence" (C. K. Barrett). But it is the man, not the flesh, who is morally responsible. In words which have become famous, flesh is "a corrupted not a corrupting element; the involuntary accomplice to the act of sin but not the criminal." [12]

"Flesh" thus indicates man in his distance from God (J. A. T. Robinson). His mind and purpose and general attitude is "enmity against God" (8:7). A particular case of this occurs in the story of Elijah at Horeb. "O Lord, they have killed thy prophets, torn down thy altars . . ." (11:3). (Cf. possibly 1:30, "hating God"; 5:10.)

This comes to its climax in the comprehensive statement that *God is sinned against*. Jews and Greeks alike are without exception accused of being under sin. There is no righteous person, not even one (3:9–10). All have sinned (3:23). Sin entered the world—an alien!—through one man and . . . all sinned (5:12).

The different kinds of sin, or perhaps rather the different ways in which sin manifests itself, are described by a number of terms which are largely the same as those used in the Epistle to the Hebrews (cf. pp. 28–30). *Sin is disobedience (parakoē)*. " . . . through the disobedience of the one man the many were constituted sinners" (5:19). (For the verb, cf. Deut. 25:6, LXX.) Cf. 11:30–32 *(apeitheō, apeitheia)*; 2:8; though there may be an undertone of "unbelief."

*Sin is lawlessness (anomia)*. " . . . you presented your faculties as slaves . . . to lawlessness making for (more) lawlessness" (6:19). The last phrase is rendered "making for moral anarchy" in the NEB. The point is that lawlessness increases, going on and on and ever reproducing itself. The different acts of lawlessness have to be forgiven (cf. 4:7 and see p. 37, note 37).

*Sin is unbelief (apistia)*. "Will their unbelief cancel the faithfulness of God? Heaven forbid!" (3:3–4). Abraham "did not waver in unbelief but was strengthened in faith" (4:20). (Cf. 11:20, 23. If the verb *apeitheō* can mean "disbelieve," "be an unbeliever," as seems likely, cf. also 15:31.)

*Sin is unrighteousness (adikia)*. "Let not sin go on reigning as king in your mortal body . . . nor present your faculties to sin as tools of unrighteousness" (6:12–13). Note the contrast: present them to God as tools of

---

11. Cf. R. M. Grant, *Gnosticism and Early Christianity* (rev. ed), pp. 136 ff.
12. W. D. Davies, *Paul and Rabbinic Judaism*, p. 19.

righteousness *(dikaiosunē)*. All men are "under sin." Not one is righteous
(3:9–10; cf. 1:18, 29; 2:8; 3:5; 9:14).

*Sin is impiety (asebeia)*. This is the sin with which a man banishes God
from his life and denies him the worship which is his due. It is perversity
in religion rather than in morality. (Cf. John Murray, 1:36; and Otto
Michel, p. 62.) Godlessness is the object of God's opposition (*epi* plus
accusative of "hostility," 1:18; cf. 11:22). It was the ungodly for whom
Christ died (5:6) and it is the ungodly who need to be, and may be,
justified (4:5). (The *epi* here is not that of "hostility"; cf. 4:24.)

*Sin is unholiness*. This is demonstrated by Paul's characteristic description
of those who have put their faith in Christ, in traditional language "the
saints" (1:7; 8:27; 12:13; 15:25–26, 31; 16:2, 15). He almost always uses
the plural *(hoi hagioi*, contrast Phil. 4:21). The new people of God could
not be called "the holy ones" in the days of their unbelief.[13]

*Sin is uncleanness*. " . . . you presented your faculties as slaves to
impurity . . . " (6:19). Arndt-Gingrich here take the word *akatharsia*
figuratively, in a moral sense, and regard it as the opposite of *hagiasmos*,
"holiness." It is perhaps best to accept the moral meaning in a cultic atmosphere. The moral use is clear in 1:24 but the impurity has a background
of, or rather arises in and because of, idolatry. Men "knew better" than to
glorify God with thanksgiving.

*Sin is ignorance*. The wealth of God's kindness and forbearance and
longsuffering is the object of human contempt because men do not know
that God's kindness is gently leading them to repentance (2:4). The
Israelites' zeal for God had no foundation in knowledge. They did not
know his righteousness and were not subordinate to it (10:1–3). Ignorance
contributed to their need of salvation.

To act in a way which does not meet the standards of knowledge must
lead to mistakes. Men (not Jews) knew God (1:21) but did not see fit to
retain him in their knowledge (1:28, cf. 32). They therefore went astray
and became guilty of error (1:27), which entails "recompence" (KJV—
*antimisthia*) or penalty (Arndt-Gingrich, p. 74). Sin is thus *error* or
wandering from the right path, the path of truth.

*Sin is transgression*. This requires the presence of law (4:15), which
brings sin into the daylight and enables it to be assessed. For transgression
*(parabasis, paraptōma)* gives precision to sin. It runs completely contrary
to a known command. (Cf. Barrett, p. 112–13.) Adam broke a clear commandment and thus transgressed in his sin (5:12–15). Between Adam and
Moses, in the period before the giving of the law, "sin was in the world"
and men sinned but they did not transgress. The argument implies that
there was nothing to transgress and is stated "in a pure form." After all,
the Gentiles have "the task required by the law written in their hearts"
(2:14–15). The drift of Paul's meaning, however, is not obscure. Sin is
transgression of the law (2:23–27), dishonors God and even "undoes"
circumcision. (Cf. 4:25; 5:15–21.) In 11:11–12 the word *paraptōma*, false
step, stumble, may well continue the metaphor in the verbs "trip" and

---

13. For a recent discussion see Owen E. Evans, "The Saints," pp. 196–200.

"fall." At the same time it sums up Jewish unbelief as a transgression as plain as murder or theft. It would be an interesting study to consider how many of the commandments of the Decalogue were broken by the Jewish rejection of Jesus: idolatry? blasphemy? spiritual adultery? robbing God? false witness? covetousness (cf. Luke 19:14)?

*Sin is weakness.* "When we were weak Christ died for the ungodly" (5:6). Perhaps the best comment on our weakness would be the celebrated seventh chapter of Romans. "When the commandment came . . . I died." "I fail to do what I want to do but I do what I hate." "Willing (is no problem and always) is at hand; it is right conduct which is never there." " . . . (it) takes me prisoner . . . who will deliver me . . . ?" (7:9–10, 15, 18–19, 23–24).

It has long been debated whether Paul is speaking in chapter 7 of his spiritual experience before or after his conversion. In spite of weighty arguments on either side it seems better to regard the whole section as a vivid description of man under the law from the point of view of man under grace.[14]

The weakness of the readers even determines the apostle's mode of expression (6:19). The weakness of Christians requires the aid of the Spirit, for we do not always know what should be the object of our prayers (8:26). The Christian can even be weak in faith (14:1–4) in spite of the example of Abraham (4:19). God still receives him (cf. 15:7). The opposite of being strong in faith is wavering in unbelief (4:20) which is much the same as the weakness in faith of the previous verse. "Weakness," whether in the Christian or the non-Christian, is sin. But "sin in believers" is covered (8:34).

*Sin is failure to realize the divine ideal.* "All . . . come short of the glory of God" (3:23). This is taken by Dodd (pp. 50–51) as a definition of sin. Man was created in the "image [eikōn] and glory of God" (1 Cor. 11:7; cf. Gen. 1:26–27; 5:1, lxx). Man's "likeness" to God may refer to his rational and moral nature or to his authority: he is to rule over the animal creation. As to the first, his reasonings are futile and his unintelligent heart darkened (1:21). This seems extravagant. As I write these words, two men are actually on the moon, an achievement which surely demands a good deal of rationality and intelligence. But where the subject of discussion is the living God, any Christian worker who has had dealings with unbelievers, especially aggressive ones, knows of the misunderstandings, sometimes deliberate and sometimes not, possible to rational men. He knows how wishful thinking can select some premises and argue from them, and reject others entirely. He knows that there is an entire spiritual realm which is foreign and unknown to those who have not the mind of Christ (1 Cor. 2:16). This is illustrated by "the problem of communication," which is not always the fault of the preacher or teacher. There are none so deaf . . .

---

14. Cf. R. Bultmann, *Theology of the New Testament*, 1:247; W. Grundmann, *TDNT* 1:311, note 157; A. Oepke, *TDNT* 1:384, note 1; G. Schrenk, *TDNT* 3:50–52. Grundmann wonders if it is only the situation of the Jew which is in view. C. K. Barrett (p. 140) says that "what Paul says of the religion of Judaism . . . is true *a fortiori* of all religion." Cf. also Michel, p. 171; and Paul Althaus, p. 80.

As to man's authority over the brute creation, it is subsidiary but real. He has domesticated, tamed or controlled (cf. Jas. 3:7). It is *natural* for man to rule and for beasts to be ruled (cf. Gen. 9:1–2). But he loses the image of God when he abandons his authority to rule and becomes subordinate to beasts. He makes images of animals as gods and worships and serves the creation rather than the Creator. The moral consequences are disastrous; the wheel comes full circle: man has an unfit mind (*adokimos nous*, 1:22–25, 28). The claim to wisdom, both intellectual and moral, is invalidated by conduct. Departure from the image of God is sin. Those who assert that in a starving country sacred cows should be eaten rather than worshiped have a case.

*Sin is spiritual petrifaction.* Those who were not of the elect remnant of Israel, and did not attain the object of Israel's search, were "hardened." They became insensitive to spiritual matters (Michel, p. 268, "unempfindlich"). Preaching to them is like preaching to stalactites. They respond as much as a block of stone would. They do not see the significance of Jesus; they are deaf to the message of the gospel. The "hardening" is the shadow cast by God's mercy. It is the climax of the offense taken at the gospel and at the same time it is God's judgment. Jewish "table-fellowship" in the law traps them in slavery (11:7–10). Cf. 11:25.

The hardening is within God's saving purpose, does not conflict with His righteousness and is not arbitrary (9:14–18). (The Greek here is *sklērunō;* in the previous paragraph it is *pōroō, pōrōsis.*) On the human level it is the final stage of a persistent impenitence (2:5). What might have been a supple, flexible and yielding heart has become rigid and unyielding. It has set—like concrete. And God's judgment is his Amen to the choice and direction of a lifetime. For his kindness has been trying to lead them [15] to repentance and they have resisted him.

## God Against Man

After this detailed description of sin it is necessary to state again what was observed when we said that God has an attitude. *God is not pleased.* We need not again discuss the concept of "flesh" (see pp. 80, 82). It is sin which excites God's displeasure. In consequence *God brings charges against men.* If this were not so, they would not be inexcusable (1:20; 2:1). There is no argument which they can produce, no fact that has been overlooked, which can be an adequate answer to the charge. They have no defense. All the world is answerable to God (3:19) but it has no answer to give. Every mouth is stopped, not because men are gagged from outside but because their lips are sealed from within. They have nothing to say.

This is a "logical" silence, for it expresses the purpose of the law. There are—or will be—those in whom the purpose is not fulfilled (Matt. 25:44–46). Their failure to observe silence is unavailing.

Related to the bringing of charges is the fact of *the divine wrath.* The final or eschatological wrath which is being stored up for themselves by

---

15. 2:4. The verb *agei* is conative present. Cf. Robertson, *Grammar,* p. 880; Moulton-Turner, *Grammar,* 3:63; C. F. D. Moule, *Idiom Book of New Testament Greek,* p. 8.

men will be manifested in the day of wrath (2:5). The wrath and anger (2:8) "describe God's attitude on the day of wrath to those whom He does not reward with eternal life" (Barrett).

God's *attitude* involves his *decision*. He renders to each man "according to his works" (2:6). This must mean that God views the works and "renders" in the light of them. If they had been different he would have rendered differently. A decision is thus implied.

What is rendered to every evildoer is tribulation and anguish *(thlipsis, stenochōria,* 2:9). This is God's *action* and it is based on his decision, because with him there is no partiality or favoritism (2:11). It does not just "happen." (The reflection is suggested that the final condition of the finally impenitent is a cramped monotony—cf. 6:19 and p. 84, "lawlessness leading to more lawlessness"—in contrast to the spaciousness of eternal life. In spite of the different manifestations of sin, evil has a deadly sameness. Goodness is infinite variety.)

The eschatological view of wrath is seen when Paul says that the justified will be saved from "the wrath" (5:9)[16] and when he exhorts his readers (in 12:19) not to take their revenge but to make room (in their thinking) for "the well-known wrath" (Moulton-Turner, *Grammar,* 3:173). Vengeance belongs to God and he will repay.

In 9:22 Paul "lets his emphasis fall . . . [on] the postponement of His wrath against men who have long since become ripe for destruction" (F. F. Bruce, p. 190). It is not always postponed. The eschatological wrath in its fullness is held back until the day of wrath but it is partially manifested in historic time. "The wrath of God is revealed [not 'will be revealed'] from heaven against all impiety and unrighteousness of men who suppress the truth in unrighteousness" (1:18).

Paul is looking at what Barrett calls "an observable situation." The sins of men associated with idolatry are plain in their hideousness for all to see. Upon them falls the wrath of God, the expression of his majesty and holiness, his aversion and resistance to malignity (cf. Michel, p. 61.)

God delivers men to the sensuality which culminates in a reprobate mind. For their physical conduct is the outcome of their mental state and attitude. Note the words expressing activities of the mind: desires (1:24, *epithumia*), worship (1:25), emotions (1:26), longing (1:27, *orexis*), thinking and knowledge (1:28).

This is not divine despair or perplexity nor is it merely divine permissiveness. God acts judicially and abandons men to their desires through which they destroy themselves. They receive their reward (1:27). "God punishes sins through sins . . . the deepest, the gravest thought of God's judgment. . . ."[17]

---

16. Cf. Michel, p. 135, n. 5. "Auch hier klingt der Begriff *orge* so verselbständigt, dass der Genitiv *theou* fehlen kann." ("In this place the concept *wrath* rings so independently that the genitive *of God* can be absent.") There is no need to ask. "Whose wrath?" in this context.

17. Althaus, p. 19. Cf. Michel, p. 67; W. Popkes, *Christus Traditus,* p. 134, "the sinner is only cast still more deeply into his sins."

"God abandons" or "delivers" means that he withdraws himself. M.-J. Lagrange, following St. Augustine, observes (p. 28) that God's judgment is executed "par la soustraction de la grâce"—by the withdrawal of grace. The principle, succinctly stated in Augustine's Sermon (LVII,9), is: *non cogendo, sed deserendo*—not by forcing but by deserting. Sinners are cast "in die Gottverlassenheit"—"into God-forsakenness" (Popkes, *Christus Traditus*, p. 287).

Lagrange regards the thrice repeated "delivered" (1:24, 26, 28 *paredōken*) not as a crescendo but as a refrain. It is an acute distinction and it emphasizes the fearfulness of what the apostle is saying. But the "reprobate mind" seems in itself to mark a climax.

A particular case of wrath is seen when the magistrate executes judgment on an offender (13:4). There can be no question here of eschatological wrath being held back until the last day. A more general statement tells us that "the law produces wrath" (4:15). Michel observes an omission and interprets: "the law produces transgression but transgression produces the wrath of God." (This recalls 7:7). It is not stated whether the divine reaction is immediate—or at any rate in historic time—or whether the wrath is being added to an existing store (2:5). The bare principle is given. Transgression is not unobserved by God. What he does, and when he does it, would seem to be determined by the context of the transgression. Is it an "isolated" offence or is it but one of a thousand transgressions which spring from a hard and unrepentant heart? If it is the latter there is a further question. Is the offender a member of a minority or are his many transgressions characteristic of a whole civilization? The wrath may be contemporary or eschatological. (Is it 1:24 or 2:5?)

The concepts of wrath and judgment overlap, but a distinction may be drawn between them. Although God's judgments are unsearchable (11:33) we do know something of them. Even in an unfathomable sea the plumb line can descend so far when soundings are taken. We therefore draw up two tables in which we seek to analyze what is meant by wrath and judgment. We have not forgotten that God is the eternal God, but there is a logical order in his mind, and with reverence we imagine him as the speaker.

| *Wrath* | *Judgment* |
|---|---|
| I see what you do and are—conduct and character. | I see what you do and are—conduct and character. |
|  | *I test it against the norm, righteousness (2:2, 12, 15), and find it wanting.* |
| I am displeased. | I am displeased. |
| I decide against you. | I give a verdict against you |
| *I will take steps to resist you.* |  |
| I will take steps to punish you. | I will take steps to punish you. |

Each italicized sentence is restricted to its own column. Thus God's wrath in history is his counteraction against men, and his judgment is not arbitrary; there are reasons for his displeasure. Thus the distinction between wrath and judgment consists of the fact that wrath manifests historical resistance and judgment is based on righteousness. It may be that wrath and judgment each imply what is explicitly peculiar to the other and that they overlap completely. If a distinction is to be drawn, it seems to be on the lines which we have indicated.

We pass on therefore to consider the evidence which shows that *God is a God of judgment*. It should first be noticed that the verb "judge" (*krinō*) may not in itself carry the thought of action. It may express an attitude or a logical implication. When Paul tells the man who judges his neighbor that he is thereby condemning (*katakrinō*), giving an adverse judgment to, himself, he is not thinking of his proceeding to carry out a sentence. Judgment here is a logical attitude and in the present instance the adverse judgment is unconscious. The man who judges his fellow does not realize that he is condemning himself (2:1). Cf. 2:27.

Paul speaks of "the day of wrath and of revelation of the righteous judgment of God" (2:5). God will judge the impenitent and will render to each man according to his works. In the meantime he is *puniendus* but not yet *punitus*. The Gentiles have the law written in their hearts, their conscience adds its testimony and in the interplay of their moral reasonings they offer accusation or even defense, "(as will appear)[18] on the day when God judges" (2:15–16).

*The judgment will be penetrating.* It is not only overt acts which come under scrutiny. God will judge the secrets of men. "The secrets" (*ta krupta*) covers the subject of their thoughts (e.g. Matt. 5:28), their unlawful enjoyments, their false ambitions and their thirst for revenge, everything in fact which they ponder deeply in their hearts without telling any man.

Thoughts are private and the judgment will thus be discriminating. Further, *the judgment will be deserved.* It is based on truth (2:2), not partiality (2:11), and will match the works of each man (2:6). It could be characterized by Paul's verdict on certain calumniators: "their judgment is just" (*endikon*) (3:8).

*God's judgment is fearful.* It is not a prospect lightly to be considered or an experience with which a man can trifle. Even on earth and in the affairs of men, long before the Day of Judgment, fear has its place. Any resistance to the civil authority, the nonclerical minister of God, will receive judgment. The wrongdoer should therefore fear: the sword is not carried in vain (13:1–7). Again, the "superior" Gentile should come down from his high horse and fear. God did not spare the natural branches and he will not spare the engrafted ones if they pass from faith to arrogance. The severity of God must not be forgotten (11:17–22).

No man should fondly think that he can escape. *God's judgment is universal and inescapable.* "God will judge the world" (3:6), which is answerable to him in its entirety. Every individual is included; every mouth will be silent in eloquent guilt (3:19). Paul challenges the individual with his pointed question, "Dost thou calculate . . . that thou wilt escape the

---

18. See Althaus, pp. 24, 26. He is able to overcome the awkward difficulty of joining the two verses by understanding and inserting "wie sich zeigen wird."

judgment of God?" (2:3). Its implementation is his (cf. 12:19). For judgment is not merely an opinion, even a divine opinion. *God's judgment involves a sentence and its execution.* It is God's ordinance that certain conduct carries with it the penalty of death (1:32). This is a particular case, or a summary of particular cases, of a general rule. Sin entered the world and through sin came death, which fanned out to all men, for all sinned. Sin was introduced by one man [19] and the result was judgment issuing in adverse judgment, condemnation. The penalty was death and men died (5:12, 16–21). Sin leads to death (6:16, 21). The pittance paid by sin is death (6:23).

It might at first be supposed that the death in question is the death we have in mind when we say that Mr. So-and-so has died. This is partly true but it is not the whole truth. For one thing it is the opposite of eternal life, which is more than a secular eudaemonism. And for another Paul's picture of the day of wrath and of God's righteous judgment (2:5) puts physical death in the shade. Death and burial are child's play compared with the Day of Judgment. And yet death held sway, for example, from Adam until Moses (5:14). Physical death seems to be the penalty of sin after all.

The problem, if it is a problem, is solved if we regard physical death as the signature tune,[20] somber indeed, to be later fully orchestrated in a dreadful dirge. For the Christian the signature tune is transposed into a less ominous key and in its later orchestration the latent joy has triumphed.

Final death is characterized by a further term, loss, waste, ruin, destruction, perdition. Men will be judged by the light which they have: those who have the law *will be judged* in its light; those not possessing the law *will perish* without it (2:12). We can hardly mistake the parallelism. There are men who are "ripe for perdition" (*apōleia*, 9:22). Such is the awful fate which awaits the finally impenitent.

## THE OTHER SIDE—GOD FOR MAN

Such is the character of God as far as our present investigation has taken us. He is the living and eternal God, invisible to men and yet by his revelation able to be known by them. He is a conscious mind and has will and purpose. He is the Creator and Sustainer of all things and is the Lord of providence. He is righteous and holy, trustworthy and consistent in his purpose. He is to be worshiped and obeyed, and he calls men to be righteous and holy, revealing his will to them in his law. Yet men, even individuals, oppose him and sin against him. His displeasure and wrath are aroused and the culmination is the judgment of condemnation. The human prospect is no less than perdition.

This majestic and awe-inspiring picture is reflected in Paul's expression,

---

19. Otto Michel sees a link between Paul (Adam—Christ; Rom. 5:12–14; 1 Cor. 15:21–23) and Hebrews (Abraham—Melchizedek; Heb. 7:10). Consult *Der Brief an die Hebräer*, p. 268.

20. I think I owe this figure of speech to Emil Brunner but the documentation is unavailable.

"the severity of God" (11:22). If this were the whole of the story the plight of men would be sore indeed.

But there is another side. In the very same verse the apostle speaks of "the kindness of God." This must not be likened to the rare act of a severe man, a sudden helpfulness which is quite out of character. God's kindness tries to lead hard and unrepentant men to repentance (2:4–5; see note 15 in this chapter). In these two verses kindness and wrath are almost as closely associated as kindness and severity in 11:22. And if the kindness of God is not rare, it is not meager. Paul speaks of "the wealth of God's kindness." When we say that a man is wealthy, we mean at the least that "he has plenty." God's kindness is thus not in short supply. There is plenty of it. There is plenty of it for the one great sinner who needs it so much; and there is plenty for the great population in which his needs are written in larger letters. (Cf. Plato, *The Republic*, II.10 368 D.)

God's kindness is manifested in his longsuffering. The emphasis here is on the "long" rather than the "suffering." God waits patiently for men. They continue in their sin against him and in their indifference towards him, and still he waits. His inactivity may be despised by men but their contempt forgets his patience (2:4). When he might demonstrate his wrath and his power, he bears "with much longsuffering" even objects of wrath ripe for destruction (9:22).

The "longsuffering" lays stress on the time element. God is indeed eternal but how otherwise can we speak of the fact that *not yet* have men repented and *not yet* has God's wrath fully fallen? From our human, finite point of view God waits. The "bearing" (*pherō*) of the objects of wrath is brought out by the use of another word, "forbearance" (*anochē*). The thought here is not so much the length of time, though in actual fact this is inevitably involved, as the delay in reaction. If a man sins, God can punish him at once. But he holds back his wrath, he does not "react" immediately in punitive action, and this gives an opportunity for repentance. The door is not shut straightway but is left open.

The divine forbearance is illustrated in the words of Psalm 50:21 (KJV), "These things hast thou done [i.e. these wicked things], and I kept silence; thou thoughtest that I was altogether such an one as thyself." [21] The offenders drew the conclusion that God was as morally indifferent as they themselves. The mills of God grind slowly and they do not always start up immediately. "It is because sentence upon a wicked act is not promptly carried out that men do evil so boldly" (Eccles. 8:11, NEB), whereas they ought to use the intervening "time for repentance and amendment of life."

The duration of God's forbearance is long. For the whole period up to the coming of Christ, "the times of ignorance" of Acts 17:30 ("except the Flood, an exceptional punishment"), "Dieu supportait le péché, il le prenait en patience"—"God tolerated the sin; he took it with forbearance." (La-

---

21. The NEB and the JB translate with a question, "and shall I keep silence?" (NEB), "and expect me to say nothing?" (JB). But see the note of C. A. Briggs, *Psalms* (ICC) 1:422, "waw coörd. emph. antith. of man's actions and God's." My point is the illustration afforded by the KJV, not the translation and exegesis of the Hebrew.

grange, p. 77; cf. Michel, p. 74, n. 3). It was this long, divine tolerance which required the revelation of the divine righteousness in the atonement (3:25–26). It should not be supposed that God's forbearance is complete inactivity, "looking on tamely" [22] at the perpetration of wickedness. As we have seen, he gently leads men towards repentance through his silent and secret influences, as well as through open proclamation. But why should God show forbearance?

God shows forbearance because he loves. The mode of its manifestation does not at the moment concern us. What is important is the fact that Paul can speak of God's love and pass on at once to his wrath (see note 16 in this chapter) without the slightest trace of embarrassment. "God brings out and brings home [Barrett] his love [23] . . . we shall be saved from wrath" (5:8–9; cf. p. 86). But the wrath will still be there (2:5). It would seem that at any rate for the moment we must accept both love and wrath, or neither. This is part of the problem.

The love of God is not only objectively shown but is subjectively experienced by men. It is present in their hearts, just as refreshing rain permeates the parched soil (5:5). The recipients of the letter are those "whom God loves" (1:7, NEB). Nothing will ever be able to separate us from it (8:38–39, cf. 37). (Cf. possibly, with due regard to exegesis, 9:13, 25.)

The apostle speaks also of "mercy" (eleos), for which the Gentiles glorify God (15:9; cf. 9:23; 11:31). If "Paul for the most part draws his quotations from the Septuagint version" and "the priority of the LXX in Pauline quotations has long been recognized," [24] it might be thought that the ground has already been covered in our study of the word eleos (pp. 36–40). Certainly the LXX yields a rich concept and it is hard to imagine Paul doing anything but rejoice in it. Even so, on occasion he "follows the Hebrew against the LXX" (Ellis). This is hardly surprising. "Ability to speak the ancient languages [Hebrew and Aramaic] was a mark of faithfulness to the old culture" (Phil. 3:5) and Paul was a Pharisee and a Hillelite.[25] We must therefore look into the background of the LXX eleos.

In its purely Greek sense eleos is psychological. It expresses the emotion which comes upon a man when he sees another stricken by some evil or misfortune. Such compassion or pity, mingled with a fear of suffering the

---

22. Cf. the Greek verb perioraō in Herodotus I.89.
23. It is not clear how to construe "to us" (eis hēmas). Lagrange takes the phrase with the noun, "son amour pour nous" (his love for us) and in the Vulgate reads in nos (with Wordsworth and White) or erga nos (toward us). Sanday and Headlam (p. 128) take the phrase with the verb, "prove to us," though in their paraphrase (p. 119) they render "God presses home the proof of His unmerited Love towards us." A. T. Robertson, Grammar, (p. 594), illustrates the use of eis "like a dative" and quotes agapēn eis; but on p. 784 he says that the phrase belongs to the verb, not the noun.
24. R. V. G. Tasker, The Old Testament in the New Testament, p. 84; E. Earle Ellis, Paul's Use of the Old Testament, p. 12.
25. R. P. Martin, Philippians, p. 142; J. Jeremias, Neotestamentica et Semitica, ed. E. Earle Ellis and Max Wilcox, pp. 88–94. A good case can be made against the view that Paul wrote in Greek but thought in Hebrew. Preachers "think in whatever language they are using currently." This is confirmed by the experience of a man who has preached the gospel in three languages. See D. H. Van Daalen, "Faith according to Paul," pp. 83–85.

same experience, is the opposite of envy. Behind the *eleos* of the LXX, however, stands predominantly the Hebrew *hesed*, a word which denotes not primarily a disposition but a helpful act. It indicates conduct which accords with a mutual relationship or covenant and so points to, and arises from, the solidarity in which the "partners" are bound together. If they are not equal the helpful act may be a rendering of service to the needy. There is thus an advance from the bare vitality of the covenant toward the concept of kindness, favor and pity. If God is a partner, he remains faithful to the mutual relationship and his attitude is that of kindness towards the members. He promised kindness when he set up the covenant, and he ever renews his promise. It extends even to the forgiveness of the sin of breaking the covenant.

As between men *hesed* is "the kindliness of feeling, consideration, and courtesy, which adds a grace and softness to the relations subsisting between members of the same society" (Driver). As between God and men it marks his faithful devotion, persistent loyalty, his steady and loyal love. His loving purpose is unswerving, unbreakable, permanent. The expression, "promptitude to help," a nomadic virtue so vital in the desert, is "raised to new powers and unexpected applications" (Robinson) when it is used to describe the activity of God.

God not only acts in accordance with the recognized tie. In his *hesed* he can create a bond where previously it had not existed.[26]

This is an inspiring view of the character of God. But a man who knows that God will judge sinners might well find himself still uneasy and troubled. "Am I included in the covenant?" he might ask. "Are all these blessings for me? Can the God who is not pleased with sinful men look with loyal love on me?" Can such a man participate in the *hesed* "which means kindness or grace on the part of Yahwe and loyal piety on the part of Israel"?[27]

Paul speaks also of the grace (*charis*) of God. We have already met this word in a LXX setting (pp. 40–43). Whereas the Hebrew background enriches the concept of "mercy" (*eleos*) by its reference to the covenant, it is not so clear that the LXX "grace" is in need of such enrichment. Even so we ought to look at the background.

In many cases the LXX *charis* stands in its own right as it is not a translation of a Hebrew word. Where it is a translation it usually renders the Hebrew *hen*. This noun, and its corresponding verb, is characteristic of the stronger either in authority or power. The disadvantages of the weaker are overcome by the action of the stronger, who takes the initiative and is

---

26. H.-H. Esser, *Begriffslex.*, 1:52–53; R. Bultmann, *TDNT* 2:479–80; T. F. Torrance, *The Doctrine of Grace in the Apostolic Fathers*, pp. 12–17; H. Wheeler Robinson, *Inspiration and Revelation in the Old Testament*, pp. 57–58, 83–87; S. R. Driver, *Deuteronomy* (ICC), p. 102. I regret that, though years ago I read Norman H. Snaith's *Distinctive Ideas of the Old Testament*, it is not at present available to me.
27. John Skinner, *Prophecy and Religion*, p. 321. Aubrey R. Johnson defends the use of the term "devotion" for God's *hesed*: *The Vitality of the Individual in the Thought of Ancient Israel*, p. 103.

quite free in his decision, though he may be moved by entreaty. Thus God in his generosity bestows unmerited favor. The motive of his supreme graciousness lies within himself. He is under no obligation. Nobody can force his favor from him and nobody can claim it as a right. It is "all of grace," [28]

## God at Work For Us—The Work of Christ For Us

This is the climax of the "other side" of God's character. It is here that his kindness is seen at its peak. But a man under conviction of sin might still have his doubts and hesitations. Is God's righteous judgment to be forgotten, even in his grace? "Judaism never solved the problem created by the tension between God's justice and His grace." [29]

The conflict between the claims of righteousness and of mercy was a problem not confined within the limits of Judaism. "Hosea reflects the conflict back into the mind of God: it is Yahwe's own heart which is torn by the antagonism of justice and affection." Skinner sees, with the prophet, that both judgment and grace express the mind of God. Muilenburg has made the same observation. "There is also conflict within Him, between the justice that demands and the grace that conquers the demands of justice." [30]

But how is the conflict resolved? Which side "wins"? (It is perhaps hardly necessary to add that *kat' anthrōpon legō*–I speak as a man.) It might be possible to infer that, if grace conquers, the demands of justice will not be met. In a sympathetic approach to the *Theological Ethics* of Helmut Thielicke, Herbert Waddams notes the tension within God himself, between his holiness and his love, a tension which Thielicke would not wish to be minimized. Thielicke is then quoted. "The point at issue is to safeguard the miracle of the Gospel by which God overcomes Himself, by which His love saves us from the threat of His holiness." [31]

My heart warms to this but I should not want to hold its author to it as his last and final word. It manifests the vividness of the eloquent preacher and recalls Thielicke's sermons on the Apostles' Creed. "He lets the father in him conquer the judge" (*I Believe*, p. 117).

But is the Judge conquered? This is how the preacher might present the good news to the troubled soul. If he puts his faith in Christ "there is no condemnation" (Rom. 8:1). But it might turn out that the Judge has not been conquered but satisfied. I feel sure that Thielicke believes this. ". . . on the Cross he submitted himself to imprisonment in the dark dungeon of ultimate loneliness. . . . he came down from heaven and descended into the deepest pits of misery and guilt." With these words, especially the word "guilt," Thielicke may be pointing to "the admitted coexistence of justice and mercy in God." It may well be that "truth lies in the recognition

---

28. Cf. H.-H. Esser, *Begriffslex.* 6:590–91; T. F. Torrance, *The Doctrine of Grace*, pp. 11–12.

29. George Eldon Ladd, *Jesus and the Kingdom*, p. 210. Cf. *TDNT* 2:198.

30. Skinner, *Prophecy and Religion*, p. 48; James Muilenburg, *The Way of Israel*, p. 23. See Hosea 6:4; 7:15; 11:8–9.

31. Herbert Waddams, *A New Introduction to Moral Theology*, p. 12.

that both aspects must be preserved in a way that it is beyond the competence of human reason to exhibit." [32]

The naked human reason will stagger before the task of such exposition. But with all the resources which are available to him, those of revelation as well as those of reason, the apostle Paul may at least have a contribution to make. The tension may be resolved.

To begin with, Paul agrees with the author of Hebrews in rejecting the law as the means of overcoming the problem. It gives the knowledge of sin, excites desire and produces wrath, but it never leads to justification. It is "incapable" (3:20; 4:15; 5:20; 7:7–8; 8:3).

*Paul has a gospel.* It is no afterthought. It was promised long ago. God made it known through his prophets and we may read about it in the Old Testament. It is "the gospel of God." He is its "originator." [33] He is also its content and indeed its owner. (Sanday and Headlam are probably right in declining to restrict the genitive to one precise classification, that of origin.) The gospel comes from God and it is about God. At the same time it finds its focus in Christ (1:1–5). As Michel finely says (p. 36, n. 6), Christ is for Paul the light which falls on God. The Jews were entrusted with the oracles of God (3:2), the oracles of promise. The gospel is their fulfillment.

For *Christ is the gospel.* Paul is the priestly minister of Christ Jesus, serving the gospel of God as a priest (15:16) and completing the preaching of the gospel of Christ (15:19). This Jesus is the Son of God (1:3–4, 9; 5:10; 8:3, 29, 32). He did not merely appear on the earthly scene. He was the One who was to come (*ho mellōn* 5:14) and "God sent his Son" (8:3). To human eyes he was a man, born of King David's line; and he was truly man. He emerged in clear outline as Son of God as a result of his resurrection from the dead. The Father (15:6) sent his Son and there was a genuine incarnation. [34] He was sinless, for it was in the likeness of sinful flesh that he came and he is the image to which his people are to be conformed (8:3, 29).

It is central to the gospel of God and the gospel of Christ that "God is for us"—this is the reason why he sent his Son—and that "he did not spare his Son but delivered him up [*paredōken*] for us all" (8:31–32). This somber verb (cf. 1:24, 26, 28) must be understood within the control of divine providence. Our Lord was delivered up by human agency: by Judas (Mark 14:10–11, 18, 42–44); by the high priests (Mark 15:1, 10); and by Pilate (Mark 15:15). But he was no passive victim and still less did he struggle to avoid the devices of men. He is the Son of God "who loved me and delivered himself up for me" (Gal. 2:20). In this he was obedient to the Father (5:19).

---

32. Helmut Thielicke, *The Waiting Father: Sermons on the Parables of Jesus,* p. 169; F. L. Cross, ed., *Oxford Dictionary of the Christian Church,* p. 683.

33. Blass-Debrunner-Funk, 163. But see U. Becker (Hannover), *Begriffslex.* 3:298.

34. Cf. Althaus, p. 10. "Nicht der Mensch ist Sohn geworden, sondern der Sohn wurde Mensch." "It is not that the Man became Son but the Son became Man."

## Righteousness and the Law

It is Christ crucified who according to Paul's gospel is the One who breaks the tension between God's justice and his grace. In speaking of the tension, we have hitherto used pairs of terms in a general way: justice and grace; judgment and grace; holiness and love; justice and mercy. We must now be more precise and start where Paul started, with righteousness (*dikaiosunē*). Unlike the author of Hebrews, Paul does not seem to have used the concept of Jesus as our high priest.

"Righteousness" is a difficult word to interpret. Apart from the meaning of the term in Greek we have to remember the Old Testament background. The waters of *tsedaqah* may flow into the river of *dikaiosunē*. The term is thus fluid and in any given context it is necessary to discover which aspect of its meaning is prominent. Great caution is necessary. The prominence of one aspect may not involve the rejection of all others. Thus David Hill (*Greek Words*, p. 98) can quote from S. Ullman's *Principles of Semantics* (Oxford, 1957): "a word may retain its previous sense or senses and at the same time acquire one or several new senses." This view is confirmed by C. H. Dodd's treatment of the term *pneuma*. According to Dodd the word means breath, wind, spirit. But a Greek would not keep to a neat separation of meanings. In translating John 3:8 ("the wind bloweth where it listeth") we have to use both "wind" and "spirit" to render the same Greek word, but in so doing we have lost something. The Greek *pneuma* has a unity of concept which cannot be reproduced in English, at any rate by a single word.[35]

We may speak in the same way, *mutatis mutandis,* about *dikaiosunē.* We must not take the risk of "losing something" from its unity of concept. We must remember the meanings and nuances which belong to the word and which seem to us merely to lurk in the background. We could do worse than heed the advice given by A. P. Herbert to a young politician. "Remember, my boy, that anything, however trivial, may suddenly emerge into the daylight and become an important political issue."

In our study of the *dikaios* group we shall not, I hope, be blind to the value of philology but nevertheless we shall look as well at the sentences and the contexts, "the living relationship which words bear to one another."[36] Etymology must exercise an ultimate control but it is within the spaciousness of the context and current use.

Righteousness belongs to God; he is righteous (1:17; 3:5, 21–22, 25–26: 10:3; and 3:26). Paul speaks of "the righteousness of God" and of his purpose to go on being (*einai* not *genesthai*) righteous.

We seek now to establish the fact that *God's righteousness is revealed in the law.*

---

35. See C. H. Dodd's important article in *The Expository Times* 72, no. 9. (June 1961): 272.

36. Muilenburg, *The Way of Israel*, p. 16. Cf. Hill, *Greek Words*, pp. 3 ff. and his reference to James Barr.

1. The law is God's law. It is not a human contrivance. It is not a device of a social contract, a necessary convenience to prevent men from tearing one another to pieces. It is "the law of God" (7:22, 25). The Jew relies on it and knows God's will because he is instructed out of the law. Because he possesses the embodiment of knowledge and truth in (the book of—Arndt-Gingrich, p. 530, under *morphōsis*) the law, the Jew stands back and looks at himself from an independent position and cries confidently, "You are a guide to the blind, a light to men in darkness, the educator of the foolish, the teacher of the immature." He glories in God because he glories in the law (2:17–23).

2. The law gives the knowledge of sin (3:20; 7:7). Disobedience to the law may or may not be a crime against society, whether society is represented by the family, the city or the state. What is certain is that disobedience to the law is disobedience to God. The law is holy and the commandment is holy, righteous and good (7:12). The law is spiritual and fine (*kalos*) (7:14, 16).

3. Transgression of the law dishonors God (2:23).

4. The law is a law of righteousness (9:31). Gentiles did not pursue righteousness but "overtook" it—surely an unusual illustration of grace! (Cf. Herodotus IX.58.) Israel on the contrary did pursue the law of righteousness but did not attain to it. It should not be supposed that Israel was in pursuit of some law or principle, whatever it might prove to be, which would give righteousness. Israel, unlike Gentiles, already had the law and all that was necessary was to obey it. Mere hearers of the law are not righteous in God's sight; the obedient will be deemed righteous (2:13).

For there are three aspects of law. It is a written word, a book, which may be put away, as we say, in a bookcase and forgotten. It is law as commandment, demanding to be obeyed. And it is law fulfilled in obedience. Law in the first two senses was already in Israel's possession. It is law in the third sense which Israel sought without avail. As we learned in Romans 7, (see p. 84), man under the law approves of the law but finds that he cannot obey it. His serious but unsuccessful struggle (7:23) is expressed in another way when Paul thinks of pursuit (9:31). Israel runs speedily after "law fulfilled" but always finds it elusive.

The loose genitive, "law of righteousness," combines three possibilities. It may be objective. If so, it means "the law which produces righteousness" (cf. 2:13). It may be descriptive, "the righteous law" (cf. 7:12). Or it may be a genitive of material, "the law which consists of righteousness (as a program to be carried out)." Probably Paul had all in mind, though not neatly separated in the manner of a grammarian.

If Israel's "pursuit" had been successful, she would not have sought in vain to establish her own righteousness (10:3). It would have been her own in the sense that it had been achieved by the sheer human effort of obedience to the law—by works, as Paul would say. But in another sense it would still have been the righteousness of God—the righteousness of God which is required by the law.

5. Men should be subordinate both to the law of God (8:7–8) and to

the righteousness of God (10:3). The law of God requires something from men—obedience. This is plain enough from the very meaning of law. But the use of the same verb, "subordinate," likewise implies that something is required by righteousness. Either we must say merely that the righteousness of God requires something and then look around to try and find out what it is, or with greater reason say that the righteousness of God requires men to be obedient to the law. It could hardly be true that God's law demands one thing and his righteousness another.

6. Analogously Paul speaks of being slaves of righteousness (6:18–19) and slaves of God (6:22). It is significant that this is in a context of obedience (6:16–17). Of all people a slave is one who should do as he is told. Righteousness commands and God commands. Is the conscientious "slave" to regard himself as trying to serve two masters? It is unthinkable. The requirement which righteousness makes is the requirement which God makes.

We thus move a step forward. Law, righteousness and God all make the same demands on men. God's righteousness is revealed in the law.

7. In theory, righteousness could come from the law. We have seen (2:13) that it is performance which counts. Hence Moses can speak of "the righteousness which proceeds from law" (10:5). There seem to be two concepts here, "the (required) righteousness (which is heard of, 2:13) from the law" and, if performed, "the (achieved) righteousness proceeding from law." "Complete conformity to God's will as expressed in the Torah may, in theory at any rate, put a man in a right relation with God" (Hill, *Greek Words*, p. 147). Even in theory could such righteousness come from a law which did not express the righteousness of God?

Perhaps some weight should be given to the fact that the word *dikaiōma* is used to express the commands of the law (2:26; 8:4) and also "a righteous deed" (5:18; Arndt-Gingrich, p. 197), as well as "the command of God" (1:32). (Cf. p. 23.)

8. The righteousness of God is attested by the law (3:21).

From the above considerations we conclude that the law reveals the righteousness of God. It might be worthwhile to bear in mind the distinction between the righteousness of God as a description of his character and the righteousness of God as a description of his requirement. In theory, if the requirement were met, we could speak of the righteousness of God achieved by men and even of the righteousness of men.

## Goodness and the Law

A further point is now advanced. *The law which reveals God's righteousness is the detailed outworking of the law of love* (13:8–10). Paul tells the Romans that they should not owe anything to anybody, except for one thing. They should love one another. To owe something means that the other man has a claim on us. We are under an obligation. We "ought" to render the debt. We ought therefore to love. If we do this we fulfill the law. Paul means that we obey the law. The man who completely obeys the law is righteous, as we have seen. Righteousness thus is a constant love, directing itself to all sorts and conditions of men in a variety of situations.

By way of illustration Paul gives four prohibitions from the law, adding "and any other commandment." Obedience to the four commandments mentioned manifests love. Let us take them in order.

If a man obeys the commandment, "Thou shalt not commit adultery," he shows love to his wife by his faithfulness to her. He shows love to "the other woman" by respecting her sexual integrity. He shows love to the other woman's present or future husband by respecting his marital rights. If the man himself is hitherto unmarried he shows love to his future wife by respecting her marital rights. (All this applies of course, *mutatis mutandis*, to a woman.) The thrust of the argument is not affected by the "depth" of adultery (cf. Matt. 5:25–26), except that the deeper the adultery avoided, the deeper is the love.

If a man obeys the commandment, "Thou shalt not commit murder," he shows love to his neighbor by respecting his life and by refusing to bring sorrow on the bereaved. He also shows love toward his own people by sparing them the sorrow at his own punishment.

Obedience to the commandment, "Thou shalt not steal," expresses love toward a neighbor by respecting his rights of property, especially if what might have been stolen is something on which livelihood or even life depends. (This is the reason why horse stealing in the "Wild West" of generations ago was so serious. A man's life depended on his horse.) Such obedience also shows love towards dependents.

Obedience to the commandment, "Thou shalt not covet," shows love toward another man by desiring him to keep what is his own. It rejoices that the other man can enjoy something that is denied to others. It shows love by refusing to poison personal relationships by a secret and perhaps sullen desire which is selfish, excessive and uncontrolled.

If a man thus obeyed the law, he would do no hurt to his neighbor. He would thus love him. All the ethical precepts of the law are summed up in the comprehensive commandment, "Thou shalt love thy neighbor as thyself." If he really loves him, he is a man of moral goodness. The word *moral* here is vital. A "good" fountain pen is one which will retain the ink, has a good nib, writes easily and so on. A "good" automobile will be reliable and take you where you want to go quickly and comfortably. But a good man is one who is morally good.

But we have seen that if a man keeps the law, which expresses the righteousness of God, he himself is righteous. We have just discovered that if he keeps the law he is morally good. We infer that righteousness must mean moral goodness.

All this is legitimate argument but it is theory. It asserts a principle. The man who keeps the law is righteous and he is morally good. Unfortunately he does not exist. Paul was well aware of this. He spoke of men's *adikia*, the opposite of righteousness (3:5), and affirms that all men are "under sin." He proves it from Scripture and his concatenation of texts is significant (3:9–18). He begins with the statement, "There is no *dikaios*, not even one." After our identification of "righteous" and "morally good," it is interesting to see that the JB translates "There is not a good man left, no, not one." This statement dominates the whole passage.

Having laid down this basic principle, Paul elaborates it. He begins with spiritual unintelligence. Nobody understands. He might here have quoted himself. "Their unintelligent heart was darkened" (1:21). (Note the cognate verb and adjective.) This is followed by impiety. There is nobody who seeks for God. They have neglected the Creator (1:25). It is this which causes all the trouble. Failure in religion means failure in morality. Paul thus follows the line which he had taken in his first chapter. He now goes on to give details of the failure in morality.

"All have swerved aside." This recalls the word "trespass" or "transgression." *To swerve* (*ekklinō*) means "not to continue in a straight line," the line which is expected or is right. Thus they have departed from a norm. This is significant, because it brings in the idea of righteousness. "From the time of his creation he is as he ought to be (that is the fundamental meaning of the Hebrew word for 'righteous')." [37]

"He is as he ought to be" implies conformity to a norm. This interpretation of righteousness goes back to Kautzsch. It is accepted by H. Wheeler Robinson and E. J. Young.[38] All who departed from the norm became morally useless.

Paul now gives examples from the realm of moral conduct. There is not one who shows kindness. Their throat is an open tomb. They are always ready to receive the unwary into an unwholesome grave. They breathe out not merely death and destruction but putrefaction. (But see H. Hanse, *TDNT* 4:57–58.) Their honeyed words deceive their listeners. What seems to be sugar is poison, for they are against their fellows, not for them: their mouth is full of cursing and animosity.

But it is not only their words which do the damage. They run swiftly with dagger at the ready. The violent death of men is their purpose and their achievement. They leave behind them a trail of ruin and misery. A peaceful errand is beyond their ken. And Paul rounds it off as he began. It is all because they had no vision of the fear of God.

Men who behave like this are not *dikaioi*. They are not righteous. They are not morally good. We come to the same conclusion if we reverse the process. If men did the opposite of what Paul has described, they would have moral and spiritual intelligence and would eagerly seek for God. They would conform to his will revealed in the law, and would be centers of moral value. Kindness to others would be their habit. Their language would be sincere and without guile. Their homes would be open to the needy and welcome would be on their lips. In everything they would try to help their fellow men. They would speed to save life. Blessings from the grateful would follow them everywhere they went. For they would have a vision always before their eyes—obedience to God.

---

37. S. Mowinckel, *He That Cometh*, p. 373; cf. pp. 383–84 "the ideally pious and moral person."

38. H. Wheeler Robinson, *Inspiration and Revelation in the Old Testament*, pp. 57, 84; E. J. Young, *The Book of Isaiah*, 1:81. Cf. also Hill, *Greek Words*, p. 97.

If even one such a man could be found Paul would call him *dikaios*. It is obvious that he would be righteous, as obedient to the law, and equally obvious that he would be morally good. Obedience would make him righteous (2:13). This is the principle of the matter. In actual fact no such man can be found (3:20). But the principle still stands fast.

It seems clear that righteousness is ethical. It may be regarded as a required program of human conduct or as obedient human conduct. But if the law, which describes the program, reveals the righteousness of God, then righteousness describes God's own character. The law is righteous because God is righteous. Hence the righteousness of God includes *ethical character*. It also includes *legislative authority:* men ought to be subordinate to it (10:3). A third element must not be forgotten, *judicial administration:* God exercises moral government of the world and he will execute judgment on the world (2:5–11; 3:5–6, 19; note the moral distinctions in 2:5–11, especially "doing evil" and "doing good," and "obeying *adikia*").

When in 3:21, immediately after his first section, especially 3:9–20, Paul goes on to speak of the righteousness of God, we ought at least to consider the possibility that the ethical element remains. And if we are tempted to regard *dikaiosunē* as abstract, we should remember that it expresses the righteousness of him who is the living God, who has mind, knowledge, wisdom, will and purpose and is consistent. When years ago I wrote an M.A. thesis on Aristotle, I found much to suggest that this word could mean something very like "moral consciousness." As equity it can judge even the law itself. It may be that it retains a certain spaciousness, for it dwells in personality. In any case we have tried to see the word, as Paul used it, in its living relationships.

The righteousness of God has been revealed (3:21–26). It is attested by the law but is now apart from the law. Two factors are here apparent: it is connected with Jesus Christ and it is concerned with sinners. Christ has done something for them and the purpose of his work for them is to demonstrate God's righteousness.

The purpose is twofold. It looks back to the past and seeks to clear up a problem; and it sees that problem in a wider setting.

In the past men have sinned. The perfect tense is significant. Not only did men sin. They have sinned and are now therefore still sinners. The point is not being made that they go on sinning. Their sins were committed in the past and they are not left in the past. The men who committed them are "men with a record." In other words, they are guilty men.

This is only repeating what Paul has just said. All the world is answerable (*hupodikos*) to God. Men are guilty sinners and it seems that God has done nothing about it. He has not intervened to punish. They seem to go scot free. But all this was the period of God's forbearance (*anoche*; see pp. 90–91). He was indeed governing the world (cf. 3:6) but his method was patience (2:4). This can be misinterpreted. Men can think that God is indifferent to moral distinctions, that the warnings of his prophets are mere bluff and conscience a liar; that God's moral character is a fairy tale and the activity of his judgment a mere quiescence. It is not so. In Christ he has revealed his righteousness.

The wider setting is "the present time," the day of God's grace. In the long period which is behind us God only passed over men's sins: this is what *paresis* implies. He did not punish them. By contrast the present time is the time, not of divine forbearance, but of grace. Its blessing is not *paresis* but *aphesis*, forgiveness.

Even in this wider setting, however, there is still a problem. The world is answerable to God, the God whose righteousness is expressed in the law. There would be no point in making the world answerable if it were never to be called to account. "Without the conception of judgment all talk of responsibility is idle chatter." [39] The righteousness of God requires obedience (6:18–20; 10:3). The wages of sin, of disobedience, is death. But God's free gift in Christ is eternal life. Has he given up his claim on men's obedience? Is he open to the charge that his moral perfection is invalid? [40]

In the order of creation the natural law must be obeyed. Men cannot trifle with it. If a man jumps out of an aircraft without a parachute, he does not break the natural law. It breaks him. If without a parachute he floated down safely, the natural order would be broken and we should speak of miracle. The natural order has been invaded. Perhaps it would not matter very much. The laws of nature are not self-existent or sacrosanct. They have no independent existence. They express the uniform way in which ultimately God is running the universe. They are external to him. They are his invention. God can work a miracle in nature but he cannot miraculously work on his own nature to change it.

The disobedience which is sin attacks the law, which is the expression of the righteousness of God. It thus opposes his personal will, and his will is not arbitrary. Sin enters into the secret shrine of God's very nature, looks around, and says, "This has no right to be." Not only is the moral order to be upheld. God himself must be vindicated.

We might try to illustrate the matter thus. Let us suppose that a man invented a game, drew up its rules and then presented a club with a field, a pavilion and all the necessary equipment. The rules might be broken or altered but it might not greatly matter. But if the players attack their benefactor personally, despise his kindness and deny his right to make a gift— what then? That would be another matter.

God may forgive, but in so doing he cannot deny himself. He cannot merely wipe the slate clean. This would be inconsistent, a contradiction of his righteousness revealed in the law as a "required program," and an affront to eternal Goodness itself. It would make him "an accessory after the fact." [41]

In the very provision for pardon God must assert his righteousness. It must be made plain that his character remains the same; that the law was

---

39. Emil Brunner, *Eternal Hope*, p. 179.

40. An apt illustration may be found in the ecumenical discussions about the "validity" of ministerial orders.

41. If murder has been committed and a man witnessed it but keeps silence, he makes himself a party to the offense and may be charged with being an accessory after the fact. In a sense he helped or encouraged the murderer. He participates in his guilt by giving the murderer the shelter of his silence.

a valid expression of his character; and the law has been obeyed and vindicated. The purpose of this demonstration of God's righteousness is that God may go on being (*einai*) righteous, even when justifying [42] the sinner.

## Redemption and Propitiation

The righteousness of God has been made plain by the work of Christ. Preachers, I suspect, have long made use of C. H. Dodd's observation (p. 56) that Paul combines three metaphors, the law court, slavery and sacrificial religion. No doubt many a three-point sermon has been thus inspired. The danger is that in an admirable desire for homiletic balance the preacher coordinates the three metaphors. But they are not coordinate. Justification (the law court metaphor) does not take place until a man believes. Redemption and sacrifice were completed by our Lord on the cross. Even if nobody ever had faith in him, his sacrifice and redemption form a "finished work." It is granted that there is an unfinished work of Christ, but it is not redemption or sacrifice.

Redemption (*apolutrōsis*) speaks of emancipation. But emancipation from what? If we say simply, "from sin" (6:17–18), it is pertinent to ask why we go on sinning. There are notable and sublime victories over sin indeed, to say nothing of the countless and unsung conquests in the lives of the humblest of Christians. But sin has not been eradicated.

Now we have seen that Paul has spoken of the wrath and judgment which await the sinner. God's indignation flames against sin "as it must if the world's pillars are not to be based on rottenness." [43] He has affirmed that the world is answerable to God but that it has no answer. In the present context it would seem that men have been redeemed from "answerableness." Their grievous responsibility for their sins, for what they have done and for what they are, has been lifted from their shoulders. Christ has undertaken responsibility for them. The work of Christ is liberation from guilt.

There are certain unsolved problems here. If Paul is influenced by 4 Maccabees 6:29 and 17:21, the liberation means "deliverance through the *substitutionary* death of Jesus." If the apostle is not so influenced, it pictures either the slave's "manumission procedure" or "the Exodus pattern" (Hill, *Greek Words*, p. 76, italics his). Whatever proves to be the final solution, the liberation was achieved through the cross and it was an emancipation from guilt. To limit it to the breaking of the power of sin as a sort of slave-master of men savors of eudaemonism. It is mercifully true that

> He breaks the power of cancelled sin,
> He sets the prisoner free,

but the cancellation is prior to the "breaking." And the whole work of Christ revealed the righteousness of God.

---

42. The meaning of this term will have to be considered later.
43. H. R. Mackintosh, *The Christian Experience of Forgiveness*, p. 32. cf. Cranfield, pp. 206–8.

The law expressed that righteousness and Christ revealed it afresh by obeying it. If ever any one loved his neighbor, Christ did. If ever in the long history of humanity someone could be found who did no ill to his neighbor, Christ is that Person. He fulfilled the law by obeying it (13:8–10). What was embodied in a book was now actualized in a Person. Words were clothed in flesh and blood. The righteousness of God dwelt among men. His character was manifested in a thousand situations. Paul can thus speak of "the obedience of the One" and of the summary "one righteous act" (5:18–19).

Christ accordingly revealed the righteousness of God both as God's character and as his requirement. In meeting the requirement Christ is himself righteous (cf. 3:10).

But the law which reveals the righteousness of God has sanctions. It is God's righteous commandment (*dikaiōma*) "that those who do such things are worthy of death" (1:32). Men are answerable to God, and as Brunner robustly observed (cf. p. 101), judgment is implied. God "moves toward" *dikaiokrisia* (2:5; cf. vv. 2, 12, 14–16). The wage of sin is death (6:23). But Christ did not earn that fearful pay; and yet he died. He died for the ungodly, for us—sinners (5:6, 8). "The death which he died [cognate accusative], he died to sin once for all" (6:10). The meaning is different from that in 6:2.[44]

Christ thus "has borne on behalf of mankind the full weight of the judgment of God, so that God remains righteous though He acquits sinners."[45] He demonstrated the righteousness of God in three aspects. He demonstrated God's character, God's requirement—both as requirement and as fulfilled requirement—and God's judgment. He obeyed the law and submitted to its judgment, though he himself was not liable to its judgment, for men. By his obedience and submission he upheld the law—for God. If the law is upheld, the righteousness of God is upheld. This norm is not apart from him. God is his own standard. God himself is vindicated. The "eternal law of righteousness" (R. W. Dale) is alive in him.

On behalf of men Christ made the only answer to God which they could have given, submission to his judgment. And by his grace men did not have to give that answer. He undertook responsibility for them.

Two observations should here be made. First, the essential nature of sin is seen in the cross. We have said (p. 101) that sin denies God's very nature. It does not so much deny that it exists; it repudiates it: "this has no right to be." In the cross this attitude is brought out into the open. Evil men, in their willfulness and wickedness, sought (successfully) to crucify the Lord and sought (unsuccessfully) to destroy him. When Absolute Goodness was within the range of sinful men, sin showed its hostility and sought to destroy it. Absolute Goodness must judge and destroy such a malignant horror. And if God is to forgive sinners, he must be vindicated.

Second, God did execute judgment. This is the force of the *paredōken*

---

44. Michel, p. 156. Michel aptly quotes Euthymius Zigabenus, "the death which he died, he died because of our sin."

45. Richardson, *Introduction to Theology of NT*, p. 77.

(p. 94). In the cross the Son of God in obedience submitted to the judgment. The divine immorality of letting off the sinner by means of the added crime of penally crushing the sinless is a charge which cannot be sustained. Dale's reply to James Martineau contains the answer *in nuce:* "He must not discuss the Evangelical theory of the Atonement on the Unitarian theory of the Person of Christ." [46]

Christ has taken responsibility for men. He gave their answer. They are accused, inexcusable, answerable and liable to judgment. Sent by the Father for this very purpose, he intervened and answered for them by taking God's judgment upon himself. Arising out of this his work for them on the cross he answers for them in another way. In an atmosphere of accusation Paul replies to his own rhetorical question, "who is the one who will condemn?" by saying that Christ Jesus crucified, risen and enthroned, "intercedes for us" (8:34). The Father will hearken to the Son because his righteousness has already been upheld. All sin, including the "sin in believers," has been judged on the cross. My sins and failures of today, as well as all the sins of all mankind that ever were or will be, were gathered together in one comprehensive accusation and condemned. And Christ submitted to the judgment. The sentence of death fell on him. If a believing man falls into sin, his Redeemer has already taken the judgment upon it. In his intercession he "speaks for the sinner" positively ( contrast Acts 25:24; Rom. 11:2). In the presence of God, he is for us *wider alle Verurteilung*— "against all condemnation." [47] The vivid imagery suggests that the Son "reminds" the Father that the case has been heard and the judgment given and executed. What it does not suggest is that the Father needs to be reminded or persuaded. Father and Son are united in love for men (8:35, 39) and in grace (5:15). The Son's submission to the Father's judgment and the Son's intercession with the Father are but the method of their united love for men.

After this consideration of redemption, judgment and the demonstration of God's righteousness, we must return to the *hilastērion*-propitiation (3:25). "By means of it is the *apolutrōsis* or redemption of the sinner and therewith the revelation of God's righteousness" (Friedrich Büchsel, *TDNT* 3: 320). The two terms, redemption and *hilastērion,* thus go together and this is our justification for our apparently moving *per saltum,* at a bound, from redemption to the demonstration of God's righteousness. In between comes the *hilastērion.*

The meaning of this term is still under discussion, and it is fashionable to think of "the means of expiating sin" (NEB). But the context is dominated by judgment and wrath. The opening chapters have been building up to this point. Other expressions in 3:21–26 relate to judgment but "there is nothing but this word to express the turning away of divine wrath" (Hill, *Greek Words,* p. 39). Does it do it?

C. H. Dodd argued (p. 54) that the LXX usage is constantly determina-

---

46. R. W. Dale, *The Atonement,* p. 454. Dale's treatment is very moving. I have not thought it necessary to comment on the mere "letting off."

47. Althaus, p. 97. "Christus hat in seinem Tode alle Verurteilung auf sich genommen"—"In his death Christ has taken all condemnation upon himself."

tive for Paul and that consequently the meaning conveyed is that of expiation, not propitiation. The cognate verb has the sense of performing an act whereby guilt or defilement is removed. "Such acts were felt to have the value, so to speak, of a disinfectant." But what has happened to the wrath?

Dodd's view has been challenged, notably by Dr. Leon Morris in his *The Apostolic Preaching of the Cross,* and more recently by Dr. David Hill. His researches lead Dr. Hill to assert that " the idea of propitiation cannot be dismissed simply on the basis of LXX usage." We are back at our starting point.

T. W. Manson (in *The Journal of Theological Studies* 46 [1945]) interpreted *hilastērion* as the "mercy seat" *(kappōreth)* of the Ark in the Holy of Holies which the high priest sprinkled with blood on the Day of Atonement. This revives "the ordinary interpretation" which Dean Alford (1810–71), following De Wette, rejected as inapplicable.[48] The *hilastērion* is thus "the place where God shows mercy to man," and the background of the thought is the Day of Atonement.[49]

The theory has appealed to many, though not to all. I disagree with the late Dr. Manson with regret. I do not think it necessary here to go over linguistic matters in detail. Dr. Hill has followed the criticisms of Dr. Leon Morris with sympathy ("his arguments are cogent") and in the light of "the remarkable community of thought between 4 Macc. 17:22 and Rom. 3:21–23," he sees propitiatory significance.

It would be difficult to undermine Dr. Hill's position. The study of the context of words suggests that the idea of propitiation belongs to the group of words cognate with *hilastērion* (*Greek Words,* p. 47). If this is not so, Paul has built up an accusation of men which can only culminate in wrath and judgment. Salvation is provided for men whereby they may escape judgment. Does the apostle leave us in doubt as to whether God's wrath has been turned away? It may be, as Barrett says (p. 78), that "expiation has, as it were, the effect of propitiation." The expiated sin no longer excites God's wrath.

The concept of expiation seems to be in danger of being only in the realm of things. Dodd's. brilliant illustration of disinfectant is very revealing. The disease germs are destroyed and perhaps the odor removed. A person coming into a disinfected room might never know that disease and smell had been there. But God knows of men's sin and his personal attitude is involved.

It would seem that our Lord has turned away God's wrath from men by deflecting it on to himself. This is a sound view, in spite of the extremes of language in which it has at times been expressed. It coheres with the Cry of Dereliction on the cross. This does not mean that the Father was personally angry with his Son, with whom he was and is always well pleased. It is only as he stood in the place of men that our Lord bore the wrath, the separation from the presence of his Father.[50]

It is sometimes suggested that an element of the unethical is here in-

48. Henry Alford, *The Greek Testament* 2:343.
49. Cf. Davies, *Paul and Rabbinic Judaism,* p. 241.
50. Cf. Cranfield, pp. 214–18, 314 ("penalty"), and 373 ("condemnation").

volved, on the apparent crude principle that "God so loved the world that he sent Someone else to suffer. . . . " Not enough consideration has been given, I believe, to what the Dereliction meant for God the Father. It is said that the Father withdrew his fellowship from the Son, and we rightly dwell on the agony which it meant for the Son—an agony with which the physical sufferings cannot be compared. Is it to be assumed that the Father enjoyed the experience? All that the Son suffered, the Father suffered at the break between himself and his beloved Son. It was not a metaphysical or ontological break but an experiential one. All that we mean when we say that a man tries to pray but cannot get through to God, multiplied by infinity, was the woe which the Lord suffered.

And the Father suffered with him. If, by comparison, the physical sufferings were as but a drop in the bucket, then it is no objection that the Father was not himself crucified. This must not be misunderstood. I am not for one moment minimizing the exquisite pain and suffering of crucifixion. What I am saying is that the holiness of Jesus was so great and real and his fellowship with his Father so intimate and unbroken, that the physical suffering, however great in itself, was slight *in comparison with* the awful desolation of being absolutely alone in the universe, cut off from the Father. If we may thus "ignore" the physical suffering, then we can say that Father and Son both experienced the same degree of suffering. The Father himself knows, no less than the Son, the infliction of his own wrath. In the Dereliction Father and Son were severed in fellowship but united still in mutual love and in love for men. Separated in experience, they were one in purpose.

The order of Paul's thought in 3:21–26 is noteworthy. All men are sinners. He thus starts in the present: sinful men may be justified. This is possible by means of the redemption and this in turn through the *hilastērion*. The latter is a sacrifice: "for Paul the term 'blood' would inevitably have sacrificial connotations whatever symbolic meaning he may or may not have imported into it." [51] The sacrifice was propitiatory. Therefore the wrath of God was turned away. Perhaps we ought to avoid the word *appeased*. Apart from its pagan associations, the wrath was exhausted rather than appeased. It was borne by the Son and the Father was not unaffected. The sacrifice opens the way to redemption. The Son bore the wrath because he took the guilt. Men are answerable to God and the Son gave the answer. He took men's responsibility and bore the judgment. [52]

This close association, if not intermingling, of sacrifice and redemption corresponds to the overlapping of wrath and judgment (see p. 87). There may be a similar connection if we may translate 8:3 "God sent his own Son . . . as a sin-offering [53] [*peri hamartias*] and condemned sin in the flesh."

51. Davies, *Paul and Rabbinic Judaism*, p. 236. Though Nigel Turner can still see in the Greek *en* the Semitic construction which renders literally the *beth pretii* (Hebrew preposition of price): "at the cost of his blood" (Rom. 3:25; 5:9). Moulton, *Grammar*, vol. 4. Nigel Turner, *Style*, p. 156. (Hereafter referred to as Moulton-Turner, 4.)

52. Cf. Althaus, p. 86. "Es ist der Tod der Sünder, den er stirbt. . . . Christus erleidet an sich die Verurteilung des Sünders." "It is the death of sinners which he dies. . . . Christ suffers in himself the condemnation of the sinner."

53. Sanday and Headlam, p. 193; Bruce, p. 161; NEB, RSV and ASV margin.

The combination of sacrifice and redemption demonstrates the righteousness of God, as we have seen. Justification can now begin, because the sacrifice has been offered, wrath and judgment endured and the answer given.[54]

Before we turn to justification, however, there are two further expressions to be considered. "Blessed are they . . . whose sins have been covered" (4:7). The verb is *epikaluptō* and the quotation is from Psalm 32:1. Now the apostle knew the Book of Proverbs and quoted it (Rom. 12:20/Prov. 25:21-22, LXX). He must have known a passage not far away, and if he did not, his spiritual common sense would have told him that "he who covers his impiety will not prosper" (Prov. 28:13, LXX). There must be two kinds of "covering" and it depends on who does it. The Greek verb is the same in Psalm 31:1 and Proverbs 28:13, LXX. In each case the Hebrew verb is a form of *kasah*. An impious man "covers" his impiety by hiding it. There is no blessedness here. That is reserved for those whose sins have been "covered" in another way—and not by themselves, but by God.

The Hebrew verb is used, as in Psalm 85:3, for the technical *kpr*,[55] a root which we have already seen in the "mercy seat" (*kappōreth*). For good reasons Dr. Hill does not go into the question of whether the basic meaning of *kpr* is "cover" or "wipe away." [56] Even if there are exceptions to its mainly cultic use, Paul must have had the sacrifice in mind in 4:7, so soon after the mention of the *hilastērion*. The implication is that God has done something in Christ before any potential believer appeared on the scene.

The other expression concerns the "removal" (aorist subjunctive middle of *aphairein*) of sins (cf. pp. 59–60), is an allusion to Jeremiah 38:33–34, LXX, and an almost perfect quotation from Isaiah 27:9, LXX. In the work of Christ sins have been removed from men as they are in the sight of God (Rom. 11:27).

We must still delay our approach to justification. We have already seen (p. 104) how our Lord at the right hand of God speaks for sinners. He need not be there alone. Through him there is access (*prosagōgē*) which we have gained into "this grace in which we stand" (5:2). The picture is of some sort of enclosure. Alexander Souter (*Pocket Lexicon*) translates it by "access," "entrée," "landing-stage." C. K. Barrett sees the approach to a holy place in virtue of a sacrifice. Access suggests the absence of barricades. Entrée implies that if you know the right people you have the privilege of moving in, say, diplomatic society, or that if someone can be found to present you it will be possible to appear at the court of the monarch. A landing stage overcomes the natural obstacle of a precipitous cliff and makes it possible to get ashore.

However we picture it there is a "place" which we can enter only in view of a sacrifice. There was a time when we had not taken the first step, but the landing stage was already in position. But what is "this grace in which we stand"? Paul himself supplies the answer. Christ has received us (15:7) and God has received us (14:3). First we had to come to Christ. When

---

54. See further Matthew Black, pp. 68–73, especially p. 73, "the very wrath of God visited on Christ for the sins of mankind was the expression of His saving love."

55. Cf. C. A. Briggs, *Psalms* 1:277.

56. Hill, *Greek Words*, pp. 30–31; but cf. E. J. Young *Isaiah*, 1:252, n. 37.

we did that we found that we had come to God. But even before we had started, the way was open. "Thou didst open the kingdom of heaven to all believers." It was "open" before a single man set foot in it.

"Access" thus implies a door already open, a door into the very presence of God. In virtue of his sacrifice the Lord leads his believing people to the Father himself, the Father on his throne. Believers do not wish to share his rule. It is enough for them in Christ to be close to God. (But cf. 5:17.)

The Lord's "leading" of his people to the Father must not be taken out of proportion. It is not a long pilgrimage but an immediate experience. Christ is the Door but the Father is not a long way in on the other side of the door. Believing men turn to Christ and find God in him. For though Paul does not use the word in Romans, his thought implies that Christ is the Mediator.[57]

We shall be saved from the eschatological wrath through him (5:9). We have *(echomen)*—or we should enjoy *(echōmen)*—peace with God through him (5:1). Through Christ crucified is reconciliation (5:10–11) and overwhelming victory (8:37, 39). The "way in" to all this, the access, is through him (5:2). Worship and thanksgiving to God are offered through him (1:8; 7:25; 16:27). It is through him that Paul can speak of our reigning and of grace reigning (5:17, 21). Grace and apostleship are received through him (1:5) and God will judge through him (2:16).

Thus the great problem of Judaism has been solved. God's righteousness continues untarnished, undiminished and absolute; and his grace is extended to sinners in Jesus Christ, who undertook the responsibility of men, bore the wrath and judgment of God and gave his life as a sacrifice. Absolute goodness can forgive and receive sinful men and it was made possible by the cross of Jesus. He was delivered up because of our transgressions and raised with a view to our justification. But when he died, justification had not yet taken place (4:25). His work *for* us was done; his work *in* us was about to begin.

### God at Work in Us—The Work of Christ in Us

It has been said that God's grace is abundant, overflowing and infinite (cf. 5:17, 20) but that admission to his grace (5:2) and the manner of admission are determined by his will.[58] It is not to be regarded as available on demand, whenever it suits the fancy of insolent men to savor it. It is not to be received in any way which men may choose. It is as spacious as the sky and as boundless as the distance between East and West, but God has willed that there should be but one door of entry. The "door" is commonly referred to as justification by faith. We must now investigate this.

### Justification by Faith

To prepare the ground we revert to the fact that words must be studied

---

57. Cf. Michel, p. 40. *"dia* ist die Präposition für Christus als Mittler"—*"dia* is the preposition for Christ as Mediator."

58. Cf. Th. C. Vriezen, *Outline of Old Testament Theology,* p. 168.

in their living context of sentences and paragraphs (see p. 95). In estimating their meaning we must be guided by their actual use as well as by their derivation. The arbitrary imposition of new meanings is ruled out by the "control of the meaning by derivation" (F. Büchsel, *TDNT* 2:661) but the control is relative. " 'The meaning of a word is to be found in the way it is used' has become a well-known slogan." [59]

We have tried to work on this principle. If our interpretation has been correct, we have found that Paul has built up an ethical meaning of the term "righteousness." What he says about the law and about human behavior (see pp. 95–100) leaves no other impression. He then moves on (3:21) to the "but now," ("like a deep breath of relief"—Althaus) and to the righteousness of God manifested apart from law but attested by it. Even if we make due allowance for background and overtones, it would be very violent to drop the ethical from the concept of the righteousness of God.

We should also note the coherence of the *dikaios* group of words. In their use they interlock. Noun *(dikaiosunē)*, adjective *(dikaios)* and verb *(dikaioō)* all appear in one verse (3:26) and they are closely linked in 3:4–5, 10. Adjective and verb are neighbors in 2:13, and adjective and noun in 1:17. Verb and noun come together in 4:2–5. Further elaboration is unnecessary.

We pass on, therefore, to consider the important word *logizomai*. Abraham's faith "was counted to him as righteousness" (4:3, NEB).[60]

The verb denotes a mental activity (2:3; 8:18; 14:14). This is true even if, with Arndt-Gingrich, we translate by the word "credit" (4:4). It may be doubted if the verb means the actual handing over of cash.

The purely mental activity is illustrated in Acts 19:27. The sanctuary of the great goddess Artemis was in danger "of being counted as nothing" *(eis outhen logisthēnai)*. But whatever men thought, there it stood in all its solidity, one of the wonders of the world. It was the "counting" in men's minds which was the point. (The NEB is disappointing here.) Even "cease to command respect" implies mental attitude.

Paul himself uses this construction in an analogous situation. If a Gentile, he argues, keep the commands of the law, "will not his uncircumcision be counted as circumcision" *(eis peritomēn logisthēsetai)*? Such a man will "count as circumcised" (2:26, NEB). It will be as if he had been circumcised, though he will continue in his natural state. He will be, so to speak, as solid and complete as the sanctuary of Artemis. The "counting" takes place in somebody's mind and only in his mind. A similar treatment can be given to 9:8.

These three cases have one element in common, and it is particularly clear in the first two instances. The two subjects are counted as being something (nothing; circumcised) *which in actual fact they are not.* (The juxtaposition of "something" and "nothing" is unfortunate but it cannot be helped. The meaning is clear.)

---

59. D. Z. Phillips, *The Concept of Prayer*, p. 4.
60. Cf. Cranfield, pp. 228–33; George Eldon Ladd, *A Theology of the New Testament*, pp. 437–50.

Now in the construction under discussion *eis* with the accusative case is used in place of a predicative accusative.[61] We can accordingly and legitimately restate the texts thus.

The sanctuary will be counted nothing.

or

Men will count the sanctuary nothing.

The uncircumcision will be counted circumcision.

or

Men will count the uncircumcision circumcision.

This type of expression is used when Paul speaks of "the man who counts something common" (*ti koinon einai*, 14:14).[62] He counts it common and to him it is so—but only to him and to others who think the same as he does. It is solely in people's thought that it is common. *In actual fact it is not.* "I know and am convinced in the Lord Jesus that nothing is common of itself" (14:14). Paul thus demonstrates the mental activity involved in *logizomai* and shows by its usage that men "count" something in their minds which is not the case in actual fact. This may have important consequences when we consider his doctrine of justification by faith.[63]

We begin with the classical statement, "Abraham believed God, and it was counted to him as righteousness" (4:3). The "it" here is undoubtedly faith, as we see in verse 5. "His faith is counted as righteousness." (Cf. 4:9). Who does the "counting"? It can only be God (4:6). If we attempt a restatement on the lines of our previous attempt, the result will be

God counts faith righteousness.

Now whatever the character of Abraham in the original story (Gen. 15:6, LXX), Paul is thinking of the gospel for the men of his own day and age. The man who exercises faith is one who does not "work" and is impious (4:4–5). He has already shown that though in theory obedience to the law will make a man righteous (2:13), in fact "works" are inadequate (3:19–20). Impiety leads to immorality (see pp. 99–100). Nobody is righteous. Everybody is unrighteous. In justification it is the impious man who believes. If it were argued that the exercise of faith in itself makes a man righteous—if, that is, faith is regarded as a "work" which merits the description "righteous"—then God would not "count"; he would not impute righteousness. He would merely recognize it. We conclude therefore that when an unrighteous man believes, God counts him as righteous.

Paul can therefore speak of "the righteousness of faith" (4:11, 13). This is still the righteousness of God. It was revealed by the law, attested by the law, but now receives a new modification. It has been revealed apart from law, that is, in Christ, but it is a righteousness of God which is given to men through faith in Christ. We thus have three aspects of the one righteousness of God (3:21–22):

---

61. Moulton-Howard, *Grammar*, 2:462–63.
62. The addition of *einai* is no problem. See W. W. Goodwin, *Greek Grammar*, paragraphs 919, 1077–80.
63. Cf. Leslie D. Weatherhead, *Psychology, Religion and Healing*, p. 341. Forgiveness is a restoration as though we had never sinned.

> the righteousness of God revealed by the law
> the character of God
> God's requirement for men
> (man's conduct—if obedient)
> the righteousness of God revealed by Christ
> the righteousness of God through faith in Christ.[64]

The third aspect may be put like this: "the-righteousness-of-God-through-faith-in-Christ, (available) for all who believe." All have sinned, Jew and Greek alike, but all who believe are justified through the redemption in Christ Jesus, the *hilastērion*. Believers are justified by God's grace and they are justified *dōrean*, as a gift, "free, gratis and for nothing."

This language (3:23-26) corresponds to that which describes the man who does not "work." When God counts a man's faith as righteousness, he counts the believing man as righteous and he does so on the basis of grace. He has no need to treat the man thus. He does not owe it to him. It is thus a gift. He counts the faith as righteousness, and he counts the man as righteous (4:4-5). This is in spite of the fact that the man is not righteous.

This appears from our study of words in their usage and in their contexts. Certain comments are now in order. The concept of justification is forensic.[65] This is not to the taste of everybody. Even so there is great advantage. If the divine requirements are committed to writing, men know where they are. It is tyrants and dictators who seek to undermine the stability of law, with its restraint on arbitrary power.[66] The decision which God gives in counting a man righteous is as clear-cut as a verdict given in a court of law. Again men—this time believers—know where they stand.

Objection is sometimes taken to the thought that God treats men "as if" they were righteous by a sort of legal fiction. "Not even He may pretend that black is white." [67] Yet Küng can say that "God treats us as though we had not sinned" (p. 203).

The objection to a legal fiction is, I think, misconceived. This is a human device to obey the letter of the law and thereby gain some advantage, perhaps by going against the spirit of the law. A man who writes his own will, for example, might say that rents falling due to his estate while his body is above ground could go to certain beneficiaries and after that everything was to go to charity. By "above ground" he meant "unburied." It gave a short interval—as he thought—in which a handful of people could benefit. But suppose that at his funeral service his body is committed to a stone tomb above the ground? As long as his body is thus above ground the rents

---

64. Cf. Michel, p. 105. The subject "righteousness of God" is taken up again, but now related to man.

65. Cf. Bultmann, *Theology of the New Testament*, 1:270–85; Hill, *Greek Words*, p. 141.

66. Cf. H. G. Wood, *F. D. Maurice*, p. 108. In the sacrifice of many lives in order to reestablish law, Wood sees a pointer to a connection between Christ's death and upholding law.

67. Barrett, p. 75. Cf. Bultmann, *Theology of the New Testament*, 1:276; Althaus, p. 37, "als ob." Karl Barth, *Church Dogmatics*, IV.1.597, quoted by Hans Küng, *Justification*, p. 65.

might continue to be paid to the beneficiaries and not to the charity. Whether this would be permitted today I do not know. But I read an account similar to the above in a parish magazine and with it was a photograph of the tomb.

Now justification is not a device of this kind. It is a positive way of saying that God does not impute sin. The latter is as much a legal fiction as counting a man righteous. We do this sort of thing ourselves frequently. Whenever in a spirit of forgiveness we say to an offender, "We'll forget about that," we indulge in a nonlegal (not "illegal") fiction. Whenever after a breach in friendship we restore the broken relationship, we pick up the threads where they were dropped, "bygones are bygones" and we continue *as if* the unhappy affair had never happened; whenever we do this we introduce an element of fiction. (Cf. Sanday and Headlam, p. 94.) We forgive and forget.

The concept of "as if" has a respectable ancestry. For example, Leon Morris can quote Hastings Rashdall: "God treated the sinless Christ as if He were guilty . . . this infliction made it possible to treat the sinful as if they were actually righteous." [68] In his chapter on "Classical Anglicanism" Dr. C. F. Allison (*The Rise of Moralism*, pp. 1–3) refers to Richard Hooker, whose argument "is typical of the position taken by Anglicans." In the *Ecclesiastical Polity* (I:21) Hooker writes thus: " . . . although in ourselves we be altogether sinful and unrighteous, yet even the man which in himself is impious, full of iniquity, full of sin . . . him God beholdeth with a gracious eye, putteth away his sin by not imputing it . . . and accepteth him in Jesus Christ, as perfectly righteous, as if he had fulfilled all that is commanded him in the law."

A number of scholars are describing justification as a "creative act" of God. This is a characterization of a wider complex, not of justification itself. For when God counts a man righteous, he is doing something in his own mind. To that extent justification is abstract. It never happens by itself. There never was a man who was justified by faith without something else happening to him at the same time. Justification has unfailing concomitants. In itself, however, it speaks of the divine attitude, an attitude of "counting" the believing man as righteous.

For what kind of a God is it whom the man trusts when he "first believes" (cf. 13:11)? He is the God who quickens the dead (4:17), that is, the man who starts to live as a result of his faith in Jesus (3:26).[69] This is the divine "creative act." It always accompanies justification but is to be distinguished from it.

Creativity is reflected in the last part of the verse to which reference has just been made (4:17). The doctrine of creation has two special emphases. The means of creation is God's Word ("God said"), and the

---

68. Leon Morris, *The Apostolic Preaching of the Cross*, p. 256, n. 2, quoting Hastings Rashdall, *The Idea of Atonement in Christian Theology*, p. 94.

69. Horst Seebass, *Begriffslex.* 5:507, translates *ton ek pisteōs Iēsou* by "den aus Glauben an Jesus Christus [Lebenden]"; "the man who [lives] as a result of faith in Jesus Christ."

sum of creation is *ex nihilo*. Both of these may be discerned in 4:17. God calls when his Word is preached. "Whom he called he also justified" (8:30).[70] Through the preacher God speaks and calls.

There is also a kind of creation out of nothing in 4:17. The listener is dead, anyway, or he could not be "quickened." In terms of creation, however, he stands for "not-being." Yet God addresses him. God gives his call to the man who is not (a believer), because He is conscious (*hōs*, subjective—see note 2 in the chapter on Corinthians) of him as being (a believer). Paul is using neuter plurals, of course, which is appropriate in a context of creation, but the application is plain.

The place of "not-being" or of "nothing" has not always been given its place in Christian thought. Elsewhere (1 Cor. 1:28) Paul tells us that God chose the "not-being" (*ta mē onta*, as in Rom. 4:17) to annul the "being," the things that are. How can God use "nothing"? We can illustrate from the parable of the prodigal son. When the prodigal had run through all his money, divine providence created a "mighty" (*ischura*) famine. It was no "weak," ineffective affair. It brought him to his senses. Now a famine is surely the classical illustration of "not-being." It connotes the absence of food. And God used it.[71] By contrast there is "being" at home. Even the workers on the estate have ample food (Luke 15:14–17).

It is sometimes pointed out that justification does not mean the acquisition of virtue. This is true, if we mean by virtue excellence of developed character, either in general or in some particular aspect, e.g. courage. But the use of the word *virtue* is setting our sights far too low. What God counts to the believer is righteousness. This, we found, is his own moral perfection. It is not the alleged artificiality of this which ought to impress us. The grace of such an imputation ought to take our breath away. God looks on an unrighteous, sinful man as if he possessed the divine perfection itself.

Paul's metaphor from clothes is relevant here. He tells his readers to "put on," to "clothe themselves with," the Lord Jesus Christ. The clothes cover the body; the bare face allows the person to be identified. Thus God looks on each believing man, knowing him and identifying him, but seeing the "clothes," Christ in all His perfection (13:14).

All this, we say, goes on in the divine Mind. As for the believing man, he is quickened from the dead. God receives him, because Christ receives him (14:3; 15:7). The imputed righteousness is his qualification to be received by God. If God did not impute the righteousness, he would not receive him.

Thus we see one complex event, of which justification is a part.
God imputes righteousness to the man who believes
—the divine attitude

---

70. Cf. Michel, p. 114. "Ohne die konkrete, zusprechende Verkündigung des Boten ist also die Rechtfertigung nicht möglich." "Without the actual exhorting proclamation of the messenger, justification is impossible."

71. I was started on this train of thought by Dorothy L. Sayers, *The Mind of the Maker*, p. 81.

God quickens and receives the man who believes
—the divine act.

These two "moments" are theoretically distinct but they happen at the same time. In the one human experience of "first faith" the forensic and the so-called mystical are united. But "forensic" belongs to justification and "mystical" to the quickening and receiving. Thus justification never takes place by itself.

In my student days a question was set in an examination in psychology on the following lines. "Pure sensation is a psychological myth. Discuss." If memory serves rightly, I think that the examiner wanted the candidate to show that every sensation on being received by the mind was immediately "worked up" into a percept. This may be old fashioned today. I do not know. But it illustrates what was meant by a "psychological myth."

So it could be said, without any allusion to "demythologizing," that "pure justification is a theological myth." It never happens by itself.

This is part of the answer to the jibe about "celestial bookkeeping." Apart from the fact that "the book of life" has an honored place in Christian tradition (Phil. 4:3; Rev. 3:5) and that our Lord told his disciples to rejoice that their names were recorded in heaven (Luke 10:20; cf. Heb. 12:23), the imputation of righteousness is not a question of records in a book. It involves the activity of the divine Mind itself. As H. W. Heidland says, *dikaioō* presents God as Judge and *logizomai* as Father (*TDNT* 4:292).

Justification is by faith alone. Martin Luther has been criticized for adding "alone" to Romans 3:28 (*allein durch den Glauben*). But he was right, both exegetically and linguistically. Justification is "apart from works of the law." And Jeremias has taught us that the Semitic mind—or rather language—omits "only" or "alone" where we should insist on its inclusion. He gives the striking example of "*only* a cup of water" (Mark 9:41). We might add, "He who is weak eats vegetables only" (Rom. 14:2). C. K. Barrett was quite right to add "only' to his translation here.[72]

It is true that "in Paul there is no suggestion of cleavage between a forensic and a mystical mode of thought. Forensic justification leads to pneumatic fellowship with Christ" (A. Oepke, *TDNT*, 1:541). It "leads" to it not by reason of justification per set but because the living God not only thinks but acts. He not only imputes but quickens and receives the believing man. It "leads" to it at once. Thus justification is part, a vital part indeed, of a wider complex which includes God's mental activity and his act of reception. "In the New Testament it [*dikaioō*] is seldom that one cannot detect the legal connexion. . . . [but] the *actus forensis* [forensic act] takes place in an act of grace from which it is not to be severed" (G. Schrenk, *TDNT* 2:214, 216). It cannot be severed in experience. Only when we analyze the experience can we sever it by making the distinction

72. Joachim Jeremias, *The Central Message of the New Testament*, pp. 55–56. In *The Parables of Jesus*, p. 28, note 35, he gives a long list of examples of this usage, and comments on its importance for Rom. 3:28 and Gal. 5:6b. But in the latter is it "faith alone" or "love alone"? This is quite tantalizing! A case could be made for either.

between God's justifying and God's quickening and receiving. There is "a juridical kernel that cannot be denied," [73] but it never stands alone.

With a renewed interest in baptism a tendency has arisen to suggest justification by baptism or justification by faith and baptism. Stauffer, for example, says that "justification takes place at baptism, or at the Last Judgment." Jeremias affirms that "it is in baptism that this bestowal [of justification] takes place." Schnackenburg feels that for Paul baptism "possesses the same importance as faith. . . . he can talk about faith or baptism according to the prevailing viewpoint. . . . faith is completed in baptism." [74] Certainly baptism is not an "optional extra." But I should prefer to say that faith is expressed, not completed, in baptism. The man who "begets through the Gospel (1 Cor. 4:15), through public preaching, not through a mystery"; [75] the man who was sent by Christ not to baptize but to preach the gospel (1 Cor. 1:17); would such a man, the champion of "justification by faith alone," have us believe that he really meant "justification by faith and baptism"?

Baptism may be regarded as the first act of the believing and justified man, if it was not long delayed—the first act of Christian obedience. Even here it might be better to say "the first sacramental act." Paul's first obedience to the heavenly vision (Acts 26:19) was not baptism. In response to his humble question, "What am I to do, Lord?" (Acts 22:10), he was told to arise and go to Damascus. For three days he was without his sight, for three days unbaptized; and he spent time in prayer (Acts 9:9, 11–12, 17–18). Are we to think that for three days Paul was not yet justified?

However we answer the question, the interval of time is significant. In the New Testament "baptism is administered to converts. This is commonly recognized now. . . ." [76] In the New Testament faith *comes* to baptism; . . . That faith is strengthened in baptism is to be expected. . . . " Baptism is thus an act of obedience. The strengthening of faith in baptism must not be regarded as a "strengthening" of justification. There are no degrees of justification. A man is either justified or he is not. A man may grow and mature in his Christian life and he may become more holy in his character. Even faith as a grain of mustard seed is recognized by God if it is genuine faith, and it will grow. But justification will not "grow." When a man first repents and puts his faith in Jesus, God counts him as righteous, quickens him and accepts him. The "counting" does not wait even for three days.

Faith is an inner attitude and baptism is its externalizing, indicating at the same time incorporation into the church. But what if baptism is long delayed? It is not enough to suggest that the New Testament does not raise such questions, and that we must not do so either. There are practical

73. Cf. Schnackenburg, *Baptism in St. Paul,* pp. 122–23.
74. E. Stauffer. *New Testament Theology,* p. 145; Jeremias, *Central Message of the NT,* p. 59; Schnackenburg, *Baptism in St. Paul,* p. 124–27.
75. F. Büchsel, *TDNT* 1:666. Does Paul mean "I alone" on the analogy of "faith alone" in Rom. 3:28?
76. Beasley-Murray, *Baptism in the NT,* p. 274. In his documentation the author lists Roman Catholic, Lutheran, Anglican, Reformed, Congregationalist and Methodist scholars.

problems which have to be answered. There are people who are immersed in the faith and life and work of the church who have not been baptized. Are they justified or not?

A personal testimony must be introduced here to show that though "faith plus baptism" is the normal it has not the validity of a natural law. "Faith alone" has its significance and value, for it is faith alone which justifies. My own experience must bear witness to this. I was a believing and practicing Christian for years before I was baptized.

There is something of a family problem about this. My father and mother were devout Christians and my debt to them is immeasurable. From them I received the Word of God. In them I saw the example of Christian faith and life, a genuine pattern of both trust and good works. From them I received the nurture and admonition of the Lord. Every day of my life I give thanks to God for them. But I was not baptized in infancy.

This is a family mystery. My parents were not Baptists. Both of them had been brought up in the Church of England, where both had been baptized and confirmed. For some reason, never satisfactorily explained, they failed to bring me to baptism. The consequence was that I gave my heart to Christ—and went on from there. Before I was twenty years old I was active in young people's groups, trying to lead them to Christ. At home we held a weekly fellowship meeting, which was something like John Wesley's "class meeting" and today's "Bible study group." I loved those warm, intimate gatherings and played the piano (or tried to!) for the hymns. In due course I read Spurgeon's sermons with delight (as I still do)[77] and took to the pulpit.

I was still unbaptized. I trusted Christ with all my heart, preached him and tried to serve him. Was I justified by faith or did it all hang precariously in the air until baptism finally put me right with God? Inner faith had been externalized many times in Christian fellowship and evangelistic enterprise, and God had owned my lay ministry.

If it is true that, unbaptized as I was, I was not yet justified, I have a theological and spiritual problem on my hands. The God I knew then is the same God as I know now. He accepted me in Christ then, and he accepts me and keeps me in him still. I know a little more now than I did then and I hope that I have grown in grace. But the essential pattern is still the same. If my unbaptized experience was that of an unjustified man, where do I stand now? I thought then that I was in Christ. Was it a ghastly mistake? If so, I may be mistaken still. My life of faith is the same.

I conclude that justification is by faith alone and that baptism is an act of obedience in which the faith is expressed.

It may be argued that all this is irrelevant and that we are concerned with the interpretation of St. Paul's writings and not with experience in the twentieth century. But God is the living God and he does not change. I submit that we have been using Romans as it was meant to be used. If it is indeed all irrelevant, what is the point of James Denney's oft-quoted

---

77. If any one raises his eyebrows he should read Helmut Thielicke's *Encounter with Spurgeon*.

statement that "it is not historical scholarship that is wanted for the understanding of him [Paul], and neither is it the insight of genius: it is despair"?
What is the value of James Moffatt's observation in his Hibbert Lectures
that "the distance of centuries between us and the New Testament age
is reduced by the essential identity of religious experience, which has
lasted in a continuity of life within the Church"? What encouragement
could be derived from Professor Hunter's remark that "it is a striking
fact that whenever there has been a really great revival in the Christian
Church, it has generally been associated with the rediscovery by someone
(Augustine, Luther, Barth) of the essential message of Romans"? If our
own experience cannot aid us in interpretation, we are brought back to the
position of F. C. Baur. One of his admirers, records Robertson Nicoll,
praised Baur after his death for "a completely objective nature. No trace of
personal needs or struggles is discoverable in connection with his investigations of Christianity." [78]

It seems to me that we must either seek to be completely objective or we
must try to enter into the spirit of the author. There is a place for the
former. Linguistic evidence, for example, should be weighed without
prejudice. As Krister Stendahl once expounded to us in an academic
"consultation," exegesis should be scientific. But when every piece of evidence has been considered and every argument weighed, it is the man
who thus equipped can enter sympathetically into the mind and heart of
the author who will penetrate most deeply into his meaning and message.
Pure objectivity will not help. Paul speaks to the student who treads where
he trod and unlocks his secrets to the seeker who finds his needs met as
Paul found them met, in Christ.

Justification, then, is by faith. It "is never to make righteous . . . but
always a declaring righteous, that determines man's standing before God." [79]

## Concomitants of Justification

"Standing" raises a question. How long does the believing and therefore
justified man "stand" before God? How long is he acceptable to God? The
answer is—forever. For justification sets up a relationship between the
believer and God. It "means the establishment of a new and permanent
relationship between God and the sinner." [80] This must now be expounded.

We have said that pure justification is the divine mental activity of
counting a man righteous, always accompanied by the divine act of quickening and receiving the man who believes. From the time of the repentant
sinner's "first faith" and for all eternity God goes on counting him righteous,
keeping him alive and finding his presence acceptable. For he is in Christ.
This is the "permanent relationship." God is always gracious to the believer, gracious in thought and deed.

---

78. James Denney, *The Christian Doctrine of Reconciliation*, p. 180; James Moffatt,
*The Approach to the New Testament*, p. 173; A. M. Hunter, *Introducing the New Testament*, p. 96; William Robertson Nicoll, *The Church's One Foundation*, p. 120.
79. Stauffer, *NT Theology*, p. 292, n. 470.
80. Stephen Neill, *Anglicanism*, p. 49.

Hence C. K. Barrett can finely say (p. 159) that "all the graces of the Christian life are the consequences of, and depend upon, justification." If God did not count a man righteous he would not quicken him and would not receive him. He would thus remain spiritually dead, cut off from eternal life and apart from God. He would not live the Christian life and therefore would have none of its "graces." But "in justification all God's gifts are included" (Michel, p. 135).

For what happens to the man himself when he believes? In consequence of the divine imputation he is quickened and accepted and as part of this experience he knows the love of God. It is not that he is merely informed about it. He may have been told a thousand times before he first believed. He now knows it, is convinced of it, feels it, experiences it. It fills his heart. "Until now I did not realize . . . " he cries. His mind grasps it; his heart warms to it; his will bows before it.

Through the Holy Spirit the love which God has for men has been poured out *(ekkechutai)* into our hearts (5:5). The perfect tense is significant. It *has been* poured out; our hearts—our whole inner nature—*are* now, therefore, steeped in the love of God. After a long heat wave with its scorching sun and weeks of drought the grass may be dry and brown and the soil like sand. Then comes a cloudburst and hours of torrential rain. The rain *has fallen;* the field *is* now in flood.

So it is with the man who believes. His soul was dry and lifeless. Now it is alive and fresh, flooded with the love of God. And it is through the gift of the Holy Spirit.

When did the "rain" fall? It was when he believed. He heard the good news preached or taught and he learnt that God demonstrates (*sunistēsin* —present tense) his love toward us in this, namely (*hoti*—dadurch, dass— Althaus), that when we were still sinners Christ died for us (5:8). The truth was driven home by the Holy Spirit—without whom all preaching is fruitless.

Two factors are thus involved in the apprehension of the love of God, the preaching of the Word and the ministry of the Holy Spirit. Paul's language here leaves no other conclusion possible (5:5, 8). It is not enough, and it can be quite misleading, to make the bare statement that "it is in baptism that the Holy Spirit is given." Converts can certainly be taught to look for a deepening experience of the Holy Spirit in their forthcoming baptism—or confirmation—but they would not be converts at all without his presence in their hearts already.

Justification, then, takes place in the divine Mind and with it, though distinct from it, are the human experiences of being quickened, of being received by God and of realizing the love of God; and all this continues. An additional concomitant is adoption.

There are two sides to adoption, the divine and the human. When a man believes in Jesus, God "adopts" him. He no longer regards him merely as His creature but as a son. He becomes what he was not before, a child of God. And on the human side the man in question is made aware of it.

There was a time when theologians spoke of "the universal Fatherhood of God" and the doctrine found its way into the hymn book. Congregations still sing "Dear Lord and Father of mankind." But God is not the Father of men merely as men; he is the Father of believing men. It ought not to be necessary to emphasize this, but much popular thinking and preaching reveals quite clearly the need of Emil Brunner's theological chemist to test the food which is publicly offered.[81] The impurity must be eliminated. God is indeed Father, not because he is our Father but because he is the Father, the eternal Father, of the eternal Son (cf. 15:6). He is responsible for men's existence, and of his grace he undertakes the responsibility for their welfare. Christ is the Son of God by nature; men become the sons of God by grace, when they repent and believe in Jesus. "Sie, die Sünder, sind nicht von Natur Söhne." [82] This is the plain teaching of the New Testament.

When God quickens and receives a justified sinner, he not only looks upon him as righteous, he receives him as a son, as one of Christ's fellow-heirs (8:17). And he tells him so. The believer is now no longer "in the flesh" (8:9) but is led by the Spirit of God. Servility, with its consequent fear, is gone. In the exhilaration and the certainty of his new experience of sonship, he cries "Abba!" The "shout" reveals the depth of his conviction. The address, "Abba," is directed to God and implies not only thought but prayer. Either the new believer is taught by the preacher or catechist that God is now his Father and the Holy Spirit so kindles the truth within him by His witness that he bursts forth in prayers and praise; or else in the newly begun life of prayer itself he receives the witness of the Spirit and knows in his heart that he is indeed a child of God. The child "speaks with his Father, simply, intimately, securely" (Jeremias). This is a deep and intense religious experience (8:14–17).

The divine imputation of righteousness gives the believer a "standing" before God. The concomitant of such justification is quickening, being received by God and grasping his love. Adoption brings justification down from heaven to earth. As long as justification goes on in the divine Mind, and only in the divine Mind, a man might not know of his status before God. Now he experiences it as sonship. His own quickening, reception and apprehension of God's love come to their focus and climax when from the heart he cries "Abba!" The imputation given in heaven has become effective on earth.

This goes a long way to answer the criticism sometimes raised that Paul's doctrine of justification creates an ethical cul-de-sac, an ethical dead-end street. It might do so, if God imputed righteousness but kept his own counsel. But when he justifies he also acts. The believing man is not left in the dark.

The doctrine of the witness of the Spirit is not heard from every pulpit in the land. Men shrink from presumption, are scared of delusion and

---

81. Emil Brunner, *Dogmatics*, 1:64.
82. Althaus, p. 90. Cf. Richardson, *Introduction to Theology of NT*, pp. 149, 263 ff.; H. F. D. Sparks in *Studies in the Gospels* (ed. D. E. Nineham), pp. 241–62; C. K. Barrett, *The Gospel according to St. John*, p. 136; T. W. Manson, *The Teaching of Jesus*, pp. 89–90, 98–113, 330–31; Jeremias, *Central Message of the NT*, pp. 26–27.

abominate cranks. But "the fact that a madman thinks he is a king does not prove that there are no real monarchs." [83]
Some men shy away from the doctrine "because it is not Anglican." This is quite wrong, as Dr. Skevington Wood shows when he retells the story of John Wesley's encounter with William Warburton, Bishop of Gloucester. Warburton did not like Wesley's teaching on the Spirit, but Wesley quoted Pearson *On the Creed,* "a classic statement of the Anglican position." Pearson had said (p. 501) that "it is the office of the Holy Ghost to assure us of the adoption of sons, to create in us a sense of the paternal love of God toward us." The dilemma was acute. Pearson and Wesley stood together. Either both were right or both were wrong. "Condemn Pearson or acquit me."

### The Blessings and Duties of Being Justified

Here, then, is a justified man who has experienced the concomitants of justification. He is a child of God and by God's grace he knows it. In the absence of pastoral guidance he might ask, "Where do I go from here?" In order to help such a person we might suggest that he consider his privileges, count his blessings and list his duties. We might ask him to accompany us in our study of Romans. What has the epistle to say?

To begin with, boasting is out of the question. The justified man can take no credit to himself. It is all of God's mercy and grace that he is now where he is (3:27). In a sense he may previously have been a seeker, though he knew not what—or whom—he sought. But at a deeper level he resembled both Israel and the Gentiles. Before his conversion he was disobedient and contradictory. At his conversion he made a discovery. "I was found by those who were not looking for me" (10:20–21).

He is no longer under condemnation (8:1). God is on his side (8:31). His calling and justification may be but yesterday, for it was yesterday when his experience began. But God's will came into it, and his will did not begin yesterday. It reaches back into eternity. God foreknew him and foreordained him to a program (8:29–30; 9:18). When he consciously stepped into God's plan he began to enjoy (*echōmen,* subjunctive) peace with God (5:1) and was reconciled to him (5:10–11; cf. 8:7). He now loves God (8:28).

For he has been liberated from a false king. Formerly sin reigned; now grace reigns (5:21) and he is under its sway (6:15). Sin must not regain its throne (6:12). He is liberated (8:2), and righteousness, God himself, claims his loyal service (6:13–22). It is not for him to be a tool of a malignant power but a royal servant gladly presenting himself for duty. The grace which reigns is God, is Christ (5:15). Sin will not "lord it" [84]

---

83. A. Skevington Wood, *The Burning Heart,* p. 258. The whole chapter should be studied.
84. Cf. the motto of the French troops at the Maginot Line, "on ne passera pas"— "they shall not pass." It was the interpretation of this as mere prediction instead of determination that led to trouble.

over him, for Jesus is Lord (10:9; 14:7–9). If sin tries to make a comeback and issues its orders, they fall on deaf, even dead, ears. If God commands, he springs to attention (6:11). For he is led by the Spirit of God (8:14) and has the mind of the Spirit and is on His side (8:5).[85] Christ dwells within him (8:9–10).

As a justified man and as a man under grace he has certain privileges. He can interpret his day-to-day experiences and even boast in his afflictions. He does not endure the advancing tide of woe with the silence of impassible pebbles on the shore. He does not merely lick his wounds like a dumb beast devoid of understanding. He knows that affliction is an opportunity and he seizes it to learn endurance. He knows—for he finds himself with the knowledge—that *Erprobtheit*,[86] testedness, has been born with endurance. Like Londoners and residents of other blitzed cities, he does not blench at the first sound of gunfire or exploding bomb. He has come through it all before. So hope lives within him and he is sure that it will not disappoint. Through all his trials, God's love has been a reality in his heart (5:3–5). Knowledge and experience make him kin to John Newton:

> His love in time past forbids me to think
> He'll leave me at last in trouble to sink;
> While each Ebenezer [87] I have in review
> Confirms His good pleasure to help me quite through.

This is knowledge and *dokimē*—character (5:4)—indeed!

For he stands under the providence of God. There is a providence of which men are quite unconscious. God raised up Pharaoh in order to demonstrate His power (9:17). The justified man, however, knows that the providence of God is at work. He may not know the details as they are being worked out but he knows that God sees him where he is, in the toils of his existing situation. The intersection of events will lead to nought but good (cf. pp. 77–78). He may or may not have been called to service such as evangelism, but he has been called and therefore "qualifies" (8:28). May we see in this word *prothesis* an echo of the *proetheto* of 3:25 (God purposed Christ Jesus to be a propitiation)?

Under the protective ceiling of God's providence, the justified man knows that he is being kept. He believes that he will live with Christ because he knows that Christ, raised from the dead, will never die again. Death is not Lord over Him. Christ is Lord. But how can the argument proceed from "Christ will never die" to "I shall live with him"? The hidden thought is, "He keeps his people with him." He keeps his people with him and he never dies. Thus the justified man is ever kept—with Christ, and by Christ (6:8–9). Even in the darkness of suffering he understands (8:17).

---

85. *ta tinos phronein.* Cf. Herodotus II.162.
86. Hermann Haarbeck, *Begriffslex.* 2:116.
87. Cf. the Hebrew of 1 Sam. 7:12. *Ebenezer* means "stone of help," a solid reminder.

He does not lack divine help and strength. The Holy Spirit takes hold of the other end of his burden and helps him in his weakness (8:26). In particular the Spirit is present in his sighs that are too deep for words and transforms them into prayers, "touching them up" as a photographer treats an indifferent portrait or a technician removes the infelicities from a tape recording. And God can and does strengthen him (16:25).

If he sins, he is not bundled out of the kingdom, to take his chance with the rest of sinful and unbelieving humanity. Christ in his ascended glory intercedes for him (8:34), with all the authority of his cross and Passion. And God listens, because he is "for him" (cf. 8:31).

He may be the victim of all the ills to which man falls heir. But the love of Christ, the love of God in Christ, breaks through them. God has not forgotten his servant even in his woe, and still less has he ceased to love him. And the servant, in whom the love of God was shed forth, does not forget either. Paul is here speaking from his own experience (*pepeismai*, "I have been persuaded" and therefore "I am now sure," 8:38). Persecutors who sought to knock the religious nonsense out of him found that they were dealing with a man who had a horizon which never changed. He was at all times surrounded by the love of God and he knew it. This is partly the indelible result of the experience of his conversion, partly the depth of his devotional life, and in it all the presence of the Holy Spirit (8:35–39). Nothing in the created universe, no person and no thing, in nature or in supernature, can erect a barrier to keep the love of God at a distance.

Not apart from these sufferings but in them the justified man is a super-conqueror. His spirit is unbowed and the gains are great, and it is all "through him who loved us." The aorist tense is startling. Did God love us in the past? We expect the apostle to emphasize the present and to use the present tense. He does not mean that the love was limited to the past. Quite the contrary: the aorist tense points to the supreme focus of the love of God in the cross, from which the warmth is radiated to the whole universe. A love like the love of Jesus, embodying as it does the love of God himself, lasts. It is the inspiration to endure, and as a loving Presence is power for positive victory.

For however hopeless the apparent odds, the justified man is a man of hope, of a hope that is surely based (5:4–5; 10:11). Whatever befalls him, the unattainable glory (3:23) is within his grasp (8:30). Meanwhile he has secret access to the source of all good and calls upon him who is rich and generous towards all (10:12). With the gift of his Son, God has in principle lavished everything upon his people (8:32).

A man in Christ not only has the abundant gifts of God; he also has weapons (13:12). He has the encouragement of the scriptures to sustain his hope (15:4). Their combination of teaching and *paraklēsis* of persuasion with authority, of "stimulus," [88] in the existing situation (cf. 15:2–3) makes

---

88. Aristotle uses the cognate verb in this sense. The smell of roast beef in the oven is pleasant to a hungry man, but after a heavy meal the "kitchen" smell of it is not pleasant. The perfumes of flowers, by contrast, are pleasant in themselves and do not constitute a stimulus to eat: *pros tēn trophēn parakalousin*. Aristotle, *De Sensu* V. (443b 28f).

for discipline. The God of hope can fill him with all joy and peace while he goes on believing, so that hope overflows (15:13). Grace is always available (16:20) and he is a saved man. Its eschatological consummation is in the future (5:9; cf. 10:9–10), it is nearer now than when he first believed (13:11) but in principle and in promise salvation is his already (8:24). Here is "the novelty and originality of the Christian soteriology, viz. that salvation is given only by and in Christ to those who are joined to Him by faith." [89]

So far we have been considering the justified man in his individual dealings with God. He was once "the godless man" (4:5) but now he is "a man justified by faith" (3:28). We must not write off such experiences as mere individualism. It is not mere individualism when a man withdraws into his private room and seeks his Father's face in secret, in obedience to our Lord's command. It is not mere individualism when a man suffers solitary confinement for righteousness's sake and nourishes and fortifies his soul by meditation and prayer. It is not mere individualism when a man repents of his sins and believes in Jesus.

Without minimizing this in the slightest but rather bearing it in mind, we must go on to point to a wider context. The justified man does not and should not stand alone. If he follows the pattern of the New Testament he will be baptized. He will be openly admitted to the fellowship of men who have traveled the same road as he has.

He will join the people of promise. As a justified man he will be a member of those whose watchword is not flesh, law and works but promise, grace and faith. He will become a son of Abraham. Put in this way it may not sound attractive to the modern ear, but it is the meaning which counts. He will have joined God's people.

The determining principle is not physical descent from Abraham but faith. Abraham is the father of those who believe. Abraham himself believed and all who likewise believe are his "descendants" (4:11, 16–18). Similarly not all who have Israelite parents belong to Israel but only those who are "children of promise" and have faith in Jesus (9:6–8, 30–31). Israel was for the most part apostate, but God did not thrust away his people. They lived in a faithful remnant according to the election of grace. Israel in general failed in her quest, but the elect attained to it (11:1–7).[90]

The remnant of Israel, then, is the people of God. But if a man becomes a descendant of Abraham by believing in Jesus, the door is flung open in principle to those who are not Jews. Salvation is for the Gentiles as well (10:12–13; 11:11). Thus believing Gentiles are engrafted, the wild olive onto the cultivated olive. The old root carries the new branches (11:17–18, 24).

The people of God thus consists of believing Jews (the faithful remnant) and believing Gentiles who by faith have become the children of Abraham.

---

89. Jacques Dupont, in *Apostolic History and the Gospel*, ed. W. Ward Gasque and Ralph P. Martin, p. 194.

90. Note the abstract and the concrete uses of the term *eklogē*, the abstract "election" and the concrete "the elect" in vv. 5, 7. Cf. Michel, p. 267, n. 2 and p. 268.

The whole is spiritual Israel, even though Gentiles predominate. This is the church, which the justified man has now joined. All such men do more than occupy their separate pigeon hole. They join the company of justified men. They each and all belong to God. In their totality they are the people of God.

The thought of the church is the convenient place to notice that the justified man has duties as well as privileges. As a "church man" he finds that his privileges are not exclusive. Others, in addition to himself, are led by the Spirit and are the sons of God (8:14). Others figure in God's long program (8:29–30). Others are no longer in the flesh but are on the side of the Spirit and have Christ within them (8:5–11).[91] Others are denied the right to claim any credit for themselves (3:27).

Certain differences within the fellowship of the church draw attention to the coexistence of privileges and duties. The strong should bear the weaknesses of those who are not strong, and should not please themselves. Each should please his fellow, with a view to the edification, the building up, of the community (15:1–3). Now a justified man might argue that others should help him, for he is weak, and should "please" him. He would not be entirely wrong, though if every member did it the result would approach dangerously near to the impossible—a "community" of the selfish. This attitude emphasizes, or overemphasizes, the privileges.

On the other hand the justified man might in a more wholesome way feel the pull to help his neighbor and to study his interests. This would point rather to the duties. What are the duties of the justified man?

His first duty is to be awake (13:11). As long as he indulges in spiritual slumber, no duty will be done. It will not even be known.

He started his Christian life with an act of obedience. He obeyed the gospel (10:16) by believing in Jesus and by submitting to baptism. Even if the baptism were delayed, it is still the rite of initiation. It is not repeated like the Eucharist and it is not the climax of the earthly pilgrimage like a Nunc Dimittis uttered over a dying man. Even baptism following a deathbed repentance marks the beginning of the Christian life.

Beginning with obedience he must continue in obedience, not in sin (6:1). The symbolism of baptism—not necessarily the "bare" symbolism—suggests the death and burial of the sinful self, *in order that* (following the pattern of the Lord's resurrection) he may "walk" in newness of life (6:4). The Hebraistic "walk" of moral conduct and behavior, "the resurrection life" as it has been called, does not follow mechanically. It is a purpose to be fulfilled. There is a real—and large—place for effort in the Christian life. If after moral and spiritual struggle the sinful self yielded to the claims of Christ and so "died," the justified man must keep his *ego* dead and must live for God (6:11). He must obey righteousness, obey God (6:12–22). He must not live on the level of "flesh" (8:12) but of spirit,

---

91. The terms "Spirit of God," "Spirit of Christ" and "Christ" seem to be used interchangeably. Each has its theological background and meaning and to that extent differs. But in the experience of the justified man they are one. Cf. Ehrhard Kamlah, *Begriffslex.* 5:486. God is present in Christ and Christ is present (though exalted) in the Spirit.

agreeing with the Spirit (8:4–10), following the Spirit's lead and not striking out on his own (8:14). The motive power for the newness of life (6:4) is the newness of the Holy Spirit (7:6). The Spirit is not a power which works *in vacuo*. He is present in the justified man (8:9–11) who has already tasted the mercies of God and knows them as a strong argument ("Therefore" 12:1–2). The moral pattern is not "this age" but the Son of God himself (8:29). Gratitude for what God has done in Christ inspires love (cf. Luke 7:47). Justified and quickened (4:17), he goes on being transformed by the renewal of his mind, the Spirit's work in him, and views the will of God in its perfection.

In simple terms, Jesus has worked for him and in him, and for him Jesus is Lord. He has been put to death to the law and so the law is dead to him. He is free to "marry Another" and thus comes under another "law of the husband" (7:1–4), the law of Christ (cf. Gal. 6:2). From this union should come (note again the *hina*) "children," moral duties fulfilled. The moral duties may be described as "the requirements *(dikaiōma)* of the law" (8:4; cf. 2:26) interpreted by Jesus the Lord through the Spirit. Meeting the requirements is not with a view to justification but a result of justification. Christ fulfilled the demands of the law *for* us; they should now be fulfilled *in* us. It should be noticed how in 8:3–4 the power of the cross is harnessed to the moral life.

The distinction between moral and spiritual or religious is not absolute but convenient. The justified man has a religious duty. Paul feels at liberty to appeal to his readers to join him in earnest prayer for specific objects (15:30–32). He does not give the impression that he is introducing something novel for which he must give an explanation or a defense. He appeals "through our Lord Jesus Christ" and through the love which has come to them through the Holy Spirit (cf. 5:5). The readers are justified and committed men and the inner life of devotion is part of their normal Christian activity. Paul, in asking for help, is merely giving "subjects for intercession."

The life of prayer is individual and private (cf. Matt. 6:6, *su*, "thou"— KJV) and public and corporate. As one man *(homothumadon)* and "with one mouth" the Roman Christians are to address God together (Rom. 15:6). In their homes and "in church" they are to pray. Paul himself sets an individual example in his "May God . . . give to you . . . " (15:5)—"a prayer for the unity of the community" (Sanday and Headlam).

The duties of the justified man are thus to be summed up in two words, *righteousness* and *piety* (cf. 4:5). The unrighteous man has been counted righteous in God's sight; he must become righteous in life. He was impious up to the time when he first believed; now in the practice of private and corporate prayer he must become pious. (*Piety* is too great a word to be dismissed with a sneer, even when we know the objections to it.)

The relation between the imputation in the Mind of God and the spiritual growth of the justified man may be illustrated by an old story. An ugly man once sought the hand of a fair lady. Realizing how slender were his chances he had a mask made. When he assumed it he appeared a handsome man. He sought and won his bride. Years of married happiness followed. Then an enemy discovered his identity and came and denounced him. In the presence of his wife he removed the mask—and the old ugliness was gone. The handsome mask had left its impress.

This is only an illustration, and every illustration fails somewhere. Otherwise it would not be an illustration but identical with the matter illustrated. Even so I find it helpful.

Perhaps we may conclude this section on the life of the justified man by quoting some wise words of the late Dr. H. Wheeler Robinson. Sin has not vanished from the cosmic record. It is still a fact that justified men once sinned. "But all the consequences of sin are transformed by the new relation to God. The consciousness of guilt is interpenetrated by that of divine forgiveness; the penalties of sin, so far as they remain, become elements of discipline; the social results of sin, though never overtaken, form a constant stimulus to Christian service." [92]

The Epistle to the Romans has painted a black picture of human sin and wickedness. On it the light of the gospel has shone. God in Christ has wrought righteous atonement for sin and offers sinful men salvation. For those who respond in repentance and faith salvation is a future certainty and a present joy. It is for men to walk with God and with his people.

---

92. H. Wheeler Robinson, *The Christian Doctrine of Man*, p. 316.

# 3

# The Epistle
# to the Galatians

THE EPISTLE WHICH WE ARE now to examine is much shorter than the one sent to the Romans, being barely a third of its length. Romans may be regarded as a more or less formal statement of Paul's doctrine, not entirely dispassionate but hardly to be characterized as emotional. This is appropriate in a letter which is sent to a church which Paul had not founded and which he had not visited. Galatians, by contrast, is written at white heat to the apostle's own children in the faith. The motive is both theological and pastoral. Paul passionately expounds and defends the gospel which he himself had earlier preached to the readers. In so doing he seeks to save them from wrecking and ruining their faith and their lives.

It is perhaps not right to say that in Romans Paul has more space at his disposal. At any rate he takes it and he is thus enabled to give his exposition at some length and in some detail. Like many an evangelist he must have drawn on his earlier preaching material. This does not mean "copying out his sermon notes." He was steeped in Christian truth and he proclaimed it in extempore utterance. He did not indulge in mere repetition. His sermons would vary according to the nature and circumstances of his audience. The point of contact in his introduction would be different in different places and his illustrations might be changed also. But in it all there would be a consistent pattern of Christian truth.

As it is with preaching, so it is with writing. Galatians could in no sense be called a formal statement of Paul's gospel. It is designed to deal with a dangerous situation. All the apostle's powers of vigorous argument and affectionate appeal, to say nothing of severity and denunciation, are manifest. He is fighting for the lives of those whom he loves. Yet in it all there is a consistent pattern. Study of the epistle will show that its theological framework resembles that of Romans.

## THE NATURE OF GOD

To begin with, *God is the living God.* This is patent in Paul's solemn

[127]

asseveration. "In what I am writing to you, I tell you in the presence of God *(enōpion tou theou)* that I am not lying" (1:20). Here we have "a favorite expression in assertions and oaths which call upon God, as the One who sees all" (Arndt-Gingrich). It is a mark of the living God that he is not quiescent or unconscious. He "worked" for Peter and Paul (2:8), and he does not (note the tense) show partiality (2:6).

*God is the only God.* There are gods indeed but they exist by what earlier Greeks might have called "convention." [1] Whoever or whatever they are, they are only gods because men think them so. They may be statues, images, the personification of some aspect of nature or just deified men. In their essential nature they are no-gods (4:8). "God is one" (3:20). From a striking Synoptic parallel we observe that "one" implies "only." "Who can forgive sins but One, God?" (Mark 2:7).[2] "Who can forgive sins but God only?" (Luke 5:21). What was the search of philosophers is the confession of Israel (Deut. 6:4).

We have already seen that *God is conscious.* The very fact that he shows no partiality, that he is not impressed by appearance or reputation, proves that he has consciousness (2:6). It is a natural inference from this to say that *God has knowledge.* He knows the reputation of men, and he knows what they merely seem to be. We do not, however, need to depend solely on an inference. Paul tells us that the Galatians were known by God (4:9). This may contain some of the richness of Old Testament interpretation and include election [3] but this can hardly deny knowledge to God.

The *God* who is conscious and has knowledge *has will* (1:4). The exercise of his will shows that *God has purpose.* The range of some human purposes is short. A man might say that he crossed the room in order to shut the window because he had suddenly felt a draft. The purpose is conceived and executed within seconds. The range of God's purpose is long. He separated Paul from birth and in due time "decided" *(eudokēsen)* to reveal his Son in him, *in order that* Paul might preach Him among the Gentiles (1:15–16). God sent his Son, *in order that* he might redeem . . . *in order that* we might receive the adoption (4:4–5). How many years elapsed between Bethlehem and Calvary? between Bethlehem and Paul's call and commission? This is *sub specie temporis,* viewed within the time-process. But how many men sustain a purpose for even thirty years? If we feel any incongruity in introducing an element of time into the divine purpose we must revert to the language of God's "eternal purpose." This does not deny his purpose but rather emphasizes it.

God's purposes are hardly likely to be frustrated. *God has power.* This is in vivid contrast to the "weak and beggarly elemental spirits" *(stoicheia)* to which the Galations were turning in a sort of conversion-in-reverse

---

1. Cf. R. L. Nettleship, *Lectures on the Republic of Plato,* p. 54.

2. "One, that is, God." C. E. B. Cranfield, *The Gospel according to Saint Mark,* p. 99. Cf. 10:18. But see Vincent Taylor, *The Gospel according to St. Mark,* p. 196.

3. Rudolf Bultmann, *TDNT* 1:700, 709–10; E. D. Schmitz, *Begriffslex.* 3:251.

(4:9; cf. 1 Thess. 1:9). The characteristics of non-Christian religionists are transferred to the objects of their worship. (Cf. Donald Guthrie, p. 123.[4]) The opposite is suggested in 3:5. God "supplies the Spirit" (RSV). From the verb used here *(epichorēgeō)* and its cognate noun elsewhere, Guthrie notes the idea of "abundant supply." God is rich. He also works miracles; an Aristotelian would say that he "actualizes potentialities." There can be no doubt that Paul has the divine power in mind. God is far from being "weak." In particular *he is the Creator*. This is implied rather than stated explicitly. But when the Jew who could quote Genesis [5] as Paul did makes reference to the "new creation" (6:15), it is at least unlikely that he was unaware of the old one.

*God is to be worshiped.* This is plain from the unexpected doxology in the introduction (1:5). At the news that their former persecutor was now preaching the faith, the churches of Judaea glorified God (1:24).

But is it morally right to worship God? Paul does not say outright in Galatians that *God is righteous* but it may be safely assumed. In so short a letter much is left unsaid. The battle is for justification and it would be meaningless apart from the righteousness of God—his character, his requirement and his gift. It is implied by the fact of the law. *God commands men* and it is unthinkable that Paul should even consider God's commandments as arbitrary or as being derived merely from his power. The summary command to love one's neighbor as oneself (5:14) does not savor of whim or naked power. The whole law is to be kept (5:3; cf. 6:13) and watchfulness is to be exercised against the temptation (note the word) to commit a transgression (6:1).

The law may be "secondary" in that it does not express God's final purpose of promise and grace. It is therefore appropriate that it was given in a "secondary" way, "ordained through [not 'by'] angels"; and there was also a human mediator, Moses (3:19). In reference to the cognate *diatagē* of Acts 7:53 Arndt-Gingrich paraphrase "by God's directing angels (to transmit it)," thus implying "the ultimate originator of the law, i.e. God Himself" (Guthrie). The law was "added," not to cancel the promise but to define sin in terms of precise "transgressions." It was temporary, a disciplinarian, the slave who took the children to school. It had this function, not "to lead us to Christ" but "until Christ" (3:24) as Althaus [6] and Guthrie (p. 114) rightly observe.

Paul had been outstanding among his Jewish contemporaries (1:13–14) in his pursuit of righteousness (cf. Phil. 3:6). When his conversion occurred with "dramatic unpreparedness" [7] he did not turn from a false god to the true God. He rather ceased to serve the true God in the wrong way and began to serve him in the right way. Part of this correction was

---

4. Where only the author's name is given, the reference is to his commentary on Galatians.

5. Cf. Col. 3:10. "The allusion to Gen 1:27 is irresistible." C. F. D. Moule, *Colossians and Philemon*, p. 120.

6. Hermann Wolfgang Beyer, "Der Brief an die Galater," revised by Paul Althaus (*Das N.T. Deutsch*, vol. 8), p. 31 (hereafter credited to Althaus).

7. William Manson, *Jesus and the Christian*, pp. 105–6.

a reassessment of the function of the law. He did not now as a Christian repudiate its divine origin. It was still God's law but it was "secondary." It was not the means to the justification of sinners.

Hence it is quite right to say that *God commands men*. Without attempting any exposition of its meaning we may here note that any reference to the kingdom of God (5:21) coheres with the idea of law. In some way God rules as King and this must mean at least that he commands. This is not the whole story of the kingdom by any means, but it must imply this if words have any meaning at all.

## Man Against God

God commands but men disobey. *God is sinned against*. Paul speaks of "our sins" (1:4) and of "sinners" (2:15–17), and of the comprehensive "sin" (3:22). To this must be added the precise concept of transgression (2:18; 6:1) and the detailed "works of the flesh" (5:19–21). Those "who keep on doing such things" are more than mere machines carried on by their own momentum. Momentum is a useful illustration [8] but the will of men is involved. Sinful men not only sin against God by disobedience to his laws. They fail to attain that to which they ought to attain. They exhibit immaturity and slavery (4:3, 8–9).

*God is not known by men* (4:8). This is especially applicable to pagans and does not contradict Romans 1:21. Neither Gentiles nor unbelieving Jews had any experiential knowledge of God. The information about God possessed by pagans was very limited, and even the truly pious Jew had not the knowledge of the glory of God in the face of Christ (2 Cor. 4:6). Such ignorance is not only unfortunate. It is part of the sinfulness of men.

## God Against Man

The seriousness of sin is measured by the fact that any one who does not fulfill all the demands of the law is accursed (*epikataratos*, 3:10). Paul here quotes Deuteronomy 27:26, LXX. This verse does not contain the word "all" in the Hebrew, though its appearance in the following verse (Deut. 28:1) goes a long way to justify the LXX insertion. But who issues the curse?

Some would rest content with the expression "the curse of the law" and deny that it is the curse of God. But if God is indeed the Author of the law the distinction is artificial. And if curse is the opposite of blessing we ought to be consistent and not ascribe the blessing to the Lord. In any case the scripture from which Paul is quoting is hardly ambiguous. Blessings and cursings are contrasted in Deuteronomy 28. Note particularly verses 15–19 and 20. "The Lord. . . . " In the LXX the succession of optatives ("May the Lord . . . ") changes to future indicatives at verse 49 ("The Lord will bring against you . . . "). The NEB begins with "May the Lord . . . " repeatedly but reverts to "the Lord will . . . " at verse 59. "Just as

---

8. Cf. Luke 11:50–51 and see Leon Morris, *The Cross in the New Testament*, p. 68.

the Lord took delight in you, prospering and increasing you, so now it will be his delight to destroy and exterminate you. . . . The Lord will scatter you . . . " (vv. 63–64). It is hard to see how we can avoid speaking of "God's curse." [9] Werner Foerster (*TDNT* 2:815) goes so far as to speak of "God's enmity against us as in Gal. 3:10." The thought here has to be considered and expressed with great care and sensitiveness. As Brunner says, God is no man's enemy. But there is a true sense in which we can say that God is the sinner's Opponent—which is not a distinction without a difference. God is not a passive observer of the human scene. He takes steps in history to resist and counteract the sins of men and to uphold his law, as we have seen in Romans (p. 87). "God's laws have both an obverse and a reverse side." The curse is "the inevitable result of divine holiness as applied to a particular mode of behaviour" (R. K. Harrison, pp. 224–25). The terminology is new, so far as our present studies of Paul are concerned, but the curse seems to mean what we have previously seen in wrath and judgment.[10]

This thought is not foreign to Galatians. The man who is troubling the readers "will bear the judgment *(krima)*, whoever he is" (5:10). (The latter clause illustrates God's lack of respect for persons stated as a principle in 2:6 and reinforces the "all" of 3:10.) Arndt-Gingrich take *krima* in the sense of condemnation (p. 451) and render "have to pay the penalty" (under *bastazō*, p. 137).

The imagery of 6:7–8 is a striking expression of judgment. God is not mocked. What a man sows he will reap. The harvest is the same as the seed. Wheat produces wheat and sin produces sin (cf. Rom. 1:24, 26, 28, "gave them up," *paredōken* and see pp. 86–87). If a man sow to the flesh, like the careless farmer who casts his seed into the thorns (Matt. 13:22; Mark 4:18), either he uses seed appropriate to the soil or even good seed is contaminated by the soil. The result is corruption *(phthora)*, the opposite of eternal life. Seed and soil alike are chosen by the will of men, and the harvest is not merely a "natural" product in the moral realm. Men are responsible and God as Judge is not mocked. The harvest is judicial.

A particular case of judgment is seen in the *anathema*, the Hebrew *hērem*, of 1:8–9. Where the truth of God is at stake Paul can call down God's wrath and judgment. There are limits to Christian tolerance.[11]

The pattern of the Epistle to the Romans has been followed, though more in outline than in detail. The living God of righteousness is disobeyed by sinful men. His opposition is aroused. Wrath and judgment lead to death.

## THE OTHER SIDE—GOD FOR MAN

But once again there is "another side." Paul speaks of the grace *(charis)*

---

9. The expression is used by S. R. Driver, *Deuteronomy* (ICC), p. 299. See also his note on pp. 248–49.

10. Cf. W. Mundle, *Begriffslex.* 4:351.

11. Cf. Althaus, p. 8; Hugo Aust and Dietrich Müller, *Begriffslex.* 4:348–49.

of God (1:3; 2:21; cf. 2:9) and of peace (*eirēnē*) and mercy (*eleos*) (1:3; 6:16). Law is matched by promise, with the prospect of blessing rather than cursing (3:8–9, 14–18). The law is still God's law but it is not his final method for dealing with men. Law is a theoretical way of attaining to life (3:12), but in practice performance of its duties falls short. There is another way to eternal life (6:8).

We are thus faced once more with the problem of the tension between God's justice and his grace. What evidence is afforded by Galatians which can be used to resolve the tension?

### God at Work for Us—The Work of Christ for Us

To begin with, *God himself is concerned with the gospel*. He who separated Paul from birth and called him resolved to reveal his Son in him for an express purpose, that Paul might make him the subject of good news to be told among the Gentiles (1:15–16). The Galatians had heard this gospel from the lips of Paul, when they had received him as if he were an angel of God (4:13–14). Now they were causing him surprise by their defection. They had "fallen for" a new teaching with a puzzling fickleness (*tacheōs* 1.6; 4:20). They had abandoned ·the realm of grace for that of law (5:4). Instead of being firmly established, they were on the move, leaving the God who had called them and making for "another gospel"— which does not exist. God has but one gospel.

The gospel is not a human invention, but human wrongheadedness can distort its verbal expression and thereby entice men away from God. So serious is this that the apostle can invoke the divine *anathema*. At his own conversion the persecuted Christians glorified God that he was now preaching the gospel (1:7–9, 11, 23–24). For the gospel is truth (2:5, 14) and Paul was deeply aware of the apostolic authority with which he preached it (2:2, 6 7).[12]

The content of the gospel is Christ, though so short a statement has to be elaborated.[13] "The gospel of Christ" (1:7) means that *God has a Son* (1:16; 2:20; 4:6).

Furthermore, *God sent his Son*. This apparently simple affirmation (4:4) has not the fullness of Philippians 2:5–11, but it coheres with it. But when did he send him? It might be possible to argue that the commission occurred at our Lord's baptism, in view of the aorist participle (*genomenon*), "born of a woman." He was born and then, afterwards, he was sent. This formal syntax is applicable in other contexts—e.g., Mark 1:31, "He approached her and took her hand and then raised her up"—but it is theologically unsatisfactory.

Can the aorist participle be interpreted as one of coincident action, like

---

12. Cf. Ulrich Becker, Hannover, *Begriffslex.* 3:296, "Im Munde seiner Boten redet Gott selbst—"In the mouth of his messengers God himself speaks" (From Gerhard Gloege).
13. Cf. R. R. Williams, Bishop of Leicester, *I Believe—and Why*, p. 27.

"He prayed and said" (Mark 14:39; cf. Acts 1:24)? This yields the picture of our Lord being sent at birth, though it seems unnatural. The best course is to take *genomenon* in apposition to "his Son." "God sent forth his Son, One born of a woman." This avoids a real difficulty. If our Lord "was sent" at his baptism, what was he doing in the world before then? How did he happen to be here? An adoptionist Christology is not the answer. It is not Pauline or biblical and it does not satisfy the Christian conscience. Where did he come from? Arndt-Gingrich (p. 272) render "send out, send away, in order to have him fulfil a mission in another place," and boldly insert "from heaven," comparing Psalm 56:4, LXX.

This coheres with the doctrine of the Virgin Birth but does not assert it. It establishes the reality of the incarnation. The Son of God became man, and he did so by the Father's will. The humanity of the divine Son is also attested by the reference to "James, the brother of the Lord" (1:19).[14]

The fact that the Son was "One born under law" implies the social setting of the incarnation. The Lord did not live on earth in isolation and he was no hermit. He moved among men and he shared their obligations. This prepares the way for the statement of God's purpose in sending his Son. The incarnation was not an end in itself. He was sent by God in order that he might redeem (4:5). From this must be distinguished the more remote purpose, our adoption.

The presence of the Son in the world as man was the decisive event in the history of the world. "Before the faith came" it was "the faith which was going to be revealed" (3:23–25). This must mean "the Christian faith." The characteristically Pauline word *faith* with its subjective emphasis has thus been made objective. It means more than "a body of doctrine to be believed." The early date of Galatians thus suggests that caution should be exercised before taking the objective use as a sign of a late date. (Cf. 1 Tim. 3:9.). "The faith" which Paul once tried to devastate and now preached was the objective Christian faith and it was in addition subjectively present in those whom he was persecuting (Gal. 1:23).

Within the decisive event was an inner decisive event. The Son who had been sent by the Father to redeem "gave himself for our sins" (1:4). This can point to nothing but the cross. Two implications should be noticed. The death of Jesus was not a mere crime of violence. The life was not taken from an unwilling victim who sought in vain for a way of escape. It was freely given. It is not enough to describe it as no more than execution or murder on the one hand or suicide on the other. The human agency was morally responsible but the Son freely and willingly submitted to it as to the will of the Father (cf. Acts 2:23). And secondly it was related to our sins.

Arndt-Gingrich (p. 846) in their entry under the preposition *huper* translate 1:4 "in order to atone for (the) sins" or "to remove them." Translation here is shading off into interpretation, though no doubt it is correct interpretation. Their view is justified or at any rate supported by the

---

14. For a discussion of the meaning of "brother," see J. B. Mayor, *The Epistle of St. James,* pp. i–lxv.

purpose which Paul states, "in order that he might rescue us from the present evil *aiōn*."

The Greek noun *aiōn* is generally translated by "age," but it is important to understand precisely what is meant. It cannot mean merely a period of time. Christians have not been taken out of the one time process which they share with non-Christians. And it may be doubted if time as such is regarded in the New Testament as evil. On the other hand Paul can hardly be thinking of "the world" (cf. Heb. 1:2). We have not been taken out of that either.

The doctrine of "the two ages" is not easy to grasp, even when we are told that "the age to come" has broken into the present age. But supposing someone said that "the Golden Age has broken in"—or "broken out" if the Golden Age is in the past—then we might have a clue. It would not mean that the clock had been put forward, or back, but that the quality of life had changed. No amount of mere waiting will bring in the age to come as it is not a matter of the elapse of time. And nobody has entered the age to come in the sense that he is already in the pure future.

In view of all this, I judge that "the present age" means "the life of humanity considered apart from God's gracious act to deal with sin." This purposely makes no reference to time. Sinful, unforgiven men do now live in a period of time which is subsequent to God's act in Christ, though they do not live in "the age to come." "The age to come" will then be "the life of humanity considered in the light of God's act." Humanity will then be in two parts, those who are believers in Christ (who have actually "entered" the age to come) and unbelievers who may enter by repentance and faith.

To some extent the time element must come in. It is an actual fact that all men now live A.D. and not B.C. Time is not, however, the vital element of itself. "The present age" and "the age to come" are a temporal framework for sin and salvation. When we say that the age to come has broken in, we mean that God has acted in Christ and that from the time of the cross and resurrection and onwards men are to be told the good news. When we say that some people have entered the age to come we mean that they have responded to God's offer to them in Christ.

Now before our Lord gave himself for our sins the life of humanity ("the present age") was "evil." All that we have said about wrath and judgment and the curse is therefore applicable. Humanity must be pictured as under the threat of divine judgment. This covers the whole human race: "all have sinned . . . " (Rom. 3:23). But Paul looked out upon, and preached to, the men of his own time, the men of his "present" age, and he saw in them an illustration and an anticipation of the eschatological judgment (Rom. 1:24, 26, 28, *paredōken*). Their "evil" is mentioned in Romans 1:29. Our Lord gave himself to rescue us from membership of this evil humanity.

The word "rescue" (*exaireomai*) means to "take somebody out of a dangerous situation": afflictions and oppression (Acts 7:10, 34), the hand of Herod (Acts 12:11) and the prospect of assassination (Acts 23:27). When the rescue has been accomplished, the rescued party is no longer in the danger but out of it. If in giving himself for our sins our Lord succeeded in his purpose, we ought to be able to say that men are now "out" of the danger.

As a matter of fact believing men are out of danger. They are still members of humanity but not members of humanity-apart-from-God's-act, humanity-under-judgment. They have entered the age to come. The rest of humanity is still under judgment, even though Christ has died. Unlike Christians, they have not been rescued. Why is this? It is because they have not come the way that Christians have, the way of repentance and faith. But in response to the preaching of the gospel and to God's call they may still come; and they may still by repentance and faith leave the present age and enter the age to come.

If we dwell on the element of time we must say that the present age and the age to come overlap. If two people live in one house, the believer lives in the age to come and at the same time the unbeliever lives in the present age. Yet Christ has died. I infer that by his death he opened the door which leads from one age to the other but that men are not rescued until they go through the door—by repentance and faith. The question must therefore be asked, what did Christ actually do in his death?

We approach this question by way of what Paul says about freedom. It is something which is already enjoyed in Christ (2:4). It was for this enjoyment that Christ set us free. Our liberation was therefore in the past. But our freedom may be lost. "Do not again be entangled in a yoke of bondage." The man who lets himself be circumcised is under obligation to perform the whole law. He is removed from where Christ operates. He is banished from grace (5:1–4).

It seems plain that we cannot make the simple statement that Christ liberated us by his cross and stop there. When Paul wrote it was still true that Christ had died and if it were a question of his death and nothing more the readers would still be free—liberated by the cross. Obviously "the benefits of his passion" have to be received and kept. Men must stay within the realm of grace and must continue to exercise faith. The context shows that in some way Christ liberated men from the obligation to keep the law. At their conversion they were "called to freedom" (5:13; cf. 1 Thess. 4:7). They are free from the law as a means to justification. We must still ask, therefore, what did Christ do in his death, considered apart from God's call to sinners and their response in faith?

Christ was sent by the Father to redeem those who were under the law (4:4–5), and he did so redeem them (3:13). Before his act they were under the law, entangled in a yoke of slavery and under a curse (3:10). This was due to the fact that they were under obligation to perform the requirements of the law and had failed to do so. Their liability to the wrath and judgment implied by "curse" can only be due to the fact that God does not turn a blind eye to their conduct. He observes it and is not pleased.[15]

---

15. The idea of pleasing God is not alien to Paul's thought in Galatians. See 1:10 and Guthrie's note.

But he does not dismiss the matter from his mind. Men should have obeyed and they are answerable. If the situation had been left to rest there, only the fearful prospect of the curse remains for men. The curse is directly related to men's conduct, to their sin, and if they are not responsible it is unjust.

But the situation did not rest there. Christ fulfilled his Father's commission and removed the curse from men "by becoming a curse for us" (3:13). If men are still answerable for their sins, they are still under the curse. But Christ has taken it away from them. The inference is that Christ has undertaken men's responsibility. He has relieved them of their accountability. He has borne their guilt. In taking the curse upon himself Christ "took upon himself with it God's judgment." [16]

At this stage, and in theory, man stands naked before God. He has been relieved of his accountability and to that extent Good Friday marks a change in the situation of the human race. But man is not yet fit to draw near to God. He stands in the unconscious enjoyment of a negative blessing—which is not *the* blessing—but he is alone in the world, without responsibility, without God, and nowhere to go.

This is the climax of the work of Christ for us. It may be summed up in the expression "the cross of Christ" (6:12). It is a stumbling-block to some (5:11) but to Paul it was his boast and glory (6:14). So captivated is he by the picture that he can use it in a surprising setting. Through the cross the world has been crucified to Paul. It has been crucified (perfect); there it is now therefore hanging, on its cross. It cannot lay its hands (crucified!) on the apostle to do him hurt or to lead him astray. For the "world" is a kind of "external flesh"; it is the scene of "the present age." For Paul its hands are tied—nailed down.

Even if the world still has the power, executed criminal thing that it is, to cast its spell on him, Paul cannot respond to its allure. For through the cross he himself has been crucified to the world. There he now hangs. The song of the Sirens may beguile him and he may want to be up and away; but he is tied to his cross.[17]

More is involved in this apostolic experience than the historic crucifixion. The cross, in fact, means the crucifixion with its meaning and its sequel, the resurrection. In thinking of the curse which our Lord bore for us and of the responsibility which has been lifted from our shoulders on to his, we have ignored the resurrection. But the living Christ has had dealings with Paul. The apostle was not "rescued" (1:4) until his encounter on the road to Damascus. Yet the curse had already been borne. On the cross Christ had done his work for us. This corresponds to the cross as an event in history and its meaning. When we think of the resurrection of our Lord we are ready to go on to consider his work in us. For without the prior cross no rescue is possible.

---

16. Cf. W. Mundle, *Begriffslex.* 4:351. This is *Stellvertretung,* substitution. I am unable to follow Mr. Whiteley here. Cf. D. E. H. Whiteley, *The Theology of St. Paul,* pp. 83–85, 99–100, 134–38.

17. Cf. of the binding of Odysseus in Homer, *The Odyssey,* XII.39,50.

## *God at Work in Us—The Work of Christ in Us*

The work of Christ is to be made known among men. *The gospel is to be preached.* It can be, and indeed must be, expressed in words, and it can be distorted. But it must be preached. Distortion is a grievous sin (1:6–9). So weighty a matter is the preaching of the gospel that Paul can see it as the purpose of God's revelation of his Son in his own conversion (1:16). When the news filtered through to the churches of Judaea that their quondam persecutor had begun to preach the gospel, a ripple of thanksgiving spread over them and they gave glory to God (1:22–24).

There is but one gospel, "the gospel which I herald" (2:2), and it is to be made known to all men. The terms "uncircumcised men" and "circumcised men," who are to be "gospeled," are collectively exhaustive: no other men exist.[18]

When the gospel is faithfully preached, *God calls the hearers.* The point here is not the human but the divine activity. The preacher ought to use all his resources of understandable (not necessarily "contemporary") language, valid argument and apt illustration. He should speak with authority rather than "from authorities." He will address his listeners directly and in this manner will give them a message from God instead of reading out loud a lecture or essay about God. And his words will be warmed from his own experience of the love of God in Christ. Even so, in the final analysis, the conversion or edification of the hearer is more than the result of human utterance. If one man by himself can convert his fellow, the next brilliant man can "unconvert" him. For though the preacher may sound the call, it is God who gives it.

It would be possible in some circumstances to speak of a call given in absence. In a time of national emergency, for example, posters might appear in every city or village bearing a portrait of the monarch and the words underneath, "Your king calls you." Many might feel it as a genuine call and flock to the colors. But the king would not be actually present. It is not so in the preaching of the gospel. It has indeed to be preached in words; but God himself owns the words as conveying his message and convinces the hearer that God is speaking to him in the preacher's words. The preacher states the gospel and gives the invitation, calling men to repentance and faith, but it is God who finally says "Come!" with convincing power.

The Galatians themselves had come to Christ in this manner (1:6; 5:13). Paul himself is a particular case of a general rule. God called him (1:15–16) and there was no human voice. But earlier witnesses had been at work and even though his conversion was "sudden" he already had heard enough of the gospel to recognize the name of Jesus (cf. Acts 9:5).

When it is preached *the gospel is to be received by men* (1:9, cf. v. 12). For God's call through the preacher is a moment of revelation. The event may be fitly compared to listening to great music. Without the organ, the piano and the violins there would be no music. But the entranced listener

---

18. 2:7. For the concrete use of abstract terms cf. Rom. 11:7 and see note 90 in the chapter on Romans.

does not listen to the instruments. He has ears only for the music. In real preaching the intellectual powers are quickened and stretched to the limit. The preacher is an agent, not an instrument. He reaches heights of personality rarely attained outside the pulpit. He does not descend to the pedestrian level of a mere machine. Yet when all is said and done, it is God who calls, not the preacher. It is the music of the gospel which is heard, not the organ. It is the voice of God which must be heeded, and is heeded. This is what it meant when people speak of "not obtruding" the personality. The real preacher's personality does not obtrude. Through it God speaks and God, living, present and active, calls. The divine Musician "plays" the preacher and only His music is heard. The message must be received—and obeyed.

When the gospel is thus heard and received *men are justified by faith* (2:15-16). The "even we" is almost sublime. "We" are Jews by nature, born to privilege. Spiritually we arrived with a silver spoon in our mouths. We are not sinners with a questionable Gentile origin. "Even we," spiritual aristocrats as we are, are justified by faith in Christ. ("By" faith is a convenient comprehensive expression. The different prepositions, *dia, ek* and *en* ["in Christ" v. 17] are variations on a single theme.)

It is not necessary to go over the ground already traversed in our study of the Epistle to the Romans (see pp. 111–16). Paul's doctrine of justification in Galatians is the same as in Romans. (Cf. Gal. 3:8, 22–24, and the significant use of "righteousness" in 3:21.)

We have already said (p. 117) that when a man is justified a permanent relationship is set up between him and God. This is reflected in Galatians. Grace and peace, as the greeting shows, continue to come from God (1:3). He did not, so to speak, shut off the supply once the man had been justified. Similarly at the close of the letter we see that mercy (*eleos*), in addition to grace and peace, streams forth from their divine origin (6:16, 18).

Other contexts show the same. "He who keeps on supplying you with the Spirit . . . , does he do it as a result of works of law or the hearing of faith?" (3:5). The thought is expressed in a simile used by Frances Ridley Havergal in her hymn,

> Like a river glorious
> Is God's perfect peace.

It is a characteristic of a river that it "keeps on rolling along." If it dries up it ceases to be a river. Nothing is left but the river bed. What is given in justification "keeps on coming." The relationship is permanent.

We are concerned, however, with more than a simile or any mere figure of speech. God himself is active in the justified man's life. He is "the One who calls you" (5:8). The present tense is important. God called the Galatians at their conversion (1:6) and he calls them still. He did not set them on the right road and then leave them. He is with them, speaking words to encourage them in the forward march of their pilgrimage, and to direct their way. When jungle warfare is their lot, with all its hazards and discomforts, they hear his voice, "Keep going!" The One who calls "is always God in Pauline theology" (R. A. Cole, p. 146).

We pass now to what we have described as the concomitants of justification (p. 112). God "*quickens*" *the man who believes and he receives him.* Such quickening is reflected in 3:21. No law can quicken but the believer finds that God can and does. He was dead; he is now, on believing, alive, a "new creation" (6:15). As to "being received," it is implied in God's call. The Galatians could not be on the move "away from him who called you" (1:6) unless they had started by being "with" him. This is possible only because God had received them.

When a man puts his faith in Christ and is justified, *he comes to know God.* Paul contrasts the ignorance of God before conversion with the knowledge of God gained in conversion (4:8–9). "At that time you did not know God . . . now you have come to know him." It is true that Paul hastily adds "rather, were known by God," but this does not cancel the knowledge which the Galatians had received. God had not enlarged his own experience when he came to know the Galatians. He rather gave them recognition. "To recognize oneself to be the centre of divine attention is one of the profounder aspects of Christian conversion" (Guthrie, p. 122). Growth in the Christian knowledge of God is not ruled out: "that they may grow in the knowledge of thee . . . " (John 17:3; cf. Phil. 3:10). The Galatians had not only been informed about God. When they put their faith in Jesus they encountered the living God; they "made his acquaintance." For the rest of their lives and for all eternity it was their privilege to deepen the acquaintance. And so it is with every justified man.

Furthermore *the man who puts his faith in Jesus receives the Holy Spirit.* The Galatians received the Spirit when the Word was preached to them and they heard and believed (3:2). They were still receiving the Spirit because, or in so far as, they were still hearing and believing (3:5). The association of the Spirit with the Word should not be unnoticed. This supports the view that the Spirit is given in conversion.[19] The gift must not be rigidly and automatically linked with water baptism. As the late Bishop of Jamaica (Dr. Percival Gibson) once told me, according to our Anglican teaching the experience may occur before, in or after baptism. If it occurs in baptism it is not due to baptism as such but to the fact that in the baptismal service the Word is heard and believed for the first time. This may be regarded as unusual. In the New Testament, faith comes to baptism (cf. p. 115). Without the Spirit there would be no faith.

In a vivid metaphor and with a decisive aorist tense Paul says that those who belong to Christ Jesus "crucified the flesh" (5:24). This is the reverse side of the coin, the human side of the reception of the Spirit. Flesh and Spirit are logically contradictory and mutually antagonistic. Each exercises desire "against" the other: note the *kata* with the genitive of hostility (5:17). When the Galatians heard the Word, the flesh "desired" them to disbelieve

---

19. Cf. Althaus, p. 23; James D. G. Dunn, *Baptism in the Holy Spirit*, p. 96.

it and the Spirit "desired" them to receive it. Each man's heart was a battle-ground. When he did put his faith in Jesus, the Spirit conquered the flesh. In human terms the *ego* crucified the flesh.

Paul links the flesh with the law (Rom. 8:3) and says that he himself died to the law in order that he might live to God (Gal. 2:19). He has crucified the flesh and is no longer "in the flesh" (cf. Rom. 8:9). He has been crucified with Christ (2:20). But when did this happen?

Paul cannot be literally referring to the crucifixion: he was not there, or at most was a spectator—surely unlikely. Was it "as if" he had been cru-cified with Christ (cf. Mark 15:32)? Then it might be argued that it is "as if" the ungodly died for themselves. It seems to me that Paul ever had the cross before his eyes (3:1; cf. 1 Cor. 2:2) and that when he thought of crucifying the flesh, the Passion of our Lord swept over him afresh. When he did crucify the flesh, he was in his Master's presence, and he bent his will to His. "What am I to do, Lord?" (Acts 22:10). "I was not (*egenomēn*) disobedient to the heavenly vision" (Acts 26:19). What inner experience lies behind that striking *egenomēn*? And so he can say that "I have been cruci-fied with Christ." The old self is nailed down—and it took place in a shat-tering spiritual event which had its points of resemblance with that of the historic crucifixion. It was "with Christ." It means that the living Christ was with him then.

It is admitted that on the Damascus road the man born *before* the due time saw by anticipation the Parousia-glory of Christ.[20] But it was none the less the crucified Jesus. "I am Jesus of Nazareth" (Acts 22:8, NEB). Because of the self-crucifixion of obedience the old "man-under-the-law," seeking self-justification, ceases to exist. Such an *ego* does not go on living any longer (2:20). Christ lives in him. (A helpful illustration here is that of the preacher who "lives" in his sympathetic interpreter. Sentence by sen-tence the one man repeats the other in a foreign language. The two per-sonalities almost fuse in their team work.) And yet the new man does go on living his human life on earth, living it in continued faith in the Son of God who loved him and delivered Himself up for him.[21]

It need not be supposed that every converted man could speak in these terms five minutes after his conversion. The apostle has given us an expo-sition of what goes on in the heart. But what he says rings true of the gen-uine convert. He has heard the Word and believed; he has repudiated self and Christ has come into his heart. As a further concomitant of justification, then, we can say that *the justified man seeks to please God rather than men, for he has become the slave of Christ* (1:10).

This is his own estimate of the situation. Though a slave he is not servile. Though he is a slave God does not treat him as a slave. Within the experience already described there is an additional factor. *The justified man is adopted by God as a son.* "You are all sons of God in Christ Jesus through faith" (3:26, cf. 29). God sent his Son in order that the redeemed

---

20. 1 Cor. 15:8. Stephen Neill, *The Interpretation of the New Testament*, p. 287, n. 2.
21. Cf. Ladd, *A Theology of the NT*, p. 132. "The taking of the cross means the death of self."

might receive the adoption (4:5-7). The thought of Paul in Galatians is parallel to that in Romans (see pp. 118–20). Adoption is the act of God, and he makes it known to believing men. *The believer knows that he is adopted.* "In proof that [*hoti*] you are sons, God sent forth the Spirit of his Son into our hearts, crying 'Abba, Father'" (4:6). ". . . adoption and the gift of the Spirit are concomitant" (Guthrie).

In spite of the similarity to Romans there is a striking difference. In Romans 8:15 Paul says that "we cry." In Galatians 4:6 it is the Spirit who cries (*krazon*). This must be given full weight. It is startling to think of the Holy Spirit shouting ("Drop Thy still dews of quietness"), and many a powerful preacher has been mistakenly directed to the "still small voice" (1 Kings 19:12, KJV). The rarity of the expression, however, must not lead us to ascribe irreverence to its use or to interpret the text as if the believer were shouting. Jesus shouted (John 7:37; 12:44) in the days of his ministry and particularly as his Passion was drawing to its close. In the parallel Synoptic accounts, is it mere coincidence that our Lord invokes his Father with a shout just as the Spirit does in Galatians? "Jesus shouted with a loud voice [Matt. 27:50] and said, 'Father . . .'" (Luke 23:46). "The Spirit (shouts), 'Abba, Father.'" The Spirit makes sure that the believer hears his voice, and instructs and encourages with no muffled sound. In consequence the believer joyously knows and invokes his Father. "Thou art no longer a slave [1:10!] but a son." This is highly individual, as the second person singular shows, and it is not the ecstasy of glossolalia.[22]

The Spirit's "shout" is logically prior to that of the believer. The former could hardly be recorded on tape. The latter might be.

The proof of adoption is in the believer's experience of the Holy Spirit. The ground of adoption is being in Christ (3:26) and the means to it is faith. How do men become "in Christ"? If we may judge from the apostle's language, it is because they have "put on Christ" (3:27). But who are those who have put on Christ?

A clue will be found in Romans 13:14, "put on the Lord Jesus Christ." The context shows that the readers had already come to first faith (v. 11) and must think of their moral walk (v. 13). In view of Romans 6:1–5 the readers were hardly unbaptized. "Put on" must therefore mean "renew your faith in, and manifest the character of, the Lord Jesus Christ." To "put on" is not therefore always and by necessity linked with baptism.[23]

We come back to adoption. It is for those who are in Christ and it is received through faith. The primary reference of the metaphor is to clothes. Those who put on (the dress which consists of) Christ are in consequence in (the dress which consists of) Christ. If the means is faith, then to put on Christ means to believe in (*pisteuein eis*) Christ (Gal. 2:16). Note the

---

22. Cf. W. Grundmann, *TDNT* 3:903. Althaus, p. 35, is very moving. "Du, jeder einzelne von Christus begnadete Mensch, du, der den Geist des Sohnes im Sohnesgebete in sich spürt—du bist Sohn und bist Erbe!" "You, each individual man begraced by Christ; you, the man who traces in himself the Spirit of the Son in the son's prayer—you are son and you are heir."

23. See my article "Quotation Marks as an Aid in Interpretation," *Southwestern Journal of Theology* 18 (Fall 1975): 69–71.

phrase *dia pisteōs,* and "to be justified in Christ" (2:17). To "put on" is a metaphor for justifying faith.

Then why does Paul call those who have put on Christ "all you who were baptized into Christ"? It is because, as we have seen, faith comes to baptism. A man believes into Christ, puts on Christ and is baptized into Christ. The clothes receive him, the Lord receives him and the baptismal water receives him.[24]

Paul does not say who baptized the Galatians, but somebody did. He baptized them in obedience to the Lord; they submitted to it in obedience to the Lord; the Lord confirmed his acceptance of them; and the church welcomed them. Baptism thus brings out into the open and attests an inner experience. It tells, in short-story form, the Lord's dealings with a believer. He emerges from the sacrament and finds as fellows all sorts and conditions of men who have traveled his road before him, who in their totality constitute one comprehensive man (3:28), clothed in one comprehensive dress, "in Christ Jesus." Yet each person in this collective "one" is covered by the clothes, has a close association with Christ, and still preserves his own identity. His personality is not lost but made. The "clothes" do not include a mask.

Baptism is not a concomitant of justification in the same sense that adoption is, as it depends on the person's own decision to submit to the sacrament. If he refused to be baptized he would not be forced. It might raise questions about the reality of his experience of adoption, though Paul does not deal with them, and the modern Quaker and Salvationist must make us exercise caution before making judgment. But baptism even so ought to be a concomitant of justification or to follow it soon.

Thus *the justified man becomes a member of a fellowship, the church.*

The church is present in the epistle even though it is not always mentioned by name. Whenever "we" or "you" appear it would be relevant to ask if the church is the background of the thought. The church is a brotherhood (6:1), a hospital for its members and a society of mutual helpfulness (6:2). It is a brotherhood which receives the grace of our Lord continually (6:18). It has some aspects of a benevolent society and even of a morally "athletic" society whose members should keep fit and not grow weary (6:9). It reaches out beyond its own frontiers but has special responsibility towards its own members. They belong to the household of the faith (6:10). Their mother is "Jerusalem above" (4:26). They constitute the society of the free, not indeed free from God but free for him (cf. Althaus, p. 21.)

This "one" (cf. 3:28) fellowship, often called the universal church, is manifested in different places. Paul can thus speak of "the churches of Galatia" (1:2) and "the churches of Judaea" (1:22–23) without losing sight of the fact of individual experience. The churches are in Christ, made up of individuals who had felt the smart of persecution ("us") and who glorified God. The justified man belongs to a fellowship which is the church of

---

24. Being baptized into Christ is analogous to being baptized into the Jordan. Cf. my article "The Semantics of Sacramental Language," in *Tyndale Bulletin* 17 (1966) 99–108.

God (1:13) and he lives his Christian life in its local presence.

In company with the other members *he is a man of eager expectation and hope* (5:5). "We eagerly await the hope (the hoped for thing) which consists of righteousness." This does not mean that after all the believer has doubts about his own justification. This would run counter to the apostle's thought. The righteousness for which the Christian hopes is the righteousness which he already has. The text therefore illustrates the faithfulness of God. Justification has set up a relationship between believing men and God. God does not take away that which he has imputed. If a man has put on Christ he need not fear a later change of clothes.

It is similar with regard to eternal life (6:8). He will inherit it but he already has it. He lives to God, because Christ lives in him (2:19–20). The old self under the law is dead. The life which he does go on living is lived in continuous faith in the Son of God. To be justified means to live (3:11), to live by the Spirit (5:25). God will not withdraw the life. The justified man may be sure that both the forensic and the "mystical" relationship will last.

It might be thought that the justified man is always "at the receiving end." The privileges of believers are indeed great but they have also their responsibilities. *The justified man has duties.* He is led by the Spirit (5:18) but he must not be without some "drive" himself. He is a man of faith but his faith is not to be quiescent. It is to be active and express itself by means of love (5:6). In the fellowship of the church each man should serve the others *(douleuete allēlois,* 5:13). It is not a question of slavishness but of gladly yielding to others as if they were owners. Let their will prevail; let their convenience and comfort be studied; let their well-being come before mine. The means to this is love. Each has been the object of the love of Christ (2:20). Each should think, feel, speak and act with love towards the others and is under obligation to do so. It sums up God's law (5:14).

This is not with the purpose of being justified but because they are justified. They are not under law (5:18). The good which each should do is not to be limited but ought to overflow to those outside the church. The immediate circle provides the closest opportunity and fellow members have thus a prior claim. But the outsider must not be forgotten. No such achievement of benevolence should be the subject of boasting, of taking the credit to oneself. For good works are not merely "works." They come from men who are led by the Spirit and are the fruit of the Spirit (5:22). They do not come from a "production line." They grow. The life of genuine piety has moral results. Effort has to be exercised by men but the credit goes to the Spirit (5:18; 6:14).

Such fruit, such active love of neighbor, fulfills the old law and the law of Christ (6:2). The latter does not imply legalism. The law of Christ is rather the old law regarded as a number of signposts to indicate the direction to be taken by those who confess Jesus as Lord. The signposts expound, if only in outline, the Lordship of Christ to those who are in Christ.

# 4

# The Epistles
# to the Corinthians

THE EPISTLES TO THE Corinthians have certain marked characteristics which make them somewhat different from the Epistle to the Romans. Unlike Romans, they do not give us a more or less ordered exposition of the content of the Pauline gospel. They do indeed contain doctrine but it is not "systematically" set forth even in the simple pattern of universal sin, salvation in Christ and the consequent duties of Christian life and behavior. Further, Paul knew the church at Corinth intimately. He had not yet visited Rome and he knew the church there only by repute.

The Corinthian letters differ also from the Epistle to the Galatians. It is true that in writing to both churches Paul is concerned with pastoral problems. Apart, however, from the question of his own apostolic authority, Paul gives the impression in Galatians that he is fighting on only one front. In Corinth, however, there were many problems. The church was split, ugly immorality had emerged and irreverence abounded. The members could not eat the Lord's Supper because each was intent on eating his own. Guidance was necessary in regard to speaking in tongues, marriage, meat offered to idols and recourse to the heathen lawcourts.

Even so, a theological pattern may be detected which is consistent with what we have found already. Under the pressure of all the many pastoral problems at Corinth and the worry about all the churches, the apostle might have reached breaking point. He would be understood, and forgiven, if it had to be said of him that "he has something on his mind." It has been said, by no means uncharitably, of nervous wrecks in the modern ministry. Their unheeding congregations—or absentees—and the personal hostilities, indifferences and sins have ever loomed before them as an intolerable cloud. Imagination sees no possible prospect but gloom.

## THE NATURE OF GOD

Now Paul did indeed have something on his mind—but it was not the burden of his ceaseless ministry. It was *the living God*. It may be a subjective judgment on my part or I may have missed the evidence in our studies up to this point, but I cannot help feeling that in composing the Corinthian letters Paul was "practicing the presence of God." He ever dwelt "in His sight." The living God was more real to the apostle than all his cares and problems.

We establish the point formally, for the purposes of our pattern, by reference to Paul's explicit use of the term, "the living God" (2 Cor. 3:3; 6:16).[1] But we must amplify this even at the cost of anticipating briefly what should, and no doubt will, appear later as the theme develops. Paul not only speaks of the living God but his language implies that God must be living if any sense is to be preserved.

To begin with, God is working in nature. He is not only the Creator (II.4:6) but "he gives the seed a body as he willed" (15:38). Again, he is working in the church. He appointed a ministry (12:28). "Through us he manifests the fragrance of the knowledge of himself" (II.2:14). (Cf II.13:3, "the Christ who speaks in me.") Different ministers are but servants through whom the Corinthians gained their faith. Paul himself planted the gospel seed and Apollos watered it but it was God "who made it grow" (3:5–7). God gave the increase in the number and the quality of the converts. Even the unbeliever who comes into the assembly of the prophetic church recognizes that "God is in reality among you" (14:25).

Finally, God is working in the individual. He urges men; he appeals to men. We are ambassadors for Christ, says Paul, "conscious that [2] God appeals to men through us" (II.5:20). God gave the Spirit (II.5:5). He listens to the man who speaks in a tongue (14:2, 28) and to the man who prays with his mind (14:15). He puts "keenness" into a man's heart (II.8:16, cf. NEB). He rescues men and will rescue them (II.1:10). He humbles them (II.12:21), perhaps even "takes them down a peg," and yet he comforts them (II.7:6) and he gives the victory (15:57). (Cf. 2 Macc. 10:38.) He loves the cheerful giver; and he can direct the full flood of grace to men, to be split up into lesser streams of good works (II.9:7–8). Not only "the love of God" but "the God of love" will be with men (II.13:11, 13).

We must now proceed with the pattern. God is *the only God*. "No one is God—except One." This is Paul's clear, uncompromising affirmation. When he goes on to admit the existence of so-called gods, he denies their divinity. "For us there is one God, the Father" (8:4–6). He would never regard the matter as subject to debate. He is not saying that "you believe in gods many and lords many, but in our view . . . ; you may possibly be right." When he says "for us" the underlying implication is that "we are right." He is not hesitantly putting forward a theory which might turn out to be wrong. "The same God" (12:6) is present (14:25) and effective in manifold situations.

---

1. Henceforth in this chapter references to the First and Second Epistles to the Corinthians respectively will be simply cited as, e.g., 15:3 and II.5:21. In the absence of "II" it should be assumed that we have the First Epistle in mind.

2. *Hōs* subjective, giving what is in the mind of the subject. It is more than "as if" (NEB) God were appealing. Paul and his companions believed that God really was appealing through them. Their deep conviction was surely right.

The same, one, living *God is conscious.* Several times the apostle confidently says that *"God knows"* (II:1:11, 31; 12:2–3). He can invoke Him as witness of his inner motive for keeping away from Corinth. God must know that he sought to spare the Corinthians (II.1:23). He knows the man who loves Him; the living God knows the living individual (8:3. cf. 13:12; cf. also p. 128 on Gal. 4:9). He "knows that the reasonings of the wise are futile" (3:20; Ps. 93:11, LXX). The *Kurios* here must be God. It is an element in proof texts used to show that the wisdom of the world is foolishness with (*para*) God (3:19).

The God who knows is also the *God* who *wills.* Paul was an apostle "through the will of God" (1:1; II:1:1) and through the same will the churches of Macedonia "gave themselves first to the Lord and to us" (II.8:5). The physical constitution of man accords with God's will. "He placed each one of the members in the body as he willed" (12:18). The planted seed does not merely evolve into full flower. "God gives to it a body as he willed" (15:38).

God's will is not the impulse of the moment, a succession of "whims" like those of the social butterfly who flutters from one aim to another and never settles. It is long range and abiding. *God has purpose.* He gave the different parts of the body their different functions and combined them so that together they form one body, *in order that* (*hina*) the body might be a unity (12:18, 24–25). Every child who is born a normal member of the human race is thus an example of the continuing will of God.

God's purpose may be immediate or remote. "He chose . . . in order that [*hina*] he might put to shame . . . and render inoperative . . . in order that [*hopōs*] no flesh might boast in the presence of God" (1:27–29). The *hopōs* expresses the remote or more comprehensive purpose. (Cf. II.8:14; 2 Thess. 1:11–12.)

In thinking of God's purpose Paul is not limited to final conjunctions. His verbs are impressive. We might paraphrase a famous passage thus:

> What eye did not see and ear did not hear
> and imagination did not conceive—
> how many things did God prepare for those who love him!
> (We know what they are.)
> For God revealed them to us through the Spirit (2:9–10).

This seems the best way to treat what is admittedly difficult to construe. The *hosa* ("how many things") is exclamatory, breaking off from the previous relative clauses; and the *gar* ("for") explains the understood sentence which we have inserted in parentheses. Paul is moved to exclamation by the thought of God's preparations. The love for God which is born in men finds him ready. The gifts which he graciously gave to us (2:12) when we turned to him did not have to be improvised. They were waiting for us. They had been prepared for us. They thus express God's long purpose.

God's hidden wisdom, "his secret purpose" (NEB), was foreordained (*proōrisen*) before time began for our glory (2:7). We may thus speak of God's eternal purpose. It was manifested in historical time, primarily in the cross. God made the sinless One to be sin and he did it for us, "*in order that* we might become the righteousness of God in him" (II.5:21). It was manifested secondly in the preaching of the gospel. "God resolved [*eudokēsen*] to save believers through the folly of the proclamation" (1:21).

Texts to which we have already referred (1:21; 2:7) show that *God has wisdom*. His wisdom is beyond the reach of unaided man. It includes knowledge but it is more than knowledge. In its broadest sense it implies a kind of anterior knowledge, the ability to draw on this item of knowledge rather than that, in order to deal with an existing situation. The inadequacy of knowledge by itself and its distinction from wisdom is vividly expressed in the famous remark, "the most learned fool in Christendom."

*God has an image.* This could be a startling statement if we had come fresh from a study of Paul's attitude to idols. But the image of God is not brute matter but living man (11:7; cf. p. 84). Thus *God is personal*. If it is objected that the image is a poor one, the answer is twofold. Even if the image is spoilt, what is left of it is still a useful pointer to the divine. And in any case there is an image which is not spoilt. The perfect Man is the perfect image. Christ is the image of God (II.4:4).[3]

The conscious, living God is not merely a spectator on the sidelines, a theorist with knowledge and the wisdom to apply it. *God has power*. The living God can do as he wills. . . . He can—but he may not; he can do, but he may not act—yet. He has a potentiality which may or may not be exercised. "God . . . will raise us through his power" (6:14). It is plain that when Paul wrote these words God had not so acted. He could act, when he willed. His power is an ability to act and it was exercised when he "raised the Lord"; potentiality and actuality are present in this same verse.

This is a clear instance and it does not lack support. "God can make all grace abound . . . " (II.9:8). The word of the cross, Christ crucified, is the power of God (1:18, 24). The human response to this preached word, faith, is grounded in the power of God (2:4–5). The medium of God's royal rule is not empty talk but power (4:20). "We are not stronger than he is, are we?" (10:22). (Cf. II.4:7; 6:7.)

The vastness of God's power may be judged by his exercise of it in creation. Paul is familiar with the recorded story and in expounding it he would agree that God exercised his power. The tense should be noted. Man was created (11:9). Everything, "the totality," derives from God (v. 12). Even a woman's tresses have been given to her (v. 15; see Gen. 2:18). The God who shines creatively in the hearts of men is the God who said, "Let there be light" (Gen. 1:3; 2 Cor. 4:6). (Cf. 1 Cor. 12:18, 24 and perhaps 2 Cor. 5:18.) Everything owes its existence to the one God (8:6). He who created the world owns it. "The earth is the Lord's and all that it contains" (10:26; Ps. 23:1, LXX).

God not only exercised his power. He still exercises it. In some respects, indeed, he holds it in reserve. He has not yet raised us from the dead. But

---

3. Cf. O. Flender, *Begriffslex.* 2:120, "Zwischen dem Bild und dem Wesen des unsichtbaren Gottes gibt es hier keinen Unterschied." "Between the image and the reality of the invisible God there is here no difference."

in other respects his power is not quiescent. He "is at work at" (*ho ener-gōn*)[4] everything (12:6). *God is the Creator* and he maintains his own property. He keeps it in existence. *God is the Sustainer.*

This is shown more by particular instances than by a universal statement. In drawing attention to the structure of the body (12:18, 24) Paul has the creation in mind. The aorist tenses of the verbs are suggestive, and "composed" *(sunekerasen)* reminds us of the *eplasen* of Genesis 2:7, LXX. Paul is thinking of the physical body and this coheres with Genesis. Man is formed of the dust and then receives the breath of life. The first man, Adam, was formed from the (dust of the) earth, "dusty" *(choïkos)*, and then became a living soul (15:45, 47).

But God as Creator did not merely create a pattern. Paul's thoughts were directed not only to Adam but to living men. "The body is not one member" (12:14). The first man was created; others are born; but the pattern is maintained. Paul, though probably unmarried, was not blind to the facts of parenthood. He can use a parental metaphor with ease: "I alone[5] begat you through the gospel" (4:15). He is equally at home with the literal: "parents should save up for their children" (II.12:14). He knows the problems (7:1–7); can see marriage as a divine *charisma* (v. 7); and realizes that children come (7:14). All normal children manifest the unity of body and members. If Paul were asked to account for this constant pattern he would say that in every case "God placed each of the members in the body as he willed" and "combined the parts of the body" with a view to its unity (12:18, 24–25). From this glimpse we can see that God is the Sustainer of the human part of the world which he created.

Again, it is God who supplies seed for the sower and bread to eat (II.9:10). Comparison with Isaiah 55:10, LXX, will show how deliberately or how unconsciously—both are significant—Paul has adapted the text to which he alludes to bring out the fact that it is God who is at work in the processes of nature and of human "manufacture." Men say that nature produces the seed for next year's crop. Paul says that God supplies it. Men bake bread, or, more strictly, transform dough into bread by baking it. Paul says that God supplies bread. Men sow the bare seed and "it" germinates and grows into the full plant. Paul says that God gives to each kind of seed its own "body," as he willed (15:38). God produces and God discriminates between the different kinds of seed.

This process of nature continues through the seasons, year after year. From the simple picture which Paul has drawn we can see God as the Sustainer of the physical part of the world which he created.

Within the world of nature and of men which God sustains, he is Master of history. The affairs of men are in his hands. He raises the dead and rescues his servants from death (II.1:9–10). He does not permit his servants to be tempted beyond their powers but with the temptation provides an escape route so that they may endure and come through (10:13). The course of nature and the life of men: continuation for both would be im-

---

4. Cf. Moulton-Turner, *Grammar* 3:244.
5. See footnotes 72 and 75 in the chapter on Romans.

possible if God were not exercising his power. All things and all men are within his control; for he is the *pantokratōr* (II.6:18). The universe itself and all that it contains cannot finally obstruct the purpose of the living God. God exercises his power in the spiritual world also. He is active in conversion: he creatively shines in our hearts (II.4:6). Men preach the gospel but it is God who creates faith (3:5–6). The body may decay but the inward man is daily renewed (II.4:16). This is not hellenistic dualism. (See H. D. Wendland's useful note, pp. 191–92.[6]) The spiritual man is a new creation (II.5:17–18). "From first to last this has been the work of God" (NEB). "We go on being transfigured" (II.3:18).

God appointed ministers in the church (12:28). They did not merely emerge. Their adequacy does not originate in their own inner resources. God qualifies them *(hikanōsen* II.3:5–7). This recalls the description of God as the Adequate One *(ho hikanos)* in Ruth 1:20–21, LXX. God appoints his ministers, qualifies them and "places" them, as the Presbyterians say (II.10:13–15).

From this series of "snapshots" we draw the conclusion that God is the Creator and the Sustainer of the whole universe, the whole realm of things, men and spiritual realities, down to the last detail.

We pass on to consider the character of God. We have already seen in this section that Christ is the image of God. God is like Christ. (This must not be taken as a denial of Nicene consubstantiality.) By drawing on Paul's language we can speak in greater detail and find what is virtually an analysis of the likeness. *God is righteous.* This points to the perfection of his moral nature. The unrighteous *(adikoi)*, who will not inherit the kingdom of God, are described in terms which imply an ethical judgment—sexual perverts, idolators, thieves, drunkards (6:9–11). The point here is not that God is not guilty of such practices but that he abhors them. Moral failure generally, not sexual laxity in particular, excludes from the kingdom of him who is utter moral goodness. (This is not the last word, as we shall see. "And such were some of you; but . . . ")

Men of this stamp have failed to meet a standard. Paul characterizes their conduct by the word "lawlessness" *(anomia)*, the antithesis of righteousness. The two have nothing in common (II.6:14). Moral failure and ethical perfection are incompatible. This ethical interpretation of righteousness has already been encountered in the apostle (see pp. 97–100).

As ministers of God, Paul and his associates seek to commend themselves by their conduct and attitude in every situation. They proclaim the truth, "working in the power of God" (II.6:4–7) (Alfred Plummer, p. 197). Their weapons are the weapons of righteousness, offensive and defensive, both sword and shield. It is through them that the power of God is exercised (II.4:7; cf. 12:9–10). Paul did not indulge in mere speech, rational argument or philosophical niceties; he was powerful in the power of God (2:1–5). For the weapons in question are not "fleshly," (like the war-

---

6. Where only the author's name is given the reference is to his or her commentary on the Corinthian Epistles.

horses of the Egyptians, Isa. 31:3) but "powerful to God" (II.10:4–5). This may mean "very powerful," an idiom going back through the LXX to the Hebrew.[7] On the other hand it may mean "powerful for God." This certainly fits the context. We tear down all towering pride that rears its battlements against the knowledge of God. Thus, servants of God in the power of God successfully defend the knowledge of God with weapons which come from God, for they are not "fleshly," but "divinely potent" (NEB; "divinely strong," Moffatt's trans.). And they are weapons of righteousness, supplied by righteousness and on the side of righteousness; "legitimate weapons [and] in a legitimate cause" (Plummer). Could God be other than righteous?

The conclusion drawn from this evidence can, I think, stand on its own feet but it is supported by the passage beginning with Romans 6:13. Through this connection "righteousness" in the Corinthian epistles is related to "righteousness" in Romans. For example, Paul can speak of "the ministry of righteousness" (II.3:9). The NEB translates by "the dispensation . . . under which we are acquitted." Plummer (p. 91) comes even closer to Romans. He interprets "righteousness" to mean "that which is attributed to man when he is justified."

Paul sees that false apostles (II.11:13–15) masquerade as apostles of Christ—who are appointed by the will of God (1:1; II.1:1). They follow the lead of their master, Satan, who masquerades as an angel of light. It is not greatly to be wondered at if his ministers take on the style of "ministers of righteousness." There may be a side glance here at the judaizing controversy but it can only be a side glance. They did not need to masquerade as ministers of the righteousness of works! Paul stands for the true apostleship, chosen, called and appointed by the will of God. If such apostles are ministers of righteousness, God himself must be righteous.

It is therefore quite in order to speak of "the righteousness of God" (II.5:21), and to regard it as coming from God (1:30). Four terms are used in 1:30: *wisdom, righteousness, sanctification* and *redemption*. They may be coordinate or the last three may unfold the content of wisdom. In either case righteousness comes from God. Can he give what he himself is not?

Paul was shocked when the "saints" did battle with each other before the heathen court (6:1–11). The judges, who are unbelievers (v. 6), are contrasted with believing brethren, but the expression of the contrast (v. 1) is not as we might have expected. The saints (*hoi hagioi*) are "the holy ones" and it would have been natural for Paul to call the judges "the unholy ones." It would have been correct, both formally and in fact. But he calls them "the unrighteous" (*adikoi*). This suggests that unholiness and un-

---

7. Cf. Jonah 3:3, LXX, and see A. B. Davidson, *Hebrew Syntax*, p. 49. A New Testament parallel is Acts 7:20, though this reference does not appear in Max Wilcox's *The Semitisms of Acts*, at any rate in the index. Cf. Ernst Haenchen, *The Acts of the Apostles*, p. 280. I cannot find any reference to Acts 7:20 in D. F. Payne, *Semitisms in Acts*, pp. 134–50 in Gasque and Martin, eds., *Apostolic History and the Gospel*. But see F. F. Bruce, *The Acts of the Apostles*, p. 167, and Moulton-Turner, *Grammar*, 4:90–91.

righteousness overlap and that a similar relationship exists between righteousness and holiness. Inasmuch as both come from God (1:30) we should add that *God is holy*. His Spirit is the Holy Spirit, "Whom you have from God" (6:19; cf. II.13:13).

The law does not figure so plainly in Corinthians as it does in Romans. What Paul does say about it, however, is enough to give us a Corinthian window on to a Roman scene. In dealing with the question of the financial support of the ministry, he uses illustrations from human life and then argues: "I am not saying this *kata anthrōpon*, am I? My point does not square with merely human principles, does it? Isn't this what the law says also? For in the law of Moses it stands written, 'Thou shalt not muzzle an ox when it is treading out the grain'" (9:7–9). Paul looks beyond the human to the divine. It would seem that he believed that *God is the author of the law*. This is confirmed by his further question: "God is not concerned about oxen, is he?" What the law prescribes, God prescribes.

In using the present tense (*melei*, "is concerned,") an insensitive townsman is not giving grounds for a meeting of protest organized by the Society for the Prevention of Cruelty to Animals. He means rather: "In this text God's concern is not solely for oxen, is it? Is not his concern more comprehensive? May not the passage be applied to men also?" (Deut. 25:4, LXX; the LXX reads *phimōseis*).

Paul goes on to draw a parallel (9:13–14). Those who engage in the ritual duties of the temple derive their food therefrom; those who as priests serve at the altar share with the altar what is sacrificed on it (Lev. 7:6–10, 14, 28–36; Num. 18:8, 31; Deut. 18:1–3). The point here is not the pleasant observation that religious workers do not have to find secular employment in order to live. This is what the law says should be done. This is what the Lord directs. "So also the Lord commanded those who preach the gospel to live from the gospel" (cf. Luke 10:7; 1 Tim. 5:18). The point of comparison is the authority which justifies the practices. The Lord and the law command; the Lord Jesus Christ commands. Behind the law is God.

We have already spoken of Paul's awareness of the living God (p. 145). He is the great background—or presence—of Paul's thought in 14:26–36. When the church gathers for worship "tongues" must be interpreted; otherwise the speaker must address nobody but himself—and *God*. If a prophet is speaking, he should break off if somebody else sitting ("in the pew") receives a revelation—and revelation comes from *God*. The two men must not each stand his ground and fight it out to gain the ear of the congregation. Prophets give way to prophets, the reason being, not that prophets are amenable to interruption, but that *God* is not a God of disorder but of peace.

Then comes the command for the wives to observe silence in the churches. Any questions can be answered by their husbands at home. Let them be subordinate, as *the law* says (11:3; Gen. 3:16). The Corinthians must not make innovations in defiance of established church practice. The Word of *God* did not start with them and did not end with them.

When Paul refers to the law he is not aware of any allusion to an inferior authority. The law is the law of God. Its "typical" events were recorded for our instruction (10:11; cf. 9:9–10). We should be instructed—and obey. The concept of transgression (II.5:19; cf. p. 83) implies sin, which is against God, and it requires law for the sin to be thus given precision. Once again we see God behind the law.

Sin gives to death its pain and its poison (15:56), if it is unpardoned sin (cf. Rom. 6:23), and the power, the vitality (Rom. 7:7–8), of sin is the law. The law gives the knowledge of sin, it gives encouragement to sin, and it is the standard by which sin is judged. The law "makes sinners of us all" (Leon Morris, p. 235). The teaching in Corinthians about law points to its fuller treatment in Romans.

Perhaps Paul's strongest statement about the divine origin of the law is to be found in 7:19. "Circumcision is nothing and uncircumcision is nothing, but keeping the commandments of God (is everything)." In harmony with this is the thought of the kingdom of God (4:20; 6:9–10; 15:24, 50). The King does not merely advise in speech. He exercises his power and rules. Men are given their program.

*God is infinitely blessed.* The Greek word used in the New Testament is *eulogetos,* an adjective, and it is used exclusively of God. When men are blessed the verb *eulogeō* is employed. H. W. Beyer (*TDNT* 2:764) finds that in the New Testament *eulogetos* is "exclusively doxological." Some epistles begin with the formula (e.g., II.1:3) and Hans-Georg Link (*Begriffslex.* 11:1124) regards as especially significant the association (Zusammengehörigkeit) of greeting and praise, attractively referring to the customary salutation which still survives in South Germany, "Grüss' (dich) Gott." He translates "Gepriesen sei Gott," "God be praised." This "understands" the missing Greek verb to be in the optative. Beyer, however, follows Blass-Debrunner. Funk's edition says that "*estin* appears to be in the mind of the NT authors" (Blass-Debrunner-Funk, para. 128 [5], p. 71).

Now Paul avoids the optative. He uses the participle of the verb to be. "God . . . who is blessed (*ho ōn*) for ever" (II.11:31; cf. Rom. 9:5). In Romans 1:25 the indicative *estin* is plain. If the apostle had sought to emphasize "for ever" in the belief, the right belief, that the praise of God would last for all eternity, he would surely have used the future tense of either participle or indicative. "God (who) will be blessed for ever." His present tense, however, suggests that "for ever" should be taken closely with the adjective, "blessed for ever." God is, now, at the moment of Paul's writing and indeed at the moment of writing and reading this present sentence: God *is* eternally blessed. The term *eulogetos* thus describes not what men do but what God eternally is in himself. He is worthy of all praise whether it is given or not, whether there are men or angels in existence to give it or not. "The adjective [*eulogetos*] implies that blessing ought to be given, the participle [*eulogēmenos*—of men] that it has been received." [8] The human dishonoring of God does not diminish his transcendent, intrinsic and unchangeable blessedness.

It follows that *God is to be worshiped.* Paul has a vivid description

---

8. Plummer, p. 7. Sanday and Headlam, *Romans,* p. 46, speak of "God's adorable perfections." Cf. John Murray, *Romans,* 1:46.

of an unbelieving man and the impression made on him by the gathered church. If the whole assembly speaks with tongues, the result will be hubbub, and he will think that they are all crazy. But if they all prophesy there will be a unanimity in their message. Under the searchlight of what they say he will be exposed to himself for what he is. His secret thoughts and plans and feelings will be brought out into the open. Moved by the reality of the divine Presence he will not delay. He will not precisely kneel. This is not fast enough. "He will fall upon his face and worship God" (14:25; cf. 2 Sam. 9:6 with Gen. 17:3, 17, LXX). His new and inner adoration is expressed by his prostrate body.

Paul may be giving a hypothetical example. Even if "all" prophesy one after another it conflicts with the apostle's own ruling (14:29–33). Prophecy should be uttered by "two or three" and "one by one." But hypothetical or not, nothing can rob the passage of the triumph of the man's conviction and surely his conversion. He reached the summit when he was brought to his knees—in worship.

As an element in worship, *God is to be thanked.* Paul himself gives thanks (1:4) and sees the church doing so, even though on occasion an uninstructed and uncomprehending man may be unable to say "Amen" to the thanksgiving (14:16–19). The apostle virtually calls on the church to join him when he exclaims in awed wonder as the sun comes out from behind the cloud, "Thanks be to God who gives to *us* the victory . . ." (15:56–57).

There are times when thanksgiving is the very purpose of prayer. Paul and his companions had hoped that God would still rescue them from death, "you also lending us your secret aid in prayer,[9] in order that [*hina*] the gracious gift meant for us may be the subject of thanksgiving inspired in many people and expressed by many" (II.1:11). The *hina* need not lose its purposive flavor here.

Paul thinks not only of "the gracious gift" but of what lies behind it. ". . . grace, by spreading increasingly through the increasing numbers,[10] swells the thanksgiving" (II.4:15). The generosity of men creates thanksgiving to God (II.9:11–12). Thanks be to God (II.2:14; 8:16; 9:15).

Thanksgiving itself is for the glory of God, because *God is to be glorified* (II.4:15). This is a clearly stated duty. "Glorify God in your body" (6:20). "Do everything for the glory of God" (10:31). Cf. II.9:13. "To glorify God" means to recognize God as glorious; to recognize him as he has revealed himself: his being, his character, his majesty and his might. It means to address him as the One who is, as righteous and holy, as majestic and mighty.[11]

*God is to be loved.* Paul does not regard men's love to God as a luxury

---

9. Michael Green's "underground assistance" is masterly. See his *Evangelism in the Early Church,* p. 235. The preposition *hupo* in the verb imparts the air of secrecy. Cf. *huphaireomai,* to pilfer, to "pinch."

10. Moule, *Idiom Book,* p. 108.

11. See further, R. A. Ward, *Royal Theology: Our Lord's Teaching about God,* chapter III (pp. 36–47).

for the few or as an additional duty for the spiritually ambitious. All men should love him. "If a man love God" (8:3) he will discover "how many things God has prepared for those who love him" (2:9).

After hearing about love to God, some people may feel a sense of shock when they learn that *God is to be feared*. But love is not to be isolated. It is not to be regarded *in vacuo*. It is the love of One who is infinitely blessed. Paul can therefore call men to join him in spiritual effort. "Let us purify ourselves . . . rounding off our holiness in the fear of God" (II.7:1). The fear in question includes reverence—we owe him everything; awe—we must give account to him; dread—lest disloyalty make us ashamed (Philip Edgecumbe Hughes, p. 258).

There is a fear of God which means no more than the usual "being afraid," and it is quite appropriate. Adam was afraid after his sin (Gen. 3:10), and Paul himself could understand. He had experienced the same fear. As a Christian man he knew that without the Spirit of adoption he would relapse again into fear (Rom. 8:15). He had felt it on the road to Damascus. The Lord had warned him, in a proverbial saying, not to "kick against the goad" (Acts 26:14), not to continue a resistance which would be futile and painful. In speaking thus, the Lord showed that he had seen the fear in Saul's heart, for the *kentron*, the poisonous sting, was "what orientals feared in the scorpion," [12] and the goad with its metal points was a fearful tool to use on animals.

We see, then, stark fear: the fear of Adam, of Saul of Tarsus and of man under the law. In distinction from this is the "godly fear," the fear of the Lord (II.5:11), in the Old Testament "the whole of piety" (Plummer). The godly fear of the man in Christ is roughly summed up thus: fear minus "afraidness" equals godly fear. But the unafraidness belongs to faith. If faith grows dim or merges into presumptuous and self-righteous confidence, "Do not go on thinking, do not cherish, 'superior' [*hupsēla*] thoughts but resume the fear (which you had before conversion); for . . . God will not spare you" (Rom. 11:20–21). John Murray (*Romans*, 2:87–88) acutely observes that "the attitude compatible with and promotive of faith is not only lowliness of mind but one of fear."

Faith fears the Lord and is unafraid of him; pride and unbelief are—and should be—afraid of him. God is to be feared.

The believing man trusts God and is unafraid, because his trust is not misplaced. *God is trustworthy and he is to be trusted*. Christ will guarantee his believing people to the end in their "unchargeableness" (1:8–9). Not only are they free from condemnation; they cannot even be charged or accused (Rom. 8:1, 33). Christ is their surety and God honors the work of his Son. For "God is faithful." "The continuance of the favours mentioned in the preceding verses may be confidently looked for. The character of God is at stake" (Morris, p. 37).

---

12. Lothar Schmid, *TDNT* 3:668. The fact that the proverb was Greek and Latin rather than Hebrew or Aramaic "does not prove that the speech was Luke's composition"—C. S. C. Williams, *Acts*, p. 264. Cf. Luke 12:4–5 and W. Mundle, *Begriffslex.* 4:416–7.

Thus God is faithful at the End. But this is no sudden change of character but a continuation of what he has been all along. He keeps his people and "intervenes" in their spiritual pilgrimage. He will not permit them to be tried and tempted above their capacity but will make for them a "way out" and a "way under" (10:13). For even in such trials he is to be trusted.

It is the same in physical as well as in spiritual danger. The evidence for this is in fact rather than in word. It is not said that "God is faithful," but he is shown to be. Paul and his friends were in grievous trouble in Asia. So great was their danger that they despaired of life itself. But their trust was not in themselves but in God—and he rescued them (II.1:8–10). It was in the certainty of the faithfulness of God that they could face the future in the hope that God would still rescue them.

It might drive the point home if we recalled 1:9 and rendered thus: "The God through whom you were (originally) called into participation in his Son Jesus Christ our Lord is faithful." The years roll by—but God is faithful. The "changes and chances of this mortal life" are many—but God is faithful. Disappointment comes—but do not blame the apostle. His plans may perforce be changed but not his principles (II.1:15–22). He may not have paid his expected visit but he is not to be charged with "lightness" (*elaphria*, v. 17). He is not a man of unsettled convictions, promising much and intending nothing, pledging anything and forgetting everything. He does not enter into solemn engagements with metal reservations. His emphatic affirmation ("Yes, yes") is not swiftly followed by an emphatic denial ("No, no").

But his defense against such accusations does not rest solely on his own character. "God is faithful, in that [*hoti*, cf. II.8:9] our word, our gospel word, to you is not yes and no" (II.1:18). The consistent apostle reflects the consistent God. And more: "the Son of God Christ Jesus, who was preached among you through our instrumentality,[13] . . . did not prove to be yes and no, but in him yes has proved to be and remains [perfect *gegonen*] true" (v. 19). The Son is as faithful as the Father. He is the "concrete" evidence of God's faithfulness, its very presence. "For in him is the yes, the fulfillment, to all the promises of God, however many they are" (v. 20).

There is an interesting and unexpected consequence. The Corinthians themselves, in their consistency, support the apostle! Through (and as a result of) the apostolic preaching they utter through Christ the liturgical "Amen," and they do it regularly. The living God promised—and is faithful. He sent his Son—and he is faithful. Paul preached Christ crucified—and Paul was faithful. The Corinthians have said "Amen" to it all—and said it to God for his glory. (Note the implication of the *living* God and the *living* Christ.) How could they be other than faithful? The Corinthians must drop the charge. And God will continue to be faithful, as they know in his gift of the earnest (*arrabōn*) of the Spirit.

In the affairs of men much prominence at times is given to groups and societies, communities and nations, and it might be thought that the in-

13. They are but secondary, only servants (3:5; cf. note 72 in the section on Romans), but not mere machines. "This *dia* is also used of Christ." See Plummer, p. 36.

dividual is submerged and lost. During World War II the island of Malta (cf. Acts 28:1, NEB), after heroically enduring the most fearful bombing, was awarded the George Cross, very much as individual bravery was recognized by the Victoria Cross or the Congressional Medal. We became accustomed to reading of "Malta, G.C." instead of merely "Malta." The island as such received the decoration. I imagine, though, that if a citizen of Malta started to put the letters G.C. after his name some questions would be asked!

King George V spent some time at Bognor in convalescence after a serious illness. The place was chosen because of the suitability of its climate and the residents manifested a kindly and loyal interest and concern without making themselves a nuisance. In consequence the town was given a new name, Bognor Regis, "Bognor of the King," on the analogy of Lyme Regis. The town received the honor. But I doubt if any person living there claims to participate in royalty.

Now God deals with communities, as we learn from such stories as the account of the Flood or the history of Israel; or from the fact that Christ loved the church and is its Head (Eph. 5:22–27). There have been times when this has been emphasized and overemphasized to the point where men have been sharply criticized for aiming at individual conversion. One would have thought that the evangelist does not start his work by inviting the heathen to participate in the Eucharist.

At this stage in our study it is necessary to point out that *God deals with individuals*. Paul at any rate thought so, if we may judge from the Corinthian letters. "If a man [*tis*] is in Christ . . ." (II.5:17); "if a man [*tis*] is convinced in his own mind that he is Christ's . . . " (II.10:7). It is similar in the First Epistle: "if a man loves God, he is known by him" (8:3); "If a man does not love the Lord, let him be anathema" (16:22). When the Lord comes he will manifest "men's inward motives (NEB); and then, at that time, praise will come to each man from God" (4:5). On the other hand "if a man tries to ruin [*phtheirei*, present conative] God's temple, this very man [*touton*] God will bring to ruin" (3:17). Paul can speak vigorously of the weak man being brought to disaster by another's "knowledge" and behavior, "the brother for whose sake Christ died" (8:10–11). Such a man has joined himself to Christ (cf. 6:17). In 7:12–16 we are given a picture of a married couple, only one of whom is a believer. The one may lead to the other's salvation. In marriage the chariot has already been boarded (Act 8:29–30). An individual may be saved. All have been redeemed; each has been called; each should obey the commandments of God (7:17–24); each should stand fast (10:12). God has distributed his varied gifts, and to each man is given the manifestation of the Spirit (12:7).

God deals with individuals (3:10–15), but *he is not known by the world*. God has shown that the wisdom of the world is foolishness. Even through its wisdom it did not get to know (aorist, *egnō*) God (1:20–21).

The Spirit is the Agent of God's revelation. He searches everything, even the profundities of God. To illuminate his meaning here, Paul uses a simple illustration. Nobody knows a man and all about him (*ta tou anthrōpou*) except the inner spirit of the man himself. (This is on the popular level and has nothing to do with psychoanalysis or anything like that. What Paul means is that, for example, "Only I know, and nobody else, whether I am feeling pain or not.") It is like that with God *(houtōs)*. Nobody knows God and all about him *(ta tou theou)* except the Spirit of God.

This would suggest at first that God is known by nobody but the Spirit. We, however, emphatically we, received not the spirit of the world but the Spirit who proceeds from God. The purpose of his coming to us was that we might gain knowledge (2:9–12). At this point Paul does not say "that we might know God" but that we might know "the things graciously given [*ta charisthenta*] to us by God." This picks up "the many things which God has prepared for those who love him," revealed through the Spirit. So far God is known in his gifts.

After a slight digression, to which we must return, Paul asks the rhetorical question, telescoping Isaiah 40:13, LXX, "who came to know the mind of the Lord . . . ?" The required—and expected—answer is: "No one" (2:16). Only the Spirit fathoms such profundity. But Paul has already said that "we" have received the Spirit. Now he says, again emphatically, that "we have the mind of Christ." This *we* is in contrast to the world which does not know God.

The parallel between the Spirit and Christ is striking, but Paul seems quite unaware of any confusion.[14] It may be conveniently seen in tabular form.

God revealed through the Spirit what
   he had prepared for us
We know through the Spirit what God      We have the mind of Christ
   graciously gave us
We have received the Spirit

The mind *(nous)* of Christ is more than "what he thinks," as when one man asks another, "I'd like your mind on this." His thought, his purpose, the plan of salvation, are included; but more than that is meant. We have received the Spirit. Paul means also that "we have received Christ." J. Behm (*TDNT* 4:953, 959) equates "the mind of Christ" with "the Spirit of God," and notes that in the LXX *ruah* (spirit) "is once transl. *nous* in Is. 40:13." Paul lets the scriptural word run on. (Cf. Arndt-Gingrich, p. 547.)

What God has prepared for us and what he has given us are not preeminently entities apart from Christ. They are summed up in him. He himself is God's gracious gift (cf. Titus 2:11; 3:4). Through the Spirit we know the "what"; but we also *have* the Spirit. Through Christ we also know the "what," the purposes of God; but we also *have* Christ. The conclusion is crystal clear. The world does not know God. We do. It would be

---

14. Cf. Wendland, p. 31, "Es gibt für ihn keine Wirksamkeit des Gottesgeistes ausser und ohne Christus." "There is for him no efficacy of the Spirit of God apart from and without Christ."

impossible to possess the Spirit of God and through him to know what God had prepared and given, and to have "the mind of Christ" as Paul understood it, without knowing God. Paul is shocked at the thought. "Some have no knowledge of God; I say this to your shame" (15:34). Either they should never have entered the church at all because at best they are nominal Christians; or their sin and their spiritual neglect of themselves has caused them to forget the "what," the plan of salvation, and to lose touch with God. It is so long since they encountered him that they need a new introduction. They do not know him now.

We must now return to the digression (2:13–15). Through the Spirit we now know what has been given to us by God. This is capable of being put into words. "We speak it." Even here the language is above that of human wisdom—which does not know God. We speak in words imparted by the Spirit. But Paul knew from his own experience what it was to be on a collision course. "The things of the Spirit" *(ta tou pneumatos)* would normally mean "the Spirit and all about him," but as Paul writes this phrase he must have been thinking of the just-mentioned language imparted by the Spirit. Paul has the gift of utterance (cf. Acts 2:4, 14). But the *psuchikos* man does not give a hospitable reception to what he hears. He is himself devoid of the Spirit (cf. Jude 19), the "natural" man. He has biological vitality and perhaps even a rich mental life, but without the Spirit a man cannot even recognize the grace of God when he sees it. He is the opposite of Barnabas, who "saw the grave of God and rejoiced . . . because he was . . . full of the Holy Spirit and faith" (Acts 11:23–24; cf. Acts 17:32; 19:9).

The natural man hears, but he does not understand because he cannot understand. He is out of his depth. He thinks it no more than foolishness. He cannot examine either the words or the preacher. He lacks the Spirit. The spiritual man, by contrast, examines everything but is himself examined by nobody. It takes a scholar to examine a student and the natural man is no "scholar." He does not know God. Even when the Old Testament (the language of the Spirit!) is read to some, there is a veil over its reading and a veil over the heart of its hearers. It is only removed when they turn to the Lord (II.3:14–16). Then in him they will know God.[15]

### Man Against God

The inability of the natural man should be kept in mind by all who are struggling with the invention of new techniques for the presentation of the gospel. The abandonment of all theological terms and indeed of preaching itself is no guarantee that the unbeliever will grasp the truth. To rely *solely* on new language and new methods would be to secularize

15. Referring to 2:11, Dr. Margaret E. Thrall thinks of a man's own spirit as his self-consciousness (p. 27). The linking of the Spirit of God with the mind of Christ suggests the profound thought that Christ is the self-consciousness of God. We sometimes say of a man that "I should like to be able to see into his mind." Wonder of wonders, what we cannot do with our fellow men we can do with God. In Christ the consciousness of God has come out into the open and has been "enfleshed."

evangelism. " . . . there is no 'problem of communication' that the Spirit cannot solve." [16]

Not only is God not known by the world, *He is unapproachable by the world.* In discussing the question of eating food which had been sacrificed to idols Paul states that "food will not present us to God" (8:8). The food is quite irrelevant. The fact of not eating will not of itself keep us out; eating will not of itself give us more divine approval (cf. Arndt-Gingrich, *perisseuō*, p. 656). As the matter of presentation to God is raised, it may be inferred that the whole problem of the approach to God lies in the background. It is not enough to say simply that God will receive anyone. Even "Israel could not take God's Presence for granted." [17] Food will not present us to him. What will?

The heathen offer their sacrifices to demons and a "not-god." [18] This seems to be the meaning of 10:20, though it has been taken as "and not to God" by, e.g., James Moffatt in his translation. The *kai ou* is inelegant Greek, unless the *ou* is regarded as a sort of prefix to its following noun. Even so "not to God" is a fair interpretation. "Or shall we provoke the Lord to jealousy?" (10:22). Obviously the Lord may not be approached by that path.

In spite of the attempt of religion to make profitable contact with the divine, might it not be argued that any member of the human race, unaided and simply and solely by his own right, is free to approach God as and when he wills? This would imply that he relies on himself. He has no need of religion of any kind. He is himself his own qualification to draw near to God. He takes the credit for himself.

But this is ruled out because ultimately it is boasting.[19] God will not permit any man to boast in his presence. He must boast only "in the Lord." (Cf. 1:29, 31; 3:21; II.10:17–18.) A man must not introduce himself to the Lord. Only the Lord can do it.

It is clear that if any man is to approach God he must do it on God's terms and not his own. For the moment we must say that God is unapproachable by the world. "Both Law and Prophets stand for a God who is holy, invisible and unapproachable, except by mediation." [20] We have not yet discovered the means of meditation. *God* is unapproachable because he *has been and is sinned against.* Paul speaks of men who had sinned in the past and not repented (II.12:21; cf. 13:2). Those who by their knowledge insist on a freedom to eat "idol meat" and thereby bring disaster on their weaker brother by their blows on his conscience are sinning against him and against Christ (8:12). In such cases as these Paul views sin as an act. This emerges when he relapses into diatribe or dialogue. "(You say that) every sin that a man commits [literally, "does"] is external to (and therefore does not affect) his personality. But he who

---

16. Richardson, *Introduction to Theology of NT*, p. 119.
17. Jakob Jocz, *A Theology of Election*, p. 94.
18. See Driver's note on Deut. 32:17 in *Deuteronomy* (ICC) p. 363; and Blass-Debrunner-Funk on asyndeton, para. 460 (1), pp. 240–41.
19. Bultmann, *Theology of the NT*, 1:315.
20. Jakob Jocz, *The Spiritual History of Israel*, p. 94.

commits fornication sins against his own personality" (6:18).[21] Similarly when the apostle says, "If you married, you did not sin" (7:28; cf. v. 36), he is regarding sin as an act.

But it is not only an act. It involves an attitude. It occurs in the mind. The wilderness experiences of "our fathers" have lessons for us (10:5–13), and warn us against being "desirers of evils" (cf. Num. 11:4, 34, LXX). The verses at the end of the passage (12–13) may possibly include a reference to trial or test (cf. NEB) but more is meant than merely "hard times." The context of the whole paragraph and the admonition to the man who thinks he is "standing" (cf. 7:37; 15:1) to beware lest he fall both strongly suggest that *peirasmos* means temptation. There is a distinction between feeling the attractiveness of something evil and actually being a "desirer" of it. "Solicitation to sin"[22] is not of itself sin but to desire the evil thing is. The overt act of sin follows up the desire and is thus the second stage.

Paul's terms to describe sin reflect the pattern which we have already seen in Romans. It is implied if not stated that *sin is disobedience*. If the experiences of "our fathers" in the wilderness (10:5–13) are really "types" for our instruction, then the exhortations are significant. The argument runs like this: they did it (desired, were idolators, committed fornication, tempted the Lord, murmured); they should not have done (look at the consequences!); do not do as they did. What they did resembles the activities of those who are in danger of not inheriting the kingdom of God but who may be justified (6:9–11). This is clearly sin. "Do not do this. If you do, you will sin." This seems to sum it up. Sin is disobedience.

*Sin is lawlessness.* "Do not . . . ; for what have righteousness and lawlessness [*anomia*] in common?" (II.6:14). This text further suggests that *sin is unbelief*. Unbelievers are not fit mates for Christians. The Christian brother (who has been forgiven) is contrasted with the unbeliever (6:6) and the Christian spouse with the unbelieving spouse (7:12–13).

*Sin is unrighteousness.* The unbelievers are the *adikoi* (6:1, 6, 9) who will not inherit the kingdom of God. (Cf. II.7:12 if we may relate to I.5:1.)

*Sin is impiety.* There is a hint of this in the contrast between the heathen court and "the saints" (6:1). The Corinthians, though justified men, are trying to get justice from the unjust. Have they forgotten God, the source of all justice, especially their own? The best example, however, is idolatry (10:7), which fails to give God his due.

*Sin is unholiness.* Before they are in Christ, men are to be described bluntly by the simple term "sinners." But now they are "the saints" (*hoi hagioi*) because they have been sanctified (1:2; 6:1, 11). Before this they were unholy.

*Sin is uncleanness.* This follows from the fact that men should repent of their uncleanness (II.12:21) when they have thus "sinned in the past"

---

21. See Moule, *Idiom Book*, pp. 196–97; W. D. Stacey, *The Pauline View of Man*, pp. 182–83, 190 ff.; C. H. Dodd, *Romans*, pp. 90–91, 190, 194; J. A. T. Robinson, *The Body*, p. 28. S. Wibbing, *Begriffslex.* 8:870–71. It is illuminating to compare Rom. 6:13 with Rom. 12:1; and 1 Cor. 6:15 with 1 Cor. 12:27. The personal pronoun and "body" seem interchanged. Body and personality are pretty well identical.

22. Alford, *The Greek Testament*, 2:557.

(NEB). There is always the danger of this sin: "touch nothing unclean" (II.6:17, NEB). This abstinence may involve effort: "let us cleanse ourselves from all defilement" (II.7:1). The weak conscience may become defiled (8:7).

*Sin is ignorance.* " . . . 'bad company ruins good character.' . . . stop sinning; for some have no knowledge of God; I say this to your shame" (15:33–34).

*Sin is error.* Paul's solemn "Do not go astray" (6:9; 15:33) is followed by a warning. A mistake in thought leads to a mistake in life. Thus the "error," the going astray, is both mental and practical. There may be wrong thoughts about God which are blasphemous. This in itself is sin. But the thoughts are followed by the actions which arise out of them, and this again is sin.

The precision already noticed in Romans is recalled in Corinthians. *Sin is transgression* (II.5:19, *paraptōma*). In contrast to the precise act of sin is the vaguer state of weakness both of a man himself and of his conscience (8:7–13). He may be sinned against by the stronger man who has "knowledge," but he would not be so likely to succumb if he were stronger in the faith and had a stronger conscience. He is to be considered and pitied rather than criticized and blamed. Even so it is hardly going too far to say that *sin is weakness.*

*Sin is failure to realize the divine ideal.* There is a hint of this in 8:8 *(hustereomai)*, but it comes out more clearly when the question of litigation between Christians arises. Brother takes brother before the heathen courts and Paul tells them that "you fall below your standard" *(hēttēma)* even in taking legal action (6:7, NEB). They ought to let wrong be done to them rather than do it themselves *(adikeo)*. They are in bad company *(adikoi)*! Finally *sin is spiritual petrification* (II.3:14). There is hope for the man of weak conscience, but it is rapidly reaching vanishing point in those who are hardened.

The inwardness of sin receives some emphasis in the expressions "the hidden things [*ta krupta*] of darkness," "the hidden things of shame," and "the counsels of men's hearts." Indeed, *sin is spiritual blindness* (4:5; II.4:2, 4).

Paul's view of sin is consistent (see pp. 82–85).

## God Against Man

*God is displeased with sin.* During the wanderings of the children of Israel in the wilderness "God was not pleased *(eudokēsen)* with the majority of them" (10:5). This use of the verb is illustrated in II:12:10, "I delight in (experiences of) weakness . . . for Christ's sake." If men refuse "to be pleasing to him" (II.5:9) God is not pleased.

For the moment we must postpone consideration of any further reaction on God's part to the sin of men and point to a significant text in the great fifteenth chapter of 1 Corinthians. Paul is working out the logical consequences of a denial of our Lord's resurrection. "If Christ is not risen, . . . you are still in your sins" (15:17).

It may be doubted if Paul means primarily that the Corinthians are logically still in the power of their sins and that he is employing the argument known as *reductio ad absurdum*. This could be very dangerous ground: the Corinthians were not the most obvious examples of sanctity. Could Paul's argument possibly run like this? "Christ is not risen. You are therefore still in the power of sin. But this is ridiculous. You are shining specimens of men who have conquered sin. Therefore Christ must be risen."

The point surely is that if Christ is not risen, God has not accepted his sacrificial death. Their faith is therefore all to no purpose. They are back where they started before they first put their trust in Christ. He was raised with a view to their justification. (Cf. Rom. 4:25.)

Now men sin from their earliest days and they go on sinning throughout life. If a man looks back from old age he might recall the schoolboy sins of youth, the undergraduate sins or the sins of early married life or of parenthood. Suppose that he remarks that "all that was a long time ago." Is it to be assumed that time in itself is enough to put away sins? Paul would deny it. Quite apart from any abiding consequences of early sins, like the loss of a fortune or a limb, the sins themselves have not disappeared. They belong to the past but they cling to a man. He is still in his sins because he is still the man who was responsible for them. He has not discharged his responsibility. He was responsible and he is responsible.

This means that men are sinners not only as men who have committed sins. They *are* guilty sinners. Thus God is displeased with sins and with sin and he holds men guilty. What, if anything, does he do?

This raises the whole question of judgment. From the evidence of the Corinthian letters it may be regarded as logical, historical, prospective or final. Paul believed that the law was given by God and expressed his will. It was a characteristic of the old covenant and was "a ministry of death," "a ministry of condemnation." He can therefore say that "the letter kills" (II. 3:6–9). This is not today's popular "letter of the law" as opposed to its spirit and intention. Paul is using the figure of speech called synecdoche in which the part stands for the whole. "The letter" may suggest the tiny, binding details which are included in the majestic sweep of the law. It is authoritative even in the smallest matters. But the primary meaning is "the letter-formulated law," "the law engraved on stone in writing, (not in pictures, but) letter by letter." Paul elsewhere calls it "the law of sin and of death" (Rom. 8:2). No man can completely obey "all that is written" in the law. Justification is not to be attained by that route. Sin occurs with its consequence of curse and death (Rom. 3:20; Gal. 3:10).[23]

The law, then, reduced to writing, is never completely obeyed and its sanctions, its penalties, are the curse and death. There is a hidden syllogism here which may be set out thus:

| All men who disobey | are | men worthy of death |
| All men | are | men who disobey |
| All men | are | men worthy of death. |

23. Cf. Bultmann, *Theology of the NT,* 1:262–63.

Paul can say that "the letter kills," but he does not mean what he literally says. The law does not kill. Swords kill; the hangman kills. The law is inert, something in writing. The truth is that, under the provisions of the law, men who have disobeyed are under condemnation and are worthy of death. As far as the law itself is concerned they are still unscathed.

The law expresses the mind of God, and the conclusion of our syllogism tells us what God thinks of men. It expresses his judgment. It is so far a logical judgment; *so far* he has done nothing. But the law itself will do nothing. It has to be implemented. Will God implement his own law?

This brings us to what we have called the historical aspect of judgment. It is illustrated in Paul's interpretation of the wilderness wanderings (10:5–11). These "typical" events are to warn us. The apostle begins with the statement that God was not pleased. How did he know? He gives the reason: "*for* they were laid low in the desert." (The passive is probably used in order to avoid the divine Name. Num. 14:16, LXX, has the active, with "the Lord" as the obvious subject.) He then hands us the key to open the purpose of the "types." The events took place to prevent us from being "desirers of evils" as the Israelites were. After a prohibition of idolatry the text falls into a scheme. Its "form" may be applied to the three sins of fornication, tempting the Lord, and murmuring in the following way:

> Do not do this or that sinful deed
> As they did
> (And excited the divine displeasure)
> And were punished.

Without the reference to the divine displeasure it is hard to see the force of Paul's line of thought. The punishment—they fell, they were destroyed, they perished—was not long delayed. It is an example of the divine judgment in history. It took place.

A third type of judgment is prospective. The word of the cross is foolishness to "those who are perishing" (1:18; cf. II.4:3). The process is going on but has not yet been completed. The NEB renders "on their way to ruin," "on the way to perdition." Similarly the end of the false apostles, the servants of Satan, *will be* in accordance with their works (II.11:15).

The prospective type of judgment looks forward to the final judgment. This is the familiar Day of the Lord (5:5). Its characteristic will be the manifestation *(phaneron)* of quality, for "the Day will bring it to light" (3:13). The Day will dawn with the sound of the final trumpet (15:52) and God will utter and implement his final judgment (3:17; 5:13). Death is not always a peaceful sinking into slumber which gives a blessed relief from pain and sorrow. It is not always true that when death comes, it comes as a friend. As the close of a human life it may be "peaceful," but with some, even in their earthly "peace" there is the sting. Unforgiven sin, the unreconciled sinful life, gives to such death its sting. Such men have judged the wisdom of the gospel to be foolishness and have consistently rejected it. Now they themselves are to be judged by the very God who had offered them his gospel. On the road to perdition even before they die they experience in death the last earthly sting (15:56) which is the first sting of God's final judgment.

This is no human "day" (4:3–5),[24] no human day of judgment. The Day of the Lord is the Day of our Lord Jesus (1:8; II.1:14).

## THE OTHER SIDE—GOD FOR MAN

We must now summarize our results so far. From our study of the Corinthian epistles we learn that God is the living God and he is the only God. He is conscious: he knows, he wills and has purpose. He has wisdom, an "image" and personality—or rather, he is personal. William Temple once said in my hearing that if God is personality, man is personality minus; if man is personality, God is personality plus. This seems very sound, but we are content with the statement that God is personal. He has power as Creator, Sustainer, Controller and as Lord of Providence. He is righteous and holy in character and is the Author of the Law. He is infinitely blessed and is to be worshiped, thanked, glorified, loved and feared. He is trustworthy and is to be trusted. He deals with individuals but is not known by the world. He is unapproachable; he has been, and is, sinned against in all manner of ways. He is displeased with sin and he judges men in history and will finally judge them at the Last Day.

On this evidence the prospect for men is not good. But as we have seen earlier, there is "another side" of the matter. We make the transition to the other side by a brief continuation of our study of judgment. Paul says that the man who eats or drinks unworthily at the Lord's Supper is guilty (enochos). He eats and drinks judgment upon himself. Because of this (dia touto) many of the Corinthians are sickly and ill and are dying in large numbers. On the surface this seems parallel to the experience of the desert (10:5–10). But the Corinthian experience (11:27–32) is not the same. It is true that "if we examined ourselves (as we do not), we should not be judged (as in fact we are)." The Corinthians are judged; yet they are not judged. "When we are judged by the Lord we are being disciplined, trained, educated, in order that [hina] we may not be condemned with the world." The course of education may be inconvenient, painful, fraught with sorrow; but it is not retributive punishment.

Illness affords an opportunity for busy men to reflect and pray. If life itself is a school of piety and virtue, if here below we are "tuning our instruments" in preparation for the heavenly worship, then with some men even death may be the final part of the process of training. It removes them from a "class," the world, and in particular from the corrupting influences of some of its members who are going to "fail" (be condemned). Others may resist the bad influence of their classmates and continue the course. Those who die are mercifully removed, in the interests of their education.

This is a different kind of judgment from that which we recently studied and it serves to introduce the "other side" of our concept of God. To begin

---

24. Cf. the Diet (Latin dies, day) of Worms, der Reichstag zu Worms, or even the Kaiser's "der Tag" (of reckoning) before World War I.

with, Paul speaks of God as *Father*. He is God the Father (8:6; 15:24).
He is the Father of our Lord Jesus (Christ) (II.1:3; 11:31). He is our
Father (1:3; II.1:2). He is Father of his people (II.6:16, 18). We do not
now stay to consider the differences between these expressions. We note that
in some way God enters into a relation with men, or with some men, which
goes beyond what we have already found in these two epistles.

Further, *God loves*. He loves a cheerful giver (II.9:7). It would seem
that he does not limit himself to cheerful givers, however, for Paul speaks
of both "the God of love" and "the love of God" (II.13:11, 13). He (or it)
will be with the Corinthians. The relationship broadens and deepens.

God is *the Father of compassions* (*oiktirmoi*) *and the God of all comfort*
(*paraklēsis*) (II. 1:3–4). The plural of an abstract noun, here "compassion,"
points to the concrete embodiments of the abstract idea. God has compassion and Paul detects it in a plurality of situations in which He acts
with compassion. As "Father of compassions" He is their "producer." Similarly God "comforts," consoles, encourages and stimulates according to the
nature of the need. "All comfort" suggests that God holds nothing back.

*God is a God of grace* (see pp. 41–43, 92, 130–31 for *charis*). It comes
from God (1:3; II.1:2) and is given (3:10; II.8:1) and as such is the
subject of thanksgiving (1:4). It is to be received by men (II.6:1). It is
surpassing and abounds (II.9:8, 14). When increasing numbers receive it
they find that it does not diminish by being shared; on the contrary, the
more the receivers the more it flows forth and swells the thanksgiving
(II.4:15; p. 153). It makes the Christian life and the Christian ministry
possible (15:10; II. 1:12).

*God has instituted a new covenant* (11:25), a covenant not of the letter
which kills (p. 162) but of the Spirit who makes alive (II.3:6). *He has
made promises* (II.1:20; 7:1). Whereas we have seen that men must not
approach God, now we learn that there is a time when they are acceptable,
yes, very acceptable (*euprosdektos*) to him (II.6:2). Thus *God receives men.*
(Cf. II.6:17.)

In particular *God may be approached in prayer.* Men may pray to him
(7:5; 11:4–5) with due decorum (11:13) and preferably with the mind
(14:13–15, cf. 19). Prayer may be offered for others (II.9:14; 13:7, 9),
even for their deliverance from danger and death (II.1:11; cf. p. 153). It
must not be thought that God does not hear (II.6:2).

Though men should fear God, they may have confidence in him. *God
inspires confidence in himself* (II.1:9; 3:4–5). He not only comforts and
encourages (II.7:6–7) but *he helps. God is the Helper* (II.6:2).

In particular he leaves gifts with them. *God is the Giver.* Though previously unseen, unheard and unimagined, God's gifts are now known (2:9,
12; pp. 156–57) to men. Both marriage and celibacy are to be regarded in
either case as a gift, a *charisma* (7:7)—a fact not always remembered in
discussion of Paul's attitude to marriage. God has given one all-inclusive
gift (2:12, 16) and within it is great diversity (12:4–11), unified by the
manifestation of the Spirit (12:7), not as a mere luxury but with a view
to the profit of others besides the bearer of the gift. A gift may be meant for

a group (*eis*, II.1:11) but the one all-inclusive gift is *offered* to men: it is not "charismatic" (II:11:7). It may be expressed in words taught by the Spirit (2:13) but is inexpressible completely (II:9:15; cf. II.8:1).

It is the last two aspects of "the other side" which seem to be so very "other." God is the One who condemns—and *God does not count men's trespasses against them* (II.5:19). He is the One who implements the judgment of the law of sin and death: e.g. "him will God destroy" (3:17; cf. 5:13)—and at the judgment *God will give praise* (4:5). He will resurrect us and bring us into his presence (II.4:14). Apostle and people will be proud of each other on the Day (II.1:14). Each will get back (*komizomai*, cf. Eph. 6:8; Col. 3:25) the achievements wrought through the body at which he had aimed, whether good or "ordinary" (*phaulon*: see Liddell-Scott; II.5:10). God is the God of judgment—and of mercy (*eleeo*, 7:25; II.4:1).

## God at Work for Us—The Work of Christ for Us

Once more the "two sides" have to be reconciled and once more we find the means to reconcile judgment and mercy embedded in the very material which we have been studying. The means is Christ and we draw a distinction between what he has done and what he still does; between an accomplished work and a continuing work; between his work for men and his work in them.

We notice, to begin with, that God is a God of revelation. He has revealed what he has prepared for those who love him (2:9–10). Without his revelation men would never have known. This accords with the failure of human wisdom and the incapacity of the natural man (1:21; 2:14). What God "prepared" and actually gave and what is the means whereby we now "know," is, in a word, Christ (2:9–16; see pp. 156–58).

There is a parallel between the God who revealed and the Christ who is the means of revelation. We read of a God of love (II.13:11, 13) and of grace (*charis*, 1:3; II.1:2; 9:14). Paul speaks also of "the love of Christ" which he has for us (II.5:14; cf. Gal. 2:20) and of "the grace of our Lord Jesus Christ" (II.8:9; 13:13).

This parallelism unfolds the fact that Christ is the image of God (II.4:4). It is God's will that Christ, his image, should be known among men, because Christ is his "message" to men: God has a word (14:36; II.2:17). This (to anticipate) is the word of the cross (1:18, 23), which is the outworking of the love and the grace of God and of Christ.

For God has a gospel (II.11:7) and there is no other gospel (II.11:4). There is no more another gospel than there is another Jesus or another Holy Spirit. This must be "the gospel of Christ" (9:12; II.9:13; 10:14; cf. 4:4; cf. Gal. 1:6). It had been preached to and received by the Corinthians. It was the safe ground on which they stood (cf. Rom. 5:2), for it was the medium of their salvation (15:1–4). In recalling the tradition which he had delivered to them, Paul singles out from the most important factors the main historic facts with a small measure of theological interpretation.

This is the primitive *kerygma*.[25] It is "to a surprising extent a factual proclamation." [26] Its center and soul is Christ. He is the fulfillment of all the many promises of God (II.1:20; p. 155).

But what is the relation between God and Christ? *God has a Son* and his Son is Jesus Christ. He is called God's Son (1:9; 15:28; II.1:19) and God is called his Father (II.11:31). God "owns" Christ (3:23) in what Alford calls "mediatorial subordination" and is the "head" of Christ (11:3). This does not detract from his coequal and eternal deity. Four lines of evidence point in this direction, for they imply his preexistence. Through him "all things came to be" (8:6). This rendering of the NEB shows him as the Agent in creation. He did not stay apart from his creation. "Though he was rich, for your sakes he became poor" (II.8:9). This cannot refer to anything like a "financial crash" in his human life. Where is he recorded as being rich on earth? He was poor from the beginning in Bethlehem. In any case "crash" would be the wrong word because it suggests an involuntary loss of possessions. But he did not "lose" them thus. It was "for your sake" that it happened. It was not his misfortune but his grace which shone in the mind of Paul.

The first man, Adam, was of the earth; he came from the soil. This is natural enough: he was made of dust (Gen. 2:7, LXX). The last Adam, "the second Man, is from heaven" (15:47). After the Exodus the Israelites in the wilderness all drank from the spiritual rock which followed them, and "the rock was Christ" (10:4). This may well be a reference to legendary, rabbinic tradition (rocks do not normally "follow") or even to Christ as the divine Wisdom.[27]

But in the context of Paul's thought generally and of the last two paragraphs in particular, to say nothing of such passages as Philippians 2:5–9, I cannot but think that the Rock which was Christ implies his preexistence. Much as I have appreciated Dr. J. D. G. Dunn's book, *Baptism in the Holy Spirit,* I cannot follow his argument here. It is no doubt true that Paul "is not talking about Christ's pre-existence here" (p. 125). It was not his explicit subject but it was the undertone, the implication. If anyone had challenged the apostle with the remark: "How can you talk like that? Christ was not yet born. Bethlehem was centuries ahead"; if any Corinthian "wise man" (3:18) had so spoken, Paul would have been astounded and would have sent him back to the catechumenate.[28]

He who is the preexistent Son is also known by the bare Name, Jesus (II.4:10–11). This is the historic Man. How is it that the preexistent Son (1:9; II.1:19) appears in history? Elsewhere (Gal. 4:4) Paul can say that God sent forth his Son, One born of a woman (see pp. 132–33). He does not

---

25. See C. H. Dodd, *The Apostolic Preaching and its Developments*, pp. 7–11 and the appendix. 1 Cor. 15:3–5 may represent the old creed of Damascus. Note *hoti* four times.

26. H. E. W. Turner, *Jesus, Master and Lord*, p. 78.

27. Cf. W. D. Davies, *Paul and Rabbinic Judaism*, p. 153. But see F. F. Bruce, *This Is That*, pp. 34–36.

28. To avoid any possible misunderstanding I ought to say that I am not accusing Dr. Dunn. I value his book too much for that. I find it rich in Christian experience. cf. H. R. Mackintosh, *The Doctrine of the Person of Jesus Christ*, p. 66.

say this specifically in Corinthians but he implies it. For God "owns" him and is his Head, and at the End he will be subordinate to God the Father (15:24, 28). He has not been a rebel in the meantime. He clearly became Man by the will of God and the incarnation was real. "Became poor" (*eptōcheusen,* II.8:9) is a very expressive ingressive aorist, and mention of "the brothers of the Lord" (9:5) "underlines the reality and completeness of the Incarnation." [29]

The incarnate Son, though born under the law with all the opportunity which it afforded (Rom. 7:7) of knowing sin, of "not merely perceiving its existence but experiencing it" (Barrett, *Romans,* p. 141), "did not know sin" (II.5:21). He did not "get to know it" (*ton mē gnonta*) in his own experience. He was no sinner.

But he was crucified (II.13:4) and his crucifixion was not just one of the many events of his earthly days, the mere termination of his life. Paul lays great stress on it (1:13, 23; 2:2, 8). "The sufferings of Christ" (II.1:5) were real. His death is to be proclaimed as well as remembered (11:26).

### Identification

For he died for all (II.5:14–15). This is the supreme expression of Christ's love for men. Christ's love "hems us in" *(sunechei)* like an enclosing force (cf. 1 Sam. 23:8, LXX; Luke 19:43) which permits no escape, "because we judged that One died for all." From this Paul draws the inference that "the 'all' died." Plummer's interpretation of this is misleading. He says (p. 174) that "His supreme act of love extinguished in (the whole race) the old life of worldly interests in which the centre of gravity was self." This is an admirable description of the flesh, which was not extinguished even in Corinthian Christians (3:1–3), to say nothing of the whole race. Plummer has anticipated Christian experience (Gal. 5:24; pp. 139–40).

It is remarkable that Paul can speak of the death of the "all" and pass on at once to an unembarrassed mention of "the living." It would seem that they did not die after all. If Plummer's view is not acceptable, we must find another.

The key is to be sought in the representative nature of the death of Christ. "Because Christ died, the sinful human race whom He represented (v. 21) has in principle been destroyed" (Thrall, p. 149). Dr. Thrall continues with "the possibility of a fresh start" (v. 17), but that is not our question at the moment. Christ died for all. In what sense can we infer from this that the human race died? If he represented them all, then he died their death. Paul might have proceeded on the lines of Romans 4:25 and have added that He rose for the purpose of justification. But he wanted to express the remoter purpose of the cross, that the living might live for Christ. He therefore states Christ's identification with sinners by means of an inversion: they died. Paul does not say that they died in order that they might live for him. It was Christ who died with this purpose, and rose

---

29. Mark 6:3. Vincent Taylor, *The Gospel according to St. Mark,* p. 249; R. J. Knowling. *The Testimony of St. Paul to Christ,* p. 266.

to carry it out. Christ died and in his death he bore all that would have been involved if they, the "all," had themselves actually died.

The "all" will die, one by one, when they first put their faith in Christ. This is the crucifixion of the self and in no sense has atoning value. If we deny this we shall have to add that the "all" die for themselves. Paul could only respond to such a suggestion with a vigorous *mē genoito*—"God forbid!"

We ought to dwell on the concept of identification and establish its strict meaning. A saddened father may observe that his son has joined a very disreputable club and may tell a friend that "he has identified himself with a queer crowd." He means that his son has joined them in their unsavory activities and has not the slightest intention of trying to change anything. On the contrary he is enjoying it all. He has joined them and become *one of them*.

Or a doctor may volunteer for service in an area where cholera is rampant. He joins, for example, the refugees from East Pakistan and lives among them in order to minister to them. He will change everything that he can. He has joined them and become *one with them*.

Finally consider a case of shipwreck. The stricken ship will shortly sink and the last lifeboat to be getting away is overcrowded. Two small people suddenly appear and cry for help. "No room, no room," is the cry. But a large man gives up his place to the two despairing little ones. Their lives are saved and he drowns. He has not become one of them and has not become one with them. *He has replaced them.*

It is the last sense of identification which we have to keep in mind when we use the word *identification* in connection with Pauline doctrine. We might complete the illustration, though not exhaust the significance of the death of Christ, by adding a sequel. Suppose the ship to have been the *Titanic* and the man who drowned a philanthropist. It is conceivable that the rescued persons might later say: "We died on the *Titanic*. We live to continue the work of Mr. X."

Christ died for all. This "collectivization" of the human race can be broken up into its constituent parts. Paul can think with pastoral care of "the brother on whose account [*di' hon*] Christ died" (8:11).

Christ died for all; he died for each. But what did he do in his death? He "died for our sins" (15:3). This decisively relates the death of Christ to the sin of men. And it is not only a question of what Christ did but of what God did in him.

Christ saw sin in men's lives as no other saw it. He penetrated to the depth of their motives and he understood the lengths to which they would go, however much they might cover it up. He saw sin, understood sin and wept over it; but he himself was untouched by it. All the more overwhelming therefore is Paul's almost violent juxtaposition in II.5:21. "Him who knew no sin God made sin for us." We must not tone this down. We must not so emphasize the truth that the riches of Christ are unexplored (cf. Eph. 3:8) and the judgments of God unsearchable (Rom. 11:33) that we decline even to begin to search. Calvary, said Spurgeon, was wrought in the dark; but we must not be so blanketed by the darkness that we refuse even to grope. For us the day has dawned and for us God has shone in our hearts (II.4:4, 6).

We should observe that the sinlessness of Christ is left intact. We should remember that he was made sin *for us*, not made a sinner by temptation. We should not forget that though he voluntarily endured the cross and did so through his grace (cf. II.8:9), it was God who made him *hamartia—sin*. Note the noun: God did not make him *to sin*, verb. We should ever bear in mind that at all times, particularly on the cross, Christ was doing the will of his Father, and that at all times, particularly on the cross, he was the Son in whom his Father was well pleased.

What, then, is the meaning here of the sin which God made him? It would be wrong to interpret it in the sense of "sin-offering." One Greek noun is used twice in close proximity and it would be unnatural, without further explanation, for Paul to mean that "him who knew no sin God made a sin-offering for us." It sounds fair enough, in English; but it strains the Greek to breaking point. And in any case it would destroy the balance of the sentence. The purpose of the cross is that we might become the righteousness *(dikaiosunē)* of God in him.

Paul's thought is coherent and the text under discussion is related to what he says about the curse (Gal. 3:10, 13). Sinful men are under a curse (cf. pp. 135–36). It is the penalty for their disobedience to God; in a word, for their sin. Christ became a curse for us (pp. 130–31). This vivid use of the abstract term sums up all that is meant, as Paul explains, by being accursed. Christ took the penalty of sin. When the apostle similarly uses an abstract term, sin, he is summing up all that made the penalty [30] necessary. Christ is therefore on the cross as a sinner, but as a sinner only in so far as it was "for us." In his private capacity, so to speak, he remained sinless, the Son in whom God was well pleased. In his representative capacity he was a sinner and accursed.

This interpretation has to be expressed, preached and taught with great sensitiveness and discrimination. In itself it is no more open to objection than the theory of vicarious penitence or inclusive penitence associated with the name of R. C. Moberly (*Atonement and Personality*, pp. 129–30, 283–84). It can suffer grievously by being distorted. Moberly himself, I venture to suggest, has failed to penetrate the depth of Paul's meaning. For example: "Could anything be more grotesquely, or even blasphemously, irrelevant to our true meaning than the thought of an obstinate Punisher, who after venting His vengeance on an innocent substitute, should consent, because someone had suffered, to treat the wicked, untruly and unrighteously, as if they were what they are not?"

I do not think that Alan Richardson would relish the idea that, because

---

30. Cf. Thrall, p. 153: Christ "voluntarily suffers death, which Paul thinks of as the consequence of sin and its punishment (Rom. 6:23)." (The word *penalty* is used on the previous page. Cf. also William Barclay, *The King and the Kingdom*, p. 188: "Jesus on the Cross bore the punishment that should have fallen on us. . . . By his death he bore the punishment that men should have borne and so opened up the door to God and the Kingdom that all may go in."

he sees Christ bearing the judgment of God, he is committed to the view that God is an obstinate Punisher. God is all holy and all righteous. "Obstinate" suggests the tenacious holding on to a position with complete disregard of moral considerations. "Venting his vengeance" in this context is sheer innuendo. Moberly has not taken into account the fact that the Father suffered (apart from the physical pain) as much as the Son. The "innocent substitute" is no mere man, chosen at random or even with the care of omniscience. He is the eternal Son with whom the Father is one. Father and Son were united in their common purpose and their common suffering but separated in their intimate communion. (See above, pp. 102–3, 105, and 117–20, "concomitant." Cf. pp. 112–13.) Moberly was no Unitarian: in the dedication of his book to the one, holy, catholic Church he refers to Jesus Christ as "very God of very God." But he is perilously near to deserving the rebuke administered by Dale to Martineau (see p. 104).

In his objection to the thought of God's treating the wicked "as if they were what they are not," Moberly has forgotten that all forgiveness treats men in this way, whether the forgiveness be human or divine; and he has given no weight to what we have earlier called the concomitants of justification. I fancy that St. Paul would want to amend the statement that our Lord "voluntarily stood in the place of the utterly contrite." Christ died not for the contrite but for the ungodly (Rom. 5:6).

It is the distortion of the Pauline doctrine which comes under heavy criticism, but the doctrine itself is both academically and spiritually worthy of respect. Wendland (p. 208) notes the "exchange" between Christ and man which takes place in the cross: Christ is made sin by God, man is made righteousness, i.e., a righteous man who passes the test in the judgment. Through his death Christ "ist mit unserer Sünde beladen und für sie bestraft worden"—"was loaded with our sins and punished for them." P. T. Forsyth (*Positive Preaching and the Modern Mind,* p. 253) ventures to say that "I never knew my sin so long as I but saw Christ suffering for me—never until I saw Him under its judgment and realised that the chastisement of my peace was upon Him."

It would not be right to accuse men of this outlook of belief in an "obstinate Punisher." If they respectively represent New Testament scholarship and theological acumen, spiritual power should not be forgotten (2:4–5). It was a great preacher who told his congregation that "a God who could pardon without justice might one of these days condemn without reason." [31]

It should be noted that the "exchange" is in two parts. On the cross Christ was made sin; but men did not become righteous there and then. The second part of the exchange has to await the preaching of the gospel and the responsive faith of men.

### Redemption

The work of Christ is also summed up in the word *redemption* (1:30).

---

31. C. H. Spurgeon, *Sermon No. 1173* (1874, p. 285).

Its Author is God and it was achieved by Christ. Paul uses here one of the *lutron* group of words, though the group is "not the exclusive means of expressing the idea of redemption."[32] Elsewhere he uses the verb *agorazō*—to buy (6:20; 7:23). There has been some discussion as to whether *redemption* as a word has worn thin and lost its reference to ransom, thus meaning little more than deliverance. With the verb just cited, however, the idea of purchase inevitably comes back. "You were bought for a price."

This may or may not reflect sacral manumission. It seems hardly necessary to investigate the question. At any rate we shall start with a consideration of the evidence supplied by the language of St. Paul.

The tense of the verb should be noticed. The aorist suggests some decisive act (cf. 2 Pet. 2:1; Rev. 5:9). Redemption is not, as some have suggested, a continuing process and the church is not the redeeming society. F. Büchsel (*TDNT* 1:125) infers from the repetition and the abruptness that we are dealing with a kind of slogan of Paul's. "Behind this slogan, though not expounded in it, is Paul's doctrine of salvation." He refers at this point to the use of the compound verb, *exagorazō*, which we find in Galatians 3:13; 4:5.

The decisive act must be the cross. Here the price was paid, though Paul does not state what it was. The Corinthian and Galatian texts can hardly represent different theological standpoints. The "price" must therefore be a figurative way of speaking of what it cost our Lord to redeem: He was made a curse for us. He took upon himself our obligation and our accountability.

This has moral consequences, which strictly ought to be considered under the subject of Christ's work in us rather than his work for us. But we must anticipate in our exegesis. When we were under the law we were under obligation. We had to do what we were told (though we did not do so). To that extent we "belonged" to the law. We were its servants, its slaves. From this we have been redeemed. We are no longer the slaves of the law. But even so "you are not your own, *for* you were bought with a price." "Do not be slaves of men."

It seems that there is a subtle duality in Paul's use of the verb *agorazō*. When he is thinking of our Lord's work on the cross in taking upon himself our obligation and our accountability, the idea of "buying" recedes somewhat: it is a way of saying that our salvation was not an accident, was not arbitrary, was not mechanically devised and is not merely the result of exhortation. The Lord had to give up something precious in order to make salvation possible. The word *buy* can be brought into service without having to raise questions often associated with price.

But when the apostle is thinking of consequences he can give more emphasis to the idea of purchase. The Lord bought you. (You have been bought and paid for—Goodspeed.) You therefore do not belong to yourselves. You belong to him. (You are like slaves who have been bought in the market.) Therefore you do not belong to any one else. You are not the slaves of any one else. Therefore "do not be the slaves of men."

Given the fact of purchase, it was natural to think of the price as the

---

32. Hill, *Greek Words*, p. 49, n. 1.

blood of Christ, as Alford did, with 1 Peter 1:18–19 in support. But this is running two categories together. If the word *life* had been used it would merely have meant that, as we still say in human events, "it was done at the cost of his life." But "blood" means more than this. It points to sacrifice. Paul interprets the death of Christ not only as his becoming a curse but as a sacrifice. By this we mean more than the frequently used figure of "giving up" something, such as "he sacrificed his day off for the sake of the boys' club." The sacrifice which Paul has in mind is cultic and is of the order of the Old Testament sacrifices. "Christ our Passover Lamb was sacrificed" (5:7).

The Greek verb in this verse (*thuō*) originally meant to sacrifice but came to mean "kill" even in a noncultic context (Luke 15:23, 27, 30; John 10:10; Acts 10:13; 11:7). Paul is not using the word *amnos*. This saves us the question of possible ambiguity, whether he meant lamb or goat, the Passover lamb or the scapegoat of the Day of Atonement,[33] or both. The noun *(to pascha)* clearly points to the Paschal or Passover lamb. Paul in fact is virtually quoting Exodus 12:21, LXX, and the verb must mean "slay in sacrifice." And we cannot make use of the interpretation given by Jeremias to the *amnos* of John 1:29, which relates the *amnos* to the Servant of the Lord (Isa. 53) and to his "substitutionary suffering of the penalty of sin."[34]

The death of Christ is a sacrifice. The "characteristic distinctiveness [of the Old Testament view of sacrifice], which is significant for the NT, is due to the manner in which the God self-revealed in history has ordered the relationship between himself and the people. In the sacrificial order of the old covenant, God wills to have personal and active dealings with his people. Sacrifice . . . is always orientated to the presence of God in grace and judgment . . . it is a means of personal intercourse between God and man."[35] From this it may be inferred that Paul saw the death of Christ as a means of bringing God and man together. The question is, how is *to pascha* to be interpreted?

It is conceivable that in addressing a group of Jewish Christians the apostle might speak to them "in their own language." You will remember, he might begin, that before you were in Christ you used to celebrate the Passover. The picture of the sacrificial lamb is still clear to your imagination. For us Christians that lamb is Christ himself. He was sacrificed.

Now if Paul ever so spoke he would have identified the death of Christ with *a* Passover. Any Passover would suit his purpose, the one celebrated by James in one city or by John in another. For the death of Christ would have been identified with the death of a lamb and in a religious festival. It would have served as a memorial, vivid and poignant indeed, but still as a mere memorial, of what God had done centuries before.

This does not seem to be "big" enough and it does not easily cohere

---

33. Cf. (on John 1:29) Aileen Guilding, *The Fourth Gospel and Jewish Worship,* p. 179.

34. Joachim Jeremias, *TDNT* 1:339; cf. Oscar Cullmann, *The Christology of the New Testament,* p. 67, 71.

35. J. Behm, *TDNT* 3:183, 185. Cf. Harrison, *Introduction to the Old Testament,* p. 409, "divinely imposed."

with Paul's thought. ". . . in Judaism the lamb sacrificed at Passover does not take away sins."[36] Bultmann apparently denies this: ". . . a passover-sacrifice, in Jewish eyes a sin-removing sacrifice."[37] It may be that the Passover was not prominently or characteristically expiatory but that "*all* sacrifices . . . effect reconciliation . . . i.e., they are the means of obtaining divine forgiveness."[38]

It is plain that the death of Christ was not *a* Passover but *the* Passover. Paul's use of the article *(to)* must be given due weight. If he had omitted it we should have had to translate "Christ was killed in sacrifice—a Passover of ours."[39] But He was *the* Passover. Paul was not thinking of celebrations which had gone on through the centuries but of the one, original Passover at the Exodus. There the blood "had a redemptive effect, and made God's covenant with Abraham operative."[40]

Paul's understanding of the Lord's death as the Passover is figurative rather than literal. He interprets it—perhaps following very old Christian tradition (Jeremias, p. 56)—by comparing the death of Jesus with the death of the Passover lamb. We must therefore ask two questions: what were the benefits, and how were they received?

According to the chapter from which Paul quotes, Exodus 12, God "passed over" his people so that they escaped the judgment which fell upon the Egyptians (Exod. 12:12–13; cf. Gen. 15:14). Note the word *ekdikēsis* (vengeance, punishment) in Exodus 12:12, LXX. Two necessary steps were involved. The lamb had to be slain; and its blood had to be "put" (Hebrew *nathan,* Greek *tithēmi*) on to the doorposts and lintel (Exod. 12:7). Even if the lamb had been slain, a house would not have been spared if the blood had not been so applied (Exod. 12:22–23).

This is analogous to Paul's doctrine that Christ had to die and the benefits of his passion have to be received by faith. The deliverance from Egyptian judgment corresponds to the fact that there is no condemnation to those who are in Christ (Rom. 8:1). What is elsewhere given in forensic terms is now given a cultic setting. "The justified have the last judgment behind them."[41] The men of the Exodus have the Egyptian danger behind them. And there is contact with the teaching of the Epistle to the Hebrews about sprinkling (cf. pp. 62, 67–69).

Ethelbert Stauffer neatly sums it up (*New Testament Theology*, pp. 132, 163). "Good Friday is the passover day of universal history." "Good Friday

---

36. Barrett, *The Gospel according to St. John*, p. 147; cf. Joachim Jeremias, *The Eucharistic Words of Jesus*, p. 146.
37. Bultmann, *Theology of the NT*, 1:296. Oscar Cullmann seems to agree. "For the Jews the purpose of sacrificing the paschal lamb is to achieve atonement for the sins of the people (Ex. 12)" (*Christology*, p. 71).
38. W. O. E. Oesterley and Theodore H. Robinson, *Hebrew Religion*, p. 335. The italic (*"all"*) is Oesterley and Robinson's. See also W. Robertson Smith, *The Religion of the Semites*, p. 401; Th. C. Vriezen, *An Outline of Old Testament Theology*, p. 286 and n. 3: "renewal of a relation."
39. Cf. Moulton-Turner, *Grammar*, 3:173.
40. Jeremias, *Eucharistic Words*, p. 146–47. See Gen. 15:14, and cf. LXX *krinō* (I will judge).
41. Forsyth, *Positive Preaching and the Modern Mind*, pp. 215, 238.

is the passover day for universal history." This leads Paul to turn his thought from the great historic occasion (Egypt, Calvary) to its celebration. The Christian life itself is one long celebration. "Let us go on keeping the feast" (1 Cor. 5:8).

Old Testament scholars will probably say that the Passover has adapted what is much older than Moses. It may be so. But St. Paul was not a modern Old Testament scholar. Like his Master, he read the Old Testament as he found it. "We must put aside all modern critical notions when we try to understand how Jesus would have read the OT." [42] And like his Master, Paul penetrated beyond the letter. "It was his theology that enabled him to divine what criticism has only verified." [43]

The concept of sacrifice is unfamiliar if not uncongenial to modern men. But it must have been part of the very atmosphere which Paul breathed, at any rate in the days before his conversion. When he entered the new atmosphere of being "in Christ," [44] he did not cease to think in sacrificial terms. F. Thiele (*Begriffslex.* 9:996) draws attention to the fact that occasionally Paul still offered sacrifice (Acts 21:26; 24:17-18; cf. 1 Cor. 9:20) though he took over the Jewish-Christian interpretation of Jesus' vicarious work of salvation on the cross as a sacrifice. This was a sacrifice to end sacrifices: the old cult was fulfilled with his death, and the Gentiles were not bound to it. W. D. Davies, (*Paul and Rabbinic Judaism*, p. 253) tends to play down Paul's sympathy with the sacrificial system and says that the channels of sacrifice "are not fully native to him, as it were."

But Davies admits, with a significant "of course," that " . . . everything covenantal had a sacrificial basis." We therefore turn to the expression given in the eucharistic passage, "the new covenant in my blood" (11:25).

These words come from the earliest literary text of the words of interpretation. Related to it but independent of it is Luke 22:15-20. The two different strands of eucharistic tradition, Mark-Matthew and Paul-Luke, are in substantial agreement and go back to preliturgical narrative tradition. "At their beginning we do not find liturgy, but a historical account." [45]

Now the matters touched on in the previous paragraph are fitting subjects for research. For our present purpose, however, it seems wiser to concentrate on the evidence supplied by the apostle himself. What can we learn from him about the meaning of "the new covenant in my blood"?

## Covenant

There could hardly have been a new covenant if an old one had not previously existed. This may seem obvious but it is important, and Paul

---

42. Richardson, *Introduction to Theology of NT*, p. 145.
43. P. T. Forsyth, *The Person and Place of Jesus Christ*, p. 174 (Gal. 3:17).
44. This is not meant to limit the meaning of the phrase to atmosphere or "surrounding element"—air for men, water for fish. See E. Best, *One Body in Christ*.
45. Joachim Jeremias, *New Testament Theology*, 1:288–89. Jeremias regards Luke's longer text as the original. Cf. his *Eucharistic Words of Jesus*, pp. 87–106; and E. Earle Ellis, *The Gospel of Luke*, pp. 253–55, following H. Schürmann. Whether the Lukan account has been influenced by the Pauline "ist noch umstritten"—"is still disputed" (Wendland, p. 97).

speaks about it (II.3:6–15). The old covenant was written, engraved on stone in writing, letter by letter. Paul refers to the contemporary "reading of the Old Testament" (II.3:14–15), as we should say, and then restricts it to the Law, "whenever Moses is read." This is a covenant of condemnation and it "kills" (pp. 162–63). But the law and death are transitory (vergänglich, Wendland, p. 180), and "only in Christ is the old covenant abrogated" (NEB).[46]

Even so it was inaugurated in glory, as Paul well knew. He alludes to Exodus 24 in II.3:3. And it was inaugurated with sacrifice. Moses narrated to the people all the words of God and the dikaiōmata. The people promised to obey and Moses wrote down all the words of the Lord. Sacrifice was offered (ethusan thusian sōtēriou), the book of the covenant was read, the people promised obedience and Moses sprinkled (kateskedasen) them with the blood of the sacrifice. His words are striking: "Behold the blood of the covenant which the Lord made [dietheto] with you concerning all these words" (Exod. 24:3–8, LXX).

But the people did not keep the covenant, in spite of their promises. The law was broken by them and their only prospect, under the old covenant, was condemnation and death. It was this situation which the new covenant was designed to meet.

This inevitably recalls Jeremiah 31:31–34 (38:31–34, LXX) which Paul cannot fail to have known. Though he had received the tradition (11:23) from "the tradent" (para), the one who actually delivered it to him, and through him from the originator (apo), as Jeremias suggests, and had passed it on, he did not do so mechanically and without understanding, as an English-speaking acolyte might follow the words of the Latin mass. (I have received illumination from a former "altar boy," still a practicing Roman Catholic, whose marriage I have solemnized.) Paul no less than we ourselves must have heard the echo of the prophecy of Jeremiah.[47] Bruce sees an explicit allusion to the new covenant of Jeremiah 31:31–33 in 2 Corinthians 3:6 (cf. v. 3) and an implicit one elsewhere, where "letter" and "spirit" are contrasted. The prophecy is "quoted in part in Rom. 11:27."

The prophecy states that the people did not abide by the covenant— they broke the law; and that God "disregarded" ("abandoned," Heb. 8:9, NEB, ameleō) them—this corresponds to Paul's "condemnation" in II:3:9. This in itself puts the people into a hopeless position. The prophecy of the new covenant, however, turns hopelessness into hope because it meets the problems raised under the old covenant. No longer are men to be abandoned by God. "I will be their God and they will be my people." They are to be acceptable to him.

No longer will men be under God's wrath. "I will be propitious to their

---

46. The different interpretations of 2 Cor. 3:14 are excellently summarized in the note given by Philip Hughes, pp. 112–13.
47. Cf. J. Guhrt, Begriffslex. 2:159. He gives an undocumented quotation from Schniewind: "Jer. 31:31–34 . . . in allen Fassungen des Kelchwortes durch(-klingt)"— "Jer. 31:31–34 . . . resounds in all forms of the saying about the cup." See F. F. Bruce, Romans, pp. 47, 161.

iniquities."[48] Thenceforth the wrath will not be renewed. The new relationship set up will be continued. "I will in no wise remember their sins any
longer." This does not mean a bare recollection, a mere mental process.
How could omniscience forget? In the biblical sense of the word, when
God remembers, He acts: "there comes a new turn in the situation." [49]
When sins are forgiven the sinner can be sure that at no time will God
resurrect them in memory and action. There will be no "new turn."

Under the new covenant men will have individual dealings with God.
Man need not exhort man, neighbor or brother, to know the Lord, because
all will know him, from small to great. Their experience of God will not
be limited to the ceremonial, the ritual or the liturgical. Mind and heart
are central, even though knees may bow. The knowledge of God will
be individual, inner, spiritual, intimate. Thus it may become universal
because every human being has mind and heart. But whereas in the old
covenant the relationship was established between God and a single people,
under the new covenant new members may be brought in who were
previously outside the covenant and not God's people (Rom. 9:25). Once
inside they will indeed individually know God.

This exposition of the prophecy of Jeremiah seems remarkably like
Paul's gospel! Men are not abandoned by God but are acceptable to him.
They are not under wrath. They have entered into a new and permanent
relationship with God. Their individual knowledge of him begins with
their justifying faith, which began when individuals received the universal
message proclaimed by the apostle to the Gentiles. All who have thus
entered the covenant know God in their hearts and have no need to
evangelize one another. They have already been evangelized. The expression, "I will write my laws on their hearts" may be due to the fact that the
prophet is struggling to express the thoughts of the new covenant in legal
language appropriate to the old covenant. Even so it leaves room in an
evangelical religion for "keeping the commandments of God" (7:19).

How does it come about that these blessings are available to men? It
is because the new covenant had to be established by God (Jer. 38:31,
LXX)[50] and God did so establish it. But just as the first covenant was
inaugurated with sacrifice, so it is with the second. "The blood of the
covenant" (Exod. 24:8) takes on a deeper meaning. The sacrificial death
of Jesus "brings into force the new covenant which was prefigured
in the making of the covenant on Sinai and prophesied for the time of
salvation" (Jer. 31:31–34).[51] The outpouring of the blood is the basis for
the establishment of the new covenant, which is "in [en] My blood."

48. David Hill uses the word *propitious* in connection with *hileōs* and suggests from
a study of contexts that the idea of propitiation belongs to its word-group: *Greek Words*,
p. 36, n. 1; and p. 47. Cf. above p. 105.

49. Otto Michel, *TDNT* 4:675. Cf. Jeremias, *Eucharistic Words*, p. 163. For illustration, see Luke 23:42.

50. Perhaps it ought to be stated that questions of authorship do not arise. Paul
would argue from the text as a *datum*. See John Skinner, *Prophecy and Religion*,
chapter XVIII.

51. Jeremias, *NT Theology*, 1:291; *Eucharistic Words*, p. 112.

Jeremias accepts the interpretation given by A. Schlatter in *Das Evangelium des Lukas* (p. 422) that the preposition is causal ("das kausale *en*"), though if it is the maid of all work of the New Testament, as Moulton said, it may have an even wider reference. It may be instrumental or may even replace the genitive of price (cf. Rev. 5:9). The maid sometimes does many tasks at the same time. It seems clear that without the shedding of the blood of Jesus no new covenant would be possible. With the shedding of the blood the kingdom is opened to all believers, "the spiritual benefits which he secured *in principle* for the whole human race as a result of His death" (Thrall, p. 77; italics mine).

Without the blood there would be no new covenant, no blessings which come with the new covenant. Without the blood men would be unacceptable to God and abandoned by him. Without the blood they would be perpetually unforgiven and under his wrath. The blood secured the blessings *in principle*. But they have to be received. Jeremiah expresses this in his words about the laws being written on men's hearts and knowing the Lord. Paul thinks of the response of faith to the preaching of the gospel and of the reception of the Spirit as a result of "the hearing of faith" (Gal. 3:2). When faith reaches out to God for forgiveness, the Holy Spirit is received, "not instead of the promised forgiveness but as the bearer of it."

In his remarks with regard to 2 Corinthians 3:3, 6, where "Paul is obviously thinking of Jer. 31:31 ff.," James Dunn goes too far in saying that "without the Spirit there is no new covenant." The Spirit is available and waiting to be received as the bearer of forgiveness by those who put their trust in Christ crucified. He is right, however, when he adds at once that "without receiving the Spirit it is impossible to participate in the new covenant."[52]

Paul himself could speak of participation, *koinōnia*, in the blood of Christ (1 Cor. 10:16). This is more than a mere partaking of, a *metochē*. A student in the privacy of his room can partake of a cake on his own, i.e., he can eat some of it; but if there is a *koinōnia* it implies that others share the cake with him. It is "common" to them and "*koinōnia* in the NT never departs from the primitive sense of sharing something in common." ". . . a common sharing in the Blood of Christ . . . constitutes community."[53]

This is true; and Paul has community very much in mind. But a man does not participate in the blood of Christ for the first time, i.e., he does not begin to participate in the blood of Christ, on the occasion of his "first communion"—his first attendance at the Eucharist as a communicant. He began to share in the blood of Christ when he first put his trust in him. Participation is not intermittent but continuous. He does not participate at the Eucharist and then cease to do so until he attends the next celebration. Once he has put his "first faith" in Christ, he goes on participating in his blood in unbroken continuity.

---

52. Dunn, *Baptism in the Holy Spirit*, pp. 80, 107–9, 135. His note 62 on p. 135 should be added to my note 47 in this chapter.

53. Davies, *Paul and Rabbinic Judaism*, p. 253. This usage goes back at least as far as Aristotle.

What it amounts to is this: Christ died for him. His faith is steadily and always directed to Christ crucified; in Him he is always acceptable to God, and as a forgiven man he is in fellowship with God. Others have the same experience as he does. Each and all trust in the same, "common" Christ and each and all receive the same, "common" benefits. This is participation in the blood of Christ.

In thinking of the new covenant and of the death of Christ as a sacrifice, with a consequent emphasis on his blood, Paul has transferred to another idiom what he has already said about redemption. Man as a sinner is under wrath, "abandoned." Christ has died, by the mercy and provision of God. In virtue of His death the believer is no longer abandoned but is acceptable to God and in Christ is in fellowship with God.

### Reconciliation

We pass on to consider Paul's great word, *reconciliation*. The relevant passages are Romans 5:10–11; 2 Corinthians 5:18–20. I did not attempt to deal with this subject when studying the Epistle to the Romans; preferring to wait until now. I hope that the postponement will lead to comprehensiveness of treatment.

There seems to be a good deal of misunderstanding of the meaning of the term. When we hear prominent ecclesiastics tell the unheeding world —the world which flouts God's laws, mocks his truth, despises his church, arrogates to itself authority in everything and manifests all the hatred which our Lord said was vented by it on himself and his disciples (John 15:18–19)—when we hear such men declare that God has reconciled the world to himself, we can only raise our eyebrows and dryly observe that the world has not yet been informed of the fact or if it has that the effect on the world has not gone down very deep. The cynical disregard of human life, the murder of whole populations, the brutal violence and the traffic in souls so characteristic of the drug pusher come ill from a reconciled world.

If indeed the world has already been reconciled, the expression can only mean that it is "as if" the world had been reconciled; and we know how "as if" is uncongenial to many. The reconciliation of the world in this sense has no "concomitants." It seems to me that we must say quite openly that the world is obviously not reconciled to God; or admit that there is some truth about its reconciliation which has so far eluded us.

We must now try to draw out the implications of the Pauline text, particularly 2 Corinthians 5:18–20. Verse 20 might be rendered thus: "We are ambassadors for Christ, conscious that God is making his appeal through us; as Christ's servants [cf. Arndt-Gingrich, p. 846] we beg (men), 'Be reconciled to God.'" The words "be reconciled to God" are not directed to the Corinthians specifically but to men in general. They summarize, so to speak, the appeal at the end of an evangelistic sermon. If men are asked to be reconciled to God, it is plain that they are not already reconciled to him.

Three points follow and we state them as if the apostle himself were speaking. "We have a ministry of reconciliation" (v. 18). The purpose of our ministry is to get men reconciled to God.

Secondly, "We ourselves have an experience of reconciliation." We were not always reconciled. "I persecuted the church of God" (Gal. 1:13). But God reconciled us to himself. The "us" must mean the apostle and his immediate circle (or the wider circle of "apostles" and missionaries), because it was to them that the ministry was given. Not all of the church consists of "ambassadors." Reconciliation to God did not come in a vacuum or through some vague religiosity. It came through Christ, and Paul did not know of any Christ except Christ crucified. The preachers know from their own experience what they are asking their hearers to do.

Thirdly, "We have a message of reconciliation." The "word of reconciliation" (II.5:19) is not mere exhortation, an appeal without content. It is not "you have been reconciled." Empirical evidence is against it, and it would be odd in one and the same breath to tell men that they have been reconciled and then urge them to be reconciled. The message is deeper.

God was engaged in the task of doing what we are trying to do, though not in the same way. Our method is preaching; his is different.

This brings us to the crucial text, "God was in Christ reconciling the world to himself." This is often taken as if it meant that God had actually done it. This would have required an aorist tense or possibly a perfect. In actual fact we have a periphrastic imperfect, ēn . . . katallassōn. Moulton declines to regard it as periphrastic. "No one would cite 2 Cor. 5:19." In certain instances (in the Acts) de Zwaan feels that "the periphrasis is not real. We might put a comma between the two parts without damaging the sense." James Denney seems to be committed to the periphrastic view because he thinks that no New Testament writer could have conceived of the sentence, "God was in Christ." This ignores such passages as John 10:38 and 17:23.

The construction is recognized as periphrastic by Howard and by Turner and we shall think of it in this way.[54] In the absence of any suspicion of Aramaic sources which might influence the Greek, as here, we must regard it as thoroughly Greek.

The periphrasis suggests a certain emphasis, with possibly a certain stress on long drawn out continuity.[55] If it were not for the fact that the subject is God, we could speak of a conative periphrastic imperfect—"God was trying to . . ." What we must not say is the aoristic "God reconciled the world." This is wrong grammatically, and is as wrong theologically as to say that "God converted the world." If this were true, conversion would be utterly valueless from the moral and spiritual point of view. What then is meant?

*Two factors are involved.* "In Christ God was reconciling . . . not imputing." The two participles are not coordinate. The first, "reconciling," is

---

54. Moulton, *Grammar*, 1:227; Moulton-Howard, *Grammar*, 2:451–2; Moulton-Turner, *Grammar*, 3:87–88. J. de Zwaan in *Beginnings of Christianity* (ed. Foakes Jackson and Lake), 2:62. Hughes, p. 208.
55. Cf. Moulton-Turner, *Grammar* 4:89.

more comprehensive and includes the latter within its process. The second, "not imputing," is negative. The grammatical structure is exactly the same as in Romans 4:6, apart from the negative: "(the man) to whom God imputes righteousness." Now God imputes righteousness when a man believes, *and not before*. Before he believes, God imputes every sinful act to him. If this were not so, no man would be guilty, answerable to God but having no answer to give. No sin would attach to him. The negative, "not imputing," therefore belongs to the stage of conversion, of receiving the gospel. But the gospel is that of Christ crucified, the divine purpose of whose death is to make it possible for a righteous God to receive unrighteous men, men no longer rebels against him but yielding to him—reconciled. God's work in Christ, then, is the comprehensive one of getting men reconciled to him, through the objective atonement (the preaching of the gospel), and the response of faith.

This interpretation helps to explain the use of the periphrastic tense. It can be said in the aorist that "Christ died" or "Christ redeemed." It can be said in the aorist that "a man believed" and that "God justified." But when the whole process is under review, the once-for-all death, the preaching in scores of cities, and the response, one after another, of hundreds and thousands of men, then we see that there must be a long drawn out process. "Was reconciling" describes such a process, and it includes within itself the cross, the preaching, the response in faith and the "not imputing," i.e., the positive imputing of righteousness.

Thus God was engaged in the task of getting men reconciled, just as we are, though the methods differ. Ours is the preaching of the gospel. This is included in God's method as he appeals to men through us (v. 20) but it is only a part of it. His method is the cross of Jesus, the word of the preacher and the influence of the Holy Spirit. In this long process Paul saw that God was reconciling men to Himself.

This understanding of Paul's thought may be supplemented by reference to Romans 5:1–11. We observe that as a result of justification we should enjoy peace with God. Before justification there was no peace but "legal strife between Judge and accused" (Barrett, p. 101). The significance of peace will be apparent as the argument proceeds.

Justification arises out of faith but it would all be unavailing apart from one great fact: Christ died. In Romans 5:8–9, Paul sees the love of God demonstrated in the fact that it was while we were still sinners Christ died for us. From this Paul develops his argument—from the greater to the less. If we were justified as sinners we shall be preserved as believers. If we are justified *now*, we shall be delivered *then*. (See p. 86.) If we have been justified now by his blood, much more shall we be saved through him from the eschatological wrath.

A parallel argument, which is also an explanation (*gar*), follows (Rom. 5:10). There is the same reference, though not formally expressed, to *now* and *then*; the same reference to God: justified (by God) and reconciled to God; the same reference to Christ: through the death of his Son and by his life, the life lived in heaven as that of the resurrected Lord. On the face of it we could easily state the argument from greater to less: if reconciled as enemies, how much more sure of preservation as friends!

This is sound—as far as it goes and only as far as it goes. It takes the word "enemies" (*echthroi*) in the sense of "hostile to God," which in fact we were. (Cf. Phil. 3:18.) In addition it regards "we were reconciled" as an experience of ours, influenced undoubtedly by the death of Christ, but still an experience in which we ceased to resist the divine call and from enemies became friends. This again is true in fact. There was a time when we were "in the flesh," "fleshly" (Rom. 7:5, 14, 18); we would not and could not obey God and we could not please him. Our attitude was hostility to God (Rom. 8:5–9). That is now past history. Far from being hostile to him we are led by his Spirit and we cry, "Abba, Father" (Rom. 8:14–15).

We must not leave the matter here. The parallelism between verses 9 and 10 merits deeper consideration. Verse 9 says that we were justified in virtue of the blood of Jesus. This has set up a permanent relationship between ourselves and God (see p. 117).

Through Jesus Christ we have gained an entry into a new territory, the territory of grace (Rom. 5:2). There we stand and there we live and there we stay. If all this came to us when were sinners, how much more shall we, believers standing in grace, be saved—and still "through him"—from the final wrath! The eschatological wrath may be anticipated in history (see pp. 86–87) and to that extent is already revealed, "though not against believers" (Barrett on Rom. 5:9). This is a massive argument from the greater to the less.

Is the parallel and explanatory argument equally massive? Look at it as we have stated it already. If when we were hostile to God we were changed from enemies to friends of God through the influence of the death of his Son, how much more, now made friends, shall we be saved by him now risen and exalted? This places almost the whole emphasis on Christian experience; and further: it looks very much as if God saves his friends. This is a long way from the characteristic Pauline doctrine.

This must not be taken as a disparagement of Christian experience. I am quite sure that Alan Richardson goes much too far in saying that "the NT writers set no store at all by religious feelings or emotions, and it is impossible to translate 'religious experience' into NT Greek." Apart from anything else this forgets that "the fruit of the Spirit is . . . joy" (Gal. 5:22).[56] Even so it may be doubted if Christian experience can bear the weight imposed on it by our present interpretation of Romans 5:10. We may assert that though "we were reconciled," in the long run it was "God who reconciled us" (2 Cor. 5:18). But this still remains in the realm of Christian experience.

---

56. Richardson, *Introduction to Theology of NT*, p. 250. I am not convinced of the inadequacy of the Greek language. We might attempt to translate "religious experience" by *ha paschō, gignōskōn ta tou theou*. The verb *paschō* here does not mean "suffer," but as the idiomatic passive of *poieō* means "what I have done to me," i.e., "how I am affected." Cf. Plato, *Apology*, 17a; Mark 5:26, *polla pathousa hupo pollōn*, "elegant classical Greek" (A. Plummer, *The Gospel According to Mark*, p. 147). Gal. 3:4, "So Grosses hättet ihr umsonst *erfahren?*"—"would you have had so great an experience to no purpose?" (Althaus, p. 23).

Now there is a text (Matt. 5:24) which in form (passive plus dative) is exactly the same as Romans 5:10, apart from the fact that the verb is *diallassō*, not *katallassō*. This need not worry us as "a distinction between [the two verbs] cannot be demonstrated" (F. Büchsel, *TDNT* 1:253). The text may be rendered thus. "If you are (engaged in the process of) offering your gift on the altar and there it suddenly strikes your memory that your brother has something against you [*kata* plus genitive of hostility], leave your gift there in front of the altar and first go and be reconciled to your brother, and then come and resume the offering of your gift."

The brother, with something "against" you, may be termed hostile to you. If you are to be reconciled to him, the ground of offense must be first removed. If this is done, the brother will cease to have anything against you and he will be reconciled; and so, presumably, will you. Notice that you must take the first step and you must remove the cause of grievance.

The setting is Jewish but the teaching is Christian, and St. Paul would have thoroughly approved. But it is teaching for the behavior of the Christian disciple. When we consider the apostle's doctrine, two difficulties arise. Sinful men did not take the first step toward reconciliation with God. Even if they sought for him they did not find him (cf. Acts 17:23, 27). Even if they had found him they would have found a God who had not waited to be found. God sent his Son. The second difficulty is almost axiomatic in Paul's teaching. Men cannot remove the grievance which God has against them. (Cf. Col. 2:14, *kath' hēmōn*.) It is the marvel of the gospel that God himself has removed the obstacle to his forgiveness of sinners. He is just and the Justifier (Rom. 3:26).

It seems clear that in Romans 5:10 the hostility is mutual and the reconciliation is mutual. Man is reconciled when he believes in Jesus, and not before. God is already reconciled in the cross, and only in the cross. That is why Paul can say with "boasting" (cf. Gal. 6:14) that through our Lord we have received the reconciliation (Rom. 5:11). We did not create it or even initiate it. In Christ it is an accomplished fact.

The enmity and the reconciliation between God and man are not on one side only. They are mutual. This is the view of Sanday and Headlam.[57] Three quarters of a century after the first publication of their famous commentary I should like to refer to the work of Canon Douglas Webster. He is one of the most devout and at the same time one of the sanest of our contemporary theologians. He observes that "some theologians fight shy of the thought that God needed to be reconciled. . . . This line of thought is so unfashionable today and yet so fundamentally right." [58]

57. Sanday and Headlam, *Romans,* pp. 129–30. Cf. John Murray, *Romans,* 1:169–77; and his *Redemption Accomplished and Applied,* pp. 33–42; R. L. Ottley, *The Doctrine of the Incarnation,* pp. 638–39; John Pearson, *An Exposition of the Creed,* pp. 552–56; Werner Georg Kümmel, *The Theology of the New Testament,* pp. 200, 203–5, 214–16, 226, 331, 161–62; Cranfield, *Romans,* p. 267; J. I. Packer, *Knowing God,* p. 198.
58. Douglas Webster, *In Debt to Christ,* pp. 89–90. It is pleasing to reflect that as Canon of St. Paul's Dr. Webster is a distinguished successor to Canon H. P. Liddon not only in the congregations who sit at his feet but in the doctrinal quality of his sermons. Almost exactly a century ago Liddon told his listeners that "Jesus crucified effects an atonement which restores to us the friendship of the holy God." See his sermon,

The point is that the wrath of God is real but it is dealt with in Christ. God is always righteous, always holy; He is always love. His reconciliation does not mean that He begins to love when He is reconciled. He is reconciled in Christ because He is eternal love. His reconciliation was not wrested from Him against His will. He sent His Son for this very purpose. The reconciliation of God means a change of relation and a change of treatment, a change in the look on the face of unchanging holy love.

This has all been well expressed by James Denney. ". . . His will to bless us is realised, as it was not before, on the basis of what Christ has done. . . . but for Christ and His Passion God would not *be* to us what He is." [59] If this were not so, "we put Christ out of Christianity altogether."

### The Resurrection of Christ

This may be regarded as a summary of the work of Christ for us. But we are not yet ready to pass on to a consideration of his work in us. His work on the cross is indeed done, and completely done. Paul, however, sees something further which on no account must be omitted. God raised His Son from the dead. If this statement proves to be false, certain dire consequences follow.

If Christ is not raised from the dead, the testimony of the apostles is untrue. Their concept of God is wrong. Their hitherto solid proclamation has nothing in it. The faith of believers is futile. They are still in their sins. All apparent victories over temptation are meaningless—and worse. The penalty of sin still hangs over their heads (1 Cor 15:4, 14–19.)

If in speaking of the Passion we emphasize, and rightly emphasize, the finished work of Christ, how is it that the resurrection of our Lord is so vital? Is not the Passion enough in itself? Could we not dispense with the resurrection, or at any rate regard it as a luxury which is no part of the Christian's iron rations? The answer to these and similar questions is to be found in the function of the resurrection in the saving economy of God and in the doctrinal understanding of the cross. The Lord's resurrection did not add to the sacrifice of the cross. What then did it do?

It is a sign of the deity of Christ. He really is the Son of God (cf. Rom. 1:4). If he were not the Son of God, our faith in him would be idolatry. If he were not the Son of God it would mean that the most holy, sinless and loving Man that ever lived was deserted by God in his darkest and bitterest hour. It would mean that God himself had not borne our sins: the Passion would be no more than the dereliction of man and not of God (see p. 171). If he were not the Son of God it would justify the cynical observation that God so loved the world that he sent someone else to suffer for our sins. The resurrection of Christ was due to the act of God. It must not be re-

---

"The Attractive Power of Christ Crucified," preached in St. Paul's Cathedral on Good Friday evening, 10th April 1868. (Sermon No. 294 of *The Penny Pulpit*, p. 429 of *Forty Sermons*, First Series.) Coming from such intellectual stature this teaching cannot be written off as crude.

59. James Denney, *The Christian Doctrine of Reconciliation*, pp. 238–39.

garded as an act of Christ. God raised him from the dead. This is the conclusive proof that God had accepted his sacrifice.

For it was the purpose of God that the work of his Son should be made known among men, in order that they might respond to the message and be justified by faith. There would be no point in telling men of the work of Christ if it were not a sure fact that God had accepted the sacrifice. The work of Christ is complete. The Father has accepted it and has testified to it in the resurrection. All is now ready. The gospel may be preached and men may be justified. "He was delivered up because of our trespasses and was raised (note the two parallel passives) with a view to our justification" (Rom 4:25).[60] Whether this text is to be traced back to Mark 9:31 is a question which need not concern us. Paul may be quoting, making an allusion to, or even unconsciously using, traditional material. The important fact is that he spoke as he did.

Justification establishes a permanent relationship between the believer and God. This is reflected in Paul's teaching about our Lord's heavenly intercession in Romans 8:34. Christ could not intercede for us if he had not died—and, "more than that" (NEB; immo vero; ja, mehr noch—O. Michel), was raised. Only a living Christ can intercede. It is the good pleasure of the living God to hearken for all time to his living Son, our Mediator.

He is our Mediator to the End—and beyond. Through him we shall be saved from the final wrath, through him the once crucified and now living for ever more (Rom. 5:9–10). The relationship between God and men established when they first believed is thus continued for all eternity.

In particular Christ is the guarantee of our own resurrection. The God who raised him will raise us (1 Cor. 6:14). He is thus the first fruits (15:20), the Leader of the procession of the dead who are no longer dead but resurrected, the first to come round the corner and emerge into full view, his people following behind him, unseen but assuredly there. The God who raised the Lord Jesus will also raise us with Jesus (II.4:14).[61] If this is not so, the permanent relationship is shattered and the cup of salvation is dashed from our lips at the very moment when we had hoped to begin to drain it. Hitherto we had sipped it, looking forward to the full draught. At our resurrection God will bid us drink deeply, for he is faithful both in life and beyond life (1:9; 10:13).

Meanwhile we do not know Christ "according to the flesh" kata sarka (II.5:16). The objective historian may do so and we should have done so, if Christ had not risen. As it is, he lives and he and his people are in fellowship. The Lord receives the prayers of his people; his grace is sufficient for them; and his power, "the power of Christ," rests on them

---

60. Cf. Popkes, *Christus Traditus*, pp. 238, 274, 276. Also p. 266.
61. "With Jesus" obviously cannot imply that our resurrection coincides with his. He has already been resurrected; we shall be. We should therefore exercise great exegetical caution when we interpret the "with" in those passages which speak of having been crucified "with" Christ or raised "with" him, e.g., Gal. 2:19; Col. 3:1. Cf. pp. 139–40.

(II.12:8–9). Christian discipleship or the Christian's "walk" is made possible only by fellowship with the living Christ. This is not unrelated to the doctrine of the Spirit, who is the Spirit of Christ (Rom 8:9).

The resurrection of our Lord thus does not add to the sacrifice of the cross. It has in itself no propitiatory power. God himself is reconciled in the cross and in the cross alone. But the resurrection makes possible the outworking of the sacrifice in the lives of men. It gives to men the knowledge that God has accepted the work of his Son. It makes permanent and eternal the mediatorship of Jesus. It ensures that men can be brought into the faith and kept in the faith, through their fellowship with the living Christ.

It is perhaps just conceivable that God might have acted otherwise and not raised his Son. He might have "informed" men that the sacrifice had been accepted, just as men were alleged to have learned of the resurrection through the notorious "telegram from heaven." He might have "told" them that Jesus was still alive and still the Mediator, and that he would still accept their prayers "through" him. If this had happened the Christian faith would have been greatly impoverished. More important, it is speculative. Paul has shown us what God actually chose to do. Given the function of the resurrection in the divine economy of salvation, to deny it is to deny along with it all that it involves.

The language of St. Paul implies the Ascension rather than explicitly asserts it and by implication it is of course associated with the resurrection. The allusion to the experience on the road to Damascus, when "last of all . . . he appeared to me also" (15:8), must point to the Ascension and all that it meant. Everything has been put in subjection under the feet of Christ (15:27). Believers are now "away from the Lord" (II.5:6–8), the distance between being bridged by faith; but this is only "until he come" (11:26). The unlimited sovereignty of the Son means once again that his mediatorship is permanent. As the living, resurrected Lord he represents men before God. As the Lord of the universe he can ensure that the preaching of the good news is not thwarted.

Paul might not have reflected deeply, if at all, on the philosophic question of the "friendliness" or otherwise of nature. He did act implicitly, however, in the assurance that as a preacher of Christ he could move and speak freely. Apart from the opposition of men he suffered intermittently from the natural dangers of sea and rivers and the cold (II.11:25–27). But there was never any question that nature in the large would or could produce some lasting disequilibrium which would make his work completely impossible. The sovereignty of the permanent Mediator makes it certain that the Mediator's message can be made known. The Ascension and Exaltation are as necessary as the Resurrection.

The work of Christ is thus finished: redemption has been accomplished, propitiation has been made and God has been reconciled. All is now ready for this good news to be preached to men, for salvation will not be theirs until at the very least they hear the gospel. Paul was willing to go to all lengths to win men, to save them (9:19–22); and the faithful spouse might likewise win the partner to a salvation not yet received (7:16). For salvation is an "advantage" (10:33), the reception of which is not to be impeded by the preacher's self-seeking.

## God at Work in Us—The Work of Christ in Us

The work of Christ has thus been done, and it has been done *for* men. We have already had to touch on his work *in* men and we must now consider it in more detail. What light is shed on this subject by the Epistles to the Corinthians?

It is plain that Paul and his companions addressed themselves to a situation. Before their arrival in the city of Corinth their hearers were Gentiles, heathen, swept away to idols which had no message for them (12:2). They were "natural" men (2:14), spiritually insensitive. Their consciences might have nothing on them to trouble them, but a clear conscience in itself is not enough (4:4). They were against the knowledge of God (cf. II.10:5). All that Paul has said about sin, judgment and perdition applies to the Corinthians before the preachers came. In a word, they were unbelievers (10:27; 14:22–24; cf. 7:39; II.6:14). When they listened to the apostle they were being given an opportunity. They might be confirmed in their death or they might pass from death to life (II.2:15). Those who "took up" the offer received something (4:7; 14:36). Before the missionaries arrived they were "have nots"; now they were "haves."

If we could ask St. Paul how he would account for the change, he could give only one answer. He had preached the gospel. This was his most important task. His medium was language uttered by the human voice. With such an instrument there were many possibilities open to him. He might have sought to demonstrate, to prove; or he might simply have revealed, relying on proclamation.[62] He chose the latter course. He did not weave arguments like a skilled philosopher and he did not seek to win men with the linguistic embellishments of a polished orator. He had a secret weapon which was effective in persuading men (1:17; 2:1–5). (For other references to preaching the gospel, see 9:14; II.10:14–16; 11:4.) The seriousness with which Paul carried out his mission of proclamation, and indeed the devotion, is attested by the dangers he was willing to encounter. He proclaimed and he testified, whatever the cost (4:9–13; 15:30–32; II.6:4–10).

What did the apostle actually say when he preached the gospel? He has not given us detailed sermons but he has outlined the important "points" which must be included in any evangelistic sermon. Note the justification for this remark. "I make known to you, brethren, the gospel which I preached to you as gospel. . . . For I delivered to you especially [*en prōtois*—Vulg. *in primis*] . . . that . . ." (15:1–8). We may arrange his points as follows:

Christ died for our sins according to the scriptures.
He was buried. (His death was real.)

---

62. Cf. Anders Nygren, *Agape and Eros*, 1:59.

He has been raised (perf. tense and therefore is still "up").

It happened on the third day.

It was according to the scriptures.

He appeared to Cephas, then to the Twelve (a title, not a number), then to over five hundred brethren at once . . . to James, to all the apostles, to the apostle Paul himself.

This includes history, doctrine, fulfilled prophecy, the possibility of confirmation from men still living, and personal experience and testimony. Such "gospel-preaching" is summed up in "the word of the cross" (1:17–18), or preaching Christ (II.1:19; 4:5; 11:4).

It should not be forgotten that preaching Christ or even preaching Jesus is not gospel preaching if it is no more than "synoptic preaching." The bare facts of history are indeed to be given, but they are inadequate apart from their interpretation. The preaching of the gospel demands the inclusion of answers to the questions of who he was and is and what he has done.[63]

The gospel is the gospel of God (II.11:7). It is also the Word of God (II.2:17; 4:2) and the manifestation of the truth (II.4:2; 6:7).

The preachers of the gospel are apostles (4:9–10), ministers of the new covenant (II.3:6; 4:1). They are the servants of Christ and stewards of God's mysteries (4:1; 9:17). The last figure is bold and suggestive. The steward does not own the property of his master but "manages" it or administers it, and he does so on his master's behalf. Paul can speak elsewhere of "my gospel" (Rom. 2:16; 16:25) but he does not thereby claim exclusive rights in it in the sense of owning it as personal property. He has indeed made it his own in his deep religious experience, and God has given to him his insights into its meaning and implications. But its owner is God, his "manager" must be one who can be trusted (1 Cor. 4:2) and he is accountable to him. The term "mysteries" suggests that when the apostle preaches he reveals what his listeners—or anyone else, come to that, outside the Christian faith—do not know and could not know, until the preacher of the gospel came to them.

Paul and his colleagues are God's co-workers (*sunergoi*, 3:9–11). Either they work with him; or they are working together, God's team, doing his work (16:10; II.1:19). Stewards do the work of their master. By a swift change of metaphors Paul characterizes the work. "We are God's coworkers; you are God's cultivated field [*geōrgion*], God's building" (3:9). The first word, *field*, suggests that there was a time when the area was just plain land and nothing else. Then the preachers came and were able to "sow the seed of eternal life in their hearts," as we pray in the marriage service. The Corinthians have been evangelized.

More remains to be done. They are God's building. First the foundation is laid, Jesus Christ. (This corresponds to the sowing.) But a building is more than its foundation. Others build upon it with their pastoral care and teaching. (This is parallel to the "watering" done by Apollos—3:6.)

Thus the Word, the message of the gospel, is preached and taught. Paul

---

63. Cf. Green, *Evangelism in the Early Church*, p. 64.

sows it (9:11) and the result of the sowing is the first fruits (16:15). He lays the foundation, i.e., he preaches Christ, and "the Word of his grace is able to build" (Acts 20:32). Without the preacher there would have been no harvest, no building. Yet the preacher is no mere dealer in words. Christ speaks in him (II.13:3). Men may put Christ to the test, as they did in the days of his flesh, and may even reject him. (Contrast the *dokimē*—proof—of II.13:3 with the *apodokimazō*—rejected—of Mark 8:31.) But they have to make their decision.

For Paul sought in his preaching to win men (9:19-27). Humanly speaking they had to be won. They were not to be coerced or mechanically manipulated. Through the preached message, foolish though it may seem, comes salvation (1:21). The day of salvation is now (II.6:2). Sometimes there is an open door into men's hearts and sometimes entrance is blocked (9:12; 16:9; II.2:12). The aim in preaching the gospel is to elicit the response which mediates salvation—faith (1:21; 15:2, 11). "Thus we preach and thus you took the step of faith."

Here we come to the heart of the subject. How do the hearers get the salvation to which we have referred? The preacher addresses the conscience (II.4:2) in what is a matter of life and death (II.2:15-16). If a positive response is received, he can say that his hearers have become his "product" (9:1). Paul here speaks of himself not as a man but as a preaching man. As such he has "produced" not men but believing men. In a different metaphor they are described as an "epistle" (II.3:2). But how did it all come about?

When he preached, the apostle offered a gift to his audience. He served the gospel banquet free of charge (9:18). It was not a "potluck supper" in which each "guest" brought his own supplies (4:7; 14:36). The gospel is a free gift (II.11:7), of indescribable worth (II.9:15). It is thus an "advantage" (10:33), for it brings enrichment (II.8:9). (Cf. I.1:4-7; II.6:10; 8:7; 9:8-11.) Though it is offered to men as a gift, its offer is accompanied by a little gentle pressure. The preacher does not violate the hearer's free will but on the other hand he does not leave the offer so "open" that he never tries to persuade. He does not speak in complete detachment. He does not leave the hearer to enjoy the liberty of indifference, as if he were Buridan's ass.[64] The gospel ought to be received (4:7; II.11:4; cf. II.6:1). Seeing that Christ is who he is, he ought to be obeyed (II.10:5). The gospel is a gift and it is also a command to be obeyed (cf. 2 Thess. 1:8).

Does the apostle then rely on the forcefulness of his character and of his utterance or on his sweetly persuasive powers? Has he mastered the problems of communication and of "hidden persuasion"? This is certainly not his method. He has what we have termed a secret weapon. As he visualized his evangelistic enterprise in Corinth, he could remember that though he himself employed the language of men it was God who had called his hearers into a participation in his Son (1:9). He bids the Corinthian brethren to "consider what happened when your call occurred" (Arndt-Gingrich, pp. 436-37). Henceforth they are *klētoi*, not exactly

---

64. Cf. Aristotle, *De Caelo*, II.13, 295 b 31-34.

"called" men (though they are such in fact) but "men with a vocation" (1:2, 24, 26; cf. 7:15–24).

The apostle's preaching was not secularized oratory. The human call is matched by the divine call. The preached cross has power (1:17–18, 23–24). It demonstrates the power of God, of Christ and of the Spirit (2:1–5; II.13:3–4). The living God owns the preached Word as his and convinces and calls the hearer.

Whatever duties the Christian is under obligation to perform in his daily "walk," the first characteristic response to the preaching of the gospel is faith. Paul and Apollos, great men as they undoubtedly were, are but servants "through whom you took the first step of faith" (3:5). The ingressive aorist is highly significant. (Cf. Rom 13:11, NEB, "when first we believed.") Wendland's text (p. 33) gives "durch die ihr gläubig geworden seid," "through whom you became believers." It is the use of the word *werden* which is significant. The hearers who had become believers were later told to test themselves to see if they were still in the faith (II.13:5). Preaching the gospel by one man and the believing response of the other are correlative (I.15:1–2—note the ingressive aorist; 15:11).

Paul probably includes repentance in the first step of faith. He certainly used the term (II.7:9–10; 12:21). A more convincing example is that given in II.3:16. A veil lies over the heart when the Old Testament is read, but "whenever a man (like Moses) turns to the Lord, the veil is removed." The allusion is to Exodus 34:34, LXX, but the verb (*epistrephō*) is taken from Exodus 34:31, LXX. Paul must be thinking of the moment of first faith in which a man "sees" the truth of God in Christ as he never saw it before. This is indeed taking the first step of faith, but *epistrephō* represents the Hebrew verb *shub*, "to return," i.e., to seek God penitently.

Given, then, that when the gospel is preached, a man believes: what happens? The answer is summed up in three aorists: washed, sanctified, justified (6:11). Paul has drawn a fearful picture of human sins and their consequences. "And such were some of you; but—washed; but—sanctified; but—justified." The contrast is vivid. The Corinthians had been on the road to exclusion from the kingdom of God; now, we must infer, they were going to inherit it. In Pauline thought the kingdom means righteousness, peace and joy in the Holy Spirit (Rom. 14:17). This combines the forensic and the mystical.

The three aorists of 1 Corinthians 6:11 indicate something done once for all rather than a process. The animated language rises in a crescendo: washed, sanctified, justified. "Washed" is negative. The earlier, ethical dirt disappeared. "Sanctified" moves forward. They were set apart for God. "justified" marks the climax. God accounted them righteous.

Paul's doctrine, which we have studied in its more elaborate form in the Epistle to the Romans, permeates the text. In particular it throws its weight backwards on to the two previous verbs. Had the Corinthians been washed? They were still not free from dirt: in this very paragraph Paul speaks of the wrong done by brother to brother (6:8). Had they been set apart for God? They were still fleshly, distant from God, mere men (3:1–4) and "walking" on the human level. (See note 13 in the chapter on Romans.

Not all the saints at Corinth were "saints.") But in spite of it all God deemed them righteous.

Paul's characteristic doctrine of justification by faith (see pp. 95–115) is shining through. This is not the only example by any means. It is implied in his contrast of the two covenants. The old covenant speaks of law, condemnation and death. The new one is not based on law but its watchwords are righteousness and the life-giving Spirit (II.3:6–9). The forensic and the mystical cannot be ruled out.

The false apostles are cunning laborers in the vineyard ("work" men, not "faith" men? cf. Phil. 3:2). They masquerade as apostles of Christ. As Satan's ministers they masquerade as ministers of righteousness (II.11:13–15). If Paul could regard himself as a minister of righteousness, it at least must make us wonder if this title is to be related to his doctrine of justification.

The doctrine is again suggested in II.5:21. On our behalf God made his sinless Son to be sin. His purpose was "in order that we might become the righteousness of God in him." The two nouns, sin and righteousness, balance each other. There is a further parallel: God made him sin—which he was not before the cross; his purpose was that we might become the righteousness of God—which we were not before our conversion. It was to be "in him"—and there was a time when we were not in Christ.

Now the righteousness of God which he purposed that we should become recalls the expression in Romans 3:21–23 (see p. 111), "the-righteousness-of-God-through-faith-in-Christ, (available) for all who believe." If a man believes, he receives it. Paul could say that it is imputed to him. He "possesses" what he did not possess before he believed. He is thus constituted righteous (*dikaios*, Rom. 5:19). Paul expresses this by the thought of our "becoming" the righteousness of God, using the noun as an appropriate contrast to the sin which our Lord was made.

Working in the opposite direction Paul can say that "Christ became for us wisdom from God, both righteousness and . . ." (1 Cor. 1:30). The Greek is deceptively simple and overlaps the constructions of Romans 7:13, "the good became death for me," and 1 Corinthians 4:5, "praise will (be) come from God for each man." The first example contains a predicate, "death" (corresponding to wisdom, righteousness); the second indicates origin, "from God," as in 1 Corinthians 1:30. It may be inferred that the source of righteousness is God (cf. "the righteousness of God," Rom. 3:21–22); that it comes to us through Christ; that we do not deserve it or earn it, as no flesh must glory in the presence of God (1 Cor. 1:29, 31); that in view of the context (1 Cor. 1:18–31) it is the righteousness of the cross (see also p. 103); and that each man will "get" it (like the praise, 1 Cor. 4:5) by imputation when he believes.

It would seem that the justification of Romans is present in Corinthians, by implication if not by exposition. At any rate Paul's language coheres with that of Romans.

There is some confirmation in the incompatibility of righteousness and lawlessness; of faith and unfaith (II.6:14–15); and in the summary description of the weapons of God's ministers as "weapons of righteousness"

(II.6:4, 7; cf. 10:3–4). The strongly ethical flavor of I.6:7–11, together with the use of *adikeō* and *adikos,* and the same flavor of II.9:9–10 (contrast Rom. 3:10, 12), add a little weight. As we have seen (p. 99), we cannot exclude the ethical from the concept of righteousness.

The evidence of the last paragraph may not amount to much in itself, but it goes along with the rest.

The view that Paul's doctrine of justification may be traced in Corinthians receives a measure of confirmation if his opponents there were Judaizers. Kümmel prefers to call them "Palestinian opponents of the Pauline mission and apostolic dignity." C. K. Barrett's discussion, however, points to Judaizers, not "pure Judaizers" indeed, as in Galatia, but still Judaizers. Paul sees in Jesus the fulfillment of the law; the Judaizers insist on legalism; hence the dispute. It may be that the opponents in question appear only in part of the Corinthian correspondence, particularly in the Second Epistle, but it hardly invalidates the argument. Paul's defense of justification by faith against legalism did not mean that he had adopted a new cause.[65]

The Corinthians, then, believed and were justified. At the same time they were sanctified. (The reference is still to 1 Cor. 6:11.) Paul writes to "the church of God in Corinth, men who have been sanctified in Christ Jesus" (1.2). They have been sanctified (perfect) or made holy; they *are* now therefore *holy.* Hence they can be called "men holy by vocation" (*hagioi*). In a reference to "all the churches of the holy ones" (14:33) Paul implies that the churches consist of holy men: the genitive is one of "material."

"Holy" does not primarily imply that men so described are of good moral character. They are rather in a certain state. "They are separated from what is profane and set in a consecrated state . . . Sanctification is not moral action on the part of man, but a divinely effected state." [66] "Holy" is thus a cultic concept. According to Procksch, Paul "maintains but spiritualises the cultic character of the holy" (p. 105). "As *hagioi* they are members of a cultic circle grounded in the sacrifice of Christ" (p. 107). "Neither in the OT nor the NT is the cultic basis of the *hagios* concept ever denied" (p. 110).

A rather unexpected illustration of the cultic appears in a passage which can be misinterpreted. In considering mixed marriages Paul affirms that the unbelieving spouse has been made holy and that the children of such a marriage are holy (7:14). The apostle does not mean that the unbeliever is saved merely by being married to a believer; nor has the reference to holy children any bearing on the rightness or wrongness of infant baptism. The "holy unbelievers" do not have the cultic qualification of approach to God. What then do they have?

As unbelievers they are strictly unholy and the unholy contaminates. Contact with the unholy spouse or parent might therefore be thought to contaminate the believer and take away the cultic qualification to approach God. This is not so, says Paul. The unholiness of unbelievers does not com-

---

65. Kümmel, *Introduction to the NT,* p. 209; C. K. Barrett, "Paul's Opponents in II Corinthians," pp. 238, 251.
66. Otto Procksch, *TDNT* 1:111–12; cf. H. Seebass, *Begriffslex.* 6:649.

municate itself to holy believers as a corpse communicates its uncleanness to those who touch it (cf. Lev. 10:10; 11:24; Num. 19:11). The unbelievers cannot "defile the sanctuary" (Num. 19:20). The temple of God, (the Corinthians believers, "you"), is holy (1 Cor. 3:17).

This truth is expressed by Paul's statement that the unbeliever "has been sanctified." He is thinking of persons but the thought is parallel to that of things. "Everything created by God is good, and nothing is to be rejected if received with thanksgiving; for it is made holy through the Word of God and prayer" (1 Tim. 4:4–5).

The believing spouse can thus go on living with the unbelieving spouse without fear of defilement by so doing, just as he or she can go on enjoying the good things of God's creation. In the same way the children of a mixed marriage cannot, in virtue of their being such, defile their believing parent.

Thus the holiness of the believer is impregnable. The *hagioi* have what Procksch calls "the static morality of innocence . . . closely linked with cultic qualification" (p. 109). If we think of Christian morality, which is active rather than static, we must say that it "does not arise on the basis of new action but on that of a new state which is best expressed as *hagiasmos*" (p. 108).

For Christ is our sanctification (1:30). We are not holy in ourselves. There was a time when we were not holy. We became holy because God called us and we responded in faith to his call. We are thus "holy by vocation" (1:2). Such an experience of becoming holy gives us a cultic qualification to draw near to God. This has points of contact with the Epistle to the Hebrews, though no mention is made of Christ as the High Priest. It is also analogous to justification. Christ is our righteousness, and we receive it when we believe; Christ is our holiness and we likewise receive it when we respond in faith to the divine call.

But are we in fact "morally innocent"? It would seem that as justification speaks of what goes on in the divine mind, which imputes righteousness to the man who believes, so likewise God regards as holy, as having a cultic qualification to approach him, the man who responds to his call. The concomitants must indeed be added; but this is the starting point.

The holiness which the believer receives in Christ and which in itself "qualifies" him to approach God has to be "completed" by his own moral action. It does not add to his "qualification." It is a practical and seemly outworking of the gift of cultic holiness. The believer, as holy, should become what he is. Thus "having these promises, beloved, let us purify ourselves from every defilement of flesh and spirit, completing holiness in the fear of God" (II.7:1). The unmarried woman whom Paul has in mind does precisely this. Instead of being concerned for the interests of the world, represented by a husband to be pleased, she is concerned for the Lord's work, "in order that she may go on being holy in both body and spirit" (7:34). She is holy in God's sight and he has received her; she manifests holiness in moral activity. Without the former even the latter activity would not be holy.

The parallelism might be expressed thus: she has been deemed righteous and she now serves righteousness; she has been given holiness and she now lives in a holy manner. The two concepts are brought together in Romans 6:19. ". . . yield (your bodies) to the service of righteousness, making for a holy life" (Rom. 6:19, NEB).[67]

When the Corinthians first believed they were justified and sanctified. They were also "washed" (1 Cor. 6:11). The middle voice suggests that they "got themselves washed." It is a somewhat inelegant expression but it reminds us of the personal interest of the subject. A comparison is sometimes made with the German *sich lassen*. The rendering "let yourselves be washed" has its dangers. It could imply that they submitted to the washing or just tolerated it—like "let yourselves be wronged" (6:7). The personal interest in fact was their initial faith.

This, rather than baptism, is the key to the interpretation. As Dr. Dunn says, "Paul is not talking about baptism at all." The man who was not sent to baptize (1:17) would hardly seize on baptism as his first thought in such a momentous context. To this must be added a fact to which White draws attention, the "curious reluctance of the apostles to baptise." [68]

The "washing" is sometimes taken (as by White, p. 202) as an experience of "a total moral transformation" (cf. Acts 22:16). The aorist tense leaves open the question of whether the transformation was maintained. "You have been washed," perfect tense, implies that "you are now clean." The bare aorist, "you were washed," would allow us to say with regret, "but you have become dirty again." This is what had happened at Corinth. In this very chapter Paul utters a rebuke (6:5; cf. p. 190).

Great issues are at stake. It is a question of inheriting the kingdom of God. Paul's animated language does not suggest that his readers have lost the privilege which they had gained when they first believed. Clearly something more than moral transformation is involved. His gospel does indeed bring such a transformation, but it is not this which opens the kingdom of heaven. The kingdom is righteousness and peace and joy in the Holy Ghost (Rom. 14:17). The believing response to the preaching of the gospel is met with the gift of righteousness and peace with God, and joy grows as the believer walks with God. The forensic and the mystical are united.

What then are we to understand by the "washing"? Paul is using an Old Testament idea figuratively and spiritually. He had preached the Word of the cross—the kingdom of God (cf. Acts 20:24–25)—and it was the power of God (1 Cor. 1:18, 24; 2:4–5; cf. 4:20). The Corinthians had believed. It was as if they had been washed, for such an "Old Testament" purification did its work. It "set man in the necessary state of holiness for encounter with God" (F. Hauck, *TDNT* 3:416). (For the purposes of illustration, cf. Lev. 11:32, 40, LXX.) Those who have traveled this road will know that encounter with God is not difficult to relate to inheriting or entering the kingdom. Faith qualifies the believer. God is ready to receive him.

Because of their fearful sins some of the Corinthians had been disquali-

---

67. With regard to 1 Cor. 7:14 and 1 Tim. 4:4–5 it may be felt that the unbelieving spouse is made holy, i.e. unable to contaminate the holiness of the believing spouse, by the believer's firm grasp of the Word of God and by constant prayer.

68. Dunn, *Baptism in the Holy Spirit*, p. 121; R. E. O. White, *The Biblical Doctrine of Initiation*, p. 114.

fied from inheriting the kingdom of God. When they believed in Jesus their disqualification was removed, they received the gift of holiness which was their qualification and God deemed them righteous. Ultimately it all expresses what took place in the divine mind. God no longer looked on their sins; God was ready to receive them; and he deemed them righteous. His attitude was determined by the Name of the Lord Jesus Christ, which the Corinthians invoked when they first believed, and still invoke (1:2). His Name means Jesus Christ himself, revealed to the Corinthians and present to them "by the Spirit of our God."

Automatically to refer such language to baptism, especially in the conditions of today, is "a sad commentary on the poverty of our own immediate experience." [69]

The finished work of Christ is preached to men and we must summarize our results so far. In what is a matter of life and death—or rather, as alternatives, of life or death—the conscience is addressed by the preacher and in the gospel a gift is offered. It is not merely the preacher who speaks but Christ speaks in him. A call from God is heard and the obedient response of faith is elicited. When the hearer thus first believes, he is washed, sanctified, justified.

We have seen that justification sets up a permanent relationship. This is reflected in the apostle's language. Each convert had been betrothed to Christ (II.11:2). Life with the "husband" should continue. At conversion, blind eyes had been made to see, and it was like the coming of the dawn—with the whole day to follow (II.4:3–4). It is expected that the converts will continue in the faith, with Jesus Christ in them (II.13:5).

At his first faith the convert is presented to God (cf. 8:8), and at our resurrection God will bring us into his presence (II.4:14)—the permanent relationship again. The convert is presented—and accepted (II.6:2, 16–17).

With all this, but to be distinguished from it, come the concomitants. When he first believes, the convert is reconciled to the already reconciled God (II.5:18, 20). He is joined to the Lord (6:15–17) and his experience is renewed when later he gives himself to the Lord (II.8:5). The Lord is his King (cf. 15:24–25) and he should seek to please Him (7:32). God adopts him and he knows it in his experience: "I will be to you as Father" (II.6:18). The language is not so rich as in Romans 8:14–17 but the central thought is clear. On the other hand Paul does explicitly say, "You will be to me as sons *and daughters.*" The new filial consciousness is a blessing for women as well as men.

The *new* consciousness: for they themselves are new. Paul is himself their spiritual father. Through the preaching of the gospel they were born. They do not have a plurality of fathers. Paul alone "begat" them in Christ Jesus (4:14–15). They thus became "babes in Christ," needing a diet suitable to their age and condition (3:1–2). So new are they that Paul can speak of a "new creation" (II.5:17). He may mean that the convert rubs his eyes like a man who has just emerged from darkness into the blaze of day. Everything is bright. Everything is new. Whereas before he had merely gazed on the physical world, the land itself as untenanted as the

---

69. Dunn, *Baptism in the Holy Spirit,* pp. 225–26.

sky above, now he gazes on his Father's world. The soft green and the colors of the countryside he now beholds with "pure eyes and Christian heart" (John Keble). All is lovelier than it had ever been.

If this is the apostle's meaning, it only draws out the consequences of what had happened to the man himself. He would not have gazed differently if he himself had not become different. Hence Paul may mean that if a man has so changed that he is now in Christ, he himself is a new creation. Everything, the recent experience involved in his first faith and the universe itself, can only come from God himself (II.5:18). This coheres with Pauline thought. The God who at the creation called light into existence by his spoken Word is the God who shone creatively in our hearts (II.4:6). The new birth is no less than a new creation.

Within such a man God dwells. We have thus passed in thought, though not in experience, from pure justification, an activity of the divine Mind.[70] He has become part of the temple of God (3:16–17). Christ is in him (II.13:5). God has given the Holy Spirit to the believing community, to its constituent individuals, for he is "in our hearts" (II.1:22; 5:5). See also 6:19; II.6:16; 11:4.

The genuine convert has freedom and is progressively "transfigured" (II.3:17–18). He should grow to maturity (2:6), avoiding "fleshliness" (3:1–3) and childishness (14:20). Faith should increase rather than diminish (II.10:15) and prayer should be planned and unhurried (7:5). There is apostolic example to be observed and teaching to be received (4:16–17). Profit may be derived from true preaching and teaching. It does not enslave but liberates; it feeds rather than devours. It does not capture but captivates. It comes humbly rather than arrogantly. When false teachers bully, the true preacher pours in oil and wine (II.11:20). Attendance at the Lord's Supper should be regular, preceded by self-examination (11:20–22, 24–25, 28) and the church should not be despised. Everything should be done for the glory of God (10:31). The imitation of Christ may be seen in the life of the apostle (11:1).

The new Christian may look for the peace of God constantly (II.1:2; 13:11), and indeed for the unceasing inflowing of blessing from God, Father, Son and Holy Spirit (II.13:13). He may thus have confidence: no accusations will be made against him in the Day of Judgment (1:8–9), for God is faithful. Even the "unsuccessful" Christian worker, even the Christian who has fallen deeply into sin, may hope (3:15; 5:5).

There is a ministry in the church to aid the convert (12:28–31) and a service to be rendered if he is "gifted." All, whether having or lacking "gifts," have before them a program of Christian love (ch. 13). It is a love to be exercised by men in Christ, who is their Mediator (8:6; II.1:20; 3:4; 5:18).

---

70. Cf. Wendland, pp. 201–2; ". . . so ist er eine neue Schöpfung. . . . die, die in Christus eine neue Kreatur geworden sind." "He is a new creation . . . those who in Christ have become a new creature."

# 5

## The Epistles
## to the Thessalonians

In the city of Falkirk in Scotland there used to be an association (and perhaps still is) for the distribution of tracts. This kind of work has often been regarded as one of the simpler forms of "church work" or Christian service. The more highly educated tend to neglect it, naturally enough, and the "superior" people may look down on it. In consequence the tracts are distributed by those whose main qualification is their loyalty and faithfulness. They get little recognition and no reward.

But on the occasion of their annual meeting they once had a visit from Professor H. R. Mackintosh (1870–1936) of Edinburgh. He spoke to them of the glory of their work. It was more than merely going from door to door in drab streets and putting pieces of paper through shabby letter boxes. They were offering gifts of immeasurable worth which would never lose their value or their luster. Mackintosh set the whole enterprise in its right perspective. Smiling faces and warm hearts attested the encouragement given by an eminent theologian to plodding disciples.

It may well be that Mackintosh availed himself of a statement made by Rainy, just as he used it in the Preface to his *Christian Experience of Forgiveness*. "The longer I live," said Rainy, "the more important and wonderful does the forgiveness of sins seem to me." If Mackintosh spoke on these lines, sooner or later he would bring in the cross. Thus we have a simple outline: sin, the cross, forgiveness—and the distribution of tracts.

A little imagination will suggest the way in which the address could have been developed, and how the content of the tracts gave a glory to their distribution. I do not know if the manuscript has survived but let us suppose that it did; and that it came into the hands of a biblical scholar or theologian. What should we think of him if he seriously contended that the address was the least dogmatic of all the writings of Mackintosh and lacked his distinctive touch? Or that it gave no systematic instruction and was devoid of originality and significant doctrinal ideas? Or that at best it contains no more than a first sketch of the doctrine associated with H. R. Mackintosh?[1]

We should very properly reply that the criticism was misconceived. Mackintosh was not lecturing on his distinctive theological ideas and still less was he writing a book. He was giving an address to encourage Christian workers. He did not elaborate his doctrine and yet the truths he most firmly believed must have shone through, in whole or in part. Those who knew him from his writings recognized him in the speaker. Professor and preacher were one man.

This rough analogy should help us to understand the Epistles to the Thessalonians. St. Paul was not writing a system of doctrine but giving encouragement and guidance to people who were young in the faith and whose eschatological expectation had become "overheated" (Kümmel). The epistles may be regarded as warm and intimate written "addresses," and it would be strange if Paul's characteristic doctrines did not shine through. At any rate we shall try to detect them. Behind a simple statement we may sense a more complex doctrine. The epistles may be but the shadow of a substance. The "pattern" may correspond to what we have found before.

## THE NATURE OF GOD

We proceed, then, to investigate the "incidental" expressions of doctrine in the Epistles to the Thessalonians. To begin with we find that Paul believes that God is *the living God*. When he preached to the Thessalonians they turned from idols to God (1:9). This in itself would prove the point. The plurality of dead objects of worship is in vivid contrast to the one, living God. But Paul goes further. Their conversion was not an absolute end in itself. They were to serve the "living and true God." "True" here means "genuine." It is implied that when the converts turned to him they did not come to a substitute God or to an inferior one. They turned to the One who really was and is—God. Thus the living God is *the one God*.

Further proof is indirect. Paul is deeply aware of being in God's presence (1:3; 3:9). He renders thanksgiving to him (1:2; 2:13; 3:9). Men ought to give thanks (II.1:3; 2:13) and Paul tells his readers to fulfill this duty for it is the will of God (5:18).[2]

God teaches (4:9), tests and approves (2:4). He witnesses (2:5, 10) and he loves (1:4; cf. II.2:13). He called (4:7; II.2:14) and he continues to call (2:12), and he is faithful (5:24).

God could hardly do all this if he were not *conscious mind*. To test or

---

1. Cf. George Milligan, *Thessalonians*, pp. lxiii f.; Kümmel, *Introduction to the New Testament*, p. 185. (Where the author's name only is given, the reference is to his commentary on the Thessalonian Epistles.) I owe the story of the Falkirk visit to Dr. F. Cawley. The glow with which he told it attested the impact made by the professor's visit and address.

2. References to the Thessalonian Epistles are given thus: when we refer to the First Epistle, only chapter and verse are given, e.g., 1:3; references to the Second Epistle are shown thus, II.1:3.

to approve is a mental activity. He has the power of choice: Paul speaks of election (1:4). God chose the Thessalonians for salvation (II.2:13) and his "keeping" is not a mechanical device (5:23–24). *God has will* (4:3; 5:18) and the long range of election points to *purpose*. God's purpose is both negative and positive (cf. A. L. Moore, pp. 77–78, 108). "God did not appoint us, destine us, for wrath but for the acquisition of salvation" (5:9–10). There is purpose in his call (II.2:14).

God is no mere theorist. He is not like a scientific genius who is frustrated by a government's unwillingness to grant funds for the expression and application of his knowledge. *God has power.* This is active in both the physical and the spiritual realm. Paul prays that God will "direct our journeying to you" (3:11). He asks for prayer that "we may be rescued from odd and evil men" (II.3:2). At the Parousia "the Lord himself . . . will come down from heaven" and "God will bring with Jesus those who fell asleep through him" (4:14, 16). We must not be slaves to literality but this must not blind us to the implications of Paul's language. Whatever eventually "happens," God manifests a mastery over the physical universe.

As Moore points out (p. 70), it is being keenly debated whether the imagery is suitable or sensible any longer. What must never be forgotten, especially by those who reject the imagery out of hand, is that an assumption is being made. It is constantly assumed, probably unconsciously, that at the Parousia the existing laws of nature will persist. How do we know? They are not necessarily eternal. And if a new heaven and a new earth are in process of formation, what right have we to assume that the old laws of nature will be again utilized by God? He might have other plans. In the meantime we should be willing to learn from the apostle's "notably restrained and unspeculative" language.

God has power in the spiritual world also. He effectively calls men (and they are converted), using the preaching of the gospel as his instrument (4:7: II.2:14). The preaching is speech but it is not mere speech. Through the influence of the Holy Spirit it becomes power, power to convert (1:5, 9). God teaches his people (4:9) and they learn (4:10). He can sanctify and keep them. He is to be trusted because he can and will act (5:23–24). He can comfort, encourage and strengthen (II.2:16–17).

In character *God is holy.* His Spirit whom he gives is the Holy Spirit (4:7–8) and it is his will that his people should be holy (4:3). Paul prays for their entire sanctification (5:23) even in the presence of God (3:13). Their characteristic name is "holy ones" (II.1:10) and even their mutual kiss of greeting is to be holy (5:26).

*God is righteous* for his judgment is righteous (II.1:5–6). His righteousness is reflected or implied in the concept of lawlessness (*anomia*) and unrighteousness (*adikia*)[3] and the consequent judgment (II.2:3, 7–8, 10, 12). Paul must have spoken at length on this subject during his stay in the city of the Thessalonians (II.2:5). It would not be difficult to make a connection with his teaching in the Epistle to the Romans. As holy and righteous, *God is trustworthy.* He is to be believed and trusted (5:24).

*God is not known by men* (4:5) though he ought to be known (II.1:8). Those who do not acknowledge him are to be punished. Their ignorance is blameworthy (cf. Rom. 1:28). It is manifested in idolatry (1 Thess. 1:9) and is vividly crystallized in the man of lawlessness (II.2:4).

If God ought to be known but is not, something has gone wrong. Paul speaks of "the tempter" (3:5) and of Satan (2:18; II.2:9). He is without doubt "the evil one" from whom we are to be guarded (II.3:3). We have already noticed lawlessness and unrighteousness. It remains to take the last, short step and speak of sin. *God is sinned against.* The concrete expression is "sins" (2:16). We might add the references II.2:4, 7. Sin is impiety, specifically against God; unrighteousness can be sin against men. Sin is a "setting aside" of God (4:8).[3]

God's knowledge of what is going on, particularly in the affairs of men, is not bare observation even when it extends to the secret thoughts and plans of the heart. *God has an attitude.* The Thessalonian Christians should "walk worthily of God" (2:12). He will undoubtedly observe their walk, but if he did not approve or disapprove, if he were entirely neutral, it would not matter whether they walked worthily or not. As a matter of fact he approves after testing (2:4). Paul speaks the Word, aware, conscious, believing that (*hōs,* subjective) he is pleasing God. Men ought to please God (4:1) though some do not (2:15). *God is pleased or displeased.*

The concept of displeasure merges into that of wrath. *God is a God of wrath.* He does not merely feel displeasure: He acts. Paul speaks of "the coming wrath" (1:10), the final, eschatological wrath. It is proleptically active in history (2:16). (Cf. A. Oepke, p. 165).

Associated with wrath (cf. p. 87) is *judgment* (II.1:5; 2:12), *the Day of the Lord* (5:2; II.2:2), *punishment* (4:6; II.1:6, 8–9; 2:11; cf. Rom. 1:21, 28) and *destruction* (5:3; II.1:9; 2:3, 8, 10).

## THE OTHER SIDE—GOD FOR MAN

Though the detail may not be so great, this follows the pattern of Pauline thought so far. And once more there is "another side." *God is the God who loves* (1:4; II.3:5). He is *the God of grace* (II.1:2, 12). The gracious God is *the God of peace* (5:23). He is *God the Father* (1:1; II.1:2). In some sense he gives grace and peace, for both are "from" him. God is not only "the Father." Paul can speak more intimately of "God our Father" (1:3; 3:11, 13; II.1:1; 2:16). He is *the God who is to be thanked* (1:2; 5:18; II.1:3; 2:13). In regarding God as thankworthy Paul is not manifesting an attitude which, to say the least, is characteristic of men who know themselves to be the objects of God's wrath, to be under his judgment, to be liable to punishment, to destruction.

The severity and the kindness of God (Rom. 11:22) are not irreconcilable. The Thessalonian epistles do not give us the fullness of treatment which we find in Romans, but at the same time we can see through them the stamp of the Roman mind. They suggest or at least are in line with our former distinction of what God has done for us in Christ and what he does in us.

---

3. Cf. Moore, p. 105; J. A. Ziesler, *The Meaning of Righteousness in Paul,* p. 213.

## God at Work for Us—The Work of Christ for Us

To begin with, God has a Son (1:10). He is in heaven but there was a time when he was on earth. He is Jesus and the Jews killed him (2:15). The human name and the human death cohere with the doctrine of the incarnation (cf. 4:14). The death of Jesus was no ordinary death. Though in part it was due to human violence—which in itself is becoming "ordinary" in these violent days—the *passio*, the suffering, the "having something done to you," does not exhaust its significance. Jesus Christ "died for us" (5:9–11). Through him, crucified, we benefit.

Three "benefits" are suggested by the apostle, the avoidance of wrath and the obtaining of salvation and of life. The statement that God did not destine us for wrath is given in explanation of the "understood" affirmation, "the hope of salvation is not a vain hope." The explanation is important. It is not a mere truism, a self-evident truth which is so obvious that it does not matter whether it is stated or not. If a man said that "God has not decreed that we should have twenty-four hours of darkness every day," it would be true but hardly worth saying. We all know it. But if he were trapped underground with some fellow miners and suddenly said that "we are not doomed to unceasing darkness. Thank God I see a light," he would be introducing a new factor. Through Christ crucified there is a way of escape from wrath. The new factor came in with him.

The "hope of salvation" is eschatological and corresponds to the "coming wrath" from which Jesus is the Deliverer (1:10). The structure of 5:9–10 should be noted. It may be set out thus:

God destined us (not for wrath but)
    for the acquisition of salvation through our Lord Jesus Christ,
      (through) the One who died for us in order that . . . we might gain
    life (ingressive) together with him.

The *hina*, "in order that," is introduced by "died." The purpose of our Lord's death was that we might live. But all this is part of a larger purpose expressed by "God destined us."

It may thus be inferred that the salvation of men was the purpose of God and of Christ; that it is made possible through Christ crucified; that in some way the wrath of God is dealt with; and that Christ still lives. There is not too much "theory" here with regard to the death of Christ. But the reference to it "in this almost passing manner," as Moore suggests (p. 78), points to the probability if not the certainty that "it must have been well understood by the converts." Paul's use of the word *wrath* indicates that the converts' understanding might very well have grasped the pattern which we have seen unfolded in Romans. The wrath of God did not just melt away. Indeed it is still "the coming wrath" but it is not coming to us for Jesus is our Deliverer. And our deliverance is linked to the cross, for he is the One whom God "raised from the dead" (1:10). This explains why we can "live together with him" (5:10).

"Jesus died and rose" (4:14). His presence in heaven (1:10; II.1:7) implies the ascension. In God's good time the Parousia will take place (2:19;

3:13; 4:15–16; 5:23; II.2:1–2, 8). This "historical" pattern is the basis of the soteriological one. The motive of the cross is the love of Christ and of God (II.2:16–17). (For a similar use of a singular verb with a plural subject, Father and Son, cf. 3:11.) The aorist, "loved," does not mean that the divine love has ceased (cf. the perfect "having been loved by the Lord," II.2:13) but it points to the one "punctiliar" act, the cross. The fact that Paul can use the word *ekdikos* of God (cf. Ps. 93:1, LXX), "the Lord punishes" (4:6, NEB; cf. II.1:8), is not without value as a sign of his more elaborate doctrine.

## God at Work in Us—The Work of Christ in Us

The simple pattern of what God has done for us in Christ is not at variance with Paul's more detailed interpretation elsewhere. We must now pass on to his work in us.

God's work in us begins with his word. *God has a Word*. It is spoken, heard and received and is active, not quiescent, in those who believe (2:13). This Word is the gospel. *God has a gospel*. The Word which the Thessalonians received, and which in turn had been sounded forth from them, was "our gospel" (1:5–6, 8). It was "the gospel of God" (2:2, 8–9) for it brought good news about God. Its content is Christ and it is thus "the gospel of Christ" (3:2; II.1:8). It has authority because it should be obeyed.

It is God's will that the gospel should be made known in speech (2:2–4). In this work he has his "helpers" (*sunergos*), like Timothy (3:2), and the "apostles of Christ" (2:7). The "speech" does indeed consist of words but it is not mere speech. It came to the Thessalonian hearers in power and in the Spirit and produced deep conviction (1:5). The Holy Spirit himself was the medium whereby the "circuit" was completed and the gap between speaker and hearer was overleaped by the spark of the gospel (cf. Oepke, p. 161.)

When the preachers spoke, God spoke in and through them. The hearers felt the powerful pull of the Holy Spirit. To reject the message as mere human speech would be to reject God, because through the preached gospel God himself gave his call (4:7–8; II.2:14). When the Thessalonians not only heard the audible Word but received it, they turned from idols to God (1:9). They were converted. The verb (*epistrephō*), particularly as used in the aorist, means "a change in the sinner's relation with God" (Arndt-Gingrich, p. 301).

Now at this point we must ask how a man can become converted. He can abandon his idols, to be sure, but what further remains to be done? If the gospel has to be obeyed (II.1:8), the preachers must have issued some orders. What did they tell their hearers to do? They must have told them to receive the Word, which in fact they did. But what does this involve? It must mean at least that they believed what the preachers were saying. They *believed*, for example, *that* "Jesus died and rose" (4:14) and had "belief in the truth" (II.2:13).

So far this is purely intellectual. It is essential but in itself inadequate. Conversion is more than bare credence or intellectual assent. For Paul the great *sine qua non* is faith or trust. He even classifies men on its basis. "Not all men have faith" (II.3:2). This trust includes the propositional element [4] but it goes beyond it. It implies an attitude to Jesus. He died and rose and is therefore living. He is not merely One of whom the Thessalonians have heard. They are waiting for him to come from heaven (1:10) and are to comfort one another with the thought that they are to be ever with him (4:17–18). Faith is the characteristic mark of the Christian. He begins his Christian life with faith (II.1:10, note ingressive aorists of *pisteuō*). He and others like him are described as "believers"—one could wish that there were such a word as "trusters" (1:7; 2:10, 13). To be without faith is to be under judgment (II.2:12).

The last text affords a clue. If to be without faith is to be under judgment, because those who take pleasure in *adikia* are devoid of righteousness, we are not far from the thought of Romans. Faith would bring the gift of righteousness and for the believer the Day of Judgment is in the past. "There is no condemnation for those who are in Christ Jesus" (Rom. 8:1). This is true "now." Paul does not use the words *righteousness* or *justify* in Thessalonians, but the man who believed in justification by faith could write 2 Thessalonians 2:12 without being inconsistent.

Paul has preserved in Thessalonians the concomitants of justification. When a man puts his faith in Christ, God receives him, quickens him and adopts him.

The Thessalonians had turned from idols to God, to keep on serving the living and true God (1:9). Had he rejected them when they directed their faith, and themselves turned, *pros ton Theon?* The evidence does not suggest it. The believing church was "in God" (1:1; II.1:1). To be in Christ is to be in God. The brethren had been, and still were, loved by God (1:4, perfect). He gave to them his Holy Spirit (4:8). At the Parousia God will bring those who fell asleep through Jesus (4:14). He gives grace and peace to the Thessalonian believers (II.1:2). Paul prays that God will completely sanctify and keep them (5:23–24). He has plainly received those who had put their trust in him.

The Thessalonian believers had life. They were "sons of the light and sons of the day." In contrast to "the rest," they were to keep awake by effort and not be spiritually insensitive. They should manifest the sobriety of daylight, not the stupidity of nocturnal drunkenness. They have put on the Christian armor in readiness for the Christian warfare.

These are marks of life, quite appropriately. For Christ died for us in order that we might gain life with him (5:5–11). Note the "you all" in verse 5. The stress is no doubt on the continuing life of believers at the Parousia, but the ingressive aorist, "gain life," can hardly mean that Christian believers are dead until the Second Advent. The Thessalonians had shown at the earliest a vitality in their service of the living God (1:8–9).

---

4. Cf. Acts 8:37. I think that this is the only example in the New Testament of *pisteuō* with the accusative and infinitive—it is a *varia lectio!* This construction is a means of expressing reported or indirect speech, like our "I declare him to be an American." It shows that faith has a content.

The third concomitant is adoption. Paul does not use this term in Thessalonians but his language implies it or at the least accords with it. He speaks warmly and intimately of prayer in the presence of "our God and Father" (1:3). Over his journeying he can see the directing care of "our God and Father himself" (3:11). Even in the majesty of the Parousia he sees the presence of "our God and Father" (3:13). His love in Christ gave us an "eternal encouragement" (II.2:16). Those who are stricken with a natural nervousness or stage-fright in the hour of death or when they come more closely into his presence can be heartened by the long lasting encouragement of no less a person than "God our Father." To be in Christ is to be in God our Father (II.1:1). By contrast those who reject the gospel do not know him (II.1:8).

A factor which should be mentioned, though it is not a concomitant, is the divine election. Paul was certain that the Thessalonian Christians belonged to the elect. He does not see divine arbitrariness here. On the contrary they were "brethren beloved by God." He was assured of their election because he had the evidence for it (1:4). The gospel had come to them in power; they had received the Word amid circumstances which could have led them away from it. They had received it with much affliction. In spite of pressure they had received it—with joy—and in an exemplary way had proceeded to proclaim it far and wide. Their conversion was the first step in a life of service to God and of eager expectation of the Parousia (1:5–10).

Paul regards these as marks of election: a decisive reception of the Word, a new joy, a spontaneous start on the work of evangelism, sustained service to God and an eager and unsecular anticipation of the end of history.

The call of the Thessalonians through the gospel was the outcome of God's election. "God chose (them) . . . for salvation" (II.2:13). This is a cause for thanksgiving. Paul is not troubled by the alleged democratic idea that it is not "fair" for God to elect and call (cf. Rom. 8:30). He is deeply thankful to God for those whom he has clearly elected. He does not explicitly deal with the question of the nonelect, who in any case have refused the gospel (II.1:8; 2:10). Election is a doctrine to build up converted men, not a subject for abstract speculation.

We must now consider the concept of salvation. It is the opposite of wrath (5:9) which is expressed in destruction (II.2:10). It is not the natural possession of men because it has to be "acquired." It cannot be achieved by their own efforts: it is "through our Lord Jesus Christ." It is not so much through his life on earth in general or what he said (cf. 4:15)[5] as through his death. He "died for us" (5:10).

But though by his death our Lord did that which was essential if men are to be saved, they are not yet saved. They have to be told about it and they have to respond. Paul speaks of the Jews who "hinder us from speaking to the Gentiles that they might be saved" (2:16). We do not have to speculate about what the Gentiles were told and what they were told to do (1:5–10). Paul and his companions preached "the Word of the Lord,"

---

5. Cf. Joachim Jeremias, *Unknown Sayings of Jesus*, pp. 4–5, 64–67.

"our gospel," to the Thessalonian Gentiles, and they received it (2:13).
God had chosen them for salvation and had linked his election to their
response, "faith in the truth"; and through the preached gospel he had
called them into the experience of receiving it (II.2:13–14). Their election
to salvation was certified to Paul by their reception of the gospel which
offered it (1:4).

Paul can therefore speak of "the hope of salvation" (5:8–9). As we have
seen (p. 201), it is not a vain hope *because* God destined us to acquire it.
But when do we acquire it?

If the reception of salvation depends on our reception of the gospel, on
faith in Christ, it seems odd to suggest that men should believe now and
should receive "only" a hope, however certain, of a future salvation. Salvation is indeed eschatological, as Paul knows full well: "we shall be saved"
(Rom. 5:9–10). Salvation in all its fullness is reserved for the time when
"we shall be always with the Lord" (4:17).

But in the interim we do not merely wait. If salvation is the opposite of
wrath, we know that wrath is not to be our experience, which should be
the source of mutual encouragement (5:11). We know *now*, even as we
wait, that we are not now and shall not ever be under wrath. We trust in
Jesus, the One who delivers *(ton ruomenon)* us from the coming wrath
(1:10). I am not convinced that the verb is timeless, with the meaning of
"Deliverer," like "Savior" for *Sōtēr*. It has an object, "us," and it balances
the wrath "which is even now approaching." [6] The empirical (Rom. 1:18)
and the eschatological wrath may be summed up by saying that as it
comes it proceeds on its course but that Jesus constantly keeps it on a
course away from those who believe in him. (The metaphor is from
aircraft.) This is not yet the fullness of salvation; but such knowledge would
entitle the believer to say that he has received salvation in principle. The
details will be known later. The full enjoyment of being always with the
Lord is yet to be. In the meantime he is "in Christ." Could there be any
doubt of the salvation of a man who is in Christ?

At one time the Thessalonians were not in Christ. Now the believing
men in their city constituted a church (1:1; II.1:1). They resembled the
local churches in Judaea not only in being persecuted (which was Paul's
point, 2:14) but in being "in Christ." It is not strict exegesis but it would be
a reasonable insight to see that when they first believed they became the
righteousness of God, i.e., righteous, in Christ (cf. 2 Cor. 5:21, p. 191).

Being in Christ is long lasting. "The dead in Christ" will rise first (4:16). [7]
Even if Paul means that the dead will rise in Christ, it is the Christian dead,
"those who sleep." They fell asleep through him, they will rise in him and
God will bring them with him. If believing men have such a program

---

6. J. B. Lightfoot, *Notes on Epistles of St. Paul*, p. 17.

7. This grouping of the words is adopted by J. E. Frame as well as by J. B. Lightfoot, G. Milligan, A. L. Moore and A. Oepke. Jeremias, *Unknown Sayings*, p. 65, takes
the *en* of the phrase "in Christ" as instrumental and the whole phrase with the verb:
"the dead will rise through Christ." But the rule about the repetition of the article
is not absolute. Cf. Rom 6:4; 10:1. Would not the apostle use "in Christ" with its
normal meaning?

before them, and such a destiny, it cannot be wrong to say that salvation is theirs in principle. They have not tasted it all but it is theirs. The eschatological End will give them precisely what they have already: they will continue to be in Christ. They wait (1:10) for what they already possess.

This illustrates a fact which we have already noticed (p. 117), that justification sets up a new and permanent relationship between God and the believer. Paul does not say this in so many words but his language implies it. All our days Jesus is delivering us from wrath (1:10). The Thessalonians are described as "brethren having been loved by God" (1:4). The perfect tense, implying as it does the abiding result of a past act, can always be reexpressed as a present. Now a widow could say that "I have been loved" and mean that she has now, in the very present, an experience and a memory of being the object of affection. But God is not dead (1:9)! Paul must therefore mean something different.

Consider the following legitimate interpretations:

| | |
|---|---|
| I have been washed | I am now clean |
| I have been hit | I am now in pain |
| I have been tricked | I am now penniless |
| I have met Jones | I am now familiar with him |
| I have been out in the rain | I am now wet. |

By analogy we may say that "I have been loved" means that "I am now in the circle of affection." Paul therefore implies that the Thessalonian brethren are still in the circle of God's love but that, unlike the world, they know it and experience it, in an experience which can be deepened (II.3:5).

God still works in the lives of believing men, answering their prayers by delivering them from odd and evil men (II.3:2). He still calls, keeps, "comforts" and strengthens (5:23-24; II.2:16-17). The Holy Spirit is still operative (5:19-20). Faith still continues (3:6-8) and God still continues to regard the believer as righteous. There may be gaps in faith which must be mended (3:10) but faith grows (II.1:3). It is not its quantity but its direction which is important. It is God's will for his people that joy should be continued always, that no season of prayer should be left unobserved and that in every circumstance thanksgiving should not dry up (5:16-18). Christians are to encourage and "build" one another (4:18; 5:11)—with doctrinal tools. They have the prospect of finally being gathered together to Christ (4:17; II.2:1).

This cannot be other than a permanent relationship with God, set up when the Thessalonians first believed.

The Christians in Thessalonica constitute the local church (1:1; II.1:1). This is the context in which they encourage and "build" one another. Over them all is an elementary form of ministry for their pastoral care (5:12-13).

The reception of the gospel, or "first faith," is not the end of the matter but rather the beginning. The believers, who make up the church of the Thessalonians, form a closely knit fellowship in distinction from those outside (4:12). They have duties as well as inestimable privileges. God's Word is still active in them (2:13). Our Lord is to be glorified (II.1:12). Doctrinal purity is to be maintained (4:13; II.2:2); the consequences are practical (4:18; 5:11). The believers are to go on "standing" (3:8; II.2:15). They should please God, "walking worthily" in response to God's continued call (2:12; 4:1; II.1:5, 11). Their aim (for it is God's will) should be holiness (4:3, 7; cf. also 5:23; II.2:13).

Though uproar and disturbance are to be avoided (4:11), quiescence is not the ideal. Faith should work (1:3; II.1:11) as well as grow (II.1:3) and its works should be good in word as well as deed (II.2:17). The church should be marked by mutual love (4:9–10) in both the local assembly and the wider fellowship; indeed love should be extended to all men (3:12). Mutual love can and should increase (II.1:3). If faith should work, love should toil (1:3). Hope likewise should endure (1:3; II.1:4). Christians should not be "shook up" or lose their heads (NEB), or be put into a flutter (II.2:2), nor should they fawn upon, or be agitated by, their persecutors (3:3).

Peace should be maintained in the community of believers (5:13; cf. II.3:16), who should not endanger it by meddling or "interfering" as busybodies (II.3:11–12). Good relations ought to be kept with those outside the fellowship by a sturdy economic independence which commands respect (4:11–12). Christians should manifest a spiritual alertness and sobriety (5:6) and show respect and love towards the ministry (5:12–13). Either the ministers or the church in general [8] should admonish, encourage, help, without acting in undue haste. Retaliation is wrong; good must always be sought for all. The glow of the spiritual life should not grow cold, and it should be mingled with a cool, critical test of everything and the retention of what is good. Negative duty must not be forgotten. Evil of every kind is to be avoided. Apostolic teaching and exhortation is to be made known to all the members (5:14–27). Prayer and evangelism go together (1:8; II.3:1). Disobedience to the apostolic word is to be remedied by brotherly discipline (II.3:14–15). The community can thus deal with the individual (tis).

This general pattern in outline of Christ's work for us, in us and through us does not seem to clash with what we have already found in other epistles.

---

8. Does the "brethren" of 5:14 address the ministers? If so, should we translate "continue your admonitions (cf. v. 12) in the direction of the disorderly"?

# 6

# The Epistle
# to the Ephesians

IT IS NOT OUR PRESENT purpose here to become involved in questions of introduction. The authorship of Ephesians is a subject of keen debate and W. G. Kümmel gives impressive lists of distinguished scholars who support or deny Pauline authorship.

If Paul is not the author, the question of the purpose of the epistle—if it is an epistle—must inevitably be raised. E. J. Goodspeed's thesis has been very influential: the document is a covering letter for the Pauline corpus. C. L. Mitton has sympathetically followed Goodspeed and speaks (p. 266) of "a comprehensive summary of Paul's message." Others suggest a post-Pauline commendation of the apostle's doctrine.

These theories are not universally accepted. Thus after giving deservedly high praise to his successor's "monumental work," the late Dr. W. F. Howard could say that he "remains unconvinced." Yet certain facts seem palpably plain. "Ephesians . . . was acquainted with the totality of the Pauline epistles" (Kümmel). "Ephesians is intensely Pauline" (Howard). "The background of Pauline theology is unmistakable" (Guthrie). [1]

In the existing state of scholarship our best course is to examine Ephesians as it stands, bearing in mind the dictum that the meaning of words is to be determined by their use and context.

It may perhaps seem a rebuff to learn that in Ephesians the death of Christ no longer holds the central position. It is now one interest among others equally important. The primary place is held by the exaltation. [2] Even Guthrie speaks of "the small attention given to the death of Christ"

---

1. W. G. Kümmel, *Introduction to the New Testament*, pp. 247–58; Donald Guthrie, *New Testament Introduction: The Pauline Epistles*, pp. 99–139; E. J. Goodspeed, *The Key to Ephesians*; C. Leslie Mitton, *The Epistle to the Ephesians*; F. L. Cross, ed., *Studies in Ephesians*; the excerpts from W. F. Howard are taken from his review of Dr. Mitton's book in *The Methodist Recorder* of the 3rd April 1952.

2. So D. E. Nineham in Cross, ed., *Studies in Ephesians*, p. 34. See also Guthrie, *Pauline Epistles*, p. 109; Everett F. Harrison, *Introduction to the New Testament*, p. 315.

in the epistle. Harrison remarks that "even the Saviour's death is subordinated to His present exaltation."

It remains to be seen whether this kind of evaluation is unduly concerned with the space given to a subject or whether the death of Christ is to be regarded as a leaven which permeates the whole. It may be that certain expressions, allusions or even hints point to the dominating position which the cross held in the mind of the author.

The answer to this problem we must try to discover as we proceed. We must follow the method previously adopted and seek some pattern, some plan of salvation, if such be implied. We begin, as before, with a study of what Ephesians has to tell us about God.

## THE NATURE OF GOD

There is but *one God* (4:6). The past tenses of verbs show that at any rate in the past God was *the living God*. He blessed . . . elected . . . foreordained . . . "begraced" us (1:3–6) and raised and exalted Christ (1:20–22). He is still *the living God*. He is at work (1:11), he may still give (1:17), he may be approached (2:18) and he has his place of dwelling (2:22). Whatever its exegesis, the expression "the life of God" (4:18) at least points to the living God.

The one, living *God is eternal.* This is suggested rather than formally stated. We may look in the direction of a past eternity, and be reminded of our election "before the foundation of the world" (1:4). The mystery was hidden in God the Creator "for long ages" (3:9, NEB). The purpose of the ages was achieved in Christ Jesus (3:11). Glory is to be ascribed to God throughout a future eternity (3:21; cf. 1:21; 2:7).

In that he chose us (1:4), *God is free.* We were not, and are not, thrust upon him, like a waif on his doorstep, neglected, forsaken, repudiated. We are not unexpectedly "on his hands" as a problem regretfully to be solved. In utter freedom he chose us, influenced by nothing outside himself.

It follows that *God has will.* "The will of God" is mentioned several times (1:1, 5, 9, 11; 6:6). A long term will is a purpose. *God has purpose* (1:11; 3:11; perhaps 1:9). It may seem somewhat naïve to say that *God makes decisions,* but the language seems to imply it.

The first chapter of the epistle "is shot through with references to the will of God" and "we have the synonyms *eudokia, thelēma, prothesis* and *boulē.*" The counsel of his will "has the final word . . . sets in movement everything which in this whole section is described as the grace present in Christ. . . . " "The term [*eudokia*] cannot be separated from the *boulē*" and expresses "a special side of this pre-temporal resolve of the divine will . . . the content of this counsel as the free good-pleasure. . . . His gracious resolution to save." [3] The "decision" may be eternal. But it is a decision, a resolve, as "sets in motion" attests. The "good-pleasure" should not be associated with "hedonic tone." It marks God's favor to men rather than his own pleasurable feeling. Within the decision indicated by "sets in motion"

---

3. The quotations are conflated from Gottlob Schrenk, *TDNT* 1:635; 2:747.

we may distinguish, *from the human standpoint*, at least three subordinate decisions. In logical order they are linked with election, predestination (both pretemporal), and the historic sending of the Son. The grace present in Christ was not present until he came.

In exercising his will *God is wise* (1:8; 3:10). He not only "thinks" or *is conscious* and "decides." *God is active* (1:11) for *he has power* beyond our ability fully to describe, a power which he actualizes as and when he wills (1:19-22; 3:7, 20). In particular he exercised his power when he formed the world, for *God is the Creator* (3:9; cf. 1:4; 4:24). The aorist of 3:9 *(ktisanti)* tells of the "moment" when potentiality was turned into actuality. *God is transcendent, immanent, intimate* (4:6), and *he may be known* (1:17). It is true that God cannot be known unless he wills to be known. It is not true that God might will to be known but could not be known because of a quality in his own nature.

*God is righteous.* The word group is not used often in the epistle (4:24; 5:9; 6:1, 14) but the righteousness of God is implied. Obedience to parents is obedience to the commandment and is *dikaion* (6:1-2). The commandment is part of the law (2:15) and the law must have been given by God. This is not a wild assumption here. For one thing Christ annulled the law. Why should he have bothered to do so if it did not enshrine the majesty of divine origin? Secondly the epistle links human desire and will with disobedience, transgressions and sins (2:1-3). Sins are against God and transgressions are against the law. The sins *in* which men walked are *forbidden* territory.

If to obey the law is righteous and to break it is sin against God, it is hard to see how God can be other than righteous.

*God is holy.* His Spirit is holy (4:30) and holy is the temple in which God dwells (2:21-22). *God is infinitely blessed.* We have already covered this ground (p. 152) and it is hardly necessary to go over it again, at any rate in detail. The term *eulogētos* (1:3) "describes the intrinsic character. . . . God is blessed, as being the absolute and proper object of blessing" (Lightfoot, *Notes*, pp. 310-11).

*It follows that God is to be worshiped and to receive thanksgiving* (1:6, 12, 14; 3:21; 5:4, 20; cf. 1:16). I believe that Dr. Wheeler Robinson once said that it is possible to add to the glory of God. Kittel would deny this. To give glory to God "cannot possibly mean giving God something that he does not have. . . . it is . . . the extolling of what is" *(TDNT* 2:244, 248). Kittel is right. But Dr. Robinson certainly draws attention to the fact that a man can decline to worship. He does not diminish the divine glory and the worshiper does not add to it; but he does add to the sum of human praise.

*God is the Observer of the human scene.* The exhortation to Christians to walk worthily of their calling would be meaningless if God did not notice what they were doing (4:1). Slaves should render honest obedience to their human masters, not acting merely to catch their eye or to please it when they are being observed. They are Christ's slaves and should do the will of God. Each will get his appropriate reward (6:5-8). God knows when his will is done.

*God makes demands upon men.* This is implied by the very existence of

the law (2:15). Men do not keep his law and *God sustains disobedience.*
"Transgression" (1:7; 2:1, 5) is the breaking of a commandment; it is to be
disobedient (2:2; 5:6). It is but a short step further to say that *God is
sinned against* (2:1; cf. 4:26).

At this point we should observe that *God deals with individuals.* The
author himself is an example of this (3:1–3, 7–8; 6:19–20). To each one of
us was given grace and each should speak truth with his neighbor (4:7, 25).
Prayer is offered that the readers may be strengthened through the coming
of the Holy Spirit into the inward man. In experience this is the same
as Christ's taking up permanent residence in the heart—through faith
(3:16–17). This can only be individual, however mediated. It can happen
to a man on his knees in the company of others or in the solitude of his
room. It cannot happen to the community as a whole without happening
to the individual who believes in Christ and receives him. The desire and
will of the flesh, characteristic of distance from God, can only be individually exercised: I desire, I will (2:3, 13). However much we speak of "the
faith of thy church," faith ultimately means "me believing" (2:8; cf. 1:15
with *kata* distributive; the faith is in *each* of them). The behavior of the
husband or the wife must be individual (5:28). The illumination of the eyes
of the heart (? imagination, 1:18) must come to an individual. The
commandment is directed to each separate child to "honor *thy* father . . ."
(6:2). Each person, slave or free, will receive his reward (6:8).

## Man Against God

God, then, is sinned against. Sin may take the form of ethical failure in
word and deed, of social disunity and of immaturity (4:1–3, 13, 25–32;
5:3–5, 18). The immaturity suggested by 4:13–14 is confirmed by the
unproductiveness of 5:11. This is so far largely a matter of overt action
but it is inspired from within. There is an inner weakness (cf. 3:16) and
deception (4:22; 5:6) from which springs the self-assertiveness of desire
and will (2:3). Forbidden company *(en hois)* on forbidden territory
*(en hais,* 2:2) involves antagonisms (2:12, 15). For the mind of men is
marked by ignorance, darkness, futility, with the culminating insensibility
which issues in moral flashiness and all impurity. Man the sinner is essentially unrighteous, unholy, Godless (4:17–24; cf. 2:12). The absence of
God from the sinner's heart has given scope to the devil (4:27; 6:11). An
interesting illustration may be seen in Matthew 12:44. "Evil cannot be
effectively *barred* out; it has to be *crowded out by good*" [4]—by the in-
dwelling presence of God.

The *mataiotēs*—emptiness—of the sinful mind (4:17) marks a departure
from the norm and is thus analogous to unrighteousness. Its world is illusion
rather than reality. It lacks a solid foundation and a persistent and good
aim and may combine both wickedness and silliness. It has been well
summarized by Schlier. Such a man "considers only himself in his thinking

---

4. L. H. Marshall, *The Challenge of New Testament Ethics,* p. 73.

and thus makes futile, as a consequence of such futility, his thinking of himself and the world." [5]

## God Against Man

God observes the human scene and is sinned against. It should follow that *God has an attitude to sin*. This may be inferred from the fact of his mind and character. He is not a mental sensitive plate, as in the old cameras, or a tape, which merely records. Given his character, he must evaluate. The aim of blamelessness (*amōmos*, 1:4; 5:27) suggests what God's attitude is. *God makes charges against men.* For because of their sin *he is displeased with them.* This is the opposite of his pleasure in goodness, righteousness and truth (5:8–11). In God's sight men are blameworthy and he is displeased.

In consequence *God is unapproachable*. Sinful men are in the world (2:2, 12). This means more than that they are on earth. They are apart from God. This in turn is more than a mere mishap, the sad story of those who have strayed far from home. They are "far off" from God (2:13, 17) not only by their own act but by God's exclusion. This is stated with special reference to certain sins. No fornicator, for example, has inheritance in the kingdom (5:5). But the exclusion applies to sinners generally. If this were not so, there would be no point in saying that in certain conditions and only in certain conditions do we have "access" to God (2:18; 3:12). Apart from these the door is closed.

The unapproachableness of God is an expression of his wrath. He reacts against sin, "for the Divine wrath operates only where sin is" (S. D. F. Salmond, 3:287). Ephesians combines Hebrew and Greek categories in the expression "children of wrath by nature" (2:3). Brooke F. Westcott (p. 31)[6] cites Deuteronomy 25:2, "a son of beating," which Driver (*Deuteronomy* [ICC], p. 279) renders "worthy to be beaten"—"by a well-known Hebrew idiom." Sinners deserve the wrath of God and it "comes (regularly; or 'is coming, is on its way') upon [*epi* plus accusative][7] the sons of disobedience" (5:6). God may be described as a *God of wrath*.

Final wrath is anticipated in history. Already the old man "is being ruined," "is sinking towards death" (4:22, NEB). Indeed men are already "dead in trespasses and sins" (2:1, cf. v. 5).

## THE OTHER SIDE—GOD FOR MAN

This completes the outline of the character of God. Once again there is "another side." Mention is made of God's love (2:4; 6:23), his mercy (2:4)

---

5. Quoted by E. Tiedtke, *Begriffslex*, 8:847, 851. I am indebted to my friend Professor J. Jocz of Toronto for help in the translation of a very awkward piece of German. Cf. O. Bauernfeind, *TDNT* 4:519–24.

6. Where only the author's name is given, the reference is to his commentary on Ephesians.

7. "inimically." Cf. Moule, *Idiom Book*, p. 49, on 1 Peter 3:12.

and his grace (1:2, 6-7; 2:7; 3:2, 7). Kindness is not absent from him (2:7). In contrast to the recent "inimical" wrath we hear of peace (1:2; 6:23). Though we were thinking of "distance" and unapproachability, now we notice "access" and "in the heavenlies" (2:6). God is God the Father (5:20). He is the One who gives (1:17; 2:8; 3:2, 7) and his gifts may be sought in prayer to him (3:14-16).

## God at Work for Us—The Work of Christ for Us

These "contradictions" in the nature of God are resolved in Christ. We must now therefore consider his work *for* us as it is described in the epistle.

The author clearly regarded his work of preaching as the greatest privilege of his life (3:8). He desired his readers to pray for him, that speech might be given to him "when I open my mouth" 8 —to make known the mystery of the gospel, for which he is an ambassador (6:19-20). Before his listeners have heard a single word the preacher has something to tell them and give them—the unsearchable riches of Christ (3:8), "the gospel of your salvation" (1:13), the Word of God (6:17). It is the preacher's hope and prayer that his hearers will "learn Christ," not merely learn about him: will hear him speaking to them and will be taught in him. (Cf. 2 Cor. 13:3, "the Christ who speaks in me." Cf. Matt. 13:37-38.) We have in this passage (4:20-21) an approximation to *kerygma* and *didachē*.

But who is the subject of the preacher's message? Who is it who speaks in the preacher to the preacher's listeners? It is Christ. But who is he?

He is the Son of God (4:13). He did not begin his life on earth. We were chosen in him before the foundation of the world (1:4). This implies at the least his preexistence and probably his eternity. (But see H. Conzelmann, p. 60 note.) The great doctrines associated with Christmas, Good Friday, Easter and Ascension Day are implied. The Son of God became incarnate. How otherwise can we think of his flesh (2:14) or his blood (1:7; 2:13)? The blood points to the cross, which is explicitly mentioned in 2:16. The resurrection is included (1:20) and the ascension and exaltation is prominent (1:20-22; 4:8-10). In regard to 4:9 Westcott (p. 61) notes that our Lord's "pre-existence is assumed."

All God's blessings are summed up in him. We bless God in words of good; he blessed us in deeds of grace (1:3). He blessed us with all spiritual blessing in the heavenlies. We may feel the impact of these words if we write them as a secular sociologist would no doubt prefer them to have been written. "He blessed us with all material good on earth." From this clue we see that the heavenlies mark the "location" of the blessing and that the blessing is the divine "instrument." With what did God bless us? With money? With food? With breathtaking scenery? No. He blessed us with all spiritual blessing.

Now the concluding *en Christō* lends itself to the interpretation "namely, with Christ." God blessed us with all spiritual blessing, i.e., with Christ. All the blessing is summed up in him. The *en* thus starts by being instrumental

---

8. A secondary semitism. Moulton-Howard, *Grammar*, 2:21, 485.

but its meaning is not exhausted by the instrumental. The phrase has behind it or in it all the wealth of the formula "in Christ."

### Grace in Christ

There follows a vast sentence which has nothing to compare with it in the whole of Greek literature.[9] Conzelmann regards the whole passage up to verse 12 (? v. 14) as commentary on verse 3, or at any rate as capable of being so interpreted. Christ thus dominates the passage, and he is the mark, even the embodiment, of the grace of God. The inclusion of all the blessings in him recalls Paul's statement in Romans 8:32, perhaps the best commentary on Ephesians 1:3. God spared not his Son . . . and with him gives everything.

Without going into detailed exegesis at this point or considering, as Westcott does (p. 5), the rhythmical structure of 1:3–14, we may set out our points in summary form thus:

Election in Christ
Adoption through Christ
    to the praise of the glory of his grace . . .
Redemption through Christ
Forgiveness through Christ
    according to the riches of his grace
The floodgates of grace opened to us by making known to us . . .
    according to his good pleasure . . . in him
Recapitulation in Christ
Destination in Christ
    to our praise of his glory (manifesting grace)
    praise from us who have already hoped in Christ
Sealing in Christ
    to the praise of his glory (manifesting grace).

All the spiritual blessing, which is analyzed into distinct blessings, is related to Christ. If it were not for Christ we should not have the blessings; if it were not for Christ they would not even be available.

The blessings are the expression of the grace of God and the "progress" should be observed. First the grace is to be praised. Then it is measured— "the riches of his grace." "Riches" is a concept which combines value with plenty. A five dollar bill has value, but there is not much of it. Counterfeit bills representing a million dollars certainly offer plenty, but they have no value. "Riches" implies the valuable and abundance of it. The grace of God is of infinite worth and there is no lack. Next it is offered. God opened the floodgates of grace by making known to us the mystery of his will. Grace is available in Christ. This is in accordance with his good pleasure which he proposed in him. (The "offering" is implied by *eperisseusen*—"lavished," RSV, v. 8—if not by *proetheto*—"purposed," v. 9). Then it is received. Our lot is cast in Christ for our response in praise. Finally, as Christians look

---

9. Cf Conzelmann, pp. 59–60. "Es folgt ein wahres Ungetüm von Satz . . ."—"there follows a real monster of a sentence."

towards their long and certain future, we see grace, standing alone in loving majesty—to be praised.

The grace already described appears again in 3:2, 7. The grace of God is given. This confirms the thought of its being "offered." It is not bought or earned, which would be a contradiction in terms. And it is given to the author "for you." As he regards himself as an apostle (1:1) and a minister, he clearly has something for his listeners which they have not yet received and will not receive if he does not preach to them. In "preparing his sermon" —in order to transmit the grace—he can draw on 1:3–14. He would hardly begin an evangelistic sermon with the doctrine of election. Where would he start? For the moment we must leave the question in suspense. The answer may emerge shortly. (Cf. 4:7.)

Note that "the surpassing riches of his grace" consists in his "kindness toward us in Christ Jesus" (2:7).

The apostle's aim is to make known the mystery (which consists of) the gospel (6:19–20 genitive of material), and with all speed.[10] This must be the grace of God which had been given to him to transmit. The mystery which consists in Christ is for all, Gentiles as well as Jews. All are to share in the promise and it comes to them "through the gospel." The writer is a minister of the gospel "according to the free gift of the grace of God which was given to me"—for others, as he has already said. How does he transmit it to them? By God's grace he has been given the task of preaching as gospel the unsearchable riches which consist in Christ (3:1–8).

The apostle preaches in words and he thereby transmits grace, the gospel, Christ himself (4:20–21). Listeners to an authentic preacher hear "the Word of truth, the gospel of your salvation" (1:13).

To this may be linked the antecedent mercy (*eleos*) and love (*agapē*) of God. God is "rich in mercy." Again we have the concept of wealth. Mercy is valuable and God has much of it. Similarly his love is plenteous (*pollēn*). Note the expression, "his ample love with which he loved us" (2:4). The present tense would surely not offend; but the aorist is chosen (*ēgapēsen*) because the author's eye looks backwards to the historic Christ and what he has done. In him the mercy and love of God were expressed and embodied, particularly in the cross.[11] The burden of the preacher's message is not therefore the exhortation, "Be quickened; be raised; be seated" (2:4–6). These events take place, when they take place, because of the response of faith to God's prior mercy and love. It is because God is rich in mercy (causal participle) and because of (*dia* plus accusative) his great love that the preacher has a message at all. He must first preach the mercy and love; he must first preach grace and gospel; he must first preach Christ. These are

---

10. See 6:15, "feet shod with the *hetoimasia* of the gospel of peace." The phrase suggests a swift mobility. Conzelmann (p. 89) translates by "Bereitschaft," a word in police circles meaning "squad." This no doubt corresponds to our Flying Squad, "ready to go" at a moment's notice. The preacher will observe the possibilities of illustration.

11. In Christ we were "begraced" and in him we have redemption; and it is not only in accordance with his grace, God's grace; it is in accordance with the riches of his grace (1:5–7).

sure and objective facts. The quickening, the rising and the session are contingent.

If then the spiritual blessing, the grace and the gospel are summed up in Christ, we should ask the question, "What is it which Christ precisely did?"

## The Love of Christ

First we should observe that "Christ loved" us (5:2). Again we have the significant aorist tense. Does he not still love us? Assuredly he does; but the context points to the cross, the quintessence of his love. Its majestic range is not indeed forgotten (3:19) but its focus is the cross. God's love was manifested in Christ's loving act—for us (cf. 5:25, aorist). But what did he actually do in the cross?

He canceled the law. The author seems to go out of his way to make his thought clear. "He canceled the law consisting of commandments expressed in decrees" (2:15). The law tells men what to do: "do this." If it is canceled, they need no longer obey it. The pressure is off, not because men have been encouraged to be rebels but because their obligation has been ended.

Now if Ephesians is steeped in Pauline doctrine, if "it appears to be almost a characteristic of Ephesians that in it some aspects of Pauline thought find their clearest expression" (Mitton, p. 263), then we must relate the cancellation of the law to what Paul has already said.

At first sight Romans seems to contradict Ephesians. "Are we canceling the law through faith? Heavens no! We are establishing the law" (Rom. 3:31). The antithesis between canceling and establishing is ancient.[12] It is still a live issue. Paul may be repudiating antinomianism (cf. 1 Cor. 7:19) but more, I think, is involved. The moot point is whether "we," that is, our system of faith-righteousness, gives due recognition to the law or not.

Paul's doctrine "establishes" the law in the sense that it is God's law and is recognized as such (Rom. 7:22, 25; pp. 95–96). Every man is answerable to God for his disobedience to it (Rom. 3:19–20). But Christ has obeyed it (Rom. 5:18–19) and obeyed it for us. Justification is by faith and not by works of the law. This is Paul's doctrine in Romans and he could have said that "we," that is, our system, has canceled the law as a means of justification. Paul himself did not "cancel" the law. He would argue that his system is God's system. Christ fulfilled the law for men, undertook to give the "answer" to God which they could not give, shouldered their responsibility and thus relieved the pressure of the law on them. Whatever precise form of words is used in Romans, the thought is plain. Christ canceled the law as a way of justification by fulfilling it for us. (See p. 104.)

Does not Ephesians 2:15 say the same? It is "not of works" (2:9). This is not antinomianism. Ephesians goes on at once to speak of good works to be done (2:10).

Further, Christ redeemed us. In him "we have redemption (apolutrōsis) through his blood, the forgiveness of trespasses" (1:7). This is the high

---

12. See Otto Michel, *Der Brief an die Römer*, p. 112; Pirqe Aboth IV.11; Matt. 5:17.

point of grace. Redemption and forgiveness are not only according to his good pleasure. They accord with "the riches of his grace." The text does not read "redemption and forgiveness." There is no "and." The two words are therefore in apposition, though it is not the normal kind of apposition like "Peter the fisherman." It is more of an analytic or consequential apposition. Redemption and forgiveness are not identical. The need for swift mobility in evangelism (6:15) and the urgency of the ambassador's task (6:19–20) forbid the assumption that when men were redeemed they were also forgiven. This would make evangelism unnecessary, or at best a luxury, and would stultify the doctrine of justification by faith or salvation through faith (2:8). Forgiveness apart from prior redemption is impossible. Redemption without forgiveness is possible: men may be apart from Christ, without hope and without God (2:12), either because they have not yet had the gospel preached to them or because they have heard the gospel and rejected it. The readers themselves had once been apart from Christ—in spite of his shed blood—but now God had forgiven (*echarisato*, 4:32) them.

For redemption is brought about "through his blood." The reference is manifestly to the cross. We have met the concept before (cf. pp. 102, 181), and no doubt 1:7 can be interpreted in the same light (cf. W. Mundle, *Begriffslex.* 3:262), especially if Ephesians is intensely Pauline. If we limit ourselves to the Ephesian text we can say that "slaves of Christ" (6:6) may point to manumission. They now have a new owner (*ho Kurios*)! But this must not be pressed. It is more convincing to link the redemption with the cancellation of the law. In the cross the Redeemer has lifted from men the responsibility which they could not discharge and taken it upon himself. To that extent they have been potentially liberated. They are actually liberated and receive forgiveness (*aphesis*) when they first believe—or why preach the gospel to them? They then "have forgiveness" because they enjoy the redemption effected on the cross. The linking of redemption thus with the law is confirmed by the use of the term "transgressions" (*paraptōmata*).

There is a distinction between redemption effected and redemption enjoyed. It is only in the latter sense that we could speak of redemption in apposition with forgiveness. We shall find an analogy when we come to think of "access," or even earlier.

"Redemption through his blood" points onward to a further concept. Christ offered his life as a sacrifice. He loved us (and thus fulfilled the law! Rom. 13:8–10). The aorist tense sums up the life and brings his love to its focus on the cross (Eph. 5:2). (It is not necessary to our present inquiry to investigate the variant readings "you" and "us.")

"He delivered himself up for us." The aorist here implies the one act. It was "for us," not for himself. The JB renders ". . . he loved you, giving himself up in our place." In predicative apposition to "himself" stand the words, "offering and sacrifice." With these nouns the phrase "to God" must be closely related. In his voluntary act Christ did not deliver himself up to God; at any rate this is not the meaning here. The thought is not that of "commending [*paratithemai*] his Spirit" into God's hands (Luke 23:46).

He delivered himself up, a sacrifice-to-God. Behind the expression stands the sacrificial system of the Old Testament.

The last phrase of the verse, "for a fragrance of a sweet smell" (*eis osmēn euōdias*), is traditional Old Testament language (Gen. 8:21; Exod. 29:18; Ezek. 20:41, all LXX). The original idea was no doubt the smell, appetizing to deity, of the burnt offering with the implication of "the acceptability of the sacrifice to God." The language and the thought persisted without the literality (cf. Ps. 50:7–15). "The LXX took no offence at the anthropomorphism of the OT expression."[13] Professor Harrison's remark about "dead verbal imagery" is applicable here.

On the face of it the Greek phrase might be translated "with a view to a sweet smell." The preposition *eis* can sustain this meaning (1:5–6, 10, 14; 4:12; 6:22). This is purposive and it might be argued that it is not stated whether the purpose has been fulfilled. On the other hand *eis* can mean "issuing in, resulting in." "They delivered themselves up to *aselgeia*, sensuality, resulting in the practice of impurity of every kind" (4:19). (Cf. 2:21–22 —contrast use of *auxō* in 4:15—and Rom. 6:19. See Barrett, *Romans*, p. 133.)

There can be no doubt of the purpose of our Lord's sacrifice. And there can be equally no doubt of its result. God raised him, seated him, subjected everything to him and gave him to the church as Head (1:20–23). Would he have done this if he had rejected the sacrifice?

The writer is not restricting the sacrificial work of Christ to "you" or to "us." He urges his readers to "walk in love" as a way of being "imitators of God" (5:1–2). They have Christ both as an Example and as One who has put them under obligation. They themselves have received the benefit and should therefore walk in love. At this point "the world" does not come into the picture (cf. 1 John 2:2; 4:14). The exhortation to believers is strangely reinforced by the simple use of *kai*. "Christ loved *and* delivered up": the *kai* both explains and intensifies.

So far the call to Christian love has been general. A little later it is directed to husbands. They should love their wives, just as Christ also "loved the church and delivered himself up for it" (5:25–27). This is again the standpoint of experience: "us" or "you" could not have been wrong. But the introduction of "the church" prepares the way for the lesson of the exemplary Bridegroom. The writer is moving towards the use of a startling (though not new, Isa. 54:5–6) metaphor. Apart from this the previous thought is repeated (5:2).

The purpose of the death of Christ is unfolded in three *hina* clauses. He died in order that he might sanctify (*hagiasēi*) the church. This has points of contact with the Epistle to the Hebrews (pp. 68–69) and with the Corinthian correspondence (pp. 190, 192–93). The problem lies in the aorist participle, *katharisas*. It is best taken as aorist of coincident action. Christ died in order that he might sanctify by purifying with the water's wash (Ezek. 16:9, LXX) consisting of the (proclaimed) Word (Eph. 6:17).[14]

---

13. A. Stumpff, *TDNT* 2:809. Cf. S. R. Driver, *The Book of Genesis*, p. 95; Kidner, *Genesis*, p. 93; Harrison, *Introduction to the Old Testament*, pp. 451–52.

14. I find Dr. James Dunn's treatment of Eph. 5:25–27 impressive. *Baptism in the Holy Spirit*, pp. 162–65.

This interpretation coheres with our earlier studies. On the basis of cultic qualification is built the edifice of the holy life (5:27), "that she might go on being holy and blameless." It belongs to that system of ideas exemplified by John 15:3, "you are clean [*katharoi*] because of the Word which I have spoken to you"; and by Acts 15:9, "having cleansed [*katharisas*] their hearts by faith." Acts makes explicit what is implicit in John.

Much discussion has centered on *en rhēmati* ("with the word," RSV). It ought to be observed that the use of the preposition *en* in the sense of "consisting in" is a mark of the style of Ephesians. We have already encountered this in 2:15, "consisting in decrees." Possible examples are as follows:

1:3   with all spiritual blessing . . . with Christ, consisting in Christ
1:17   a spirit of wisdom and revelation consisting in the knowledge of him
1:18   his inheritance consisting in the saints (the NEB is hard to understand here)
2:7   the wealth of his grace consisting in kindness
(2:22   a habitation of God consisting in [not bricks, and mortar but] spirit)
4:14   every wind of doctrine consisting in the trickery of men, in readiness to do anything
4:19   all impurity consisting in greediness (cf. 5:3)
5:9   the fruit of the light consists in nothing but (cf. Jas. 1:2) goodness and righteousness and truth.

It would seem that the translation "consisting in the Word" cannot be summarily ruled out.[15]

With the expression, "water's wash," the apostle moves a step nearer to the open use of his metaphor. The allusion may well be to the prenuptial bath of the bride. This must not be overemphasized: it merely sustains the motif. It is not a weighty criticism to say that the bridegroom does not normally give the prenuptial bath to the bride. For one thing we are not considering an ordinary bridegroom: most grooms do not die for their bride before the wedding! Further, if not long before the ceremony the bride fell into the river and her life was saved by her bridegroom, it would not necessarily be a vulgar comment to say that he had given her the prenuptial bath. It could be vulgar; it need not be. It depends on who makes the remark and how he makes it.

The second purpose of the death of Christ looks forward to the wedding. He died "in order that he might present [cf. 2 Cor. 11:2] the church to himself in her glory" (cf. 1:18). The juxtaposition of *autos heautōi* is very Greek and confirms the view that the Bridegroom is no ordinary bride-

---

15. 4:21 may possibly be added to the list, "according as truth exists (not located in but) consisting in Jesus." With this interpretation, the *e* of *estin* retains the acute accent. See Simpson's note 45 on p. 102 of E. K. Simpson and F. F. Bruce, *Ephesians and Colossians*. This follows the text of Westcott and Hort. Westcott himself (p. 67) seems to point in this direction. "There is Truth—we can find it—in Jesus." This he imagines his disciples to say—"just as the Lord said, 'I am the Truth.'" Cf. Goodwin, *Greek Grammar*, p. 32, para. 144, 5; and Moulton-Howard, *Grammar* 2:54.

groom either in person or activity. The "presentation" seems to refer to the Parousia. The amplification of the purpose, "not having stain or wrinkle . . . ." continues the idea of purification and sustains the metaphor also. It is the cleansed church which is to be the bride at the wedding ceremony; and she is to be a bride, young and radiant still. The "youthfulness" of the church is not a matter of age. There are women, young in age but haggard in look, their very wrinkles recording the life of sin. It is not to be so with the church. The bride, according to the purpose of the Bridegroom's death, is to continue in holiness, blameless.

Without waiting for the ceremony the Bridegroom nourishes and cherishes the bride. We individual Christians are already parts of his body (5:28–32; Gen. 2:24, LXX). This mystery is indeed great. It is partly due to the fact that Christ is viewed as Bridegroom and indeed Husband before the actual wedding ceremony at the Parousia. The author may have been influenced by the custom of betrothal.[16]

Another factor lies in the writer's perspective. He tends to link, even to intermingle, objective and subjective, past, present and future, fact and purpose. Note in 1:3–14, for example, "elected," "foreordained," [17] leading up to redemption and forgiveness which link the objective and the subjective; then the subjective "made to abound . . . by making known to us." There follows the *proetheto* and then the close association of "in whom our lot is cast, having been foreordained." The apostle prays that "God may give . . ." (1:17–19, subjective) and then brings in the objective "raised . . . seated . . . subordinated . . ." (1:20–22).

Notice again the leaning towards the objective in 2:4, "God, being rich in mercy, because of his great love with which he loved us." This is followed at once by the subjective "he quickened us together with Christ." In the epistle there is a kind of oscillation between subjective and objective; between the statement of a principle and its application. "Walk in love, as Christ also loved you (us) and delivered himself up . . ." (5:2).

This feature, together with the uniqueness of the Bridegroom, may help to explain any apparent "inconsistencies."

From the point of view of a member of the believing church it can be said that the purpose of the death of Christ was sanctification-purification by the response of faith to the preached Word. On analysis the work of Christ, objectively considered, proves to be his deliverance of himself to death for us, a sacrifice (cf. 5:2) which was in itself an act of purification analogous to that of Hebrews 1:3 (cf. p. 60). The Bridegroom (to return to the metaphor) did something for the bride before she had even been approached. Apart from the "wooing" note of the evangelistic appeal and such factors, the content of the preached Word is what Christ has done on the cross.

### Christ Our Peace

The passage 2:11–22 is a further illustration of the "oscillation." In verse

---

16. Cf. A. C. Bouquet, *Everyday Life in New Testament Times*, p. 147; *NBD*, p. 788; C. K. Barrett, *The New Testament Background: Selected Documents*, pp. 37–38.

17. Or "decreed." See Leslie C. Allen "The Old Testament Background of (pro) horizein in the New Testament," pp. 104–8.

11 "you" seems addressed to the Ephesian readers. But as the translation should be "you, *the* Gentiles," rather than "you Gentiles," it could be argued that the writer is addressing the Gentiles as a whole, particularly as he contrasts them with the Jews as a whole. There are two distinct groups, the so-called uncircumcision and the so called circumcision. The whole Gentile world was "apart from Christ" and alien in regard to Israel. Yet in verse 13 it is restricted to the Ephesian believers or at any rate to Gentile believers. It would seem that in verse 11 "you" means "you Ephesian believers as representatives of the Gentiles as a whole." The apostle is leading up to the thought of the admission of the Gentiles, through the gospel, into the people of God (3:6).

Now Christ "made both parties one" (2:14). This must mean "Gentiles and Jews" in general. It refers to Christ's objective work on the cross and implies "potential unification" because his purpose is to create one new man out of the two and to reconcile both parties to God. This would be unnecessary if Christ has already "made both parties one" empirically. Such an interpretation is consonant with the objective canceling of the law of commandments and the slaying of the enmity in the cross (2:16). When Christ died on the cross Jews and Gentiles were not yet actually reconciled to each other and made one. The enmity is illustrated by the well-known "middle wall of partition" with its notice forbidding Gentiles, on pain of death, from going beyond the Court of the Gentiles into the Temple. Jewish exclusiveness, *as a principle*, was as smashed in the cross, as was the Temple itself in A.D. 70.[18]

The opposition between Jew and Gentile is continued when it is said that "he came and preached (as gospel) peace to you who were distant and peace to those who were near." The allusion is to Isaiah 57:19, LXX, used apart from the original context for the sake of the concept of distance. The prophet was thinking of Jews still in exile and those who have returned.[19] (Cf. Isa. 52:7, LXX.)

Now the gospel message which he "preached" is not a mere exhortation to stop fighting. (Cf. Acts 7:26 with its conative imperfect: "he was trying to reconcile them.") It implies a peace already achieved and it is available for those who are afar off (Gentiles) and for those who are near (Jews). Jews, *as such*, are not automatically "in." Privileged they are indeed, as we learn from Romans 3:1–2; 9:4–5. But they are like the scribe who was not far from the kingdom of God.[20]

Ephesians 2:13 now awaits interpretation. The present is contrasted with the past. "You" were at one time apart from Christ, outside of Israel, in the world, hopeless and Godless. Now "you" are "near." The disabilities of the past are summed up in the word "distant." The blessing of the present lies in being "near." Either the "near" corresponds to the "near" of verse 17, i.e., they are as qualified to hear the gospel as the Jews are. Being Gentiles does not shut them out from being evangelized. Or "near" has a deeper mean-

---

18. See Bruce, *Acts*, p. 395; A. Deissmann, *Light from the Ancient East*, p. 75; *NBD*, pp. 1246–7, Plate XVa.

19. See J. Skinner, *Isaiah*, 2:161–62.

20. Mark 12:34. For an illustration of the spatial metaphor cf. Lord Eccles, *Half-way to Faith*.

ing: they are actually in the kingdom. The second view coheres with 3:6 and 5:5. The Gentiles are co-heirs through the gospel, but it must be preached to them and they must repent and believe; otherwise their characteristically Gentile sins keep them out. And the readers seem to have believed: "you" who were once apart from Christ have now become near "in Christ Jesus." This must surely be more than merely "open to be evangelized." The two views of "near" tally with what we have observed of "oscillation." The peace which had been preached to them (2:17) and their present position, their "nearness," in Christ were both due to the blood of Christ. (Cf. 4:17–20; 6:15.)

"He is our peace" with God (2:14). This explains the present "nearness." ("*For* he is our peace.") On this basis he made the two parties in principle to be one. When each party, Jews and Gentile, responds in faith to the gospel and is thus reconciled to God, each finds a fellow. Each by faith is in the one body. Believing Jew and believing Greek each rubs his eyes in wonder as he looks upon the other: he is in Christ through the cross! Each finds that he can no longer treat the other as an enemy.

When the Lord died on the cross, he brought the divine hostility to sinners to an end. God was now at peace with men, with the totality of Jews and the totality of Gentiles. They must be told the good news of the new situation created by the blood of Christ (cf. 2:17; 6:15). As individual Jews and Gentiles repent and believe, they receive God's peace and are reconciled to him. In Christ both Jew and Gentile find that they have converged on a single goal. Thus they discover each other. Reconciled to God in Christ, they are reconciled to each other in him.

This is a continuing process. More and more Jews and Gentiles are converted and become reconciled to one another. This is the continuing work of Christ, who "goes on making peace" (*poiōn eirēnēn*, 2:15) between Jew and Gentile. It is based on, and would be impossible without, the prior peace of God toward men due to the cross.

For before the cross God was not at peace with men. All men were "children of wrath" (2:3). God therefore kept them at a distance from him. Even the privileged Jews, the men who were "near," were not "near enough." They could not be. Neither Jew nor Gentile, as a sinner, had the right of access to God. But through Christ the way has been thrown open. Through him both have the access previously denied to them (2:18). "Our 'access' is gained only through Him. Compare John 14:6; Heb. 4:14ff" (Westcott). The access of 2:18 may be fittingly contrasted with the exclusion of 5:5–6.

The work of Christ on the cross has opened up a way for men to come to God. Will they tread that path? It will depend on Christ's work in us as well as on his work for us.

### God at Work in Us—The Work of Christ in Us

In our attempt to find out precisely what our Lord has done for us, we have already had occasion to think of what he has done in us. This is because the author of Ephesians has interwoven his material—an aspect of what we have called "oscillation." We had to disentangle the evidence with regard to "for us" from that concerned with "in us." Inevitably we have been guilty of some anticipation. We must now concentrate on Christ's work in us, even, if necessary, at the cost of a little repetition.

We begin with the observation that the author of Ephesians regards himself as an apostle of Christ Jesus (1:1). He holds this office "through the will of God." It is a fair inference from this that God sent him out into the world for the performance of a specific task. As an apostle he has something to say to the world. His characteristic work is speech. As a free man and a personality he would undoubtedly choose his own words and frame his own sentences and paragraphs. Study of what he said would reveal his own traits of style. Even so he asks for prayer that speech may be given to him when he opens his mouth (6:19). The Giver can be none other than God. God has an interest in what he says and how he says it. It is a matter of urgency (cf. 6:15) and a great privilege to speak (3:8).

The apostle has something not only to say but to give. The grace of God had been given to him "for you" (3:2). He is a sort of steward or manager, a "factor," as the Scottish people say. He did not create the grace and he does not own it; and he does not keep it exclusively for himself. He "distributes" it. His commission ranges far. It had been revealed to him (and to other apostles and prophets) and he had a shrewd understanding of the position, that the Gentiles at large were to be included in his ministry. They were to be offered the gospel. If they received it they would gain large benefits: an open door of entry into the inheritance, membership of the body, participation in the promise. These are included in the grace which the apostle offers or "distributes" to those who will welcome it. It is the unsearchable riches which consist in Christ. The apostle has Christ—to give (3:1–9), for Christ is the embodiment of grace. (Cf. 4:7, 32.) The thanksgiving for everything (5:20) will include thanksgiving for the grace from which everything flows.

The "something to give" is conveyed in words. This may come as a surprise to those who limit the means of grace to the sacraments. But the evidence is clear and we ought not really to be surprised. "In Catholic theology the sermon is more and more described as a quasi-sacrament." [21] We therefore turn our attention from the speaker to the hearer.

The preacher spoke; and the listeners "heard the Word of truth, the gospel of your salvation" (1:13). The preacher spoke; and the listeners did not hear him. They heard another voice, the voice of Christ. They "heard Him" (4:21). Speech had indeed been given to the preacher (6:19), for Christ spoke in him (cf. 2 Cor. 13:3). This may be regarded as a partial fulfillment of Ephesians 2:17.

Even so something was said. There was a verbal content. Hearing Christ and being taught in him (4:21) suggests *kerygma* and *didachē*. The three infinitives of 4:22–24 are often taken as dependent on the verb "taught" in 4:21. "You were taught in him . . . that you should put off . . . be renewed

---

21. Hans Küng, *Justification*, p. 336. Cf. my *Royal Sacrament: The Preacher and His Message*, pp. 22–26. Cf. Eph. 4:29! See Jaroslav Pelikan, *The Christian Tradition*, 1:162.

. . . put on." Given the fact of this dependence it was natural for scholars to regard these and subsequent verses as catechetical material, derived (like similar passages in other epistles) from a common tradition. The church had to teach its converts the elements of Christian life as well as of belief.[22]

Now the passage 4:17–19, 4:25–6:18 is plainly addressed to Christians: "no longer go on walking as the Gentiles walk . . ." (4:17); "members of one another" (4:25); "give grace" (4:29); "sealed" (4:30; cf. 1:13); forgiven (4:32); "saints" (5:3); "once darkness, now light in the Lord" (5:8); "giving thanks . . . in the Name" (5:20); "members of his body" (5:30); "training and admonition of the Lord" (6:4); Christian slaves (6:5) and owners (6:9); the Christian warfare (6:10–12); prayer (6:18).

But are the verses 4:22–24 typical of teaching given to converts? Of the activities indicated by the three infinitives, putting off, renewal, putting on, Westcott remarks (p. 67) that "the first and third are acts done once for all." The aorist infinitives confirm the rightness of this interpretation. The hearing and the teaching must therefore be taken closely together as describing the content and the thrust of the message which the Ephesians heard at the very first. (See note 23 in the chapter on Galatians.) When the gospel was first preached to them, they heard Christ himself (4:20) telling them (the Word of truth, 1:13) and commanding them. To "put off the old man" is another expression for repentance, the repudiation of the old deceived and selfish *ego* which is on the road to ruin.

To "put on the new man" contains great depths for the imagination. If the old man is gone, the new man could well be Christ, the new robe of righteousness. This is true spiritually and it might have been in the mind of the author at first. But it is exegetically wrong or at least inadequate. Christ was not created. Even so the thought may be a sound clue. If a man is in Christ, he is a new creation (2 Cor. 5:17; cf. Gal. 6:15). A man becomes "in Christ" when he first believes in Jesus. Thus the command to repent is followed by the command to believe. When a hearer responds in repentance and faith he becomes a new man in Christ and begins the process (present infinitive) of being renewed in the spirit of his mind. The work of sanctification has begun.

This, then, is to learn Christ as he himself speaks in the preacher. It is to renounce sin, to trust Christ, to become a new creature and to start off on the road of holiness. The Ephesian readers have done this. They must not therefore go on walking their old, Gentile way in illusion and darkness, alien, ignorant, insensitive, immersed in impurity. Not so did they learn Christ when they first encountered him in faith.

In this encounter we have observed that he informed them and commanded them. Christ told them the truth of the gospel and summoned them to obey in repentance and faith. The "information" and the command together constitute the "call." The apostle urges his readers to walk worthily

---

22. See Philip Carrington, *The Primitive Christian Catechism;* A. M. Hunter, *Paul and his Predecessors;* E. G. Selwyn, *First Epistle of St. Peter,* pp. 363–466; G. B. Caird, *The Apostolic Age,* pp. 109–113; C. H. Dodd, *Gospel and Law.*

of "the call with which you were called" (4:1; cf. 1:18; 4:4). The aorist tense marks the decisive act,[23] the act of response. It is true that during the sermon or during several sermons Christ is "calling" all the time; and the individual hearer in question may be postponing or evading decision. Finally he yields. The aorist marks the moment in which (for him) the invitation crystallized and he was effectually called.

The context of 1:18 suggests that the call of Christ is the call of God. For the hearer the effectual call is a matter of deep spiritual experience. It may later, that is, the response may later be "externalized" in baptism. But the call and the decisive response of repentance and faith are prior to baptism. Or why should anyone submit to baptism?

The hearer, then, takes the first step of faith. We must now ask what happens when he thus begins to believe. The purpose of God's election is that he might be holy and blameless "in his sight" (*katenōpion autou,* 1:4). This can hardly mean merely that God stands looking on or that the man just happens to be in his presence. What does the phrase mean?

In their treatment of the ethical dative, Blass-Debrunner-Funk cite Barnabas 8:4, *megaloi tōi theōi,* "great in God's eyes." Then, quoting our phrase from Ephesians 1:4, (and Col. 1:22), they say that "the dat. can also be equated with this circumlocution. . . ."[24] The nearest parallel which I can find in the LXX is Joshua 3:7, which the NEB (from the Hebrew) renders, "Today I will begin to make you stand high in the eyes of [this is literal] all Israel." The JB gives ". . . a great man in the eyes of. . . ." Brown-Driver-Briggs (p. 744) translate the idiom by "in the view, opinion, of."

This evidence suggests that the purpose of God's election was that men should be holy and blameless "in his opinion." His purpose was that he might regard them as holy and blameless. Its fulfillment is not postponed until the Day of Judgment or afterwards. Christ died to make the church holy by purifying it with the water's wash consisting in the Word, in order that it might really be holy and blameless (5:25–27). The church is not yet empirically holy and blameless; but it has been sanctified and purified. It has the cultic qualification to approach God and it has it now. It has "the static morality of innocence" (cf. pp. 192–93).

But it is far from perfect. If we study the church as exemplified by the Ephesian readers we find much room for improvement. There is room for reminder (2:11); room for more knowledge (1:17–18; 3:18–19); for more strength (3:13, 16; 6:10); for ethical encouragement (4:1, 17, 28, 30); for more growth and stability (4:14–15); for constant renewal (4:23); and for warning (5:6, 15). The Christian life is a struggle (6:12), open to attack (6:16) and in need of persistent prayer (6:18). A study of the negative adverb *mē* and the present imperative ("do not go on doing this") yields

---

23. Cf. Westcott, p. 56. "The tense carries back the thought to the decisive moment when they accepted the Gospel." He speaks (p. 24) of the call as "divine invitation." The punctiliar aorist points to *id punctum temporis,* i.e., the very moment, of the acceptance. See also Blass-Debrunner-Funk, para. 337(1), p. 173, "the *new* life of the Christian, corresponding to the divine call which creates a new beginning. . . ."

24. Blass-Debrunner-Funk, para. 192, p. 103; cf. para. 214(5f), p. 115, "in the eyes of someone." Cf. possibly Acts 6:5; Heb. 13:21; 1 John 3:22.

significant results. The readers are to stop sinning, giving scope to the devil, stealing, using "rotten" instead of edifying speech, grieving the Holy Spirit (4:26–30). We might add 5:3, 6–7, 11, 17–18; 6:4. A positive commandment must be quoted (6:2) and slaveowners told to "give up using threats" (6:9, NEB).

The believing church is far from being holy and blameless. Yet in virtue of the death of Christ and the believer's faith the member is holy and blameless "in God's opinion."

In other words, God regards him as holy and blameless. To recall the Epistle to the Romans, God counts him as righteous. Ephesians does not use the word *dikaioō*, but it would seem that justification by faith has come in, in the disguise of different language. Romans uses the word *logizomai*. God does not regard a man's sin if he is a believer but counts his faith as righteousness (Rom. 4:6, 8). In Ephesians such a man is holy and blameless in God's sight. In both cases we are concerned with what goes on in the divine Mind. And in both cases "works" do not come into consideration at all (cf. Eph. 2:8–9).

This theory of "justification in Ephesians" receives some slight confirmation in the expression "the breastplate consisting of righteousness" (6:14).[25] Now the breastplate is part of the defensive armor and guards a vital part of the body. The ancients need not be credited with knowledge of the heart and the circulation of the blood. They knew the consequences of a deep wound in the place where the breastplate should have been! Life is at stake when the attack is launched by the devil, the evil one, the accuser (6:11, 16). For "the work of the adversary implies always an attempt on the part of the *diabolos* to separate God and man." "The goal of Satan's activity is man's destruction in alienation from God."[26]

The separation of God and man is complete and absolute when man stands entirely alone. It is ended through the work of Christ and the man's response of faith. He has "access" to God in and through Christ because righteousness has been imputed to him. As long as he thus is clothed in righteousness he is not separated from God. The defense against the devil's attack is the righteousness. In the martial figure it is natural to speak of the breastplate of righteousness. Every attack which seeks the believer's destruction by separation from God is inevitably smashed when it encounters his imputed righteousness.

What it amounts to is this: in the spiritual life a Christian may be tempted to "doubt of himself," to wonder if after all he is on the right road, to question the reality of the forgiveness of his sins. As long as he remembers the work of Christ for him and the result of his own response in faith, he will know how God looks upon him—holy and blameless! Thus there will be no separation from God. But his "remembrance" must be more than mere thought and reflection. It must be in a context of alert prayer (6:18). Then doctrine will be alive in experience.

---

25. R. R. Williams refers to Isa. 59:16–17 and thinks of "the armour which God wears, the weapons with which God does battle." But does God wear the shield of faith? See F. L. Cross, ed., *Studies in Ephesians*, p. 95.

26. Werner Foerster, *TDNT* 2:73, 79. Cf. H. Bietenhard, *Begriffslex.* 10:1057–60.

This example (6:14) might not carry much weight if it stood alone. It is more cogent in the light of 1:4.

So far, then, we can say that when a man responds in first faith to the preaching of the gospel he is justified. We have earlier spoken of the concomitants of justification. The same pattern is apparent in Ephesians. When a man first believes, he is accepted by God. He has "access" to God through faith (3:12; cf. 2:18). Once he was "far off." Now he has come near (2:13). Not only has God thrown open the door; the believer has entered it. He understands the experience of those who say that they are "in Christ, in whom our lot is cast" (1:11; Arndt-Gingrich, p. 436). God has seated him in the heavenlies (2:6). "Seated" implies that he is there to stay. "In the heavenlies" means "with God." [27] This is where his blessing is, where Christ crucified now is (1:3, 20). He belongs to God and is a member of His household (2:19), no longer excluded as an alien (cf. 4:18) or just admitted as a temporary visitor or "tourist" who does not really "belong." He is *in*—accepted.

A further concomitant is the "quickening." He was once dead in trespasses and sins. When he first believed he was made alive; when he "woke from the sleep of death" he found himself alive—with the living Christ (2:1, 5–6); he had been "raised." This theme is repeated, transposed into another key or expressed in another figure. The man who was once dead and is alive again is the product of God's creative activity—he is God's *poiēma*. He (the former Gentile citizen!) has been created in Christ Jesus (2:10). He has put off the old man and put on the new. The old was on the road to ruin. The new was created *kata theon* (4:22–24). The old was once the embodiment of darkness; now he is light itself—in the Lord (5:8; cf. 4:18). The motifs of life and light are united in what may be part of an early Christian hymn (5:14).[28]

Associated with acceptance and quickening is adoption. God foreordained us, decreed us, "for adoption to himself through Jesus Christ" (1:5). There is no explicit teaching in Ephesians comparable with Romans 8:15 and Galatians 4:6, but the experience is beyond doubt. The readers had once been apart from Christ and without God (2:12); in the world and not in Christ; darkened in mind and excluded from the life of God (4:18). Now, as forgiven men in Christ, they are called to show themselves as imitators of God. Conscious of the divine love which has made them the children of God, they are to "walk in love" (4:32–5:2; cf. 2:4). Adoption is the awareness in experience of the justification which took place in the divine Mind. It is the experience, not the mere theory, belief or doctrinal truth, of "acceptance." Other expressions reflect the experience. God dwells in the believer (2:22; 4:6). Christ dwells in him—through faith (3:17). The empowering Spirit dwells within (3:16). The experience grows and deepens with the years but it is real from the beginning.

Finally we come to salvation. The word is not liked by some. Men hesitate

---

27. Cf. A. T. Lincoln, "A Re-examination of 'the Heavenlies' in Ephesians," pp. 468–83.

28. See Ralph P. Martin, *Worship in the Early Church*, pp. 47–48, 104, 108–9.

to claim that salvation is already theirs, either through fear of presumption or because they have been "put off" by some of "the saved." But the evidence is plain to see. The perfect tense of 2:5, 8 is highly suggestive. "By grace you have been saved through faith." Grace was the instrument. Grace did the work. Faith is the channel through which it is received. Now the perfect tense expresses the abiding result of a past act. "You have been saved" may therefore be expressed afresh as "You are now safe." Full weight must be given to this assertion. It must not be laid aside and ignored.[29]

J. H. Moulton in his famous *Prolegomena* (*Grammar* 1:127) has a comment to which Dr. Moule calls attention. Moulton speaks of "a work which is finished on its Author's side, but progressively realised by its objects." Everything here turns on the meaning of "realised." If it means that God has yet more blessings to give to His people, including heaven itself, or if it means that the believer is constantly being refreshed by the Holy Spirit (cf. 5:18, "keep on being filled with the Spirit") and therefore empirically becomes more and more holy and more and more sanctified, then there is no problem. Sanctification is a process. But if it is implied that a believer has, so to speak, half a salvation, a quarter of a hope concerning his final destiny or one tenth of the forgiveness of his sins, then we must demur. He is safe. This is absolute. We have here the difference between contrary and contradictory propositions. For example, a man may be standing on firm dry ground, in mud or in a pond. There are differences of degree in the firmness or the wetness. "In the mud" is roughly halfway between the extremes of "firm dry ground" and "in a pond." This points to contrariety. But a man is either on firm dry ground or he is not. There is no middle course possible. The "not" may cover any depth of mud, any depth or kind of pond, in fact anything and everything which is not "firm dry ground." This is contradiction: there is no midpoint between yes and no. A man may be half-sanctified but he cannot be half-saved. He is either saved or he is not. And the Ephesians were saved—and safe.

This is the objective position or "status" as Dr. Moule calls it, of the believing man. The question is sometimes asked of a Christian, "Will you go to heaven when you die?" He ought to be able to reply—humbly, because it is God's gift, his grace and "not of works," and he does not deserve it; and with conviction, because he has been redeemed and forgiven and he ought not to doubt the love and the righteousness of God—he ought to be able to reply that he will go to heaven because he is safe. This is surely the point of the theological affirmation that salvation is eschatological.

The perfect tense of 2:5, 8 brings certainty to the believing person. He ought therefore to have boldness and confidence (3:12). He must never presume and let boldness become familiarity or flippancy. He must ever bow in utter adoration before the Most High. But—he knows his Father. In principle, if not in the actual "handling," he possesses all that God has

---

29. Professor Moule gives alternatives, both making good sense, "you are safe" and "you have been saved (and therefore enjoy your present status)." *Idiom Book*, p. 19.

given to believers. He is in Christ and Christ is the Savior (5:23; cf. 6:17). Even the Holy Spirit is but the first installment (*arrabōn* 1:14; cf. 4:30), the pledge and certainty of blessings yet to come.

We have earlier stated that justification sets up a relationship between the believer and God. As we have found traces of justification in Ephesians it is pertinent to ask if there are also traces of the permanent relationship. A point of departure would be the question just discussed—being safe. We then notice the sealing of the Spirit and the "first installment" (1:13). When they believed they were sealed: the aorist is one of coincident action. The Ephesians believed: and they were justified, accepted, quickened, adopted —and given a sure future. In the interim between the present and the End, the believing church is nourished and cherished by the Bridegroom (5:29). Believers can go on being filled with the Spirit (5:18). Prayer is always possible (6:18). The body of Christ is constantly being built up, with the vision of final attainment for the totality of its members (4:12–13, 15–16). The existence of pastors and teachers implies a constituency, which itself in turn has a ministry (4:11–12). The believing church continues and God dwells in it (2:22). There may be some small significance in the use of the word "habitation" (*katoikētērion*). It hints at a permanent dwelling place. A word cognate with *paroikeō* might have suggested no more than a visit.

The Christian has duties, as the catechetical material shows, and he lives his Christian life in the fellowship of the church.

# 7

## The Epistle
## to the Colossians

It is widely held that Ephesians is dependent on Colossians. We have preferred to examine it in itself, trying to bear in mind the ideal of finding the meaning of words in their use and context. Thus in considering Ephesians 1:4 (cf. pp. 225–26) we did not bring in Colossians 1:22 to our aid, though the resemblance is striking. We shall proceed in the same manner with Colossians.

### THE NATURE OF GOD

We begin, as before, by looking at the passages in which the apostle speaks of God. We may find the same "duality" of severity and kindness and their resolution in Christ.

The expression, "the fullness of deity" (Col. 2:9), prepares us for what is to follow. The abstract noun *theotēs* is used for *theos* (cf. Arndt-Gingrich, p. 359). *God is invisible* (1:15). The condemnation of idolatry (3:5) is more than a protest against material images as objects of worship. It objects to anything (in the present instance greed) which takes the place of God in human thought and aspiration. This points to monotheism. There is but one God. *God is One.*

*God is in heaven.* Human slaveowners have their own Owner in heaven (4:1). The reference may be to Christ as their Lord. But he is "above" and he is seated there on the right hand of God (3:1–3). God himself must therefore be in heaven.

*God is conscious* because he "thinks." He has his "opinion" (*katenōpion autou,* 1:22). We have already used this word (p. 225) in connection with Ephesians 1:4. It is anthropomorphic but hardly more so than the Hebrew "in his eyes." God is, however, more than a Thinker. (I hope that it will not be assumed that God is ratiocinative.) He is not quiescent, wrapped up in his "thoughts." *He is active.* The Aristotelian distinction between power (*dunamis*) and its actualization (*energeia*) is not inapplicable to God. He

[230]

can act (cf. Rom. 4:21) and he does act. He raised his Son from the dead (2:12). He may open a door for the apostle to preach (4:3).

The "door" might be small, though opening on to a large area. But it should not be thought that God's activity is necessarily on a small scale. Paul speaks of "the might of his glory" (1:11). *God has mighty power* and he has exercised his power. *God is the Creator.* In Colossians 3:10 "the allusion to Gen. 1:27 is irresistible" (C. F. D. Moule, p. 120).[1] And he still exercises his power. History itself, with its physical background, lies within his domain. How otherwise could he "open a door" for a preacher? Of what avail would it be for God to open the doors of men's hearts if the apostle could not first get within range of their ears? *God is the Lord of Providence.*

These divine acts are not to be compared with the start of a mechanism. *The conscious God has will.* Paul accordingly speaks of "the will of God" (1:1, 9; 4:12). In its long range His will is purposive. *God has purpose.* The Word of God, the mystery, lay hidden (not nonexistent) for long ages and then God willed (almost "decided"—aorist) to make it known (cf. 1:25–27). He "resolved" to reconcile all things (*eudokēsen* 1:19–20). This has not yet been accomplished. To say that it has is to fly in the face of the evidence: *si monumentum requiris, circumspice.*[2]

Will, purpose, resolve: *God has freedom of choice.* "The elect of God" (3:12) are the people whom God has chosen. Having made his choice, God does not abandon men, or ignore them. He is "interested" in them. *God has an attitude.* He is *to be worshiped* (3:16), thanked (1:3, 12; 3:17; 4:2), approached in prayer 1:3, 9; 4:3) and *pleased* (3:20). *God has authority,* implied by the fact that Christ is seated at the place of authority, at God's right hand (3:1); and *he has a kingdom,* a royal rule (4:11). *God may be known* (1:10; 3:10).

The fact that men commit trespasses (2:13) implies a law. If it is God who forgives, it must be God's law which has been broken. *God has a law for men.* This has implications which are not explicitly worked out in the epistle. The word "trespasses" is a keyhole through which we may view the large room of Paul's thought. The law is God's law and it reveals God's righteousness (cf. pp. 81–82, 95–97). Hence *God is righteous;* and *he requires righteousness from men.* God's ethical character and requirements may be seen in 3:5–14, 18–24. The exhortation to children to obey their parents recalls the commandment, in thought if not in language (Exod. 20:12), and the use of the word *dikaion* may have some significance (Col. 3:20; 4:1).

The description of God's people as *hagioi* (1:2, 4, 12, 22, 26; 3:12) re-

---

1. Where only the author's name is given, the reference is to his commentary on Colossians.

2. "If you seek a memorial, look around you"—on a tablet in the crypt of St. Paul's in memory of its architect, Sir Christopher Wren. I was tempted to alter *monumentum* to *documentum*, but the diabolic edifice in the world of today allowed it to stay as it is. Cf. F. F. Bruce in E. K. Simpson and F. F. Bruce, *Ephesians and Colossians*, p. 210. "The peace . . . may be freely accepted, or it may be compulsorily imposed." Paul includes here in reconciliation "what we should distinguish as pacification."

flects the fact that *God is holy*. But *he is sinned against*. This is implied in "trespasses" (2:13), illustrated in the former life of the readers (3:7 and context), and explicitly mentioned in the "sins" of 1:14. *God has enemies* needing to be reconciled (1:21), whose deeds are "evil," and *he makes accusations against men*. This is implied by the fact that in his "opinion" (p. 230) certain people are now not to be accused (1:22). The use of the cognate verb is illuminating (Acts 19:38–40; 23:28–29; 26:2, 7; Rom. 8:33), especially in its context.

God's accusation is logically followed by his ethical reaction, "*the wrath of God*" (3:6). It "comes" (*erchetai*). "This may refer either to the present and continuous dispensation, or to the future and final judgment" (J. B. Lightfoot, p. 213). We have already met the distinction between historic and eschatological wrath (pp. 85–88). In favor of the historic interpretation is the fact that the readers had been "dead" in trespasses (2:13)—even while walking and living in them (3:7)! The eschatological is not, however, ruled out. "The reward of the inheritance" (3:24) points forward and the parallel case does likewise in the following verse. "He who does wrong will get back the wrong which he did, and there is no partiality."

Once more we see that *God deals with individuals* as well as with broad movements of history: "he who does wrong. . . ." Paul likewise is concerned not only with the masses but with individuals also. "We proclaim (Christ), admonishing every man and teaching every man . . . in order that we may present every man mature in Christ" (1:28). The thrice repeated "every man" is neither a crescendo nor a refrain. (Cf. p. 87 above for Lagrange's comment on Rom. 1:24, 26, 28.) It is more to be likened to three successive blows of a hammer, with which St. Paul is driving home the message of individual responsibility. Each man must respond to the preached gospel and the apostolic admonition and teaching if he is to enter the light. Otherwise he remains in darkness (1:12–13) with its fearful consequences.

## THE OTHER SIDE—GOD FOR MAN

The apostle has not gone into lengthy detail; but so far the pattern is recognizably the same as we have seen before. Again there is "the other side." When we think of God we must think of grace and of peace (1:2, 6; 4:18), and of his purpose to reconcile his enemies to himself (1:20).

The severity and the kindness of God are brought together in Christ, who is significantly the image of the invisible God (1:15). We must keep this in mind as we proceed to consider Christ's work for us. What he did could hardly be against, or apart from, the will of him whose image he is. If Christ "went off on his own" he would surely be departing from the image, which would indeed become marred.

### God at Work for Us—The Work of Christ for Us

We start with a familiar concept, the Word of God (1:25–26). It is the mystery, long hidden but now manifested. As "word" it means speech (cf. 4:3, 6). God has something to say. But what did he say?

St. Paul uses the expression, "the Word of Christ" (3:16). The genitive has received a variety of interpretations—subjective, objective or possessive—and it is not easy to say that any one of them is wrong. Christ himself speaks (cf. 2 Cor. 13:3), his people speak of him, and the message belongs to him. Even the great apostle himself has but a stewardship (1:25). If asked, he would probably decline to choose one interpretation rather than another. But one view in particular must not be forgotten. The genitive can be one of material—"the Word which consists of Christ." This accords with 1:27, "Christ in you." But it is not Christ *in vacuo*. It is Christ as understood in his Person and work. Those in whom he dwells can thus "teach one another." J. B. Lightfoot (p. 224) says that the phrase "denotes the presence of Christ in the heart, as an inward monitor."

God spoke—and what he said was Christ. Christ is "the hope of glory" (1:27) and the same hope ("stored up for you in heaven"—NEB) was heard "in the Word of the truth of the gospel" (1:5). The gospel came to the Colossians. They heard it and in it they heard and recognized truly the grace of God (1:6–7). Thus "what God said" was Christ, the gospel, the grace of God.

But who is Christ? He is the beloved Son of God (1:13).[3] If it be insisted that we have here no more than a metaphorical Semitism, it is sufficient to answer that God is "the Father of our Lord Jesus Christ" (1:3). The word "Lord" itself is highly significant, representing as it does the Old Testament Yahweh (Exod. 6:2–3; Ps. 82:19; Isa. 12:2; 26:4, all LXX).

He is the preexistent Son. He could not be otherwise. The whole universe has been created through him and for him and its present coherence as a system is due to him (1:15–16). In this context "Firstborn" could not be understood in any Arian sense. In him are hidden all the treasures of wisdom and knowledge (2:3) and indeed the whole fullness of deity dwells permanently (*katoikei*) in him (2:9). He is more than the shadow (cf. 2:17) of his Father. (Cf. 1:19.)

The term "bodily" (*sōmatikōs*) hints at the incarnation.[4] Paul's language implies the doctrine. He has not ceased to use the name, Jesus, and "blood" (1:20) would be inappropriate for deity as such. "The afflictions of Christ" (1:24) must have the incarnation as background. The text calls for some examination. "Now I am rejoicing in my sufferings for you, and in my flesh I am filling up the gaps—the afflictions of Christ which are not taking place. It is for his body, which is the church."

Exposition here is notoriously difficult. One problem may be removed at once. Speaking of Christian individuals Lightfoot (p. 166) affirms that "St. Paul would have been the last to say that they bear their part in the atoning sacrifice of Christ." In our search for what he really meant we attempt the following observations.

Paul is suffering "for you," "for his body." "You" are included in "his body" because the church is the body of Christ (cf. 1:18). The body, that

---

3. Cf. Moulton-Howard, *Grammar*, 2:441.
4. Cf. Lightfoot, p. 182; Moule, pp. 93–94. Michael Green significantly comments "in the historical Jesus" in expounding Col. 2:9. See his *I Believe in the Holy Spirit*, pp. 154–55.

is, the church, must suffer. (Cf. Acts 14:22; 1 Thess. 3:3–5; 2 Thess. 1:5.) Its sufferings are "edificatory" (Lightfoot), not piacular.

Is Christ a member of the church? He surely must be, if he is a part of the body. (Obviously we need not discuss terms of entry.) He is the Head of the body. Then if the body (the church) must suffer, the Head must suffer.

Two approaches are now possible. When believers suffer they can comfort themselves with the thought that it does not matter if the fingers drown, provided the head remains above water. But suppose the legs are cut off? In ancient thought the head might or might not feel pain, but it is clear in any century that without legs the head could not "go." The head could not tell the feet that it had no need of them. If one member suffers, all the members suffer along with it (cf. 1 Cor. 12:21, 26).

St. Paul would understand and sympathize with the suffering saint. The "fingers" might indeed drown but the Lord dies no more (cf. Rom. 6:9). But it is this which *in the present context* constitutes the problem for the apostle. The church must suffer. The Head ought to suffer with it.

But it is precisely suffering which is impossible to the Head. Admittedly at his conversion St. Paul heard the voice asking "Why persecutest thou me?" (Acts 9:4), but the exalted and glorified Lord was *in himself* beyond persecution.[5] He has no flesh on earth in which to receive the kindly ministries or the blows of men. "You have the poor with you always . . . me you have not always" (Mark 14:7).

But Paul has flesh on earth and he seizes on the idea. We may paraphrase him thus: "in my flesh I am replacing him [*anti-*] and am suffering the afflictions which the Head of the church ought to suffer but cannot." This inspires and sustains him in his sufferings "for you." Its characteristic is not irreverence but discipleship. It accords with his exhortation to men to imitate him (cf. 1 Cor. 4:16; 11:1). Its motive is not to relieve the Lord, for he has already suffered (cf. Acts 17:3). The *hysterēmata* (things absent) do not stand for defects but for absence (cf. 1 Cor. 16:17).

The cumulative evidence of the name Jesus, of the term *blood,* and the reference to the afflictions of Christ point conclusively to the incarnation of the One through whom the universe was created (Col. 1:16–18).

The Son, then, became incarnate. We shall not at the moment linger on the death of Christ but we note it. The death upon the cross (1:20, 22; 2:14) was followed by the resurrection (2:12) and the exaltation ("above") to the heavenly session. He sits at the right hand of God in hidden majesty. He will be manifested in glory (3:1–4). This is the Parousia.

Now as the ground of thanksgiving Paul affirms three great acts of the Father. He qualified . . . delivered . . . translated (1:12–13). We may find that the last two are more closely associated with the work of Christ in us. At present we concentrate on the first.

The allusion is to ancient Canaan. The people of God were promised the land as their inheritance. This is used as an illustration and is spiritualized. "God qualified you for a share in what was allotted to the saints in

---

5. The text may reflect the doctrine of corporate personality or the divine attitude expressed in Matt. 25:40, 45.

the light." Paul is obviously referring to the blessings of the gospel, but it should be observed that a man must be "qualified" to receive them. They do not come automatically to all and sundry. We attempt, therefore, to find out the nature of the qualification.

A vast field of inquiry is opened up in 2:14, the "handwriting" passage. The *cheirographon*, in the literal sense of handwriting or written document, is not easily construed with the dative, *tois dogmasin*. Deissmann has shown, however, that in the papyri the technical signification of "certificate of debt" is very common.[6] The expression then flows on: "the adverse certificate of debt to the decrees." "Adverse" loses something when it replaces "against us" but facilitates the translation. The thought is emphasized by the addition of the relative clause, "which was hostile [*hupenantion*] to us." The LXX background of *hupenantion* is instructive [7] and the idea of divine opposition is biblical (e.g., Ps. 34:16; 1 Pet. 3:12).

The term "decrees" includes the Old Testament law and its reflection in the mind of Gentiles (cf. Rom. 2:14–15). God has made demands on all men.

The certificate of debt is at the same time "handwriting." In a sense it was written by "us." This may or may not mean that we acknowledge our debt. "The task of the law written in their hearts" might suggest that we do acknowledge it. On the other hand this particular piece of writing was not done by us and some men repudiate it. We must not lay undue stress on our personal signature on the IOU. Paul uses this figure in order to bring out human responsibility, whether acknowledged or not.

"The certificate of debt" implies that we ought to have obeyed God's law, whether we are Jews or Gentiles, but that we have not obeyed it. The fact that it is "against us" is a form of accusation. We are guilty men. The sins listed in 3:5–9 can be fitted into the Decalogue and they entail the wrath of God. The IOU in the ordinary sense of the term is an expensive investment; as pointing to human responsibility it involves disaster. As Moule says, Christ "discharged [this debt] by accepting the death-warrant which the bond constituted."

The discharge is described in three movements. He obliterated it, removed it, nailed it to the cross. Without being unduly fanciful in interpretation we may see three truths here expressed.

The obliteration recalls the ancient method of writing on wax tablets. But would a creditor accept an IOU written in so risky a manner? A. R. C. Leaney follows Lagrange in regarding the *pinakidion* of Luke 1:63 as a tablet of wood covered with parchment. It is all the more significant, therefore, that Paul uses a word appropriate to wax. The writing is not merely crossed out; it is erased, no doubt smoothed out with a sort of rolling-pin. We do not say that the charge has been withdrawn. It has been withdrawn from sinners for reasons which will follow, and it was done at the cross.

This is important if only because the same imagery is used in Acts 3:19

---

6. A. Deissmann, *Bible Studies*, p. 247. Cf. J. A. T. Robinson, *The Body*, p. 43; Moule, p. 98.

7. See E. Hatch and H. A. Redpath, *Concordance to the Septuagint*, 2:1407, and particularly 2 Chron. 20:29; Wisdom 11:8; 18:8; Nahum 1:2, all LXX.

for the erasure of sins as a consequence of repentance and conversion. In Colossians 2:14 the erasure takes place at the cross. (Cf. p. 368.)

Even if obliteration has occurred, the tablet itself remains. But Christ "has removed it from the midst." The perfect tense should be given its proper weight. If the accusation *has been removed*, it *is now* out of sight. In other words the charge has gone and the reminder of the charge has gone also. Even the discarded tablet is no longer to be seen. The believing Christian may not forget his "sins done aforetime"; perhaps he cannot forget; perhaps he should not forget. What he should forget is the fact of being charged with them. The accusation has been blotted out and even the reminder has been taken away. There is no condemnation . . . (Rom. 8:1) and there is no accusation.

Finally Christ "nailed it to the cross." The aorist participle indicates the manner of the removal. It might be thought that this was giving publicity to the accusation on the lines of the "demonstration" of Romans 3:25–26, but this misses the apostle's point. For him there is a deep chasm between guilty sinners on the one hand and the cross on the other. The accusation is removed out of the midst of the sinners, taken right away from them, and nailed to the cross.

The reference can hardly be to the superscription on the cross. Pilate wrote it (John 19:19) and "they" put it above His head (Matt. 27:37). The nails were driven into Jesus (John 20:25). An alternative interpretation must be sought.

Paul's statement, "He nailed it to the cross," has certain implications:

Our Lord died by crucifixion: He was nailed to the cross.

His death was voluntary: He nailed. . . .

He was the embodiment of human guilt: He nailed "it."

Paul has telescoped the nailing of a body and the nailing of an accusation in one vivid expression. This is a "daring metaphor." ". . . the body of Christ, nailed to the cross, does in some sense represent humanity's guilt" (Moule).

All this was done at the cross. The accusation was taken away from men, to prevent a reminder of what had been obliterated; but it was not merely withdrawn. It was laid on Christ.

The subject is somewhat obscure. God "quickened you with him" (2:13), and it might be God who obliterated, removed and nailed. But we seem to have a *constructio ad sensum*, construction according to the sense, or a change of subject. Christ must be the subject of verse 15 and probably earlier. The "vagueness" coheres with the thought of Christ as the Image of God and of the unity of Father and Son.

The readers at one time "walked" in sins (3:7) and were dead (2:13). During the period of time between the cross of Jesus and their first hearing the gospel they were still dead. The obliteration, removal and nailing took place before they could receive the benefits therefrom. The guilt of men was obliterated and removed as an obstacle to God's forgiveness, and it was laid on Christ. But the Colossians had to hear the gospel to receive the forgiveness and its concomitant blessings. If this were not so, they would have ceased to be dead and would have been made alive without knowing anything about it. This is both an impossibility in itself and contrary to the tenor of the New Testament.

In taking upon himself man's "answerableness," his guilt, Christ has wrought redemption. The expression, "in whom we have redemption, the forgiveness of sins" (1:14), closely resembles that in Ephesians 1:7 and does not call for further comment (see pp. 216–17; cf. pp. 102; 135–36; 171–72).

Finally, "he made peace through the blood of his cross" (1:20). The subject is God. The question immediately arises, who was hostile? It seems to be "you" (1:21–22). But men did not put an end to their hostility to God the moment our Lord said "It is finished" (John 19:30) on the cross. And we have already seen in Colossians a divine "opposition." The handwriting which was against us (2:14) expresses far more than a guilty conscience. It is the divine accusation and its logical outcome, apart from the cross of Christ, would have been the wrath of God (cf. 3:6–7). The peace which was made through the blood of the cross was in God himself. (Cf. pp. 179–84; 231.)

The "blood" is cultic and the death of Christ was a sacrifice for sin. There are points of contact here with Hebrews 1:3 (cf. pp. 59–61).

In his cross Christ did something for men which they could not do for themselves. He bore their guilt; he reconciled the Father; he made a purification from sins. But not yet are men "qualified." They must first receive the benefits which flow from the cross. Hence we must pass on from Christ's work for us to his work in us.

## God at Work in Us—The Work of Christ in Us

As a preliminary we must notice the contrast in the lives of the Colossian readers between "then" and "now." They had once "walked" in all manner of sins and idolatry (3:7). Now they were to walk differently (1:10; 2:6). Once they had been alienated and hostile but now they were reconciled (1:21–22). Their life had been in the world (2:20) but it was now in Christ (2:6), in God (3:3). They had been subject to divine accusation (2:14). Now they knew forgiveness (1:14; 2:13; 3:13). Once they were dead (2:13). Now they were resurrected and made alive (2:12–13). Once they did not "belong," uncircumcized (2:13). Now they were part of the church (1:24), circumcized with a spiritual circumcision (2:11). What has happened to them?

In their day a new movement had emerged in the Roman Empire. Men went from place to place with a message. The outstanding example was St. Paul himself, an apostle of Christ Jesus (1:1). He does not seem to have visited Colossae himself but Epaphras had come to them (1:7). His coming was the occasion of a change in the Colossians.

God has now revealed what had hitherto been hidden and it is to be made known among men (1:25–2:2; cf. 4:3–4). Something "came" to the Colossians which they had not known before. They learned it from the lips of Epaphras, for they "heard" (1:5–7, 23) the truth of the gospel and came to know the grace of God. When they thus heard they were not merely informed. An atheist may be informed from the pulpit and may remain an atheist. The Colossians heard the voice of Epaphras and the message which he gave, and in it they heard more than a human utterance. God was speaking to them in Epaphras, inviting and summoning them. He was calling them and they were called (3:15) effectively.

For they had responded to the call. They had put off the old man with his deeds. They had stripped off the clothing of the old Adam. ". . . you have discarded the old nature with its deeds" (3:9, NEB). They had repented.

At the same time they had believed; they had exercised their "first faith." In that faith they must abide, not shifting from the hope of the gospel, which gospel they had heard (1:23). Though the apostle did not refrain from warning, he rejoiced at the solidity of their faith in Christ (2:5). It was not an evanescent thing. It was to be kept firm, "just as you were taught" (2:7) by the evangelist. So vital is faith that it must be "consolidated" (cf. Acts 16:5).

Repentance and faith were the response of the Colossians to the preaching of the gospel (cf. Acts 20:21). What happened when they repented and believed?

They were forgiven (3:13; cf. 1:14) and it was a lasting forgiveness. In Christ "we have . . . the forgiveness of sins." The apostle does not say here "we had" though he does use the aorist tense in 3:13; and he does not say "we shall have." We were given pardon when we believed and we still possess the pardon. (The difference between *aphesis* in 1:14 and *charizomai* in 3:13 is not material. They differ mainly as two distinct figures of speech. The "release" is due to the "grace.")

The doctrine of justification by faith is not formally or explicitly stated, but there is a hint of it in 1:22. If the readers are to be "free from accusation"; and if they are so free not in virtue of their own life and behavior but because it is "in God's sight," "in God's opinion"; and if there is a condition attached, "if you continue in the faith . . ." (1:23); then we have something very much like "justification in Colossians" (cf. pp. 225–26).

And the concomitants of justification are not absent either. God receives the believer. Instead of living in the world (2:20; cf. 2:8) he is now "in God" (3:3). This can be none other than "access." Further, he is no longer dead but "quickened" (2:13). If justification takes place in the divine Mind, quickening is an experience of the believing man. He is alive from the dead. This is expressed in other idioms also. Even if in some way it is associated with baptism, his experience is of being raised through faith (2:12; 3:1). He has "put on the new man" (3:10). This is a beginning, as decisive as the donning of a new garment. A believing man does not spend the whole of his Christian lifetime in putting on the new man. Note the aorist tense. In other language, his Christian life is not a process of conversion or regeneration, of being born again. But once the new man has been put on (once the man has been converted to Christ) he goes through a constant process of renewal which issues in a knowledge of his Creator characteristic of unfallen man. Justified by faith in Christ, he knows the work of grace in his heart and ever more deeply knows God.

For he has received Christ Jesus the Lord (2:6). These words must be given their full weight. He has not merely received the tradition, the form of words in which Christ was preached.[8] He has indeed received them and believed them. But this is so far on the level of intellectual assent. He has intellectually assented but he has done more. He has received Christ into his heart. I believe that this statement can stand on its own feet and therefore refer to Ephesians 3:17 not to find support but solely for the purposes of illustration. A text which cries aloud to be quoted is John 1:11–12, ". . . his own people did not receive him. But to all those who did receive him. . . ."[9]

If Christ is in a man's heart and if he with Christ is in God, we have what Paul elsewhere called (Rom. 8:15; cf. Gal. 4:5) the spirit of adoption. For consider the situation of a man in whom Christ dwells. In a sense we can say that two persons dwell in him. Christ lives in him. And although St. Paul (Gal. 2:20) says that he himself no longer lives, he goes on to speak of "the life which I am now living in the flesh." So that we may say after all that Christ lives in a believing man and the man himself lives ("in himself," as it were). This experience is not unique to the apostle. He differs from many other Christians in the intensity of his experience but not in its essential quality.

Now in the unity of a believer's consciousness it would not be right to affirm that Christ within him looks up to the Father with filial consciousness but that the believer himself does not. Hence the presence of Christ in his heart means that he has the spirit of adoption. In any case God has received him and he is "in God."

The fact that the believer has received Christ is confirmed by the expression, "Christ in you" (en humin). This is more than "among you," as the thrice affirmed "every man" attests (Col. 1:27–28). Similarly "the Word which consists of Christ" is to dwell "in you" (again en humin) and you are to sing to God in (or "with") your hearts (3:16). Christ in the individual heart inspires the song even of individuals gathered in community (cf. p. 233).

Thus we see in Colossians, though not always in the same language, something which approximates to justification and its concomitants. The fact that justification sets up a permanent relationship between God and the believer is shown by the fact that he continues to give thanks to God through Christ (3:17). He is the permanent Mediator.

In regard to the "quickening" which is a concomitant of justification, we ought perhaps to add that this is to be taken in relation to the previously "being dead in trespasses" (2:13). The "dying" of the Christian refers to the crucifixion of the old ego as the culmination of a spiritual struggle which ends in conversion. Within the limits of the figure of speech, crucifixion, the new life of the new believer is a resurrection (cf. pp. 139–41).

The crucifixion of the ego, an inner, spiritual experience, is followed by

8. See Moule, p. 89; and C. F. D. Moule, *The Phenomenon of the New Testament*, p. 26, n. 9.
9. For the repetition of the compound verb in simple form, see C. K. Barrett, *The Gospel according to St. John*, p. 136; Moulton, *Grammar*, 1:115.

public "burial" (2:12). In submitting to the rite the man who has already begun to believe "externalises" and makes permanent the inner experience of crucifixion which he has already had. The resurrection in Christ (*en hōi*)[10] through faith did not start in baptism but in baptism was symbolized and confirmed. As the candidate emerged from the water in which he had been immersed, he knew and the congregation knew that his old, sinful ego was dead and that he was alive in Christ. The baptism itself told a story. Who knows what joyous and "living" thoughts swept through the mind of the candidate?

The circumcision of 2:11 is a description of spiritual experience rather than an allusion to baptism. It is the circumcision of the heart. It could hardly be associated with baptism because it is *acheiropoiētos*. This adjective elsewhere means "not made with hands," and is appropriate to, or used of, a temple (Mark 14:58). But circumcision is not "made" but "done." The verb *poieō* has this meaning (Col. 3:17). A circumcision "not done with hands" can hardly refer to baptism, especially baptism by immersion, which "buried" (2:12) requires. Paul surely was not thinking of se-baptism, in which a man baptizes himself.

We have spoken of inner struggle and its outcome, the final (and initial!) decision of faith. When a man thus first believed he ceased to be hostile to God. He responded with faith to the preaching of the cross and "through the death" of Christ thus preached and believed he was reconciled (1:21–22). If we were correct in seeing justification by faith in Colossians, we have its analogy in God's regarding men as holy, as having the cultic qualification to approach him, "the static morality of innocence" (p. 225). "The holy ones" is a characteristic description of Christians (1:2, 4, 12, 26; cf. 3:12), but they still need the exhortations of 3:1–4:6. Though holy "in God's opinion," they still need positively to seek the things above. There are goals not yet attained even by holy men. Though holy in God's sight, they are still to dwell in thought on things above. The earthly glitter may obscure the vision of heavenly glory (3:1–2).

Christian believers belong to the church, which is distinct from non-members (4:5, 15–16), and they have a glorious prospect (3:4, 24). In the meantime they are already in the kingdom of God's Son and in its light. They have been rescued from an old authority and consciously transferred to a new one. Their "qualification" for this privilege was the response of repentance and faith to the preaching of the cross. Presiding over the cross, the preaching of the cross and the response to the cross was the sovereign grace of God (1:12–13). For they are part of God's beloved elect (3:12).

---

10. See Dunn, *Baptism in the Holy Spirit*, p. 154, n. 7. The whole discussion on pp. 153–57 is instructive.

# 8

# The Epistle
# to Philemon

THIS SHORT LETTER comprises only twenty-five verses. It might therefore be thought that it could safely be omitted from our consideration. It might indeed be safe to disregard it. Such a document could hardly upset the balance of our findings. Even so we shall examine it, partly in the interests of thoroughness and partly through curiosity. A generation or so ago scholars like Hoskyns and Davey, and William Manson, showed that the individual *pericopai* which are the constituents of the Synoptic Gospels are steeped in messianic material. We may find that the Epistle to Philemon is similarly colored with the Pauline gospel.

In view of the shortness of the letter and the absence of any great risk we shall reverse our previous method. We shall not begin by considering the evidence for the character of God and then go on to examine the work of Christ for us and in us. We shall rather start with the existing situation and work backwards. (A bare number in parentheses will indicate a verse in the epistle.)

## God at Work in Us—The Work of Christ in Us

Paul refers to Philemon and to others as "fellow-workers" (1, 24). What are they working at? Archippus is called a "fellow soldier" or "comrade-in-arms" (2). What are they fighting for? The answer is summed up in the one word, "gospel" (13). The expression, "the fetters of the gospel," means that Paul is in prison because of his activities as an apostle and evangelist. His fellow workers share with him the task of making the gospel known.

One result of this work of evangelism is seen in the story of Onesimus, the runaway slave. He must have encountered the apostle in prison. Whatever the circumstances of the meeting, St. Paul took advantage of the opportunity. He preached the gospel to him. Philemon's slave became Paul's own child, "whom I begat in bonds" (10; cf. 1 Cor. 4:14–15). Philemon should understand the experience through which Onesimus had gone.

He himself had also been converted through the apostle's ministry. He owed his very self to Paul (19), his new, believing self.

For obviously Philemon had a "self" before he met Paul. The new self is not unrelated to "the new man" (Col 3:10), which "replaces" the old, crucified ego (Gal. 2:19–20). Philemon has been "quickened" (Rom. 4:17). He cannot be excluded from "your prayers" mentioned in verse 22, which Paul hopes will be answered. Philemon has access to God. God has received him. God has quickened him. This is remarkably like some of the concomitants of justification!

For the God whom Paul knows is the God who deals with individuals. He gives thanks to "my God" and he does it "in my prayers" (4). We must therefore ask at what point Philemon gained his new "self."

It can only be when he first put his faith in Jesus. The structure of verse 5 is almost certainly a chiasmus. (See note 39 in the chapter on Hebrews.) Faith and love are sufficiently important for the apostle to give thanks for them. Philemon has faith "directed towards" (pros) the Lord Jesus and love "to" (eis) all the saints. Faith in Christ is sustained; and it is expressed in love.

It may be inferred that Philemon has not always had faith. He has it now. It is a living faith, expressed in love. It is important. Is it farfetched to see in Philemon an experience which Paul elsewhere described as justifying faith?

Philemon has a love for all "the saints" (5) and they have been refreshed by him (7). There is nothing in the epistle to suggest that he is no more than a sympathetic outsider, like the worthy centurion who "loves our nation and himself built our synagogue for us" (Luke 7:5). On the contrary Philemon very much "belongs." He is not excluded from the company of the "saints." But there was a time when neither he nor Onesimus could be counted in their number.

When did they become saints? When did they become holy? This raises the whole question of the cultic qualification to approach God (cf. p. 225). As unbelievers they were without the qualification. Now they possess it. They were surely given it when they first believed in Jesus.

Paul is far from speaking here about justification by faith or sanctification by faith. The spiritual experience of Philemon and Onesimus, however, even though briefly described, can be interpreted in accordance with the Pauline doctrine. If this view is rejected we have to explain their experience in another way. This is not easy. Has Philemon a new self? If he has not, what has happened to him? If he has, and if he joins in the prayers, what is to be put in place of his being quickened and his having been received by God—concomitants of justification? And how does Onesimus differ from those "begotten" in 1 Corinthians 4:14–15? If they have not been given a cultic qualification to approach God, what have they in its place?

We have been thinking of individual experience, the exercise of faith. It appears again in the expression, "thy faith" (6). Even so this very verse suggests that we are concerned with more than merely individual experience. The interpretation is not easy but we shall attempt it.

We notice first that Paul is preparing the way, step by step, for his request to Philemon. It was a serious business for a slave to run away, but Paul wants his owner to welcome him as he would welcome the apostle himself (17). He does not mention this dangerous topic at once but leads up to it. Notice the progress.

The apostle begins with thanksgiving for Philemon's faith and for his love to all God's people. Hitherto there are no exceptions. Then he prays for a certain recognition on the part of Philemon, of which we shall have more to say shortly. At this point (7) he recalls his own joy and encouragement inspired by Philemon's love to God's people, which he has shown by "refreshing" them. The *gar* in this verse may explain the thanksgiving for the love of verse 5 or, perhaps better, the suppressed clause after verse 6. "I pray that. . . . (I have high hopes that this prayer will be answered.) *For* I gained much joy . . . at your love: you have already put new heart into God's people, my brother." Still treading cautiously the apostle acknowledges his right to command, but rejects it in favor of an appeal to the Christian love which Philemon has already shown. Only then, and with a side glance at his own imprisonment for Christ's sake, does he mention the slave by name, linking Onesimus to himself as a convert (like Philemon! 19), virtually promising good behavior in a playful pun and almost putting Philemon under obligation voluntarily to welcome Onesimus as a brother beloved. It might be thought a tall order, but Paul has broached the question with great skill and feeling.

Paul has referred to "the fellowship of your faith" (6). We can hardly translate *koinōnia* as "participation" in your faith. The word "your" stands in the way. It is better to take "your faith" (*tēs pisteōs*) as a subjective genitive. "Fellowship" implies something held in common. Philemon already, like Paul and Onesmimus, has faith in Jesus (5) and Jesus is "common" to them all. They have a joint participation (*koinōnia*) by faith in the Son of God (1 Cor. 1:9). Paul can therefore speak of "your faith's joint participation" without specifying Him in whom he participated.

This *koinōnia* is primarily a relationship. Two men in different parts of the world, unknown to each other, as believers participate in their common Lord. The relationship can become an experience when they meet in Christ's Name and an activity when it is expressed. Paul prays that the relationship may be expressed, the quiescent stirred into action, the potential become the actual. The adjective *energēs* suggests the Aristotelian concept of actuality. Even the potentiality of a door may be actualized when it lets men in (1 Cor. 16:9). Fellowship is a relationship, an experience, an activity.

What does Paul want Philemon to do, according to his prayer? In common with other Christians he is a believer. Paul desires this faith to be actualized and expressed, to be shown for what it is: a faith in Christ which others exercise also. It will show itself in the recognition (cf. Rom. 3:20) "of everything good in us—for Christ." The "us" means Christians other than Philemon, in particular Paul and Timothy and perhaps even just Paul himself. As a partner, a "commoner" (cf. 17) of the believing community, Philemon should recognize as good all that other partners do in the service of Christ. Paul is leading up to what he has done in the conversion of

Onesimus (this must be good) and what he is going to ask of Philemon. This also is good and Paul prays that Philemon may so recognize it.

We have discussed this at some length in order to bring out the presence of Christian community or fellowship in the epistle. The individual has a social context. He is "in Christ," "in the Lord" (16, 20, 23), in the church, certainly in the local church "in thy house" (2). If we ask how Philemon managed to enter the church, we have as background all that Paul has ever taught on the subject: the preaching of the gospel, the divine call, repentance and faith, justification and sanctification, and the rite of initiation, baptism. The Christian, the "church man," is described by the term "brother," and Philemon himself is so addressed (7, 20). It is distinct from the relationship of blood or social tie (16). A female Christian is a "sister" (2).

Now Philemon loved all his fellow members (5). If we ask why he was so deeply aware of his relationship to his brothers in the Lord, we can only say that he was deeply aware of their common Father, "God our Father" (3). This points to Paul's doctrine of adoption and the testimony of the Holy Spirit (Rom 8:15–16; Gal 4:6–7).

Theology is veiled in the apparently simple statement of verse 15: "Perhaps he was separated (from you) for a while for this purpose, namely in order that you might keep him for ever." Here is an overruling Providence, planning and purposing, controlling the affairs of history and the decisions of men, seeing and loving and aiding individual men. If Onesimus is to be kept permanently as a brother beloved (16) it would seem that the Christian life of both Philemon and Onesimus is to continue. This accords with the fact that justification sets up a permanent relationship between God and the believer, a relationship which is exemplified in the prayers (22). The hope that the prayers will be answered confirms the belief in Providence. When Paul spoke of keeping the former slave "forever" (*aiōnion*) his primary thought was that "he will never run away again." A believer could not fail, however, to notice the choice of a word. When he sees *aiōnios* he is reminded of the long range of the joyous Christian prospect. This does not "prove" immortality or, better, resurrection but it serves as a reminder.

## God at Work for Us—The Work of Christ for Us

So far the Epistle to Philemon is colored with Paul's teaching about the work of Christ in us. We must now consider the evidence, if any, for the work which Christ has done for us. There is no formal statement of doctrine. But Paul would not have been the man he was if it could not be said concerning him that "thy speech bewrayeth thee" (Matt. 26:73, kjv). The evangelical accent abides.

To begin with, his attitude toward God is one of thanksgiving (4). Apart from mere social courtesies, thanksgiving is the recognition of something received without payment. At the end of the week an employed man does not normally burst into his employer's office with tears of gratitude for his pay envelope. Paul has received something beyond his wildest imagination.

He has not bought it, earned it or deserved it. It was God's free gift—the gospel (13). It is summed up in the words *grace* and *peace* (3, 25). This is no formal salutation or farewell, like "Goodbye," from which the "God be with you" has been removed. Full weight must be given to both words. Behind them lies all the apostle's teaching about grace and God's attitude of peace toward men through the work of the cross. The grace and peace are still "coming." The cross has altered the situation for men and the offer of the gospel is still open. Father and Son are united in this work. In particular if grace still comes from Christ, he must be able to give it. He is no longer in the tomb. His resurrection and exaltation are necessary if he is still to give grace. The full title is significant. Jesus is the Man of Nazareth. As Christ he fulfills the Old Testament prophecies and promises. As Lord he shares in deity and has the preeminence.

It is probably true that if the Epistle to Philemon were the only Pauline document to have survived, it would be hard if not impossible to reconstruct the apostle's teaching. If, however, we have deeply studied his major epistles, we cannot miss the color of what is almost "a note to a friend." Unless we are colorblind, we shall see the scarlet of the blood of the cross.

# 9

## The Epistle
## to the Philippians

THERE IS A WARMTH in the Epistle to the Philippians which is to be distinguished from the heat which may be felt in the Epistle to the Galatians. Even in his imprisonment the apostle Paul is sustained by his joy in Christ. It would be going too far to say that he had mellowed with the years, as if an earlier crudity had been refined and a pugnaciousness laid to rest. Paul is indeed mellow and he has the heart of a pastor. Yet he can still express himself strongly and can still contend vigorously for the faith.

It is not necessary for our purpose to discuss the unity of Philippians. Some scholars have felt that two distinct letters are to be discerned, apart from the question of Paul's possible use of an existing Christian hymn (2:5-11). If the two letters are separated by only a year, it is likely that the character of the apostle is consistent in both. His theological and spiritual development has already taken place.[1]

We revert now to our earlier method, which we temporarily abandoned when considering the Epistle to Philemon, and direct our attention to the character of God as we find it in Philippians.

## THE NATURE OF GOD

God exists (2:6) and he is *the living God*. "God is my witness" (1:8). The reference to "the form of God" (2:6) suggests that *God may be characterized*. Something may be said of him. (We shall have to speak further about "form" later.) *God has consciousness*. There would be no point in the exhortation to "let your requests be made known to God" (4:6) if he were unconscious. Consciousness implies at least a minimum of knowledge. God's mind is not to be regarded as a *tabula rasa*, a blank sheet of paper, until our requests are made known to him. In the context of Paul's thought it is not stretching the evidence to say that *God has knowledge*.

---

1. See Gerhard Friedrich, pp. 95, 116, 128; F. W. Beare, pp. 1-5. Phil. 2:5-11 is given exhaustive treatment by R. P. Martin in *Carmen Christi*. Where only the author's name is given in the text or notes, the reference is to his commentary on Philippians.

For within his consciousness we may discern will. *God has will* (2:13) and *purpose* (2:27). Epaphroditus fell grievously ill, but "God had mercy upon him . . . in order that [*hina*] I might not pile sorrow upon sorrow." Through the act of God the patient was saved from death. Thus *God has power*. It is part of his wealth (4:19) in accordance with which he will fully meet our every need.

From this it may be inferred that *God is active*. He exalted Christ (2:9), he is active in his people (2:13) and he will give them a further revelation (3:15).

In character *God is righteous*. In 3:4–9 there is a clear echo of Romans. There is a righteousness in the realm of law and a righteousness which is given by God. As "holy" is the mark of God's people (1:1; 4:21–22), we may add that *God is holy*. It is unthinkable that the author of Philippians should repudiate the righteousness and holiness of God.

*God is to be worshiped* (4:20; cf. 2:11; 3:3). Within worship are prayer and thanksgiving (4:6; cf. 1:3, 9). *He is to be obeyed but is not*. On the one hand we see the example of Christ (2:8) and on the other the behavior of men. They serve a false God; their interests are earthly. It is not that they are degraded without knowing it. They are themselves the objects of their own endeavor and they glory in their shame (2:3–4; 3:18–19).[2] They may be downright pagans or they may be "semi-Christians" (Beare, p. 134), not legalists but antinomians. But are semi-Christians Christians? However we answer the question, Paul looks out on a crooked and perverse generation (2:15). Morally they are not "straight" but "crooks." They "live" in the dark and in death.

In all the affairs of men *God has an attitude*. The ideal of blamelessness (2:15) points in contrast to those whom *God does blame*. In other circumstances an action may please him (4:18). *God deals with individuals*. Paul speaks of "my God" (1:3; 4:19).[3] God dealt with Epaphroditus by the mercy of sparing his life and with Paul in the same incident by sparing him sorrow upon sorrow (2:27). The final issue of men's sin is *perdition* (1:28; 3:19), the opposite of salvation—from God. The God who blames and who deals with individuals does not stare helplessly at men on the road to perdition, nor does he weakly acquiesce. "Perdition and salvation both refer to the final destiny of men as it will be appointed to them in the day of judgment" (Beare, p. 68).

We have earlier noticed the proleptic or historical occurrence of God's wrath and judgment (cf. Rom. 1:24, 26, 28). Friedrich (p. 106) observes with regard to Philippians 1:28 that "the final judgment of God throws its shadow forward, so that what the Last Day will confirm is already taking place in the present." It is not dissimilar in 2:15–16. The shining of the Christian "stars" implies a surrounding darkness, ominously suggested by

---

2. For "unconscious degradation" cf. J. Alexander Clapperton, *The Essentials of Theology*, pp. 447–49. He impressively quotes Robertson of Brighton in support of his theory. But hell is more than "stripping off the epaulettes of an officer" or the unfrocking of a priest.

3. Cf. Friedrich, p. 98, "die Innigkeit des Verhältnisses zu Gott"—"the intimacy of the relation to God."

"in the world." They hold out the Word of life, offering it to those who are devoid of life. (Cf. Rom. 1:21; 5:12; 6:23; Col. 1:12–13; 2:13.)

## THE OTHER SIDE—GOD FOR MAN

The pattern which has emerged is not so full or detailed as in some of the epistles previously examined but it is recognizable and clear. Its outline corresponds to what we have previously found with regard to the character of God.

As in the earlier epistles there is also "another side." God fully meets every need (4:19). From him come grace and peace (1:2; 4:7, 9). He shows mercy (2:27), is described as Father (1:2; 2:11; 4:20) and he has children (2:15). Though we have heard of perdition, we learn also of salvation (1:19, 28; 2:12).

Men "are heading for destruction" (3:19, NEB) and yet there is salvation. How is this brought about?

### God at Work for Us—The Work of Christ for Us

It is clear that God has a Word (1:14) and it is to be "spoken." It is the Word of life (2:16). In the context of the epistle this is the gospel, and Paul is at his post to defend it (1:16; cf. 1:7). It must be told to men. But this is no other than preaching Christ (1:15, 17–18). Hence the gospel is Christ himself. But who is Christ?

He is One who is alive, for in Paul's view "to go on living is Christ" (1:21; cf. Gal. 2:20). But there is something far better in store. He desires the gain which death will bring, to slip his cable and be with Christ (1:23). Thus not only is Christ alive but he will also go on living. He lives; he will live; because he has lived. Paul implies the preexistence of Christ.

### The Form of God

Christ was in the form of God. The verb *huparchō* (2:6) has more significance than is sometimes realized. As E. M. Cope says, "the verbs *huparchein, einai, gignesthai,* stand to one another in the relation of past, present and future; to be already in existence, to be (simple and absolute being, independent of time), and to become, to come into being from a state (if that be possible) of non-being." "To be already . . ." involves two elements, continuity and relevance. *Continuity* means the opposite of a flash in the pan. The verb *huparchō* thus means "to be in a state arising out of the previous same state." *Relevance* requires us to add "and be a factor in the situation and one to be reckoned with."

The spirit of the verb is best brought out by an illustration. If a man suddenly fell off a high bridge into a deep river we could describe him by the phrase "being in the river" or "having become (*genomenos*) in the river." Now it might happen that in the river in question and at that very time, the half-mile swimming race was in progress and that just as we were despairing of the life of the drowning man one of the competitors appeared. We could describe him as "being in the river." But suppose we said "*huparchōn* in the river"? This would imply (1) that he was already in the water (and had not dived in to the rescue); (2) that he continued to be in the water; and (3) that he was in the place, i.e., the water, from which a rescue was possible. In other words he had been swimming for, say, a quarter of a mile, he kept on swimming without a break, and he was a factor in the situation and one to be reckoned with.[4]

This is a weighty way in which to begin the *locus classicus* on the Person of Christ. At the beginning of our story, so to speak, our Lord was in the form of God already and he continued so to be without a break—a crucial factor in the situation. We can take the illustration further and draw a parallel between the Lord and the swimmer. If the latter enjoys swimming, is confident of winning the race and is keenly looking forward to winning, and makes some sacrifice in turning aside to an unseemly struggle in midstream with a desperate man, we can say of him: "*huparchōn* in the river, he did not count getting first to the winning post as something to snatch." The force of the participle is plain. He was "all set" to win.

We must now consider the meaning of "form" (*morphē*). Modern interpretation may be said to begin with J. B. Lightfoot, whose commentary on Philippians is still well known and used. In Lightfoot's view *morphē* implies the "essential attributes." "It is used in a sense substantially the same which it bears in Greek philosophy" (pp. 110, 132).

The value of Lightfoot's work here was challenged by H. A. A. Kennedy (3:435–37), who was influenced by a trend away from classical studies as a tool of New Testament interpretation. He has little place for the minute investigation of the refinements of Greek metaphysics. The word *morphē* had come to receive "a vague, general meaning, far removed from the accurate, metaphysical content which belonged to it in writers like Plato and Aristotle." Paul uses it here "in a loose, popular sense, as we use 'nature.'"

Kennedy weakens his case, however, by asking what other terms the apostle could have used to express his conceptions. Could he have written *hos toioutos huparchōn hoios ho Theos*? Kennedy would have been horrified at the encouragement given to the Homoiousians, the men who from the Council of Nicaea (A.D. 325) onwards have regarded our Lord as being of like substance, not of one substance, with the Father. The apostle "means in the strictest sense that the preexisting Christ was Divine. For *morphē* always signifies a form which truly and fully expresses the being which underlies it." Christ possesses "the same kind of existence as God possesses."

The last sentence betrays Kennedy. The "kind" may be attributed to both God and Christ. It is thus a universal. The word *morphē* "is often identified with *eidos* and *ti ēn einai*. . . ."[5] We refrain from speculating whether in this case the form is to be identified with the substance, or how far St. Paul was conversant with Aristotelianism. Who knows what he might have picked up in Tarsus? We merely observe that *form* is one of the terms which "like

4. E. M. Cope, *The Rhetoric of Aristotle,* 1:65; R. A. Ward, "Aristotelian Elements in the Philosophical Vocabulary of the New Testament," pp. 454–90.
5. W. D. Ross, *Aristotle's Metaphysics,* 2:165.

ideas, gradually permeate society till they reach its lower strata. Words stamped in the mint of the philosopher pass into general currency, losing their sharpness of outline meanwhile, but in the main retaining their impress and value. The exclusive technicalities of the scholastic logic are the common property of shopmen and artisans in our own day" (Lightfoot, p. 130). I have read Dr. R. P. Martin's survey (*Carmen Christi*, pp. 99–133) with appreciation and admiration but cannot help feeling that the scholars whose work is described have been engaged in a speculative task. For example Hatch and Redpath in their *Concordance* cite only about a dozen instances of *morphē* in the LXX, and the proof that it is synonymous with *eidos* and *homoiōma* is precarious. Further, to identify "visible form" with "glory" draws attention to the "shining light" around God to the neglect of the other conception of glory, God's revealed being, character, majesty and might.[6] The reference to the myth of a heavenly redeemer lacks cogent proof and even an allusion to Adam is but an undertone.

We shall therefore try as far as possible to understand the text from the text itself. The word *morphē* appears again almost immediately (2:7) and it affords a clue. It would require very strong proof to convince us that it occurs twice in close juxtaposition with two different meanings.

### The Form of a Slave

St. Paul says that Christ "emptied himself by taking [*labōn*—aorist of coincident action] the form of a slave." If we ask the question, "What slave?" it is apparent at once that the answer is "any slave," or "a slave as such." In other words we are dealing not with an individual slave but with a class name which is applicable to every member of the class. Thus "slave" is a universal.

Whether or not the apostle could expound the meaning of *form* is at the moment irrelevant. He was at home with the idea. He can use a generic singular without any trouble: "the Jew" or "the weak man" (Rom. 3:1; 14:1).[7] It is much too weak to think of "a visible form . . . by which the slave is recognised and known."[8] Who would look at Jesus of Nazareth and from his appearance characterize him as a slave?

The term *slave* may be defined as "a human being without any rights whatsoever." It may be that humanitarianism made the lot of individual slaves comparatively happy and that the definition as a result is unduly severe. This hardly affects our argument. We are concerned with a metaphor which admirably describes our Lord's attitude. " . . . slave of all. For the Son of Man did not come to be served but to serve and to give his life as a ransom for many" (Mark 10:44–45). "I have come down from heaven not to do my will but the will of him who sent me" (John 6:38). (Cf. Luke 22:27; John 4:34; 5:30.)

There was nothing slavish about our Lord: we have only to think of his

---

6. Cf. R. A. Ward, *Royal Theology*, pp. 36–47.
7. Cf. Moulton-Turner, *Grammar*, 3:22. Note that "the Jew as a Jew" is followed in Rom. 3:2 by "*they* were entrusted with. . . ." 2 Tim. 3:17 should be contrasted with 1 Tim. 6:11.
8. Vincent Taylor, *The Person of Christ in New Testament Teaching*, p. 75.

ability to inspire men to follow him or of his coolness under examination or in controversy. His being a slave, or rather his taking the form of a slave, vividly expresses his willingness to serve, to give up his rights. "Do you think that I cannot appeal to my Father and he will at once send to my aid more than twelve legions of angels?" (Matt 26:53). Or consider the whole story of the Temptation (Matt. 4:1–11 and parallels).

Thus we should observe the parallelism. He was in the form of God; he took the form of a slave. The significance of the "form" is brought out if we ask ourselves, "Was he a slave?" The answer must be a decided negative and therefore he could have been a slave only figuratively. Take the figure as a metaphor and we must say that "he was a slave—metaphorically." Use a simile and the statement reads that "he was like a slave." There is no question of his being like to any particular slave. The term must therefore be generic. (Notice that though "slave" is generic, "God" is not.)

Paul does not say that in taking the form of a slave Christ abandoned the form of God. He does, however, mention two "steps," one negative and one positive. First, "he did not deem equality with God a matter of snatching." Equality with God was not yet within the grasp of the preexistent Christ. This seems to conflict with his being in the form of God, but in fact it does not. The Greek behind "equality" should be noted: *to einai isa theōi*. Paul does not say *ison* (or *isos*) but *isa*. This adverbial accusative does not have to be regarded as an adjective. A natural translation would be "to exist in a manner of equality with God."[9]

The comparison with John 5:18 is, I think, a false trail. Here Jesus is "making himself equal to God," i.e., independent of God. The Rabbinic Hiphil of *shawah* (the Hebrew behind the Greek verb of John 5:18—cf. Isa. 46:5) speaks of equating, but Paul speaks of being equal or rather of existence in a manner of equality. Even Schlatter (on the "making himself equal" of John 5:18) is content with the succinct "Siehe [See] Matt. 20:12."[10]

Now Christ was already in the form of God and to that extent was already equal to God. What could he possibly lack? It could hardly be cosmic dominion. He was the Agent of creation (Col. 1:15–17), and we cannot suppose a sort of "Christ-deism." He did not create the universe and then leave it until he resumed power and authority over it at his exaltation. What he lacked was existence in a certain manner of equality with God. What was the "manner"?

St. Paul himself supplies the answer. The worship which has hitherto been addressed to God is now to be offered on a universal scale to Jesus (Phil. 2:9–11). Paul alludes to Isaiah 45:23, a passage which he knows full well ascribes worship to God (cf. Rom. 14:11). Now it is to be given to

9. Cf. M. R. Vincent, pp. 58–59. The use of *einai* in the sense of "exist" is not foreign to Paul. See Rom. 4:17; 1 Cor. 1:28; 8:5; and Arndt-Gingrich, p. 222. I have since come across Gerard Manley Hopkins's "no snatching-matter"—*New Testament Studies* 18, No. 2 (Jan. 1972): 152.
10. R. P. Martin, *Carmen Christi*, p. 148; A. Schlatter, *Der Evangelist Johannes*, p. 147.

Jesus, hitherto unknown to men. To him is given the Name of Lord, the Old Testament Yahweh. "He hath changed the ineffable name into a name utterable by man, and desirable by all the world; the majesty is all arrayed in robes of mercy, the tetragrammaton or adorable mystery of the patriarchs is made fit for pronunciation and expression when it becometh the name of the Lord's Christ."[11]

So much for the negative "step": our Lord did not regard the adoration of men as a prize to be seized. On the contrary "he emptied himself." This is sometimes referred to Isaiah 53:12, "He poured out his soul unto death," and it may be an undertone. But it is more instructive to examine Paul's use of the two words, *heauton ekenōsen*. It will not perhaps take us far to notice that it is possible to empty a pail and to empty water. But when Paul uses the verb *kenoō* he seems to imply the result that "there is nothing in it." If certain conditions apply, there is nothing in faith (Rom. 4:14), the cross (1 Cor. 1:17) or his own "boast" (1 Cor. 9:15; 2 Cor. 9:3). What happens, then, if there is nothing in self? Paul speaks of not living for self (2 Cor. 5:15) and of Christ who did not please himself (Rom. 15:3). He had himself entered into the experience of making the self nothing. "I [note the strong *egō*] am no longer living . . . " (Gal. 2:20).

It would seem that the clause "he emptied himself" is a kind of summary or anticipation of the explanatory phrase, "by taking the form of a slave." At the incarnation, self was nothing and all "rights" abandoned even though the form of God persisted. The word *ekenōsen* "does not indicate a surrender of deity, nor a paralysis of deity, nor a change of personality, nor a break in the continuity of self-consciousness."[12]

### The Likeness of Men

As if to make doubly sure, the apostle adds to the phrase, "by taking the form of a slave." Literally we might go on to render "having become [*genomenos*] in the likeness of men." The verb denotes a transition. Something new has happened. He *became* incarnate. The meaning might also include "being born" (cf. Rom. 1:3; Gal. 4:4). "Likeness" must not be interpreted in the sense of "mere likeness." Paul was no docetist. He uses the word elsewhere (Rom. 8:3) and "it leaves room for the thought that the human likeness is not the whole story" (Beare, p. 83).

Paul is quite insistent on the humanity of Christ. He was found, appeared, as a man in *schēma*. The LXX does not help us in elucidating the meaning of this word. It appears there only once (Isa. 3:17) and then as the equivalent of the Hebrew *pōth*, which Holladay translates by "forehead."[13] We must extend our search.

Scholars have tended to emphasize outward appearance, but this neglects the fact that *schēma* can be an object of thought as well as of sense—if it

11. Jeremy Taylor, *Works*, 2:72, quoted by Kennedy, 3:439.
12. Vincent, p. 89. But see G. Braumann, *Begriffslex.* 5:541; E. Beyreuther, *Begriffslex.* 6:579. Reference should be made to Eugene R. Fairweather's "The 'Kenotic' Christology," an appended note to Beare, pp. 159–74.
13. William L. Holladay, *Concise Hebrew and Aramaic Lexicon of the Old Testament*, p. 300.

can be an object of sense. A basic meaning is "shape," but this needs qualification. The term *schēma* means "shape without size" or in Aristotelian language "form minus measurement." It may include "geometrical shape" like that of a circle, however large or small the radius may be. It may mean "logical shape" like that of analogy, an equality of ratios, or that of the syllogistic "figure" (determined by the function of the middle term), or that of the "figure of predication" or category—the ten ultimate genera. "Shape without size" may cover "social shape" like outward show or fine airs, the "cut" of clothes or the "style" of a man (or even of his speech, "literary shape"). In the plural the word means "gesture," a succession of shapes, as a slow motion film shows. We should notice once more the absence of size or measurement. Gesture is possible to a tall or a short man, fat or thin as the case may be. An interesting modern parallel may be found in the fact that in Ireland a person who goes about putting on airs (the Irish say "swanking") is said to be "shaping." [14]

In all these examples size or measurement is at a discount. The word is applicable to a man of any stature and includes such ideas as style, carriage, figure, address, gait, attitude, expression and bearing. Paul is extending the range of the bare "likeness of men." In all the different circumstances of his life and in all the varied situations Christ appeared as a man. (If we need to emphasize "appearance," we have all we need in the verb *heuretheis*.) There were times when he acted on the grand scale, magnificently, as when he stilled the tempest. There were times when it was the very reverse of this, as when during the same incident he was asleep. He displayed a majestic moral authority during the cleansing of the Temple and a pathetic submission when he said, "I thirst."

The apostle implies that in these and in all other incidents, in matters of greater and of lesser moment, in dealing with crowds and with individuals, in the Transfiguration and on the cross, on a grand scale and in the details of life, Christ exhibited the *style* of a man. This is the force of "shape *without size*." [15]

### The Death of the Cross

Having asserted that the One who was in the form of God took the form of a slave and became man, Paul describes the next step downwards. His language is paradoxical. "He humbled himself—by becoming obedient" (2:8). The self-abnegation was continued and it was voluntary. We are forbidden to see the alien forces closing in on an unwilling victim, forced to endure what he could not escape. He humbled himself, of his own free will; but it was at the same time an act of obedience.

The obedience was rendered to God (cf. Rom. 5:18–19) rather than to the elemental spirits. Christ obeyed his Father throughout his life, up to and including his death. This must be the hidden history conveyed by the word *mechri*, "to the length of."

---

14. I owe this information to Professor E. H. Warmington.
15. See further Ward, "Aristotelian Elements": for *morphē*, pp. 601–637; for *schema*, pp. 562–600.

Death itself is not the lowest point of his descent. There is a further phrase which some scholars regard as Paul's addition to an existing hymn. If it is such an addition, it is all the more significant. Christ was obedient not only to the length of death but of death of a cross. This is the nadir of his incarnation.

The death on the cross is the expression of perfect obedience (Friedrich). We ought to be very careful before we say that Christ obeyed death or obeyed the elemental spirits. Obedience implies that "they told him what to do." Had they the right so to command him? Obedience in the abstract is neutral. In some instances obedience can be highly immoral.[16] In the trial after World War II of the German leaders and their subordinates, it was established that it was no defense merely to plead obedience to orders. The perfect obedience of Christ derived its merit from the fact that it was obedience to God.

Friedrich observes (p. 110) that the cross belongs to the vocabulary of Pauline preaching (1 Cor. 1:13, 17, 18, 23; 2:2, 8; 2 Cor. 13:4; Gal. 3:1; 5:11; 6:12, 14). It represents the sum and substance of his message, his very glory. He can therefore speak of Christ as having breathed out his life in complete solitariness, "von Gott und Menschen verlassen"—"abandoned by God and men." Martin (*Carmen Christi*, pp. 221–22) notes the suitability of the phrase "death of a cross" in a letter to a Roman colony (Acts 16:12) and its "agreement with attested apostolic doctrine." It means "an extra humiliation." Christ descended not only to death but to "a death which placed him under the wrath of God." The tears which Paul shed over "the enemies of the cross of Christ" (Phil. 3:18) reveal the heart of the man—and of his doctrine.

### The Power of His Resurrection

The sufferings of Christ were real (3:10) and they were followed by his resurrection. Paul speaks of "the surpassing greatness of personal acquaintance with Christ Jesus my Lord [Arndt-Gingrich, p. 848] . . . of knowing him and the power of his resurrection" (3:8, 10). How did Paul know of its greatness? It can only be because he knew Christ already. We must therefore be cautious in interpreting "knowing" (*gnōnai*). The verb may be ingressive, "of making his acquaintance," provided it is understood that the apostle is not thinking of an absolutely new beginning. He is not meeting a stranger for the first time. This would be analogous to the use of such a verb as *noseō*. It could be an ingressive aorist to express "I fell ill (for the second, third, . . . time)." Paul is thus thinking of a further step into the knowledge of Christ and of the power of his resurrection. It corresponds in spiritual experience to his prayer, "May the Lord direct your hearts *into* the love of God . . . " (2 Thess. 3:5).

On the other hand the aorist may be constative. Paul may be summing up his life's pilgrimage in the vision of a moment. The focus of all his gain is this, to know Christ and the power of his resurrection. . . .

For Paul the resurrection is a historic event, but it is more. He is "being

---

16. Cf. Prince Hubertus zu Löwenstein, *Towards the Further Shore,* p. 88.

conformed to his death, in case I shall attain to the resurrection of the dead." [17] His own future resurrection, if it occurs, depends on Christ. He is the guarantee of the resurrection of Christians (1 Cor. 15:20-22). In the meantime Christ really is deity, the permanent Savior, Intercessor and Mediator. To live is Christ (1:21), the One who empowers for every situation (4:13). (See pp. 184-86.)

Paul does not state in Philippians all that he had earlier asserted about the place of the resurrection of Christ in the economy of salvation. But it seems to shine through. We are listening to the same man, who has the same faith and the same Lord. He does not contradict himself.

The resurrection was followed by the ascension. The risen Christ is now in heaven (3:20). How did he get there, if not by the ascension? This was the first step to his exaltation (2:9-11). From heaven he will come in due time (3:20) at his Parousia, the Day of Christ (1:6, 10; 2:16; 3:11).

So far the pattern is consistent. But we still have to ask precisely what Christ has done. It is clear that everything depends on the cross. It is the crucified Christ who is central (2:21; 3:3). Our boast is in him and he is to be magnified (1:20). But it is God who is to be glorified (4:20). Christ was obedient to the length of death of a cross (2:8) and God therefore (dio) exalted him—for his own glory (2:11). It must be inferred, therefore, that God sent him to do his will on the cross.

On the cross Christ opened the way for sinners to approach God. Paul himself was externally blameless in legal righteousness (3:6-7) but it was of no avail. It was only after his conversion that he could say that our politeuma, seat of citizenship, is in heaven (3:20). We are in fact on earth but we "belong" elsewhere. We are surrounded by a crooked and perverse generation (2:15) but we are not "one of them." There are saints even in Caesar's household (4:22).

Now to belong to heaven means to belong to God. Our civic rights or freedom of the city (Bürgerrecht—Friedrich) are stable (huparchei—cf. pp. 248-49). This can only mean that God has accepted us and keeps us: he is not going to turn us out. For Christ our Savior is in heaven also and he is going to transform our bodies to match the body of his glory (3:21). He would not do this against the will of his Father! In other words he entered heaven himself and opened its door to us; and he remains there as our Mediator and Intercessor.

This illustration, brilliantly rendered by James Moffatt as "a colony of heaven," is Paul's doctrine of "access" in another idiom (Rom. 5:2; cf. Eph. 2:18; 3:12). It emerges in another way also. For the apostle "to go on

---

17. Conditional and purposive constructions are telescoped. ". . . (in order that) I may attain, if by some means (I may attain), to the resurrection of the dead." In such instances the "if" is sometimes translated by "in case," "in the hope that." Cf. Mark 11:13; Acts 8:22; 17:27; 27:12; Rom. 11:14. This is not Pauline pessimism or doubt about his own destiny. His resurrection would be impossible if the Parousia occurred before he died. But if he dies first—and it is still not yet decided by the court—he will be particularly conformed to the Lord's death, in order that, if it so be, he may attain to the resurrection of the dead. See W. W. Goodwin, Syntax of the Moods and Tenses of the Greek Verb, p. 180, para. 487 and n. 1.

living is Christ and to die is gain." He actually desires to die and be with Christ, for it is far, far better (1:21–23). But Christ is in heaven. If Paul were asked what would happen if God objected to his presence, he could and probably would answer that he himself would say nothing but that Christ would say that "he is with me."

The same thought of "access" is present in the reference to "the book of life" (4:3). The names in the book are clearly those of believing people. They were part of a company which included the apostle himself and the two women, Euodia and Syntyche (who were "in the Lord"). They had worked together in the evangelistic struggle. Beare (p. 145) defines the book of life as "the roll of those whom God has 'appointed to obtain salvation' (1 Thess. 5:9)." He draws attention to Psalm 139:16 and to the book as "a figure of predestination." In the view of Friedrich (p. 123) the book of life means that "God has accepted them and chosen them for life." In the context of Philippians this must imply that God has accepted them in Christ and not apart from Him. This is "access."

But why should God accept them in Christ? It is because he is "the God of peace" (1:2; 4:7, 9). For Paul this implies more than the calm and unruffled attitude which comes to those whose trust is in God. It does mean this, to be sure. Many a tried Christian has had cause for thankfulness that he has been sustained by the peace of God. But it is based on a prior peace, the peace which God himself exercises towards men. Paul cannot have changed his mind. The reconciled Father is at peace with men through Christ who is our peace (see pp. 179–84, 221–22).

But again a question must be asked. Why is God at peace with men? It is because they have been redeemed. Paul speaks of himself and Timothy as "slaves of Christ Jesus" (1:1). Paul does not here characterize himself as a servant of God or as simply a slave but as a slave of Christ Jesus, "for Jesus Christ has redeemed the Christian (1 Cor. 6:19f.) and made him His property" (Friedrich, p. 96). K. H. Rengstorf would agree (TDNT, 2:276). "Even as a self-designation the phrase [slave of Jesus Christ] cannot be separated from the understanding of the relationship of Christians to Christ in terms of an interpretation of the work of Christ as redemption." (Cf. Beare, p. 51.)

If "slave" recalls redemption, "saints" (1:1; 4:21–22) speaks of purification (cf. 1 Cor. 6:11). "Holy men are not perfect men (cf. Phil. 1:6, 9; 3:12)," as Friedrich (p. 97) observes. They are "set apart for God" (Beare). Paul does not explicitly state his doctrine but his use of "saints" implies it (cf. pp. 192–94). It has contact here with the Epistle to the Hebrews (cf. pp. 59–61, 67–69). In virtue of the cross of Christ, believing men, still imperfect, are God's people, accepted by him.

This ends our survey of the work of Christ for us, as it is presented in Philippians. It lacks the detail of Romans but the framework remains. The outline of doctrine is distinct and it accords with Pauline doctrine hitherto studied. The man himself appears as the same man of living faith and coherent doctrine. The full and characteristic Pauline doctrines are not expressed but they are reflected. Even a crooked and perverse generation may have the Word of life offered to them (2:15–16). If we ask whether their crookedness and perversity can be forgiven, there can be but one answer—the cross of Christ. If we observe the perdition which threatens many (3:18–19) and ask if and how it may be averted, there is again but one answer—the cross of Christ. The doctrine is implicit but real.

## God at Work in Us—The Work of Christ in Us

We must now turn from the objective work to the subjective work. The work of Christ on the cross was done "outside of" us. There is a work within us which demands attention.

To begin with, it has a beginning. There was a time when no work had yet started within us. There was a "first day" in which a "good work" was begun (1:5–6). We might here profitably refer to Acts 16:13–15, 20–21, 33–34, 40 and to Galatians 3:3. The work has to be finished, and it will be, but it has indeed begun.

For the Philippians it all started when the gospel was preached to them. There is an intense evangelistic activity pictured in the epistle (1:12–18; 2:22, 30a; 4:3, 9, 15) and it was in the exercise of such a ministry that Paul spoke in Philippi. If he spoke, they must have heard. What happened then? God began a good work in them. This is the apostle's description of what is put elsewhere in another idiom. "The Lord opened Lydia's heart" (Acts 16:14; cf. 2 Macc. 1:4). It corresponds to Paul's doctrine of the divine call (Rom. 8:30; 1 Thess. 4:7), the call at the initial stage. Once given, it continues (1 Thess. 2:12), as Paul implies in the Philippian epistle: " . . . the call '(come) up' addressed to me by God in Christ Jesus" (Phil 3:14).[18] The initial call came to the Philippians and they answered decisively.

How did they answer? Paul describes them as "my fellow participators in grace" (1:7). To them it had been graciously given to believe in Christ and to suffer for him (1:29). The believing must have been prior to the suffering, or they would have lacked a motive. Hence God began a good work in them by giving them the grace (*charis, charizomai*) to believe in Christ. What happened then?

The apostle's teaching in Philippians is a clear echo of that in Romans. There is a righteousness, in theory at any rate, created by obedience to the law, as we have seen (p. 97). At one time Paul possessed it (Phil. 3:6). But it was external, legalistic and devoid of love. It was not in the deepest sense the righteousness which the law demands. After his conversion he repudiated a righteousness of his own which originated in law (3:9). He had given up seeking to establish his own righteousness (Rom. 10:3). He had instead "the righteousness (which comes) through faith in Christ, the righteousness (which comes) from God on the basis of faith."

My friend Professor Beare thinks that Paul "uses the word [righteousness] in two different senses." The righteousness in the realm of law, his own righteousness, is "an approved conduct and character, a level of moral achievement which God as the Judge of men will approve." The righteousness from God "rests upon the thought that God has 'justified' him; that

---

18. Cf. L. H. Marshall, *The Challenge of New Testament Ethics*, p. 308.

is to say, has pronounced him righteous, has reckoned to him a righteousness which he does not possess. . . . righteousness has here had forced upon it a meaning which is not really proper to it. . . . "

I dissent from Dr. Beare with regret. But the contrast is not between two meanings of righteousness but between the two origins of righteousness. The one is the result of moral achievement in obeying the law; the other is the gift of God. But the meaning of righteousness is sustained. The significant expression, "a righteousness which he does not possess," recalls our discussion of the word *logizomai*. God counts believing men as having a righteousness, as being righteous, *which in actual fact they are not* (pp. 108–12). And if the meaning of a word is to be determined by its use and context (pp. 95, 108), the usage of the terms *righteous, righteousness,* in Romans has been shown to be ethical (pp. 95–100).

All this is recalled by Philippians 3:9. It comes from God; it is based on faith; it comes through faith in Christ. It is to be inferred that when a man puts his trust in Christ (cf. Rom. 3:22) God gives him righteousness (cf. Rom. 3:24, *dōrean*), he counts him righteous. If the brief passage in Philippians does not ultimately point to this, it is hard to see precisely what it does mean.

The few instances of the word group in Philippians seem to accord with our interpretation. "It is indeed only right that . . . " (1:7, NEB). In 4:8 *dikaia* appears in what is a list of virtues. The fruit of righteousness (1:11) implies that the imputation of righteousness is in a context (the concomitants) and that through Jesus Christ (in the power of his resurrection, 3:10) the justified man must "produce." From the experience linked with justification should come Christian character and activity. There may be an allusion to Paul's doctrine of justification in his reference to the bad "work men"—not "grace and faith men"—and to "mutilation" (3:2). An appropriate comparison would be Galatians 5:1–12. Conduct without perpetual complaint, "in order that you may prove to be blameless [*amemptoi* . . . *amōma*]," is another example of spiritual "production" (2:14–15). Those accounted blameless in justification should show themselves blameless in life.

We must now consider the concomitants of justification so far as they are noticed in Philippians. We have observed Paul's doctrine of access. Christ has through his cross opened the way to God. But the way has to be entered, the path trodden. Otherwise perdition stares sinners in the face (3:19). When a man first puts his faith in Christ, God justifies him. This is an activity of the divine mind. At the same time God accepts him. The figures of heavenly citizenship and the book of life apply only to believing men. Further, would God give a revelation to those whom he had not accepted (3:15)?

When a man repents and believes, God "quickens" him. It is not in mockery that the Word of life is held out to a crooked and perverse generation (2:15–16). Even if the participle means "holding fast" (*epechontes*), the readers were to hold fast to what they had not always possessed. The Word of life had been preached to them and they had believed. They had been quickened no less than the persecuting Pharisee himself (3:6), for whom to live was Christ (1:21). God himself was active in them (2:13). When they believed they became the children of God (2:15) and in Christ brothers (1:14). (Cf. Moule, *Idiom Book,* p. 108. Cf. also 1:12; 2:25; 3:1, 13, 17; 4:1, 8, 21.) The term *brother* must be taken quite seriously. Paul is not "jollying along" his readers. They are all brethren because they are in Christ and in him the children of a common Father, "our Father" (1:2; 4:20). They were not "children" and were not "brethren" in this deeper sense until they were in Christ—when they believed and were justified. "Justification and being in Christ belong together (2 Cor. 5:21; Gal. 2:17)" (Friedrich, p. 119).

Paul does not in Philippians expound his doctrine of adoption (cf. Rom. 8:14–16; Gal. 4:4–7) but the experience of adoption is plain to see. A man who is justified and in Christ could hardly have the supply (or "support") of "the Spirit of Jesus Christ" (1:19) without being aware of his sonship.

There is no explicit statement to compare with Romans 5:5, "the love of God has been poured out in our hearts through the Holy Spirit given to us." But the text is illustrated. Love should ever grow and abound and show itself in increasing knowledge, sensitiveness, discrimination, sincerity and blamelessness—to the glory and praise of God (1:9–11). Such a prayer must have been addressed to One who was known as a God of love.

Christ was obedient to the length of death. He obeyed his Father and the commandment was not arbitrary. It must have been "for us" and its consequence (*dio*) was the exaltation. God exalted Christ, for his own glory. Could Paul have been insensitive to the love of God here? He saw the mercy of God in providence. Epaphroditus was restored to health and Paul also shared the blessing (2:25–28). God himself gives righteousness to the man who believes in Christ (3:9).

We are familiar with the thought that justification sets up a permanent relationship between God and the believer. This also may be detected in Philippians. The good work begun in believers will be completed (1:6). Final salvation is not to be regarded as hanging precariously in the balance (1:19, 28).[19] God still calls and will still reveal. From heaven itself we await a Savior who will transform even our bodies (3:14–15, 20–21). God may be approached with the prayer of petition, and worry can thereby be hushed (4:6). His peace will guard the believer's heart (4:7). He notices, and is pleased with, a kindly act of thoughtfulness on the part of his people and will meet their every need (4:18–19). Grace and peace still come from him (and from the Lord Jesus Christ) (1:2) and glory is to be ascribed to him for ever (4:20)—our Father! In the meantime the prospect invites to progress—and joy—in the faith (1:25). (Cf. 4:9.)

The adaptability of the apostle to all the vicissitudes of life which he has learned in the school of experience and into which he has been

---

19. Cf. Friedrich, pp. 103, 106; Beare, pp. 62, 67–68. "The Christian gladiator does not anxiously await the signal of life or death from the fickle crowd," J. B. Lightfoot, pp. 91, 106.

"initiated" is strongly reminiscent of the *pepeismai,* "I am sure," of Romans 8:38. He carries his resources within, for he is *autarkēs*—he is "self-contained." The Stoic word has been baptized into Christ.[20] Nothing that the present or the future holds can separate him from the love of God in Christ Jesus our Lord. The permanent relationship abides (Phil. 4:11–12). God knows that he can long for his readers with the very love of Christ Jesus himself (1:8, *splangchna*).

For the sake of completeness it ought to be stated that Paul's reference to "the saints" (cf. p. 256) is consistent with the "cultic" approach. In his cross Christ effected purification. Impure sinners are made holy when they put their faith in Christ.

Paul has no place for the "lone wolf" type of Christian. He is strong on fellowship (the *koinos* group—1:5; 2:1; 3:10; 4:15) and his attitude to the church, both universal and local (3:6; 4:15), is almost that of Luther—a child of seven knows what it is. At any rate he does not go into too many details in Philippians. He does permit himself the observation that "we (believing men, Jew and Gentile) are the circumcision" (3:3). We are the people of God.

If the "lone wolf" has no place, the "armchair Christian" is a contradiction in terms. Believing men have duties. Paul lays great stress on behavior. Christians are to live in a manner which is worthy of the gospel. They should be one in steadfastness, spreading the gospel and never suffering from failure of nerve in the presence of their adversaries. God has given them the grace of suffering for the sake of Christ (1:27–30). In their moral "walk" God is ever to be their God, worshipped and served. The very shame of it should prevent their absorption in earthly pursuits (3:17–19). Moral excellence should be their standard, the tone of all their thinking high (4:8). They should press on to perfection (3:12–14, 17); even the mature have further to go. Those who do not see it like this will receive the divine illumination. In the meantime the level already reached should be maintained. At least walk in the light which you have! (3:15–16).

Stiffness and rigidity in social life are to be avoided (4:5). In private, worry is to be banished through prayer (4:6). Yet doctrinal purity and the distinctiveness of the church must not be forgotten (3:2–3). The Advent hope is a real one (3:20–21). Christian workers are to be honored (2:29). Christians should stand out in distinction from the world, always ready, always willing, and never grumbling and arguing (2:14–15). The gospel light should not be dimmed by darkened souls; the saving music should not be marred by sullen growls (2:15–16). The unity of the church should be preserved: Christians should be one in thought and love, humbly looking up to one another and seeking the others' interests, not looking down on one another in selfish rivalry. They are, and they should be, kindred spirits. The attitude which they have to one another should manifest the spirit which they show in their relations to Christ. Roughly, "have the same mind in company as you have privately when on your knees." They have a Great Exemplar (2:2–6).

---

20. Cf. R. A. Ward, *Hidden Meaning in the New Testament,* pp. 121–22.

In a word, in matters individual and social, moral and spiritual: stand; walk; progress; behave. Tell others the gospel by lip and show it to them in life. Serve the Lord humbly and for his sake humbly love and serve his people.

The Pauline pattern of doctrine is not slavishly repeated but is vitally reflected. We are still dealing with the same man.

# 10

# The Pastoral Epistles

THE THREE EPISTLES which form this group (1 Tim., 2 Tim., and Titus) belong together and we shall so treat them. Matters of "introduction" are still under dispute, and distinguished names can be quoted for and against the various theories advocated. The Pauline authorship has been assailed on historical, ecclesiastical and doctrinal grounds. Perhaps the heaviest attack has been in the field language. Much contemporary discussion has been influenced by P. N. Harrison's *The Problem of the Pastoral Epistles* (1921) and there has been no lack of counterattack. The problem has been surveyed and recent trends assessed by E. Earle Ellis (*Paul and His Recent Interpreters*, pp. 49–57). He lists (p. 57) nearly a dozen scholars who favor the genuineness of the Pastorals and finds such a "minority report" to be "not unimpressive." He conjectures that "the future trend will lie in their direction." This guess was followed within two years by J. N. D. Kelly's *Commentary on the Pastoral Epistles*. Kelly assigns a high degree of probability "in favour of the traditional theory of authorship" (p. 34), and even characterizes the "fragments hypothesis" as "a tissue of improbabilities" (p. 29).

These issues are not our immediate concern. We shall try to let the epistles speak for themselves and to enter into their spirit. If we do this we may find that it is unjust to say that they are orthodox rather than inspired; we may find that the Christian life is more than rational and ethicized, a mere "bourgeois Christianity"; we may discover more than "a somewhat faded Paulinism."

## THE NATURE OF GOD

We begin, as in earlier studies, with what the epistles have to tell us about God.[1] He is *the living God* (3:15; 4:10). His approval is to be sought

1. In giving references we shall refer to the First Epistle to Timothy without mentioning the "First," thus 3:15; to the Second thus II.2:15. Titus will have to be mentioned.

(II.2:15). Prayers are to be offered to him (2:1–4): only a living God can hear and answer. The salutations, particularly that to Titus (Titus 1:1–4), do not make sense if God is not living. He promised, he manifested, he entrusted, he commanded; grace and peace still come from him.

*He alone is God* (1:17). There is one God (2:5; cf. 6:15). *He is unseen* (1:17) and indeed *invisible*. No man can see him (6:16). *God is eternal.* If we look to the past, we must say that there never was a time when there was no God. He existed "from all eternity" (II.1:9, NEB). I wonder why the NEB translates the same Greek phrase by "long ages ago" in Titus 1:2? If we look forward into the future, honor and glory are to be ascribed to him "for ever and ever" (1:17, NEB). He is imperishable (*aphthartos*). He will never go out of existence. Merkel sees the term (*Unvergängliche*) as part of a doxological confession. Without denying the doxology Spicq considers the probable application of the term to God as a contrast to the imperial pretensions. The rule of the Caesars was not eternal.[2] Whether the term already existed in a doxology or was here inserted is immaterial. It has a fine Aristotelian ring and recalls Romans 1:23. Still looking to the future we may say that God alone possesses immortality (6:16). His existence from all eternity and his being the sole possessor of immortality can point in only one direction: *God is self-existent.*

This is confirmed by the fact that *God is blessed.* The adjective *makarios*, so well known from the Beatitudes, is applied to God only twice in the New Testament (1:11; 6:15). In this context it seems to mean "blessed *par excellence.*" It has a synonym, *eulogētos* (see p. 210), though Spicq (p. 29) holds that *makarios* is the stronger term. It conveys the idea that God "contains all blessedness in Himself and bestows it on men" (Kelly, p. 51).

God's blessedness is not to be thought of as a sort of meditative content, an inactive self-sufficiency. *God has power.* The expressive phrase, "the power of God" (II.1:8), is meant to inspire Timothy to take his share of suffering for the sake of the gospel. He is to be empowered (cf. 1:12; II.2:1; 4:17), that is, he is to draw on the power of God. But God's power is not thereby exhausted. He is the "sole *dunastēs*" (6:15). He is more than the feudal overlord of lesser lords and lesser kings. He is the great Sovereign of the cosmos (cf. 2 Macc. 12:15). His might is eternal (6:16). The kings and lords do not go on as kings and lords for ever!

God has power and he exercised it, for *he is Creator.* This might have been inferred by reference to the story of creation (Adam, Eve, 2:13–14) in particular and to the scripture (5:18) in general. But the word *create* is specifically used, both verb and noun (4:3–4). The Creator is not quiescent but active. He supplies us with everything (6:17). Wealth which has been amassed may disappear. Hope should not therefore rest upon it but upon God. From him comes a constant flow, and on a rich scale. He gives life to all (6:13), both as Creator and Redeemer.[3] The reason for describing God as the Life-giver, according to Guthrie, is "to bring out the ever-present character of the divine witness." *The Creator is thus the Sustainer.*

---

2. Friedemann Merkel, *Begriffslex.* 12:1258; C. Spicq, pp. 44–45. Where only the author's name is given, the reference is to his commentary on the pastorals.
3. Cf. Joachim Jeremias, p. 40. Donald Guthrie, p. 115.

*God the Creator and Sustainer is conscious.* He must have consciousness because he "knows" (II.2:19). *God also has will* (II.1:1). (The meaning of *thelei* in 2:4 will be considered later.) When anything is persistently willed over a long period of time, will merges into purpose. *God has purpose* (II.1:9). In implementing his will *God commands* (1:1; Titus 1:3). In the exercise of his will *God is free.* He chose certain angels (5:21) and men (II.2:10; Titus 1:1), restricted, hampered, influenced by nobody but himself.

Such a *God is to be worshiped.* This is clear from the doxologies (1:17; 6:16), prayers (2:1-3, 8; 4:5; 5:5) and the references to piety (2:2; 4:7-8; 6:3,5-6; Titus 1:1; 2:12). Notice that prayer is good and acceptable in the sight of God (2:3). It almost escapes our notice that *God is to be loved* (II.3:4).

Further, *God has given his law* (1:7-10). Study of the passage in question will show that it approximates to the Decalogue. Both Tables are represented, duty to God and duty to man—piety and righteousness. The law is "good" (cf. Rom. 7:12, 16) but it must be treated as what it is, law. It is not enacted for the righteous, for two reasons, one theoretical and one practical. It is a principle that if a man keeps the law, he is righteous. Such a man may not exist but the principle holds. He has kept the law and is righteous, as Paul teaches elsewhere (Rom. 2:13; 10:5). From the practical point of view the believing man is already righteous (Rom. 5:19). This is Paul's doctrine of justification, reflected in the Pastorals (Titus 3:7). The law is not aimed at those who are righteous by faith.

The law is for the lawless—not those who lack the law (cf. Rom. 2:12) but those who oppose it by disobedience—and for the insubordinate (cf. Rom. 10:3), for the impious, unholy and profane. It is for those who fail to discharge their duty to God and to man. All the commandments are included with the possible exception of the last, though even covetousness is covered by "anything else which conflicts with wholesome teaching."

The enactment of the law implies that *God has revealed himself.* This is attested by the existence of the holy scriptures and their authoritative position (5:18; II.3:15-17). They do not mislead because *God is true:* he cannot lie (Titus 1:2). The demands of the law—and of God—and the nature of scripture shed light on the character of God. *God is righteous and holy.* Scripture is useful for training in righteousness. It is the man of God who is thereby equipped—for every good work.

The righteous character of God is also shown by the fact that those who name the Name of the Lord should depart from unrighteousness (II.2:19). The servant of the Lord should pursue righteousness (II.2:22-24) and the bishop as God's steward should be righteous and holy (Titus 1:7-8). It is the grace of God himself which, when manifested, trains us to repudiate impiety and live righteously and piously (Titus 2:11-12). The Christian's award is the crown of righteousness, given by the righteous Judge (II.4:8). Even if the Judge is Christ, he cannot but reflect or express the righteousness of God. Both God and Christ are Savior and from both come grace and peace (Titus 1:3-4).

In spite of his righteousness and holiness *God is opposed.* This is implied by the reference to demons (4:1), the devil (3:6), the adversary and Satan

(5:14-15). The devil sets snares for men because he has will (II.2:26).
But it is not only the devil. The significant word "transgression" is used
(2:14) of what followed Eve's deception. This means the breaking of the
specific commandment of God. Eve fell into transgression and she does
not stand alone. *God is disobeyed.* Men are disobedient (Titus 1:16; 3:3)
and lawless (Titus 2:14). They are not only tempted (6:9-10) but commit
evil. In fact men are evil (II.3:13) and their character comes out in what
they do (II.4:18). They can speak blasphemously about God (1:13, 20;
6:1; Titus 2:5) and act outrageously towards men (1:13). They are guilty
of impiety (II.2:16; 3:5; Titus 2:12) and their priorities are wrong: they
love pleasure rather than God (II.3:4; cf. Titus 3:3). They are corrupt in
mind (II.3:8; cf. Titus 3:3) and defiled (Titus 1:15). *God is not known*
(Titus 1:16).

In short, *God is sinned against* (1:9, 15; 5:20, 22, 24; II.3:6; Titus 3:11).
He is far from being indifferent. *God has knowledge of what men do* (5:21;
6:13; II.2:14-15; 4:1). He is neither uninterested nor disinterested. *God has
an attitude.* Some deeds are acceptable to him (2:3; 5:4). Sinful acts cannot
be. And sinners are not acceptable to him either. *God is unapproachable
by sinners.* The strong word *bdeluktos,* "detestable" (Titus 1:16, NEB),
"abominable," recalls the language of the Old Testament. Investigation of
the evidence has shown that when God "abominates" we have a concept
which includes distance, wrath, hatred, opposition, destruction.[4] God is
not only unapproachable metaphysically but morally and spiritually. This
is the undertone of 6:16. The result is judgment (5:24; cf. 5:12 and ?3:6).
"That day" (II.1:12, 18) is coming, the day of the Lord's final epiphany
(II.4:8). The end is ruin and perdition (6:9).[5]

If this is all, how could any man have any joy whatsoever (II.1:4)? But
it is not all. The picture is relieved by contrasted statements about God.
From him come mercy, grace and peace (1:2; II:1:2; Titus 1:4; 2:11; 3:5),
not to mention kindness and "philanthropy" (Titus 3:4). He is Savior (1:1;
2:3; 4:10; Titus 1:3; 2:10; 3:4) and Father (1:2; II.1:2; Titus 1:4). He is
the object of hope (4:10; 5:5; 6:17). He has a church (3:5, 15; 5:16) and
even a man (6:11; II.3:17). He makes gifts (II.1:6; cf. I.4:14), sometimes
special and sometimes general (6:13, 17), life and "everything." His scale
of giving is rich and he gives for the purpose of men's enjoyment (6:17; cf.
4:3-4). There is no "catch" in it: what he gives is good.

## THE OTHER SIDE—GOD FOR MAN

This pattern is not new to us. It raises once more the whole question of
God's "two attitudes" to men. Does he judge and destroy or does he continue to give? The answer is found in Christ and in particular in his work
for us and in us. We begin with his work for us.

---

4. Cf. Ward, *Royal Theology,* pp. 75-87.
5. Cf. Jeremias, p. 39, ". . . dann endet der Lebensweg im ewigen Verderben"—
"then the path of life ends in eternal ruin."

## God at Work for Us—The Work of Christ for Us

At the outset we notice again what we have just observed, that God is Savior. It is said that he wills all men to be saved (*thelei sōthēnai*, 2:4). This is not universalism. God's will is not to be viewed as naked might, sheer abstract will, a bulldozing mechanism. It may not be thwarted but it is not mere coercion. It acted by fiat in creation ("God said") but God extends his methods in dealing with men. This is a profound subject and we must be content with studying the uses of the verb *thelō*.

It is used in Mark 12:38 in the sense of "liking." "Beware of the scribes who like to walk in long robes. . . ." In the parallel passage (Luke 20:46) the meaning is even clearer by association. ". . . who like to walk . . . and love greetings. . . ." (Cf. Col. 2:18, and Lightfoot and Moule, *ad loc.*) This way of using the verb reflects or follows the LXX, where *thelō* is employed in a number of instances to render the Hebrew verb, *haphētz*, "to delight in," "have pleasure in." (See Judg. 13:23 [B text, the Vatican manuscript]; 3 Kings [equals 1 Kings] 9:1; 10:9, all LXX.) The spirit of the verb is brought out in Micah 7:18 AV, KJV, "He delighteth in mercy."

It would be infelicitous to say that God "likes" it when men are saved. The point is that the range of prayer ("for all men"—1 Tim. 2:1) is justified by the range of the divine benevolence. The question of universalism is here irrelevant. The text really applies to God the words of Jesus: "Him that cometh unto me I will in no wise cast out" (John 6:37).[6] Some have already come and "God saved us" (2 Tim. 1:9).

God, then, is Savior. He saves "in accordance with his purpose" (II.1:9). The context shows that the purpose was eternal. If this is not so, the gift of grace in Christ in a past eternity was no more than an accident. The purpose began to be realized in the divine election (II.2:10) and in the eternal promise of eternal life (Titus 1:1–2). Thus in eternity we see three logical steps: purpose, election, promise. This was "followed," still in eternity, by yet another step. Salvation is in accordance with God's grace as well as with his purpose and his grace was given to us in Christ Jesus in eternity. This reflects the preexistence of Christ. It does not imply our own. If we prefer an illustration from human life, we can point to a rich man setting up a trust and "settling" sums of money on grandchildren yet unborn. This view rests on the fact that the New Testament does teach the preexistence of Christ elsewhere; it does not teach ours.

In the implementation of God's saving purpose, the scene now changes. We pass from eternity to history. "Christ Jesus came into the world to save sinners" (1:15). This is preexistence again (cf. Kelly, p. 163). The incarnation is implied. He was "manifested in flesh" (3:16) and was "of the seed of David" (II.2:8).

Hitherto the grace of God had been hidden in the divine Mind from

---

6. The use of *thelō* in relation to the Hebrew verb has of course already been observed, but it does not seem to have been applied to 1 Tim. 2:4. Cf. Gottlob Schrenk, *TDNT*, 3:45–47: *thelō* is used in 1 Tim. 2:4 "of God's gracious and majestic will to save all." See also D. Müller, *Begriffslex.* 13:1399–1400. Micah 7:18, LXX, says that God is a *thelētēs* of mercy.

all eternity. It was now "manifested through the 'epiphany' of our Savior Christ Jesus" (II.1:10). And more: it was not only "through"; the grace of God itself appeared ("made its epiphany," *epephanē*), remedial (*sōtērios*) for all men (Titus 2:11). "The kindness and 'philanthropy' of God our Savior (similarly) made its epiphany" (Titus 3:4–5).

The remarkable parallelisms should be carefully observed. They may be tabulated thus:

| | |
|---|---|
| God is Savior | Christ is Savior |
| Christ was manifested | Grace was manifested |
| Christ appeared | Grace appeared |
| Christ came to save | Grace is saving (*sōtērios*) |

This can only mean that Christ came to implement in history God's eternal purpose.[7] But what precisely did He do?

"He gave himself for all as an *antilutron*" (2:6). Any emphasis on "all" must not deflect us from the doctrine implied. Prayer should be offered for all because of the divine benevolence toward all, a universal benevolence which is shown by the work of Christ for all (2:1–6).

The fact of the One Mediator between the One God and men carries with it the unexpressed thought that Christ Jesus "the Man," incarnate, is doing the work which God assigned to him to do. There is not the slightest suggestion that Christ seized the mediatorship. It is thus God's work; but he "gave himself." It is thus Christ's work as well. It was not a mere silent endurance, an enforced obedience or a submission to superior human forces. Both Father and Son may be called "Savior."

This leaves *antilutron* to be explained. This is its only occurrence in the New Testament. We hear possibly an echo of a primitive creedal formula or community-confession, and Hill accordingly turns to Mark 10:45 where the simple, uncompounded (*lutron*) form is used. His expectation is that "our understanding of 1 Tim. 2:6 will be clarified by it." His final interpretation is "atoning substitute." Jeremias affirms that the Markan ransom saying "relates word for word to Is 53:10f, and indeed to the Hebrew text." The word *lutron* therefore "has the wider meaning of substitutionary offering, atonement offering. . . . " He sets out the Greek words of Mark 10:45 right across the page with 1 Timothy 2:6 immediately underneath, word or phrase corresponding to word or phrase. He thereby shows that "1 Tim 2:6 has given Mark's Semitic wording a more pronounced Greek flavour in every word."[8]

Now if we dwell on the factor of substitution—and Jeremias uses the word *stellvertretend*—we must observe that in his work for the "all" Christ did something which they did not themselves do. Are we to consider this as the making of atonement in no more than general terms? It seems to me that some color of the original "ransom" idea must remain. We need not

---

7. It could be an attractive thought for preachers that *philanthropy* can bear the sense *hospitality* (Acts 28:2). This is the translation given in the (Black's) Commentary of C. S. C. Williams. The God who in wrath and judgment keeps sinners out now opens the door to them in Christ. And what a reception and "entertainment" he gives!

8. David Hill, *Greek Words*, pp. 76–81; J. Jeremias, *NT Theology*, 1:292–94, 299; and his commentary already cited, p. 17.

insist on matters of price and certainly not on questions as to whom the ransom was paid. But at least there continues some thought of release, deliverance, freedom. But deliverance from what?

It is not enough merely to say "from sin." The "all" are far from being so delivered, if we may judge from these epistles. The picture of sin (1:9–10) is too vivid to be purely imaginary; the "world" (*aiōn*) still allures (II.4:10) and "worldly" (*kosmikos*) desires still arise (Titus 2:12) to tempt (6:9). If we analyze the "atonement offering" and find deliverance from wrath, judgment and destruction, it can not unreasonably be objected that we have moved a long way from the original figure, if we started by questioning the whole idea of ransom.

There is much to convince us in the view of W. Mundle (*Begriffslex.* 3:261–62) that the *lutron* has a liberating character. The ransom saying answers the question posed by Jesus, What is a man to give "to buy that self back?" (Mark 8:37, NEB). He has nothing to give, but Christ Jesus gave himself. And he is the One Mediator. Unless we take the preposterous view that as Mediator he is a dispensable luxury, we are forced to admit that without him we are in trouble with God. This opens the door to the ideas of liberation from guilt, wrath, judgment, death and destruction, as Mundle sees. The last four would never arise if it were not for the fact of guilt. If we come back now to the thought of substitution, Christ has taken upon himself man's accountability, his "answerableness."

This he has done in his cross and he faces his Father to make answer for men. But the benefit does not come to men until they receive it. This is supported by two pieces of evidence in the Pastorals. God gave his grace to us in Christ Jesus in eternity, but it was manifested in history (*nun*) through the appearing of our Savior Christ Jesus. He is One who canceled death and brought life and immortality to light through the gospel (II.1:9–10). The cancellation represents the word *katargeō*, and I have long thought of Christ as the One who for the believing man puts the horrors of physical death out of action. The Christian still has to die, but the horrors have been switched off. This is still true. But protracted study of the text has shown that it rests on a prior "cancellation." First the death was canceled. That leaves us, so to speak, in a no-man's land. Where do we go from here? In addition, life and immortality have been brought to light through the *preached* gospel. If it were not preached, nobody would know about life and immortality. It is offered to men when Christ is preached to them and it depends on Christ's finished work. When he put death out of action he did it on the cross. It was the death which threatened men. He took it upon himself, the death of judgment. This is what he did when he gave himself as an *antilutron* for all.

Secondly, Christ our Savior gave himself for us in order that he might redeem us from all lawlessness and purify for himself a "peculiar" people (*laos periousios*, Titus 2:14). At the time of the cross such a people did not exist. They were constituted God's special people, his particular treasure, when they believed in Jesus. (We still speak of a man "joining the church.") How then did Christ purify them? It takes us back once again to Hebrews 1:3. The act of purification was performed on the cross and men become "saints" when they repent and believe in Jesus (see references on p. 256). So "our" redemption from lawlessness is more than an improvement in our behavior. This should follow. But first is the Lord's shouldering responsibility for our guilt. He took it upon himself when he died on the cross.

The cross is implied in 6:13, whether we translate "before Pontius Pilate" or "in the time of Pontius Pilate" (cf. Mark 2:26 and 13:9 for the two uses of *epi* plus genitive). Christ Jesus gave his testimony to the good confession *epi* Pontius Pilate. Even when we read Luke 3:1 the mention of Pilate reminds us of the cross.

The phrase, "slave of the Lord" (II.2:24), which means "slave of the Lord Jesus" (Jeremias, *ad loc.*), is a silent pointer to the fact of redemption (see p. 256).

We might summarize by translating II.1:9–10 thus: "God saved us . . . according to . . . his grace, given to us . . . in eternity but manifested in history through the appearing of our Savior Christ Jesus, *seeing that* he canceled death and brought to light life and immortality through the preached gospel." God's grace was manifested when Christ canceled the death of judgment by assuming our guilt and taking our responsibility. This gives expression to the word already noticed, *substitution*. The passage recalls Colossians 2:14. (See pp. 235–36 and Moule's statement on p. 236.)

The human life or "career" of Christ is outlined in the hymn quoted in 3:16. "Justified in spirit" seems to refer to the resurrection (cf. Rom. 1:4). The resurrection of Christ is vital in Pauline thought (cf. pp. 184–86) and in the Pastorals receives an emphasis which is not to be measured by the space devoted to it. "Keep on remembering Jesus Christ risen from the dead" (II.2:8). The constant remembrance is balanced by the permanence of the result. "He has been raised" (perfect tense) means that he is still "up." The perfect participle carries the same force. This may be early creedal material of Jewish-Christian origin ("of the seed of David"), and if so, the addition of the phrase "according to my gospel" is of great weight. "The resurrection of Christ . . . contains the guarantee of all other aspects of the work of Christ" (Guthrie, p. 143).

If this comment is inappropriate, it is hard to understand why the author of the Pastorals is so insistent. The background (see again pp. 184–86) is surely not entirely invisible.

Thus on the cross Christ redeemed men and made purification for them. In the meantime, between the present and his final epiphany (6:14; II.4:1,8; Titus 2:13), these facts as good news must be brought to men. "Preach the Word" (II.4:2). But what happens when this Word is preached? This brings us to a consideration of Christ's work in us.

## God at Work in Us—The Work of Christ in Us

We start with a situation which is illustrated by the Apostle Paul. He was a blasphemer and persecutor and guilty of outrageous conduct (1:13). He was an unbeliever but had received mercy. Up to that time Jesus Christ had shown toward him "all his longsuffering" (1:16). The "all" does not mean that the longsuffering has been exhausted and cannot therefore be repeated. We might think rather of a test pilot from an aircraft factory flying a new supersonic plane and finding out "how much it can do." He does everything he can to coax the highest speed out of the machine. And if it can be done once, it can be done again. Hence Blass-Debrunner-Funk (para 275 [7], p. 144) boldly translate "the utmost patience of which he is capable."

Paul did not stand alone. Christians are to be like their Master in showing "all" gentleness toward all men. The reason given is important. "For we also were once senseless, disobedient, astray, slaves to desires and various pleasures, spending our time in malice and envy, hated and hating one another" (Titus 3:3; cf. 1:14–16).

Something has happened to them. "We," including the author, were all in the same boat. And what happened to the author happened to all. The conversion of Saul of Tarsus is often regarded as an exception, as abnormal. The contrary is the case. He is the typical example, the model, the prototype, of those who are going to believe in Jesus Christ and thereby gain eternal life (1:16).[9]

The change would not have been possible if they had not encountered the gospel (1:11; II.1:8, 10; 2:8). The author describes himself as a preacher (of the gospel), an apostle and a teacher (II.1:11), and he is very conscious of the fact (2:7). He looks out on the world and he has a message for the world. Each word has some slight emphasis in distinction from the others. "Preacher" or "herald" (kērux) makes us think of the people to whom he goes, whereas "apostle" suggests rather from whom he comes and the authority with which he comes (1:1; II.1:1; Titus 1:1–3). "Teacher" reminds us of the content of the message, the promised life (II.1:1; Titus 1:2).

The message, which has already been preached and is still to be preached, is summed up in various ways. Christ was preached (3:16). The Word is to be preached and when an evangelist preaches it he must preach the evangel (II.4:2, 5). This is the Word of God (Titus 2:5) which is credible and is to be believed (Titus 1:9), and is manifested in the proclamation (Titus 1:3; cf. II.4:17).

Author and readers (note the plural "you" with which each letter ends) constitute or are part of a fellowship which faces the world with a message. It was not always so. At one time they were the receivers, not the givers, of the message. Paul himself received the message directly, with no human intermediary. This point does not need to be labored. The others received it when human messengers came to them. This is the occasion which marks the transition from their former life (Titus 3:3) to their present position. What precisely "happened"?

Preaching and teaching imply speech. First, then, the readers *heard* the preached Word (II.4:17). There is an allusion to hearing also in 4:16; II.1:13; 2:2, 14; 4:3–4. This is all pretty obvious though it has some importance. There are still people who hear with their ears and the message gets no further. Even so it is absolutely necessary that the message be heard. (Cf. Rom. 10:14.)

---

9. I have attempted to work this out in my *Mind and Heart*, pp. 78–86.

So far we are at the tape recorder stage. Men just "hear." But some hear more than the voice of the speaker. Some have heard in the speaker's voice the voice of God, who "called" them (II.1:9). Kelly (*ad loc.*) characterizes this as "the first stage in the process of salvation" (cf. 6:12; Rom. 8:30). Men heard and were called.

Now when Christ is preached it is the grace of God which is preached, as the parallelisms (p. 267) suggest. The man who is called finds that grace is present (cf. 1:14), grace which instructs and trains. The call of grace says, "repudiate impiety and worldly desires . . . " (Titus 2:12). The aorist expresses "une rupture décidée avec le passé"—"a resolute break with the past" (Spicq). This can be no other than repentance, a concept with which the author is familiar (II.2:25). Timothy (like grace!) is to train his opponents in case God may give them repentance. This is a practical step and goes beyond a mere rational apprehension which is the most that can be expected from bare "hearing."

Associated with such repentance is "coming to the knowledge of the truth" (2:4; 4:3; II.2:25; 3:7). This is related to "the Word of truth" (II.2:15). Men should not turn away from the truth (Titus 1:14). There is a Hellenistic touch in the expression which can be deceptive. The truth might be regarded as propositional statement and no more. It might be thought that Christ the truth, the complete revelation of God, has been reduced to a form of words. This is going too far, for a number of reasons.

Whenever preaching is under discussion the question is sooner or later raised, "What is the man saying?" Is he a blind leader of the blind or ought we, for our souls' good, to pay attention to him? Is what he says true? This is a valid inquiry but it by no means implies that preacher or listener thinks that truth is limited to statements. What the preacher says "describes" Christ, so to speak, and he urges men to turn to him as so described. In a situation where there are those who do not give "sound teaching" (1:10; II.4:3–4; Titus 1:9; 2:1) it was all but inevitable that the message should be summed up as "the truth." The readers first heard it from human lips but it was more than merely human utterance.

If this does not carry conviction, the apostle himself can be criticized. He is very near to tying salvation to an implied accusative and infinitive and a dependent statement (Rom. 10:9)! The mouth confesses Jesus to be Lord and the heart believes that God raised him from the dead. It is all very propositional. The point surely is that the statements point to him who is the truth. When we say that Christ is the truth we mean that he is the final truth about God: He does not merely say it; he is it. In calling both God and Christ "Savior" the Pastorals must have this in mind.

If the truth is only propositional, it is only rationally apprehended and believed. As the saying is, a man believes it "with his head." But in Romans 10:9 St. Paul avoids criticism by speaking of believing "with the heart." This includes not only the "head," the cognitive factor, but also the feeling, the will and the conscience. In particular the will is practical and "the faith of the will," when first exercised, marks the beginning of discipleship, of following, of obedience to a Person.

Now the Pastorals are not unaware of "the heart." They speak of love "out of a pure heart" (1:5) (what purified it?). Even more important is the reference to "those who invoke the Lord from a pure heart" (II.2:22). The religion of the heart involves the invocation of a Person—this is more than mere propositions. The Lord is described by the propositions, which are believed, but it is as a Person that he is invoked.

There is yet another consideration. There is a striking expression, "the truth that is in accordance with piety" (*kat' eusebeian,* Titus 1:1). It is a temptation to render this "the truth which is in the latitude (cf. Acts 16:7; Herodotus I:76) of piety," a translation which grants a certain spaciousness without losing the control of a standard. Such truth is not purely speculative or profane but essentially religious, based on religion. "La vérité venue de Dieu conduit à la vie avec Dieu"—"Truth come from God leads to life with God" (Spicq, p. 221). Similarly teaching in the same latitude encourages the life with God (6:3), for the words of faith and good teaching have the power to train (4:6).

"To come to the knowledge of the truth" (2:4), then, implies an initial ignorance and indeed a distance and a change which is no less than conversion.[10]

This ultimately means beginning to know God. This seems to be "standard" for the Christian. Others profess to know Him but their deeds belie their profession (Titus 1:16). Side by side with knowing God is knowing Christ (II.1:12). As Christ is the Mediator (2:5), God is known in Christ. This supports our interpretation of "the knowledge of the truth."

"I know whom I have believed" (II.1:12) can be a trap for the unwary. It looks like a dependent question. Although a relative pronoun is not uncommonly confused with an indirect interrogative, it is specifically ruled out here by A. T. Robertson.[11] He analyzes the dative relative pronoun, the result of a telescoping process, into an accusative antecedent, *auton,* object of "I know," and a dative relative pronoun, indirect object of "I have believed." If we were concerned with no more than a dependent question, Paul would be doing no more than asserting a knowledge of the identity of the object of his faith. "I know his identity; I know who it is." In fact he is saying—"I know him." And "he" is the One "whom I have trusted since the day I first encountered him and who is now still the object of my trust."

So far what has "happened" is this: men have heard, have been called, have repented, have come to know the truth, and in Christ they meet and know God. They have put their faith in Christ.

We must pause here on this exercise of faith in Christ. At one time "we" (Titus 3:3) did not have such faith. It must therefore have had a begin-

---

10. Jeremias, p. 17, "sie sich bekehren (vgl. Heb. 10:26 und auch 2 Tim. 2:25; 3:7)" —"they become converted (cf. Heb. 10:26 and also 2 Tim. 2:25; 3:7)"; H. G. Link, Begriffslex. 13:1350, "Die Formel kann . . . das Christwerden umschreiben"—"The formula can . . . paraphrase 'to become a Christian'"; Kelly, p. 62, "equivalent to 'be converted to Christianity.'" Spicq, p. 57, quotes Dibelius: "c'est presque une formule de conversion"—"it is almost a formula of conversion," and says that the thought is that of John 17:3. Spicq's comments are, as frequently, broad and warm.

11. Robertson, *Grammar,* pp. 720–21, 726; cf. Moulton, *Grammar,* 1:93.

ning. This is illustrated in the examples of Timothy, his mother Eunice and his grandmother Lois (II.1:5). Faith "took up its abode" (cf. Arndt-Gingrich, p. 266–67), took up residence, in them. The perfect, *pepisteuka* (II.1:12), expresses the abiding result of the past act of putting faith in Christ for the first time. Titus is a true child of the apostle in virtue of a common faith (Titus 1:4). The two engaged in the same activity, believing; the content or object of their faith was the same, Christ; and their believing in the same Person set up a relationship between them. Titus was not the child of Paul by natural generation, which does not need the assent of the child. Spiritual birth requires the agreement of father and child.[12] Titus gave his "agreement" when he first put his faith in Christ.

Reference is made to the younger widows who, though enrolled in the "order of widows," desire to marry again. They thereby incur judgment "because they set aside their first faith" (5:12). This is sometimes taken to mean "their first pledge"—"leur engagement envers le Christ . . . [le] fiancé divin (2 Cor. 11:2)"—"their promise to Christ . . . the divine betrothed." As Spicq (p. 171) attractively suggests, in their early widowhood they have formally pledged themselves to Christ and his service. Their sin is deficiency rather than apostasy.

However sound this interpretation is, it is not the last word. The subsequent career and behavior of the young widows is ominous and with some it culminates in a new discipleship, "after [*opisō*] Satan" (5:15). The NEB rendering, "gone to the devil," is vigorous and "popular," but it cannot do service as a reminder of its opposite: "Come after [*opisō*] Me" (Matt. 4:19); " . . . he who does not . . . follow after [*akolouthei opisō*] Me . . . " (Matt. 10:38). The "first faith" must therefore contain at least some allusion to their original commitment to Christ in faith.

Faith is of vital importance. There are those "who are going to believe in him (and so gain—*eis*) eternal life" (1:16). A characteristic word for Christians (and they were not Christians always!) is "believer" (5:16), "believers" (6:2), and some have "believing children" (Titus 1:6). Christ "was believed in within the world" (3:16). Faith must be pursued (6:11; II.2:22), and kept (II.4:7). Some, in contrast, have been shipwrecked in their faith (1:19) or become "reprobate" (II.3:8): they fail to meet its tests. The faith of some has been "upset" (II.2:18). It does not stand erect but collapses; it has no muscle. Faith is a norm, from which some have gone astray (6:10; cf. 6:21). It is a mystery to be kept (3:9), the spur and the secret of boldness (3:13). It is a cause which demands energy in overcoming opposition (6:12; cf. II.4:7), for which its words and teaching afford nourishment and training (4:6). It has claims on men though they may desert or revolt from it (4:1) or even deny it (5:8). Men should be healthy in the faith (Titus 1:13; 2:2) with a health promoted by wholesome teaching (1:10; II.4:3; Titus 1:9; 2:1) or by the wholesome words of our Lord Jesus Christ (6:3; cf. II.1:13; Titus 2:8). To be worse than an unbeliever (5:8) is condemnation indeed!

---

12. "Partus fidei, et gignentis et geniti consensum requirit"—"the birth of faith needs the agreement of both parent and child." From Theodoret, quoted by Spicq, p. 223.

Now in some of these examples it may be asserted that "faith" is not so much a personal commitment to Christ and an attitude of trust toward him but a system of doctrine or even Christianity itself—"the faith." This need not be denied. But why was the word originally chosen? It seems to me that the characteristic activity of Christians was taken to summarize the whole, whether of doctrine or Christian life generally. This cannot but point to and emphasize the importance of faith in the Christian life.

We are, however, at the first stage, the stage of "first faith" in Christ. What happens when in response to the preaching of the Word a man believes? We have seen that faith is important. What does it do?

The various pieces of evidence in the Pastorals converge on one point, justification by faith. To start with, works are ruled out completely. It is not "in virtue of our works" (II.1:9). It is not "arising out of works in the field of righteousness which *we* did" (Titus 3:5). (The reference to salvation will be considered later.) In the empty talk of men who wish to be teachers of the law (1:6-7) we may detect in some measure a repudiation of legalism.

The motive of God in his dealings with men is the grace (1:14) of Christ and of God (II.1:9), which "appeared" (Titus 2:11). It was likewise his kindness and "philanthropy" and mercy (Titus 3:4-5). But how does grace or mercy make itself effective in men? Either they must do something in order to get it, which has been ruled out, or we are left with a choice between two alternatives. Men must either be completely quiescent or they must have faith. No other way seems possible. Quiescence can have no place where evangelism is urgent and a reponse is sought. Faith is therefore the only answer.

In view of these considerations, full weight must be given to the word "justified" (Titus 3:7). But a further factor now comes in, that of salvation. With works and quiescence both ruled out and faith of sole importance, justification by itself is not enough, at any rate according to the Pastorals. "God is the Savior of all men, especially of believers" (4:10). This cannot be universalism. He is Savior of all in that he has made provision in Christ for all and offers salvation to all. This is the point of urgent evangelism. It is the divine benevolence (2:4, pp. 265–66). He is the Savior of believers especially in that they have accepted his gift of grace. Faith, then, means not only justification but also salvation. This is confirmed by the Holy Scriptures, "which can make you wise for salvation through faith in Christ Jesus" (II.3:15). Two points should be noticed here. "The Scriptures *can* . . . [*dunamena*]." But will they? They will not, unless one condition is fulfilled. This is the second point, explicitly made. The salvation in question is given through faith in Christ Jesus. Until a man believes, the Scriptures only "can." When he believes, they "do." In other words, salvation is through faith.

Hence the past tense of the verb "to save" is quite appropriate. "God saved us" (II.1:9, Titus 3:5). It does not say "them." The "us" means "us who believe." The object of the proclamation of the church is that hearers may do precisely this, may believe. If this is not so, evangelism is stultified. Consequently, "I endure everything for the sake of the elect (those chosen for salvation by God's eternal predestination 'who have not yet responded to His call'—Kelly, p. 178), in order that they also (in addition to those who have responded) may obtain salvation, the salvation in Christ Jesus, with eternal glory" (II.2:10).

The salvation is plainly a present possession of believers—the aorist tense, twice used, is proof of this. And it is eternally guaranteed. The crown of righteousness is stored up in readiness, to be given by the Lord to all, including the apostle, who have loved his appearing. It will be given "on that day" (II.4:8). "The Lord will save me for his heavenly kingdom" (II.4:18).

We have spoken in earlier chapters about justification and its concomitants. The Pastoral Epistles, speaking as they do so frequently about God our Savior, Christ our Savior, and teaching as they do the doctrine of salvation by faith, now suggest a further explicit statement. Justification and its concomitants in their totality constitute salvation. In greater detail we might put it thus:

Justification plus its concomitants = Salvation

or

$$\left. \begin{array}{l} \text{Justification} \\ \text{Acceptance} \\ \text{Quickening} \\ \text{Adoption} \\ \text{Certainty} \end{array} \right\} = \text{Salvation.}$$

This thesis we must now examine.

"The house of God" is not a building but is "the church of the living God" (3:15). It is a striking fact that the God who is unapproachable (6:16) and for whom sinful men are an abomination (Titus 1:16—p. 265) now has his spiritual house among men. The church is made up of believers; otherwise they would never have been baptized. God has come to men in Christ and when they turned to him in faith he accepted them. Or how does he dwell in the church?

Again, the faith of some is overturned. But God's solid foundation is not overturned. It continues standing. Not all believing men are "upset." "The Lord knows those who are his"—those who go on believing, those whose faith is not overturned (II.2:18–19). He must have accepted those who are now his. And he continues to accept them. There is no suggestion that Timothy will be turned away if he eagerly presents himself to God in service (II.2:15).

Or consider the concept of the "peculiar people" (Titus 2:14). The sequence, deliverance from lawlessness and purification, follows the pattern of Ezekiel 37:23, lxx. In the purification Kelly (p. 247) sees an allusion to the cleansing blood (Exod. 24:8, lxx) (cf. pp. 268–69). The divine object is to create a *laos periousios,* a lxx rendering of the Hebrew *segullah* (Exod. 19:5; Deut. 7:6; 14:2; 26:18), rendered by Holladay as "personal property." In civic as opposed to spiritual matters the word implies the private possessions of a king in distinction from state property which may be in his hands to be administered but is not strictly his (cf. 1 Chron. 29:3). Study of the relevant Old Testament passages already mentioned suggests certain leading ideas: the divine choice, mutual acknowledgment, distinctiveness, value and obligation to live according to God's will. The choice is "out of all peoples" and God and his chosen people "recognize" (Deut. 26:17–18, NEB) each other.[13]

The "peculiar people" are prized by God. The spirit of the word would be conveyed by the cry of a slave over his *peculium*—his personal possessions or private savings—or of a boy over his first boat: "you are my very own!" In particular we must notice the mutual acknowledgment. When the people "recognize" God, he "recognizes" them. What is this but faith and acceptance? Hidden in Titus 2:14 is justification and one of its concomitants, acceptance by God.

In case any objection is raised by the apparent fact that it is Christ and not God who accepts, we ought to point out some counterarguments. It was the grace of God which appeared, with saving purpose. It was this same grace that "trained us to . . . live . . . in eager expectation of the blessed hope and appearing of the glory of our great God and Savior Christ Jesus . . ." (Titus 2:11–13).[14] The appearing of Christ is the appearing of God. If it is insisted that the words must be construed as "the glory of the great God and of our Savior Christ Jesus," the glory is one. Both God and Christ are Savior. In view of these considerations it is unthinkable that Christ should accept and God should not.

Still in the realm of "acceptance" we pass on to the cultic. The author in no way treats of the subject in the manner of the Epistle to the Hebrews, but he is at home here. We have just seen his use of the word "purify" (Titus 2:14) and he can link the ideas of defilement and unbelief with one article in a context of purity (Titus 1:15). He knows something of sanctification: "salvation will be enjoyed (by women) through the period of childbearing, if they abide in faith and love and sanctification with sobriety" (2:15; cf. II.2:21). He speaks of a "holy calling" (II.1:9) and of "holy hands" (2:8), and of keeping the commandment without blemish (6:14). Christians are "the saints" (5:10), and Christians are those who believe. Faith is linked with a pure heart and a good conscience (1:5; cf. "pure conscience," 3:9).

The whole idea of piety really comes within the field of the cultic. An example of piety would be "those who invoke the Lord out of a pure heart" (II.2:22), for piety is duty done to God. It holds the promise of life both now and in the future (4:8). The life of piety is in Christ Jesus (II.3:12) and has power (II.3:5) and profit (4:8; 6:6–7). We shall take nothing with us when we leave this world; are we to find ourselves in an untenanted sky or to be denied entrance? No, for we are in Christ. In the meantime if we say our prayers (2:1–3) we shall meet with God. Piety is the expression of the holiness, the qualification for approach, which God has given to those who believe in Christ. They have been accepted.

This is the answer to a profound question once posed by Sir Edwyn Hoskyns (*Expository Times*, July 1955). "The one fundamental moral

---

13. See S. R. Driver, *Deuteronomy* (ICC), pp. 100, 293.
14. For Christ as God, see Cullmann, *The Christology of the NT*, pp. 313–14.

problem is what we should still possess if the whole of our world were destroyed tomorrow and we stood naked before God." If we are believers, though we had lost our all we should still have everything. For in Christ we should have—God (1 John 2:23).

The second concomitant of justification we have found to be quickening. Piety has the promise of the present life (4:8). The promise of life is fulfilled in Christ Jesus (II.1:1; Titus 1:2–3) and such life is enjoyed by those who are in fellowship with him. Thus piety has already the promise which consists of life. An interesting picture is given to us which contrasts the presence and the absence of life. The "real" widow in her isolation has her hope based on God and never ceases from the life of prayer, public and private. If ever a person manifests eternal life, she does. On the other hand the widow given to self-indulgence, pleasure and comfort "is dead while she 'lives' " (5:5–6). She obviously has not really put her faith in Christ (1:16).

Evidence of the presence of eternal life in the believer may be drawn from the statement of II.1:7. "God did not give to us a spirit of fear but of power and love and sobriety." Pedestrian virtues, it may be objected. But think of the outworking of this new spirit. The person of natural timidity overcomes his fear. The drunkard, the harlot, the gossip, the malicious and every other type of weak person who used to say "I cannot" now says "I can." He is no longer enslaved to desires and pleasures of every kind (Titus 3:3), absorbed in malice and envy. Instead of being hateful and hating he now loves. He could not stop himself from going to extremes; now he exercises self-control. Pedestrian?

The new spirit which he has is due to the Holy Spirit who dwells within him (II.1:14). Through his presence a believing person taps the source of divine power (II.1:8; 2:1; cf. 3:5).

All this is evidence of the possession of eternal life, which is given to a man when he puts his faith in Christ (1:16). Just as a man can "pursue" faith even though he already has it, so he can tighten his grip on the eternal life to which he was called and which he possesses (6:11–12, 19).

The object of the present discussion is to draw attention to the difference between, for example, the "dead" widow and a person who shows the vitality described. It began when he first believed. Eternal life is not only a status, not primarily a status at all, but a state, a condition. A person who has "just believed," i.e., is very new in the faith, is "newly planted" (neophutos, 3:6). There is ample scope for development and in fact he ought to "grow." But he is alive and he began to live when he put his faith in Christ.

For he has undergone a rebirth and a renewal created by the Holy Spirit (Titus 3:5). A man is born into this world once and only once; he is born into the spiritual world once and only once. If the later condition is compared with the former it is appropriate to speak of renewal. Renewal can be repeated or continued (cf. Rom. 12:2) but rebirth cannot. It is an oversimplification to describe rebirth as "the result of baptism," as Büchsel does (TDNT 1:688). More convincing is the line taken by Dr. Dunn (Baptism in the Holy Spirit, p. 168), who sees here "a spiritual washing which is effected by the Spirit." We should be impressed "by the reality and not by the symbol" (Schnackenburg, *Baptism in the Thought of Paul*, p. 13).

Dr. Dunn's exegetical treatment in general and of this text in particular, the fact that the New Testament itself provides evidence of baptism without rebirth—for Simon Magus can hardly be regarded as an example of spiritual birth (Acts 8:21–23), and the empirical facts about "indiscriminate baptism"—all this should caution us against accepting a bald statement like "baptism regenerates." It is of significance that the term "poured out" (Titus 3:6) recalls the Day of Pentecost and the use of the same word (Acts 2:17–18, 33). The author must have known of the tradition. As Dunn says, the outpouring then "was wholly independent of the water-rite."

Büchsel remarks (p. 687) that the word "rebirth" *(palingenesia)* seems to have become "part of the heritage of the educated world." As supporting proof he refers to Cicero's *Ad Atticum* (6.6), where return from banishment is characterized as rebirth. This points to the doctrine of access. When a man believes, he has "come home" and the Father welcomes him (Luke 15:20).

This fitly introduces another concomitant of justification, adoption. The evidence for this is not plentiful but it can be detected. There is a clear distinction in the Pastorals between the familiar "us" and "them." Within the latter are included "the nations" or "the Gentiles" (2:7; 3:16), "the whole pagan world" (II.4:17, NEB). In a limited environment they are "those outside," "the non-Christian public" (3:7, NEB). They bear the characteristics of "this world," "the present age" *(ho nun aiōn,* II.4:10; Titus 2:12), whose impiety and worldly *(kosmikos)* desires Christians should already have repudiated. They were once like them (Titus 1:12–13; 3:3). Disobedience is an abomination (Titus 1:16).

By contrast "we" are believers; we have come to the knowledge of the truth. We are "his" (II.2:19), his "peculiar people" (Titus 2:14), "elect" (II.2:10; Titus 1:1). God has saved us (II.1:9; Titus 3:5). Mention can therefore be made of "our people" (Titus 3:14), for they are members of the church of God (3:5, 15). This emphasis on "our" distinctiveness is not arrogance or boasting. It is realistic because it states the facts. It is not exclusive because the door is always open to the repentant. And in any case it is all of grace.

Now in this Christian community, so clearly marked off from the world, the titles will repay study. "Paul . . . to Timothy, my true son in the faith" (1:2; cf. 1:18; II.1:2; 2:1; Titus 1:4). The best comment here is 1 Corinthians 4:14–15. Paul does not call himself Timothy's spiritual father (or father of Titus; cf. p. 273), but he undoubtedly was. Similarly Christians are not called the children of God in these epistles, but they certainly are his children. It is implied by the title "brethren" (4:6; 6:2; II.4:21). And God is called Father (1:2; II.1:2; Titus 1:4)! The right question is not, "Why is the word *our* omitted?" or "Why is no explicit reference made to adoption?" It is rather, "What reply would the author have given if he had been asked if a believer is a child of God?" On the evidence of the present paragraph, against the background of the whole teaching of the

Pastorals, there can be only one answer. The believer in Christ has God as his Father.

This impression may be checked by a careful rereading of the three epistles to find out what traces there are of "personal" religion. The clearest example is the writer's own intense experience of Christ, to which Timothy is no stranger (4:6–7; 6:11–12; II.1:5, 14; 2:1–8, 15).

We come finally to that concomitant of justification which we called "certainty" (p. 275). By this was meant the knowledge and experience of the love of God (cf. Rom. 5:5). Once again the truth is implied rather than asserted. Certain facts may be regarded as "given," as data for our present purpose. First we have the life of prayer (2:1–4, 8; 5:5). Then comes the fact that "God has given us . . . a spirit . . . of love" and that we should be willing to suffer hardship for the gospel (II.1:7–8). Thirdly, this same God has been active in our lives and has saved us (II.1:9–10). Fourthly, why should men be expected to love God (*philotheoi*, II.3:4) except in response to his overwhelming love to us in Christ? Finally God our Savior, whose kindness and "philanthropy" appeared in Christ and whose mercy saved us in disregard of our works, poured out his Holy Spirit upon us richly through Jesus Christ our Savior (Titus 3:4–6). The Christ in whom God's love appeared is the Mediator of the rich gift of the Spirit. Could any believing man thus blessed, a receiver of salvation and of the Spirit, both through Christ, fail to know in the depths of his heart the love which God has for him?

Justification by faith—and as we have seen it has concomitants—sets up a permanent relationship between God and the believer. This truth is not absent from the Pastoral Epistles. Christ is the permanent Mediator (2:5; cf. Titus 3:6). The Holy Spirit continues to dwell in believers. They will be kept to the end (II.1:12) and the crown of righteousness awaits them (II.4:8).

The life of Christians is lived in the fellowship of the church. There is an elementary form of ministry to encourage the guide believers. Decision and effort are necessary to live the Christian life, the duties of which may be summed up in the words piety and righteousness, love to God and love to men.

The pattern, explicit or implicit, does not greatly diverge from our earlier studies. What is relatively new is the equating of salvation with justification and its concomitants.

The suggestion is sometimes made that the Pastorals are on a lower level than the Pauline literature generally; that they are pedestrian, ecclesiastical, orthodox and ordinary, lacking a certain spirit of creativity. I find it hard to sympathize with this. The ground may be familiar, the truths not new. But protracted study of the Greek text has inspired in me feelings akin to those in Professor Beare when he wrote his commentary on Philippians (p. vii). The experience has been most rewarding and my conviction of the truth and reality of the Christian faith has been constantly deepened. There are depths in these epistles still unplumbed and they speak to us if we begin by being *en rapport* with them. For example, Dr. Kelly can discern "heights of emotion" (p. 55) after "a sudden outburst of self-abasement" (p. 54); he can feel the impact of the author's "moving terms" (p. 161) and warm himself at "a glowing expression" (p. 246). If we approach the Pastorals in this spirit I am sure that they will allow us to unlock treasures yet undiscovered.

In the meantime we leave them, confident that they reflect, if they do not always fully express, the pattern of the plan of our salvation.

# 11

# The Epistle of James

As WE PASS FROM EVERYTHING which in any sense of the word could be called Pauline we may be tempted to think that we have entered another world. Martin Luther must have shared such sentiments. For him the Epistle of James was no more than "a right strawy Epistle" (cf. 1 Cor. 3:12). It lacked the evangelical touch.

Superficially there is much to be said for Luther's position. If we are looking for an evangelistic tract, we shall be disappointed. If we wish to see a theological theme developed with the profundity and the warmth of an Epistle to the Romans, we shall search in vain. To that extent Luther was correct in his assessment.

But this approach misconceives the purpose of the Epistle. Its aim is not to teach doctrine but to give ethical exhortation. It may be that the behavior desired should be based on the doctrine, but at the moment this is the most that we can expect. We must study the Epistle. It may perhaps betray here and there a doctrinal flavor; "the New Testament Amos" may show that he is not a moralist and nothing else but a man with a gospel which he proceeds to apply.

It may serve as an encouragement to begin with two observations of R. W. Dale, first made a century ago in his book *The Atonement*. If, argues Dale, the categories of sin and sacrifice and priesthood and the like were so embedded in the Jewish mind that on conversion it had to clothe the new truth in ancient dress, if it was thus inevitable that Paul and the writer to the Hebrews should retain the accent of their earlier days, then why does not James speak in the same way? He, Christian though he was, did not cease to be a Jew of Jews. Why did he not give us another Epistle to the Hebrews? The fact that such a man could fail to mention, for example, the blood of Christ, is proof that when it is mentioned it is not due solely to the Jewishness of its author. They did not "have to" speak of it and we must not dismiss it as an archaism.

The second observation is this: James is attacking antinomian heresy, a heresy which can arise in a context of the grace of the cross and justification by faith but never where the work of Christ is interpreted by some form of moral influence theory. If the work of redemption consists solely in making bad men better, the charge of antinomianism cannot be leveled against men who have received the benefits of redemption. It may be that James will prove to be a defender of Paulinism and an opponent of pseudo-Paulinism. Walter Bauer cites James 2:14–26 as "evidence of how difficult it was to retain an undistorted recollection of the Apostle to the Gentiles." [1] The Jewish Christians, "with their bitter hatred of Paul" (Bauer), may have distorted his message or may have failed to understand it through receiving it in a distorted form; but it is not certain that James distorted it or failed to understand it.

## THE NATURE OF GOD

After these introductory words we must proceed to consider the doctrine of God for which there is testimony in the epistle. It may not be the whole story and James would wish to add much more, but it is still true that *God is One* (2:19). It was basic Jewish monotheism (cf. Deut. 6:4). See 4:12. The present tenses show that *God is the living God:* He gives (1:5) and he is untempted (1:13). The prohibition of swearing by heaven (5:12) may point to the transcendence of God. (Cf. Matt. 5:34.)

The one, living *God is conscious.* The faith of Abraham was "counted to him" as righteousness (2:33) and the "counting" can only have been done by God. The God who "thinks" does not merely think. *God has will* (1:18)—a fact confirmed by the *condicio Jacobaea,* the stipulation of James, "if the Lord will" (4:15)[2]—and *he exercises choice.* "God chose the poor . . . " (2:5). "The twelve tribes" (1:1) accords with the fact of the divine choice (cf. Deut. 7:6). *God is free* because *he discriminates.* He gives and he withholds (1:5–7) and he tests (1:12). The fact that he can and does make promises (1:12; 2:5) implies in human terms a look toward the future: *God has purpose.* He is the Giver of wisdom (1:5; cf. 3:15, 17) and he could hardly give what he himself does not possess. *God is wise.* The wisdom which he gives is free from insincerity (*anupokritos*) and does not tell lies against the truth (3:14–17). He himself is concerned with truth on earth (1:18; 5:19–20). *God is true.*

*God does not change.* The word *parallagē* (1:17) means quite generally "change" or "alteration" and is not a technical term of astronomy (Martin Dibelius, p. 131; cf. Mussner, p. 92, n. 1). The sun goes down or "turns" at the solstice and the shadows may deepen and lengthen; but the Father of Lights is not one of them. The stars may set and men may change but

---

1. Walter Bauer, *Orthodoxy and Heresy in Earliest Christianity,* p. 213, n. 32. See also R. W. Dale, *The Atonement,* pp. 236–50. I have tried to summarize Dale's arguments in my own words.

2. Cf. Franz Mussner, p. 191: "mit *kurios* ist wohl Gott gemeint"—"with *kurios* [Lord], God is probably meant." Where only the author's name is given, the reference is to his commentary on James.

God does not change. He is unvaried in nature and consistent in character. He is exalted above all temptation and feels no pull towards evil (1:13).[3] *God has power.* He is "the Lord of Hosts" (*Sabaōth,* 5:4). We do not have to decide whether the hosts refer to the armies of Israel, the heavenly armies consisting of the stars and the forces of nature, or the armies of angels. They all symbolize power, the executive of him who issues the orders. He "can save and destroy" (4:12).

In particular God exercised his power in a specific way: *God is Creator* (1:18). James clearly refers to the story of creation (3:9) and briefly conflates Genesis 1:26–27, an echo of which may also be heard in 3:7.

The fact that God is exalted above temptation should have prepared us to learn that *God is righteous.* "The righteousness of God" (1:20) is the righteousness required by God from men. Could such an exalted Being, in the context of the whole epistle, be other than righteous himself? The God who can save and destroy (4:12); the God who does and does not answer prayer (1:5, 7): this God attaches great weight to the prayer of a righteous man (5:16). Dibelius (p. 142) distinguishes between "righteousness from God" and "righteousness before God." James is thinking (1:20) of a righteousness brought about by human activity. And yet it is not a mere secular morality. For consider the context.

Human wrath does not produce the required righteousness. The man who is to "produce" it is to be "slow to wrath." In an explosive situation he needs to pacify, to be yielding and amenable; he should not be angry but compassionate, showing a kindness which makes no invidious distinctions and adopts no pose. These are large demands on a man who is sorely tried and perhaps on the verge of losing his temper. They are remarkably like the wisdom which comes from above! It is such a wisdom which produces such qualities. James could well have said that "the fruit (or product) of wisdom is (originally) sown in peace for those who make peace" (3:17–18).

But he did not say this. He spoke of "the fruit of righteousness," which is "the fruit of that righteousness as it is characterized in the foregoing verse 17 as expressions of the 'wisdom from above'" (Mussner, p. 175). There is thus a link between wisdom and righteousness. Wisdom comes from above; it expresses itself; and what appears is righteousness. Righteousness cannot thus be purely secular. It goes back ultimately to the wisdom which has come from above. Thus we have a series: wisdom from above; wisdom expressed as righteousness; and from this a whole harvest of righteousness.

The man who through love to God endures temptation and thus passes the test, a test not imposed by God but observed by Him, is blessed both in his present activity and in his prospects (1:12–13, 25). His "prospects"— what God will eventually give to him—depend on love to God, the activity of endurance and—faith (2:5). The "unsecular" activity which is righteous-

---

3. Cf. A. Schlatter, p. 127. "Er will und wirkt, was er selber ist"—"He wills and effects what He Himself is."

ness has God's approval. Can God be other than righteous? Schlatter (pp. 50–51, 142) can go as far as to say that the phrase "righteousness of God" is common to Paul and James and retains the same sense. The righteousness is God's, not man's. As R. Hensel says (*Begriffslex.* 4:401), with Paul the good deed is the fruit of faith, of righteousness, effected by God himself, by Jesus Christ or the Holy Ghost. It is the fruit which is "effected." Hensel refers to Philippians 1:11 and James 3:18. (See pp. 258–59 above.) We shall again encounter this connection of faith with works.

We have already observed that *God demands righteousness in men* (1:20) and approves of it (5:16). This means that men are to be in subordination to him (4:7, 10). *God is to be obeyed.* His will has been made known, because *God gave the law.* Disobedience to it is sin, which the law exposes as a precise transgression. The law will be the standard of judgment (2:8–12). James regards the moral law with the utmost seriousness. It is an indivisible unity, originating in the one divine will. Hence failure at one point, and only at one point, means breaking the whole law. This apparently "hard saying" is illuminated by Johannes Schneider's helpful treatment of the passage. "The man who climbs over the fence in *one* place has climbed over the fence" (p. 17). The law must be obeyed by men, not judged by them. God is the one Lawgiver (4:11–12).

Obedience to God must be rendered not only by man but by Christian man. The implanted Word which can save must also be "done." A word, even a gospel Word, which should be done is a law (cf. Schlatter, p. 150). Here (1:21–25) the Jewish Christian uses the ancient term to describe the demands even of the liberating gospel. It is "the norm of Christian piety" (Dibelius, p. 148). The reference to the kingdom (2:5) accords with the thought of obedience to the rule of God.

James would not dissent from the statement that *God is holy.* He speaks of a ritual which in the sight of God is pure and undefiled (1:27). J. B. Mayor (p. 77) speaks of "the heavenly standard" and refers to the righteousness of God (1:20) and *enōpion* in 4:10. A Jew, if anybody, would understand the cultic approach to God and understand, though not approve, John 18:28. Cultic words flow naturally from James (3:6; 4:8).

### Man Against God

*God is to be worshiped* (3:9) and *he is to be loved* (1:12; 2:5). *Even so he has his enemies* (4:4), the devil (4:7) and the world (1:27; 3:6; 4:4). *God is sinned against.* The author's insight into the nature of sin is profound. James is impatient of compromise and has no time for "the man of two minds" (1:8; 4:8). Even so he can make use of the idea. As he sees it, a man begins by being tempted (1:14–15). When this happens the ego is tempted by the *desire.* It all takes place in the unity of consciousness of the man in question, for the desire is his. Yet in a sense he is a man of two minds. The desire is a harlot and he succumbs to her allure. In consequence she conceives and bears a child, sin.

The development should be observed. Desire first appears as a pleasant picture, a "neutral" object of perception, very much like a beautiful woman passing in a crowd on the sidewalk. This is swiftly followed by "a picture pleasant for me." We may imagine that after all the woman stops and retraces her steps and the man stops as well. At the third stage the man says "I will have her." This is still no more than an activity of the mind, but he has made his decision, *whatever the cost*. This is sin, and apart from the figure of speech it corresponds to intention. No deed has yet been done but it is the man's policy.

The child, sin, grows up. The man's decision, in other words, is implemented. He does what he had decided to do. The figure is sustained in the remark that sin gives birth to death. The presence of sin in the intention, the circumstances ("whatever the cost"), and the action seem to correspond to the teaching of historic Catholicism.[4] The "individualism" should not be unnoticed. *God deals with individuals.* Sin as action is recorded in 2:9, 11, and desire and action in 4:1–2.

Sin is characterized as unrighteousness (3:6) and as the bad quality of being "untamed" (3:8). It is uncleanness of thought ("hearts") and deed ("hands") and therefore hinders the approach to God (4:8). At the heart of sin is the arrogant assertion of the self against the will of God, the taking of credit for oneself and, in short, pride. It may take the form of failure to do what is known to be the immediate duty, "sins of omission" (4:15–17). Note again the individual (*eidoti*).

Sin as "wandering" (5:19–20) implies the deviation from a norm and may therefore be related to righteousness (3:6). It has its effect on the sinner. By this is meant more than, for example, the resultant weakness in the face of further temptation. The perfect tense is significant. The man who is told, "you have become a transgressor," has become, and therefore now is, guilty (2:10–11). If a man has committed sins (5:15), they have not become lost or nonexistent in a remote past. He is and remains a guilty sinner.

## God Against Man

Sin is by definition sin against God. God observes and *he takes action against the sinner.* The essence of sin is pride and "God resists the proud" (4:6). This resembles the Pauline doctrine of wrath. Associated with wrath is judgment. God decides and he acts. *God is Judge,* and he alone is Judge (Dibelius, p. 273; 4:12). The judgment is imminent without necessarily being immediate. At this very moment "the Judge stands before the doors" (5:8–9). His judgment will be executed "in the last days" (5:3), at the time of the Parousia (5:7–8). It is eschatological but it is also operative in history. James (5:5) has deftly altered Jeremiah's phrase, "for [*eis*]a day of slaughter" (Jer. 12:3, LXX), to read "in [*en*] a day of slaughter."

The judgment is to be taken seriously by men. They are to speak and

---

4. Cf. John A. Hardon, *Christianity in the Twentieth Century*, p. 402.

act "in the consciousness that [*hōs*, subjective] . . . they are going to be judged. (This must be given due weight.)[5] *For judgment is merciless on him who showed no mercy*" (2:12–13).

This seems unduly harsh. In actual fact it is not. It recalls our Lord's own teaching (Matt. 5:7; 18:33–35). It is literally true. Judgment *as such* is merciless. If it were not, it would not be judgment. It would be judgment modified, judgment tempered with mercy. It would not be judgment but "judgment plus." Even this is not the last word, for "mercy exults, triumphs, over judgment." (Cf. 5:12.)

Judgment passes the sentence of death (5:20), the finality of which is suggested by the word "Gehenna" (3:6) or hell. Perhaps the rust (5:3) which will be evidence is likened to the leprosy of hell. The condemned are consumed. (See Mussner, p. 195; Lev. 13:24; Num. 12:12.)

The evidence of the rust on the gold and silver of the negligent wealthy reveals that they have had too much wealth to handle. They fail to pay their workmen yet possess so much that they cannot look after it. This points to a connection between sin and punishment. Sin gives birth to death (1:15). There is a rationality in God's judgment which should not be forgotten. Dorothy L. Sayers once drew the distinction between "If you whistle, I shall whip you," and "If you touch the fire, you will be burned." There is no necessary connection between whistling and whipping. Whistling might be followed by a reward of money or being sent to bed. It depends on whether the hearer likes it. But the inevitable burning depends on the touching. It is not imposed arbitrarily. Who created the nature of fire?

Thus judgment manifests a coherent connection between sin and death. The consequence of sin is death but it is not automatic or mechanical. God implements the consistent choices of men.

## THE OTHER SIDE—GOD FOR MAN

All that we have said is balanced by other truths about God. James himself seems to have sensed the tension involved. If mercy triumphs over judgment they must have started by being opposed in some way. It is the turn now for the triumphant mercy to be considered.

God is a Giver of grace (4:6). He is compassionate and merciful (5:11; cf. Ps. 102:8; 110:4, lxx). He gives to all (1:5, 17). Sacrifices have been known to be acceptable to him (2:21) and prayers may be offered (1:5; 4:2–3; 5:13–18). He is responsive to an approach (4:8). He has made promises (1:12; 2:5). Forgiveness and healing are derived from him 5:15–16). The term "Father" is used of him (1:27; 3:9; cf. 1:17).

We have hitherto found these two "sides" reconciled in the cross. In an ethical treatise not unlike a diatribe we might well be pessimistic about Christ's work for us and in us. We must examine the epistle minutely to see if it yields any clues. Though its explicit statements may be few, its implications may be many.

---

5. Cf. Mussner, pp. 126–27, for the "Zwischengedanke"—the unexpressed but implied "intermediate thought."

In view of the apparent paucity of material we shall adopt the procedure which we found useful in considering the Epistle to Philemon. We shall first see if James has anything to tell us about Christ's work in us. If he has, it may throw light on what Christ did for us.

## God at Work in Us—The Work of Christ in Us

We notice, to begin with, that God can save and God can destroy (4:12). He is not impelled in either direction. He can save. But will he? We next observe that "the implanted Word . . . can save your souls" (1:21). If we ask the similar question, "Will it?" we are nearer to an answer. For the Word is to be received. This may actualize the potentiality.

The Word is to be received with gentleness. This is not flabbiness but restrained strength. The receiver is not to react with force of words, which would be bluster, or of deeds, which would be violence. Gentleness suggests thus a receptivity, a willingness to be told. He who receives the Word will not oppose it or argue against it. He is willing to be informed, and to believe. An offer is made to him, and he goes to meet it.

Associated with this is "laying aside, finishing with, all moral uncleanness and evil in its abundance." This is a decisive step of renunciation and it looks very much like repentance. Its sincerity and reality can be seen in wretchedness and mourning and weeping. "Let your laughter be turned into mourning and joy into gloom" (4:9). This is appropriate in a call to "sinners." If it is objected that James is here addressing the church, whose prayer is wrong, who are "adulterers" from God and yet are "brethren," although their life and behavior leave so much to be desired (4:1–4), it may be countered by saying that a strongly evangelistic sermon to sinners is a fruitful way of renewing the life of a sinful church.

Other expressions of James are in tune with repentance. Men are told to humble themselves before the Lord. If they do, he will exalt them, for "he gives grace to the humble" (4:6, 10). They are to be subordinate to God. In a decisive act they are to renounce their own will and accept God's will. They are to cleanse their hands and purify their hearts. The only contribution which sinful men can make to such cleansing is to abandon once and for all their evil thoughts and deeds. They are to draw near to God and he will draw near to them (4:7–8).

James has been describing human activities. To repent, to humble oneself, to be subordinated to God, to cleanse oneself and to draw near to God are all part of the one act which we call conversion. James uses this term and his approach is again on the human side (5:19–20). Somebody converts a man who has wandered, a sinner, and thereby saves him from death. As it is God or the implanted Word which can save, the man who converts the sinner is but the means and not himself the Savior (cf. 1 Cor. 9:22).

James has said little about the preaching of the Word. But somebody must have "planted" it, if it was going to be received. If it is received in the manner already described, the receiver turns to God in conversion. What then happens? The man is a sinner: he has sinned and his sins cling to him as guilt. The right translation is suggestive. It is not, "his sins will be forgiven" or "he will be forgiven." We must say that "forgiveness will be made to him" (5:15). The emphasis is on God's act of forgiveness.[6]

God not only forgives; by a deliberate act of will he used the Word, the preached Word, as an instrument to bring us to birth (1:18). This was to make us "a sort of firstfruits [*aparchēn tina*] of his creatures." The rest of creation has not yet reached the point that "we" have reached. Some may yet do so, when men respond to the preaching of the gospel. That is not the question here, however. James is ultimately indicating a classification of all being.

At the lowest level we have brute matter, without prejudice to how matter is to be defined. Above it is vegetable life, a sort of rooted animal. Higher still is animal life, the moving plant, though with a brain and consciousness. At the top is man, the crown of creation, endowed with rationality and a moral consciousness. From this highest plane of personality comes something yet higher. It does not merely "emerge"; it is not the result of development. By God's act it is brought into being. Now the higher "includes" the lower. For example, the vegetable is matter (it "includes" it) and yet has life. The animal has matter, life and an elementary mind. Man has all this, with an added rationality and moral consciousness. The man whom God has brought to birth by the Word has all the qualities described. That is why Alexander Hodge (*Prayer and Its Psychology*, pp. 180–81) could describe the human soul as "a unitary, psychic being . . . the ground of the unity of consciousness and of psychical individuality." It is why such students as Robert Ferm and Owen Brandon can investigate the phenomena of conversion from the psychological point of view. But the Christian who prays, the man who has been converted or brought to birth, has all the human qualities plus an extra. Otherwise he is still "in the flesh," as Paul would say (Rom. 7:5; 8:8–9). The "extra" is sometimes termed "spirit" (cf. 1 Thess. 5:23). Whether the "spirit" is a constituent part of the new man or whether it is his soul with a new vitality we do not stop to ask. The man is different from the man as he was before God brought him to birth. He is different from men who have not been so brought to birth. He is different not only in his behavior but in his essential nature.

We must retrace our steps. In varied language one event has been described. A man has gently received the Word. He has humbled himself, has subordinated himself to God, has cleansed himself, has repented, has drawn near to God and has been converted. When he did this, God drew near to him, gave him his grace, forgave him, exalted him and brought him to birth. This cannot be other than what has been previously observed as the divine acceptance and the divine quickening—concomitants of justification! Whether adoption and certainty (see p. 275) are to be added has yet to be shown.

If adoption is present in the epistle, it has not the richness of expression

---

6. The question may be raised whether at the end of the epistle James is speaking of reclamation or conversion. I have tried to deal with this in my commentary on the Epistle of James in *The New Bible Commentary Revised*, p. 1235.

which we observed in the Pauline writings. Even so James may point to it. Even a man of austere life and a strongly moral message may know God as his Father. James uses the term twice (1:27; 3:9) and we ought perhaps to include also "the Father of lights" (1:17). Why should James call the immutable Creator, the source of gifts and the One who "begat" us in conversion: why should James call him Father unless he is so?

Stronger proof lies in the fellowship which James enjoys. He addresses his readers as "brothers" (4:11; 5:7, 9–10), "my brothers" (1:2; 2:14; 3:1, 10; 5:12, 19) and "my beloved brothers" (1:19; 2:5). Would a man who had been "begotten" by God (the Father of lights) by the instrumentality of the Word and who stood out against the rest of men by being part of "a sort of firstfruits" and was addressing men of similar experience ("us," 1:18)—would such a man repeatedly use the word "brother" and that in the context of the fellowship of the church (5:14) and mean no more than "fellow humans" or "fellow Jews"? James knows about and experiences adoption even if he does not talk much about it.

By "certainty" we meant the consciousness of the love of God "shed abroad in our hearts" (Rom. 5:5). James does not specifically mention this. But the richness of the experience of conversion as it has been described, the fact that God gives his grace, and the fact that he gives liberally and does not upbraid (*oneidizō*) (1:5), all point to the treatment received, to the divine acceptance and to the new attitude of the converted man. Could he go through all this without knowing in his heart the love of God? Could he receive his grace and still not know? Would he love God (1:12; 2:5) without knowing already that God loved him?

It would seem that James knows at least all about the concomitants of justification.

We have spoken about repentance and other attitudes but have omitted one activity which is present in all of them. It deserves treatment by itself. Without it repentance, subordination, self-cleansing, humbling and drawing near; without it the one comprehensive reception of the Word would be impossible. I refer to faith.

For James, faith has an importance which is sometimes overlooked. It is important enough to be tested (1:3). The trials of an unbeliever may test his courage, his patience, even his outlook on life, his philosophy. They test the courage and patience even of a believer. But James seizes on the word *faith*. His encouragement would be, "Hold on to your faith; by it you will endure." Believers must go on believing. They must not "let go." This at once brings faith into the forefront of the thought of James.

Next comes its presence in prayer, particularly petitionary prayer. Men must pray in faith (1:5–8). They must be utterly single-minded. They must be men of one attitude, that of trust in God. They should look to him—and nowhere else. This would be "wavering." The term (*diakrinomenos*) suggests "making distinctions within onself." It is aptly illustrated by Peter when he walked on the water. He "came towards Jesus." His eyes and his thought must have been fixed on Him. But he "saw the wind" and fear assailed him (Matt. 14:29–30). Now the wind cannot be seen though its effects can. Peter turned his thought away from Christ to the wind. Then, in danger of sinking, he turned his thought back to Christ: "Lord, save me." In this incident Peter was "double-minded." This again shows the importance of faith. It affects the moral life. The "man of two minds" is restless, vacillating, in all his ways. A fickle faith means fickle conduct. "This one thing I do" (live the moral life) depends on "This One Person I trust," all the time. This brings us back to temptation or trial. "It is taken for granted that the natural effect of *peirasmoi* is to imperil persistence in faith." "Faith is the fundamental religious attitude, not an incidental grace of character. . . ." (J. H. Ropes, pp. 135, 140). The readers should go on having faith but not with partiality. This would be double-minded (2:1, 4 *diekrithēte*).

Throughout the epistle, according to Ropes (p. 187), faith is the "subjective" faith, not a body of doctrine to be believed. Yet for James it has an intellectual content. "You believe that God is One? Good!" (2:19). The comment is meant to be taken literally and seriously. James would not deny the monotheistic faith of his fathers (cf. Deut. 6:4) and would have been scandalized at the thought of Christian faith vaguely and experientially abandoning it. It is only as he proceeds that he criticizes. The monotheistic creed is held here merely as an intellectual tenet, perhaps no more than a popular belief; and it is shared by the demons. Even the devil is correct in some things—but not enough.

Thus faith is, for James, a *sine qua non*. It is a monotheistic faith and at the same time faith in our Lord Jesus Christ (2:1).

We must now consider the notoriously difficult question of faith and works (2:14–26). This is not a commentary and we shall try to make interpretive comments on relevant texts without trying to be exhaustive. James begins with an abstract contrast under the guise of a man making a statement. It is a stark contrast between faith and works in the abstract. No man ever lived, apart from the penitent thief (Luke 23:42–43) and such cases, who had faith and absolutely no works at all. Even James seems near to recognizing such a thing as a deathbed repentance (5:15, 19–20). The man who speaks does not claim to have been just converted. The time factor comes in. James is considering the existence of faith without works over a period of time. Such a faith is not saving faith, any more than the mere words of an official of a charitable institution are charity. It is lifeless, not only in relation to other people but in itself. In dealing with others it manifests no sign of life for the simple fact that it is dead. It was never alive.

The factor of evidence is now considered. Faith is an inner attitude towards God. It cannot be "seen." A man may kneel, to be sure, and try to make us believe that he is praying in faith. But it falls short of demonstration. He may be a hypocrite or just mistaken. The vitality of inward faith can be demonstrated only by outward act. "Show me your faith apart from works." It cannot be done. (James is not taking into consideration the external act of witness which is baptism.) In a previous passage (1:27) the "externals" of religion consist of works of kindness as well as the maintenance of faith ("unspotted from the world").

Faith as intellectual monotheism is inadequate. In the absence of works faith is idle, lazy (cf. Matt. 20:3, 6; 1 Tim. 5:13; Titus 1:12). The time factor has again come in. Conversion lies in the past—and nothing has been done. James boldly asks if Abraham were not justified by works in offering up Isaac his son. The Old Testament passage from which James quotes (Gen. 22:1–12) will repay study. Abraham was not newly converted. He had worshiped (v. 5). He assured his inquiring son that God would provide the sacrificial offering (v. 8). He offered Isaac in intention, not in actuality. (James amends the LXX text by inserting "offered" from v. 13 in place of "laid" in v. 9.) The angel of the Lord who restrained him from slaying his son did so because "now I know that you fear God" (v. 12). The attempted offering of Isaac was an act of obedience. It was not abstract "works."

James recognizes this fact. "Faith cooperated with his works." We expect it to be the other way round but James means that faith and works were both active. Faith was not absent, for it determined the work (cf. James 1:8; pp. 289–90). As a result of the work faith flowered. Hence "Abraham believed God (see the LXX story!) and it was counted to him as righteousness."

Again note the time factor: "you see that as a result of works and not of faith alone a man goes on being justified" (present tense). Two points should here be noted. The quality of living faith is opposed to the mere abstract concept: faith obeys. And the fact that a man goes on being justified by an obedient faith reflects our previous observation that justification sets up a relationship between God and the believer. With a living faith expressed as the days go by in obedient deeds he is all the time regarded by God as righteous. James rounds off his argument with a robust example from history. Rahab certainly had works. She rescued the spies. But she recognized the Lord (Josh. 2:9–11). The author of Hebrews sees faith in her act (Heb. 11:31) and James would not have dissented. It worked with works (James 1:8; 2:22) and James was concerned to lay stress upon the works.

There is ultimately no conflict between James and Paul because Paul is as insistent on works as James is (1 Cor. 7:19; Gal. 5:6). God's commandments are to be kept and faith is actualized through love. As a result of controversy or of pastoral needs their standpoints differ. Paul has to dwell on the beginning of the Christian life, James on its continuation. In the view of James if a man has faith and literally no works at all, his faith is not faith and he is not converted.

We might put any difference like this. Paul and James would ask two questions with regard to faith. Paul would ask: "What happened when you got it?" He would expect the answer, "I was justified." James would ask: "What have you done with it?" He in turn would hope to hear the reply, "I have used it." James would not deny salvation to the penitent thief. But if the news suddenly came that in spite of all the reports he had survived his crucifixion, James would want to know what he was now *doing* in the church in Jerusalem.

We notice further support of the permanent relationship set up in justification. The believer has prospects. The man whose living faith has survived the test and inspired him to endure (1:3, 12) is blessed and will receive the crown of life. God chose those whom the world regards as poor to be rich "in faith" (2:5). It may be true that they have ample supplies of faith and are therefore "rich in faith," on the analogy of a man who is called "rich in books" or "rich in friends." This, however, is not the meaning here. The *en* is both instrumental and figuratively local.[7] The poor have been made rich by their faith. Schlatter remarks (p. 169) that James has given the name of riches to what the poor man possesses as a believer. None of it would be his if he were not a believer. This can be interpreted as the whole conversion experience as we have seen it, culminating in being brought to birth and being made a member of the "sort of firstfruits of his creatures" (1:18).

Further, the poor have been made rich "in the realm of faith." Here they have not only the wealth of their own experience, as just mentioned, but also all the treasures of fellowship with others who have traveled the same road. This is their present position and they have "prospects." They are "heirs of the kingdom." They are going to inherit. This forward, indeed eschatological, reference implies that the believers are "in good standing." Justification has set up a relationship between them and God.

It would seem that James would have no difficulty in settling down in a truly Pauline church. His language points to religious experience which in essentials is that of Paul. An abstract, idle, lazy faith will not save; a living faith will. The believer is committed to "walking in newness of life" (Rom. 6:4). This is what James has been saying.

"The fair Name which was invoked over you" (2:7) is probably a reference to baptism. Christians are members of the church (5:14) and its elders act "in the Name of the Lord." When presbyters of the church so act, could the Name be other than the Name of Jesus? It must surely point to him as the Mediator.

The evidence of the Epistle of James leads us to think that the author was a Jewish Christian who wrote an ethical exhortation against the background of the gospel. But the "background" was not mere scenery. The Word is to be heard, received and done (1:21–22). The work of Christ in us starts with our reception of the Word; it includes all that is comprised in the conversion experience and being brought to birth; in fact it may be summarized by the expression, "justification and its concomitants." But what is the Word? What is the gospel which is implied by the epistle? How are we to describe Christ's work for us?

### God at Work for Us—The Work of Christ for Us

We start by recalling that God is Lawgiver and Judge (4:12). But men sin against him (1:15, 2:9; 4:8, 17; 5:15–16, 20). His resistance of the proud (4:6) may be taken as typical of his resistance to sinners generally, for the essence of sin is self. Pride is taking pleasure in oneself and praising oneself, and sometimes telling others about it also. Such boasting is evil

---

7. Cf. Mussner, p. 120. The use of *en* is "etwas schillernd"—"somewhat iridescent," playing from one color to another.

(4:16). The climax of God's resistance is death (1:15). God can destroy (4:12).

Now God does not change (1:17). His character is consistent. His attitude to sin is constant. The fact that he is Judge shows that whether he acts or not ("he can destroy"), he condemns it in his mind. He is against it. His "resistance" is the expression of his attitude, which is itself the expression of his unchanging nature. The God who requires righteousness (1:20) is righteous.

But in addition "God can save" (4:12). This must not be regarded as a change of roles. It does not mean that, if God saves, we are to say that at one time God was Judge but that now he is Savior. God does not change. He is still Judge. He is still against sin.

There is yet another factor. We must not leave grace out of our reckoning when we are speaking of God. He is gracious and "he gives grace" (4:6). Grace is thus not only something to do with the mind of God. He acts graciously, without ceasing to be Judge. He has something to give and he gives it.

We have said that "God can save." So can the implanted Word if it is received (1:21). Somehow God who can save and is gracious must be working through the Word which saves. The Word is his instrument (1:18). What is the content of this Word?

As it has to be received, and as James gives such prominence and importance to faith, it is not going too far from the evidence to say that it has to be received by faith. But James speaks about faith in our Lord Jesus Christ (2:1). The last two words of the verse *(tēs doxēs)* are not easy to construe. If the genitive is dependent, we must translate "faith in our Lord (Jesus Christ) of glory." The word "glory" then connects with "Lord," "the Lord of glory," but its position makes it rather awkward. We might repeat the title and say "faith in our Lord Jesus Christ, the Lord of glory," but we should not do so unless we are forced. Is there no way out?

"The Lord" is objective genitive governed by "faith." (This should be noticed because it is important. It is a construction of nouns corresponding to the verbal "men trust him." We must not therefore render "faith of our Lord. . . .") "Jesus Christ" is in the genitive in apposition to "Lord." There is no reason why we should not adopt Bengel's interpretation, which takes the genitive *tēs doxēs* in apposition to "Lord." Hence the text reads: "faith in our Lord, Jesus Christ, the glory."

The Word is to be received by faith. Christ is to be the object of faith. But why is he to be trusted? What has he done?

For a Hebrew the use of the Septuagintal *Kurios* is of the highest significance. If James had been a profane writer we need not have taken too much notice. Roman emperors could be given the title, or even Pilate (Matt. 27:63)! But in the LXX it is the Name of God. James is following the custom of the primitive church ("Jesus is Lord," 1 Cor. 12:3). He links the title with Jesus, the historic Man of Nazareth. God and Man: James has not "proved" the doctrine of the incarnation but at the least he has not deviated from it and in some sense he has pointed to it.

Now this Lord, Jesus Christ, actually is "the glory." This may imply the

Shekinah (Mayor, pp. 80–82), in contrast to the dazzling appearance of the rich man with his gold ring and gorgeous apparel (2:2–3), who impresses the congregation as if he were the Epiphany itself (cf. Mussner, p. 116). The other meaning of "glory" is relevant also. Glory means God as he has revealed himself (his being, character, majesty and might) in nature and in history. Now he has revealed himself in Jesus. Jesus is the very glory of God. Is it mere coincidence that the universal worship of Jesus as Lord is to the glory of God the Father (Phil. 2:11)?

We assemble the evidence gained so far:

| | |
|---|---|
| God can save ⎱<br>The Word can save ⎰ | God uses the Word as his instrument |
| The Word is received by faith ⎱<br>Jesus is trusted ⎰ | God "uses" Jesus in his saving purpose |
| Jesus Christ the Lord, the glory, is the revelation of the unchanging God | God "uses" Jesus to give his grace. |

I was about to write something about "from judgment to grace," but I withdraw it before it is written. Because the unchanging God is still the God of judgment. Jesus has revealed him also as the God of grace. We are now ready to try to answer the question which has been raised but held in suspense. What did Jesus do?

James tells us by suggestion and implication rather than explicitly. He begins his epistle by calling himself "the slave [*doulos*] of God and the Lord Jesus Christ" (1:1). This unites God and Jesus, quite naturally if Jesus is the glory, the revelation of God. But further: the term, "slave of the Lord Jesus Christ," implies redemption.[8] It is not really an objection to say that James goes beyond the bare "slave of Jesus Christ." God and Christ, "the glory," are one in the work of redemption.

In Christ the unchanging God of judgment and of grace has redeemed. Believers (in the fullest sense of the meaning to James) do not "fall under judgment" (5:12). James had been a slave of the law but in the broken law he could find nothing to help him. What did help him was grace, which he found in Jesus. This is what the cross of Jesus meant to James. For him it was the revelation of the divine mercy. (See Schlatter, p. 183.)

James does not expound his doctrine of redemption but he reveals his heart. If we were inclined to take the view that he knew nothing of redemption we should have to explain how he can believe in an unchanging God and in the salvation of sinners. The broken law and the judgment cannot be conveniently forgotten, at any rate by James. He knows what it is for the unchanging God to avert his judgment and to forgive. He is the slave of *our* Lord Jesus Christ. He has been redeemed. This is what Jesus did.

There is in addition another category to which our attention should be directed. James tells his readers to "draw near to God" (4:8). Would an austere Jew, steeped in the Old Testament, lightly think of man's approach

---

8. See the valuable quotations from G. Friedrich and K. H. Rengstorf given on p. 256.

to God and take it for granted? Surely through the centuries the Jews had learned more than that. In the absence of some deeper reason James would think of priests "as possessing the right of access to God" (Moffat; see Lev. 21:21, 23; Ezek. 40:46; 44:13, lxx). It may be true that drawing near to God may be a description, as Bauder and Link suggest, of participation in divine worship (Isa. 29:13, lxx),[9] but James is saying far more than "go to church." Sinners must cleanse their hands and men of two minds must purify their hearts. They must indeed repent. But does repentance *in itself* qualify men for the solemn approach to the unchanging God of righteousness and judgment? I do not think that James, Jew as he is, could possibly think so. Mitton is not happy about the reference to priesthood here and sees "the general privilege of Christians that they have at all times through Christ 'access to God'" (C. Leslie Mitton, p. 159).

"Through Christ" is the "deeper reason" of which we have just spoken. The cultic terms remind us of the Old Testament and of the Epistle to the Hebrews. How did James know that God would receive those who approach him and would indeed draw near to them? At some time in his spiritual pilgrimage which led to his conversion to Christ he must have learned that Jesus had made a purification for sins (Heb. 1:3). This was the ground of his call to men to purify themselves and to draw near to God. Apart from the cross the unchanging God will not receive them. In the cross judgment and grace are present together and through Christ crucified men may draw near to God. When they so approach him they find that he forgives them (5:15). This is the message of the Word which the preacher and teacher must proclaim. The sinner can be rescued from death when he receives the Word which tells him that his sins have been covered (5:20; cf. Ps. 84:3, lxx).

James has manifested a strongly ethical purpose. It is based on the gospel, the "pattern" of which does not materially diverge from that which we have hitherto discovered in the New Testament.

---

9. James Moffatt, *The Epistle to the Hebrews*, pp. 125, 144; W. Bauder and H. G. Link, *Begriffslex.* 13:1486–87. Bauder and Link draw attention to the solemn prohibition to Moses at the burning bush, "Do not draw near" (Exod. 3:5, lxx), and also say: "Der nahe Gott wird vor allem im israelitischen Gottesdienst erfahren (vgl. Ps. 145:18)"—"The near God is experienced first of all in Israelite worship."

# 12

## The First Epistle
## of Peter

IN VIEW OF THE FACT that the First Epistle of St. Peter "presupposes Pauline theology" and its author "stands in the succession of Pauline theology," [1] we embark on our study of its doctrine with a measure of optimism. We hope that we shall find a "pattern" which is consistent with the results already attained. We therefore begin at once to seek what it has to tell us about God.

### THE NATURE OF GOD

The prohibition of idolatry and its deeds unlawful (*athemitos—nefas,* cf. Acts 10:28) implies that *God is One* (4:3). He is in heaven (3:22) and therefore transcendent. *God is conscious* because he *has knowledge* (1:2). He sees and he hears (3:12). *God has will* (2:15; 3:17; 4:2, 19). If, with anthropomorphism as marked as in God's seeing and hearing, we think of his planning long in advance to implement his will, we can notice that *God has purpose.* This is suggested by "grace destined [*eis*] for you" and "sufferings destined for Christ" (1:10–11). *God has power* (1:5; cf. 4:11) and indeed *he is the Creator* (4:19; cf. 1:20). His hand is in control and to that extent *he is the Sustainer* (5:6; cf. 4:11; 5:11, *kratos*). He "sustains" the universe continuously but can and does act intermittently (1:3, 21): he raised Christ and he begets Christians. *God is active,* not quiescent.

The terms "excellence" and "light" (2:9) appropriately describe him, because *God is holy* (1:15–16). *He is righteous* because he judges righteously (2:23) and his eyes are upon the righteous and his ears attentive to their prayer (3:12: cf. Num. 6:25–26, LXX). *He is trustworthy* (4:19) and *may be known* (2:19; cf. 3:16, 21). *He has revealed himself,* as the appeal to Scripture shows (1:16; 2:6) and *he makes demands on men.* God's holiness requires a corresponding holiness in men (1:15–16). He is to be feared (2:17), whatever spiritual relationship these words mean.

---

1. W. G. Kümmel, *Introduction to the New Testament,* p. 297.

He is to be the object of hope (3:5; cf. 1:21) and of trust. *He is to be worshiped* (1:3; 2:12; 4:11, 16). *God deals with individuals* (3:4). *He has enemies*, the devil and the world (5:8–9).

*God is sinned against* (2:24; 3:18; 4:1, 18). He is neither blind nor unconcerned; *he has an attitude*. He values (*para* with dative); and certain activities are acceptable to him (2:4–5, 20; 3:4). See also perhaps 4:6; 5:2 (*kata theon*). But by no means are all activities acceptable to him. *He is the divine Opponent*. He is "against those who do evil" (3:12)[2] and "God resists the proud" (5:5). "Where will the impious and sinner appear?" (4:18). The divine holiness repels the sinner and bans him from the Presence. He has nothing in himself to commend him and has to be brought near (cf. 3:18). Apart from this, judgment awaits him (1:17; 2:23; 4:5).

## THE OTHER SIDE—GOD FOR MAN

This is not, however, the whole story. The impartial Judge is also the Father (1:17; cf. 1:2–3). He is concerned for men (5:7). Mercy (*eleos*)—and he has much of it—is the standard of his activity (1:3; cf. 2:10). He is the God of all grace, which is given to men (4:10; 5:5, 10, 12). He repels the sinner and yet has his people (2:9–10; 4:17; 5:2).

Once more we have to resolve the contradiction between the divine repulsion and the divine acceptance. We turn, therefore, to the work of Christ for us as it is described in this First Epistle.

## *God at Work for Us—The Work of Christ for Us*

We start by noticing that there is such a thing as the Word of God (1:23, 25). It is living and lasting; it lasts indeed forever, yet it was "preached as gospel" to the readers. (Cf. 2:2; 3:1.) It commands obedience though there are those who disobey "the gospel of God" (4:17). The "content" of the gospel of God must be Christ himself. The readers to whom the gospel had been preached (1:25) and who were believers (1:8, 21: 2:6–7) had the duty to "recognize and reverence Christ in [their] hearts as Lord" (3:15). The allusion is to Isaiah 8:13, LXX and the word "Christ" is inserted. In the Hebrew it is the Lord of Hosts who is to be "treated as holy."[3] Who is this Person, the content of the gospel, who is thus quietly placed alongside the Lord of Hosts?

He is the Son of God (1:3). His Spirit testified to the prophets (1:11) and he was known before the foundation of the world (1:20). He is thus the pre-existent Son. (Cf. J. Schneider, pp. 48, 55.)[4]

The incarnation of the Son is implied. He was manifested (1:20) and he

---

2. The preposition *epi* with the accusative here means "*against* (inimically)." See Moule, *Idiom Book*, p. 49.
3. W. L. Holladay, *Lexicon*, p. 314 on Num. 20:12. Cf. A. B. Davidson, *Theology of the Old Testament*, p. 156; E. J. Young, *The Book of Isaiah*, 1:311; Arndt-Gingrich, p. 9.
4. Where only the author's name is given, the reference is to his commentary on First Peter.

had a body, flesh and a mouth (2:22–24; 4:1), though the readers had not seen him themselves (1:8). He did no sin (2:22) but was rejected by men (2:4) and reviled (2:23). He suffered (4:13; 5:1) and died (3:18) but God raised him from the dead (1:3, 21; 3:21). He is now alive, though unseen (1:8), for he ascended into heaven and is at the right hand of God in authority (3:22), glorified (1:21). The Second Advent or Parousia is implied (1:7; 5:1).[5] The outline which we have disentangled from the epistle resembles the primitive *kerygma*.

Central to this *schema* is the death of Christ. His sufferings were destined (*eis Christon*, 1:11). It was the rejected "stone" which was elect and precious (*entimos*) in God's sight, the value (*timē*) of which was and is gain to believers. This points to the cross (2:4, 7), which is concerned with the salvation of men (1:9–11). The grace of God destined for sinners is linked to the sufferings destined for Christ. "Christ suffered for you" (2:21).

In describing the work of Christ the author combines two concepts, the commercial and the cultic, redemption and purification. We have already met these and it is not perhaps necessary to go over the old ground in detail. The "commercial" idea of deliverance by payment is not rejected but amended. The stress is not on a repudiation of payment as such but on the nature of what was paid. It was not with the cash of the normal transactions or even with the most precious of transitory things, silver or gold, but with the precious blood of Christ that we were redeemed (1:18–19).

We were redeemed from a futile, unoriginal manner of life. Even the most hardened advocates of the avant-garde are embedded in tradition. It is not only this, that or the other sin from which we have been redeemed, but our whole life. The description sums up our darkness (2:9), ignorance and folly (2:15), our distance (2:25), our state of being unreconciled (3:1), and the absence of Christ from our hearts; in short our impiety and our sin (4:18). We followed the path of Gentile sins and idolatries (4:3) and we needed to be saved (3:21).

Now the "life" which we lived may be summed up in the word *sin*. As sinners we were under judgment (4:17–18). But Christ bore our sins in his body on the tree (2:24). It is plain that we did not bear them. If, then, he bore them and if in so doing he redeemed us, it can only mean that he assumed responsibility for us. He bore our guilt. Dean Selwyn will not, I think, be accused of fundamentalism or of an excessively conservative evangelicalism, and his words will therefore have all the more significance. He says (p. 180) that Christ bore our sins "in the sense that He took the blame for them; suffered the 'curse' of them (cf. Deut. 21:23, quoted in Gal. 3:13), which is separation from God; and endured their penal consequences." Similarly Schneider (p. 73) says that the death of Christ signifies the liberation of humanity from its guilt (*Sündenschuld*). He ob-

---

5. In 5:1 it is implied that Peter *is already* a participator (*koinōnos*) in the glory which *will be* revealed. The reference is to the Transfiguration. The glory of the Parousia was revealed in advance to Peter in the Transfiguration and to Paul at his conversion. An abortion is one born *before* the due time (1 Cor. 15:8). See E. G. Selwyn, pp. 228–29 and his reference to G. H. Boobyer, *St. Mark and the Transfiguration Story*; and Stephen Neill, *The Interpretation of the New Testament 1861-1961*, p. 287, n. 2.

serves a difference, however, from St. Paul. Peter does not link his doctrine of the cross with doctrine about justification. In the present text (2:24) "only the objective effect is emphasized." (Cf. F. W. Beare, p. 124; Num. 14:33.)

But what is the objective effect? "Christ died once for all for sins, the Righteous for the unrighteous, in order that he might bring you to God" (3:18). But did he bring them to God? If we think of his death by itself, we can only say that he did not. Men have to come to him (2:4) and it is incredible that they should have been brought to God before they come to Christ. The point is that the way to God has been opened for sinners. God does not now bar them out. We are therefore approaching a doctrine of access. Through the death of Christ, in which he took responsibility for sinners, God is ready to accept sinners.

In the phrase "for sins" there may be an allusion to the sin-offering, "which was propitiatory," though the plural "makes the phrase less technical" (Selwyn, p. 196; cf. Charles Bigg, pp. 159–60). In any case we have the cultic reference to sacrifice. We were redeemed by "the precious blood of Christ, as of a Lamb without blemish and without spot" (1:19). Schneider (p. 55) sees a close relationship to the views of Paul and a primary reference to the passover lamb (1 Cor. 5:7; cf. pp. 172–75 above). There is also contact with the Epistle to the Hebrews. By the shed blood a purification from sins has been made (Heb. 1:3) but a man has to be sprinkled with the blood and so sanctified (1 Pet. 1:2), that is, qualified to draw near to God. This again is "access" and we shall have to look again at sprinkling when we consider the work of Christ in us. We ought, perhaps, to notice that "without blemish and without spot" corresponds to "did no sin" and "righteous" (2:22; 3:18). It is this which gives value to his death.

Thus in his work on the cross for us our Lord assumed our responsibility and our guilt. God is free to receive sinful men and they are free to approach Him. A purification from sins has been made (cf. pp. 59–61) and the world is potentially purified. Sinful as it is, it need not be shut out from God. For God himself is affected by the cross. His character and purpose have not changed but his treatment of men can change. Judgment has been held up. God is willing to forgive. But what must men do to be forgiven? This brings us to the question of Christ's work in us. We should observe that either he is the only One who can bring us to God (3:18) and that he does it in virtue of his work on the cross; or that some other way is possible also. If we believe that the latter is true, we have successfully put Christ out of Christianity—destroyed Christianity. We have made him unnecessary, if we can approach God without him. This violates the principle of "exclusiveness" or "intolerance" which permeates the New Testament. But what is his work *in* us?

## God at Work in Us—The Work of Christ in Us

We should notice first the state we were in before he began to work in us. We were in the dark, ignorant and foolish, distant from God and unreconciled (p. 298). It is plain that some vital, transforming experience had occurred in the readers. Femininity is not normally prepared even to listen to the suggestion of substituting an inner gentleness of spirit for the outer adornment of attractive dress, jewelry, and the "hairdo" (3:3–4). It is made possible by the contrast of the past and "now" (2:10, 25; 3:21). What has happened?

The readers had stood in the path of some movement of God towards them. Grace had been destined for them (1:10; cf. 3:7) and Christ had been manifested for their sakes (1:20). The gospel had been preached to them (1:12, 25). In the voice of the preacher they had heard the call of God (1:15; 2:9; 3:9; 5:10).

Now the gospel, as preached, is information but it is more than information. It is good advice, but it is more than good advice. It is a call, a summons, a command. It must be a command. How otherwise could men disobey it (4:17)? Notice the concept of obedience in the epistle (1:2, 14, 22; 2:8; 3:1). When the gospel was preached in the power of the Spirit (1:12) the readers had heard the call and the command of God and had made their response.

They had obeyed. This implies first that they had repented. Note the context of 2:1. The Word had been preached to them as gospel. Therefore, having laid aside all wickedness (*kakia*) . . . and its expression in word and deed (*dolos*), as newly born babies they should long for the milk of the Word. The particle is not imperatival. (There is a similar sequence in 1:22. Cf. NEB.) They had already "changed their minds."

Further, they had begun to believe (1:8–9, 21). They would find in their continuing Christian life that in their sustained commitment to their Creator he would prove to be trustworthy. They should continue what they had begun (4:19).

Obedience, repentance, faith: these are the first steps in salvation; or perhaps it would be better to say that in their unity in experience they constitute the one first step. A variey of figures of speech is used by the author to describe it. They have come to Christ, the living Stone (2:4). They have tasted that the Lord is kind (2:3). From their distant wanderings they have returned to their Shepherd (2:25). They have passed to a marvelous light which makes them rub their eyes in wonder (2:9). Hitherto they had lived in darkness and had been accustomed to it (1:18, "traditional"). They had been given a new purpose: they had died to sins in order to "begin to live for righteousness" (2:24, NEB). They had been healed. They had been "won"—had been reconciled (3:1). (The reference in the context [3:4] to "the hidden person of the heart" suggests individual experience.) They had received Christ into their hearts (3:15).

One particular aspect of the response of obedience should be observed. In their obedience to the truth, "i.e., the Gospel" (Selwyn), they had purified their souls. This is not strictly self-purification. They did not purify themselves *simpliciter*. The purification was brought about when they obeyed. The obedience of 1:22 is to be linked with "the obedience and sprinkling of the blood of Jesus Christ" (1:2). This reflects the ideas of the Epistle to the Hebrews. The sacrificial blood of the cross is "sprinkled" on the man who makes the response of obedience to the preached gospel.

The implication is that the man who so obeys is now qualified to approach God. His "purity" or "holiness" is a divine gift and it should be followed by human achievement: human, or why the command or exhortation? "Be holy in all your behavior" (1:15–16). The gift of the "qualification" is to be worked out in the strenuous moral and spiritual life of the qualified man. By God's gift he may approach God. As a result of his obedience to the message of the cross, Christ has brought him to God (3:18).

This is not far from the concept of God's "reckoning" (*logizomai*) or "counting" him as holy. When he obeyed the gospel he had no holiness of his own. Admittedly he has now to work at it: "be ye holy." But at this initial point he has had no time, to say the least, to be holy by his own effort. If anyone objects to "his own effort" on the ground that "without Me ye can do nothing" (John 15:5, KJV), we reply that the Lord's aid is indeed necessary to make empirical holiness possible and human effort necessary to make it actual. Christian men are not machines.

We pass now to the *dikaios* concept and note that it is largely ethical. The Lord did not sin and used no trickery in his speech. He did not meet reviling with reviling. When He suffered he did not threaten. He himself would not deal with his mockers and persecutors. That was left for "him who judges righteously" (2:22–23), for him "who judges impartially according to each man's work" (1:17). (Once more we observe that God deals with individuals.) This is ethical. Christ bore our sins "in order that we might die to sins [ethical!] and begin to live for righteousness" (2:24), "to follow in his steps" (2:21).

Who will harm the readers if they are zealous for goodness? But assume the remote contingency. If they were to suffer on account of righteousness, they would be blessed (3:13–14), "religiously fortunate." [6] This is parallel to the suffering *adikōs*, to being knocked about even when they have done what is right (2:18–20). If in this unfairness they endure, it is "a gracious act pleasing to God" (Selwyn, p. 176). "Doing good" and "righteousness" are parallel, and "religiously fortunate" is balanced by "pleasing to God." The ethical atmosphere can hardly be denied.

We now have to ask what the author meant by "righteous" in 3:12. "The eyes of the Lord are upon the righteous and His ears are attentive to [*eis*] their prayer." They are contrasted with "those who do evil." To which group do the readers belong? Before they heard the gospel and responded to it in obedience they were undoubtedly the latter, evildoers (cf. p. 298; 1:14). Where do they stand now? We ought to be able to call them "the righteous," but if the word is ethical, could we go so far? The presence of exhortations in the epistle suggests that righteousness is what the readers have to achieve or at least to perfect. They still have some way to go. To that extent they are not yet righteous. But this would deny to them God's favorable look. (See Moule, *Idiom Book*, p. 49), and his hearing of prayer. This cannot be correct. In the preached gospel God came

---

6. Selwyn, p. 192, from Montefiore: enjoyment of "a peculiar divine blessing or favour."

to them with a favorable look, even when they were evildoers. He can hardly have changed now that they are believers and in some measure trying to do what is good. How then can the not-yet-righteous be called righteous?

For God is treating them, believers, favorably. He is not against them. An inheritance is being kept for them in heaven and they themselves (through their faith and not their works) are being guarded. They are within God's protective power, preserved for a salvation ready to be revealed at the End (1:4–5). It would seem that though they are not righteous in achievement they are being treated by God as righteous. His eyes are indeed favorably upon them.

The implication should be set out with care. Peter does not use the word *justify* and there is no exposition of a doctrine of justification by faith. The epistle, however, affords certain pieces of evidence which we can assemble and from which we can infer the doctrine. It manifests the experience of justification by faith if not its elaboration, its exposition or even an explicit statement. Men are under obligation to be righteous and they need the exhortation; but before they have fully attained, God treats them favorably, keeps them and will mend them, establish them, give them strength and a firm foundation (5:10). He treats them as if they were righteous, keeps a loving eye on them and listens to them. The life of the Christian is beset with difficulty and there are not absent factors even of judgment;[7] but God is faithful to those whose lives are committed to Him (4:18–19). The greater the emphasis on judgment, the greater is the "difficulty." But "the righteous" even if an object of judgment is yet saved. God treats him as righteous.

If this interpretation is incorrect, where do the readers stand? If they are plain evildoers, God is against them. If they are not righteous, they cannot expect God's favor. It is not enough to be "half righteous," or just "trying" (cf. 2:24). Yet they may pray (3:12; 4:7)! They must be accounted righteous.

At the start of their Christian life, described in various figures, they had gained new knowledge (1:14) and had come under God's favorable eye (3:12). This can all be summed up in the statement that they had begun to put their trust in Christ. Faith has an importance in the epistle which we have not yet remarked. When it is real [8]—its genuine "part" as opposed to any lingering superstition or a mere willingness "to go along with the others"—it is more precious than refined though perishable gold and at the End will lead to praise and glory and honor (1:7), "bestowed by God upon man" (Selwyn, *ad loc.*). This looks like justification by faith, especially if justification is eschatological. In the meantime they are already "getting" the object and goal (*telos*) of faith, salvation, though the unfading crown of glory they will only "get" at the appearing of the Chief Shepherd (1:9; 5:4).

Faith and its opposite are sharply contrasted (2:6–8). Individual faith in the Stone does not meet with disappointment, for it is the believers who

---

7. Cf. Derek Kidner, *The Proverbs*, p. 95, with regard to 1 Pet. 4:12–19.

8. Cf. Adolf Deissmann, *Bible Studies*, pp. 259–62. Schneider renders *dokimion* by *Echtheit*, "genuineness." Cf. 2 Cor. 8:8. Cf. Nigel Turner, *Grammatical Insights into the New Testament*, pp. 168–69.

gain (cf. p. 298) and the unbelievers who stumble. Faith in Christ, the Stone, is faith through him in God and indeed faith in God (1:21). Believers not only "get" salvation through faith but through faith are guarded for salvation (1:5). They should stand up to the devil and not let him swallow them; they should be firm, "solid," in faith (5:8–9).

The different figures which describe the beginning of the Christian life—coming to Christ, returning to the Shepherd, entering the light, tasting the kindness of the Lord, being healed, being won, being given a new purpose and receiving Christ in the heart—have one element in common. Not one of them is possible without faith. The experience behind the language can hardly be other than justification by faith. If we ask what God "thinks" of men who begin to believe, we can give only one answer. His eyes are turned favorably upon them (3:12) because he counts them as righteous. But what happens then?

We have to raise again the question of the concomitants. Justification in itself is not an experience; it is what God "thinks." But there is evidence in the epistle that when God thus deems a believer righteous he accepts him. A man believes in God, in Christ. He has gained a new taste; he has discovered that the Lord is gracious, is kind (2:3). How does 'he know? How did he come to "taste"? Surely he found that God had received him. He knew that now God's favorable eyes were upon him (3:12). God had called him out of darkness into his wondrous light, and he now knew the difference between his former darkness and the present light. One of the "excellences" of God which he was to proclaim was the fact that when he entered the light God did not, as it were, switch it off. He had received him (2:9).

This is eminently reasonable. The believer finds himself part of a fellowship, one with men who have been treated as he has been. God chose them—only to reject them? He made them a holy race—only to refuse to recognize their "qualification" to approach him? He made them a holy priesthood, a priesthood in royal service, to offer spiritual sacrifices acceptable to him through Jesus Christ (2:5, 9)—only to decline to accept the acceptable? The author actually calls his readers to prayer (4:7; cf. 3:7). He at any rate did not think that it would be all in vain. To crown the argument: Christ died once for all and died for sins to bring the readers to God (3:18). Would the Father block the purpose of the Son and refuse to receive the very men who loved the Son and believed in him (1:8–9)? Their faith was deeply spiritual, for they had not seen the incarnate Son and did not see him now, but it gave them unspeakable joy as it progressively realized its goal in them and gave them their salvation. Why, God himself looked upon them as his very own, his "peculiar people" whom he prized (cf. p. 276). (The *laos eis peripoiēsin* [a people as a special possession, 2:9] is "a very good paraphrase" [Selwyn, *ad loc.*] of *laos periousios* [a people especially possessed].) They belong to God in time and eternity (Schneider, *ad loc.*). Even the individual who serves him may expect to receive strength from him. Even individuals may receive a "gift," a *charisma,* from him and be "administrators" of the variegated grace of God (4:10–11; cf. 2:16).

When the gospel was preached to the readers they obeyed it, the truth.

Through the Word of God thus received they were born again (1:22–25) when they were "purified." In virtue of his great mercy they received a second birth when God "begat" them (1:3). The place of the resurrection here corresponds to Pauline thought (1 Cor. 15:14–19; cf. pp. 184–86). Those who had been born again were thus like very young babies. They needed nourishment and should have an appetite. They ought to "cry" out for the Word in order that thereby they might grow up (2:2) for a salvation yet to be revealed openly but already received (1:5, 9). I am not sure that Bigg (p. 127) is right in saying that "in St. Peter's eyes the Christian is always a babe." There is indeed much to be said for "the faith of a little child," though this is not the faith of a baby. In any case the words "behavior" (1:15, 18; 2:12; 3:1–2, 16) and "conscience" (3:16, 21; ? 2:19) are used of Christians. Do babies "behave" and have they a conscience?

We have thus passed from the first concomitant of justification, acceptance, to the second, quickening (pp. 275, 277–78). The categories differ: quickening or lifegiving is not precisely the same as rebirth; but the experience is the same, the fundamental *Heilserfahrung*—experience of salvation.[9]

The third concomitant, adoption, is really implied by the equivalent of the second as we have just been studying it. The readers have been born from "seed" (1:22–23) or "parentage" (NEB). This fact, together with the word *philadelphia* (love of the brotherhood) in the context, points to an "arrival" in the family of God. God is the Father of the man who believes. He is the Father of our Lord Jesus Christ (1:2–3) and of us in Christ. Believers may therefore be regarded as brothers in the family of God, like Silvanus (5:12). The spiritual family is a cohesive fellowship, aware of "one another" (1:22; 4:8–10; 5:5, 14). If Christ is in the heart of the believing man, he can hardly be unaware of his sonship (3:15). In actual fact he invokes the impartial Judge of individuals as Father (1:17). He knows that he is a son. This accords with his experience of the Holy Spirit, in whose power the gospel first came to him (1:2, 12) and who rests upon him (cf. 4:14).

The thought is not so full as in Romans 8:14–16 or Galatians 4:5–7, but the experience is the same. The brotherhood is to be loved (2:17), and is loved by the author (2:11; 4:12), because Christ is loved (1:8), and in him (3:16; 5:10, 14) they all have a common Father. (Cf. 3:8; 5:9.)

. A fourth concomitant of justification we have called "certainty." By this we do not mean the wider sense of certainty but rather the "impressiveness" of the love of God and the fact that the believer knows and experiences it (Rom. 5:5; cf. p. 118). The approach of First Peter differs from that of Paul but in essence the same truth is expressed. This is clear from the passage 1 Peter 1:3–9. As we consider it we shall work backwards.

The readers are already "getting" the goal of their faith, salvation. They therefore exult with unspeakable joy. This arises from their love of, and trust in, Jesus Christ. Though beset and pained by varied trials they do not cease to exult: their genuine faith is precious and it will bring them

---

9. Schneider, p. 57. "Christlich leben heisst wiedergeboren leben"—"Christian life means regenerate life" (p. 58).

praise and glory and honor from God. For through their faith they are being guarded, preserved within the protective power of God himself for the open revelation of their salvation. They have an imperishable inheritance, untainted and fadeless, kept in heaven for them. There it waits for them, far beyond the range of any earthly vandal. Their hope is high, indeed it never dies. It lives as surely and as long as the risen Christ lives. They never cease to hope, for they are not as other men, secular, pessimists, a prey to doubts and fears and devoid of knowledge. They have been born again. This fundamental and decisive change in them is no mere development; it is not to be traced to education from without or to the will within. It sprang from God's great mercy (*eleos*).

What should be the feelings of such men? Selwyn (pp. 28–29) speaks of "the exhilaration . . . [which] vibrates through this passage" and, even more significantly (p. 121), of "this outburst of praise." "Blessed be the God and Father of our Lord Jesus Christ, the God who in virtue of his great mercy. . . ." Such praise can only come from men who know that they have received the very love of God. For they had been sinners of the darkest hue, standing under judgment (4:3–5). They now have more than "the security which faith gives them for salvation" (Selwyn). They have learned and believed and known and felt the love of God and it filled their hearts, inspiring praise.

For God had given them his grace (*charis*). He plans to exalt them. He can and will shoulder the burden of all their anxiety, for their care is his. In regard to his believing people he is "the God of nothing but grace" (5:5–7, 10).[10]

The term "salvation" is used in the epistle and it seems to sum up all that is meant by "justification and its concomitants." Salvation is both present and future. It is received here and now and is also kept for the final End (1:5, 9–10). It was "planned" in the past. (Cf. 2:2; 4:18.)

A text which has caused difficulty (3:20–21) may be best expounded by a paraphrase. ". . . (the ark) into which a few people, i.e., eight, entered and were safely brought through the threatening water. This same water now no longer threatens you but correspondingly as baptismal water saves you—the point is not the removal of dirt from the body but the prayer to God for a continued good conscience . . ."[11]

The readers should be encouraged even in persecution. The threatening element no longer threatens! This is an illustration and the author guards against misinterpretation. In the situation envisaged, the believer (he is a believer, purified—1:22) already has a good conscience and prays that

---

10. Cf. James 1:2, "nothing but joy." The Greek *pas*, "all," here has the sense of the German *lauter*.

11. They were not brought safely "through the water" but "through the threat of the water." For the believer, threats have lost their power: in baptismal immersion he emerges from the "threatening" water. Blessed are ye (3:14)! Selwyn (p. 299) inclines to the view that *antitupon* is a predicative adjective added to the relative pronoun. Thus: "Which (i.e., water), antitypically (to the type the Flood water), as baptism, now saves you." The RSV pushes "baptism" rather violently to the front and makes it the antecedent to "which." For *eperōtēma* as "prayer" or "request," cf. Matt. 16:1 with its use of the cognate verb. Cf. H. Greeven, *TDNT* 2:688.

it may so continue (cf. 3:16), i.e., that he may not sin. The "point" of the illustration is the contrast of functions, threatening and saving. But water *as such* does not save.

The reference to the resurrection of Jesus Christ should not be kept apart from that to the heavenly session. In the background is the thought of Christ as living, exalted and Intercessor (3:22). For he is the Mediator. We believe in God through him (1:21). As in 3:21–22, just noted, the resurrection and exaltation are linked—though not identified. We approach God through him, for we are a priesthood, and we worship God through him (2:4–5) and we glorify God through him (4:11). It was in Christ that God called us into his eternal glory (5:10).

To sum up: I think it can be said that the First Epistle of St. Peter corresponds to the epistles which we have already studied. The thought and language overlap. This should not be given too much emphasis. The earlier equation of "justification plus concomitants equals salvation" is implied or reflected. We shall realize this with more and more conviction as we ourselves enter more and more deeply into the experience of author and readers. Their experience was not a vague religiosity but had a content, a doctrinal content which is sometimes implied rather than stated. Ultimately the plan of salvation is unaltered. Our optimism at the beginning of this chapter was justified.

The Christian faith, according to this epistle, is individual but not individualistic. The church is entered by the believer, the church which is the spiritual house or temple, the holy priesthood which is elect and royal. It is a holy nation (almost, by oxymoron, "the holy Gentile"), the people of God (2:4–10) and his family. It is scattered throughout the earth and is here but for a season (1:1; 2:11). It has a form of ministry (5:1) and its members have duties to God and man (2:13; 4:2 *et passim*).

The word *church* is not mentioned in the epistle but the church is there. Likewise the word *justify* is not used, but the experience of its concomitants, with the language also, implies its reality. A permanent relationship has been set up between God and the believer. Grace and peace still come—multiplied (1:2; cf. 5:14).

# 13

# The Second Epistle
# of Peter

This epistle is apparently regarded by some as a sort of second-class citizen when compared with its fellows in the New Testament. One or two others may stand with it in its lowly position. It may be felt that I am embarrassed by having to say at least something about it in the present investigation. The attitude is appreciated but the task must be attempted and I feel no embarrassment.

For one thing it is canonical scripture. In this regard it is analogous to Mark 16:9–20.[1] We must consider it. If it is thought that it affords very little material for our purpose, we answer that quantity is not determinative and that quality may be valuable. There may not be much that is new but the old may be in line with and therefore confirm what has already been found elsewhere. A document does not have to be rejected because it does not contain a great deal of matter which could be strictly called evangelical. In a remarkable sermon to doctors, entitled "Reverence for Human Life," the Rev. John Stott dealt with such problems as abortion and euthanasia with but a couple of paragraphs devoted to the doctrine of redemption. We cannot infer from this that he obviously could not have written the sermon or that it is one of his less successful efforts. On the contrary it is highly relevant to our times; and the doctrine of redemption puts the whole sermon into perspective.

Ultimately the question of the authorship of the epistle does not concern us. Nor does the literary relation to the Epistle of Jude. The widespread view that Second Peter is dependent on Jude may be true but our business is to discover the contribution of Second Peter as it stands. We may find more than we have anticipated.

## THE NATURE OF GOD

We begin, then, with the evidence of the epistle concerning God. In clear distinction from man stands "the divine nature" (1:4). This is very Greek.

---

1. Cf. R. H. Lightfoot, *The Gospel Message of St. Mark,* p. 116, final note.

There is no Hebrew word for "nature" [2] and to that extent the term, "divine nature," "belongs rather to Hellenism than to the Bible" (Charles Bigg, ad loc.).[3] "The divinity" (to theion) was therefore appropriately used by Paul on Athenian soil as a synonym for "God" in one and the same verse (Acts 17:29). In the absence of any trace of polytheism we can affirm that God is One. His voice came from heaven (1:17-18) and he is therefore transcendent. The brief quotation from Psalm 89:4, LXX, "a thousand years as one day," rebukes human impatience not by suggesting that God's timetable has been upset or that he cannot "tell the time," but by the implication of his eternity. God is eternal. He is Lord of time and not subject to it (3:8-9). It cannot make him late or early.

God has power, for his Word is a mighty instrument (3:4-7). He is indeed the Creator and the Sustainer. He is conscious, for He has knowledge (2:9). The fact that God has purpose is attested by the evidence of vocabulary. "Kept for judgment" (2:4; cf. 2:9; 3:7); "object-lesson" (2:6, NEB); "promise" (1:4; 3:13); all these in their context are unintelligible if God does not have purpose. Purpose reflects the fact that God has will (3:9).

God has revealed himself, transcendent as he is, partly in a vocal utterance and over a longer period in the words of the prophets (1:17-21). The prophetic Word did not come merely because men willed it and no prophecy of scripture arises as a prophecy carrying its own interpretation. It is not self-enclosed. Men spoke (?words) from God in ancient time because, like ships, they were driven (cf. Acts 27:15, 17) by the wind of the Holy Spirit, and the same Spirit is needed still. Where there is no Spirit there is no prophecy; and where there is no Spirit there is no interpretation: only the spiritual doldrums or "prophecy brought by the will of man," false prophecy (2:1).

God does more than speak. He is not quiescent. God is active. "God did not spare, but . . ."; "he rescued Lot" (2:4-5, 9). Here it may be noted that God deals with individuals. Lot was an individual and "the day dawns" only "in the hearts" of individuals. In character God is holy. His Spirit is holy (1:21), his prophets are holy (3:2) and the conduct of his servants should be holy (3:11). It should be added that God is righteous. It was Noah, the preacher of righteousness, whom he preserved and righteous Lot whom he rescued; and it is the unrighteous who are kept for the Day of Judgment (2:5, 7-9). In the new heavens and the new earth, which we expect according to his promise, righteousness has its permanent home (3:13; cf. Rev. 13:12).

Righteousness leads on to the question of law. God makes demands on men. This is implied by the term "lawless" (anomos, 2:8). The juxtaposition is striking. "By what the righteous man saw and heard day after day as he dwelt among them he tormented his righteous soul with their lawless deeds." The commands of God may be inferred similarly from the "lawlessness" (paranomia, 2:16) which is an infringement of law and from the

---

2. H. Wheeler Robinson, Inspiration and Revelation in the Old Testament, p. 1.
3. Where only the author's name is given, the reference is to his commentary on Second Peter.

conduct (in contrast to that of righteous Lot) of unprincipled men (*athesmos* 2:7). They have no regard for what has been "laid down." Related to such behavior is the concept of departure from a norm. "They abandoned the straight path and followed the path of Balaam and so they went astray" (2:15; cf. 2:18 for the "error"). It (*planē*) belongs to the unprincipled (3:17). "Slaves of corruption" are in bondage to what has mastered them. They take their orders from the wrong authority (2:19).

God makes his demands but they are not met. *God is sinned against* by angels (2:4) and men (2:14). Sin is regarded in a variety of ways. It is ignorance, if not irrationality (2:12), deception or "pleasant illusion" (2:13; cf. A. Oepke, *TDNT* 1:385), culpable madness (2:16). On the resulting "practical" side, sin is "wandering" (2:15, 18; 3:17), unrighteousness (2:9, 13, 15) and impiety (2:5–7; 3:7). When it is appraised it is a stain or defilement (2:10, 13, 20; 3:14) and a blameworthiness (2:12–13; 3:14). Its seat is in the mind, in "desire" (1:4; 2:10, 18; 3:3), and is a kind of "discipleship of the flesh" (*opisō sarkos*).

God is not indifferent to the sins of men. If sins are blameworthy, he blames them—and their authors. If they are a stain, they disqualify from the approach to God and he keeps sinners away. That is to say, *God is a God of Judgment.* His judgment includes both attitude and action. He condemned the cities—and reduced them to ashes (2:6). "He did not spare" angels when they sinned; "he did not spare" the ancient world of men (2:4–5). His attitude and action were consistent. Sin is followed by punishment (2:9). The verb *kolazō* can hardly be remedial or educational in this context.[4]

Judgment and destruction may be empirical and historical or eschatological and final. A combination of the two is suggested in 2:9. The Lord knows how to keep the unrighteous "under punishment" (NEB, *kolazomenous*) until (or "for," *eis*) the Day of Judgment. The prospect is not bright. The distinction between "now" and "then" applies to both judgment and destruction. Since long ago the judgment for some men has not been idle (2:3) and the Flood and the burning of the cities did not wait for the End (2:5–6). On the other hand, judgment is still future and comes on the Day of Judgment (2:4, 9, 17; 3:7). Destruction may be swift and is not drowsy (2:1, 3), as the Flood attests (3:6). Yet in the future the Day of Judgment will be the Day of Destruction (3:7) for impious men (cf. 2:12). Note that destruction may originate in the distortion of the scriptures (3:16), if men are ignorant and unstable.

The awful divine attitude and action may be summed up in the word "curse" (2:14, *katara*). "God's curse is on them" (NEB). "The curse is a judicial action of God, or a consequence of human sin," with the emphasis "on the ineluctability of this consequence of sin, which is determined once and for all by the divine judgment" (F. Büchsel, *TDNT* 1:449).

Of particular importance is the word *hupodeigma* (2:6). Elsewhere it

---

4. Cf. F. Selter, *Begriffslex.* 3:273.

signifies an example to be followed (John 13:15—note *hina kathōs*) or avoided (Heb. 4:11), or an illustration to be considered (Jas. 5:10). Here (2 Pet. 2:6) it is not quite "a warning example to" or "an object-lesson for" future impious men. This rather strains the genitive case. We must think of the word *pattern*. The sentence in which it occurs begins in verse 4, introduced by the significant "for" (*gar*), thus being linked with the preceding long sentence (2:1–3). God set up a pattern of future impious men, a pattern which is a kind of universal. It is the same as the pattern of past impious men. They sin; they are observed; they are judged; they are not spared; they are punished; they are kept for future judgment; they will be destroyed. The divine immutability and consistency could hardly be expressed in briefer compass. The pattern of impious men is consistent because God is himself consistent. Sin is followed by judgment.

## THE OTHER SIDE—GOD FOR MAN

It is an austere and somber picture. But shining on the murk and gloom is a light. It may be small but it is powerful and penetrating. The epistle speaks also of God as Father (1:17) and of grace and peace (1:2; 3:14, 18). The holy God who reserves men for the Day of Judgment also chooses men, makes promises to them and calls them (1:3–4, 10). We must look for a clue, however small, to explain the dual attitude and action.

The evidence in the epistle, which constitutes the "clue," is not more ample than the evidence for redemption in Mr. Stott's sermon. But, as in the sermon, we have enough.

We begin by recalling the actual situation. There are different kinds of sin, mental and gross, and they may be grouped under the general description of impiety and unrighteousness. Men are godless and immoral. As such they stand under the curse and under judgment. The "pattern" is reproduced in every one of them. If we stopped here, we should have to leave them to their fate. There is no sign that they will "develop" into something else. But all the while that they are sinning, God is long-suffering. He does not wish any to perish but that all should come to repentance (3:9). This implies that the threat of judgment and destruction is not absolute. There may be a way of escape.

Everything has been given to "us" which makes for life and piety (1:3–4). If the "us" means the apostles, the gift is not meant for them alone (cf. 3:9). But the author may mean "us Christians." "Life" is the opposite of the depravity which involves destruction and "piety" the opposite of the impiety which leads to the divine rejection.

The apostle (1:1) has a message. He is the apostle of Jesus Christ.

### God at Work for Us—The Work of Christ for Us

In considering Jesus Christ we should observe two outstanding features. He is a Figure of power and majesty, of honor and glory, attested by God the Father himself. A Voice came from the magnificent glory, from heaven. He is the Son of God, the One in whom God is well pleased. He is God's beloved Son, his only Son.[5] He is "our Lord," not "a Lord of ours" (1:12–21). Secondly, he is a historic Person. Peter and his companions have not taken as their authority fables fabricated by sophisticated men according to their own will (cf. 1:21; 2:3). "There is within [the term *myth*] an inherent antithesis to truth and reality which is quite intolerable on NT soil" (G. Stählin, *TDNT* 4:794; cf. 1:12.) The author was an eyewitness; the Lord had spoken to him clearly about his decease (1:14; cf. John 21:18–19); and he, with others, had been with the Lord "on the holy mountain" of the Transfiguration. They now had the prophetic Word in surer form: not in words only but in the Son of God made man. For the incarnation is implied. How otherwise could we account for the language?

But the author does not stop here. The incarnation by itself is not enough. The fact that the author is looking beyond the Incarnation is suggested by his use of the word *parousia* (1:16). This may possibly refer to the Lord's first coming. The cognate verb is used of the "coming" of the truth (1:12; cf. John 11:28). But it is more natural to take it of the Second Advent (cf. 3:4, 12). What happened between the Incarnation and the Parousia?

So far we have touched on the human life of the Incarnate One up to and including his transfiguration. If the Second Advent meant anything to the author, he must have wondered how to get the Lord from the Mount of Transfiguration up to heaven and back again—unless he had some events in mind which he would regard as truth rather than myth. Now there is evidence which points to this.

The author claims that the Lord told him about his death. If it is Peter himself to whom He "made it clear" (1:14), it is natural to think that he is recalling John 21:18–19. We should not overlook the sustained metaphor of clothing, "gird" and *apothesis* (cf. verb Acts 7:58). If on the other hand we are concerned with a pseudo-Peter, it is equally natural to refer to the Johannine passage. This would imply the resurrection. In any case some form of ascension is required.

It is plain, apart from these considerations, that the author knew of something between the transfiguration and the Parousia. He speaks of men who will "deny the master who bought them" (2:1). "Bought" is a redemption word (*agorazō*). "Master" is relevant to the slavemarket (*despotēs*). "Deny" (*arneomai*) is "almost technical," [6] like "confess" (*homologeō*), and is thus a confessional word.

The author does not elaborate. In compact language he speaks of what is vital and he speaks as if the subject is well known. He does not need to explain or expound. The readers know what is meant. Redemption is not beyond their ken; it is their very life.

The false teachers, because they are false teachers, deny what the church teaches. This means that they repudiate, disown, the Lord of the church.

---

5. The word *agapētos* may mean "beloved" (3:1, 8, 14–15, 17) or "unique." Cf. H. E. W. Turner, *Jesus Master and Lord*, pp. 216–17; and Vincent Taylor, *The Gospel according to St. Mark*, p. 161, and the authorities there cited. The usage goes back to the LXX and to Aristotle. James Denney, *The Death of Christ*, p. 14, points out that "a voice from heaven does not mean a voice from the clouds, but a voice from God."
6. C. H. Dodd, *Historical Tradition in the Fourth Gospel*, p. 299, n. 1.

The propositional and the personal belong together. Whereas the believer says "I believe that . . . " and "I trust Him," the false teacher says "I do not believe that . . . , I regard as untrue that . . . , I deny that . . . ," and implicitly if not explicitly says "I do not trust Him, I repudiate Him." (Cf. 1 John 2:22–23.)

Now the false teachers incur a penalty, destruction. They constitute a particular case of sinners and they reject the only remedy. They, like all sinners, are subject to destruction because they are guilty; they are responsible for what they have done and for what they are. Redemption signifies that destruction has been averted from sinners. Christ has taken their "answerableness" upon himself.

If the consistent "pattern" (2:6) were followed, God would indeed be "against" sinners, as Paul would say (Rom. 8:31). But in Christ the Redeemer he is "for" us. This coheres with Peter's words about "peace" (1:2; 3:14).

There is a further factor. The author calls himself the slave (*doulos*) of Jesus Christ (1:1). He has a new Master (contrast 2:19) for he has been redeemed. (See especially p. 256.)

We pass from the field of redemption to that of the cult. The "purification from sins" (1:9) is strongly reminiscent of Hebrews 1:3. This does not imply literary dependence but doctrinal coherence. Sinners as such are not qualified to draw near to God but they gain their qualification through the purification given by Christ. It is not certain whether Peter is thinking of the cross by itself, as in Hebrews 1:3, or of something analogous to the sprinkling of 1 Peter 1:2 (pp. 299, 300–301). In any case the sprinkling or its equivalent is based on the cross. A doctrine of access is thus implied (2:10, 13, 20).

We may sum up Christ's work for us in the words "redemption" and "purification." The author has not explained at length but for a moment he has drawn aside the curtain in order that we may look inside. What we see resembles what we have seen before.

### God at Work in Us—The Work of Christ in Us

It is now necessary to find out if the epistle has anything to say about Christ's work in us. The author calls himself an apostle of Jesus Christ (1:1), and he therefore has something to say. What he said was truth. If he himself was not the man who originally evangelized the readers, he may be taken as representative of them. What the first preachers told them was truth. Through their lips it came to them (1:12). In consequence they have knowledge. At the very least they have been informed, not of sheer fabrications, but of truth (2:2–3). Knowledge has some emphasis (1:5–6).

But it was not merely a set of propositions, however attractively presented. A gift was offered (1:3), mediated "through the knowledge." It first came to the apostles and then through the preachers was offered to the world at large. It offered everything which makes for life and piety, which the heathen certainly did not possess already. It looks very much like the offer of the gift of grace (cf. 3:18). Grace comes increasingly in deeper knowledge (1:2).

The offer was made in the words of truth but it was not made impartially, in a colorless, neutral way. It was indeed offered impartially to all but it was not given as mere information. The preachers were not indifferent to the reception accorded to their message. There is a savor of "telling the listeners what to do." "It would have been better not to know . . . than having come to know to turn away from (not knowledge but) the holy commandment which had been delivered to them" (2:21; cf. 3:2).

The preachers inform their listeners; they offer them the gift of grace; and they command them to receive it. This inevitably requires decision. The hearers must either accept or reject.

The apostles, and by implication the readers, had not rejected the message. The voice of God as well as of men had been heard. They had been "called" (1:3), and they had made their response. This is described in a number of different ways.

Men are faced with destruction. God does not want them to be destroyed. How can they avoid it? The epistle speaks of coming to repentance (3:9). It may therefore be inferred that the readers had responded to the preached message by repentance. In principle they had renounced sin (cf. 2:14). In accordance with this is the concept of escape. When men come to know the Lord they escape "the defilements of the world" (2:20). This does not mean that they reach an unsullied ghetto. They have abandoned the sins which would hold them fast, the sins which defile and which incur the destruction of the sinner.

There is a vivid picture of men still in the valley of decision who are "barely escaping from those who conduct themselves in error [planē]" (2:18). "Their heathen environment" (NEB) lacks exegetical precision. The readers were no doubt still living in their heathen environment but they had got away from being members of a society which was astray and lived in the wrong moral "territory." The picture of the church emerges faintly here, though this is not our point. The idea is surely that of renouncing a way of life—repentance. The change of mind involved is suggested by the word "desire" (1:4).

But if they escape, where are they heading? The factor of faith enters at this stage. The readers' faith was equal to that of the apostles or at any rate that of the author and his circle (1:1). The stress in these opening words of the epistle may be laid on the content of faith rather than on personal commitment. (Cf. Schneider, p. 102.) But the latter is not absent from the author's thought. The false teachers deny the intellectual content of the faith (2:1) and repudiate or disown him who is the object of faith. It follows that genuine believers not only believe the content but do the opposite of repudiating the Redeemer. When the message of the truth first came to them, the readers received the knowledge, heard the command and the call, repented of their sins, committed themselves in trust to Christ and received the gift of grace.

Though complex this is one experience. Their repentance from the defilements of the world is associated with knowledge of the Lord and Savior Jesus Christ (2:20-21). This is more than the "information" which a continuing unbeliever may have. It is the personal, intimate knowledge of the Lord; it is "knowing the Lord" as opposed to "knowing about the

Lord." It is part of the experience of trusting him. Now knowing the Lord is connected with the purification from sins (1:8–9). When the readers first put their trust in Christ they received the gift of grace: they were made pure or holy and thus were qualified to approach God. This is a matter of status. At this point they have renounced defiling sins but have nothing of their own achievement to replace them. It is indeed the gift of grace.

The one initial experience, then, brings purification. The men in question as conscious persons have "experience" in that they are the people who decide, repent, trust. But the purification is not something which they do. They may experience it in the sense that they have a flush of realization of its meaning. But strictly, purification has to do with God. He purifies in the sense that he regards the men as qualified to approach him, now that they believe. Their repentance did not make them pure. God's mental activity comes in. He looks upon them as pure.

But we are not finished with human experience. The initial, decisive step, represented by repentance or "escape," brings something further. The epistle speaks of "becoming participators of the divine nature by escaping . . . " (1:4). In a Christian context this is not metaphysical deification. Peter means that all believers, when they first believe, begin to draw on a common source, God. The thought is analogous to that of participation in the Holy Spirit (2 Cor. 13:13; Phil. 2:1). The initial experience is not kept on the human, secular level, with men preaching and men listening, learning, repenting and believing—and no more. They do all this; and they hear the call of God and when they respond God himself comes to them. They experience what Emil Brunner called "the divine encounter." They meet with God.

But this is what the heathen did not and could not do. Something has happened, not only in the Mind of God but in the hearts of men; and not only their repenting and believing. We are in the realm of conversion or of being born again. And being born again the believers must not stay "just being born again." They must "grow" (3:18). This might mean that they must increase in grace and knowledge, i.e., receive more (cf. 1:2). This, however, is not entirely satisfactory. If, to change the metaphor, they were regarded not as newly born but as plants, we could render "grow in the soil of grace and knowledge. . . . " Perhaps, as newly born, they could grow in the atmosphere of grace and knowledge. It is hard to grasp the author's metaphor, even supposing that he had one. The point is that the believers should not stay precisely as they were when they first believed.

One metaphor is clear, that of the dawning of the day or the rising of of the morning star (1:19). The author's thought implies the first step of faith. In Christ we have the prophetic Word in surer form. It is good to attend to the Word of the prophets. Attend to it, remembering that it is a lamp shining in a dark place. Keep your attention on it, but only until the greater light comes which puts forth a fuller power, only until the day dawns and the morning star rises—in your hearts.

The author is referring to Christ. Until they believed the readers were in heathen darkness. When they believed and encountered God in Christ, something happened to them. In their hearts the dawn broke. Dawn means the beginning of the day. They were therefore different people. They were different from what they had been before their conversion. In yet another metaphor they were now for the first time on a straight road (cf. 2:15). They had begun a new discipleship, no longer going "after [*opisō*] the flesh" (2:10; cf. Luke 21:8//9:23; 14:27).

We must now face a difficult problem. In earlier chapters we have spoken of justification and its concomitants. It has been our hope that we should find the same here. But it seems to be absent; at any rate it is not obviously present. The epistle does not use the word *justify*. Is it to be assumed that it contains nothing of justification at all? We must consider such evidence as there is.

The word "righteousness" in the epistle "has the ethical associations which we find given to it in the Old Testament" (Michael Green, p. 60). The readers have obtained a faith which is *isotimos* (1:1). The first part is an adjective (*isos*) which describes the second part but does not govern it. The meaning is not "equal to the value" but "the value is equal." The compound is "a political word" (Green), "of equal standing" (RSV). The emphatic idea is equality.[7] The equality of status is due to the righteousness of God. To the faith of an apostle and to that of a simple, ordinary believer God gives an equal status. In theory it could be argued that naught equals naught and that the status in question is precisely nothing, but it would be bare, abstract theory, quite unrelated to the spirit of the epistle.

God, then, gives a status to believers. He "refuses to make distinctions" (Green). In other words, in his own Mind he regards all believers as being of equal standing. He must count them (*logizomai!*) as equal in status. Peter does not use Paul's terminology but his thought is akin if not the same. The important factor is faith, and God recognizes it. He regards its possessor, or, better, the one who exercises it, as one who now, in virtue of his faith, has certain "rights or privileges." The quotation marks convey an apology for the use of the words in relation to God. The point is this: it is the unrighteous who are kept under punishment for the Day of Judgment (2:9), and the readers who have a Savior in the knowledge of whom grace and peace may be increased, not decreased (1:1–2). It would seem that the readers are no longer unrighteous. What can they be then, except righteous in the eyes of God?

Justification by faith seems indicated if not implied. In association with such concomitants as we may find, the language points to the religious experience which we have previously observed.

Beyond manifesting an ethical flavor, the adjective "righteous" in 1:13 ("I deem it right") does not greatly advance our present purpose. But the reference to Noah and to Lot is interesting (2:4–10). Notice first the structure of the long sentence. We have a long and involved elaboration but its conditional nature is clear. "If God . . . did not spare . . . but preserved Noah . . . and condemned the cities . . . and rescued righteous Lot . . . (then—apodosis) the Lord knows how to rescue the pious out of trial. . . ." First the condition; then what is "granted."

Both Noah and Lot were in danger but they were delivered. This calls

---

7. Cf. Moulton-Howard *Grammar*, 2:276, 291–92; James H. Moulton and George Milligan, *Vocabulary of the Greek Testament, sub voc.*

for some "technique" ("the Lord knows how to . . . "); it did not merely occur. Noah was "a preacher of righteousness" (by life or by lip, or both) in contrast to the world of impious men. Lot was righteous in contrast to outrageous and lawless behavior and also in contrast to the impious (the "pattern"; cf. pp. 309–10). In some sense both men were therefore righteous but their righteousness is to be contrasted with impiety. Both then in some degree may be called pious. This is justified by the apodosis (2:9). If God rescued the righteous (Noah and Lot), he knows how to rescue the pious— the pious who are contrasted with the unrighteous, and especially with those who follow a false discipleship: they desire that which defiles (and keeps them from God; pp. 312, 313–14) and they despise lordship. The thought is suggested that Noah and Lot may be called righteous in contrast to the sinners who surrounded them. They acknowledged God, their discipleship was correct, they did not desire what would keep them from God and they bowed to God's sovereignty.

This is far from being a bare secular morality, even a perfect morality. They acknowledged God. Within their piety was something which the New Testament would call faith. And Noah found grace (Gen. 6:8, lxx) and Lot was spared and found mercy (Gen. 19:16, 19, lxx). This is God's "technique." His grace and mercy went forth to meet their faith.

The author alludes to Noah and Lot as to well known characters. He does not need to go beyond the barest essentials. The readers were familiar with the stories. They are used for the purposes of practical instruction and exhortation. False teachers will be judged; believers will be spared.

We cannot argue that the author's treatment of the Old Testament stories "proves" the doctrine of justification by faith. But it is legitimate to point out that Noah and Lot were but men, living amid a sinful world. Their own righteousness was not absolute moral perfection. The author's attitude thus coheres with the doctrine. He knows how God deals with sinners: He does not spare them. He also knows of a Redeemer; he knows that God spares men who acknowledge him. Justification by faith is reflected in his language. God did not spare angels when they sinned. He does spare men.

"The way of righteousness" (2:21) may give a measure of support. In the initial Christian experience, "knowing the Lord" involves an escape from the defilements of the world which separate from God (2:20). If a man becomes entangled in them again, he is worse off than before. The author might well have said of such people that "it would have been better for them not to have known the Lord and the escape from the defilements which separate from God." Instead of this he says that "it would have been better not to have known the way of righteousness." "The way of righteousness" thus corresponds to "knowing the Lord and escaping from the defilements." "The way of righteousness" is more than just ethical behavior. It means that through knowing the Lord the defilements no longer keep him from God. God does not keep him at a distance. This is at least analogous to regarding him as righteous. It is admitted that from the moment of his first faith a man is committed to good behavior, to the ethical or righteous life. But he does not start under a handicap. He starts with a clean sheet. He has escaped the defilements. Accounted righteous, he should live righteously, in accordance with the "holy commandment" which told him both to repent and believe and to live righteously.

The promised (not threatened!) new heavens and new earth (3:13-14) are the objects of believers' expectations, not their fears. They should speed the day of their establishment (cf. 3:12). In them righteousness has its home. There is no indication that believers will not be there. Until then they should live lives of holy behavior and piety, combining the moral and the spiritual (3:11), eager to be found religiously unspotted and morally blameless (3:14; cf. 2:13). And if they fail to attain perfection? They will not be shut out. Their entrance does not depend on their own achievement. God is not against them. Already they are "in peace."

The author of the epistle may or may not have reflected on the doctrine of justification by faith. What is clear, however, is that his own religious experience depended on it. Defiled men had been purified by God, given a qualification to approach him; unrighteous men had been given a status. The Christianity of Second Peter is the Christianity of the New Testament as we have found it so far.

In writing the last few paragraphs about justification I have constantly felt that we were in danger of encroaching on its first concomitant. Now the subject must be brought out into the open. When God justifies a man he receives him, he accepts him.

This is implied by the purification. The removal of defilement "qualifies" a man to approach God, and God would not repudiate what he himself has given. It is implied by the whole concept of piety, which is not intelligible if God does not accept the pious man. In fact he more than accepts him; he rescues him (2:9). It is implied by the concept of escape. Believers escape the defilements which keep them from God as they come to know the Lord and Savior Jesus Christ (2:20; cf. 3:18). To know him (1:8) is to know God (1:2).[8] The effectual calling (1:3) is the beginning of acceptance, and knowing God is more than knowing about him. It suggests the intimate interplay of persons. God cannot be known by men if he does not accept them.

The second concomitant of justification is quickening. Parallel to this in Second Peter is. "life" (1:3), significantly joined with "piety." We did not always possess it but we have been given all that makes for (pros) life and piety. Once given it, we should "grow" (3:18). Such life is not unrelated to our becoming participators of the divine nature (1:4; cf. p. 314). This rather emphasizes "direction." When we "know" God, we go to meet him; when we "participate" in him, he comes to meet us. It is a living fellowship, and it was not ours until we had believed.

When we thus know and encounter him, what does he prove to be? We are no longer unrighteous, being preserved for judgment (2:9). He has received us and we intimately know him as we know Jesus Christ. He does not keep us at the level of bare creatures (cf. 2:12) or even of servants. For he has received us as if there were nothing wrong about us and never

---

8. For Christ as God, cf. note 14 in chapter 10 on The Pastoral Epistles; and Bigg, Green, and Schneider on 2 Pet. 1:1.

had been. He has received us as if he were well pleased with us: this is what happens when a man is justified, by whatever name we call it. But being well pleased is God's attitude to his Son (1:17). He thus treats the believer as a son, and he himself is Father.

Those who share this experience find themselves part of a fellowship which is distinct from their heathen environment. They are part of a brotherhood (1:10; 3:15) marked by mutual love (1:7; 3:1, 8, 14–15, 17), and in Christ God is their Father. This is the third concomitant of justification.

The fourth has to do with the "impression" of the love of God, and certainty with regard to it. This is given in the knowledge of his grace (1:2; 3:18). It is deepened by the strenuous living of the Christian life. God does not ever become "less enthusiastic" about the election he has made or the call he has uttered, but individual Christians can make their convictions more certain by their own obedience. The more a man obeys, the more sure he becomes that he was elected and called. God does not need to be made more sure (1:10–11; cf. Rom. 11:29). If the readers follow this exhortation their entrance into the final kingdom will be "rich"—in contrast to some who will enter emptyhanded (cf. 1 Cor. 3:15).

The author is surely here guided by his own experience. In his service to Jesus Christ (1:1) he has grown in grace and become more and more assured of his original certainty. All that he has known of justification and its concomitants is due to him whom he calls "Savior" (1:1, 11; 2:20; 3:2,18). Until the day of the Parousia these themes can be preached to men. The Lord's longsuffering which causes the delay is thus an opportunity for men. If they hearken and respond, it will mean their salvation (3:15).

We have not exactly "proved" a similarity of doctrinal pattern. Second Peter is not an Epistle to the Romans. But the Christian faith as evidenced in Second Peter coheres with Romans. We are concerned with the same God, the same Savior, the same evangelism, the same need for living faith. A believer from "Second Peter," if he entered a "Roman" church, could feel at home in the fellowship. He might increase his knowledge but he would be nourished at the same table.

# 14

## The Epistle
## of Jude

WE HAVE ALREADY STUDIED an epistle which is quite short, the Epistle to Philemon. Though it is not a theological treatise or even a brief theological summary, we found a doctrinal consistency. Given the actual situation, it is the sort of letter in thought and atmosphere which we can well believe the apostle Paul wrote.

Here in the Epistle of Jude we have a similar brevity though a somewhat different spirit. It manifests a good deal of indignation and judgment. This must not blind us to the value of the epistle or make us insensitive to the character of the author. He is certainly fiery in denunciation. But his epistle is not, like the Book of Nahum, "this small prophecy of doom" (Harrison). We could not say, with the Oxford Dictionary, that "the prophecy . . . makes no specific allusions to any future hope and destiny connected with the Messiah" (cf. Jude 24–25). We should not characterize the epistle as Pusey characterized the Book of Nahum. "As a whole, there is no place more for repentance. . . . The office of Nahum is to pronounce [Nineveh's] sentence. That sentence is fixed. . . . Nothing is said of its ulterior conversion or restoration." [1] Jude is fiery in denunciation, but he has a gospel and is warm in pastoral care. But what is his gospel?

In seeking an answer to this question we shall follow our earlier route. We shall try to discover what Jude has to say about God, about the work of Christ for us and the work of Christ in us. Sympathetic to Nahum Jude undoubtedly was; but he may prove to be more than a New Testament Nahum. We proceed to examine his teaching about God. (The epistle is not divided into chapters, and verses to which reference is made will be indicated by a number in parentheses.)

---

1. R. K. Harrison, *Introduction to the Old Testament*, p. 930; F. L. Cross, ed., *Oxford Dictionary of the Christian Church*, p. 937 (article on the Book of Nahum); E. B. Pusey, *The Minor Prophets*, 2:105.

The Epistle of Jude

## THE NATURE OF GOD

*God is One.* There is but one God. He alone (*monos*, 25) is God. *God is eternal.* If we look backwards or forwards into eternity, or concentrate our gaze on the present time, the story is always the same. Praise is ever due to God. There never was or will be a time without his existence; and he is Lord of time. *God is to be worshiped.*

This is not idolatry, for God is God and *he is personal.* This is implied by the recognition of his *exousia*, his authority (25). It is exercised only by persons (O. Betz, *Begriffslex.* 9:926–27). The word denotes the power which decides and acts and has the right to do so. It is illustrated in civic affairs by officials who rule not by naked compulsion (even if force is used) but because they have the right to rule, not shared by men who do not hold office. The "right" is held by God in virtue of his own inherent nature (W. Foerster, *TDNT* 2:566–67).

*God is* thus *free* and *he is powerful* (24–25). "He is able" and he has *kratos*, power to overcome opposition, power "over" something or somebody. It is illustrated by the power of the police to arrest or detain. God exercises his power, because *God is active.* He delivered his people from Egypt and then destroyed those who did not believe, thus showing his freedom of choice and action; and "has kept the angels . . ." (5–6). The fact that he chose the unbelievers to destroy is a sign that he knows the depths of the human heart. *God has knowledge and is* therefore *conscious.* His keeping of the angels for judgment shows that *God has purpose.*

The concept of defilement (8, 12, 23) and impiety (15), and of moral behavior which is outrageous, *aselgeia* (4), to which God is opposed, suggests that *God is holy and righteous.* His holiness and righteousness constitute the ground of his *exousia.* The fact that he judges men for their conduct points to the fact that *he makes moral demands on persons,* not intermittently but always. The punishment of the cities, whose immorality was similar to that of the angels (*ton homoion tropon*, 7) if not precisely the same, was a demonstration (*deigma*) of God's attitude to such men and of the treatment which He accords to such. The "wandering" of Balaam (11) is a deviation from God's requirement and therefore also deserved the Lord's "rebuke" (cf. 9).

But *God is opposed:* by the devil (9) and by men. They speak defiant (*skleros*, NEB) words against him (*kat' autou*) as well as commit godless deeds (15). In fact *God is sinned against.* The impiety in word and deed is characteristic of the "natural" man (19). It is more than merely uttered words or outward action; it goes back to desire itself (16, 18), murderous, self-seeking and rebellious (11).

The inner attitude and the overt action are alike observed by God, together with the character, the godlessness, which they express. The author's comment is more than his own private judgment. He gives his readers the mind of God, his reaction to men's sin. "Woe to them!" is better rendered "Alas for them!" This is not a curse, a wish that evil may befall. It is a "highly emotional statement of fact" (Manson), "a lamentation filled with wrath" (Delitzsch) which "expresses burning condemnation" (Filson), "especially preparatory to a declaration of judgment" (Brown-Driver-Briggs) "in prophetic threat" (Holladay).[2]

The emotion belongs to the author. In the mind of God a fact is observed, a situation assessed; wrath is felt and judgment is on the way.

As men had spoken against God (*kat' autou*), so he is against them (*kata pantōn*, 15) in judgment. The judgment is against all sinners and remembers all their deeds and words—note the repeated "all." As defiled they are repelled from the divine Presence. Judgment, punishment, destruction sum up their end (4–7, 10, 13, 15). Judgment in history is the pattern of the Day of Judgment itself. Sinners have "set aside" (cf. pp. 57–58) the sovereignty of God. In judgment and destruction he shows that authority is still his. He is still Lord, vindicated.

## THE OTHER SIDE—GOD FOR MAN

We can only say that it would be a terrifying experience to fall into the hands of the living God. We turn with relief to "the other side." Jude can speak of love and of God in the same breath, swiftly followed by mercy and peace and even of grace (1–2, 4). He knows of a God who saved his people (5) and of prayer which may be offered (20). He can even bring himself to think of the power of God to view men as blameless (24). If Jude has a gospel which can meet all that he has said about judgment, it must be a gospel indeed. But has he?

We must ask if Jude has anything to tell us about the work of Christ for us.

### God at Work for Us—The Work of Christ for Us

We start by noticing that even Jude who thunders judgment can speak of the grace of God (4). As he looks towards the eschatological End with all its possible terror, he is filled with eagerness. As first this seems surprising; but he sums up the End as "the mercy [*eleos*] of our Lord Jesus Christ" (21). The grace of God is present in the mercy of Jesus. What might have been climactic perdition is pure mercy.

This is not a divine change of mind at the last moment, or a last minute intervention by our Lord. "Mercy" is "an allusion to the atonement he wrought upon the cross" (Green, *ad loc.*). This is indicated by Jude's description of Jesus Christ as "our only *despotēs* and Lord" (4). There is but one Figure in the picture and we are his. He is our new Owner, for he bought us. On the cross Christ redeemed us.

That this is the right interpretation of Jude's words is confirmed by his description of himself. He is the slave (*doulos*) of Jesus Christ (1). He has been redeemed by Him. (See again p. 256.)

We shall thus be saved from the judgment. We now look forward not

2. T. W. Manson, *The Sayings of Jesus*, pp. 29, 97; F. Delitzsch, *Biblical Commentary on the Prophecies of Isaiah*, 1:60; Floyd V. Filson, *Commentary on St. Matthew*, p. 244; Brown-Driver-Briggs, pp. 222–23; W. L. Holladay, *Lexicon*, p. 77.

to judgment but to mercy. But we already have the mercy, which reaches us like an incoming tide (2). Hence Jude was going to write about "our common salvation" (3). Judgment has been averted through the grace of God and the mercy of Jesus. "Peace" is a not unfitting word in these circumstances. For we have been relieved of our guilt.

The designation "the saints" (3, *hagios*), "the holy ones," against the background of defilement (8, 12, 23), suggests Christ's work of purification on the cross (cf. p. 256). The entrance closed to sinners has now been opened by him. God's attendants at the judgment will be "myriads of his holy ones" (14), possibly angels but still holy. The faith of Christians is holy, just as they themselves are (20). Even the praises, given to God by holy men throughout the ages, are "through Jesus Christ our Lord" (25), the Lord who is the new and eternal Owner—because he has redeemed.

The picture of the judgment was dark but the light of the gospel banishes it. Great is the judgment but greater still is mercy. Jude has not devoted much space to the work of Christ but it does not matter. A small diamond can cut the large and hard substance.

Christians are "holy." But how do they become holy? We must consider the work of Christ in us.

### God at Work in Us—The Work of Christ in Us

Jude knows of "the apostles of our Lord Jesus Christ" (17). These men spoke, because they had a message. There was a time when the readers had not heard them or any other evangelists. At the time of writing, mercy, peace and love may come to them increasingly. There must have been a time when it all started. It may be inferred that the first preachers heard by the readers offered them mercy, peace and love. They may not have expressed themselves in this way but it describes what they said.

In making the offer the preachers were using words. In actual fact they were offering Jesus Christ for their hearers to receive. This must be so: they did not offer Christ in order that they might repudiate him (cf. 4).

When the listeners heard the words they heard also the voice of God, calling them. They must have responded because they are still *klētoi* (1). They are "men with a vocation still." How did they respond?

The significance of faith in the epistle suggests that their response was the decisive step of believing in Jesus. God saved his people and then did not preserve but destroyed those who did not believe (5). (Perhaps we should interpret in the spirit of an ingressive aorist, "those who fell into unbelief.") Faith was vital. Faith is the foundation (20): "building . . . on your most holy faith." This is more than doctrine, more than even apostolic teaching. It is Christ in his doctrinal truth as experienced by believing men. Such faith is most holy. Any tampering with it is therefore sacrilege (cf. Schneider, *ad loc.*). The characterization of the revelation as "the faith" emphasizes what is characteristic of Christians (3). They are to spend themselves in effort for its defense and maintenance. It was delivered (*paradidōmi*) once and for all to the "holy ones." This is a "tradition" word. Apostolic teaching is to be "handed over," horizontally so to speak, to contemporaries and "handed down" from one generation to another.

Faith, then, is decisive. But what happens when a man does begin to believe? If faith is holy and tampering with it is sacrilegious, then the believing man is holy. He is no longer divinely repelled. God looks upon him as qualified to approach him, and he began so to look upon him when he first believed. This corresponds to "the sprinkling of the blood of Jesus Christ" (1 Pet. 1:2; pp. 300–301). The effect can last until the Day of Judgment itself (24). "God is able . . . to present you . . . blameless *(amōmous)*." The word may be cultic, as in 1 Peter 1:19 (cf p. 299), but in Jude 24 it can hardly mean a sacrificial victim without blemish. It points rather to the forensic. Unless Jude meant that God would keep his people in moral perfection and thus present them in their achieved moral perfection at the Day of Judgment, which is doubtful, there is at least a flavor of "God's counting them as blameless." Thus as far as we can see into the mind of Jude, when a man believes, God looks upon him as holy and blameless. Grace calls for a life of piety and righteousness indeed (4)—from the redeemed.

If the interpretation given corresponds to justification by faith, then we have already discovered its first concomitant. Obviously God will accept the man, the believer, whom he regards as holy.

Jude also makes reference to having the Spirit and praying in the Holy Spirit (19–20). This is not possible before conversion. Deep experience is implied. It is in line with the "quickening" or being born again which has been noticed before—the second concomitant.

The men of faith who have a vocation have been kept for Jesus Christ (1). They are a distinctive, cohesive group, not existing before men believed, augmented as men begin to believe, bound together in love of one another (3, 17, 20) because each has been offered and has received the divine grace and love. God is Father, they are kept for Jesus Christ, they possess the Spirit and pray in the Spirit. Can they be other than sons of God and can they fail to know it? The third concomitant, adoption, cannot be far away.

"They have been loved in God the Father" (1). The expression is unusual and has proved somewhat puzzling. We should observe that men can be loved without being in God the Father. When they were "in the world" or "in the flesh" it was true that "God so loved the world. . . . " Again, we have seen the phrase, "in the Spirit." It points to Christian experience. To be loved in God the Father thus means to be loved by God but, unlike the world, to be loved by him within Christian experience. Such experience has to be maintained. "Keep yourselves in the love of God" (21). No Christian can ever fall outside the love of God. Jude therefore means "keep yourselves in the consciousness of the love of God." Perhaps the best comment would be to refer to John 8:31; 15:4,9.[3]

This is the fourth concomitant, "certainty." Believing men who pray in the Spirit and have been loved in God resemble those in whose hearts the love of God has been poured out through the Holy Spirit (Rom. 5:5).

Taken all together justification and its four concomitants amount to sal-

---

3. Cf. R. A. Ward, *Royal Theology*, pp. 202–3. "Abide in me": maintain the spiritual life. "Abide in my Word"—in Christ as he has described himself: maintain the spiritual knowledge. "Abide in my love": maintain the spiritual obedience.

vation (3, 23). It is the deep awareness of the whole that inspires believing men to speak of "our God" (4, 25) and "our Lord Jesus Christ" (17, 21). God is "our God" because Jesus is "our Lord." In him God is for us and in him he is graciously present to us; for he is the Mediator. All that we have in God and all that we offer to God is "through Jesus Christ our Lord" (25).

The Epistle of Jude does not expound the New Testament way of salvation, but it reflects what we have already discovered. At the very least it can be interpreted without undue violence on the lines of our previous studies.[4]

---

4. I have not found it necessary to our purpose to consider Jude's possible use of the *Book of Enoch* or *The Assumption of Moses*. See R. H. Charles, *Apocrypha and Pseudepigrapha of the Old Testament*, 2:163–277, 407–424.

# 15

# The Epistles of John

IN CONTRAST TO THE Fourth Gospel which is the product of a lifetime, the First Epistle of John "seems to have been written to meet a special situation . . . [and] is a pastoral letter dealing with the practical needs of the hour." [1] The doctrinal statements are not concentrated but scattered and are applied in the "life situation." We must therefore disentangle these elements and try to set them forth in logical order. The resultant pattern is then available for comparison with what we have already found.

## THE NATURE OF GOD

We begin with what John says about God. (References are from the First Epistle, unless otherwise stated.) *God is real.* "The true God" (5:20) means that God really is God. "True" here means "genuine." It is striking that in the following verse the readers are told to guard themselves from idols, from substitute gods, from imitations which are not, as we say, the genuine article. It follows that *God is One.*

*God is invisible.* No man has ever seen God (4:12, 20). This recalls the statement that "God is spirit" (John 4:24; not "a spirit"). The invisible *God knows everything* (3:20). This is not the "knowledge" of the computer but of the divine consciousness. It is not the so-called "theoretical consciousness" which in a detached way is aware of all things. When we say that *God is conscious* we are thinking of the moral consciousness as well as the theoretical, though with God there is no awareness of obligation. God has no duty.

*God has moral perfection.* "God is light." There is not a wisp of darkness in him. Men who would have fellowship with him must not walk in darkness but in the light and must "do the truth" (1:5–10). For God himself is

1. W. F. Howard, *The Fourth Gospel in Recent Criticism and Interpretation* (revised by C. K. Barrett), pp. 283–84. This is from an article in Appendix B, "The Common Authorship of the Johannine Gospel and Epistles," reprinted from the *Journal of Theological Studies,* old series 48 (1947):12–25.

"in the light" and what fellowship can light have with darkness (cf. 2 Cor. 6:14)? The "walk" means the walk of life, conduct or behavior. The life of Jesus is summed up in the aorist, "as he walked" (2:6). It is a moot point whether it is appropriate to speak of the "walk" of God but the meaning is clear. God is morally perfect and his people should correspond to him.

It is implied that if a man is in the light he should not hate but love (2:9–11). If he loves God, he will not love the world with its blandishments and its appeal to the eye and to feelings (2:15–17). The worldly life is the immoral life and it cannot be inspired by him who is morally perfect, any more than murder can (3:15).

Thought and language of this kind seems to fall within the province of righteousness. Righteousness has to be done; it is an activity (2:29; 3:7–12). It is the opposite of sin and may be observed when a man loves his brother in deed as well as in word or feeling. In some degree it reflects the righteousness of God. It may therefore be inferred that *God is righteous*.

We should add that *God is holy*. John speaks of "the holy One" (2:20) and it is not easy to determine whether he refers to the Father or the Son. Brooke (p. 56)[2] regards it as "immaterial whether the writer speaks of God or of Christ as the immediate source of their holiness." The problem arises elsewhere in the Epistle (e.g., 1:9) and is well known. Its seriousness should not be overemphasized. John is not guilty of lack of clarity. The difficulty of making the distinction calls attention to the unity of Father and Son (cf. 2:23; 2 John 9). Dodd (p. 53) seems to refer the title of "holy One" to God for he speaks of the "anointing" as "something given by God." It cannot be wrong to say that *God is holy*.

*God is true and should be believed* (1:10; 5:10). The unbeliever does not actually "make" God a liar, but he logically implies that he is one and thus "represents" him to be such. The verb *poieō* bears this meaning in John 8:53, 10:33 and 19:7, 12. John rejects the "representation." God ought to be believed. He is credible.

It accords with God's perfect moral consciousness that *he has will* (2:17; 5:14–15). As an extension of his will it should be added that *God has purpose*. He has sent his Son into the world in order that we may live (4:9; cf. 4:14). This points to the fact that *God has power*. God sent his Son into the world and the world could not stop him. Sinful men could not prevent him. No prescient Herod (cf. Matt. 2:3–4, 13, 16) could have kept him out. No "unfriendly" universe could impede. God is "greater" (4:4). His ability to answer prayer is a sign of his power (5:14–15).

The fact that he hears and approves (cf. 3:22) and answers indicates that *God is the living God. God is knowable* (2:14) *but is not known* (3:1).

The will of God implies that *he makes requirements of men*. He is the *Giver of commandments* (2:3–4; 3:22, 24; 5:2–3) and they direct the moral "walk" (2 John 6). Failure to keep God's commandments is lawlessness (*anomia*, 3:4). This is sin.

---

2. Where only the author's name is given, the reference is to his commentary on the Johannine Epistles.

## Man Against God

*God is sinned against.* Three "parties" may be distinguished. There is "the evil one" (2:13–14; 3:12; 5:18–19), the devil (3:8–10). He "produces," for he has his works, the results of his activities (*erga*—"products of work") and he has his children. The devil has sinned from the beginning.

Secondly, John speaks of "the world," the sum total of unsaved sinners. Much is said to describe "it" or "them" in John's Gospel. In the Epistle there is less but it is very pointed. "The whole world lies in (the power of) the evil one" (5:19). It is occupied territory, like France during World War II; a sort of spiritual East Germany or Eastern Europe. It "goes along" with its rulers. Its desires spring from a heart unreconciled to God ("flesh"). It is captivated by what it sees, with all its glitter. It wants to stand independent, self-reliant, boastful and braggart. It is not prompted or inspired by God and does not love God. In its social or collective aspect it stands over against the eternal life of God, for it is passing away, desires and all (2:15–17).

Thirdly, the world may be regarded as the individual sinner writ large, or "flesh" on the grand scale. The individual is a miniature world. God in his moral perfection has the right to make demands on men. He does make such demands but men reject them. We err if we say that we have not sinned (1:8, 10). We are sinful in nature and sinful in our deeds. We act against God's known will by committing lawlessness (3:4). The sinner, as sinner, not merely "copies" the devil but originates in him (3:8). He belongs to him. This ties in with the thought of the world as being "occupied."

Sin is both lawlessness and unrighteousness (*adikia*, 1:9; 5:17). It is so heinous, vile and alien that it has to be removed (3:5). As a particular case of sin or rather as the permanent attitude of the sinner it should be added that *God is not loved.* To love God is to obey him. Lawlessness and lovelessness overlap (4:10, 19–20; cf. 5:1–3).

## God Against Man

In all this *God has an attitude.* The living God who knows everything does not view behavior in detachment. We read of keeping his commandments and doing what is pleasing to him (3:22). It is a safe inference that disobedience, sin, is not pleasing to him. The thoughts and deeds of men do not come before God's eyes in an undifferentiated mass. He makes distinctions: some deeds please him and some do not.

Although the word is not used, the divine displeasure is to be regarded very much in the same way as *the wrath of God.* It is implied in the use of the word *hilasmos* (2:2; 4:10), especially as "there are signs that the meaning 'propitiation' should be retained" (Hill, *Greek Words*, p. 37).

It follows that *God passes judgment.* He may not execute his judgment at once or he may do so only partially. John, however, looks ahead and sees finally the Day of Judgment (4:17). He has not repudiated the eschatology of primitive Christianity. (Cf. Schneider, pp. 155–56, 159.) Related to the

Day of Judgment is "the last hour" (2:18) and the Parousia (2:28; 3:2). But John does not wait for the End. Even now there are those without life (5:12). They "abide in death" (3:13–14). Thus for some there is present death and the future Day of Judgment.

The displeasure of God, then, issues in judgment and death—a present state and a future destiny.

## THE OTHER SIDE—GOD FOR MAN

Such a picture of God may well inspire fear (cf. 4:17–18). But there is another picture which ought to be placed beside it. *God is love* is in itself a deceptively simple statement but it stands firmly in the text (cf. 2:5; 3:1; 4:7–11, 16, 19). From God comes judgment and death; and God is love. How can the two sides be reconciled? How can the same God be both Judge and Father?

### *God at Work for Us—The Work of Christ for Us*

We seek to solve the problem by considering once more the work of Christ for us. It will be convenient to begin with the concept of the Word of God. God has spoken and men must not "make" him a liar (1:10; cf. 5:10). He has in fact a Word (2:14; cf. 2:5) and it has been heard (2:7; cf. 2:24). If the Word of God "abides in you," it must at the very least be remembered. But more is involved.

The Word is prominent in the first paragraph of the epistle (1:1–4). The text ought to be read twice. The first time we should translate, rightly, "That which was from the beginning. . . . " The second time we may translate in the same way but we should remember that by the end of the paragraph John has revealed that the "it" ("that which") is a "he." The great Original was audible, visible and tangible: was manifested, was made subject to our awareness. This is strongly reminiscent of John 1:1–5, 14, 18.

The subject is the Word of life. The life was manifested: was seen, attested and proclaimed. Yet it is true to say that it was "with [*pros*] the Father." It corresponds to "that which was from the beginning" and means "him who was from the beginning" (2:14). This is the preexistent Son of God, known to men as Jesus. Reference is made to the Son in every chapter of the First Epistle (cf. 2 John 3, 9). He is the only begotten (4:9).[3]

For love of men God sent him into the world (4:9–10, 14). He was seen by men as Jesus. He is the Christ (2:22; 5:1), righteous (2:1, 29; 3:7) and sinless (3:5). It was possible for men to hear and see and touch him because he became incarnate (4:2; 2 John 7; cf. 5:6–8).

The Son of God, then, was sent by the Father into the world. Hence he came, with lasting results (5:20, "has come"), and was manifested (3:5). The hidden life of the preexistent Son was laid open to men's apprehension

---

3. C. K. Barrett, *The Gospel according to St. John*, pp. 60, 139. Cf. R. H. Lightfoot, *St. John's Gospel*, p. 90; E. C. Hoskyns, *The Fourth Gospel* (edited by F. N. Davey), pp. 149–50.

when he came "in the flesh." "Apprehension" includes the realm of sense and the realm of mind.[4] But there was a purpose in his coming which was more than being thus "apprehended."

The Son came, first, to destroy (*luō*) the works of the devil (3:8). It is not correctly formulated to say that He came to put an end to his activities. The devil is still active, or tries to be (5:18–20), and the whole world still lies in his power. The young men have indeed conquered him (2:13–14), a fact which shows that he had not been put out of action before they engaged him in battle. In any case the perfect "you have conquered" does not imply the present "he is now dead, prostrate or in bondage" or anything like that. It means, as John says, that "you are (now) strong." They now know their enemy and have taken his measure; they know their own weapons and resources. They are not raw recruits but seasoned veterans, men of experience (cf. Rom. 5:4). John is not secularizing the young men: the Word of God abides in them.

The "works" (*erga*) of the devil are not his activities but what he has produced. "He has sinned from the beginning and still sins" (3:8).[5] He thus "produces" children (cf. 3:9–10), sinners. His children are in direct contrast to those who are born of God and do not sin.

Now the "products" are viewed in their collective cohesiveness. They resemble the solid structure of a temple (cf. John 2:19) but not the true temple of God (cf. Eph. 2:21–22). They are like a heathen temple of idolatry (2 Cor. 6:16; 1 John 5:21). The Son came to pull it down. Or they may be viewed as being tied together by a common bond (cf. John 5:18; 7:23). Whatever metaphor appeals to us, we should observe that the Son came not to destroy the sinners but to deal with something which was common to them all and which linked them. It is not a question of his healing them or restoring them (or whatever figure we prefer) one by one. He came for the negative task of dealing with the situation in which all sinners had their part.

But what was "the situation"? He came "in order that we might gain life through him" (4:9). For we were dead (3:14) and there is no life apart from him (5:11–12) who is the life (1:2).

But why were we dead? We must not think merely in terms of the empirical lack of spiritual vitality. Deadness certainly characterized us and we brought it on ourselves: we failed to love (3:14–15). But we had broken God's law; and we had failed to meet his requirements. Our deadness was not only our condition, our state; it was the expression of the wrath and judgment of God. The Son came to put an end to such wrath. The love of God was made subject to our rational awareness (and we ought to draw the inference) in the fact that God sent his Son in order that we might gain life; he sent him to be the propitiation (*hilasmos*) for our sins

---

4. The word *phaneros* means "visible," even if nobody is looking at it, and also "clear to the reasoning mind," even if nobody is reasoning about it—sometimes "inferable." To summarize: the word means "subject to sensuous or rational awareness." See my unpublished M.A. thesis, "Aristotelian Antecedents of the Philosophical Vocabulary of the New Testament," pp. 123–31.

5. Moulton-Turner, *Grammar*, 3:62.

(4:9–10). This is not limited to "our sins." It is for the whole world (2:2). Some of the sins had not been committed when the Son was on earth; some had not been committed when John wrote; some have not been committed yet.

The wrath and judgment of God was directed towards the sum total of sinful humanity in its "collective cohesiveness." The Son came, sent by the loving Father, to divert the wrath.

But how did he divert it? He came, says John, in order to remove (*airō;* Vulgate, *tollo*) sins (3:5). He has not removed them in the sense that he has banished them from the earth. They have not only been committed already; they are still a possibility and John writes to guard against it. Even so it is still a "live" possibility: "and if a man sin . . . " (2:1). The sins of the "little children" have been forgiven (2:12). Why single them out? It is because the sins of some others have not been forgiven. There are still people who sin (3:4, 6, 8), and are still unforgiven. In what sense, then, did the Son remove sins? Or did he fail in his mission?

The point is important and attention has recently been drawn to it by Professor John M. Rist.[6] "A sin may be forgiven, but as a 'happening' it remains for ever. To talk of sin being redeemed makes no sense if we think that redemption means a wiping clean of the slate of history such as to imply that what has been done can be undone and the world can be as if sin had never occurred. The forgiveness and salvation of a sinner does not entail the blotting out of the fact of a sin."

Now the verb *airō* means to "lift" or to "shift." Both meanings can be relevant here. "We have sinned" and therefore we now "have sin" as guilt (1:8, 10). It is a burden resting on the shoulders of humanity. Christ came to lift the burden. Its weight is not to be felt by humanity. He came also to shift it. If it has been taken away, humanity is no longer exposed to the wrath and judgment of God.

So far we have a stay of execution. Even so the "memory" remains. The omniscient God (3:20) cannot forget the fact of human sin. We are therefore concerned with the divine Mind. The Son came in order that sin might be removed from the Mind of God *as an obstacle to his forgiveness*. This is crucial. It cannot be removed from his Mind *simpliciter*. Once it has been removed as an obstacle, God is free to forgive. Whether he does or does not forgive depends on whether men meet the conditions, for example, confession (1:9). They may or may not confess. But he who is morally perfect and is displeased with men's sins, he who is consistent with himself and will express his displeasure at the Day of Judgment if not before—he, if the purpose of the incarnation is accomplished, is free to forgive.

But what has happened to the sin and guilt? God is not inconsistent and it is far too shallow to say merely that he has changed his mind. " . . . fellowship with God is moral in character . . . the conversion of the sinner is not an adequate ground for fellowship with God" (A. Oepke, *TDNT* 4:303). If our interpretation has hitherto been sound, it would seem that the Son assumed the sin and guilt and stood under the divine displeasure. The holy

---

6. *Journal of Theological Studies,* new series 23, part 1 (April 1972):99–100.

and righteous God has expressed his attitude; the Son has sustained it; and God is free to forgive. This is the purpose of the incarnation and it makes plain the love of God.

John has not expounded his doctrine. What we have said seems to be implied by his language. It coheres with our earlier studies and lends itself to be interpreted in a way which is not alien to them. It should be observed that the ultimate source is the love of God and that Father and Son were united in purpose: grace, mercy and peace come from both Father and Son (2 John 3).

The purpose of the incarnation may thus be summarized. Negatively, the Son came to destroy the works of the devil. Positively, he came that we might gain life; that he might be the propitiation; that he might remove sins. To summarize the summary, he came to be the Savior of the world (4:14).

How did he set about his task? At the end of his earthly days, in which he showed himself to be righteous (2:1, 29; 3:7) and without sin (3:5), "he laid down his life for us" (3:16). He thus manifested his own love for us as well as that of his Father (4:8-11, 16).

The death of Christ was voluntary (cf. John 10:11, 15, 17-18); and it was "for us." Obviously we have an interest in his death. It must have accomplished something for us. Logically there are two possibilities. Either it achieved something quite unrelated to the purpose of the incarnation; or its aim was the implementation of that purpose. If we isolate the death from the purpose of the incarnation, it is difficult to see what it accomplished. There was a purpose in the death: it was "for us." It is conceivable that it might have resulted in benefit for us, unknown in advance to him who died. This, however, hardly fits in with "laying down his life." It is a purposive action, as purposive as taking off one's clothes (cf. John 13:4, 37; 15:13). Then either its purpose is unknown to us; or it contains in itself the whole purpose of the incarnation.

It is surely as certain as anything can be that the death of Christ was the one great means to the diversely expressed end. He embodied and shared in the loving, divine purpose. He was sent, he came (cf. 5:20) and he died in order that he might destroy the works of the devil: to obtain life for us, to be the propitiation, to remove sins—to be the Savior of the world.

But how did the death "work"? John gives us a clue. "If a man sin, we have a Paraclete with the Father . . ." (2:1-2). The fact that a Paraclete, an advocate (a "Fürsprecher") is needed implies that a man cannot sin with impunity. Even if we are dealing with a case of "sin in believers" the matter is serious. It may not be passed over, ignored or forgotten. In a sense the individual sinner reverts to the status quo—or he would do so, if there were not some other factor. Sin exposes a man to the wrath and judgment of God, and he will be judged, if no satisfactory answer can be given. An answer is given, and given by the Paraclete.

In the New Testament the word *paraklētos* occurs only in John's Gospel and Epistle (cf. John 14:16, 26; 15:26; 16:7). Braumann calls attention to the fact that although originally it meant the passive "one called to the side of the speaker," this meaning will not fit the New Testament texts. He is not called in but sent, given and received; and he not only intercedes but is an active helper.[7] The reference is to the Holy Spirit in John's Gospel but the parallel with Jesus Christ, though not to be unduly pressed, is noteworthy. As our *Paraklētos* with the Father, Jesus Christ is the One who has been sent (1 John 4:9–14) and given (1:2; 5:11; John 3:16); and we cannot doubt that he has been received by the Father (cf. Acts 3:21). Whence could he "start out" at the Parousia (1 John 2:28) except from the Father's side? In other words, he is our Paraclete by the will of the Father. He is our Helper because he is our Intercessor or Advocate.

We should notice that John is not thinking solely of a particular case. He is applying a general principle, as we see from the wider and wider extension of his thought. A man may sin, but others in addition, "we," have an Advocate, and the propitiation relates to the whole world. The man who sins is not a special example or a man with a special privilege. All of "us" have the privilege and it is always in operation; in particular it operates when a man sins and it may operate even before he knows about it.

Christ is our Advocate by the will of the Father; and he is the Son, the righteous Son of the righteous Father, one with him in his loving purpose. He does not therefore "venture to suggest," like a timid clerk who dares to try to put a new idea into the head of a dominant superior. He speaks to the Father by the will of the Father; he speaks for us and as the propitiation he speaks about the cross.

But what entitles him to speak for us? It is because he has taken our responsibility, our "answerableness," upon himself. This must be so. If it is not so, he could be asked, "What is this to do with you?" He took the responsibility and he stood where we should have stood; He "has borne on behalf of mankind the full weight of the judgment of God."[8] But what entitles him to expect that God will listen to him? It is because by the will of God he has taken our responsibility. He can therefore speak for us, assured of the Father's ear.

He speaks, even before we confess (1:9). When we confess, God is faithful and just to forgive and cleanse. He is faithful to his promise and faithful to the Son whom he had sent into the world. He does not repudiate the Son's completed mission. Hence in listening to his Son, and in forgiving and cleansing the repentant man, God is just. The responsibility has been transferred; the human obligation has been met. The Son has already endured the judgment. God can and does forgive.

Thus when Christ speaks to the Father on our behalf, we must not think of love pleading with justice. It is the reverse: it is justice pleading with love. For "God is love" (4:8, 16). And the loving Father has good reason to give pardon: he forgives the sinner for whom Christ died—for the sake of his Name (2:12). Thus God is both faithful and just when he forgives.

The implication that Christ has taken our responsibility upon himself suggests that John has a doctrine of redemption. He does not use the stock metaphors or the word *Lord* (*Kurios*) but the thought is present.

---

7. G. Braumann, *Begriffslex.* 4:414.
8. Richardson, *Introduction to Theology of NT*, p. 77.

He has also the cultic approach. Brooke (pp. 28–29) speaks of "the dominant idea . . . of the absolute holiness of God, Who dwells in the light to which no man can approach. . . . " No man can approach—except the cleansed man. John's language is significant. "If we walk in the light as he is in the light, we have fellowship with one another and . . ." (1:7). If we were to read this verse with some degree of unfamiliarity and inattention or to try to quote it in spite of a bad memory, it would be very easy to continue "and the light cleanses." But the light does not do this. According to Johannine thought it exposes (John 3:20–21). It is the blood of Jesus, God's Son, which cleanses us from all sin. "Cleanse" is a cultic word, recalling Leviticus 16:30, lxx and the teaching of the Epistle to the Hebrews.

John attaches considerable importance to this. It is not the incarnation as such which has cleansing power. Obviously the death could not have taken place if the incarnation had not occurred, and John insists on the reality of the incarnation (4:2; 2 John 7). But without the death the incarnation would have no power to cleanse. John's insistence is marked in 5:6–8 even without "the heavenly witnesses." He seems to be using the language of local controversy, and he may be paraphrased thus: "He is the One who came through the water of baptism, according to you incipient Gnostics. But he did not leave before the crucifixion. He came through water—and blood. He came in the flesh (4:2) and there on earth he stayed—not only in the water but in the water and in the blood."

John continues the construction and lets the prepositions run on for the purposes of correction. He came through water? Through blood as well! He came in the flesh? Yes—in the water *and* in the blood. The water may testify to the Father's testimony (5:9; John 1:32–34); the blood testifies to the sacrifice of Jesus on the cross. (A reference to ecclesiastical baptism and the Eucharist seems ruled out: John does not say "water and wine.")

The death of Jesus was a sacrifice. A detailed theory has not been worked out, but we cannot help being reminded of the Lamb of God which lifts and shifts the sin of the world (John 1:29, 36). We do not at present consider the question of when the blood cleanses. If it cleanses, for example, when a sinner first believes, it can do so only in virtue of something prior, Christ's objective work of purification on the cross (cf. p. 256). We should observe that the validity of the sacrifice is not undermined by the imperfection of the Victim: he was righteous and sinless (p. 328).

John does not make explicit mention of the resurrection and ascension but they do not conflict with his thought. It would be impossible to abide in Christ if he were not living; and it is said clearly that he laid down his life for us (3:16). John did not leave him in the tomb. And the Parousia (2:28) would be impossible without the prior ascension.

The work of Christ for us may thus be regarded in a twofold way. He removed from humanity the load of guilt by taking the responsibility upon himself; and by an act of sacrifice he made it possible for sinful men to be "qualified" to draw near to God. These "benefits of his passion" stand firm in their objective security; but they have to be received by men before they are effective in them. If they are not received, it is still true that he has accomplished his mission on our behalf. If they are not received by anybody, all his toil and his tears, his agony and his shed blood, are all to no final purpose and are wasted. He might as well never have come. We therefore have to pass on to a consideration of Christ's work in us.

## God at Work in Us—The Work of Christ in Us

Before he did anything "in" us we were outside of the realm of benefit. We were members of "the world" (2:15–17; p. 327). We did not love God or do his will. Our center of interest was ourselves. We did not know God (3:1) or his Son (3:6). The world inspired our talk and gave us our audience (4:4–6). We were deaf to any who spoke for God. We were in the power of the evil one (5:19). As sinful men, as sinners—in contrast to the abstract "mere men"—we sprang from the devil and were his children (3:8, 10). The Day of Judgment (4:17) had cast its proleptic shadow upon us and we were dead (3:14).

Then something new came into our lives. John speaks of a "message" (1:5; 3:11). Men came to us and spoke, and we heard (2:24) what they had to say. We heard words but not only words; we heard the Word (2:7), which included, but was wider than, a commandment. We heard "his Word" (1:10). The speakers, in fact, were teaching and preaching Christ (cf. Acts 5:42) the Word (1 John 1:1–3). It was on behalf of his Name that they had come at all (3 John 7). They came with an invitation to us. Hitherto we had been "outside" (1 John 1:3).

They told us all about Christ. But they gave more than information. They gave us a commandment. We were told to believe in the Name of him in Whose behalf they had come (3:23). He is the Christ (5:1), the Son of God (5:5). It was a question of believing God himself (5:10; cf. 1:10). We found ourselves under obligation not to disbelieve God, for he was calling us (3:1).

We did not turn away. We received the Word of God (2:14). For we confessed our sins (1:9); we admitted that we were indeed sinners. We acknowledged that the Son of God is Jesus (4:15), come in the flesh (4:2). Our attitude was more than intellectual. We did indeed "acknowledge that" certain propositions were true; but we did more. We did not "deny that" the Christ is Jesus and we did not deny him: we did not repudiate or disown him. We rather welcomed him, received him, "confessed" (not only propositions about him but) the Son himself (2:22–23).

And so we came to know the truth (2:20–21), not only as propositions but as a Person. We came to know "him who was from the beginning" (2:13–14).[9] When we thus came to the Son we found the Father (2:23; 2 John 9). To confess the Son is to have, to be in fellowship with (cf. Schneider, ad loc.), the Father also. When we belonged to the world we did not know him (3:1). Now we do know him (4:6–7; 5:20).

Thus we entered the light (1:5–7; 2:8–11) and began to see. We began to "abide" (cf. p. 323): in Christ (2:28; 3:6); in God (4:15–16); in the Son and in the Father (2:24; 5:20). We passed from being "in the evil one" (5:19) to being in Christ and in God.

---

9. Cf. Barrett, *The Fourth Gospel* . . . , p. 68: " . . . knowledge itself implies relationship in addition to cognition. . . ."

We became guests in a new home. We also became hosts. What we heard began to abide in us (2:24). The "anointing" (*chrisma*) (2:27) and the Word of God (2:14) abide in us. God abides in us (3:24; 4:12–13, 15–16) and we know that he does because he has given us his Spirit (3:24; 4:13; cf. 5:6, 8).

It may be asserted that "abide in me" (John 15:4; p. 323) is a command and is therefore something which we ourselves must do; whereas it is not said that we are to "abide in my hand" (cf. John 10:28–29). This is true; but the point is that we had not even made a beginning before the preachers came and offered us the Word of God.

If we now give a brief "progress report" we must say that we have confessed, have believed, have taken the first step of faith. What else was involved?

We were cleansed. We had entered the light and had begun to walk in it and from that moment the blood of Jesus, God's Son, was cleansing us from all sin (1:7). Up to the moment of our first faith we had been sinners, unclean, disqualified from approaching the holy God. When we believed, God regarded us as qualified to approach him, as clean. The continuous present tense of *katharizō* does not mean that the process takes a long time, in the sense in which a woman may say that "I am cleaning the house and it is taking me all week." It rather indicates the fact that when we first put our faith in Christ, a permanent relationship with God was established in which he kept on regarding us as qualified to draw near to him.

Confirmation of this view is found in 1:9. "If we confess our sins, he is faithful and just to . . . cleanse [aorist] us from all unrighteousness." God "cleanses" us when we first believe. He gives us the "qualification" to approach him.

The text is thus appropriate to the time of conversion. It is relevant also if the converted and established Christian sins.[10] If he sins, God does not cast him out. He is still in God's home but there is a barrier between him and God. The barrier, raised by a Christian man (in distinction from the earlier barrier raised by the holy God against sinful men), will not be swept away until confession of sin is made. When he confesses, God cleanses him there and then. This is a "reapplication" of the same blood. God tells the believer who has sinned: "you are already 'qualified'; you are already in my home; you are as welcome now as on the day when you first came." And Keble's "cloud" is gone.

The cleansing of the man who exercised his "first faith" is analogous to the sprinkling of the blood (cf. pp. 300–301).

When a man believes, he is forgiven. His exercise of faith is not abstract but part of a unified experience which includes confession of sin—which is very like repentance. Confession of sin is the "agreement" of the sinner with the judgment of God and in forgiveness the annulment (*Nichtigmachung*) of the sin takes place.[11] Now if Professor Rist is right (See above p. 330), and I think he is, the sin has not been "annihilated." God still

---

10. Cf. John Wesley, *Sermon XIII*, "On Sin in Believers"; and John Keble's hymn, "Sun of My Soul": "O may no earthborn cloud arise/To hide Thee from Thy servant's eyes."

11. H. Vorländer, *Begriffslex.* 12:1265–66.

knows about it but he adopts an attitude to it. He acts as if sin had not occurred. We are close to Paul's doctrine of justification and his use of *logizomai*. And God so acts in virtue of the cross of Christ. Sins have been forgiven "on account of his Name" (2:12).

When a man puts his faith in Jesus, knowing who he is and what he has done, he conquers the world (5:4-5). He may go on doing so throughout his Christian life but there must have been a first time. This was when he first believed. But what does John mean by conquering the world? It seems to be more than the bare overcoming of temptation.

The world is the flesh writ large, godless, egocentric, self-willed (2:15-17). When the gospel is preached to a man there is a struggle within him between his sinful ego, writ large in the glittering world around him, and the call of God to repent and believe. When the decisive moment comes at which he puts his faith in Christ, he "crucifies the flesh" (Gal. 5:24) in spite of its appeal (cf. Gal. 5:19-21). Thus in his believing response to the preached cross, "the world is crucified" (Gal. 6:14) and thereby conquered. Christ, the living Christ, is present in his experience and in his company the ego itself is crucified (Gal. 2:19-20). From that time onwards he lives, believing in the Son of God, still conquering the world. "The mind of the flesh (the inner world) is enmity towards God" (Rom. 8:7) and the believing man "has conquered the evil one" (1 John 2:13), who also is God's enemy.

John is not rewriting Paul. He is describing in his own language the same authentic spiritual experience.

"From that time onwards he lives." For he has been born again. It is the believer who has been "begotten of God" (5:1). He goes on believing but he does not go on being born again. "He has been begotten" (perfect tense; cf. 2:29; 3:9; 4:7; 5:4). He is now "of God" (4:4, 6; 5:19).

When a man first believes, the purpose of the incarnation (4:9) is fulfilled. Eternal life was manifested (1:2) and it has been given to him (5:11-12, 20). It is for those who believe (5:13). On this subject John is all black and white; he knows no gray. He who is in fellowship with the Son has the eternal life of which John was speaking. He who is not in fellowship with him has not the life.

Note that John does not say "will have" and still less anything of the nature of "will have if he is lucky." We know that we have it now (5:13). We have passed from death to life (3:14); we are alive.

It follows that at "first faith" a man has taken the first step in a new moral life, a new "walk." He is a committed man, "from the beginning" (3:11; cf. 2:7, 24; 2 John 4-6). He has commandments to keep (2:3-5; 3:22-24; 4:21; 5:2-3), the breaking of which impairs the spiritual life. He has a Savior (4:14) who keeps him (5:18) and a prospect and destiny to inspire him (3:2). This looks very much like John's way of saying that a man has entered the kingdom of God. In such a kingdom the King rules. John just speaks of commandments.

It should be observed that John's spiritual experience and his teaching involve justification by faith. The initial response to the preached message is complex, as we have seen. Central to this is the act of faith, and faith is very important in John's thought. It is commanded by God (3:23). It is the believer who has been born again (5:1); and it is by faith that he overcomes the world (5:4–5). Through faith he gains fellowship with the Son and with the Father (2:22–25; 5:10–12) and receives the gift (not the reward or the pay) which consists of eternal life. It was to believers that John wrote so that they might know (not guess or hope) that they had eternal life (5:13; cf. John 20:31) and he wrote to men who already knew the truth (2:20–21).

It was because of faith that men received the gift. Similarly as a result of faith they received the gift of cleansing, the "qualification," and the gift of forgiveness. Light is thrown on this matter by John's reference to "boldness in the Day of Judgment" (4:17). The ground of such boldness exists already. "As He [ekeinos] is, we also are—in this world." The likeness does not refer to the moral example of Jesus. John is thinking of the exalted Christ (Schneider, p. 178) and the Day of Judgment. We are not now, and shall not be then, "like" him enough to give us boldness. In that forensic situation, as now "in this world," we have a likeness given to us. We are one with the Father, and are his children, not by nature but by grace; not from all eternity but from the time when we first believed. God knows our state full well. Even if love has flowered and we have no fear of our Father, we do not manifest the matchless sinlessness of his Son. Yet he treats us as if we were indeed Christ his Son. This is the "likeness." It is a daring description of justification.

And it is by faith. For John it must be a living faith. Paul (and James!) would have agreed. He has devised a system of tests.[12] But whatever language he chooses to employ, John is no stranger in thought and experience to justification by faith.

But has he room for its "concomitants"? It must be clear from what has already been said that God accepts the man who believes. He cleanses him and thus qualifies him to draw near. He does draw near, for example in prayer (5:14–15), and God hears him. For he is in fellowship with the Father (2:23). He has begun to abide in Christ—and in the Father (2:24; 4:15–16; 5:20). He is no forceful and unwelcome guest who cannot be removed. He is accepted by the Father.

He certainly is quickened. "We have passed from death to life" (3:14). The purpose of the incarnation is realized (1:2; 4:9) every time a man begins to believe. For eternal life is given to him (5:10–12). Before his "first faith" he was in the world and did not know God or love Him (2:15; 3:1). Now he knows him (4:6–8). He has been given a faculty of perception (dianoia) whereby he may know him (5:20). This is perhaps more than a natural disposition and less than the Holy Spirit. (Cf. J. Behm, TDNT 4:967.) Even so he has been given the Holy Spirit (3:24; 4:13; 5:6ff). The presence of the Holy Spirit is not only the sign that God abides in him; it is the method of his presence. Such a man is an example of a familiar expression, "the life of God in the soul of man." He has indeed been quickened.

12. Cf. Robert Law, The Tests of Life.

He has been accepted and quickened. He has also been adopted. John does not use the Pauline word *adoption*, but he knows the experience. He exults in the permanent gift of God's love in giving us the truly descriptive name of "children of God" (3:1–2). We really are that—now—and we manifest it by doing righteousness and loving our brother (3:10). We were not always thus. Before we believed in Christ we were "of the world" (2:16), "of the evil one" (cf. 3:12), and "of the devil" (3:8).[13] Hence we were "children of the devil" (3:10). Now we are "the children of God" because we "have been born of God" (2:29; 3:9; 4:7; 5:1, 4, 18) and are now therefore "of God" (4:4, 6; 5:19).

God has many children (*tekna*) but only one Son (*huios*). In the Johannine circle the word "Son" is always reserved for Christ. This is John's way of saying that "men are not by nature the children of God . . . Only by receiving Christ do they gain the right to *become* children of God."[14] Those who receive him are those who believe in his Name.

To "become children" expresses more than a change in the divine attitude to certain men. It is an experience. Its fruit is doing righteousness (2:29), avoiding sin (3:9) and loving one another (4:7).[15] Hence the children of God are manifest (*phanera*, 3:10; see p. 329), though the world does not "draw the inference." "The world does not know us" (3:1). It knows us as bankers or farmers but not as children of God. The text does not mean that the world withholds recognition, like a government which refuses to recognize and have diplomatic relations with some new nation. It means rather that "the world sees us, children of God, and does not know us when it sees us."

Adoption therefore implies not only an experience but a distinctiveness. For John the distinction is absolute, though by repentance and faith a member of the world may cross the border and join the "children." "We" are different. "We know that he abides in us from the Spirit whom he gave to us" (3:24; cf. 4:13). The Spirit is an abiding Presence (*dedōken*). The context (3:21–24) is instructive: clear conscience, boldness, prayer and its answers, obedience, pleasing God, faith and love. Add to this the "mutual abiding." The child of God in the Johannine scheme and experience knows his Father.

We should observe that John has more in mind than the collective experience of the church. God is indeed in the assembled community (cf. 1 Cor. 14:25). But in addition "God abides in him" (1 John 4:15–16). John spoke of his abiding "in us" (4:12) and he could have rephrased verses

---

13. The phrase, "of the [*ek*] . . . ," indicates origin, dependence, attachment. See C. H. Dodd, p. 66, n. 1.

14. Barrett, *The Fourth Gospel* . . . , pp. 136–37 (on John 1:12). The italics are Barrett's. Cf. John Marsh, *The Gospel of St. John*, p. 107; Leon Morris, *The Gospel according to John*, p. 98.

15. "He cannot go on sinning" (3:9) may well be taken literally, if we notice the present (continuous) tense. The life of the genuine believer is not characterized by a persistent course of sin. We may also translate "he is not at liberty to. . . . " Cf. Luke 11:7. The man in bed was not trussed up or strapped down as if he had been kidnapped! To get up out of bed would at least have disturbed the children and might have created an uproar. He was not "free" to move.

15–16 accordingly. It remains that he wrote "in him." As we have seen before, God deals with individuals. He does not turn them into hermits. Each exercises his faith and enjoys his sonship, loves his fellows and does his deeds of righteousness—and he is bound together with "us."

There is always the possibility of sin (2:1). But as a sort of counterbalance to the natural man's bias toward it the regenerate man has a new tendency or driving force against sin. "God's seed abides in him" (3:9). Biologists speak of a law of heredity. John is thinking of spiritual heredity. The man who is born of God has some of the characteristics of his Father. Apart from the fact that he lives after, not before, the Fall, he is like "Adam, son of God" (Luke 3:38).

The believing man was once a child of the devil; he is now a child of God. He must have been "adopted."

Accepted, quickened, adopted: has such a man that which we previously summarized as "certainty" (pp. 275, 279)? When he believed, did he come to know and to experience the love of God (Rom 5:5)? A short answer would refer to 1 John 4:16 and its context. "We have known and have believed the love which God has" for us. The context is that of the mutual abiding, which we know from the permanent gift of the Spirit. The *en hēmin* may therefore have some significance and may go beyond "for us." We have thus the mission of the Son as Savior, with lasting results; the mutual abiding; and the presence of the Spirit, with a distinctive experience of adoption. Could John and his fellow believers, the "brethren" (3:13–16; 3 John 3, 5, 10), fail to be at home in Paul's language and experience?

The mutual abiding, made known to us by the Spirit (4:13), is of importance here. If we say that we abide in God, we imply that our status in Christ, our "qualification" to approach God, is realized and exhibited in our experience. God is not only accessible to us in Christ; we have actually approached him—and "stayed there." If, on the other hand, we say that God abides in us, we imply the divine Presence. The holy God has not repelled us. He is not only accessible in Christ; he has come to us—and not as Judge.

This mutual abiding is the quintessence of eternal life. It is not something which is given to us by Christ apart from himself, as if he gave it to us and then left us. This would be no more than a form of eudaemonism. He himself is the life (1:1–2) and to have, i.e., to be in fellowship with him is to have that same life (5:11–12), to have indeed the Father himself (2:23).

The status of the believer is an objective fact. God regards him as "qualified" to draw near. Paul would say that God counts him as righteous. In the mutual abiding, with all that it involves, the objective fact is subjectively realized.

The initial act of justification or cleansing—we may use other language to describe it if we will—sets up a permanent relationship between God and the believer. This is implied by what John says. "We" are "of God" and no longer, like the world, "in the evil one" (5:19). John's use of the perfect tense implies a present possession or enjoyment. We have been forgiven (2:12); we have conquered (2:13–14); we have received the Spirit (4:13).

We have eternal life already (5:11–13). In contrast to the world we shall abide for ever (2:17). John visualizes a continuation in the light (1:7) and in love of the brotherhood (2:10). He sees a life of prayer (5:14–15) and of protection from the evil one (5:18). The Parousia is anticipated, welcomed and prepared for (2:28; cf. 4:17), with its further blessings (3:2–3). And if meanwhile a man fall into sin, he is not expelled and sent back into the world. "We have an Advocate with the Father" (2:1), the very One who will come for us to make us like to himself. For we shall see him as he is.

It is hardly necessary to retrace our steps in detail in order to prove that for John the believer has both privileges and duties. As a privilege he has the fellowship (1:3, 6–7) of the church (3 John 6, 9–10) and the benefit of pastoral supervision. The ministry at this stage is young and fluid, far from the development of the second century. But the epistles manifest an affectionate pastoral concern. We see an elder or presbyter (2 John 1; 3 John 1) and apparently traveling evangelists (3 John 7). The fellowship or church is distinct from the world and is conscious of itself: some apparent members do not really "belong," and some others must not be received (1 John 2:19; 2 John 10–11). The truth is known (2:20–21, 27). The "privileges" include everything which has been given in Christ, from "first faith" up to the Parousia. The "abiding" Christian will not be caught by surprise at the Parousia (2:28). The Christian hope is no mere dream. We shall see him and be like him (3:2).

The duties, as John sees them, are those of regenerate and forgiven men who are called to abide in Christ. It is enough at this stage to say that we are not concerned with natural or secular ethics but with the moral behavior of the man who walks with God. He is to walk in the light, to love his brethren, to do God's will, to keep his commandments and to do righteousness. Negatively he must not sin or forget the need of self-purification. His "outreach" is not limited to an ecclesiastical closed shop. "The statements of 1 John about brother-love seem not at all to be restricted to one's *Christian* brother (e.g., 1 John 3:17)." [16]

These duties, broadly speaking, may be termed moral. There are others which are spiritual or religious. John does not use the word "piety" (*eusebeia*) or its cognates but he implies it. If moral duties involve love of neighbor, religious duties mean love to God (4:20–21; 5:1–3). Loving God should not occur in a vacuum but it should still occur. John would include under this head the whole life of prayer and "abiding in Him." The imperative (2:28) should not be missed. The Christian should "walk" as Christ walked (2:6). This includes the spiritual or religious as well as the moral (cf. John 17:1–26; 2 Cor. 5:7; Col. 2:6).

If we have interpreted the author rightly, it would seem that his expression of "justification and its concomitants" describes the same spiritual

---

16. Rudolf Bultmann, *Theology of the New Testament,* 2:82. The italics are Bultmann's.

outlook and experience as we have already found in the New Testament. In their totality they amount to salvation. This we might have expected. "The Father has sent the Son to be the Savior of the world" (4:14). We have found him to be our Savior. We once belonged to the world and were members of a false fellowship: the world is in the evil one (5:19) and the evil one is in the world (4:4). Now we belong to God and are members of a true fellowship: we abide in God (4:15–16) and God abides in us.

# 16

## The Revelation of John

THE BOOK OF THE REVELATION has not always been valued as it should; it has not always been treated as what it is. If we regard it as a coldly calculated blueprint of the future, we miss its deepest message. The author speaks of becoming "in the Spirit" (1:10; 4:2). This must not be interpreted as entering a trance. "Rapture" is not quite the word. We should think rather of spiritual exaltation (cf. H. B. Swete, pp. 12–13, 66),[1] of "the prophet under inspiration."

This at first may seem somewhat elusive. But all Christians *are* "in the Spirit" (Rom. 8:9). When the prophet *becomes* "in the Spirit" he travels further along the road on which "ordinary" Christians are already traveling. If we think of the deepest moments of the life of prayer, we have at least a clue. When prayer is not ejaculatory but unhurried, when the believer is not straining to finish his prayer in order to get back to his work, when he is so far "in" that he lingers with God as if he had all eternity before him—then we have something which approximates to the prophetic experience.

The imagery of the book is alien to us. And yet most of us from time to time see the strangest of images and absorb them all without concern. The oddest sights appear to us in dreams and we accept their incongruities without question. I do not mean that the author was dreaming but that we ourselves ought at least to be sympathetic to what he saw. We have seen strange things too.

The author is a genuine visionary with authentic prophetic consciousness. His book is "closer to the prophetic tradition than to the apocalyptic" and it is written with authority.[2] In style and imagery it leans on the Old Testament and apocalyptic but it is nonetheless original. Its aim is the interpretation of history.

But the writer is no academic essayist. His purpose is practical. He seeks

---

1. Where only the author's name is given, the reference is to his commentary on Revelation.

2. Cf. David Hill, "Prophecy and Prophets in the Revelation of St. John," pp. 401–418.

to warn, to encourage and to strengthen the Christian congregations in their struggle with political absolutism. His ultimate concern is pastoral care. (Cf. G. B. Caird, pp. 3, 188). Whether or not he "wrote in code to deceive the secret police," his imagery must have thrown dust into the eyes of some literal-minded officials.

We might observe that any apparent sternness comes within the author's loving, pastoral care and is not opposed to it (cf. 3:10). God preserves his people and one of his methods is to warn them of the consequences of faithlessness. "He who conquers will inherit . . ." (21:7). John clearly belongs to the long line of Christian pastors, a fact which is confirmed by his farewell (22:21; cf. Rom. 16:20; 2 Thess. 3:18; for Rom. 16:24 see RSV, note 6). His book is therefore not primarily a puzzle to be solved (though it has its problems) but the fruit of an experience in which we share.

If the author is thus a believing man and a pastor charged with the cure of souls, in this respect he does not differ greatly from the writers whom we have already encountered. It is therefore natural for us to ask if his message is the same as theirs or at least if it coheres with it. We begin our search for the answer to this question by study of his doctrine of God. What does John believe about him?

## THE NATURE OF GOD

God is *the living God* (4:9–10; 7:2; 10:6; 15:7) and *he is eternal* (1:4, 8). *He alone is God,* metaphysically and ethically *transcendent* (4:1–11). John has no use for idolatry (2:14) and he is no henotheist. God is the Alpha and the Omega (1:8; 21:6–7). *He has great power* (11:17; 12:10; 15:3, 8; 19:1). We see it illustrated all around us, for *God is the Creator* (3:14; 4:11; cf. 13:8; 17:8) of all things, including men (cf. 16:18).

To say, as John does, that God has "great power" seems to be the understatement of the century, if not of eternity! But it should be understood in the light of the fact that God is Creator and that *he is almighty* (1:8; 4:8, et al.). The omnipotence of God ("God can do anything") is sometimes used by critics to raise questions which are really irrational: "can God make wet dry?" Apart from the fact that the doctrine means that God can do everything that he wills—an important qualification—the word *pantokratōr* means "all-controlling." A police officer arrests and detains. The prisoner may walk about in his cell or take exercise in the yard but his freedom is limited. He is under control. Similarly all things in heaven and earth, "free" though they may be, are subject to God's control. With him no prison riots can ever get out of hand.

Nature, history and even the mind of man are in the control of God. The language of cosmic catastrophe (6:12–14) "illustrates the transcendence of God and the dependence of His creation upon its Creator." History (5:1) has no ultimate independence. "The whole story of human history rests in the hand of God" (G. E. Ladd, pp. 82, 107; cf. his *Jesus and the Kingdom,* p. 85). He controls the very minds of men. He "has put it into their heads [*kardias*] to carry out his purpose" (17:17, NEB). "He sees to it that the kings have the unity they need for their act of destruction" (Leon Morris, p. 213).

*The purpose of God* implies that "the future has been decreed in the predestining purpose of God . . . a purpose as old as the world and as ultimate as the crack of doom" (Caird, pp. 290–91). It is clear that *God has will* and *God has freedom* to implement his long term will. It was because of God's will that the universe existed in thought and was materially created (4:11; cf. Swete, *ad loc.*).

Before it was created the universe existed in the thought of God, because *God is conscious.* He remembers (18:5). The fact that he has an identity is confirmed by his possession of a Name (3:12; 11:18; 14:1). *God makes demands on men:* He has given commandments which should be kept (12:17; 14:12). *He is to be worshiped* (4:8; 11:16; 15:4; esp. 14:7; 19:10; 22:8–9) and he will be worshiped (7:15; 22:3); and *is to be thanked* (4:9; 7:12; 11:17).

*God deals with individuals* as well as with states and civilizations (2:23; 6:11; 20:13; 21:7; 22:4, 12). *He is righteous and true* (15:3–4). "The justice of your decrees stands revealed" (Caird, p. 199). "A *dikaiōma* is a concrete expression of righteousness, whether in the form of a just decree (e.g., . . . Luke 1:6), or a just act, as here and in 19:8" (Swete, p. 194). The word "*dikaiōmata* here means the judicial sentences of God in relation to the nations either in the way of mercy or condemnation" (R. H. Charles, 2:36). (Cf. 16:5, 7; 19:2.) The ethical flavor is brought out in the command for the righteous man still to *do* righteousness (22:11).

*God is holy* (4:8; 6:10); He is *the* holy One (16:5) and *he alone is holy* (15:4). *God has authority* (16:9). (Cf. W. Foerster, *TDNT* 2:566–67.)

Charles (1:127) comments that the trisagion of 4:8 "confines itself to the holiness, omnipotence and everlastingness of God." The praise of creation (cf. Isa. 6:3) is not voiced. He adds significantly that "on the essential nature of God our author bases his assurance of the ultimate triumph of righteousness." In simple terms: God will act—because of his holiness; he can act—because of his omnipotence; he has time to act—because of his everlastingness. He will not be impeded by his own inability or thwarted because the time runs out.

## Man Against God

For *he has opposition,* omnipotent though he is. However earlier Jewish thought regarded him (cf. Job 1:6), John did not look on Satan or the Devil with any kindly eye (2:9–10, 13, 24; 3:9). The scale of his operations is vast: he seeks to deceive the whole world of nations (12:9; 20:2–3, 7–8, 10). He is the serpent which appeared at the beginning of the Bible (Gen. 3:1, 13–15) and his final punishment is certain. His efforts have not been in vain, for *God is sinned against by men* who have become his dupes.

John speaks of sin in both general and specific terms. He uses the noun "sin" (1:5; 18:4–5, *hamartia*) and in a more or less moral sense the noun *adikēma,* "act of unrighteousness" (18:5), and its cognate verb *adikeō,* "to act unrighteously" (22:11). All sin is against God and the unrighteous act is also against man. It is failure to love one's neighbor. There is in addition the specific sin of not loving God. Broadly speaking this is impiety, *asebeia*, though John does not use the Greek term or its cognates. The concept, however, is present.

God alone is to be worshiped (19:10; 22:9; cf. 20:4) and to divert worship from him is the sin of impiety (13:4–8, 12, 15; 14:9–11; 16:2; 19:20). This is a form of idolatry, which may be crude or refined (2:14, 20; 9:20; 21:8; 22:15). John makes plentiful use of the concept of fornication or whoredom, taken over from the Old Testament. In Israel "every dalliance with paganism was fornication."[3] What may be a literal sin of unrighteousness is taken as a type of impiety, of hostility to God. Its object of worship may be the crude, cultic image; or the call of God may be replaced by "the economic seductions of the omnicompetent state" (Caird). John similarly speaks of adultery in a figurative sense (2:22).

The call to repentance and the threat of punishment imply that men are held responsible for their sins. *God holds men accountable.* This is because *God has an attitude to men.* It is suggested by John's use of the terms of cultic defilement: *molunō* (3:4; 14:4; cf. Lev. 15:16; Deut. 23:9–14); *akathartos* (16:13; 17:4; 18:2) and *koinos* (21:27). Being defiled, unclean or "common" really expresses what God thinks of a man. If he rolls in the mud, he is literally unclean. If he breaks some law of ceremonial purity, it may be hard if not impossible to find anything "wrong" with him. But he is unholy in God's sight. Ceremonial purity or defilement may symbolize moral and spiritual qualifications or their absence. "Nothing unclean shall enter" (21:27, NEB).

The attitude of God is confirmed by the appearance of the *bdelugma* group. By "abominations" (17:4–5; 21:8, 27) is meant everything that God detests and repels; everything with which he is angry; everything which he hates, opposes and will destroy. The awful concept of abomination implies the divine detestation, "distance," wrath, hatred and opposition culminating in destruction.[4] John was quite justified in using the phrase, "in the sight of God" (3:2; 16:19).

## God Against Man

In particular, God's attitude towards sin is that of wrath. *God is a God of wrath.* John's use of both *orgē* and *thumos* and his richness of language show that he took the wrath of God with the utmost seriousness. It is God's wrath (11:18), the wrath of the living God (15:7). It is directed against sin (14:8), the sin of the individual (14:9–10) no less than that of the state. It is "undiluted," "sheer," and perhaps still fermenting (Ladd, p. 196; Charles, 2:16–17). "It will be drunk full strength."

For John likens the wrath of God to wine. This in itself, apart from the possibility of its still fermenting, implies that it takes time for it to be produced. The grapes are cut from the vine (14:18–20) and put into the wine-

---

3. Caird, pp. 212, 294. Cf. H. Reisser, *Begriffslex.* 13:1508–9. Reference should be made to Moulton and Geden's *Concordance* under *porneia* and its cognates.
4. Cf. Ward, *Royal Theology*, pp. 75–87.

press. Here men "press" them by trampling on them, and cause the juice to run down into a lower container. (Cf. G. Bornkamm, *TDNT* 4:254. Cf. 19:15.) The wrath of God is not a sudden flash of temper. It matures, if we may put it so, in the divine reflection (cf. 15:1; 16:19). The wrath of God is inflicted. It "comes" (11:18; cf. 6:17) in response to a situation (cf. Ps. 2:1, 5; 98:1, LXX). "The futile violence of men is answered by the effective judgments of God" (Swete, p. 140). It is "poured out" (16:1). It is "given" (16:19). It is "fearful and final" (Ladd on 14:9–11).

For when the divine attitude issues in act, it becomes judgment. *God is Judge.* He executes judgment upon sin (18:8), based upon a divine "survey" of accumulated wrong (18:5). It is a *true* judgment (16:7; 19:2). The evidence is not inadequate or false. It was "written down" at the time of each sinful act (20:12f), and judgment is in accordance with the acts. It is therefore *just* (16:5, 7; 19:2) and it is executed upon individuals (20:13, "each"). It cannot fail: the Lord God who judges is mighty (18:8).

The fact that the evidence has been written down and that there is a record of sins committed is John's simple way of saying that God's memory is reliable. His judgment cannot miscarry.

It is sometimes said that evil is self-destructive. This may well be true but it is not the whole truth. God may indeed use in history the self-destroying power of evil but in the Revelation "the imminent historical judgment is seen as a type of, or a prelude to, the eschatological judgment" (Ladd, p. 13; cf. Caird, p. 295). The final judgment "comes" (14:7; 18:10). At that Day the sinner will be finally fixed in his character. Improvement or repentance is out of the question. It is an impossibility; and the opportunity has gone forever. "He which is filthy, let him be filthy still" (22:11, KJV). This is the death and destruction of the finally impenitent (Cf. Swete, p. 301).

## THE OTHER SIDE—GOD FOR MAN

In vivid contrast to this stern picture of God there is another one of the utmost tenderness. From him come grace and peace. He is described as Father. Far from being repelled, men may approach him (1:4–6). They have "access," to use Paul's term (7:15). Salvation is ascribed to him (7:10; 12:10; 19:1). Every tear will be wiped away by him (7:17). He speaks of "my people" (18:4; cf. 21:3–4). The curse is gone and his people see his face (22:3–4).

It might almost seem that we are concerned with two Gods, One who judges with severity and One who does not forget a single falling tear (cf. Matt. 10:29; Luke 12:6). But John would agree that "we believe in one God" and it is this fact which constitutes the problem. We have met it before and in the Revelation we find the same answer as before. The problem is solved in Christ. (Cf. G. R. Beasley-Murray, p. 242—"judgment and redemption"; p. 318—"the unity of the justice of God and the grace of God.")

We shall have to see what the Revelation has to tell us or show us about

Christ's work for us and his work in us. For the sake of convenience we shall consider first his work in us.

## God at Work in Us—The Work of Christ in Us

John lives in a doomed world, but in that world are churches (1:4, 11, 20; chaps. 2 and 3 *passim*; 22:16). They had not always existed but they were there now. Each of them is made up of individuals (2:23) whose inmost thoughts come under the divine scrutiny. John is "your brother and partner" (1:9; cf. 19:10). Each church may be an "it" but John uses the plural, "you" (cf. 6:11; 12:10). They are the objects of the love of Christ (1:5). He who loves can also hate (2:6) and kill (2:23). There must be something distinctive about them. They endure for the sake of his Name (2:3). They form an inner kingdom in the world (1:6), with each member a priest with access to God. They want to give the glory to Christ, not to themselves—in contrast to "Babylon" (18:7). They are indeed "different," and called to be different (18:4; [5] cf. 1 John 3:10).

They were not always like this. At one time they were part and parcel of Babylon, caught up in its pagan immorality and economic seduction, blithely unaware of the dark cloud of judgment which overhung them. How is the change to be explained?

### Faithful Witnesses

The necessary evidence may be found in the Revelation. John knows of the existence of "apostles" (2:2; 18:20). The word here may be used in the wider sense and we need not dogmatize about it. He is not, however, unaware of the narrower meaning. He speaks of the "twelve names of the twelve apostles of the Lamb" (21:14). This goes back to the historic Jesus and his significance. "The Twelve" were men sent out by him with a message. They were not settled pastors but itinerant preachers, constantly traveling to places and peoples where the Name of Jesus had hitherto been unknown. They were always breaking new ground. But what did they say when they reached yet another city or town?

They said what was said by their co-workers and successors. (We are not here thinking of "apostolic succession" but of the work of preaching and teaching done by the apostles and by others.) John speaks of men who had been martyred "for the sake of the Word of God and for the sake of the testimony which they bore" (6:9). In some way they had been declaring the Word of God: not inferring it but stating it as a witness states his evidence. As the same group of people both keep the commandments of God and bear their testimony, such witnessing can hardly be against the will of God. It is witnessing to Jesus (12:17). "The Word of their testimony" (12:11) is not a bare reference to Jesus; the significance of Jesus is included. They spoke of, because inspired and strengthened by, "the blood of the Lamb."

Thus they declared the Word of God. It was testimony to Jesus Christ

---

5. For a very interesting study of "difference," cf. W. Barclay, *Ethics in a Permissive Society*, pp. 17–20.

(1:2, 9). Preaching Christ is preaching the Word of God, for he is the Word of God (19:13). To preach Christ is to catch the very spirit of the prophets, to reproduce their essential characteristics (cf. Luke 9:55, variant reading; Eph. 1:17). It is to say what God wills to be said and gives to be said; and it is to be said for God's glory and worship. "Worship God. *For* testimony to Jesus is the spirit of prophecy" (Rev. 19:10). It demands faithfulness and endurance even unto death; and the living Christ is concerned with the work of his servants (3:8, 10; 12:11).

But what happens when the Word of God is thus preached? Obviously sounds are heard, significant intelligible words (3:3). They may be disbelieved and rejected. We are not at the moment, however, concerned with the spiritually deaf but with those who do not reject the spoken Word. They may conceivably be part of a mass movement but even so it is individuals who hear and do not reject. "He who has an ear" (2:11) is subject to searching scrutiny of the heart (2:23).

Within the voice of the preacher the hearer detects the voice of Christ. "If any man hear my voice . . . " (3:20). This text has been used many times in evangelistic services, not incorrectly, though it is really addressed to the church in Laodicea. But the members are being taken back to their first Christian days. They are receiving an appeal as if they were a virgin evangelistic field. It is not the rough "Open up!" of the secret police, to be followed if necessary by the smashing of the door. It is the call of Christ, spoken through the closed door: he calls for it to be opened. Those who open the door are "the called" (17:14). They are called to a final banquet in which they are not in the position of host (3:20; 19:9).

The hearers of the Word are thus called by Christ. When they are so called, they repent. In summoning the church in Ephesus to repentance John takes the members back to their beginning (2:5). "Keep in mind whence you have fallen and repent and do the first works." When slipping, "a useful counter is to go back in thought to the first days" Morris, *ad loc.*). "The first works" are hardly "the important works" (cf. 1 Cor. 15:3). John means "repent and do as you did before" (Caird). They have "later" works of toil and endurance (2:2). Back to square one: repent!

John returns to the theme of "first repentance" (3:3). Repentance is important in his thought (2:16, 21–22; 3:19; 16:9). It covers both the religious and the ethical, impiety and unrighteousness, sin against God and sin against man (9:20–21). There is a sense in which a Christian should be always repenting and a sense in which he should not. If he sins, he should repent; if he does not sin, he should not repent. *He has already done it.*

For if repentance means a change of mind, he should stay in that mind. If it means returning to the Lord, then having returned to him he should stay with him. For the man who hears the Word, is called and repents, comes to the Lord. John expresses this with a spatial metaphor. "Remember whence you have fallen" (2:5). You are not staying with him.

The thought of coming to the Lord is the opposite of going away from him and being distant from him. It is suggested by the concept of fornication (2:14, 20), of "whoring after false gods." An Old Testament prophet would call men to return to the God of Israel. A Christian preacher correspondingly summons them to come to Jesus.

When, then, the Word of God is preached, a man hears, is called, repents and comes to Jesus. Other factors are also involved.

John knows of the faith of Christians (2:19)—just as the Son of God knows, but in a different way—and of "keeping" it (14:12). Those who keep it are those who have come to him and are still "with him" and "faithful" (17:14). Those who are without faith are mentioned in the company of men who have clearly not repented (21:8). Christ calls the objects of imminent persecution to be faithful unto death (2:10). When did it all start?

Obviously men are not born believing; and they do not drift into faith without knowing what they are doing. They could not believe in Christ before they had heard of him. They must have started to believe either when they first heard the Word or later, after deliberation or mere procrastination. It is most likely to have been associated with their repentance and coming to Jesus. John knew of men who had continued to believe and had not denied their faith in Christ even when a faithful witness was slain in persecution (2:13). "Deny" is the opposite of "confess." What is more natural than to think that men heard the Word preached and then and there, or later, responded to the call of Christ by repenting, by coming to him and by believing in him?

## Clothed in White

But what happened when they believed? John does not use the word *justify*, and still less does he speak about justification by faith. His language, however, can be interpreted in accordance with the doctrine. For example, the complacent and spiritually lukewarm Laodiceans are "naked" and are counseled by Christ to obtain from him "white clothes." This should achieve a double purpose. They would clothe themselves; and they would not only cover up their nakedness but cover up the shame of their nakedness.

This is not the Jewish abhorrence of exposing the naked body. The nakedness comes under Christ's censure. It is not immodesty but sheer shame. And he can supply the clothes. According to Albrecht Oepke (*TDNT* 1:775) "naked" means "without the preparedness of the inner man." For H. Weigelt (*Begriffslex.* 1:80) it indicates "an inner poverty." Clearly the Laodiceans lack something which only Christ can supply— "without money and without price" (Isa. 55:1). He is not calling them to a secular moral renewal but to repentance and to an openness to him. This is a call to a glowing faith in him. If they put their faith in him, he will give them "white clothes." What do the white clothes symbolize?

John himself gives us the clue a little later (7:9, 13–15). The white-robed men who with joyous shouts ascribe salvation "to our God . . . and to the Lamb" have maintained their faith through the great tribulation. They washed their robes and made them white in the blood of the Lamb. This gives them their qualification. "Because of this" (*dia touto*) they enter the very Presence of God (contrast 21:27). "The purification of the conscience and character derived in their lifetime from faith in the Blood of Jesus Christ (Acts 15:9; Heb. 9:14) had fitted them for the Presence of God" (Swete, p. 101).

The "clothes," pure and white as they are because of the blood of the

Crucified, are analogous to the Pauline imputed righteousness. "Put on (as clothes) the Lord Jesus Christ" (Rom. 13:14; cf. Gal. 3:27). John is not giving a formal lesson in imputed righteousness but consciously or unconsciously he has transposed it into another idiom. The doctrine is reflected in his language and agrees with his own spiritual experience.

For imagine a situation in which John secretly overheard a conversation between a Christian minister and a dying heathen. "I am afraid," says the man; "afraid to meet your God with all these scars on me. I have had many a fight and have always killed my man. Your God will see me in all my nakedness. What will he do to me?" "You need not go like that," says the minister. "Those scars can be covered up. Repent of your murders and all your other sins and put your faith in Jesus. He will give you a set of new clothes. God will see the clothes and will not think of the scars."

"What clothes?" asks the man, "And where can I get them?" "If you repent and believe in Jesus, if you hand yourself over to him in trust, God will dress you in what we call his robe of righteousness. He will dress you in the character of Jesus. In fact you will be dressed in—Christ himself. He is all the raiment you need."

How would John react to this unusual conversation? Would he—not the heathen [6]—understand? Or would he be completely out of his depth? I think that he would understand. Spiritually he would have to be extremely dull not to see the connection. It is the clothes which qualify. They were made white in the blood of the Lamb and because of this their wearers are in the presence of God. It is because of this and only because of this. And the white clothes are only for those who believe in Jesus.

The idiom is gently maintained in "the bride adorned for her Husband" (21:2). It is not really disturbed when John identifies the pure, shining linen with the *dikaiōmata* of the saints (19:7-8). These are often regarded as "righteous acts." But the clothes were given to the bride, supplied to her but not by her. We must therefore say either that the righteous acts spring from faith—it is the acts of the saints—and that it is John's way of referring to a living faith; or, with Leon Morris (*ad loc.*), that the term means "sentence of justification" pronounced on individual believers.

The metaphor of the clothes has further implications, but we must first consider a passage in which men are under a charge, are being accused. Their accuser is Satan. At the beginning of his "career" he is morally neutral as the prosecuting attorney in heaven. He gathers his evidence on earth and presents it at the heavenly court (Job 1:6-7). His indictment of sinners is just but he goes too far, and in the "war in heaven" (Rev. 12:7) Michael, the defending lawyer, defeats him in a legal battle. Satan is turned out of heaven and continues his accusations on earth. But he is again defeated; in particular the martyrs conquered him "because of the blood of the Lamb and because of the Word of their testimony, and they did not love their

---

6. "It is often said that to speak of 'justification by faith' is to use language which, to the modern man, is meaningless. What is often forgotten is that such language was as meaninglesss to ancient man also, apart from the gospel which gave it significance." G. O. Griffith, *St. Paul's Gospel to the Romans*, p. 106, quoted by Leon Morris, *The Apostolic Preaching of the Cross*, p. 262.

life unto death" (12:10–11). The sacrifice of the cross "silences Satan's accusing voice" (Swete, p. 153).[7] The martyrs' testimony to Jesus and their "loyalty to him" (Swete) implies a living faith in him as the Crucified.

It is significant that the reference here to martyrdom is proleptic; "the fall of Satan precedes the age of persecution" (Swete). "The work of salvation was fully accomplished on the Cross. . . . It [needs] for its completion only that [sinful men] should accept in faith what [God] has offered in love" (Caird).

This is very much like justification by faith, especially in view of the forensic situation. In the light of this passage our interpretation of the "white clothes" seems to gain in cogency.

In speaking of clothes, John blends the forensic concept of justification with the cultic one of purification. Sinners as such are defiled and barred from God's presence (21:27; 22:15; cf. p. 345). The language of ceremonial defilement symbolizes moral and spiritual disqualification. But robes may be washed (22:14) in the blood of the Lamb (7:14) and blessed are they who so wash them. It gives them the right to the tree of life and entrance into the city of God.

When did they wash their robes? The blood of the Lamb takes us back to the cross. There the blood was shed but the robes were not washed there. This would obliterate the distinction between the believing church and the unbelieving world. Even Babylon would have been washed and freed from her impending judgment! In fact "they" wash their robes. When they so wash them they become holy (*hagios*). This qualifies them to draw near to God.

Obviously we have here points of contact with the Epistle to the Hebrews. Purification from sins is objectively accomplished on the cross and sinners are purified or sanctified when they believe. This is the moment when they wash their robes. " 'The saints' (*hoi hagioi*)," says Swete (on 11:18), "are, as always, the faithful in general."

Those who wash their robes in the blood of the Lamb, those who put their faith in Jesus, become holy. They are qualified to approach God. This is expressed by John when he calls them priests. "We" collectively are a kingdom but "we" individually are priests (1:6; 5:10; cf. 20:6). The individual believer can draw near to God.

But what happens when he does in faith begin to draw near to God? Does God receive him? This raises the question of what we have called the concomitants of justification. John draws moving pictures which must certainly imply that God accepts believing men. "They washed their robes. . . . Because of this they are before the throne of God" (7:14–15). The loud voice from the throne says "Behold the dwelling [*skēnē*] of God is with men" (21:3). "The throne of God and of the Lamb will be in it and his servants will worship him" (22:3).

Two points should be observed. It is the unrepentant and unbelieving who are "outside" and not received (21:8, 27; 22:15). And the mention of "the throne" is significant. It stands for the rule and authority of God and

---

7. I have here been indebted to Caird's illuminating treatment of the subject.

for his power, not only in the physical but in the moral realm. The right-eous Ruler receives men who believe.

It is instructive to see what is said about the throne of God. It repels: from it proceed flashes of lightning and peals of thunder. It stands in isola-tion, fenced off by a protective sea of glass like ice, fiery to behold (4:5–6; 15:2). It inspires a ghastly fear, terror, panic (6:16–17). In vivid contrast are those who stand before the throne and before the Lamb (7:9), for the Lamb is "at the heart of the throne" (7:17, NEB). Indeed it is "the throne of God and of the Lamb" (22:3) and from it come the summons and the invitation to "praise our God, all you his servants" (19:5). They are the called, the saints, those who have maintained their witness to Jesus (19:8–10). They each sit with him on his throne as he sits with his Father on his Father's throne (3:21). And the throne is one (22:1, 3), the throne of God and of the Lamb. It is situated in the holy city which comes down from heaven in her newness, adorned as a bride (21:2, 9–10). The separating sea is gone (21:1) and the throne is in the believing church. God does accept men who believe.

It may be argued, not without reason, that much of this moving picture is of the future heaven and the consummation of all things. But are be-lievers to wait in uncertainty until they discover in heaven that God has indeed accepted them? Caird (on 21:3) is surely right in saying that "the voice from the throne gives the permanent guarantee of those privileges which have always been enjoyed by those who, refusing to be at home in the old order, have lived as citizens of the city whose builder and maker is God (Heb. 11:8–16; cf. Gal. 4:26)." He finely states (on 21:2) that "this is a future which interpenetrates and informs the present."

If we need formal confirmation, it may be found in the Revelation. John speaks of "the prayers of the saints" (5:8). They rise with incense (8:3–5) and the fragrant smoke cloud is "the symbol of Divine acceptance" (Swete, ad loc.).[8] The prayers of all the saints are mightily answered!

Thus the future divine acceptance of believing men is but the intensifica-tion of what they have already experienced. We might have expected that the man who repents and puts his faith in Christ will be at once received by God; for he himself has opened the door to Christ and has received him (3:20). Would God decline to accept a man in whom Christ dwelt?

### The Book of Life

The second concomitant of justification is quickening. It is expected that men who believe are made alive. The church in Sardis, before it was a church, when it was isolated and merely unrelated individuals, "has re-ceived and heard" in a certain way. The members ought to be alive and indeed have the reputation of being alive but are severely censured for being dead. They are told, somewhat surprisingly, not to rise from the dead but to wake up before life becomes finally extinct. (An apt illustration would be the example of a man whose heart stops beating and thus dies but is given the emergency treatment of resuscitation. I have seen this done in

---

8. Cf. S. R. Driver, *The Book of Genesis*, p. 95.

hospital.) Something has gone wrong and it must be put right. It is a characteristic of a believer to be alive (3:1–6).

This is part of the divine plan. There is a "book of life" (3:5; 20:12, 15), "the Lamb's book of life" (13:8; 21:27). The names were written in it in eternity (17:8). This implies a doctrine of election. The excluded emerge as the defiled and abominable (21:27). They have clearly not been washed in the blood of the Lamb and are the unrepentant and unbelieving. To believe in Jesus is to be made alive.

A number of metaphors express the general concept: the tree of life (2:7; 22:2), the crown of life (2:10), the spring of the water of life (21:6; cf. 7:17), the river of the water of life (22:1). The right to the tree of life is given to those who wash their robes but is denied to the unrepentant and faithless (22:14–15). Life is offered as a gift to anyone who is willing to take it (22:17). The figure of "thirst" implies that until he receives the gift a man is without life. It is received when he puts his faith in Jesus (cf. 2:10). Life is offered here and now to any who will believe in Jesus. Some have already received the gift. How otherwise can God take away a man's share in the tree of life (22:19)? We conclude that the second concomitant of justification is quickening.

The third concomitant is adoption. It is not expounded in the Revelation but the experience is present (Beasley-Murray, pp. 313–14). If quickening is linked with justification, adoption is linked with quickening. "I will freely give . . . life to him who is thirsty. . . . I will be to him who conquers [12:11 !] his God and he will be my son" (21:6–8). Note that God is the God of individual experience and that the receiver of the blessing is not called "worshiper" but "son." Those who are not adopted are unrepentant unbelievers, guilty of sins against both God and man.

It may be argued that all this is in the future. But "he who goes on conquering" is the man of persistent faith. If he has Christ in his heart, if he shares his throne, and if the throne is in the believing church, then would it be unexpected if he felt, not repelled from the throne, but a son in his Father's house? When a man believes, he is adopted.

The fourth concomitant is the elusive "certainty," "the love of God shed abroad in our hearts" (Rom. 5:5). Are John and his readers strangers to the experience? He does not speak explicitly about it but it can be detected. The believers knew the life they had lived before the gospel came to them. They knew the judgment to which they had been liable. They knew that they had been redeemed by him who is the very Word of God. They knew that they had repented and believed. They knew that Christ was in their hearts and that they shared the throne of God and of the Lamb. And they persisted in their faith and in their testimony to Jesus and did not shrink from dying for their faith. They did not love their own lives (12:11). What made them? What inspired them? What sustained them? Was not their negative love of their own lives a positive love to God in response to his love in their redemption?

Their love to Christ, which had not always existed (2:4), was as real as their faith in him and their works and service and endurance for him (2:19), and it was a response to his love to them. It cannot be that they believed and knew Christ's love and disbelieved in or were ignorant of God's love for them. Christ is the Utterance of God and the blessings of his love are related to God. They knew that Christ loved them (3:9) and his benefits link them to "my God" (3:12)—his temple, name and city. How could they fail to know the love which God has for them? (Cf. 1:5.)

John has expressed himself with matchless art, in figures tender, stern or bizarre. He has revealed what was given to him to see rather than expounded an argument which he has followed. Yet justification and its concomitants are to be found in his book. They are either implied by his language or reflected in his experience. Thus as far as the work of Christ in us is concerned, John and his readers would be at home in the churches of God which are in Christ Jesus. At heart their doctrine and their experience are one. Justification and its concomitants together point to the salvation which is to be ascribed to God on his throne and to the Lamb (7:10; cf. 19:1). "The salvation . . . of our God" is forever joined with "the authority of his Christ" (12:10).

### God at Work for Us—The Work of Christ for Us

The "response" which we have attempted to describe and the preaching of the Word which called it forth would never have taken place without some great anterior fact. This is the work of Christ for us, to which we now turn.

John begins his book with a series: God—Christ—angel—John—his servants. His subject is the unveiling of Jesus Christ, the removal of the veil or curtain which hides him. The revelation was given by God to Christ. Christ gave it to his angel to give to John, who in turn gave it to "his servants" by means of the book. It is a record of "all that he saw" (1:2), of visions or "images." [9] John thus "testifies" as he writes (the aorist is epistolary) and what he gives is the Word of God. He has given it before (1:9), though not necessarily in writing. As he knows of "apostles" (2:2; 18:20; esp. 21:14) his message will probably overlap theirs. He will further unfold the same subject.

He gives the Word of God, testimony, and prophecy. It is to be read aloud. It is to be heard, for it gives information. It is to be obeyed, for the Word of God is command as well as statement.

The Word of God has an intellectual content or it could not be written down in the book. Even the "images" are described in words. But it is more: it is Christ himself (19:13). As the "content" of testimony he is preached. He is not "reduced" to words, but through the preached words he is present (20:4). He is the gospel (14:6)[10] even on its sterner side. He is one with God in wrath (6:16–17; 19:15); the throne is "the throne of God and of the Lamb" (22:3); and salvation is ascribed to God and to the Lamb (7:10). "What must soon happen" (1:1) is thus related to the Word

---

9. See Austin Farrer's *A Rebirth of Images: The Making of St. John's Apocalypse.*
10. Cf. Caird, pp. 181–83 for a spirited defense of the essential meaning of "gospel" in this text.

of God, to Christ. He is the subject of the book, which is written for
"normal" Christians who are addressed in some familiar terms, grace and
peace (1:4; 22:21).

The pre-existence of Christ is implied. He is the First and the Last (1:17;
2:8), the Alpha and the Omega, the Beginning and the End (22:13). He
is the Principle of God's creation (3:14). He is the Reason or intelligibility
in the universe—i.e., the *Logos*—and is recognized by all creation (5:13).
He is the key to history and destiny, the meaning of all things. The search
for a philosophy of history is ended in him.

For he, the Son of God (2:18), is man as well as God. He is the Lion
of the tribe of Judah (5:5; cf. Gen. 49:9; Heb. 7:14), the Root or Scion of
David (cf. 22:16; Isa. 11:1, 10; Rom. 15:12). He is thus the Christ. Even
this does not go far enough. He is "his Christ" (11:15). "The speakers are
representatives of creation" (Swete, *ad loc.*). Jesus is not somebody who
emerged as a world figure and has caught the imagination of history. He
was sent by his Father into the world in fulfillment of a promise, and in
order to carry out a plan. (Cf. 12:10.) He was obedient to his Father, for
he was the "faithful Witness" (1:5: 3:14) even unto death (cf. 2:10).

He died (1:5, 18; 2:8); he was pierced (1:7; cf. John 19:37); he was
slaughtered (5:6, 9, 12; 13:8); he was crucified (11:8). This is not docetism
but harsh reality. But he rose from the dead (1:5; 2:8). The fact that he
became dead and is now living for ever and ever (1:18) corresponds to
Paul's perfect tense (1 Cor. 15:4). "He has been raised" and is now therefore permanently "up." He ascended (12:5) to his Father's throne (3:21)
and there he exercises his rule (1:5). For he is Lord of lords (note the
significant *Kurios*) and King of kings (17:14; 19:16) and has authority
(12:10). He is proclaimed to the world, received in the hearts of those
who put their trust in him, worshiped by his church and is coming again
(1:6–7; 22:7, 12, 20).[11]

We have thus surveyed, from the evidence in the Revelation, the pattern
of the life of the Son of God: his preexistence, incarnation, life of obedience,
death, resurrection, exaltation and Parousia. It corresponds to the primitive
*kerygma*. We now have to direct our attention particularly to his death.
Any theory which asserts that the incarnation by its very nature elevates
the whole human race is foreign to John's thought. At best it is an inference, peripheral and precarious. The human race has not been so elevated
that it does not need the preaching of the gospel. John can rightly use an
aorist tense for the death of Christ (5:9) but he cannot forget its abiding
result. Hence his perfect tense. And the death was in the eternal purpose
of God, "from the foundation of the world" (13:8; Beasley-Murray, pp.
213–14).

Christ was indeed slain. But it is more than past history, gone without
a trace. "He has been slain" (5:6, 12; 13:8) and the results abide. We can
express this pictorially if we wish. In his glorified body he still bears the
scars of his death. The point, however, is not the picture but the meaning.

---

11. See Swete's note on pp. 83–84 on the "comings" of God or of Christ in the
Revelation.

The effect of his death remains. It has accomplished something permanent. What is it?

Consider the situation. There was a time when we were the objects of accusation before God (12:10). If events had merely taken their course, we should have settled down in permanent sin and final judgment (22:11; cf. pp. 345–46). But something intervened. We did not merely "improve." The "something" is associated with "the blood of the Lamb" (12:11). We were "loosed" from our sins (1:5). This is more than liberation from the power of the sins which so easily beset us. It is liberation from the sins of which we have been accused, the sins for which we are responsible. It is liberation from guilt. For Christ redeemed *for God* (5:9). Apart from his work God would have kept us at a distance and judged us. Instead, his work made it possible for us to draw near to God, as priests. We can have access into the presence of God (cf. Ladd, pp. 27, 92, 268). "The members of the Church, a Kingdom in their corporate life, are individually priests" (Swete, pp. 8, 80). God makes this gift to us in Christ. He can accept us instead of judging us. But we have to receive the gift. As Swete says, "the 'new song' refers only to those in whom redemption has become effective by their incorporation in the body of Christ." It is already effective in God: he is ready to receive; it is effective in men when they repent and believe. Hence the story must be told and the Word must be preached (cf. 12:11).

So far we have stayed on the forensic level. Every statement that men have acted against God's will and sinned must involve something of the forensic sooner or later, however unpopular the word. We have accordingly drawn the inferences from the concept of redemption in this way. But John does not keep his concepts separate. They interpenetrate, intermingle, are "fluid." When he speaks of "blood" or of "the Lamb" we are in the realm of the cultic and of sacrifice.

Guilt and accountability are involved in redemption. Defilement and unholiness are related to sacrifice. The unholy disqualifies from the approach to God (p. 345). The death of Christ is therefore not only a solution to the problem of men's accountability to God, an answer to the accusation, a claim that the Redeemer has relieved them of their answerableness. It is a sacrifice. John does not work out the details. He does not use the word *thusia* (sacrifice) but he is familiar with temple (7:15, ?priests), altar, censer and incense (8:3–5). In any case the use of the terms "blood" and "Lamb" seems to be decisive. As the benefit has to be received ("washed," 7:14), the death in itself as a sacrifice had an atoning power.

The death of Christ, considered as a sacrifice, is thus a "purification from sins" effected before the Ascension took place (cf. Heb. 1:3). When unholy, and therefore disqualified, men put their faith in Christ, they become holy, qualified to draw near to God.

John thus blends the concepts of redemption and sacrifice. (Cf. Beasley-Murray, p. 203, "redemptive sacrifice.") The accused, and accountable, find their salvation in that which frees them from unholiness, "the blood of the Lamb" (Rev. 12:10–11). Jesus stood trial "on behalf of those He represents. . . . His death is . . . the judgment of all men. . . . Because He has identified Himself with all men where they are, under the judgment of God, He draws all men through His death into unity with Himself where He is, in the bosom of the Father. . . ." These impressive words are Caird's (p. 155). Men are relieved of their accountability and judgment because he bore the judgment; they may respond to his drawing power and reach the Father's side because of his act of purification. They are not judged; they are not kept out. Redemption and sacrifice are one.

It is clear that as a result of his work Christ is the Mediator between God and men. He holds "the key of David" (3:7; cf. Isa. 22:22). The expression "has apparently a Messianic significance. . . . [The] scope [of the words] is universal" (Charles, *ad loc.*). It is he who can lock the gates of death against his believing people (cf. 1:18). It is he who retains their names in his book of life (3:5; 13:8). It is he who confesses their names before his Father (3:5). He is one with the Father in sovereignty (22:1, 3) and in wrath (6:16–17). (John can even speak of "their wrath.") Yet he is God's Christ (11:15; 12:10) and has authority. The kingdom is the Father's; and the kingdom is the Son's. For ever and ever, royal rule is exercised in the unity of Father and Son (*basileusei*, singular, 11:15). Salvation is ascribed to God and to the Lamb (7:10). Both temple and illumination are to be found in God and the Lamb (21:22–23; cf. Beasley-Murray, p. 327). It is because of the blood of the Lamb that believers are in the temple (7:15). For he has made them priests (1:6; 5:10; cf. 20:6). All this evidence points in one direction. Christ is the Mediator.

The prayers of the faithful suggest that justification sets up a permanent relationship between God and the believer (8:3–5).

We conclude that John's teaching about Christ's work for us and in us does not differ essentially from that of other New Testament writers whom we have studied.

# 17

## The Acts of the Apostles

WHEN WE TURN FROM the Book of the Revelation to the Acts of the Apostles we find ourselves in another world. No longer are we in heaven, gazing in awestruck wonder at solemn magnificence or listening to voices which ripple like the sound of many waters or deafen us with their thunder. We are very much on earth, encountering all sorts and conditions of men and visiting many diverse scenes.

But both books are concerned with the authentic gospel either in its beginning or its end. In these days of redaction criticism "the stress is on Luke as a theologian" (Marshall). As Haenchen says, "he has a theology of his own." Indeed he can "make free with tradition." Marshall agrees that he has his own distinctive ideas and points of view but holds that "basically he builds upon tradition and treats it faithfully." [1]

Now we are not concerned with the theology of Luke himself or of the anterior tradition which he may or may not have amended or edited. Our interest is in the Acts of the Apostles as a whole and as it stands. Sectional matters must yield to the whole. What Christian beliefs and doctrines does the book express or reflect? According to Haenchen (p. 92), "Acts does not contain a doctrine of vicarious atonement." There is but an echo of it in 20:28. This is a continuation of what I have heard flatly and dogmatically asserted in a North American "consultation" of scholars: that there is no *theologia crucis*, theology of the cross, in the Third Gospel.

If such a view could be substantiated, it would seriously affect our thesis. We must therefore press on to an examination of the text of the Acts. We shall put ourselves into the position of a man who "wants to know the message of Christianity" and is given the Acts and told to search it for the evidence. We follow our precedent in trying to find out what the Acts has to tell us about God.

---

1. I. Howard Marshall, *Luke: Historian and Theologian*, pp. 18–20; Ernst Haenchen, pp. 91, 110. Where only the author's name is given, the reference is to his commentary on the Acts.

# THE NATURE OF GOD

*God is the living God* (14:15). Actions take place in his sight (*enōpion*, 4:19: 10:31, 33). *He is the Most High* (7:48; 16:17) and is *One* in contrast to the futile pluralities of idolatry (14:15). *He is conscious*, for he remembers (10:4, 31). *He has will* (18:21; 22:14). A series of "things willed" (13:22) points to the fact that *God has purpose*. David was hardly "a man after mine own heart" in the usual sense of the words, but he was one "according to my purpose." [2] God's purpose is emphasized in Acts in the use of the word *boulē* (purpose, decision, 2:23; 4:28; 5:38–39; 13:36; 20:27). In implementing his purpose *God has freedom of choice* (1:24; 13:17; 15:7, 14). (Cf. pp. 209–10.)

God is self-sufficient and self-existent, needing nothing (17:25). If he asks for, and accepts, any service, it is not because of any lack in himself. *He is the eternal Ground of his own eternal existence.* He does not live in temples made with hands, wherever they may be. In principle they might be built anywhere in the material universe or even flung into orbit in space. He would not dwell in them. For *God is spiritual and transcendent.* Heaven is his throne and earth his footstool; yet he is not extended in space (7:48–49; 17:24). On the other hand *he is immanent*, not far from any one of us. We live "in" him (17:27–28).

*God is the Creator* (4:24; 7:50; 14:15; 17:24) *and Sustainer* (14:17; 17:24–25), Lord of heaven and earth. The story of Cornelius in Acts 10 illustrates *his overruling providence*. He is *the Controller of history and geography* (17:26). For *he has authority* (1:7; cf. 26:18), symbolized by "the right hand of God" (2:33–34; 5:31; 7:55–56).

God is not quiescent. *He speaks* (2:17; 3:21; 7:3, 6) *and he acts* (2:22, 24; 7:8, 10). *He is to be obeyed* (5:29; cf. 4:19), a fact which is recognized by conscience (23:1; 24:16). *He is to be worshiped* (10:25–26): thanked (27:35; 28:15), praised (2:47; 3:8–9), "hymned" (16:25) and glorified (4:21; 11:18; 21:20). The duty was recognized in synagogue (13:14–15, 43; 18:13) and temple (22:17), in the church (13:2) and in heathenism (14:11–13; 17:22–23). Idolatrous worship is not acceptable to him (7:40–43; 14:14–15; 17:16, 29; 19:26). He, not the idol, is to be sought (15:17; 17:27), and *he calls to holiness* (7:33).

*God is the Author of the law.* It was received by the Jews in ordinances given by angels (7:53). Saul of Tarsus was trained in fine detail in the law—and had a zeal for God (22:3). The law is to be believed (24:14; cf. 26:27). Critics of Stephen said that he made blasphemous statements against Moses and against God, incessantly speaking against the law (6:11, 13–14). It was venerated and not to be changed. Paul denied that he had sinned against the law in any way (25:8). Its divine origin obviously gave it a preeminence.

*God is righteous.* Obedience to him is righteous in his sight (4:19–20;

---

2. "Heart," standing for volition or purpose (1 Sam. 2:35), "is one of the most characteristic usages of the term in the O.T." H. Wheeler Robinson, *The Christian Doctrine of Man*, p. 22. Cf. H. P. Smith, *The Books of Samuel* (ICC), p. 97 on 1 Sam. 13:14.

5:29). Hostility to righteousness is to be a son of the devil (13:10) and a perversion of God's ways, deserving and receiving punishment. *God keeps his word* (3:18; 13:32–33). He will judge the world with righteousness (17:31), "with retributive justice" (Haenchen, p. 526). (Cf. Ps. 9:5, 9.) *God is the Observer.* He sees what is going on (7:34). Men may lie to him (5:4) but he knows their hearts (15:8; cf. 1:24). *God has an attitude.* He does not merely "take a photograph." He assesses and evaluates. An act may be righteous in his sight (4:19). If the Twelve abandoned the ministry of the Word for social service, it would not be proper in the sight of God. It would displease him (6:2; cf. Haenchen, p. 262). We may find that his displeasure leads on to action, but for the moment we notice that in past generations, though no doubt displeased, God "permitted" all the nations "to go their own way" (14:16, NEB); he disregarded the periods of ignorance (17:30; cf. Rom. 3:25). But he knew about them and he knew what he thought about them.[3]

### Man Against God

God's attitude ought not to surprise us. For *he is opposed.* He is opposed in words. This is suggested by the concept of blasphemy (6:11, 13; 26:11) and by telling lies to God (5:4). Opposition in deeds is apparent in any attempt to hinder him (11:17) or in "tempting" him (15:10); in the whole life of idolatry (14:15) and in the activities of the devil (10:38; 13:10) or Satan (5:3; 26:18). The thought of defilement (21:28; 24:6) means that men have failed to attain to God's requirement and are unclean (15:9) and at a distance from him (15:19; 26:20), needing to turn to him. In fact *God is sinned against* (2:38, et al.) and sins need to be forgiven, blotted out, washed away.

*God is not a Respecter of persons,* a partisan (10:34). All men need to repent (17:30). Their *adikia* (unrighteousness) is vividly illustrated in Judas (1:18) and Simon Magus (8:23). For their sins *God holds men responsible.* If this were not so, Stephen's dying prayer would be unintelligible: "do not charge this sin to them" (7:60). The high priest believed in the doctrine of human responsibility. "You wish to bring [*epagō*] upon us the blood of this man." "You are trying to make us responsible for that man's death" (5:28, NEB). The apostolic accusation (4:10) "is taken by the High Priest to mean that the Christians seek divine retribution for the killing of Jesus" (Haenchen, p. 251). Haenchen observes in a note that "the frequent *epagō* of LXX is mostly said of God bringing on man the punishment for his sin." (Cf. 18:6; 20:26 for the responsibility of "blood on your own head.")

### God Against Man

But if men are thus responsible for their sins, what does God do? *God*

---

3. The rendering, "God winked at" (17:30), of the KJV must obviously not be interpreted in the modern spirit, but even so it has more in its favor than is generally recognized. "God closed his eye to" is a possible translation. But it should be noted that it is only one eye which is closed. With the closed eye God "disregards" but with the other he sees. This might be helpful to those preachers who still use the older version.

*is Judge.* He acts to punish. When Simon offered money in return for authority to confer the Spirit by the laying on of hands (8:18–19), Peter replied in robust biblical language. "To hell with you and your money." This is the rendering of Prebendary J. B. Phillips, who regrets the obscurity caused by modern slang. Haenchen repeats this translation and refers to Daniel 2:5 (Theodotion). The "hell" is literally "destruction" or "perdition" (*apōleia*). With this we may compare the "disappearance" (*aphanizō*) of 13:41.

But when does God's judgment take place? It may be empirical or eschatological. It may take place in history or come at the End. The empirical judgment is evident in several examples: Judas (1:25); Ananias and Sapphira (5:1–11); the history of Israel (7:7, 42–43); and Herod (12:23). (Cf. 23:3.) The *paredōken* of 7:42 reminds us of Romans 1:24, 26, 28. (Cf. 28:26–27).

The empirical judgment is individual or corporate and may occur at different times and in different places. The Final Judgment will be directed to every individual but it will take place at one and the same time. "God has appointed a day in which he will judge the world in righteousness" (17:31). No wonder that Felix became alarmed when Paul spoke of righteousness and self-control and coming judgment (24:25)! The apostle might have warned him that his blood would be on his own head (18:6; 20:26).

Judgment looks back over the whole of a past life. The sins of that life occurred in the past but they are present at the Judgment nonetheless. Men are responsible and their sins persist as guilt. Their social effects may have petered out in history; they *may* have; but their guilt remains. In the absence of any overriding factor the sinners will be punished. In punishment judgment is executed.

## THE OTHER SIDE—GOD FOR MAN

This pattern of the character of God does not diverge in any marked way from what is already familiar to us. And once more the night of coming judgment is pierced by a gleam of light. God the Judge is also the Father (1:4, 7; 2:33). He remembers men's deeds of compassion (10:4, 31). The man who breathed in (not "out," *empneōn*, 9:1) threatening and murder; the man, that is, to whom threatening and murder was the breath of life (cf. Josh. 10:40, LXX): this man later found that God had graciously given to him (to him!) the lives of all who sailed with him the turbulent sea (27:24). The ship was wrecked but their lives were spared—for him.

This is not the first sign of the grace of God in the Acts. God gave Joseph grace and wisdom in the sight of Pharaoh (7:10). David found grace in his sight (7:46). Barnabas rejoiced to see the grace of God (11:23). It is no transient phenomenon (13:43; 14:26). The gospel itself is "the gospel of the grace of God" (20:24).

This raises the old problem. Do we have to choose between God the Judge and the God of grace; or is there a mediating position which does justice to both sides? So far we have found the answer in Christ. We must therefore look again at the Acts and see if there is any evidence to help us.

## God at Work in Us—The Work of Christ in Us

If we had to find a short title to sum up our impressions of the book or of its impact on us, we might think of "Upsurge and Outreach." This characterization of a mightly movement introduces us to a study of Christ's work in us. The spirit of the Acts prompts us to begin here and thus to postpone for the present a consideration of his work for us.

### The Work and Message of the Apostles

We first observe the existence of apostles. They are chosen men (1:2; 15:7) and as commanded men they are under orders (1:2; 10:42; 13:47). Directions, even negative ones, still come (16:6–7), for they are "servants [douloi] of God" (16:17) and recognized as such even in unlikely quarters. Their work is to be witnesses of Jesus with an ever widening range (1:8, 21–22; 2:32; 8:25; 10:39; 13:31; 18:5; 20:20–21, 24; 22:15; 26:16; 28:23). Such giving of testimony is an act of obedience (4:19–20; 5:29–32; 10:41–42; 13:47). The divine call to service (13:2; 16:10) reinforces the original command (1:2, 8), obeyed at times at great hazard (15:26).

The work of the apostles is thus prayer and the ministry of the Word (6:2, 4). But it should be noted that just as the range of witness widens, so the membership of the apostolate is extended. At first it is the Twelve (1:2; 6:2). Then Barnabas and Paul are included (14:14). The work of witness is also done by Philip (6:5; 8:5, 12, 35), a "deacon" or at any rate "one of the Seven," who became "Philip the evangelist" (21:8–9). His four unmarried daughters "possessed the gift of prophecy" (NEB). The process is completed in "the apostolate of the laity." The bulk of the church was scattered from Jerusalem and gave their witness on the way (8:1, 4; 11:19). The upsurge and outreach was real and widespread.

How did they give their witness? It was by means of speech, indicated by Luke in a variety of terms. The simplest is legō (8:6; 28:24), though laleō is more frequent. Sometimes they teach (didaskō) and sometimes they proclaim (katangellō, anangellō) or preach (kērussō). They "evangelize" (euangelizomai), prove (sumbibazō, 9:22)—"put (two and two) together to prove"—exhort (parakaleō, 2:40) and persuade (18:4; 19:8, 26; 28:23). This is not silent evangelism, the appeal of the moral life. "We cannot not-go-on-speaking . . ." (4:20). But what did they say?

Once more we find variety. Just as "Luke is always changing the designation for 'Christians'" (Haenchen, p. 319), so he rings the changes on the content of the message given. It may be set out thus:

The Word (4:4; 8:4; 11:19; 14:25; 16:6; 17:11).

Thy Word (4:29).

The Word of the Lord (8:25; 13:48–49; 15:35–36; 19:10).

The Word of God (4:31; 6:2; 8:14; 13:5, 7, 44; 16:32; 17:13; 18:11).

The Word of the gospel (15:7).

In 6:7; 12:24; 19:20 the word loomed larger, like a waxing moon. It did not objectively "increase." The kingdom was extended (8:4, 12).

The Word of his grace (20:32).

The Word of this salvation (13:26).

The Way of salvation (16:17).

All the words of this life (5:20).

The speakers are obviously not speaking for themselves or giving their own inventions. In the use of the term *euangelizomai* two ideas are combined, the bringing of good news (14:7) and the giving of a commandment, "we bring you the good news (commanding you) to turn to God" (14:15). The content of the good news is the Word (8:4) or the Word of the Lord (15:35). It is also Christ Jesus (5:42) or "that the Christ is Jesus"; or the Lord Jesus (11:20); or Jesus and the resurrection (17:18), possibly understood by the Athenians as the foreign divinities called Jesus and Anastasis. We should also include the kingdom of God and the Name of Jesus Christ (8:12), and the promise made to the fathers (13:32), fulfilled in the resurrection of Jesus. The good news is brought to "you," to "them" (16:10), to "many villages of the Samaritans" (8:25) and to "all the cities" (8:40; cf. 14:21).

When the term used is *kērussō* they preach the Christ (8:5), Jesus as the Son of God (9:20), Jesus (19:13) and the Kingdom (20:25; cf. 28:31). In the last mentioned text, Paul taught "all about" (*ta peri*) the Lord Jesus Christ. He had long "carried his name" (9:15) before men.

If we thus study the Acts in depth and handle it day after day and week after week, we are impressed not only by the versatility of the author in style and vocabulary but by some peculiarity of throbbing power which he seems to impart to his writing. As J. B. Phillips said in his preface to *Letters to Young Churches*, we feel "rather like an electrician re-wiring an ancient house without being able to turn the mains off." He has said the same thing in the title of another book, *The Ring of Truth: A Translator's Testimony*. His public discussion with Dr. E. V. Rieu revealed that they had a common mind and experience (See pp. 55–56 of *Ring of Truth*.) The power is still on. If this is true of the language, what must it have been like in the company of the characters described? Their contemporaries may suggest an answer. We must consider their attitude to this surge of speakers let loose in the world.

They were people who had long been permitted to go their own way. Now they were pulled up short by the call to repentance (14:16; 17:30). Divine judgment threatened them and a divine way of escape was offered to them. Some were perhaps seeking the Lord (15:17) and were not "against" him (4:26). Others were "stiffnecked and uncircumcized in heart and ears" (7:51). They would not be led and they would not listen (7:57). Yet others merely procrastinated (17:32). Obviously there must have been a divided response. Some listeners raised their opposition and others did not. "The multitude of the city was split" (14:1–2, 4; 18:6–8; 19:9). A city would be evangelized and many people would become disciples—but not all (14:21).

## The Results of Receiving the Message

We are now concerned with those whose response was not negative, who were not "against." What happened when the Word was preached to them?

First of all they "heard." This was inevitable, unless they were stone deaf

(19:10, et al.). Those who were not "asleep," like a dull schoolboy ("Wake up, Jones!"), paid attention to what was being said (8:6; 16:14). It is here that the "split" began. Some felt the smart and were minded to kill (5:33; 7:54, 58) but others felt it in another way. Their conscience was pricked and they asked the question, "What are we to do?" (2:37). Lydia's heart had been opened by the Lord and she drank in the message.

Clearly there was more at work than a human speaker. In the voice of the preacher God was speaking. These particular listeners were called by him (2:39). The aorist vividly suggests the impact of the divine call.

The call of God is elsewhere implied by Luke though in other terms. In the work of evangelism "the hand of the Lord was with them" (11:21; cf. 2 Sam. 3:12, LXX). A report is given of what God had done "with" (*meta*) or "through" (*dia*) them (15:4, 12) or "through his ministry" (21:19). The testimony is given not only by the preachers but by God who knows men's hearts (15:8) and by "the Lord who testifies to the Word of his grace" (14:3). The Holy Spirit adds his testimony to that of his servants (5:32) and through his *paraklēsis* the church grew in numbers (9:31). *Paraklēsis* means broadly "persuasion with authority." According to context it may be rendered exhortation, appeal, encouragement, comfort, stimulus. It was he who drove the message home into the hearts of the listeners. This can be no other than God's call. The men who "stopped their ears" and refused to listen to Stephen were resisting the Holy Spirit (7:51, 57; cf. 14:27). Christ himself is ultimately the Preacher (26:23; cf. 2 Cor. 13:3).

Those who were called obeyed. "I was not disobedient to the heavenly vision" (26:19). In the special circumstances of his call Paul is not usually regarded as a typical convert. But he so regarded himself, "typical of all who were in future to have faith in him and gain eternal life" (1 Tim. 1:16, NEB). He would have all his hearers be such as he was—"except these bonds" (Acts 26:29). They can all have their own Road to Damascus.

Those who were not disobedient (14:2; 19:9) "received the Word of God" (8:14; 11:1; cf. 17:11; ?2:41). What was the result?

God was calling for repentance from all men (17:30). This was a general proclamation which was taken up by his preachers and repeated as a command (2:38; 3:19; 20:21; 26:20). Notice the use of the same verb in 17:30 and 26:20. The command to repent is accompanied by the opportunity. There will be a time when it will be too late. The command and the offer will be withdrawn. In the meantime God gives the privilege of repentance to Israel and to the Gentiles (5:31; 11:18). "Those who received his word," which included the command to repent, were baptized (2:38, 41). It may be inferred that the obedient received the Word of God and repented.

For God had surely opened their hearts (16:14) when the Word of God (16:32–33) was preached to them. In washing the wounds of Paul and Silas the Philippian jailer certainly did "works worthy of repentance"—he proved his repentance by deeds (26:20, NEB).

Those who received the Word of God and in repentance thus obeyed it were clearly "persuaded." Earlier in this chapter we have seen in evangelism "the exercise of suasion" (cf. 18:13). The present and imperfect tenses imply that the speaker was "working" on his listeners. Some people would say that he was "twisting their arm." But these tenses leave open the question whether the process of suasion was successful or not. It did not always attain its object (19:8–9; 28:23–24). Success was not universal but it was vast. Demetrius the silversmith recognized this. Throughout almost all Asia Paul had persuaded (*peisas*, aorist) a great crowd of people and had thereby caused them to change their position (19:26). Similarly at Thessalonica a great number "were persuaded" (17:4). The same must have happened with those who "received the Word with nothing but eagerness" (17:11). The suasion was not apparently effective with Agrippa. "You are persuading me to play the Christian" (26:28; cf. 1 Kings 20:7, LXX). This metaphor belongs to the theatre and may possibly be discerned in John 8:53, "You are playing yourself as whom?"

They were thus "persuaded." But persuaded to do what? They believed. The verb (*pisteuō*) is used a number of times absolutely, in an ingressive aorist. "All who had begun to believe" (2:44) is a characteristic expression. The NEB translates the verb by "became believers" (4:4; cf. 11:21; 13:12, 48; 14:1; 15:7). In 19:2 (NEB, "became believers") the Canadian Book of Common Prayer (1959, p. 558) gives "Did ye receive the Holy Spirit when ye believed?" This is a "coincident aorist participle" (Moulton, *Grammar*, 1:131). In the case of Simon Magus the difficulty is perhaps relieved by the judicious use of quotation marks. "And Simon himself also 'believed'" (8:13). (See note 23 in chapter 3 on Galatians.)

There are certain developments from the absolute use. "They believed Philip when he was evangelizing concerning the kingdom of God and the Name of Jesus Christ" (8:12). Philip was speaking and they believed what he said. There is an intellectual content to faith. Paul and Silas had spoken the Word of God and the Philippian jailer had believed God (16:32–34). The perfect tense here (cf. 15:5) suggests that he is continuing what he has started.

Other constructions come in: "set their faith on [*epi*, plus accusative] the Lord" (9:42; 11:17; cf. 16:31); "set their faith in [*eis*] . . . Jesus" (19:4; cf. 10:43). It is a summary of the apostolic command when Paul speaks of "repentance toward [*eis*] God and faith in [*eis*] our Lord Jesus" (20:21). Christians are described as "believers" (10:45; 16:1, 15), their characteristic activity since they first began to believe.

For faith is a *sine qua non*. The churches were "consolidated" in it (16:5) and it was "grounds of faith" which God had given to all men by raising Jesus from the dead (17:31).[4]

Associated with repentance (26:20) and faith (11:21) is "turning" or conversion. The term may be used absolutely (3:19; 28:27) but more frequently it has a phrase attached: "to the Lord" (9:35; 11:21) or "to God" (14:15; 15:19; 26:20) or "to light" (26:18; cf. 15:3). When the hearers repented and believed, they "turned" and were converted. If the distinc-

---

4. The word *pistis* here does not mean "faith" or "assurance" but that which can produce it, "evidence" or "proof." "Sufficient grounds for faith" shows the connection. For references to this use in Aristotle, Longinus and Josephus see my *Royal Theology*, p. 52.

tion of tenses is to be pressed, the aorist points to the decisive reversal of direction and the present to the succession of individuals who take this step.

In spite of the absence of the actual word, conversion is suggested in "being added to the Lord" and in "holding fast to the Lord" (11:23–24). Demetrius was wrong in attributing the work to Paul instead of to the divine agency but otherwise right when he saw that he had (by his persuasion!) "translated" a great number from one position to another (19:26; cf. Col. 1:13;[5] cf. also Acts 14:22–23).

Those who turned to the Lord did not do so in dead silence. Believers are described as those who call upon, who invoke, the Name (9:14, 21). There must have been a first time and this must surely be at their conversion. (Cf. 2:21; 7:59; 22:16.)

### The Advantages of Receiving the Message

If the Gentiles "go in" through the door which God has opened to them when they believe (14:27), and go in with an invocation, they receive an advantage (20:20, 24), "the gospel of the grace of God."

To determine in greater detail what the "advantage" is, we must assemble the evidence from the Acts. To begin with, we notice the striking expression, "Your blood on your head!" (18:6). Apart from the plural "your" in place of the singular "thy," this is an exact quotation, consciously or unconsciously given, of 2 Samuel 1:16, LXX. "Blood" has the meaning, following Hebraic usage, of "the guilt of bloodshed." [6] Now in Acts 18:6 Paul, absorbed in preaching the Word, was testifying to the resisting Jews. As far as may be seen they were not guilty of shedding blood. Paul is using a vivid figure for plain guilt. If divine punishment comes to them for their sins, he himself is not the guilty party. He has preached the gospel to them. Murder or no murder, they are guilty sinners.

Similarly in 20:26 Paul is clear of the blood of all. They have heard the gospel from him. If they have rejected it, he bears no blame and they remain guilty.

For in their sins they are guilty of disobedience to God. This is a "general" disobedience, a particular case of which would arise if Christian preachers allowed themselves to be silenced (4:19–20; 5:29). Now to be obedient to God is to be righteous and to oppose him is to be an enemy of righteousness, like Elymas the sorcerer (13:10). For God demands righteousness, as the many converted priests knew full well (6:7), and guilty sinners do not possess it. It was this which made Felix "tremble" (24:25, KJV). Paul undoubtedly reasoned with him about the righteousness of God's character and demand, and of the self-control which Felix had unrighteously failed to display [7] and of the judgment which was certain to come. In spite of his alarm, Felix procrastinated, even though he had heard about faith in Christ Jesus from Paul. Punishment was on the way.

---

5. A bishop may be "translated" from one diocese to another.
6. Cf. A. H. McNeile, *The Gospel according to St. Matthew*, on 27:25, p. 413.
7. Felix had taken his "wife," Drusilla (24:24), from her husband.

A more pleasing character is the Roman centurion, Cornelius. This pious "God-fearer" did many works of mercy and to that extent was a "righteous" man (10:1-2, 22). It might be thought that such a man who "worked righteousness" was acceptable to God (10:34-35). And so he was—as a target for evangelism. For Peter proceeded to preach the gospel to him, "the apostolic Kerygma in a nutshell" (F. F. Bruce, p. 224; see also C. H. Dodd, *The Apostolic Preaching and Its Developments*). He spoke the Word (10:44). This included a reference to Jesus as Judge and to the receiving of the forgiveness of sins by everyone who believes in him (10:42-43). Even the "righteous" and "acceptable" Cornelius needed to be saved (11:14) and Peter's words showed him how. It is "through his Name" for "every one who believes in him."

Through his appointed Judge, Jesus, God will judge the world in righteousness (17:31). He is no Respecter of persons. Nobody can escape on the grounds of privilege or race. But even so there is a way of escape. Through Jesus (the Judge!) there is forgiveness of sins. There must be some explanation of this (13:38). The disobedient, and therefore unrighteous, and therefore guilty man does not get rid of his unrighteousness and gain righteousness by way of the law. At the very least his sins have to be washed away (22:16). If his faith is in Jesus, he is justified (13:39). When he believes in Jesus he has the righteousness which before he lacked. This clearly implies the "reckoning" (*logizomai*) in the divine Mind which we have seen as a feature of Paul's doctrine of justification.

Thus the "advantage" which a man receives when in faith he turns to the Lord and "goes in" is the benefit which the gospel brings. By the grace of God he is given a righteousness to replace his own unrighteousness. It does not come as a result of works of the law or of his own deserving. This is an advantage indeed!

The "advantage" of justification has its parallel in cleansing, a concept which is related to the holiness of God (7:33). There was a time when both men and things were regarded as common, unclean, defiled (10:14, 28). The people of God had to avoid the unclean thing, the defiled person—the Gentile—for fear of contamination and the consequent loss of qualification to approach God. This has now come to an end. God has ceased to regard things as unclean (10:15; 11:9) and Peter is not to say ( =Palestinian "think") that any man is common or unclean (10:28), because God has forbidden him. The Spirit told him "not to make any distinction" (11:12) between men. Notice the slight stress on mental activity. "What God ruled [aorist] to be clean, you stop [imperative] regarding as unclean" (cf. Mark 7:19).

The Gentile is not to be shunned merely because he is not a Jew (10:34-35). He is a proper field for evangelism. He needs to be saved, like all men, because in another sense he is unclean. At this point we must refer again to "your blood on your head!" (18:6; 20:26). Paul says that "I am clean." The implication is that "you are not clean." Men have rejected the only message which tells them how they may cease to be unclean. God regards them as unqualified to draw near to him.

Other men became "qualified." God who knows the hearts of men "cleansed their hearts by faith" (15:9), and it is by faith in Jesus (26:15, 18) that they have been made holy. The perfect tense, "(they) have been sanctified" (cf. 20:32), implies that "they are now holy." And this is a characteristic description of believing men! Christians are traditionally called "the saints" (9:13, 32, 41; 26:10). As justified (13:38–39) they are accounted righteous— as Jesus is (3:14; 7:52; 22:14); and they are holy—like Jesus (3:14; 4:27, 30) and the Holy Spirit. Such holiness cannot be an inherent quality or even an expression for moral renewal. The renewal is associated with justification and purification but is not part of their definition. Holiness in fact tells us what God thinks of a man: he is prepared to receive him. Thus both justification and sanctification tell us of what goes on in the mind of God. He counts a man righteous and he regards him as holy, "qualified" to draw near to him. And it starts when he begins to believe.

When he thus for the first time puts his faith in Jesus he is forgiven. The forgiveness of sins is not to be taken for granted, like the average height of men or anything else belonging to the nature of man. It is something to be obtained (26:18). Men, as men, do not possess it already. They must be told that it is proclaimed to them (13:38) and in the proclamation it is offered to them as a gift (5:31). It is not on sale and it cannot be obtained by "doing" anything. It can only be received. It comes through Jesus, it is offered to all and it is received by "every one who believes in him" (10:43). The reality of faith is attested by a willingness to be baptized in the Name of Jesus Christ (2:38).

By way of comment on the forgiveness of sins we refer to 3:19. Men are to repent and be converted in order that their sins may be obliterated. The sins are clearly not "erased" until they repent and are converted. This is in sharp contrast to the obliteration of Colossians 2:14 which is already completed. The benefit of the cross has to be received. (Cf. pp. 235–36.)

Men who have not yet received the benefit are guilty sinners. If simple justice were the only factor, they would be judged. But the message of the gospel tells the story of the grace of God (20:24). God is gracious in his attitude to men, in what he did for them in Christ and in sending them his preachers to tell them the good news. Those who welcome the message "have begun to believe (and remain believers—perfect tense) through grace" (18:27). It can only have been through grace that they were antecedently "marked out" (NEB) for eternal life—before they became believers (13:48). It can only be through grace that their hearts are opened to attend to the message when it is proclaimed (16:14). It is through grace that the preachers are "used" ("the hand of the Lord") to lead men to faith (11:21; 14:3; pp. 363–64). The work and its results are visible to the eye of faith (11:23-24).

Grace makes demands on believers. They have entered its realm, so to speak, and should "attend upon it" (13:43; cf. Wisdom 3:9) with loyalty and "purpose of heart" (cf. 11:23–24). They have been added to the Lord. They should not seek to emigrate. Before some great venture men are "handed over," entrusted, to grace (14:26; cf. 15:40). As they are already in grace, the meaning must be that they are left there for safekeeping (12:4!). The figure is changed with "full of grace" (6:8) and perhaps even more fruitfully with the use of the preposition *epi*—"great grace was upon them all" (4:33), manifesting itself in the care of fellow believers. This is in contrast to the fear which might have been upon them (5:5). When grace is "upon" believing men, their blood is not upon their heads (18:6). Again, when men have heard the Word of the gospel (of grace, 20:24) and have begun to believe, it is wrong to impose upon such disciples the yoke of the law (15:7–10). They do not bear it yet; they ought not to be made to bear it.

The implication would be made plain if a disciple were asked a leading question. What is *upon* you? Is it your own blood? No, my guilt is gone; I believe in Jesus and have been justified and sanctified. Is the law *upon* you, a grievous weight to be borne (cf. 15:28)? No, I could not bear it and in any case salvation is for believers, through grace (15:11). Is grace *upon* you? Yes.

In fact you are not under law but under grace (Rom. 6:14; cf. Gal. 5:18). You are not under law and God does not therefore accuse you of breaking it (pp. 360-61). God has accepted you. He accepted you when you first put your trust in Jesus and were justified (13:38-39); but it was not in the sphere of the law of Moses but "apart from law" (Rom. 3:21).[8] A concomitant of justification is acceptance.

### The New Life of Believers

So far our emphasis has been largely on what the hearers of the Word did. They responded to God's call, received his Word, repented, were persuaded—or "decided"—believed, turned to the Lord, invoked him and received an advantage. When they so acted, God gave his "thought" to them: he justified, cleansed and forgave them; in fact he accepted them. We must now think more of what God did to them and in them.

Something "happened" to the new believers which is described in a number of metaphors. They came to the light and their eyes were opened (13:47; 26:18). They are in direct contrast to those who are hostile to the gospel and refuse to respond to its offer. They close their eyes to it. Their heart is "fat," insensitive, "watertight," unlike the heart of Lydia (16:14; 28:26-27; cf. 7:51, 57). Three particular cases are given in Acts. Scales fell from the eyes of Saul of Tarsus (9:18) and spiritually he continued to "see." For the eyes of the new believer remain open. Stephen saw Jesus standing on the right hand of God (7:55-56) and Barnabas saw the grace of God (11:23).

The experience—for it is experience—of hearing, repenting, believing and invoking is thus extended. The believer not only "sees"; he is healed (28:27); and he enjoys "seasons [note the plural] of refreshing" (3:20). (Cf. C. S. C. Williams, p. 80; " . . . when *or before* the Messiah would return," italics mine.) He sees because his eyes have been opened. He is healed but not self-healed. The seasons of refreshing come from the Lord. They are not bursts of optimism, intermittent resolutions or the cultivation of the

---

8. Cf. Marshall, *Luke*, p. 191. "The Pauline position is surely not essentially different from that of Luke."

spiritual life. Something has affected him from outside himself. He is an example of *pathos*, not *praxis*. He himself did not "do it." It was "done to him." It is a sign of new life.

This might have been expected. God gave repentance with a view to life (11:18). The NEB even renders "life-giving repentance." It comes from the Originator of life (3:15) and is made known by the apostles. "Go and take your stand in the Temple and tell the people all the words of this life" (5:20). It is "this life," not "the coming life." It must not be "pushed aside" (13:46; cf. 7:27) with the preached Word of God which offers it, for it is "eternal life," received when a man believes (13:48). "This life" is the life which a man has in Christ. We should beware of the modern usage here. We say that "this life is short" or that "secularism is limited to this life." The meaning in Acts is different, as we have just seen.

Thus a man believes and is justified (13:38–39). He believes and is given eternal life. A second concomitant of justification is quickening.

The "extended experience," as we have called it, is profound, going down into the depths of a man's soul. It follows from his responsive obedience, for the preaching of the gospel is command as well as information (14:15). In his first act of faith he is "experientially" related to God (cf. p. 364). In particular as an obedient man he has received the Holy Spirit (5:32). How can we describe the continuing relation to God of such a man?

He possesses the Holy Spirit. Whose son is he? An enemy of righteousness is a son of the devil (13:10). Can a man who has the Holy Spirit be other than a child of God? Now the expression, "men and brethren," which is not infrequent, "seems to have belonged to synagogue phraseology" (Bruce). It is a sign of the "family" relationship of the Old Testament people of God. It is noteworthy that apart from the synagogue and in addressing the heathen Paul does not speak in this way. He says "Men of Athens" (13:15, 26; 17:22; Bruce, p. 76; cf. W. Günther, *Begriffslex.* 2:148). But even men who were guilty of the crucifixion, though in ignorance, may be addressed as "brothers" (3:17) within the Jewish family.

The consciousness of membership of a family is deepened among Christian believers. The old term, "brothers," is retained, but it is now used within the Christian community. It has been baptized into Christ. Thus Paul can take leave of, say goodbye to, the brothers in one place and go on in another to greet the church (18:18, 22).

This is no secular "family spirit." Each member of the believing church has found God in Christ and found him as Father. He is the Father (1:4, 7). From him the risen and exalted Jesus received the promised Holy Spirit and poured forth the gift (2:33). The Holy Spirit proceeds from the Father and the Son.

In practice it means that Jesus is preached; in obedience men turn to him in faith (11:20–21); and they receive the Holy Spirit (5:32). But Jesus is still active and to him men turn (9:34–35). To him they are added and with him they stay (11:23–24). But they have turned to God (15:19).

This evidence can point in only one direction. If a Christian were cross-examined, there could be no doubt of his answer. Is he a child of God or only a servant? Is he a son or a slave? The answer could be on the following lines. "I turned to Jesus and discovered that I had come to his Father, who received me not as a Judge but as Father. I stayed with Jesus and was with the Father still. My guilt is gone and the burden of the law is gone. I have the Holy Spirit through whom I still have Jesus and the Father. Is there anything I can be but a son?"

The proof is not formal and statements are not explicit. But the experience can be recognized. Christians are to be distinguished from unbelievers (13:46; 19:9). Men in general are the *genos* of God (17:29; cf. Luke 3:38) by the fact of their creation.[9] They bear his image, even though it is marred. They are kin to him in rational and moral consciousness. But they do not know him; certainly they do not know him as the God of grace. They do not know him in Jesus and they have not turned to him. Christians do know him. They have met him in Christ and still know him in Christ, who is present through the Holy Spirit. Christians are thus more than the *genos* of God. They are God's children and they know it.

Thus in the Christian experience reflected in the Acts we see that adoption is the third concomitant of justification. Adoption began when belief began—or rather, adoption took place when belief began. God regarded the believer as a son and treated him as a son.

Could the men who have been described in detail as they have, who have experienced all the (perhaps simultaneous) stages of their conversion, who are possessed of the Holy Spirit—could such men fail to know, through this same Spirit, the love which God has for them? The Acts points to Romans 5:5 and Paul is not the only Christian who has obtained help from God (Acts 26:22). Paul was "in grace" and "in afflictions" (Rom. 5:2-3) and in Acts the church was persecuted and scattered. But they did not feel that they had received a raw deal. They joyously went on spreading the good news of God's grace. The further they went, the more they preached (8:1, 4; 11:19-24).

Th parallel should be noted. Paul is in grace and in afflictions and he certainly continued the joyous work of preaching Christ. The church was in grace and in persecution and it likewise continued to evangelize. Paul knew—and his knowledge sustained him—the love of God through the Holy Spirit. Was not the church sustained through the same knowledge?

It all started when they first believed. The fourth concomitant of justification is what we have called "certainty." It comes to expression when men glorify God (cf. 11:18; 13:48; 21:20; cf. also 4:28-31).

We have gone into considerable detail in describing the positive response to the upsurge and outreach of the young church. Men were obedient to God's call and they received the Word of God. They repented, were persuaded, made a decision, believed. They turned to God in conversion and invoked him. They received an advantage. They were justified, cleansed, forgiven. They were brought under grace. They were accepted, quickened, adopted and impressed with the certainty of the love of God for them.

---

9. Luke can handle *genos* quite easily as a "class" term referring to members of a distinctive group, family, nation or city. See Acts 4:6; 4:36; 7:13; 7:19; 13:26; 18:2; 18:24.

It might be objected that our method is illegitimate. We have "added up" the various modes of response and made one grand total and then said that this one "total" is what happens when one man responds to the gospel.[10] We ought, it might be said, to have avoided the addition and left everything in its separation. When Luke said one thing, he meant that and no more. When he said something else, he meant something else. Leave it as he left it.

There are two possible answers, one concerning the practice of Luke and the other concerning that of today. First we should observe a feature of Luke's style. It is natural in any good writer to use synonyms—apart from technical terms—but Luke uses synonyms not only of words but of phrases and concepts. We have seen (pp. 362–63) the varied ways in which he described the outreach of the church. The members "spoke" and in so doing preached, taught, evangelized, persuaded. To some extent Luke was indicating an identical activity. The content of what they said is summarized in a number of different phrases such as "the Word," "the Word of God" and so on. The designation of those who have received the gospel, Christians, is constantly altered.

Luke is consistent in his practice. He varies the way in which he speaks of the response made to the gospel but the different terms all point to the same, one experience of conversion. Repentance indeed means repentance but points also to the other elements. The part is used for the whole.

Secondly, Luke has his imitators. They probably do it unconsciously but still do it. They use words and concepts which may be quite simple and yet point beyond themselves. The terms retain their meaning but are not restricted to their meaning. They are pointers, indicators, symbols of a comprehensive whole.

In my student days a friend set off one evening to "hear" a minister at one of the great Methodist halls in London. (We were "sermon-tasters" then.) On his return I inquired how he had fared. With the omniscience which characterizes the theological student of all generations, he summed up his story. "He preached on the Prodigal Son. Man! There was nothing in it. There were nine conversions."

But there was something in it. That good man, the preacher, had received a theological training. I think that he would have agreed that in his sermon he had implicitly called for the response which we have elaborated in detail. If the conversions were genuine—and I do not for one moment question them—the Lord was witnessing to the Word of his grace (14:3); the Holy Spirit was a Witness in the hearts of the nine converts (5:32) and by his stimulus the church was increased (9:31). The simple words of the preacher "meant" nothing less than "all the words of this life" (5:20).

If, then, we accept the fact that (in the Acts) the response has been made as we have indicated and in particular that the new believers have received justification with its four concomitants, what do they possess? This brings us to the question of salvation.

---

10. Cf. James Barr, *The Semantics of Biblical Language*, p. 218.

## The Nature of Salvation

First of all there is a way of salvation (16:17). Not every one knows it. Not every one finds it. There are wrong ways, wrong roads. The road may lead to salvation or the road itself may be salvation—as opposed to the ditch alongside.

The "way" in fact is not a method which men devise and use for their own attainment of salvation. The "way" is a Person, Jesus (5:30–31) and he is the only way. Salvation is not to be found anywhere but in him. Men may plan schemes of social betterment and improve the material conditions of millions. But the salvation which comes through Jesus is a given salvation, not a humanly devised salvation. And it is in him and in him alone that we must (*dei*) be saved, if we are going to be saved at all (4:12). This is the logical use of *dei*. In his search for eudaemonism man may be successful but eschatological salvation will be sought in vain outside of Jesus. The word *dei* is not only logical. It savors of the ethical also. It conveys something of the divine imperative. God's universal proclamation says that all men everywhere should repent (17:30). This is an early step in the direction of salvation.

For Jesus is the only Savior. He is the only One commissioned by God to carry out the work of salvation, the only One capable of doing it and the only One who has actually done it. Salvation has been given. It may be received without charge. And it is available, because it has been sent (28:28). Its availability must be made known and made known at once.

God has therefore appointed messengers to bring the light of salvation to the nations at large (13:47) by his command. The Jews are not ruled out, for the Word had to go to them first. Thus it is not only salvation itself which has been sent. The very message about salvation was sent also. "The Word of this salvation was sent out" (13:23, 26; cf. 10:36–39). Simon Peter accordingly "will speak words to you by which you will be saved" (11:14).

Peter's "words" might well have been those used by Paul and Silas to the Philippian jailer. "Set your faith on the Lord Jesus and you will be saved . . . " (16:31). They need not be, and probably were not, the only words, but they form the core of a context or the climax of a story. The way to salvation is faith. Do it now! (Note the urgent aorist imperative.) The Word of God was spoken to the jailer, who was overjoyed at having believed God (16:34). He may very early have called on the Name of the Lord (cf. 2:21). Some great change in him is required to explain the joy which he showed in spite of the circumstances.

Faith and salvation are likewise connected in 14:9. Paul and Barnabas were evangelizing in Lystra. A lame man who had never walked was listening to Paul. Something about him must have caught the speaker's eye, rapt attention, eager anticipation or a change in expression from resigned hopelessness to vivid expectation. At any rate Paul fixed his eye on the cripple and saw (cf. 11:23, "seeing the grace of God," p. 368) that he had faith to be saved. Now in the light of the situation and of our knowledge of the apostle and his dominant determination to evangelize, is it likely that he would break off his sermon with the thought that "I must stop preaching and get this man healed"? *He continued his sermon.* "Stand up on your feet—upright!" (Cf. 26:16!)

"The thought possibly flashed across him that an act of bodily salvation would be the best explanation to his hearers of his doctrine of spiritual salvation . . ." (R. B. Rackham, pp. 231–32). This interpretation is the most appropriate, though we shall not observe it unless we give due attention to the fact that it is Paul the preacher who is at the center. The authentic preacher does not care for interruptions and seeks to handle them effectively. "When a speaker feels, 'I am master of the situation,' he usually is so." [11] When the interruption of his thought came, the "master" continued his sermon in word and deed.

There is a symbolism here and it raises the question of when salvation comes to the man who believes. The cripple leapt up and began to walk when the apostle gave the word of command. His name was not merely added to a waiting list. It is to be inferred that he received salvation there and then. If this applies to him, it applies also to the Philippian jailer and indeed to Cornelius (11:14, 17). Salvation is salvation from judgment and it is possible to be saved now from a judgment which is to come. "Be saved from this crooked generation" (2:40) which is ripe for judgment for the rejection of the Savior (2:36).

This view is confirmed by the statement that "the Lord was adding those who were being saved" (2:47). The relative-equivalent *tous sōzomenous* is an iterative present participle. It does not mean "those who were in the process of being saved" as if they were like children still in the bath and still "being washed." It is almost "those who were saved one after another." Hence C. H. Rieu in his translation of Acts can render by "new converts." The cripple of Lystra would not have entirely relished a one-legged salvation.

The symbolism of another lame man follows this line. He "has been saved" (4:9) and therefore walks (3:8–9). In Egypt "God was offering salvation through Moses" and it was accepted when "he led them out" (7:25, 35–36).

More difficult is the assertion that *pisteuomen sōthēnai* (15:11). Interpreters have been slow, I think, or even reluctant, to take this expression at its face value. "We believe we have been saved" or more vividly, to be true to the aorist, "We believe we were saved," has not commended itself to all. Three points may be advanced in its favor. The context is concerned with disciples, men already cleansed by faith and possessed of the Holy Spirit. If the infinitive had been *baptisthēnai* there would have been no trouble. "We believe we were baptized." And, thirdly, the cripple of Lystra would have rejoiced to say, "I believe I was saved."

It would seem that it is not far-fetched to say that the equation, salvation equals justification plus its four concomitants, is reflected in the Acts.

We have already observed in earlier chapters that justification sets up a permanent relationship between God and the believer. This is illustrated in

---

11. C. H. Spurgeon, *Lectures to my Students* (First Series), p. 163; repeated in Helmut Thielicke, *Encounter with Spurgeon*, p. 186.

the Acts. Believers are "men of the Way" (9:2) and they exercise a certain persistence (2:42, 46). They are called "disciples" in both singular and plural, masculine and feminine (9:1, 10, 19, 25, 26, 36, 38). It was "the disciples" who were given the name of "Christians." Some received a strengthening inspiration for their persistence (14:22). One certainly showed it, for he was a disciple who "had come in at the beginning" (21:16). He manifests the grace of grit.

The disciples constitute the church (11:26). It is local (5:11–12; 8:1, 3; 11:22; 13:1; 15:41) or particular and general or universal (9:31). It is built up in spiritual strength, is led by its fear of the Lord in moral conduct and increases in numbers by reason of the stimulus of the Holy Spirit. For this purpose it has pastoral supervision, given by the Holy Spirit. It belongs to God because he purchased it (20:28). At times it is scattered by persecution (8:1, 4; 11:19) or by the obvious need of earning a livelihood, but it may be gathered together for a local meeting (14:27). The word *homothumadon* suggests a certain inner coherence and enthusiasm of numbers (1:14; 2:46; 2:24; 5:12; 15:25). The phrase *epi to auto* (1:15; 2:1, 47) conveys something of "central rallying point." It is not a fixed place but varies from time to time. In fact the "pull" comes not from the place but from the people themselves. The church is centripetal.

We read finally of the breaking of bread (2:42, 46; 20:7, 11). At the very least Christians were reminded of the Cross and its meaning. This says nothing about whether the Eucharist is "only" a remembrance or not.

Thus we see individuals, societies and a society of men and women who belong to one another, disciples of a common Lord and walking in the fear of the Lord. It is unthinkable that the relationship with God set up when they were justified has not continued. We could only ask "how they are faring" (15:36) in that relationship.

## God at Work for Us—The Work of Christ for Us

We started with a heathen world, under the judgment of God, with at best synagogues scattered about it in various places which were in more or less close relation to the "people" in Israel, a people willful and disobedient and a people which had rejected its Messiah. We ended with the new People of God, scattered throughout the Roman Empire and present at its heart, Rome. What produced the change? It was the preachers who had been let loose in the world. But what started them off and what sustained them in what at times was an arduous, painful and dangerous task?

We are brought back to the work of Christ for us. Without it there would have been no church, because there would have been no mission to the world.

We start therefore to gather and to classify all the evidence on this subject which is to be found in the Acts. We seek answers to the question, "Who was Jesus and what did he do?" We notice at the outset that there is a large body of material which is available but which it is not our purpose to examine as it is outside the scope of the present inquiry. Behind the Acts stands the Gospel of St. Luke. Acts (1:1) is linked with the

Third Gospel (Luke 1:1–4), the Preface of which shows the spirit in which Luke wrote. In view of his gifts as a historian and his ability to discover, sift and formulate the evidence, to say nothing of his honesty, a scholar ought at least to be slow to believe that in writing the Acts Luke "made it up." What, then, has the Acts to say about Jesus?

## The Person of Jesus

He was a man (17:31) and he had a mother and brothers (1:14). He was a descendant of David (2:30–32), and the Christ (2:36; 3:20 [cf. Josh. 3:12]; 9:22; 17:3; 18:5, 28). (Cf. 10:38.) The promised Deliverer had come. He was "his Christ" (4:26–27); the expression suggests that he was sent by God. He appeared in history, opposed by Herod and Pontius Pilate "in this city." He was "the holy One" (*hagios*, 4:27; *hosios*, 2:27), "thy holy One." He was "the righteous One" (3:14; 7:52; 22:14). His coming was foretold (3:24; 13:27–29, 32–33), and he was *the* Prophet (3:22–23; 7:37; cf. Deut. 18:15, 18–19).

He is the *pais* of God (3:13, 26; 4:27, 30). Haenchen translates this by "Son" but refers to Isaiah 52:13. In view, however, of the clear quotation in Acts 8:32–33 from Isaiah 53 and the fact that, beginning from this text, Philip preached Jesus to the Ethiopian eunuch, it is likely that *pais* refers to the Servant. Admittedly *pais* can mean "boy." But in France a waiter is called *garçon*, whatever his age. Jesus is the Servant of God. (Cf. Marshall, *Luke*, p. 171; J. Jeremias, *TDNT* 5:700–717.)

As the Servant of God, Jesus exercised his public ministry, beginning at the time of "the baptism of John" (1:21–22; 2:22; 10:37–39). He went about doing good and healing all who were under the domination of the devil. This does not actually prove but points to his sinlessness and opposition to evil. *He* did the good and *he* did the healing. It was because God was with him, "demonstrating" him. In fact it was God who performed the deeds, "through him." The relationship between Jesus and God was close. The Holy Spirit had foretold the betrayal of Jesus by Judas, and its scriptural anticipation had of necessity to be fulfilled (1:16). The act of Judas was an act of unrighteousness (*adikia*, 1:18). Even so Jesus was a Man of Destiny: a program was being followed. Or why did the Holy Spirit make the prophecy or God work through Jesus?

He was brought before the Roman governor, Pilate, who decided to release him as an innocent man. But his own people disowned him and asked instead for a murderer to be released. "You killed him." "You crucified him" (2:36; 3:15; 4:10; 5:30; 10:39).

The deed was done in ignorance (3:17: 13:27) but not all ignorance is innocent. This was culpable. When Jesus was in your hands, "you" used lawless men to crucify and make away with him (2:23). It was a wicked act, but foreseen in the program.

The death of Jesus was not the end. God raised him from the dead (1:3, 22; 2:24, 31–32; 3:15; 4:2; 5:30; 10:40; 13:30–31, 33–34, 37; 17:18, 31; 25:19). His resurrection was prophesied in scripture, proved to his followers by his manifestation to them in food and drink and conversation, and attested by them to the world to which they preached.

At intervals the risen Jesus appeared to his disciples during a period of forty days. This particular activity ended with his ascension and exaltation (1:2ff, 9ff, 22; 2:33ff; 5:31) though later events revealed "the enduring activity of Jesus" (Bruce, p. 95; 3:6; 4:10). He has become "the Head of the corner" (4:11). As exalted he is Lord (2:36; 9:10-11, 15, 17; 26:15) and gave the Holy Spirit (2:33), the mode of his own continuing ministry. Just as he himself is thus sent by God with blessing (*eulogounta*, present) for individual men in their conversion, so he sends men to serve his overruling purpose (3:26; 9:17; 10:19-20; 26:17). He is thus both absent and present; it all depends on the mode.

This duality of operation will not continue forever. This Jesus will come again, finally (1:11; 3:20-21), for the Judgment (17:31).

## The Death of Jesus

This Jesus, so described, is the burden of the apostolic message. The various "parts" cohere, for it is one Christ, but there is great emphasis on his death. It is more than just another stage of his earthly ministry or his long "career." He is the Son of God (9:20) and he died. There must be some reason for his death, which we seek to discover in the Acts.

We observe that the Son of God is "his Christ" (3:18). Long in advance God proclaimed the sufferings of the Christ. It is not merely that "all the prophets" spoke of them, though this of course is true. It is God who prophesied, a fact which sets the matter in the right perspective.

God not only spoke; he acted. During the earthly ministry God "demonstrated" Jesus with mighty works, wonders and signs (2:22-23); nor was God absent from the cross. Jesus was delivered up by the definite *boulē* (p. 359), the precise resolution and foreknowledge of God. The Jews ("you") affixed him to the cross and did away with him, using lawless men as their agents. Long beforehand God knew about it and he decreed it. In a sense he carried it out.

This does not detract from human responsibility. It was a wicked deed and the Acts clearly recognizes it as such. But God was also at work. Men gathered together in concentrated hostility to Jesus—to do what ("all the things that," *hosa*) "thy hand and resolution [*boulē*] had decreed should take place" (4:26-28). The zeugma is striking but the meaning is clear. "Thy hand" did not decree, but it expresses God's power. In the unity of his omnipotence and wisdom "God's hand—an image of his power—and his counsel guided the course of the Passion" (Haenchen, p. 227).

Men may be "against the Lord and against his Christ" and they may fight against God and resist his *boulē* (5:38-39). But they cannot thwart it. Christ had (*edei*) to suffer (17:3) and he did suffer, for he was subject to suffering (*pathētos*, 26:23)—"ordained for, charged with, suffering" (W. Michaelis, *TDNT* 5:924). In the sufferings of his Christ, it was God who fulfilled his own prophecy (3:18).

God fulfilled it. The cross was not divinely unforeseen and the event itself tolerated. The crucifixion is not merely the prelude to the resurrection. It was God who foreknew, planned, decreed and acted, all in the context of human freewill and responsibility. It would seem unwise to say that the doctrine of the Acts is primitive and simple. It is profound.

If, then, God decreed the cross and ensured the implementation of his decree, it must have some great purpose in the divine Mind. It can hardly be fortuitous that Jesus, who suffered, is connected with the forgiveness of sins (2:38). Peter made the connection in his reply to a question arising out of his sermon, a sermon which contained the reference to the divine decree (2:23). It is the Christ of the cross whom God raised and exalted to give the forgiveness of sins (5:30–31). Forgiveness is not to be found elsewhere. God's gift is concentrated in him, the Christ of the cross (4:9–12). Salvation is in him and in him alone. The healing, which is an image of salvation, was a "sign" (4:22). All spiritual cripples can find their salvation in the Crucified (3:13–16), for the blessing in him is for all and after the resurrection God sent him with the blessing to bestow (3:25–26).

Christ is the only Savior. Rejection of him implies more than the mere negative absence of salvation. Penalties are attached to rejection. For he is "that Prophet" and everyone who refuses to listen to him will be destroyed (3:22–23).

The crucifixion was decreed by God and carried through by God and it is only when men repent and turn to Christ crucified that their sins are blotted out (3:19). Note the sufferings of Christ in the previous verse. When they follow the normal pattern they find themselves in the church and take part in the breaking of bread (2:42, 46; 20:7). The language of 27:35 cannot fail to remind the reader of the Eucharist, though the local conditions are against this interpretation. Paul may have felt at the time that it was a sort of private communion. However that may be, the breaking of bread must inevitably remind the communicants of the cross.

To put it in summary form, we can say that God decreed the Cross, carried it through, offers forgiveness and salvation solely through the cross, and bids his people ever to remember the cross. What is the explanation?

A fruitful line of investigation would be to examine the concepts of law, the tree and redemption.

Study of the Acts reveals that the law was a living factor in the life of men. It was no mere literary survival from the past, to be studied in much the same way as men today study the pre-Socratics. It had been given by God (7:38, 53). The "living oracles" were living in that they came through a living voice. Though afterwards reduced to writing they did not begin as a document. They were spoken. They were still "living" in the sense that they still spoke to men even from the written page. The law was meant to be obeyed.

There was such a person as a teacher of the law (5:34). The eminence of Gamaliel suggests that there was no small body of public opinion which regarded the law with respect and reverence. There were priests who carried out their ministry in accordance with its provisions. We may meet them later (6:7). Any question of the abolition of the law would become a live issue, not a merely academic one (6:11, 13–14; 18:13, 15). It had an authority which gave it credibility (24:14; 28:23; cf. 26:27) and a proper administration (23:3). It still held the respect of the apostle Paul (25:8). Ananias was devout according to the law (22:12); not so perfectly righteous that he needed no salvation (he was a believer, 9:17) but a Jew who had sincerely sought to walk with God under the old dispensation and who still seems, as a Jewish Christian, to have followed the Jewish customs. At any rate he was held in esteem by all the local Jews.

There were still many who were zealous for the law and to deal with a difficult situation Paul as a Jew could observe the law without forcing its observance on Gentiles or abandoning his doctrine of free grace (21:20–26). The law was still "live" enough to provoke animated controversy (23:29), and to be present in the Jewish cultus (cf. p. 359).

Yet in spite of the zeal of many, the law was not universally kept (7:39). The rejection of Moses implied the rejection of the law, and disobedience was followed by punishment (7:42–43). And still the law was not kept (7:53). It was an intolerable burden (15:10, 19, 28), in spite of which there were men who insisted on its observance. But the law brought no justification (13:39–41; 15:5). It could not be adequately obeyed.

This leaves men in a dangerous condition. The Acts recognizes the fact of human responsibility (5:28; 7:60; 18:6; 20:26). Disobedient men are guilty men and there will be a resurrection of both righteous and unrighteous (24:15). Men with the blood of millions on their hands will not escape the punishment of their enormities by annihilation. The dead will be judged as well as the living (10:42). The very day has been set for universal judgment (17:31). It is an alarming prospect (24:25; cf. 8:20–24).

Here, then, is the law, a factor to be reckoned with in the life of men. It cannot be conveniently dropped. What did the church say to any of the priests who entered its fold, steeped in ancient sacrifice and perhaps wondering what the present position was (6:7)? What did it say to the heathen who asked why God could not let them go on in their own way (14:16)? Why the universal call to repentance? Why could he not still overlook everything as before (17:30)? It is not enough to say simply that the situation is changed because Jesus is risen from the dead. If this is said, and no more than this, we ignore the cross and all its meaning (pp. 377–78), and our Lord might as well have died in his bed. For on these premises the effect would have been the same. The problem of the law has to be solved.

We pass then to "the tree." A number of verbs are used to describe the crucifixion: "kill" (3:15), "crucify" (2:36; 4:10), "affix to (the cross)" (2:23), with others like *anaireō*, "do away with, liquidate," (2:23; 10:39; 13:28) and *diacheirizomai*, "lay violent hands on" (5:30). The guilty are "murderers" (7:52) and their Victim was "led to the slaughter" (8:32). It might be supposed that the linguistic resources have been sufficiently used in their variety.

But there is a significant addition. They killed Jesus, "hanging him on a tree" (*xulon* 5:30; 10:39; cf. 13:29). The allusion is to Deut. 21:22–23, which commands that a body should not hang on a tree overnight, but be buried. After the execution of the criminal, his body was exhibited "on a tree" for the remaining hours of the day. For a Jew, therefore, the Deuteronomic text would invest the word "tree" with the ideas of humiliation, degradation and curse.[12] The allusion was caught in the early church (cf. Gal. 3:13). The curse is the consequence of the broken law, as Deuteronomy 27:26 goes on to say.

So Jesus, who went about doing good and was "demonstrated" by God, ended his life in the position of a man under the divine curse. Is this a clue? Consider the position which we have now reached. The law is a factor to be reckoned with and cannot simply be forgotten. It is not obeyed and men are faced with the fearful prospect of judgment. Now we learn the full penalty of the law, the malediction of God. Instead of rushing throughout the Roman Empire with warnings of judgment and the curse, however, the early preachers joyfully spoke of the forgiveness of sins in the Name of One who had occupied the position of one accursed, a position, moreover, which had been brought about by God himself (pp. 377–78). It was a woe which Jesus himself never personally deserved. Does the Acts supply any explanation?

It does. St. Paul told the elders of the church of Ephesus that (1) he was clean from the blood of all. (If any rejected his message, they were still guilty sinners.) (2) He had declared the whole *boulē*, counsel, of God. (3) God had acquired as his own "the church of God," and he had done it by means of the blood of his Own (20:26–28).

We cannot say that Paul had 2:23 in mind. It is hardly likely to be an allusion consciously made. Even if it were, we could not prove it. But this is not the point. We cannot be sure that Luke in his own mind connected 2:23 with 20:27. But that is not the point either. We are not concerned with the theology of Luke as such. We are seeking evidence from the Acts as a whole (cf. p. 358). In 2:23 we learn that it was by the definite resolution of God that Jesus was delivered up for crucifixion; in 20:27 Paul claims that he omitted nothing: he preached and taught the whole purpose of God. Within that purpose we can discern "purpose fulfilled." God acquired as his own. . . .

The most satisfactory translation of a text of well-known difficulty is "through the blood of his Own." The term *ho idios* is used absolutely in 4:23, 21:6, and 24:23. Through "his Own," God "acquired as his own." Did not the church, in common with everybody else, belong to God anyway? Of course, by creation. But here is something added. God was concerned "to get . . . a people for his Name, i.e., for himself" (15:14). In Corinth the Lord encouraged Paul to continue his work there, because "I have a great many people in this city" (18:10). They are waiting to be won, "predestined for the faith" (Haenchen, p. 535, n. 4, from Loisy). They will be won by the preaching of Christ crucified; and Christ crucified shows the means through which God acquired the church as his own.

For before its individual members were converted to Christ they were guilty sinners. They had not kept God's law. They were therefore accursed. But it was Christ who was hanged upon a tree. It would seem that he has occupied the position which they should occupy.

---

12. Cf. P. W. Evans, *The Cross as a Tree*, pp. 14–15; J. Schneider, TDNT 5:39.

"Blood" obviously refers to the cross. If we dwell on guilt and the curse, then Christ has taken our guilt and curse upon himself. Then men can be free from guilt and curse. God has now no curse for them. They can turn to him when they hear the gospel and he can and does receive them. This all points to redemption.

But if we think of the blood of sacrifice, we remember that men are cleansed or sanctified by faith (15:9; 26:18). As sinners they are unclean and cannot approach God. Christ's shed blood was an act of purification (cf. Heb. 1:3) which was the basis of their being cleansed by faith. As cleansed they can draw near to God. When they so draw near in Christ, God receives them and they become part of the church which God has acquired as His own. Redemption and sacrifice are united in the word *blood*.

It might seem that we have made a good deal of an "echo" (p. 358). But it is more than an echo. Indeed it is not an echo at all. It is a key. There is a double door before us when we study the Acts. The law makes itself strongly felt; and the cross is God's deliberate act. The blood of Christ, as Paul speaks of it in 20:28, is the one key which will open the door. Without the cross the law is not satisfied and the gospel has no foundation. The blood of Christ is the grace of God in operation, the base from which the preachers go forth to preach the forgiveness of sins.

It is sometimes said that the germ of later doctrines, more fully developed in the epistles, is found in the gospels. It might be similarly said that from the acorn of the Acts the oak of the epistles grew. It may be true. I should not wish to deny it. But I am more inclined to the view that one turn of phrase indicates or "means" the whole (cf. pp. 371-72). This applies to the work of Christ for us as well as to his work in us.

Those who have studied the sermons of John Wesley, particularly the "official" ones, must be struck by his close reasoning, his theological interest and use of theological terms and the lack of illustrations. It might be wondered why such crowds listened to him, especially as "the bulk of the congregation consisted of the poor." He was the apostle of the proletariat. The coal miners at Kingswood "were coarse in the extreme." But listen they did. "Wesley's style was marked by simplicity and sincerity. His sermons were meant for the people, and they were couched in language which the people could grasp." [13]

I suggest that Wesley's language in all its simplicity "meant" the doctrines which he set out in the official sermons. Similarly the varied expressions in the Acts all point to the one overwhelming fact of "the blood of his Own." The work of Christ for us and in us, as described in the Acts, is recognizably the same as his work as it appears elsewhere in the New Testament.

13. A. Skevington Wood, *The Burning Heart*, pp. 137, 142, 156.

# 18

## Conclusion

WE HAVE COME TO THE END of our survey of the New Testament literature (apart from the gospels). Before we try to sum up our results a few preliminary words are in order.

As we have progressed from epistle to epistle my impressions have grown clearer and sharper. At some point "crystallization" took place. From then on I recognized a distinctive pattern. The work of Christ for us consists of purification and redemption. On the cross he performed an act of atonement in virtue of which unholy men who are barred from God's presence may be received by him. By the divine mercy in Christ, unholy men may be "qualified" to approach the holy God. On the cross Christ redeemed men. He bore their guilt, stood under God's judgment and assumed their responsibility, taking their "answerability" on to his own shoulders. He ever speaks for men, and in him unrighteous men may be received by the righteous God. The experience of the work of Christ in us is apparent in the richness of vocabulary employed, and we found a summary in the equation, salvation equals justification plus its four concomitants.

Once this had been established, it might have been possible to revise the earlier chapters and made them conform more closely to the pattern of the equation. For example: I could have shown "quickening" in Hebrews by emphasizing more the tasting of the heavenly gift and becoming participators of the Holy Spirit, or by drawing more attention to the eleventh chapter. If faith meant so much to the Old Testament saints, what a chapter the author could have written on faith in the life of Christians! Such believers in Christ must have been quickened indeed!

It seems wiser not to revise the earlier chapters but to leave them as they are. This avoids the charge of forcing them into a pattern and lets them speak for themselves. And it may be more honest to let the reader see how the thought developed and how the pattern "emerged." For I am convinced that there is in the New Testament a pattern of our salvation. Details may vary and figures of speech may differ; but the framework abides and the individual books cohere with it.

[382]

To summarize the pattern, then, we shall try to set out four points:
The character of God
The "other side"
The work of Christ for us
The work of Christ in us.

1. God is the living God. He is eternal, self-existent and self-sufficient. He is the only true God, invisible, transcendent and immanent. He is conscious and has, or is, Mind. He is conscious and has knowledge and wisdom. He has will and is free to exercise his will. He discriminates and he chooses. He has purpose and is consistent: he does not change his mind; he does not lie and he is trustworthy.

He has power and he exercises his power. He not only speaks; he acts. In particular he is the Creator and Sustainer of all that is other than himself. He created everything and keeps it in being and is the ultimate Controller of all. He can "intervene" as he wills.

God is righteous and has authority. He is holy and he requires holiness. He is to be worshiped, loved and obeyed. He is the Lawgiver. He deals with individuals and he has an attitude: he may be pleased or displeased. He may be known and he should be known.

But he is the object of hostility and revolt by the devil, the world and individual men. He is thus sinned against. The heinousness of sin is attested by the variety and extent of the language which describes it. Sin is self-assertive desire and disobedience. Sinners are lawless and they transgress. They are deceived, erring or "wandering," ignorant and blind. In their weakness they fail to attain to the ideal—they "fall short." Sin is unrighteousness, impiety, unholiness; it is uncleanness and defilement. Sin "hardens" into fixed character and is marked by utter unbelief.

God is not pleased and he accuses and blames men. He is the One to whom they are responsible and to whom they must render account. God's attitude, decision and action is one of wrath and he is unapproachable. He is a God of judgment and his judgment may be inflicted in history or it may await its fullness at the Day of Judgment. It is his personal prerogative and is logical, deserved and just. It is penetrating, inescapable and terrifying. It culminates in death, destruction, perdition.

2. On the other hand judgment may be postponed or even avoided. There may be a day of salvation when God invites men to come to him. For he loves them. He is a God of longsuffering, kindness, grace, mercy and peace. He is Father as well as Judge.

3. The problem of the coexistence of Judge and Father in the one God is solved by the work of Christ for us. In the love, grace, mercy and righteousness of God a way out has been found. Its method is not law but gospel. For God has a gospel and it is not an afterthought. God has a Son, an eternal Son. He sent him into the world and he became incarnate as Jesus. He was obedient and sinless. He voluntarily endured death on the cross and his sufferings were real. This was the climax of his obedience, for the cross was God's purpose and plan, and indeed his achievement.

On the cross Jesus, as high priest with a superior and permanent ministry, gave himself as a sacrifice for sin and made purification for sin. As Bearer of sin and curse he redeemed men. He bore their sins, removed their sins and set aside their sins. He made propitiation and made peace. He reconciled God to men.

After the death on the cross came the resurrection, ascension and exaltation. The Crucified appears before God for us in permanent intercession by the will of God. He has opened a way into God's presence for men. He is thus the Mediator between God and men. He will appear finally at the Parousia as Judge.

4. The way into God's presence lies open. But before men can walk in it they have to be told. The story of the cross must be brought to them. This is the Word of God. Christ must be preached, Christ crucified, with a clear emphasis on fact, meaning, offer and invitation. In the response of men may be discerned the work of Christ in us. For he is able to save. Whether they are saved depends on their positive response to the Word of the cross.

Four "movements" may be distinguished in the work of Christ in us: (a) what the preachers do; (b) what the hearers do; (c) what God does in himself; and (d) what God does in the hearers.

(a) The preachers speak and tell a story. They preach, teach and proclaim. They expound the meaning of the cross and on the strength of it, the gospel, they offer a gift. They persuade, sound a call, utter a command.

(b) The work of Christ has a beginning in the hearers. They hear the Word preached in words, they pay attention and understand. They learn the truth and hear the divine call in the human voice of the preacher. They are persuaded and they "decide." They obey and receive the Word. They repent, confess and invoke the Name of the Lord. They believe the statements of the preacher and they put their trust in Christ. Thus they come to know Christ. For they have turned to him and in turning to him they have turned to God and drawn near to him.

(c) When a man first puts his trust in Christ, God counts him as righteous or justifies him; he regards him as qualified now to draw near to him, or sanctifies him. These are activities solely in the divine Mind. Varied expressions are used to describe them: God justifies, sanctifies, sprinkles, cleanses, forgives.

(d) When a man first believes, God not only "thinks" about him. He acts towards him and in him. He receives him and does not turn him away. He quickens him and makes the dead to live: he enlightens him, gives him a taste of the heavenly gift and makes him to participate in Christ and in the Holy Spirit. He adopts him as his son, tells him he has adopted him and treats him as a son. He puts certainty into his heart by impressing on him the fact of his love. He thus gives him a lasting possession, starts him on a heavenly pilgrimage and calls him to live the life of a disciple. For he has already called him to believe.

The work of Christ in us, which we have summarized as justification and its four concomitants, is salvation. It all depends on the cross, the work of Christ for us. This is the plan of God's salvation, a consistent pattern in the New Testament.

## DETACHED NOTE

Some words are certain to provoke easily anticipated reactions. If mention is made of *wrath, propitiation, penalty, substitution,* we hear that the idea is crude, clumsy, immoral. (Cf. the discussion above on pp. 170–71 of R. C. Moberly's book.) An enthusiastic evangelist may be crude or clumsy, especially if he is uneducated. On the other hand, if he is educated, he may be brilliantly overcoming the problems of "communication" in the immediate context. Rough people may need rough speech. Even apart from practical matters, if the gospel is to be preached and taught and if its prior theology is to be formulated, the categories are necessary. Vincent Taylor has said that "no good alternative has been suggested" for the word *penal* (*The Cross of Christ,* p. 94; cf. A. M. Hunter, *Interpreting Paul's Gospel,* pp. 31–32).

Many theologians—and preachers—have long given up speaking of, or believing in, penal substitution, vicarious punishment or the reconciliation of the Father in the cross. It is fashionable to despise the doctrine. But it keeps creeping in. These concepts, together with those of wrath, judgment, condemnation suffered by our Lord and the propitiation achieved by him, are related and the presence of one suggests the latent presence of others. It is surprising to find that scholars who are not reputed to "dig in their heels" in defense of penal substitution seem somehow to betray its presence by implication.

I have been struck by the use of the word *substitution* in Kittel (e.g., F. Büchsel, *TDNT* 1:450–51; 3:322–23); and by J. Jeremias (*The Central Message of the New Testament,* pp. 36–39; *New Testament Theology,* 1:293, "substitutionary offering"). The Greek Orthodox Church has not withheld its contribution. With distinguished Orthodox encouragement, my friend and colleague Dr. C. J. de Catanzaro has translated from the Greek the work of a man born in Thessalonica in about 1322. I judge that more than merely historical interest is involved. We are meant to see a living faith. In *The Life in Christ,* Nicholas Cabasilas speaks of our Lord's "dying on the cross. By this he paid the penalty for the sins which we had audaciously committed" (p. 53; cf. pp. 59, 78, 202). "It is the Father who is reconciled, the Son who reconciles . . . " (p. 74).

We have already quoted a number of scholars in our text and it will be enough to refer to them. Matthew Black, note 54 in the chapter on Romans; C. E. B. Cranfield, note 50 in the same chapter, and note 57 in the chapter on Corinthians; Margaret E. Thrall and William Barclay, note 30 in the chapter on Corinthians; W. G. Kümmel and Douglas Webster, text and notes 57 and 58 in the same chapter; J. K. Mozley, E. G. Selwyn and F. W. Beare, text and notes 50 and 51 in the chapter on Hebrews; text on pp. 298–99 in chapter 12 on Peter.

Other names should be mentioned. David Hill, *Greek Words and Hebrew*

*Meanings*, pp. 38–48, 158; G. E. Ladd, *A Theology of the New Testament*, p. 450; Michael Green, *I Believe in the Holy Spirit*, pp. 85, 127; R. H. Lightfoot, *St. John's Gospel*, p. 129; James Moffatt, *Hebrews*, p. 134 (". . . vicarious suffering; He took upon Himself the consequences and responsibilities of our sins"); Allen Cabaniss, *Evangelical Quarterly* 48, no. 3 (July-Sept. 1976): 166 (God reconciled); Emil Brunner, *The Mediator*, p. 474 ("the Mediator must bear the punishment instead of him . . . "). In addition there are the Germans, with their use of the word *bestrafen* (e.g., H. D. Wendland, p. 311, n. 2). Lewis B. Smedes *(The Incarnation: Trends in Modern Anglican Thought*, p. 160, n. 6) observes that though our Lord's substitutionary death is not everything in redemption, nothing else is enough without it.

Leon Morris, in *The Cross in the New Testament*, quotes a number of scholars whose language is explicitly or implicitly that of penal substitution: J. P. Hickinbotham, J. K. S. Reid and D. H. C. Reid (pp. 48–49); F. Delitzsch (p. 280); T. F. Torrance (p. 302); L. S. Thornton (p. 348): "He took our place [in the dock] and was willing to suffer the consequences."

I do not think that men of this caliber ought to be accused of crudity, clumsiness or of framing an immoral theory. God's "morality" is not to be judged at the bar of our own rationalistic prejudices. Matthew Black's moving tribute to Toplady's "Rock of Ages" (*Romans*, p. 73) rings true.

There is a perceptive article on the subject written by Dr. J. I. Packer in the *Tyndale Bulletin* 25 (1974).

# Practical Postscript

THE PLAN AND ACHIEVEMENT of salvation which we have found in the New Testament raise large questions of a practical nature. Is the church today proclaiming the message entrusted to her? The answer is twofold. There are sections of the church, and individuals, whose proclamation is faithful to the message. And there is still truth in Brunner's observation that it was the sacraments which preserved the gospel when the pulpit was in danger of losing it. The sacraments are still celebrated and they enshrine the message.

But they preserve it, so to speak, unconsciously. I have known men, and have had fierce arguments with them, who celebrate the service of Holy Communion and proceed to deny what they have sacramentally proclaimed. The table says one thing and the pulpit another.

This may be partly a failure of intellect. They may not have been taught the gospel or, if they have been taught it, they have failed to grasp it. But more than intellect is involved. It all savors of a failure of faith. There is widespread turmoil and confusion and the trumpet of the Church Hesitant gives forth an uncertain sound. Men are so impressed by the secular world view that they "cannot" nowadays believe.

It would seem that they start at the wrong end. They listen to the world and test the message of the church by the secular theories. They ought to start with the gospel. It is a datum, not a discovery or an invention of men. If Christ has laid hold of them, they should press on to know him and make him known.

The public utterances of some men make us wonder if they have ever read the New Testament. At any rate they do not seem to have studied it, pondered it, let themselves be nourished by it. Its deepest notes are unheard. It is not believed. In consequence the church has become identified with the oddest of activities.

We claim that we have the one remedy for which the world yearns; we claim that we offer life from the dead. And then men advocate, agitate for, contribute to, violence and revolution. They forget that all they that take the sword shall perish with the sword. Men limit their gospel to loud cries for social justice, unmindful of the fact that the kingdom of God is not eating and drinking but righteousness, peace and joy in the Holy Ghost. Their ideal for the church is service to the community, ignoring the fact that a permissive society may take them at their word and call for their support in sheer wickedness.

The church in many of its representatives seems blind to its priorities. We are exhorted to "feed the hungry" on a massive scale which may be beyond the power of governments. We are reminded of the "Inasmuch" and of the Feeding of the Five Thousand, strange proof texts from those who have otherwise muted the solemn warning of judgment and have rejected miracles. Has it never been noticed that our Lord did not spend all his time on earth in feeding the multitudes; that he told men not to work for perishable food but to prefer instead his gift of eternal life; that he himself rejected the temptation to feed the hungry?

In a time of economic stress when, if ever it did, the situation cried out for a social gospel, the apostles insisted that it was not pleasing to God for them to abandon his Word and serve tables. Other men must be appointed to care for the needy. They themselves must concentrate on their vital task, prayer and the ministry of the Word. Even so, one of the appointed men could not limit himself to feeding the hungry. It was his preaching which led to Stephen's martyrdom. "Thou art a minister of the Word. Mind thy business."

It is at times said that the church has too long thought of the saving of the soul. "The soul is saved. Good! Let us now proceed to the saving of the body." It is then said that illness is never the will of God and that the task of the church is therefore to "save" the body. There have been some notable, even miraculous, cases of divine healing and we praise God for them. But two points should be kept in mind. According to St. Paul, illness may be God's way of dealing with those of his people who do not "discern the Body" at the communion. Further, "saving the body" in distinction from saving the soul misunderstands New Testament anthropology.

Human personality is a unity of body and soul. It is an animated body rather than a soul within a body. If therefore a man receives the gospel and is saved; if we may truly and rightly apply to him the words "By grace you have been saved through faith," and he is indeed "safe"; then the whole man, body and soul, is saved. *He* is saved. If we insist on saying that his soul is saved, we ought to add that his body is saved also. It is a constituent part of his personality.

The church should therefore not speak of saving the body but of caring for it. There is a ministry to the sick and diseased and an important ministry. But what point would there be in patching up a body if its "owner" were unreconciled to God? The illness of Christians, even the permanent illness, may be within the loving purposes of God. Some flowers of character will never grow except in the soil of illness. Some ministries have been far more effective, more "used of God," from a bed of permanent pain than ever they were in the days of health. The church must ever have an eye on priorities.

There is a practical test which is not irrelevant. For years I have inevitably worked in church and university with men whose denominational and theological doctrine has not been entirely the same as mine. Many times I have quoted such a colleague, who told me once that he could not accept an invitation to preach in a synagogue ("as some of these fellows do") unless it had been made perfectly clear from the beginning that he was free to preach the gospel. I cannot refuse to cooperate with such a man.

But a new test has been forced upon me, the test of prayer and devotion. When men say in all seriousness that God is dead and repudiate "a God who exists in himself"; when a leading ecclesiastic publicly says that such views contain valuable insights for the church; when the resurrection of our Lord is taken to mean no more than that what is essential and new in his preaching is still valid; and when it is suggested that the abandonment of the gospel is thus ruthlessly carried out in order to rescue the gospel, because the men who do it are believers; then my eyebrows are raised and I wonder if, for such, prayer is at best no more than meditation. Gone is Brunner's "divine encounter." Vain is the cry, "My soul thirsteth for God, for the living God." "Walking with God" is but an exercise in solitude. What can be the devotional life of such "believers"?[1] How can they cry, with the dying Stephen, "Lord Jesus, receive my spirit"?

We live in a world of sorrow and suffering, of increasing violence and bitter poverty, of frustration and of blind groping. I live and minister in a city which brings it all into a sharp focus and constantly run into these ills.[2] The church has need of constant and renewed compassion. But we must not omit the fact that the world is a sinful world and a doomed world. There is a Day of Judgment and there is the proleptic judgment in history. The churches here give away thousands of dollars annually to relieve distress and I have first-hand acquaintance with this ministry. I doubt if there is ever a tragedy, a sorrow, without a clergyman's swift response to a known need. But when all is said and done I wonder if the best service to this stricken world is not for the *church* to remember her priorities.

Let us suppose that there is some old tub of a ship, some tramp steamer still in service on the oceans. And let us further suppose, as a datum, that it is known in advance that on her next voyage she will blow up in mid-ocean with the loss of all hands. Which would be the wisest and the kindest course of action: to agitate for "better conditions for the men," for shorter hours of work at sea, for more recreational facilities, better food and less cramped surroundings; for a change of captain and first lieutenant; in short, for a "new deal" for the men; or to move heaven and earth to persuade them not to sail in that ship?

This is the situation which faces the church today. If the New Testament is true; if it is not reinterpreted, misinterpreted or replaced; then there looms before men the judgment to come. And the church is the one body which has the answer. There is salvation in Christ and in him alone.

Those who have thrown judgment overboard will not be convinced. The

---

1. Cf. Heinz Zahrnt, *The Question of God*, pp. 269–84; Carl F. H. Henry, *God Revelation and Authority*, 1:57.
2. These words were written while I was still rector of a historic city parish.

universalist will not worry. But those who feed upon the New Testament and have already tasted the heavenly gift of salvation will want to share with others the amazing grace which they have received. They will lovingly warn men of what is in store; and they will point them to the Savior of the world.

# Appendix

# Pointers to the Plan of Salvation

In the accompanying chart I have tried to indicate the plan of salvation as we find it in the New Testament. The parallel texts should not be regarded as manifesting literary dependence. They are rather parallels of doctrine or of Christian experience. As a general rule the references have been given in their order in the book from which they come. Where certain references have to be taken together they may have to be arranged in the order which best expresses the development of thought. For sometimes the "proof texts" are cumulative and the unit is not the single text but the group. In any case, study of the context should be instructive. At times the references overlap: a text may appear in one place and yet support more than one point. On occasion the evidence may be sparse or nonexistent; at other times a selection has had to be made. In some instances an inference has to be drawn. For easier reference, I have listed below the one hundred one points of the chart, showing how they develop the four main points of the pattern of salvation. The chart itself begins on page 394.

*The Character of God*
1. Living
2. Eternal
3. One, Alone
4. Invisible
5. Conscious
6. Knows
7. Wise
8. Has power
9. Creator
10. Sustainer
11. Has will
12. Has purpose
13. Does not change his mind
14. Righteous

15. Does not lie; trustworthy
16. Holy
17. Requires holiness
18. To be worshiped
19. Has an attitude
20. Deals with individuals
21. To be obeyed; Author of law
22. Has enemies
23. Sinned against
24.    Self
25.    Deception
26.    Disobedience
27.    Lawlessness
28.    Transgression
29.    Error; wandering
30.    Ignorance
31.    Weakness
32.    Miss
33.    Unrighteous
34.    Impiety
35.    Unholiness
36.    Uncleanness
37.    Defilement
38.    Hardening
39.    Unbelief
40. God not pleased
41. Blames
42. Answerable to
43. God of wrath
44. Judge
45.    His judgment: in history
46.         at End
47.         logical
48.         penetrating
49.         prerogative of God alone
50.         deserved
51.         just
52.         inescapable
53.         terrifying
54.         final
*The "Other Side" of God*
55. Kindness
56. Love
57. Mercy
58. Grace
59. Peace
*The Work of Christ for Us*
60. Not by law

61. But by grace (see "other side" no. 58)
62. God has a gospel; no afterthought
63. God has a Son
64. Preexistent/Creator
65. Purposively sent
66. Jesus
67. Incarnate
68. (High)priest
69. Obedient
70. Sinless
71. The Cross: real suffering
72.     sacrifice/once only
73.     God's will
74.     voluntary
75.     for others
76.     bore sins; set aside sins; removed sins
77.     made propitiation
78.     made purification
79.     redeemed
80.     made peace/reconciled God
81. Exaltation; before God for us; intercession
82. Opened a way for us
83. Mediates

*The Gospel Preached: The Work of Christ in Us*

84. Able to save; power
85. The Word heard: invited; called
86. The Word received/truth learnt
87. Obey
88. Repent
89. Turn to the Lord/invoke him
90. Faith begins
91. Confess
92. Sprinkled; cleansed; sanctified; justified
93. Enlightened; tasted gift; partook of Christ, Spirit; quickened
94. Draw near
95. Forgiven
96. Received by God
97. Adopted
98. Permanent relationship established
99. Salvation
100. Certainty
101. Discipleship begun

| | Heb. | Rom. | Gal. | 1 & 2 Cor. | 1 & 2 Thess. | Eph. | Col. |
|---|---|---|---|---|---|---|---|
| **The Nature of God** | | | | | | | |
| **1. Living** | 3:12<br>9:14<br>10:31 | 1:9f<br>8:26,34<br>14:11 | 1:20<br>2:6,8 | II.3:3<br>II.6:16 | I.1:9 | 1:3-6<br>1:11,17-22<br>2:18,22 | 1:25ff |
| **2. Eternal** | 1:8-12 | 1:20<br>16:26 | 1:5 | I.2:7<br>II.9:9<br>II.11:31 | I.4:14 | 1:4,21<br>2:7<br>3:9,11,21 | |
| **3. One, Alone** | 1:3<br>6:13<br>7:1<br>8:1 | 1:21<br>3:30<br>11:33ff<br>16:27 | 3:20<br>4:8 | I.8:4ff<br>I.12:6<br>I.14:25 | I.1:9 | 4:6 | 3:5f |
| **4. Invisible** | 11:27 | 1:20<br>2:22 | | I.11:7<br>II.4:4 | | | 1:15 |
| **5. Conscious** | 2:6<br>6:10<br>8:12<br>10:17 | 8:27<br>11:34 | 2:6 | I.2:16 | I.2:4 | 1:4 | 1:22 |
| **6. Knows** | 1:1f<br>2:4<br>4:12f<br>11:4 | 2:16<br>8:29<br>11:2<br>11:33 | 4:9 | I.3:20<br>I.8:3<br>II.1:23<br>II.12:2f | | 1:4,16f<br>2:10<br>3:14ff<br>5:20 | |
| **7. Wise** | 12:5-11 | 11:33f<br>16:27 | | I.1:21<br>I.2:7 | | 1:8<br>3:10 | |
| **8. Has power** | 2:4<br>6:5<br>11:19<br>13:20f | 9:17,22<br>11:23 | 3:5<br>4:9 | I.1:18,24<br>I.2:5<br>I.4:20<br>I.6:14<br>I.10:22<br>II.4:7<br>II.6:7<br>II.9:8 | I.1:5,10<br>I.3:11<br>I.4:14,16<br>II.3:2 | 1:11<br>1:19<br>3:7<br>3:20 | 1:13<br>2:12<br>4:3 |
| **9. Creator** | 1:2f<br>3:4<br>11:3 | 1:25<br>11:36 | 6:15 | I.8:6<br>I.10:26<br>I.11:9-15<br>I.12:18,24<br>II.4:6<br>II.5:18 | | 1:4<br>3:9<br>4:6 | 3:1ff<br>3:10<br>4:1 |
| **10. Sustainer** | 1:2f<br>2:10<br>6:7 | 8:28<br>11:36<br>13:1-7 | | I.15:38<br>II.6:18<br>II.9:10 | | 4:6 | 1:15ff |
| **11. Has will** | 2:4<br>10:5-10<br>10:36<br>13:21 | 1:10<br>2:18<br>12:2<br>15:32 | 1:4 | I.1:1<br>I.12:18<br>I.15:38<br>II.1:1<br>II.8:5 | I.4:3<br>I.5:18 | 1:4-11<br>6:6 | 1:1<br>1:9<br>3:12<br>4:12 |
| **12. Has purpose** | 1:2<br>2:4<br>11:39f | 3:25f<br>8:28ff<br>9:11<br>9:17 | 1:15f<br>4:4f | I.1:21<br>I.1:27ff<br>I.2:7,9<br>I.12:24f | I.1:4<br>I.5:9<br>II.2:13f | 1:9-12<br>3:11 | 1:19f<br>1:25ff |
| **13. Does not change his mind** | 6:17f<br>7:21 | 9:11<br>11:7<br>11:29 | | | | | |

Chart [395

| Phm. | Phil. | Pastorals | James | 1 Pet. | 2 Pet. | Jude | 1 John | Rev. | Acts |
|---|---|---|---|---|---|---|---|---|---|
| 4 | 1:8<br>3:15 | I.3:15<br>I.4:10 | 1:5<br>1:13 | 1:5 | 1:17 | 1 | 3:22<br>5:14f | 4:9f<br>7:2<br>10:6<br>15:7 | 4:19<br>10:31,33<br>14:15 |
| | 4:20 | I.6:16<br>II.1:9<br>Tit.1:2 | | 4:11<br>5:10f | 3:8f | 25 | | 1:4<br>1:8<br>15:7 | 15:18<br>17:25 |
| 4 | 4:9 | I.1:17<br>I.2:5<br>I.6:15 | 2:19<br>4:12 | 4:3 | 1:4<br>1:17 | 25 | 5:20 | 4:1-11 | 7:48<br>14:15<br>16:17 |
| | | I.1:17<br>I.6:16 | | | | | 4:12<br>4:20 | | 17:27ff |
| | 4:6 | II.2:19 | 2:23 | 1:2 | 2:9 | 5f | 3:20 | 18:5 | 10:4<br>10:31 |
| 4<br>22 | 4:6 | II.2:14f<br>II.2:19 | 4:10 | 1:2<br>3:12 | 2:9 | | 3:20 | | 1:24<br>7:34<br>15:8 |
| | | | 1:5<br>3:17 | | | | | | |
| | 2:27<br>4:19 | II.1:8 | 4:12<br>5:4 | 1:5<br>4:11<br>5:6 | 1:3 | 24f | 4:4<br>5:14f | 11:17<br>12:10<br>15:3<br>15:8<br>19:1 | 1:8<br>2:22ff<br>2:32f<br>10:38<br>19:11 |
| | | I.2:13f<br>I.4:3f | 1:18<br>3:9 | 1:20<br>4:19 | 3:4f | | | 3:14<br>4:11<br>13:8<br>17:8 | 4:24<br>7:49f<br>14:15<br>17:24 |
| 15<br>22 | 2:10f | I.6:13,17 | | | 3:6f | | | 1:8<br>4:8 | 14:17<br>17:24ff<br>18:21 |
| | 2:13 | I.1:1<br>II.1:1<br>Tit.1:3 | 1:18<br>2:5<br>4:15 | 2:15<br>3:17<br>4:2<br>4:19 | 3:9 | 6<br>18 | 2:17<br>5:14f | 4:11 | 1:24<br>13:17<br>18:21<br>22:14 |
| | 2:27 | II.1:9 | 1:12<br>2:5 | 1:10f | 1:4<br>2:4,9<br>3:7<br>3:13 | 6 | 4:9<br>4:14 | 17:17 | 2:23<br>4:28<br>13:22 |
| | | | 1:13<br>1:17 | | | | | | |

| | Heb. | Rom. | Gal. | 1 & 2 Cor. | 1 & 2 Thess. | Eph. | Col. |
|---|---|---|---|---|---|---|---|
| **14. Righteous** | 1:8f<br>6:10<br>11:4 | 1:17<br>3:5<br>3:21<br>3:25f<br>9:14<br>10:3 | 2:16f<br>3:6-12<br>3:24<br>5:4f | I.1:30<br>I.6:9ff<br>II.3:9<br>II.5:21<br>II.6:14<br>II.11:15 | I.2:10<br>II.1:5f<br>II.2:3-12 | 4:24<br>5:9<br>6:1f<br>6:14 | 2:13<br>4:1 |
| **15. Does not lie**<br>**Trustworthy** | 6:18<br>10:23<br>11:11 | 3:1-4<br>3:7<br>15:8 | 3:14-22<br>3:29<br>4:28 | I.1:9<br>I.10:13<br>II.1:18 | I.5:24 | 2:12<br>3:6 | |
| **16. Holy** | 3:1<br>9:3-9<br>12:10 | 1:2-4<br>6:19<br>6:22<br>7:12<br>12:1<br>15:16 | | I.1:30<br>I.6:19<br>II.13:13<br><br>{I.1:2<br>{I.7:34} | I.3:13<br>I.4:3f<br>I.4:7f<br>I.5:23<br>II.1:10 | 2:21f<br>4:30 | 1:22 |
| **17. Requires**<br>**holiness** | 9:6-9<br>10:1f<br>12:10<br>12:14<br>13:12 | 6:19<br>6:22 | | I.1:30<br>I.6:11<br>I.8:8 | | | |
| **18. To be**<br>**worshiped** | 8:4f<br>9:1<br>12:28<br>13:15 | 1:21,25<br>15:6,9<br>16:27 | 1:5<br>1:24 | I.10:31<br>I.14:25<br>II.1:3 | I.1:2<br>II.3:1 | 1:3,6<br>1:12,14<br>1:16<br>3:21<br>5:20 | 3:16 |
| **19. Has an**<br>**attitude** | 11:5f<br>12:28<br>13:16<br>13:21 | 8:8<br>12:1<br>14:18 | 1:10 | I.10:5 | I.2:4<br>I.2:12<br>I.2:15<br>I.4:1 | 1:4<br>5:6-10<br>6:18f | 3:20 |
| **20. Deals with**<br>**individuals** | 3:12f<br>4:1<br>4:10ff<br>6:11<br>12:14ff | 2:1-6<br>3:10f<br>3:28<br>4:5<br>8:9<br>9:13<br>9:18 | 2:16<br>6:7f | I.3:17<br>I.6:17<br>I.7:16<br>I.10:12<br>I.8:3<br>II.5:17 | I.2:11f<br>I.4:3-8<br>I.5:15<br>II.1:3<br>II.3:14f | 3:2ff<br>3:7f<br>3:16f<br>4:7<br>6:8 | 1:28<br>3:25 |
| **21. To be obeyed**<br>**Author of law** | 7:5<br>7:11<br>8:4f<br>9:19f<br>10:28 | 7:22<br>7:25<br>8:7 | 3:12<br>3:19<br>5:3<br>5:14<br>6:13 | I.7:19<br>I.9:8f<br>I.10:11<br>I.15:56 | I.1:9<br>II.2:3f<br>II.2:7f | 2:15<br>6:2f | 2:13f |
| **Man Against God**<br>**22. Has enemies** | ( 1:13)<br>3:12<br>(10:13)<br>(12:3) | 5:10<br>8:7<br>11:3 | | I.15:25-28<br>II.10:5 | I.2:18<br>I.3:5<br>II.2:9<br>II.3:3 | 4:18<br>6:11f<br>6:16 | 1:21 |
| **23. Sinned**<br>**against** | 3:17<br>5:1<br>8:12<br>10:26<br>11:25<br>12:1 | 3:9f<br>3:23<br>5:12 | 1:4<br>2:15ff<br>3:22 | I.6:18<br>I.8:12<br>I.10:5-13<br>I.15:17<br>I.15:34<br>II.12:21 | I.2:16<br>I.4:8<br>II.2:4<br>II.2:7 | 2:1f<br>4:26f | 1:14 |

Chart [397

| Phm. | Phil. | Pastorals | James | 1 Pet. | 2 Pet. | Jude | 1 John | Rev. | Acts |
|---|---|---|---|---|---|---|---|---|---|
|  | 3:6<br>3:9 | II.2:19<br>II.3:16<br>II.4:8<br>Tit.2:12 | 1:13<br>1:20<br>1:25<br>2:23<br>5:16 | 2:23<br>3:12<br>3:14 | 2:5<br>2:7ff<br>3:13 | 25 | 1:5f<br>1:9<br>3:10 | 15:3f<br>16:5<br>16:7<br>19:2 | 4:19<br>5:29<br>17:31<br>24:25<br>26:18 |
|  |  | Tit.1:2 | 1:18<br>3:14<br>3:17<br>5:19 | 4:19 |  |  | 1:10<br>5:10 | 15:3<br>19:9<br>21:5<br>22:6 | 3:18<br>13:32f |
|  | 1:1<br>4:21f | I.5:10<br>II.1:9<br>Tit.1:8 | 1:27<br>3:6<br>4:8 | 1:15<br>2:9 | 1:21<br>3:2<br>3:11 | 3<br>20 | 2:20 | 4:8<br>6:10<br>15:4<br>16:5 | 20:32<br>26:18 |
|  |  |  |  | 1:15f |  |  |  | 21:27 | 7:33 |
| 4 | 2:11<br>3:3<br>4:20 | I.1:11<br>I.1:17<br>I.6:16 | 3:9 | 1:3<br>2:12<br>4:11<br>4:16 |  | 25 |  | 4:9ff<br>14:7<br>19:10<br>22:9 | 10:25f |
|  | 2:15<br>4:18 | I.2:3<br>I.5:4 | 1:27<br>4:3<br>4:8 | 2:4f<br>2:20<br>3:4 | 2:11 | 7<br>11 | 3:22 | 3:2<br>16:19<br>17:4 | 4:19<br>6:2 |
| 4<br>6<br>10<br>19 | 1:3f<br>2:27<br>4:19 | I.6:11f<br>II.1:5f<br>II.1:12<br>II.3:15 | 1:14f<br>4:17 | 1:17<br>3:4 | 1:19<br>2:7 |  | 2:5f<br>4:15f | 2:23<br>6:11<br>14:9f<br>20:13<br>21:7<br>22:4<br>22:12 | 8:38f<br>16:14<br>16:30f |
|  | 3:5f<br>3:9 | I.1:1<br>I.1:7-10<br>Tit.1:3 | 1:25<br>2:8-12<br>4:11f | 1:14 | 2:7f<br>2:16 |  | 2:3ff<br>3:4<br>3:22ff<br>5:2f<br>(II.4ff) | 12:17<br>14:12 | 5:29<br>7:38<br>7:53<br>22:3<br>24:14<br>25:8 |
|  | 3:18f | I.3:6f<br>I.4:1<br>I.5:14f<br>II.2:26 | 1:27<br>4:4<br>4:7 | 5:8f |  | 9<br>15 | 2:15f<br>3:8<br>5:18 | 2:9f<br>2:13<br>2:24<br>3:9<br>12:9<br>20:10 | 4:26<br>5:3<br>10:38<br>13:10<br>26:11<br>26:18 |
|  | 3:19 | I.1:9<br>I.1:15<br>I.5:20<br>I.5:22<br>I.5:24<br>II.3:6<br>Tit.3:11 | 1:15<br>2:9<br>4:8<br>5:15f<br>5:20 | 2:24<br>3:18<br>4:1<br>4:18 | 2:4<br>2:14 | 15 | 1:8ff<br>3:9 | 1:5<br>18:4f | 2:38<br>3:19<br>7:60<br>10:43<br>13:38<br>26:18 |

| | Heb. | Rom. | Gal. | 1 & 2 Cor. | 1 & 2 Thess. | Eph. | Col. |
|---|---|---|---|---|---|---|---|
| **24. Self** | 10:26ff<br>11:25<br>12:3<br>12:16 | 2:21ff | 5:16<br>6:8 | I.10:6 | I.2:5f<br>I.4:5f | 2:3<br>4:19 | 3:5 |
| **25. Deception** | 3:13 | | 6:3 | I.10:12 | II.2:10 | 4:22<br>5:6 | 2:8 |
| **26. Disobedience** | 2:2<br>3:18<br>11:31 | 2:8<br>5:19<br>11:30ff | 3:10 | I.10:5-13 | | 2:2<br>5:6 | 3:7 |
| **27. Lawlessness** | 1:9<br>10:17 | 4:7<br>6:19 | | II.6:14 | II.2:3<br>II.2:7f | | |
| **28. Transgression** | 2:2<br>9:15 | 2:23-27<br>4:15,25<br>5:12-21 | 2:18<br>6:1 | II.5:19 | | 1:7<br>2:1<br>2:5 | 2:13 |
| **29. Error<br>Wandering** | 3:10<br>5:2 | 1:27 | 6:7 | I.6:9<br>I.15:33 | II.2:11 | 4:14 | |
| **30. Ignorance** | 3:10<br>5:2<br>9:7 | 1:21,28<br>2:4<br>10:2f | 4:8 | I.1:21<br>I.2:14<br>I.15:34<br>II.4:4 | I.4:5<br>II.1:8 | 4:18 | 1:13 |
| **31. Weakness** | 4:15<br>5:2<br>7:28 | 5:6<br>6:19<br>8:26 | 4:3<br>4:8f | I.8:7-13 | I.5:14 | 3:16ff | |
| **32. Miss** | 4:1<br>12:15 | 3:23 | | I.6:7<br>I.8:8 | | 2:12<br>4:17 | |
| **33. Unrighteous** | 8:12 | 1:18,29<br>2:8<br>3:5,9f<br>6:13 | 4:12 | I.6:1<br>I.6:8f<br>II.7:12 | II.2:12 | 4:24 | 3:25 |
| **34. Impiety** | 2:1,3<br>12:16 | 1:18<br>4:5<br>5:6 | 4:3,8 | I.10:7 | | | |
| **35. Unholiness** | 12:14 | 6:19,22 | | I.1:2<br>I.6:1,11 | | 4:24 | |
| **36. Uncleanness** | 9:13f<br>9:22f<br>10:2 | 1:24<br>6:19 | | II.6:17<br>II.12:21 | | 4:19 | |
| **37. Defilement** | 9:13<br>12:15 | | | I.8:7<br>II.7:1 | | | |
| **38. Hardening** | 3:8<br>3:13<br>3:15<br>4:7 | 2:5<br>9:18<br>11:7-10<br>11:25 | 4:29 | II.3:14 | I.2:15f | 4:18f | |
| **39. Unbelief** | 3:12<br>3:19<br>4:2 | 3:3f<br>4:20<br>11:20,23<br>15:31 | | I.6:6<br>I.7:12f<br>II.6:14f | II.2:11f | | |
| **God Against Man** | | | | | | | |
| **40. God not pleased** | 3:8<br>3:15f<br>10:6ff<br>11:6 | 8:8 | 5:21 | I.10:5<br>II.5:9 | I.2:15 | 5:10f | |

# Chart

[399

| hm. | Phil. | Pastorals | James | 1 Pet. | 2 Pet. | Jude | 1 John | Rev. | Acts |
|---|---|---|---|---|---|---|---|---|---|
|  | 2:3f 2:21 | II.3:6 Tit.3:3 | 1:14f 4:1f 4:16 | 1:14 4:2 | 1:4 2:10 2:18 3:3 | 16 18 | 2:16 | 3:17 | 7:39 7:51 8:9 16:19 |
|  |  | Tit.1:10 | 1:26 |  | 2:13f 2:18 |  |  | 18:23 | 17:32 |
|  | 3:19 | Tit.1:16 Tit.3:3 | 3:8 4:15 | 2:8 3:1 3:20 | 3:5 |  | 2:4 | 12:17 14:12 | 7:39 7:53 |
|  |  | Tit.2:14 |  |  | 2:7,16 3:17 |  | 3:4 |  |  |
|  |  | 2:9 2:11 |  |  |  |  |  |  |  |
|  |  | I.4:1 Tit.3:3 | 1:16 5:19f | 2:25 | 2:15 2:18 3:17 | 11 | 1:8 4:6 (II.7) | 12:9 18:23 20:10 |  |
|  |  | Tit.1:16 |  | 1:14 2:15 | 2:12 3:5 | 10 | 3:1 3:6 | 3:17 | 3:17 13:27 17:30 |
|  |  |  |  |  |  |  | 5:19 |  |  |
|  |  |  | 1:18 |  |  |  |  |  |  |
| 3:19 |  |  | 3:6 | 3:18 4:3 | 2:9 2:13 2:15 | 11 | 1:9 5:17 | 18:5 22:11 | 1:18 8:23 |
| 3:19 |  | II.2:16 II.3:5 Tit.2:12 |  | 4:3 4:18 | 2:5f 3:7 | 15 | 2:15 | 13:4-15 | 7:40f |
|  |  |  |  |  |  |  |  |  | 26:18 |
|  |  | Tit.2:14 | 4:8 |  |  |  | 1:7 1:9 3:3 | 22:11 | 15:9 |
|  |  | Tit.1:15 | 3:6 |  | 2:10 2:13 2:20 3:14 | 8 12 23 |  | 3:4 16:13 21:27 | 21:28 24:6 |
|  |  |  | 4:16f | 3:16 4:4 4:14 |  |  |  | 2:21 9:20f 16:9,11 | 7:51 7:57 19:9 |
|  |  | I.1:13 I.5:8 Tit.1:15 |  | 2:7 |  |  |  | 21:8 | 13:8ff 19:9 |
|  |  |  |  |  |  |  | 3:22 |  |  |

| | Heb. | Rom. | Gal. | 1 & 2 Cor. | 1 & 2 Thess. | Eph. | Col. |
|---|---|---|---|---|---|---|---|
| **41. Blames** | 8:7f | 1:20<br>2:1 | | I.10:11 | | | 2:14 |
| **42. Answerable to** | 2:17<br>4:13<br>5:1<br>13:17 | 3:19<br>14:10ff | 5:3 | | | | |
| **43. God of wrath** | 3:10f<br>3:17f<br>4:3<br>12:25 | 1:18<br>2:5-8<br>4:15<br>5:9<br>9:22 | 3:10 | | I.1:10<br>I.2:16 | 2:3<br>5:6 | 3:6 |
| **44. Judge** | 10:30<br>12:23<br>13:4 | 11:33 | 1:8f<br>3:10<br>5:10<br>6:7f | I.5:13 | I.5:2<br>II.1:5<br>II.2:2<br>II.2:12 | | |
| **45. His judgment<br>in history** | 3:17ff<br>8:9<br>11:28f | 1:24<br>1:26<br>1:28<br>9:17f<br>13:2ff | | I.10:5-11 | | 2:1<br>2:5<br>4:22 | 2:13 |
| **46. at End** | 10:27ff | 2:5<br>2:16 | | I.1:8<br>I.3:13<br>I.5:5<br>II.1:14 | I.5:2<br>II.2:2 | 4:30 | 1:22f<br>3:4<br>3:24f |
| **47. logical** | 11:7 | 2:1<br>2:27 | | II.3:6-9 | | | |
| **48. penetrating** | 4:12 | 2:16 | | I.4:5 | I.2:4 | | |
| **49. Prerogative<br>of God alone** | 10:29f | 12:19 | | I.3:17 | | | |
| **50. deserved** | 2:2 | 2:2,6<br>3:8 | | II.11:15 | II.1:6 | | |
| **51. just** | | 1:27<br>2:5<br>9:14 | | | II.1:5f | | 3:25 |
| **52. inescapable** | 2:3<br>10:27<br>12:25<br>12:29 | 2:3<br>3:6<br>3:19<br>12:19 | 6:7f | | I.5:3<br>II.2:12 | | |
| **53. terrifying** | 4:1<br>10:27<br>10:31 | 11:20f<br>13:3f | | | I.5:3 | | |
| **54. final** | 10:28f<br>10:39 | 2:12<br>5:12<br>6:23<br>9:22 | 6:8 | I.1:18<br>I.15:21f<br>II.2:15f<br>II.4:3 | I.5:3<br>II.1:9<br>II.2:3<br>II.2:10 | 4:22 | |
| **The Other Side—God for Man** | | | | | | | |
| **55. Kindness** | 4:6f | 2:4<br>11:22 | | | | 2:7 | |
| **56. Love** | 12:6 | 1:7<br>5:5,8<br>8:39 | | II.9:7<br>II.13:11<br>II.13:13 | I.1:4<br>II.3:5 | 2:4<br>6:23 | |

# Chart [401

| Phm. | Phil. | Pastorals | James | 1 Pet. | 2 Pet. | Jude | 1 John | Rev. | Acts |
|---|---|---|---|---|---|---|---|---|---|
| | 2:15 | | | | 3:14 | | | 12:10 | |
| | | | 4:5 | | | | | | 5:28 7:60 18:6 20:26 |
| | | | 4:6 | 3:12 4:18 5:5 | | 11 | | 11:18 14:8ff 15:7 | |
| | | I.5:12 I.5:24 | 2:12 3:1 4:12 5:9 5:12 | 1:17 2:23 4:5 | 2:4ff 2:9 2:14 | 4 6 | 4:17 | 14:7 16:7 18:8 19:2 | 17:31 |
| | | | 1:7 1:11 | 4:17 | 2:5f | 11 | 2:17 3:14 5:12 | 19:2 | 5:1-11 7:7,42f 12:23 23:3 |
| 1:6 1:10 2:16 3:11 3:20 | | II.1:12 II.1:18 II.4:8 | 5:1ff 5:7ff | 4:7 4:18 5:4 | 2:4 2:9 2:17 3:7 3:10ff | 6 13ff | 2:18 4:17 | 20:11-15 22:11 | 17:31 |
| | | | | | | | | | 13:46 |
| | | | | 3:4 | | | 3:20 | 2:23 | 1:24 15:8 |
| | | | 4:12 | | | | | | 17:30f |
| | | | | 1:17 | | | | 2:23 20:12f | 8:20 |
| | | | | 2:23 | | | | 16:5ff 19:2 | 17:31 |
| | | | | | | | | 6:10 6:15ff | |
| | | | 2:13 | | | | 4:17f | 6:15ff | 5:11 8:24 24:25 |
| 1:28 3:19 | | I.6:9 | 1:15 3:6 4:12 5:20 | | 2:1 2:12 3:7 3:16 | 5ff 13 | | {21:27 22:15} 14:11 19:3 | 8:20f 13:40f |
| | | Tit.3:4 | | | | | | | |
| | | | | | | 1f | 2:5 3:1 4:7-11 4:16,19 | | |

| | Heb. | Rom. | Gal. | 1 & 2 Cor. | 1 & 2 Thess. | Eph. | Col. |
|---|---|---|---|---|---|---|---|
| **57. Mercy** | 4:16 | 9:23<br>11:30ff<br>15:9 | 6:16 | I.7:25<br>II.1:3<br>II.4:1 | | 2:4 | |
| **58. Grace** | 2:9<br>4:16<br>10:29<br>12:15 | 1:7<br>3:24<br>5:15<br>5:20 | 1:3<br>1:15<br>2:9<br>2:21 | I.1:3<br>I.3:10<br>I.15:10<br>II.1:2,12<br>II.6:1<br>II.8:1<br>II.9:8<br>II.9:14 | II.1:2<br>II.1:12<br>II.2:16 | 1:2<br>1:6f<br>2:7f<br>3:2<br>3:7 | 1:2<br>1:6<br>4:18 |
| **59. Peace** | 13:20 | 5:1<br>14:17<br>15:13,33<br>16:20 | 1:3<br>6:16 | I.1:3<br>I.14:33<br>II.1:2<br>II.13:11 | I.5:23<br>II.1:2 | 1:2<br>6:23 | 1:2 |
| **The Work of Christ for Us**<br>**60. Not by law** | 7:11<br>7:18f<br>9:8f<br>10:1-4 | 3:20<br>8:3 | 2:16<br>2:21<br>3:2,11<br>3:19ff | I.9:20<br>I.15:56f | | 2:8f | |
| **61. But by grace**<br>(see "other side") | | | | | | | |
| **62. God has a gospel**<br>No afterthought | 1:1f<br>1:6-12<br>4:2,6<br>10:5<br>11:12,18<br>11:40 | 1:1f<br>1:16<br>15:16 | 1:6<br>1:15f<br>1:23f<br>2:2<br>2:5,7<br>2:14 | I.15:1<br>II.11:4<br>II.11:7 | I.2:2<br>I.2:4<br>I.2:8f<br>II.2:14 | 1:13<br>3:6<br>6:15<br>6:19 | 1:5f<br>1:23 |
| **63. God has a Son** | 1:1-8<br>4:14<br>6:6<br>10:29 | 1:9<br>5:10<br>8:29<br>8:32 | 1:16<br>2:20<br>4:6 | I.1:9<br>I.15:28<br>II.1:19<br>II.11:31 | I.1:10 | 4:13 | 1:3<br>1:13 |
| **64. Preexistent/**<br>**Creator** | 1:2f<br>9:26<br>10:5 | 1:2f<br>8:29 | 4:4 | I.10:4<br>I.15:47<br>II.8:9<br>I.8:6<br>(II.4:4) | | 1:4<br>4:9f | 1:15ff<br>2:3<br>2:9 |
| **65. Purposively**<br>**sent** | 3:1<br>10:5-9<br>10:37 | 5:14<br>8:3 | 4:4 | | | | |
| **66. Jesus** | 2:9<br>3:1<br>4:14 | 3:26<br>5:1<br>10:9<br>16:20 | 1:3<br>3:1<br>3:22<br>6:17 | II.4:5<br>II.4:10f | I.1:10<br>I.2:15<br>I.4:14<br>II.1:1f | 4:21<br>5:20<br>6:23 | 1:1-4<br>2:6<br>3:17<br>4:12 |
| **67. Incarnate** | 2:9f<br>2:14-18<br>5:7 | 1:3<br>8:3<br>9:5 | 1:19<br>4:4 | I.9:5<br>II.8:9 | I.2:15<br>I.4:14 | 1:7<br>2:13<br>2:14 | 1:20<br>1:24<br>2:9 |
| **68. (High) priest** | 5:5<br>7:21f<br>9:11<br>10:21 | | | | | | |
| **69. Obedient** | 5:8<br>10:7 | 5:18f<br>8:32<br>13:8 | ⎰4:4<br>⎱5:14<br> 2:20 | | | | |

Chart [403

| Phm. | Phil. | Pastorals | James | 1 Pet. | 2 Pet. | Jude | 1 John | Rev. | Acts |
|---|---|---|---|---|---|---|---|---|---|
| | 2:27 | I.1:2<br>II.1:2<br>Tit.3:5 | 2:13<br>5:11 | 1:3<br>2:10 | | 2 | II.3 | | |
| 3 | 1:2 | I.1:2<br>II.1:2<br>Tit.1:4<br>Tit.2:11 | 4:6 | 4:10<br>5:5<br>5:10<br>5:12 | 1:2<br>3:18 | 4 | II.3 | 1:4 | 7:46<br>11:23<br>13:43<br>14:26<br>20:24 |
| 3 | 1:2<br>4:7<br>4:9 | I.1:2<br>II.1:2<br>Tit.1:4 | | 1:2<br>5:14 | 1:2<br>3:14 | 2 | II.3<br>III.15 | 1:4 | 10:36 |
| | 3:9 | II.1:9<br>Tit.3:5 | | | | 3f | 5:11f<br>II.7,9 | | 13:38f |
| 13 | 1:5,7<br>1:12-17<br>1:27<br>2:22<br>4:3,15 | I.1:11<br>II.1:8<br>II.1:10<br>II.2:8 | | 4:17 | | | | 14:6 | 8:12<br>13:32f<br>16:10<br>20:24 |
| | | | | 1:3 | 1:17 | | 1:3<br>2:22ff<br>3:8,23<br>5:5 | 2:18 | 9:20 |
| | 2:6 | I.1:15<br>II.1:9 | | 1:20 | | | 1:2<br>2:14 | 1:17<br>2:8<br>3:14<br>22:13 | |
| | 2:8f | II.1:10<br>Tit.2:11<br>Tit.3:4 | | 1:20 | | | 4:9f<br>4:14 | 11:15<br>12:10 | 3:22-26<br>4:26ff |
| | 2:10<br>2:19<br>4:23 | I.1:1f<br>I.6:3<br>I.6:14<br>Tit.1:1 | 1:1<br>2:1 | 1:1<br>2:5<br>3:21 | 1:1f<br>1:8<br>3:18 | 1<br>17<br>21 | 1:7<br>2:22<br>4:3<br>5:1,5 | 1:9<br>14:12<br>22:16<br>22:21 | 1:1,11<br>7:55<br>11:17<br>17:7 |
| | 2:7 | I.1:15<br>I.2:5<br>I.3:16<br>II.2:8 | (5:7f) | 1:21<br>2:4,7<br>2:23<br>4:1 | 1:14-18 | | 1:1ff<br>4:2<br>5:6,20<br>II.7 | 5:5<br>22:16 | 1:14,21f<br>2:31<br>10:38<br>17:31 |
| | 2:8 | I.2:6<br>Tit.2:14 | | 1:11<br>2:21 | 1:17 | | 4:2,9 | 3:14 | 3:13f,26<br>4:27,30 |

| | Heb. | Rom. | Gal. | 1 & 2 Cor. | 1 & 2 Thess. | Eph. | Col. |
|---|---|---|---|---|---|---|---|
| **70. Sinless** | 1:8f<br>4:15<br>7:26f<br>9:14 | 8:3<br>8:29 | | II.5:21 | | | |
| **71. The Cross:**<br>**real suffering** | 12:2<br>5:7f<br>13:12 | 8:34 | 6:12<br>6:14 | I.1:18,23<br>I.2:2,8<br>I.11:26<br>II.1:5<br>II.13:4 | I.2:15<br>I.5:10 | 2:16 | 1:20<br>1:22<br>2:14 |
| **72. sacrifice/**<br>**once only** | 7:27<br>9:14<br>9:26ff<br>10:10,12 | 6:10 | 1:4 | I.5:7<br>I.11:25f | | 5:2 | 1:20<br>2:14 |
| **73. God's will** | 5:6ff<br>5:10<br>7:21f | 5:8<br>8:32 | 1:4 | I.1:4<br>I.1:18<br>I.1:23f | I.5:9f | 5:2<br>(1:4) | 1:19f |
| **74. voluntary** | 7:27<br>9:14 | 5:7f | 2:20 | | I.1:10 | 5:2<br>5:25 | 2:14 |
| **75. for others** | 6:20<br>7:27<br>9:24 | 5:6<br>5:8<br>14:15 | 2:20<br>3:13 | I.1:13<br>I.8:11<br>II.5:14f<br>II.5:21<br>II.8:9 | I.5:10 | 5:2<br>5:25 | 2:14 |
| **76. bore sins**<br>**set aside sins**<br>**removed sins** | 8:12<br>9:26,28<br>10:4,11<br>10:17<br>12:2 | 11:27 | 3:13 | I.15:3<br>II.5:21 | | | 2:14 |
| **77. made**<br>**propitiation** | 2:17<br>8:12<br>9:5 | 3:25 | (3:13)<br>(4:5) | | I.1:10<br>I.5:9f | 2:3f | |
| **78. made**<br>**purification** | 1:3 | | | I.1:30<br>I.5:7f<br>I.6:11 | | 5:25f | |
| **79. redeemed** | 9:11f<br>9:15 | 3:24 | 3:13<br>4:5 | I.1:30<br>I.6:20<br>I.7:23 | | 1:7<br>2:15 | 1:14 |
| **80. made peace/**<br>**reconciled God** | | 5:9f | | II.5:18ff | | 2:14,17<br>6:15 | 1:20 |
| **81. Exaltation**<br>**Before God**<br>**for us**<br>**Intercession** | 1:3<br>6:20<br>7:22-26<br>9:24 | 8:34 | 1:1<br>1:12 | I.15:23<br>I.15:25ff | I.1:10<br>II.1:7 | 1:20ff<br>4:8ff | 3:1-4<br>4:1 |
| **82. Opened a way**<br>**for us** | 6:20<br>9:8<br>10:20 | 5:2 | 1:6 | I.8:8<br>II.3:4 | | 2:18<br>3:12 | 3:3 |
| **83. Mediates** | 7:25<br>8:6<br>9:15<br>12:24<br>13:15<br>13:21 | 1:8<br>2:16<br>5:1<br>5:11,21<br>7:25<br>16:27 | 2:16<br>3:14<br>3:16<br>3:22<br>3:26<br>3:29 | I.1:4f<br>II.1:20<br>II.3:4<br>II.5:18f | I.4:14<br>I.5:9 | 1:3-14 | 3:17 |

Chart [405

| Phm. | Phil. | Pastorals | James | 1 Pet. | 2 Pet. | Jude | 1 John | Rev. | Acts |
|---|---|---|---|---|---|---|---|---|---|
| | | | | 1:19<br>2:22<br>3:18 | 1:17 | | 3:5 | 3:7 | 3:13f<br>10:38<br>22:14 |
| | 2:8<br>3:10<br>3:18 | I.6:13 | | 2:21<br>3:18<br>4:13<br>5:1 | | | 5:6 | 1:7<br>1:18<br>5:6<br>5:9<br>11:8 | 3:15<br>5:30<br>10:39 |
| | 2:8 | Tit.2:14 | | 1:19<br>3:18 | | | 1:7<br>5:6 | 7:14<br>12:11 | 2:23 |
| | 2:7f | II.1:9f | | 1:11<br>1:20 | | | 4:10<br>4:14 | 13:8<br>14:6 | 2:23<br>3:18<br>4:27f<br>20:28 |
| | 2:6ff | I.2:6<br>Tit.2:14 | | 2:23 | | | 3:16 | 1:5<br>3:9 | 8:32<br>8:34f |
| | | I.2:6<br>Tit.2:14 | | 2:21<br>3:18 | | | 3:16 | 1:5<br>5:9 | 20:28 |
| | | | | 2:24 | | | 3:5 | | |
| | 3:18ff | | | 3:18 | 2:1<br>2:4ff | 11<br>24 | 2:2<br>4:10 | 6:16f<br>21:3f<br>22:3f | |
| | 1:1<br>4:21f | Tit.2:14 | 4:8 | 1:2<br>1:19 | 1:9<br>2:20 | 3<br>14 | 1:7 | 1:5f<br>7:14 | 20:26ff |
| | 1:1 | I.2:6<br>Tit.2:14 | 1:1 | 1:18 | 1:1<br>2:1 | 1<br>4 | | 1:5<br>5:9 | |
| 3 | 1:2<br>4:7,9 | I.1:2<br>II.1:2 | | 1:2 | 1:2<br>3:14 | 2 | II.3<br>III.15 | | 10:36 |
| | 2:9<br>3:20 | I.3:16<br>I.6:14<br>Tit.2:13 | 5:7f | 1:7<br>1:21<br>3:22<br>5:1 | 3:4<br>3:12 | | 2:1<br>2:28<br>3:2 | 1:12-18<br>3:21<br>12:5 | 2:33-36<br>3:13<br>5:31<br>7:55,59f |
| | 3:14<br>3:20f | I.2:5<br>I.6:16 | 4:8 | 5:10 | | 1 | 4:15 | 1:6<br>5:10<br>7:15 | 7:55f,59f |
| 5 | 3:3<br>3:9 | I.2:5 | 2:7<br>5:14 | 1:21<br>2:5<br>4:11<br>5:10 | 1:11<br>2:9 | 25 | 2:12<br>2:23<br>3:23<br>5:11f | 1:18<br>3:5<br>3:7<br>7:15 | 5:31<br>10:43<br>13:38f |

| | Heb. | Rom. | Gal. | 1 & 2 Cor. | 1 & 2 Thess. | Eph. | Col. |
|---|---|---|---|---|---|---|---|
| **The Gospel Preached** | | | | | | | |
| **The Work of Christ in Us** | | | | | | | |
| **84. Able to save** | 2:4 | 1:16 | | I.1:18,24 | I.1:5 | 1:19 | 1:29 |
| Power | 7:25 | | | I.2:5 | | 3:2,7 | |
| | | | | I.4:20 | | 3:20 | |
| **85. The Word heard** | 2:3f | 8:30 | 1:6 | I.1:9 | I.4:7 | 1:13 | 3:15 |
| invited | 6:20 | 9:24 | 1:15 | I.7:17-23 | II.2:14 | 1:18 | |
| called | 13:7 | 10:20f | 5:8 | II.13:3 | | 4:1 | |
| | | | 5:13 | | | 4:4 | |
| | | | | | | 4:21 | |
| **86. Word received** | 10:26 | 16:17f | 2:5 | I.15:1 | I.2:13 | 1:13 | 1:5f |
| truth learnt | | | 3:1 | II.4:2 | II.2:13 | 4:21 | 3:16 |
| | | | | II.6:7 | | 6:14 | |
| | | | | II.7:14 | | | |
| **87. Obey** | 5:9 | 1:5 | 5:7 | II.10:3-6 | II.1:8 | 2:2f | |
| | | 15:18 | | | | 5:6 | |
| | | 16:19 | | | | | |
| **88. Repent** | 6:1,6 | 2:4 | 5:13 | II.7:10 | | 4:22 | 3:9 |
| | 12:1 | | 5:16-21 | | | | |
| **89. Turn to the** | 4:1,11 | 10:12ff | 4:14f | II.3:16 | I.1:9 | 5:19f | 3:16 |
| Lord | | | | II.8:5 | | | |
| invoke Him | | | | I.1:2 | | | |
| **90. Faith begins** | 4:2 | 4:5 | 2:16 | I.1:21 | I.2:13 | 1:13 | 1:23 |
| | 6:1 | 10:9ff | 3:2 | I.3:5 | I.4:14 | 2:8 | 2:5 |
| | 10:22 | 13:11 | | I.15:11 | II.1:10 | 3:12,17 | |
| | 10:39 | 15:13 | | II.13:5 | II.2:12f | 4:5 | |
| | 11:6 | | | | II.3:2 | 4:12f | |
| **91. Confess** | 4:14 | 10:9f | | II.9:13 | I.1:8 | | 4:6 |
| | 10:23 | | | | | | |
| | 13:15 | | | | | | |
| **92. Sprinkled** | 2:11 | 3:28 | 2:16 | I.1:2 | II.2:12 | 1:4 | 1:12 |
| **Cleansed** | 9:13f | 4:3-6 | 3:8 | I.1:30 | II.2:13 | 5:26 | 1:22 |
| **Sanctified** | 10:10,14 | 4:11ff | 3:22ff | I.6:11 | | 6:14 | 1:28 |
| **Justified** | 10:22,29 | 5:9 | | II.3:9 | | | 3:12 |
| | 12:24 | | | II.5:21 | | | |
| | 13:12 | | | | | | |
| **93. Enlightened** | 3:14 | 4:17 | 3:2,5 | I.2:12 | I.5:5 | 1:13,18 | 1:13 |
| **Tasted gift** | 6:4f | 8:9 | 3:11 | I.15:45 | I.5:10 | 2:5 | 2:6,13 |
| **Partook of** | 11:1,3 | 8:16 | 5:24f | II.1:22 | | 5:8,14 | 3:1-4 |
| **Christ, Spirit** | 12:2 | | 6:15 | II.4:6 | | | 3:15 |
| **Quickened** | | | (3:21) | II.5:17 | | | |
| **94. Draw near** | 4:16 | 5:2 | | I.8:8 | | 2:18 | 4:2f |
| | 7:19 | | | | | 3:12 | |
| | 7:25 | | | | | | |
| | 10:1,22 | | | | | | |
| | 11:6 | | | | | | |
| | 12:22ff | | | | | | |
| **95. Forgiven** | 9:22 | 4:7 | | | | 1:7 | 1:14 |
| | 10:18 | 8:1 | | | | 4:32 | 2:13 |
| | | | | | | | 3:13 |

Chart [407

| Phm. | Phil. | Pastorals | James | 1 Pet. | 2 Pet. | Jude | 1 John | Rev. | Acts |
|---|---|---|---|---|---|---|---|---|---|
|  | 3:10 | II.3:15 | 1:21<br>4:12 | 1:5<br>1:23ff<br>2:2 | 1:3<br>1:16 | 24 | 1:3 | 5:12<br>12:10f<br>19:1f | 4:33<br>10:38<br>20:32 |
|  | 3:14 | I.6:12<br>II.1:9<br>II.4:17 | 1:21 | 1:15<br>2:9<br>3:9<br>5:10 | 1:3<br>1:10 | 1 | 3:1f | 2:23<br>3:3<br>3:20<br>17:14<br>19:9 | 2:39<br>19:10 |
|  | 1:5-11 | I.2:4<br>I.4:3<br>II.2:25<br>II.3:7 | 5:19 | 1:14<br>1:22<br>5:12 | 1:12<br>2:2f<br>2:21<br>3:18 |  | 1:8<br>2:20ff<br>3:19 | 3:8<br>14:5 | 2:41<br>14:3f<br>14:21 |
|  |  | Tit.2:12 | 1:22-25 | 1:14<br>3:1<br>4:17 | 2:21 |  | 3:23 | 12:17<br>14:12 | 6:7<br>19:9<br>26:19,29 |
|  |  | II.2:25<br>Tit.2:12 | 1:21<br>4:9f | 1:14<br>2:1 | 3:9 |  | 1:9 | 2:5<br>2:16,21<br>3:3,19<br>9:20f<br>16:9,11 | 2:38<br>11:18<br>20:21<br>26:20 |
|  |  | II.2:19 | 4:8<br>5:19f | 2:4<br>2:25 |  |  | 2:28<br>3:6 | 2:14,20<br>5:8 | 2:21<br>9:35<br>11:21<br>14:15 |
| 5f | 1:25<br>1:27ff<br>2:17<br>3:9 | I.3:16<br>I.5:12<br>II.1:12<br>Tit.1:4 | 1:3<br>1:6ff<br>2:1<br>2:19f | 1:7ff<br>1:21<br>4:19<br>5:9 | 1:1 | 3<br>5<br>20 | 3:23 | 2:13,19<br>14:12 | 2:44<br>4:4<br>14:1<br>19:2<br>20:21 |
|  | 2:11 | I.6:12<br>Tit.1:16 | 2:7 | 3:15 |  | 4 | 2:23<br>4:15 | 2:13<br>3:8 | 9:19f |
| 5<br>7 | 3:9<br>4:21f | II.1:9<br>II.2:21<br>Tit.2:14<br>Tit.3:5,7 | 2:22ff | 1:2<br>1:22 | 2:20<br>1:9 | 20<br>24 | 1:7<br>1:9<br>4:17 | 7:14<br>22:14<br>3:18<br>12:10f | 15:9<br>20:32<br>26:18<br>13:38f |
| 10<br>19 | 1:19<br>1:21<br>2:1<br>2:13<br>2:15f | II.1:1<br>II.1:7<br>II.1:9f<br>II.1:14<br>Tit.3:5f | 1:18<br>4:10 | 1:3,23<br>2:3<br>2:5<br>2:9<br>3:7,15 | 1:3f<br>1:19 | 19ff | 1:5ff<br>3:9,24<br>4:7,13ff<br>5:1<br>5:11f | 2:7<br>3:1f,5,20<br>7:17<br>21:6<br>22:17 | 5:32<br>9:17f<br>13:46ff<br>26:18 |
| 22 | 1:9<br>4:6 | I.2:1ff<br>I.2:8<br>I.5:5<br>II.2:19 | 4:8 | 2:4<br>3:18 |  | 20 | 2:5f<br>3:21f<br>5:14f | 1:6<br>5:10<br>22:17 | 9:11 |
|  |  |  | 5:15 |  |  |  | 1:9<br>2:12 |  | 5:31<br>10:43<br>13:38f<br>26:18 |

| | Heb. | Rom. | Gal. | 1 & 2 Cor. | 1 & 2 Thess. | Eph. | Col. |
|---|---|---|---|---|---|---|---|
| **96. Received by God** | 4:16 7:25 10:19 10:35 | 14:3 15:7 | 1:6 | II.6:17 | I.1:1 II.1:1 | 2:6 2:13 | 3:3 |
| **97. Adopted** | 2:10ff 12:4-10 | 8:14f | 3:26 4:5ff | II.6:18 | I.1:3 I.3:11ff II.1:1 II.2:16 | 1:5 5:1 | 1:13 2:6 3:3 3:16 |
| **98. Permanent relationship established** | 10:34 13:5f | 5:1f 5:21 6:15,23 8:26,31 | 1:3 3:5 5:5,8 6:16 | I.1:8f I.3:16f II.4:14 II.13:13 | I.1:4,10 I.4:17 I.5:23f II.2:16 | 1:13f 4:13-16 5:29 | 1:5 3:17 |
| **99. Salvation** | 2:3f 5:9 9:28 | 5:9f 8:24 11:11,14 | | I.1:21 I.9:22 II.6:2 | I.2:16 I.5:8f II.2:13 | 2:5,8 5:23 6:17 | |
| **100. Certainty** | 10:23,35 12:6 | 5:1-11 8:28,38f | 6:14f | I.6:2f II.5:1 | I.4:18 II.1:10 | 3:12,18f 6:16 | 1:6,10f 1:27 |
| **101. Discipleship begun** | 12:4-11 | 12:1f | 1:10 5:6 | I.2:6 I.7:32 | I.1:3 II.1:11f | 4:17,20 5:15 | 1:13 3:24 |

Chart [409

| Phm. | Phil. | Pastorals | James | 1 Pet. | 2 Pet. | Jude | 1 John | Rev. | Acts |
|---|---|---|---|---|---|---|---|---|---|
| 22 | 3:15<br>3:20<br>4:3 | I.3:15<br>II.2:15<br>II.2:19 | 2:23<br>4:6<br>4:8 | 2:5,9<br>3:7<br>3:12<br>3:18 | 2:9 | 1 | 2:24<br>4:15f | 7:14f<br>21:3<br>22:3 | 10:35,43ff<br>11:14-17<br>14:27<br>15:7ff |
| 3 | 2:15<br>4:20 | I.1:2<br>I.6:2<br>II.4:21<br>Tit.1:4 | 2:5 | 1:17 | 1:10<br>3:15 | 1 | 3:1f<br>3:10 | 21:7 | 2:33<br>13:9f<br>18:18 |
| 15f<br>22 | 1:6<br>3:14<br>3:20f<br>4:19 | I.6:17ff<br>II.1:12<br>II.2:1<br>II.4:8 | 1:3,12<br>2:5 | 1:2<br>2:24f<br>5:14 | 3:18 | 2 | 2:17<br>3:2<br>5:18ff | 3:10 | 3:19ff<br>14:22f<br>15:36<br>21:16 |
| | 1:19<br>1:28<br>2:12 | I.1:15<br>II.2:10<br>II.3:15 | 1:21<br>4:12<br>5:20 | 1:5<br>1:9<br>2:2 | 1:11<br>3:15 | 3<br>23<br>25 | 4:14 | 7:10<br>12:10<br>19:1 | 4:12<br>14:9<br>16:31 |
| 3<br>25 | 1:23<br>4:13 | II.1:7-12<br>II.3:14 | 1:5<br>4:6f | 1:3-9<br>5:6f,10 | 1:10f<br>3:18 | 1<br>21 | 4:16<br>5:13 | 3:9 | 7:59f<br>20:17-38 |
| 1f | 1:9ff<br>1:27 | I.6:11f<br>II.4:7 | 1:1<br>2:1 | 1:15<br>2:21 | 3:11 | 3<br>17 | 2:6<br>3:3 | 2:4f | 6:1,7<br>14:21ff |

# Bibliography

Alford, Henry. *The Greek Testament*. London, Oxford, and Cambridge: Rivingtons; Cambridge: Deighton, Bell. Vol. 1, 6th ed., 1868; vol. 2, 6th ed., 1871; vol. 3, 4th ed., 1865; vol. 4; 3d ed., 1866.

Allen, Leslie C. "The Old Testament Background of *(pro)horizein* in the New Testament." *New Testament Studies* 17, no. 1 (October 1970): 104–8.

Allison, C. F. *The Rise of Moralism: The Proclamation of the Gospel from Hooker to Baxter*. London: SPCK, 1966.

Althaus, Paul. *Der Brief an die Römer. Das Neue Testament Deutsch*, vol. 6. 10th ed. Göttingen: Vandenhoeck & Ruprecht, 1966.

Althaus, Paul, et al. *Die kleineren Briefe des Apostels Paulus. Das Neue Testament Deutsch*, vol. 8. 11th rev. ed. Göttingen: Vandenhoeck & Ruprecht, 1965.

Althaus, Paul. See Beyer, H. W.

Barclay, William. *Ethics in a Permissive Society*. London: Collins, 1971; New York: Harper & Row, 1972.

——. *The King and the Kingdom*. Edinburgh: Saint Andrew Press; Philadelphia: Westminster Press, 1969.

Barr, James. *Biblical Words for Time*. 2d rev. ed. London: SCM Press; Naperville, Ill., 1969.

——. *The Semantics of Biblical Language*. Oxford: Oxford University Press, 1961.

——. "Trends and Prospects in Biblical Theology." *The Journal of Theological Studies*, New Series, vol. 25 part 2 (Oct. 1974): 270–71.

Barrett, C. K. *A Commentary on the Epistle to the Romans*. London: Adam & Charles Black, 1957; New York: Harper & Row, 1958.

——. *The Gospel According to St. John*. London: SPCK; Naperville, Ill., 1955.

——. *The New Testament Background: Selected Documents*. London: SPCK; New York: Harper & Row, 1956.

——. "Paul's Opponents in II Corinthians." *New Testament Studies* 17, no. 3 (April 1971): 238, 251.

Barth, Karl. *Church Dogmatics. Vol. 4. The Doctrine of Reconciliation*. Edinburgh: T. & T. Clark; Naperville, Ill., 1956.

Bauer, Walter. *Orthodoxy and Heresy in Earliest Christianity*. Philadelphia: Fortress Press, 1971.

Beare, F. W. *A Commentary on the Epistle to the Philippians*. London: Adam

& Charles Black, 1959. (The 2d. ed. is also published by Allenson, Naperville, Ill., 1969.)

————. *First Epistle of St. Peter.* Oxford: Basil Blackwell, 1947.

Beasley-Murray, G. R. *Baptism in the New Testament.* London: Macmillan & Co.; New York: St. Martin's Press, 1962; Grand Rapids: Wm. B. Eerdmans, 1973.

————. *The Book of Revelation.* New Century Bible. Greenwood, S. C.: Attic Press; London: Oliphants, 1974.

Best, Ernest. *One Body in Christ.* London: SPCK, 1955.

Beyer, H. W. "Der Brief an die Galater." Revised by Paul Althaus. In Paul Althaus, et al., *Die kleineren Briefe des Apostels Paulus.*

Bigg, Charles. *A Critical and Exegetical Commentary on the Epistles of St. Peter and St. Jude.* International Critical Commentary. Reprint. Edinburgh: T. & T. Clark, 1910; Naperville, Ill.: Allenson.

Black, Matthew. *Romans.* New Century Bible. London: Oliphants; Greenwood, S.C.: Attic Press, 1973.

Blass, F. and Debrunner, A. *A Greek Grammar of the New Testament and Other Early Christian Literature.* Translated and revised by Robert W. Funk. Chicago: University of Chicago Press, 1961.

Bonhoeffer, Dietrich. *Letters and Papers from Prison.* Rev. ed. London: Collins, Fontana Books; New York: Macmillan, 1967.

Boobyer, G. H. *St. Mark and the Transfiguration Story.* Edinburgh: T. & T. Clark, 1942.

Bouquet, A. C. *Everyday Life in New Testament Times.* London: B. T. Batsford; New York: Charles Scribner's Sons, 1953.

Briggs, Charles Augustus, and Briggs, Emilie Grace. *A Critical and Exegetical Commentary on the Book of Psalms.* International Critical Commentary. 2 vols. Edinburgh: T. & T. Clark; 1927, 1925. Naperville, Ill.: Allenson.

Brooke, A. E. *A Critical and Exegetical Commentary on the Johannine Epistles.* International Critical Commentary. Reprint. Edinburgh: T. & T. Clark, 1957; Naperville, Ill.: Allenson.

Brown, Francis; Driver, S. R.; and Briggs, Charles A. *A Hebrew and English Lexicon of the Old Testament.* Boston and New York: Houghton Mifflin, 1906.

Bruce, F. F. *The Acts of the Apostles: The Greek Text with Introduction and Commentary.* London: Tyndale Press, 1951; Grand Rapids: Wm. B. Eerdmans, 1953.

————. *Commentary on the Epistle to the Hebrews.* London & Edinburgh: Marshall, Morgan & Scott; Grand Rapids: Wm. B. Eerdmans, 1964.

————. *The Epistle of Paul to the Romans.* Tyndale New Testament Commentaries. London: Tyndale Press; Grand Rapids: Wm. B. Eerdmans, 1963.

————. *An Expanded Paraphrase of the Epistles of Paul.* Exeter: Paternoster Press, 1965.

————. *This Is That: The New Testament Development of Some Old Testament Themes.* Exeter: Paternoster Press, 1976.

Bruce, F. F. See Simpson, E. K., jt. author.

Brunner, Emil. *The Christian Doctrine of Creation and Redemption. Dogmatics,* vol. 2. London: Lutterworth Press; Philadelphia: Westminster Press, 1952.

————. *The Christian Doctrine of God. Dogmatics,* vol. 1. London: Lutterworth Press, 1949; Philadelphia: Westminster Press, 1950.

————. *Eternal Hope.* Translated by Harold Knight. London: Lutterworth Press; Philadelphia: Westminster Press, 1954.

————. *The Mediator.* London: Lutterworth Press, 1934; Philadelphia: Westminster Press, 1947.

Bultmann, Rudolf. *Theology of the New Testament*. 2 vols. London: SCM Press, 1965; New York: Charles Scribner's Sons, 1970.

Cabaniss, Allen. "The Gospel According to Paul," *Evangelical Quarterly* 48, no. 3 (July-Sept. 1976): 164–67.

Cabasilas, Nicholas. *The Life in Christ*. Translated by C. J. de Catanzaro. New York: St. Vladimir's Seminary Press, 1974.

Caird, G. B. *The Apostolic Age*. London: Gerald Duckworth; Naperville, Ill.: Allenson, 1955.

————. *A Commentary on the Revelation of St. John the Divine*. Black's New Testament Commentaries. London: Adam & Charles Black; New York: Harper & Row, 1966.

Carrington, Philip. *The Primitive Christian Catechism*. Cambridge: University Press, 1940.

Charles, R. H. *The Apocrypha and Pseudepigrapha of the Old Testament*. 2 vols. Oxford: Clarendon Press, 1913.

————. *A Critical and Exegetical Commentary on the Revelation of St. John*. International Critical Commentary. 2 vols. New York: Charles Scribner's Sons, 1920. Reprint ed., Naperville, Ill.: Allenson.

Clapperton, J. Alexander. *The Essentials of Theology*. 2d ed. London: Epworth Press, 1924.

Coenen, Lothar; Beyreuther, Erich; and Bietenhard, Hans, eds. *Theologisches Begriffslexikon zum Neuen Testament*. 13 vols. Wuppertal: R. Brockhaus Verlag, 1966–71.

Cole, R. A. *The Epistle of Paul to the Galatians*. Tyndale New Testament Commentaries. London: Tyndale Press, 1965.

Conzelmann, Hans. "Der Brief an die Kolosser." In Paul Althaus, et al., *Die kleineren Briefe des Apostels Paulus*.

————. "Der Brief an die Epheser." In Paul Althaus, et al., *Die kleineren Briefe des Apostels Paulus*.

Cope, Edward Meredith. *The Rhetoric of Aristotle: With a Commentary*. 3 vols. Edited and revised by John Edwin Sandys. Cambridge: University Press, 1877. Reprint ed. New York: Irvington Pubns.

Cranfield, C. E. B. *A Critical and Exegetical Commentary on the Epistle to the Romans*. Vol. 1, Romans 1–8, International Critical Commentary. Edinburgh: T. & T. Clark; Naperville, Ill.: Allenson, 1975.

————. *The Gospel According to Saint Mark*. Cambridge: University Press, 1959.

Cross, F. L., ed. *The Oxford Dictionary of the Christian Church*. London: Oxford University Press, 1957.

————, ed. *Studies in Ephesians*. London: A. R. Mowbray, 1956.

Cullmann, Oscar. *The Christology of the New Testament*. London: SCM Press, 1959.

Dale, R. W. *The Atonement*. 27th ed. London: Congregational Union of England & Wales, 1924.

Dalman, Gustaf. *The Words of Jesus*. Edinburgh: T. & T. Clark, 1909.

Davidson, A. B. *The Epistle to the Hebrews*. Edinburgh: T. & T. Clark, n.d.

————. *Hebrew Syntax*. 2d ed. Edinburgh: T. & T. Clark, 1896.

————. *The Theology of the Old Testament*. International Theological Library. New York: Charles Scribner's Sons, 1904.

Davies, W. D. *Paul and Rabbinic Judaism: Some Rabbinic Elements in Pauline Theology*. London: SPCK; New York: Seabury Press, 1955.

Deissmann, Adolf. *Bible Studies*. 2d ed. Edinburgh: T. & T. Clark, 1909.

————. *Light from the Ancient East*. London: Hodder & Stoughton, 1910; New York: Harper & Bros., 1927.

Delitzsch, F. *Biblical Commentary on the Prophecies of Isaiah*. 2 vols. Edinburgh: T. & T. Clark, 1890.

Denney, James. *The Christian Doctrine of Reconciliation*. London: Hodder and Stoughton, 1917; Naperville, Ill.: Allenson.

——. *The Death of Christ: Its Place and Interpretation in the New Testament*. London: Hodder and Stoughton, 1909. (A revised edition, edited by R. V. G. Tasker, was published by Inter-Varsity, London, Chicago, in 1951.)

Dibelius, Martin. *Der Brief des Jakobus*. Meyer's Critical-Exegetical Commentary. 11th ed. Göttingen: Vandenhoeck & Ruprecht, 1964.

Dodd, C. H. *The Apostolic Preaching and Its Developments*. London: Hodder and Stoughton, 1963.

——. *The Epistle of Paul to the Romans*. The Moffatt New Testament Commentary. London: Hodder and Stoughton, 1934.

——. *Gospel and Law: The Relation of Faith and Ethics in Early Christianity*. New York: Columbia University Press, 1951.

——. *Historical Tradition in the Fourth Gospel*. Cambridge: University Press, 1963.

——. *The Johannine Epistles*. Moffatt New Testament Commentary. London: Hodder and Stoughton; New York: Harper & Row, 1946.

Dods, Marcus. "The Epistle to the Hebrews." In *The Expositor's Greek Testament*, vol. 4, edited by W. Robertson Nicoll, 5 vols.

Douglas, J. D., ed. *The New Bible Dictionary*. Grand Rapids: Wm. B. Eerdmans, 1962.

Driver, S. R. *The Book of Genesis*. 5th ed. London: Methuen, 1906.

——. *A Critical and Exegetical Commentary on Deuteronomy*. International Critical Commentary. Edinburgh: T. & T. Clark; Naperville, Ill.: Allenson, 1902.

Dunn, James D. G. *Baptism in the Holy Spirit*. London: SCM Press; Naperville, Ill.: Allenson, 1970.

Eccles, (Lord). *Half-way to Faith*. London: Geoffrey Bles, 1966.

Ellis, E. Earle. *The Gospel of Luke*. The Century Bible, New Edition. London: Nelson; New York: Attic Press, 1966.

——. *Paul and His Recent Interpreters*. Grand Rapids: Wm. B. Eerdmans, 1961.

——. *Paul's Use of the Old Testament*. Edinburgh and London: Oliver and Boyd, 1957.

Evans, Percy W. *The Cross as a Tree*. London and Edinburgh: Marshall, Morgan & Scott, 1946.

Evans, Owen E. "The Saints." *The Expository Times* 86, no. 7 (April 1975): 196–200.

Fairweather, Eugene R. "The 'Kenotic' Christology." An appended note to F. W. Beare, *A Commentary on the Epistle to the Philippians*. pp. 159–74.

Farrer, A. M. *A Rebirth of Images*. Westminster: Dacre Press, 1949; Boston: Beacon Press, 1963.

Filson, Floyd V. *A Commentary on the Gospel According to St. Matthew*. Black's New Testament Commentaries. London: Adam & Charles Black, 1960; Naperville, Ill.: Allenson, 1971.

Forsyth, P. T. *The Cruciality of the Cross*. London: Hodder & Stoughton, 1909.

——. *The Person and Place of Jesus Christ*. London: Congregational Union of England and Wales; and Hodder & Stoughton, 1909; reprint, Grand Rapids: Wm. B. Eerdmans, 1964.

——. *Positive Preaching and the Modern Mind*. London: Independent Press, 1964.

414]                          Bibliography

Frame, James Everett. *A Critical and Exegetical Commentary on the Epistles of St. Paul to the Thessalonians.* International Critical Commentary. Edinburgh: T. &. T. Clark, 1966; Naperville, Ill.: Allenson.

Friedrich, Gerhard. "Der Brief an die Philipper." In Paul Althaus, et al., *Die kleineren Briefe des Apostels Paulus.*

Gasque, W. Ward, and Martin, Ralph P., eds. *Apostolic History and the Gospel: Biblical and Historical Essays Presented to F. F. Bruce on His 60th Birthday.* Exeter: Paternoster Press; Grand Rapids: Wm. B. Eerdmans, 1970.

George, A.; Mollat, D.; et al. *Baptism in the New Testament: A Symposium.* London: Geoffrey Chapman, 1964.

Goodspeed, Edgar J. *The Key to Ephesians.* Chicago: University of Chicago Press, 1956.

————. *The New Testament: An American Translation.* Chicago: University of Chicago Press, 1923.

Goodwin, William W. *A Greek Grammar.* Reprint. London: Macmillan and Co., 1924; New York: St. Martin.

————. *Syntax of the Moods and Tenses of the Greek Verb.* London: Macmillan and Co., 1889; New York: St. Martin.

Grant, R. M. *Gnosticism and Early Christianity.* Rev. ed. New York: Harper & Row, 1966.

Green, Michael. *Evangelism in the Early Church.* London: Hodder and Stoughton, 1970; Grand Rapids: Wm. B. Eerdmans, 1975.

————. *I Believe in the Holy Spirit.* London: Hodder & Stoughton; Grand Rapids: Wm. B. Eerdmans, 1975.

————. *The Second Epistle General of Peter and the General Epistle of Jude.* Tyndale New Testament Commentaries. Grand Rapids: Wm. B. Eerdmans, 1968.

Griffith, Gwylim Oswald. *St. Paul's Gospel to the Romans.* Oxford: Basil Blackwell, 1949.

Guilding, Aileen. *The Fourth Gospel and Jewish Worship: A Study of the Relation of St. John's Gospel to the Ancient Jewish Lectionary System.* Oxford: Clarendon Press, 1960.

Guthrie, Donald. *Galatians.* The Century Bible, New Series. London: Nelson; New York: Attic Press, 1969.

————. *New Testament Introduction: The Gospels and Acts.* London: Tyndale Press; Chicago: Inter-Varsity Press, 1964.

————. *New Testament Introduction: Hebrews to Revelation.* London: Tyndale Press; Chicago: Inter-Varsity Press, 1962.

————. *New Testament Introduction: The Pauline Epistles.* London: Tyndale Press; Chicago: Inter-Varsity Press, 1961.

————. *The Pastoral Epistles.* Tyndale New Testament Commentaries. Grand Rapids: Wm. B. Eerdmans, 1964.

Guthrie, Donald, and Motyer, J. A., eds. *The New Bible Commentary Revised.* London: Inter-Varsity Press; Grand Rapids: Wm. B. Eerdmans, 1970.

Haenchen, Ernst. *The Acts of the Apostles: A Commentary.* Oxford: Basil Blackwell; Philadelphia: Westminster, 1971.

Hanson, Anthony Tyrrell. *The Wrath of the Lamb.* London: SPCK; Naperville, Ill.: Allenson, 1957.

Hardon, John A. *Christianity in the Twentieth Century.* New York: Doubleday and Co., 1971.

Harrison, Everett F. *Introduction to the New Testament.* Grand Rapids: Wm. B. Eerdmans, 1956.

Harrison P. N. *The Problem of the Pastoral Epistles.* Oxford: Oxford University Press, 1921.

Harrison R. K. *Introduction to the Old Testament.* Grand Rapids: Wm. B. Eerdmans, 1969.

Hatch, E. and Redpath, H. A. *A Concordance to the Septuagint.* 2 vols. Graz, Austria: Akademische Druck-u. Verlagsanstalt, 1954.

Henry, Carl F. H. *God, Revelation and Authority.* 2 vols. Waco, Texas: Word Books, 1976.

Héring, Jean. *The Epistle to the Hebrews.* London: Epworth Press; Naperville, Ill.: Allenson, 1970.

Hill, David. *Greek Words and Hebrew Meanings: Studies in the Semantics of Soteriological Terms.* Cambridge: University Press, 1967.

————. "Prophecy and Prophets in the Revelation of St. John." *New Testament Studies* 18, no. 4 (July 1972): 401–418.

Hodge, Alexander. *Prayer and Its Psychology.* London: SPCK, 1931.

Holladay, William L. *A Concise Hebrew and Aramaic Lexicon of the Old Testament: Based upon the Lexical Work of Ludwig Koehler and Walter Baumgartner.* Leiden: E. J. Brill; Grand Rapids: Wm. B. Eerdmans, 1971.

Hooker, Richard. *Of the Laws of Ecclesiastical Polity.* Everyman's Library. 2 vols. London: J. M. Dent & Sons; New York: E. P. Dutton, 1958.

Hoskyns, Edwyn Clement. *The Fourth Gospel.* 2d rev. ed. Edited by Francis Noel Davey. London: Faber and Faber, 1947; Naperville, Ill.: Allenson, 1956.

Howard, Wilbert Francis. *The Fourth Gospel in Recent Criticism and Interpretation.* 4th rev. ed. London: Epworth Press; Naperville, Ill.: Allenson, 1955.

Howard, Wilbert Francis. See Moulton, James Hope.

Hughes, Philip Edgcumbe. *Paul's Second Epistle to the Corinthians.* New International Commentary. Grand Rapids: Wm. B. Eerdmans, 1962.

Hunter, A. M. *Interpreting Paul's Gospel.* London: SCM Press, 1954; Philadelphia: Westminster Press, 1955.

————. *Introducing the New Testament.* 2d ed., reprint. London: SCM Press, 1965; Philadelphia: Westminster Press, 1968.

————. *Paul and His Predecessors.* London: Nicholson and Watson, 1940. Rev. ed. Philadelphia: Westminster Press, 1961.

————. *The Unity of the New Testament.* London: SCM Press, 1943.

Jackson, F. J. Foakes, and Lake, Kirsopp, eds. *The Beginnings of Christianity: Prolegomena II and Criticism.* Vol. 2. London: Macmillan and Co., 1922.

Jeremias, Joachim. *The Central Message of the New Testament.* London: SCM Press; New York: Charles Scribner's Sons, 1965.

————. *The Eucharistic Words of Jesus.* Oxford: Basil Blackwell, 1955; New York: Charles Scribner's Sons, 1966.

————. *New Testament Theology: Part One, The Proclamation of Jesus.* London: SCM Press; New York: Charles Scribner's Sons, 1971.

————. *The Parables of Jesus.* London: SCM Press, 1954.

————. *Unknown Sayings of Jesus.* London: SPCK, 1957.

————. "Paulus als Hillelit." In *Neotestamentica et Semitica: Studies in Honour of Matthew Black,* edited by E. Earle Ellis and Max Wilcox. Edinburgh: T. & T. Clark, 1969.

————. *Die Briefe an Timotheus und Titus.* In *Das Neue Testament Deutsch,* vol. 9. 8th rev. ed. Göttingen: Vandenhoeck & Ruprecht, 1963.

Jocz, Jakob. *The Spiritual History of Israel.* London: Eyre & Spottiswoode; Naperville, Ill.: Allenson, 1961.

————. *A Theology of Election: Israel and the Church.* London: SPCK; New York: The Macmillan Co., 1958.

Johnson, Aubrey R. *The Vitality of the Individual in the Thought of Ancient Israel.* Cardiff: University of Wales Press, 1949.

416] Bibliography

Käsemann, E. "The Problem of a New Testament Theology." *New Testament Studies* 19, no. 3 (April 1973): 235–45.

Kelly, J. N. D. *A Commentary on the Pastoral Epistles.* Black's New Testament Commentaries. London: Adam & Charles Black, 1963.

Kennedy, H. A. A. "The Epistle to the Philippians." In *The Expositor's Greek Testament,* edited by W. Robertson Nicoll.

Kidner, Derek. *Genesis: An Introduction and Commentary.* London: Tyndale Press, 1967; Chicago: Inter-Varsity Press, 1968.

———. *The Proverbs.* Tyndale Old Testament Commentaries. London: Tyndale Press; Chicago: Inter-Varsity Press, 1964.

Kirk, J. Andrew. "Apostleship since Rengstorf: Towards a Synthesis." *New Testament Studies* 21 (1975): 249–64.

Kittel, Gerhard and Friedrich, Gerhard, eds. *Theological Dictionary of the New Testament.* 9 vols. Grand Rapids: Wm. B. Eerdmans, 1964–1973.

Knowling, R. J. *The Testimony of St. Paul to Christ.* London: Hodder and Stoughton, 1905.

Kümmel, Werner Georg. *Introduction to the New Testament.* London: SCM Press; New York and Nashville: Abingdon Press, 1966.

———. *The Theology of the New Testament.* Nashville and New York: Abingdon Press, 1973.

Küng, Hans. *Justification: The Doctrine of Karl Barth and a Catholic Reflection.* New York: Thomas Nelson & Sons, 1964; London: Burns & Oates.

Ladd, George Eldon. *A Commentary on the Revelation of John.* Grand Rapids: Wm. B. Eerdmans, 1972.

———. *Jesus and the Kingdom: The Eschatology of Biblical Realism.* London: SPCK, 1966.

———. *A Theology of the New Testament.* Grand Rapids: Wm. B. Eerdmans, 1974.

Lagrange, M. J. *Épître aux Romains. Études Bibliques.* Paris: J. Gabalda et Cie, 1950.

Law, Robert. *The Tests of Life: A Study of the First Epistle of John.* Edinburgh: T. & T. Clark, 1909; reprint ed., Grand Rapids: Baker Book House, 1968.

Leaney, A. R. C. *A Commentary on the Gospel According to St. Luke.* Black's New Testament Commentaries. London: Adam & Charles Black; Naperville, Ill.: Allenson, 1958.

Liddell, Henry G. and Scott, Robert. *Greek-English Lexicon.* 2 vols. 9th ed. London and New York: Oxford University Press, 1940.

Liddon, H. P. *Forty Sermons: On Various Subjects.* First Series. London: Charles Higham, 1886.

Lightfoot, J. B. *Notes on Epistles of St. Paul: From Unpublished Commentaries.* 2d ed. London: Macmillan & Co., 1904.

———. *St. Paul's Epistles to the Colossians and to Philemon.* 2d ed. London: Macmillan and Co., 1876. Reprint ed. Grand Rapids: Zondervan Publishing House, 1957.

———. *Saint Paul's Epistle to the Philippians.* London: Macmillan and Co., 1885. Reprint ed., Grand Rapids: Zondervan Publishing House, 1957.

Lightfoot, R. H. *The Gospel Message of St. Mark.* Oxford: Clarendon Press, 1950.

———. *St. John's Gospel: A Commentary.* Edited by C. F. Evans. Oxford: Clarendon Press; New York: Oxford University Press, 1956.

Lincoln, A. T. "A Re-Examination of 'the Heavenlies' in Ephesians." *New Testament Studies* 19 (1973): 468–83.

Löwenstein, Prince Hubertus zu. *Towards the Further Shore*. London: Victor Gollancz, 1968.

Mackintosh, H. R. *The Christian Experience of Forgiveness*. London: Nisbet, 1927.

——. *The Doctrine of the Person of Jesus Christ*. Edinburgh: T. & T. Clark, 1931.

Manson, T. W. *The Sayings of Jesus*. London: SCM Press, 1954.

——. *The Teaching of Jesus: Studies of Its Form and Content*. Cambridge: University Press, 1951.

Manson, William. *Jesus and the Christian*. Grand Rapids: Wm. B. Eerdmans, 1967.

Marsh, John. *The Gospel of St. John*. Pelican New Testament Commentaries. Harmondsworth, Middlesex: Penguin, 1968.

Marshall, I. Howard. *Kept by the Power of God: A Study of Perseverance and Falling Away*. London: Epworth Press, 1969; Minneapolis: Bethany Fellowship, 1974.

——. *Luke: Historian and Theologian*. Exeter: Paternoster Press, 1970; Grand Rapids: Zondervan, 1971.

Marshall, L. H. *The Challenge of New Testament Ethics*. London: Macmillan & Co.; New York: Martins, 1946.

Martin, Ralph P. *Carmen Christi: Philippians 2:5–11 in Recent Interpretation and in the Setting of Early Christian Worship*. Cambridge: University Press, 1967.

——. *The Epistle of Paul to the Philippians*. Tyndale Bible Commentaries. Grand Rapids: Wm. B. Eerdmans, 1965.

——. *Worship in the Early Church*. London and Edinburgh: Marshall, Morgan and Scott, 1964; Old Tappan, N. J.: Fleming H. Revell, 1965.

Mayor, Joseph B. *The Epistle of St. James*. 3d ed. London: Macmillan and Co., 1913.

Michel, Otto. *Der Brief an die Hebräer*. Göttingen: Vandenhoeck & Ruprecht, 1966.

——. *Der Brief an die Römer*. 13th ed. Göttingen: Vandenhoeck & Ruprecht, 1966.

Milligan, George. *St. Paul's Epistles to the Thessalonians*. London: Macmillan and Co., 1908.

Mitton, C. Leslie. *The Epistle of James*. London and Edinburgh: Marshall, Morgan & Scott; Grand Rapids: Wm. B. Eerdmans, 1966.

——. *The Epistle to the Ephesians: Its Authorship, Origin and Purpose*. Oxford: Clarendon Press, 1951.

M'Neile, Alan Hugh. *The Gospel According to St. Matthew*. Reprint. London: Macmillan and Co., 1938.

Moberly, R. C. *Atonement and Personality*. Reprint. London: John Murray, 1932.

Moffatt, James. *A Critical and Exegetical Commentary on the Epistle to the Hebrews*. International Critical Commentary. Edinburgh: T. & T. Clark; Naperville, Ill.: Allenson, 1924.

——. *The New Testament: A New Translation*. New York: Harper & Row; London: Hodder & Stoughton, 1964.

Moore, A. L. *1 and 2 Thessalonians*. The Century Bible, New Series. London: Nelson; Greenwood, S.C.: Attic Press, 1969.

Morris, Leon. *The Apostolic Preaching of the Cross*. London: Tyndale Press, 1955; Grand Rapids: Wm. B. Eerdmans, 1956.

——. *The Cross in the New Testament*. Grand Rapids: Wm. B. Eerdmans, 1965.

———. *The First Epistle of Paul to the Corinthians.* Tyndale New Testament Commentaries. Reprint. London: Tyndale Press; Grand Rapids: Wm. B. Eerdmans, 1964.

———. *The Gospel According to John.* New International. Grand Rapids: Wm. B. Eerdmans, 1971.

———. *The Revelation of St. John.* Tyndale New Testament Commentaries. London: Tyndale Press, 1969.

Motyer, J. A. "Idolatry." In *The New Bible Dictionary,* edited by J. D. Douglas. Grand Rapids: Wm. B. Eerdmans, 1962.

Moule, C. F. D. *The Epistles of Paul the Apostle to the Colossians and to Philemon.* Cambridge: University Press, 1957.

———. *An Idiom Book of New Testament Greek.* 2d ed. Cambridge: University Press, 1959.

———. *The Phenomenon of the New Testament.* London: SCM Press; Naperville, Ill.: Allenson, 1967.

Moulton, James Hope. *A Grammar of New Testament Greek.* Vol. 1. *Prolegomena.* 3d ed. Edinburgh: T. & T. Clark, 1919.

———. *A Grammar of New Testament Greek.* Vol. 2. Moulton, James Hope and Howard, Wilbert Francis. *Accidence and Word-Formation.* Reprint. Edinburgh: T. & T. Clark; Naperville, Ill.: Allenson, 1960.

———. *A Grammar of New Testament Greek.* Vol. 3. Turner, Nigel. *Syntax.* Edinburgh: T. & T. Clark; Naperville, Ill.: Allenson, 1963.

———. *A Grammar of New Testament Greek.* Vol. 4. Turner, Nigel. *Style.* Edinburgh, T. & T. Clark; Naperville, Ill.: Allenson, 1976.

Moulton, James Hope, and Milligan, George. *The Vocabulary of the Greek New Testament.* Grand Rapids: Wm. B. Eerdmans, 1949.

Moulton, W. F., and Geden, A. S. *A Concordance to the Greek Testament.* 4th rev. ed., reprint. Revised by H. K. Moulton. Edinburgh: T. & T. Clark, 1967.

Mowinckel, Sigmund. *He That Cometh.* Translated by G. W. Anderson. Oxford: Basil Blackwell; New York: Abingdon Press, 1956.

Mozley, J. K. *The Doctrine of the Atonement.* London: Duckworth, 1927.

Muilenburg, James. *The Way of Israel: Biblical Faith and Ethics.* New York: Harper & Row, 1961.

Murray, John. *The Epistle to the Romans.* New International Commentary. 2 vols. Grand Rapids: Wm. B. Eerdmans, 1959, 1965.

———. *Redemption: Accomplished and Applied.* Grand Rapids: Wm. B. Eerdmans, 1955; London: Banner of Truth Trust, 1961.

Mussner, Franz. *Der Jakobusbrief.* Freiburg, Basel, Vienna: Herder, 1964.

Neill, Stephen. *Anglicanism.* London: Penguin Books, Pelican, 1958.

———. *The Interpretation of the New Testament 1861–1961.* London: Oxford University Press, 1964.

Nestle, Erwin, and Aland, Kurt, eds. *Novum Testamentum Graece.* 25th ed. Stuttgart: Württembergische Bibelanstalt, 1963.

Nettleship, Richard Lewis. *Lectures on the Republic of Plato.* 2d ed., reprint. London: Macmillan and Co., 1937.

Nicole, Roger. "'Hilaskesthai' Revisited," *Evangelical Quarterly* 49, no. 3 (July–Sept. 1977): 173–77.

Nicoll, W. Robertson. *The Church's One Foundation: Christ and Recent Criticism.* London: Hodder and Stoughton, 1902.

Nicoll, W. Robertson, ed. *The Expositor's Greek Testament.* 5 vols. London: Hodder & Stoughton, 1897–1910. Reprint ed. Grand Rapids: Wm. B. Eerdmans, 1952.

Nineham, D. E., ed. *Studies in the Gospels. Essays in Memory of Robert H. Lightfoot.* Oxford: Basil Blackwell; Naperville, Ill.: Allenson, 1955.

Nygren, Anders. *Agape and Eros.* Part 1. London: SPCK, 1932; New York: Harper & Row, 1969.

Oepke, Albrecht. "Die Briefe an die Thessalonicher." In Paul Althaus, et al., *Die kleineren Briefe des Apostels Paulus.*

Oesterley, W. O. E, and Robinson, Theodore H. *Hebrew Religion: Its Origin and Development.* 2d rev. ed. reprint. London: SPCK, 1944.

Ottley, Robert L. *The Doctrine of the Incarnation.* 8th ed. London: Methuen 1946.

Packer, J. I. *Knowing God.* London: Hodder & Stoughton; Downers Grove, Ill.: Inter-Varsity Press, 1973.

————. "What Did the Cross Achieve? The Logic of Penal Substitution." *Tyndale Bulletin* 25 (1974): 3–45.

Payne, D. F. *Semitisms in the Book of Acts. Apostolic History and the Gospel.* Edited by W. Ward Gasque, et al., pp. 134–50.

Peake, A. S. *Hebrews.* The Century Bible, old edition. Edinburgh and London: T. C. & E. C. Jack.

Pearson, John. *An Exposition of the Creed.* London: George Bell & Sons, 1893. First ed., 1659.

Pelikan, Jaroslav. *The Christian Tradition: A History of the Development of Doctrine. 1. The Emergence of the Catholic Tradition (100–600 A.D.).* Chicago: University of Chicago Press, 1971.

Phillips, D. Z. *The Concept of Prayer.* London: Routledge and Kegan Paul, 1968.

Phillips, J. B. *Letters to Young Churches.* The New Testament Epistles. London: Geoffrey Bles; New York: Macmillan Co., 1947.

————. *Ring of Truth: A Translator's Testimony.* London: Hodder and Stoughton; New York: Macmillan, 1967.

Plummer, Alfred. *A Critical and Exegetical Commentary on the Second Epistle of St. Paul to the Corinthians.* International Critical Commentary. Edinburgh: T. & T. Clark, 1915. Reprint ed. Naperville, Ill.: Allenson.

————. *The Gospel According to St. Mark.* Cambridge Greek Testament. Reprint. Cambridge: University Press, 1926.

Popkes, Wiard. *Christus Traditus: Eine Untersuchung zum Begriff der Dahingabe im Neuen Testament.* Zürich and Stuttgart: Zwingli Verlag, 1967.

Pusey, E. B. *The Minor Prophets.* 2 vols. New York: Funk & Wagnalls, 1885. Reprint ed. Grand Rapids: Baker Book House.

Rackham, R. B. *The Acts of the Apostles: An Exposition.* 11th ed. London: Methuen & Co., 1930. Reprint ed. Grand Rapids: Baker Book House, 1964.

Rashdall, Hastings. *The Idea of Atonement in Christian Theology.* London: Macmillan & Co., 1925.

Richardson, Alan. *An Introduction to the Theology of the New Testament.* London: SCM Press, 1958; New York: Harper & Row, 1959.

Rieu, C. H. trans. *The Acts of the Apostles.* Harmondsworth, Middlesex: Penguin Books, 1957.

Robertson, A. T. *A Grammar of the Greek New Testament in the Light of Historical Research.* 4th ed. New York: Hodder & Stoughton, 1923. Reprint. Nashville: Broadman Press, 1947.

Robinson, H. Wheeler. *The Christian Doctrine of Man.* 2d ed. Edinburgh: T. & T. Clark, 1913.

————. *Inspiration and Revelation in the Old Testament.* Oxford: Clarendon Press, 1946.

Robinson, J. A. T. *The Body: A Study in Pauline Theology.* London: SCM Press; Naperville, Ill.: Allenson, 1952.

Rodgers, John. *The Theology of P. T. Forsyth.* London: Independent Press; Naperville, Ill.: Allenson, 1965.

Ropes, James Hardy. *A Critical and Exegetical Commentary on the Epistle of St. James.* International Critical Commentary. Reprint. Edinburgh: T. & T. Clark, 1961; Naperville, Ill.: Allenson.

Ross, W. D. *Aristotle's Metaphysics.* 2 vols. Oxford: Clarendon Press, 1924.

Russell, Jeffrey Burton. *A History of Medieval Christianity.* New York: Thomas Y. Crowell, 1968.

Salmond, S. D. F. "The Epistle to the Ephesians." In *The Expositor's Greek Testament,* edited by W. Robertson Nicoll.

Sanday, William, and Headlam, Arthur C. *A Critical and Exegetical Commentary on the Epistle to the Romans.* International Critical Commentary. 5th ed. Edinburgh: T. & T. Clark, 1925.

Sayers, Dorothy L. *The Mind of the Maker.* London: Religious Book Club, 1942.

Schlatter, Adolf. *Der Brief des Jakobus.* 2d ed. Stuttgart: Calwer Verlag, 1956.

————. *Der Evangelist Johannes: Wie er spricht, denkt und glaubt.* 3d ed. Stuttgart: Calwer Verlag, 1960.

————. *Das Evangelium des Lukas.* Stuttgart: Calwer Verlag, 1960.

Schnackenburg, Rudolf. *Baptism in the Thought of St. Paul.* Translated by G. R. Beasley-Murray. Oxford: Basil Blackwell, 1964.

Schneider, Johannes. *Die Kirchenbriefe (Die Katholischen Briefe): Die Briefe des Jakobus, Petrus und Johannes. Das Neue Testament Deutsch,* vol. 10. 9th ed. Göttingen: Vandenhoeck & Ruprecht, 1961.

Selwyn, E. G. *The First Epistle of St. Peter: The Greek Text with Introduction, Notes, and Essays.* 2d ed., reprint. London: Macmillan & Co., 1952.

Simpson, E. K., and Bruce, F. F. *Commentary on the Epistles to the Ephesians and the Colossians.* New International Commentary. Grand Rapids: Wm. B. Eerdmans, 1957.

Skinner, John. *The Book of the Prophet Isaiah.* Cambridge Bible. 2 vols. Reprint. Cambridge: University Press, 1925.

————. *Prophecy and Religion: Studies in the Life of Jeremiah.* Cambridge: University Press, 1963.

Smedes, Lewis B. *The Incarnation: Trends in Modern Anglican Thought.* Kampen: J. H. Kok, n.d.

Smith, H. P. *A Critical and Exegetical Commentary on the Books of Samuel.* International Critical Commentary. Edinburgh: T. & T. Clark, 1912.

Smith, W. Robertson. *The Religion of the Semites.* 3d ed. London: A. & C. Black, 1927.

Sorley, W. R. *Moral Values and the Idea of God.* Cambridge: University Press, 1930.

Souter, Alexander. *A Pocket Lexicon to the Greek New Testament.* Oxford: Clarendon Press, 1925.

Spicq, C. *Les Épîtres Pastorales (Études Bibliques).* Paris: Librairie Lecoffre, J. Gabalda et Cie, 1947.

Spurgeon, C. H. *Lectures to My Students.* First Series. London: Passmore and Alabaster, 1876, 1881. Reprint ed. London: Marshall, Morgan & Scott, n.d.

Stacey, W. David. *The Pauline View of Man.* London: Macmillan & Co.; New York: St. Martin's Press, 1956.

Stauffer, Ethelbert. *New Testament Theology.* Translated by John Marsh. London: SCM Press; New York: Macmillan, 1955.

Stott, John. "Reverence for Human Life." *Christianity Today* 16, no. 18 (9 June 1972): 852–56.

Strathmann, Hermann. *Der Brief an die Hebräer.* In *Das Neue Testament Deutsch,* vol. 9. Göttingen: Vandenhoeck & Ruprecht, 1963.

Swete, Henry Barclay. *The Apocalypse of St. John*. London: Macmillan and Co., 1906. Reprint ed. Grand Rapids: Wm. B. Eerdmans, 1951.

Tasker, R. V. G. *The Greek New Testament: Being the Text Translated in The New English Bible*, 1961. London: Oxford University Press, 1961; Cambridge: University Press, 1964.

———. *The Old Testament in the New Testament*. Grand Rapids: Wm. B. Eerdmans, 1963.

Taylor, Vincent. *The Cross of Christ*. London: Macmillan; New York: St. Martin's Press, 1956.

———. *The Gospel According to St. Mark*. London: Macmillan & Co.; New York: St. Martin's Press, 1952.

———. *The Person of Christ: In New Testament Teaching*. London: Macmillan & Co.; New York: St. Martin's Press, 1957.

Thielicke, Helmut. *Encounter with Spurgeon*. London: James Clarke, 1964. Reprint ed., Grand Rapids: Baker Book House, 1975.

———. *I Believe: The Christian's Creed*. Translated by John W. Doberstein and H. George Anderson. Philadelphia: Fortress Press, 1968.

———. *The Waiting Father: Sermons on the Parables of Jesus*. Translated by John W. Doberstein. London: James Clarke; New York: Harper & Row, 1959.

Thrall, Margaret E. *The First and Second Letters of Paul to the Corinthians*. The Cambridge Bible Commentary. Cambridge: University Press, 1965.

Torrance, Thomas F. *The Doctrine of Grace in the Apostolic Fathers*. Edinburgh: Oliver and Boyd, 1948. Grand Rapids: Wm. B. Eerdmans, 1959.

Turner, H. E. W. *Jesus, Master and Lord: A Study in the Historical Truth of the Gospels*. London: A. R. Mowbray, 1953. Naperville, Ill.: Allenson, 1954.

Turner, Nigel. *Grammatical Insights into the New Testament*. Edinburgh: T. & T. Clark; Naperville, Ill.: Allenson, 1965.

Turner, Nigel. See Moulton, James Hope.

Van Daalen, D. H. "'Faith' According to Paul." *The Expository Times* 87, no. 3 (Dec. 1975): 83–85.

Vincent, Marvin R. *A Critical and Exegetical Commentary on the Epistles to the Philippians and to Philemon*. International Critical Commentary. Edinburgh: T. & T. Clark; Naperville, Ill.: Allenson, 1897.

Vriezen, Th. C. *An Outline of Old Testament Theology*. Oxford: Basil Blackwell, 1966. Newton Centre, Mass.: Charles T. Branford, 1969.

Waddams, Herbert. *A New Introduction to Moral Theology*. Rev. ed. London: SCM Press; New York: Seabury Press, 1965.

Ward, R. A. "Aristotelian Antecedents of the Philosophical Vocabulary of the New Testament." Masters Thesis. Deposited in University of London Library, 1947.

———. "Aristotelian Elements in the Philosophical Vocabulary of the New Testament." Ph.D. thesis. University of London. A copy is deposited in the Angus Library, Regent's Park College, Oxford.

———. *Hidden Meaning in the New Testament: New Light from the Old Greek*. London: Marshall, Morgan & Scott; Old Tappan, N.J.: Fleming H. Revell, 1969.

———. *Mind and Heart: Studies in Christian Truth and Experience*. London and Edinburgh: Marshall, Morgan & Scott, 1965. Grand Rapids: Baker Book House, 1966.

———. "Quotation Marks as an Aid in Interpretation." *Southwestern Journal of Theology* 18 (Fall 1975): 69–71.

———. *Royal Sacrament: The Preacher and His Message*. London and Edinburgh: Marshall, Morgan & Scott, 1958.

————. *Royal Theology: Our Lord's Teaching about God.* London and Edinburgh: Marshall, Morgan & Scott, 1958; Greenwood, S.C.: Attic Press, 1964.

Weatherhead, Leslie D. *Psychology, Religion and Healing.* 2d. ed. London: Hodder & Stoughton; Nashville: Abingdon Press, 1952.

Webster, Douglas. *In Debt to Christ: A Study in the Meaning of the Cross.* Reprint. London: Highway Press, 1957; Philadelphia: Fortress Press, 1964.

Wendland, Heinz-Dietrich. *Die Briefe an die Korinther. Das Neue Testament Deutsch,* vol. 7. 12th rev. ed. Göttingen: Vandenhoeck & Ruprecht, 1968.

Wesley, John. *Sermons: On Several Occasion.* Reprinted from 1771 edition. London: Wesleyan-Methodist Book-Room.

Westcott, Brooke Foss. *Saint Paul's Epistle to the Ephesians.* London: Macmillan & Co., 1906. Reprint ed. Grand Rapids: Wm. B. Eerdmans, 1950.

White, R. E. O. *The Biblical Doctrine of Initiation: A Theology of Baptism and Evangelism.* Grand Rapids: Wm. B. Eerdmans, 1960.

Whiteley, D. E. H. *The Theology of St. Paul.* Oxford: Basil Blackwell; Philadelphia: Fortress Press, 1964.

Wilcox, Max. *The Semitisms of Acts.* Oxford: Clarendon Press, 1965.

Williams, Charles B. *The New Testament: A Private Translation in the Language of the People.* Chicago: Moody Press, 1949.

Williams, C. S. C. *A Commentary on the Acts of the Apostles.* Black's New Testament Commentaries. London: Adam & Charles Black, 1957.

Williams, R. R. *I Believe—and Why.* London: A. R. Mowbray, 1971.

Williamson, Ronald. "The Background of the Epistle to the Hebrews." *The Expository Times* 87, no. 8 (May 1976): 232–37.

Wood, A. Skevington. *The Burning Heart: John Wesley, Evangelist.* Exeter: Paternoster Press, 1967; Grand Rapids: Wm. B. Eerdmans, 1968.

Wood, H. G. *Frederick Denison Maurice.* Cambridge: University Press, 1950.

Wordsworth, John, and White, Henry Julian, eds. *Novum Testamentum Latine: Secundum Editionem Sancti Hieronymi.* Oxford: Clarendon Press; London and New York: Humphrey Milford, 1931.

Young, Edward J. *The Book of Isaiah.* Vol. 1. Grand Rapids: Wm. B. Eerdmans, 1965.

Young, Frances M. "Sacrifice." *Expository Times* 86, no. 10 (July 1975): 305–9.

Young, Norman H. "C. H. Dodd, 'Hilaskesthai' and His Critics." *The Evangelical Quarterly* 48, no. 2 (April-June 1976): 67–78.

Zahrnt, Heinz. *The Question of God: Protestant Theology in the Twentieth Century.* Translated by R. A. Wilson. New York: Harcourt Brace & World, 1969.

Zerwick, Max. *Analysis Philologica Novi Testamenti Graeci.* Rome: Sumptibus Pontificii Instituti Biblici; Chicago: Loyola, 1966.

Ziesler, J. A. *The Meaning of Righteousness in Paul.* Cambridge: University Press, 1972.

Zuntz, G. *The Text of the Epistles.* London: British Academy, Oxford University Press, 1953.

# Scripture Index

This index lists references to verses from biblical books other than the one under discussion in a chapter. The chart on pages 394–409 lists the main references from each biblical book discussed. Since each chapter follows the outline of the chart, it should be relatively easy to find the discussion on a particular verse or passage.

**Old Testament**

| *Genesis* | | | | | | | |
|---|---|---|---|---|---|---|---|
| 1 | 16 | 24:12 | 36 | 17:1–3 | 37 | | |
| 1:3 | 147 | 24:14 | 36 | 17:2 | 31 | | |
| 1:26–27 | 84, 283 | 24:44 | 36 | 17:7 | 26, 31 | | |
| 1:27 | 129, 231 | 25:33–34 | 37 | 19:1–6 | 44 | | |
| 2:7 | 148, 167 | 27:36 | 41 | 19:5 | 275 | | |
| 2:18 | 74,147 | 31:1 | 47 | 19:12–19 | 37 | | |
| 2:20 | 74 | 32:6 | 41 | 20:6 | 37 | | |
| 2:24 | 220 | 33:3 | 41 | 20:12 | 231 | | |
| 3:1 | 344 | 33:10–11 | 42 | 21:31 | 24 | | |
| 3:10 | 154 | 37:28 | 42 | 23:20–33 | 44 | | |
| 3:13–15 | 344 | 37:36 | 42 | 24 | 176 | | |
| 3:16 | 151 | 39:1–2 | 42 | 24:1–8 | 25 | | |
| 5:1 | 84 | 39:20 | 42 | 24:3–8 | 176 | | |
| 5:24 | 24 | 39:21–22 | 42 | 24:6–8 | 37 | | |
| 6:5–8 | 42 | 40:19 | 59 | 24:8 | 177, 275 | | |
| 6:6 | 21 | 41:42 | 60 | 25:1 | 25 | | |
| 6:8 | 316 | 45:5–8 | 48 | 25:18–19 | 25n | | |
| 8:21 | 218 | 49:9 | 355 | 25:40 | 25n | | |
| 9:1–2 | 85 | *Exodus* | | 29:18 | 218 | | |
| 14:17–20 | 51 | 3:5 | 295n | 30:10 | 60 | | |
| 14:18 | 14 | 31:7–8 | 48 | 34:7 | 59 | | |
| 15:6 | 110 | 3:10–18 | 48 | 34:9 | 59 | | |
| 15:14 | 174 | 5:22 | 47 | 34:31 | 190 | | |
| 17:3 | 153 | 6:2–3 | 233 | 34:34 | 190 | | |
| 17:17 | 153 | 7:16 | 47 | *Leviticus* | | | |
| 19:16 | 316 | 12 | 174n | 7:6–10 | 151 | | |
| 19:19 | 316 | 12:7 | 174 | 7:14 | 151 | | |
| 22:1–12 | 291 | 12:12 | 174 | 7:28–36 | 151 | | |
| 22:16–17 | 36 | 12:21 | 173 | 8:6 | 67 | | |
| 23:4 | 37 | 12:22–23 | 174 | 8:30 | 67 | | |
| | | 15:25–26 | 24 | 10:10 | 193 | | |

# Index of Authors